MIKHAIL BULGAKOV
THE LIFE AND TIMES

ИНСТИТУТ ПЕРЕВОДА

AD VERBUM

Published with the support
of the Institute for Literary Translation, Russia

MIKHAIL BULGAKOV:
THE LIFE AND TIMES

by Marietta Chudakova

Translated from the Russian by Huw Davies

© 1988, 2019 by Marietta Chudakova

Published by arrangement with ELKOST Intl. Literary Agency

Published with the support
of the Institute for Literary Translation, Russia

Introduction © 2019, J.A.E. Curtis

Proofreading by Kevin Bridge

Publishers Maxim Hodak & Max Mendor

© 2019, Glagoslav Publications B.V.

www.glagoslav.com

First published in 2019 (abridged)

ISBN: 978-1-78437-980-3

A catalogue record for this book is available from the British Library.

This book is in copyright. No part of this publication may be reproduced, stored in a retrieval system or transmitted in any form or by any means withoutthe prior permission in writing of the publisher, nor be otherwise circulated in any form of binding or cover other than that in which it is published without a similar condition, including this condition, being imposed on the subsequent purchaser.

MARIETTA CHUDAKOVA

MIKHAIL BULGAKOV
THE LIFE AND TIMES

Translated by Huw Davies

GLAGOSLAV PUBLICATIONS

Mikhail Bulgakov

(1891-1940)

CONTENTS

INTRODUCTION:
Marietta Chudakova and *Mikhail Bulgakov:*
The Life and Times 7

PREFACE 17

    CHAPTER ONE
    The Kiev Years: the Family; Grammar School and University.
    The War. Medicine. Revolution 24

    CHAPTER TWO
    The First Moscow Years 162

    CHAPTER THREE
    A Theatrical Five Years (1925-1929) 318

    CHAPTER FOUR
    The Crisis Years (1929-1931) 391

    CHAPTER FIVE
    A Return to the Novel.
    New Plays and Hopes (1932-1935) 459

    CHAPTER SIX
    A Fresh Failure. "What Can I Say,
    It's a Libretto Like any Other!" 539

    CHAPTER SEVEN
    "The Final, Twilight Novel".
    The Final Play. (1938-1940) 580

ACKNOWLEDGEMENT 620

INDEX 621

MARIETTA CHUDAKOVA AND *MIKHAIL BULGAKOV: THE LIFE AND TIMES*

In order to understand the huge importance that this biographical study of Mikhail Bulgakov written by Marietta Chudakova had when it was first published in 1988, we need to remind ourselves of the difficulties which faced literary scholars and other intellectuals in the late Soviet period. Since the death of Stalin in 1953 the USSR had gone through a period of cultural 'Thaw', a period when it had become possible to denounce Stalin (in official circles, but only behind closed doors) for his crimes against members of the Communist Party, but not to spell out in full the extent of the criminal horrors perpetrated against the Soviet people as a whole during the Terror. The Thaw period initiated by Nikita Khrushchev's 'secret speech', which revealed Stalin's actions to the XXth Party Congress in 1956, was only ever a partial thaw. True, in 1962 the sensational publication of Solzhenitsyn's short novel *One Day in the Life of Ivan Denisovich* had for the first time lifted the veil of silence which had up until that moment concealed the history of the Gulag from public view. But this brief glimpse of life in Siberian labour camps did not signal the opening of floodgates, and it was not followed by a rush of other such publications. On the contrary, literary censorship seemed to regroup and reassert itself, and further controversial works by Solzhenitsyn and others failed to be granted permission to be published.

This largely repressive regime continued under Khrushchev's successor, Leonid Brezhnev, who from 1964 onwards came to preside over what is now known as the 'era of stagnation', when Soviet Communism became more and more bureaucratic at home, while its foreign policy came to be defined by the aggressive and wary attitudes of the Cold War. As often as a relatively outspoken or liberal work of literature was published, so equally often were intellectuals harassed or put on trial for spurious offences: and so the dissident movement was born, with liberally-inclined intellectuals banding loosely together to outwit the authorities where possible, often with the connivance - or at least the tacit encouragement - of westerners interested in Soviet culture.

One such figure on the literary scene was Marietta Chudakova, who joined the staff of the Manuscript Department of the Lenin Library (now known as the Russian State Library) in 1965, after completing her literary studies at doctoral level at university. Not long after this the Library acquired a sizeable archive from Yelena Sergeyevna Bulgakova, the third wife of the writer Mikhail Bulgakov. After a career which had sparkled into celebrity in the mid-1920s, when he had been the most controversial and sought-after playwright in the early years of the Soviet régime, Bulgakov had suffered increasing defeats as he attempted to publish or stage further works. By the time he died of a hereditary disease of the kidneys in 1940, at the early age of 48, he had become entirely frustrated in his literary endeavours. He had also come under the close and personal scrutiny of Stalin and other members of the Politbiuro, who on several occasions discussed whether to permit his works, but regularly concluded that they were too subversive. Bulgakov was perhaps lucky to escape the physical torments of the Terror, but his reputation as an essentially anti-Soviet figure remained after his death. Through the years of World War II in Soviet Russia (1941-45), and until well after Stalin's death, he was virtually written out of literary history, and there could be no question of publishing his many unpublished works. Yelena Sergeyevna, like other 'literary widows' in the USSR, devoted herself to the courageous and difficult task of gathering his papers and manuscripts together and preserving them discreetly, in the hope that his works might eventually see the light of day.

This situation began to change, however, with the Thaw. By the mid-1960s – a quarter of a century after the author's death - a number of his works, including several of his plays, had at last been published. The next most exciting event of the Thaw after the 1962 publication of Solzhenitsyn was the publication – for the time being only in part – of two portions of Bulgakov's masterpiece *The Master and Margarita* by the journal *Moskva*, in late 1966 and early 1967. It would take until 1973, however, three years after Yelena Bulgakova's own death, for the novel to be published in full, in a volume also containing his earlier novel *The White Guard* and his unfinished *Theatrical Novel*. This was the literary sensation of the decade, which launched the cult following of Mikhail Bulgakov and his works which has persisted to this day, very belatedly turning him into Russia's most popular writer of the twentieth century.

Marietta Chudakova's task, after the acquisition of the archive around the time of the *Moskva* publication, was to sort and catalogue the manuscripts, letters and papers in the archive. This was an enormous responsibility, which she undertook with passion and ferocious dedication. It involved her in unceasing investigation, over many years, of the context of these documents, to establish the biographical facts which lay behind the events alluded to, and to trace the writing history of Bulgakov's entire oeuvre. She not only applied to the task her own extraordinary erudition and knowledge of the literary scene in the 1920s and 1930s, but she also undertook numerous trips to interview surviving members of Bulgakov's family, contemporaries of his dating back to Bulgakov's schooldays in Kiev in the 1890s and the early part of the twentieth century, and literary figures who had known him personally. She also got to know all three of Bulgakov's wives, eliciting from them candid and illuminating stories of their lives with this brilliant - but not always easy - man.

Chudakova's task as an archivist in the late 1960s and early 1970s was to write up her investigations in scholarly form, as a description of the archive's contents according to the exacting library conventions of the day. Strictly speaking, she was not meant to stray into biographical narrative, or to offer any evaluative commentary on the works. But with a writer of this calibre the norm would have been to make appropriate references to already published biographies or interpretative studies, whereas in this case none had yet been written, so there was nothing else for her to refer to. And so she found herself essentially writing his biography as she went along, compiling as she did so an astonishing resource for herself in the shape of an exhaustive chronology of his life. Some moments remained unexplained for the moment, however. As she once reported it, she was obliged in this extremely lengthy article about his archive, published in 1976, to state simply that in 1920 Bulgakov had lived in the town of Vladikavkaz, in the northern Caucasus. Neither Bulgakov's sister Nadya nor any of his three wives was prepared to tell her what he was doing there, for fear of the possible repercussions even several decades later; for, as it subsequently emerged, Bulgakov had gone there with the White Army to serve as a medical officer during their retreat from the advancing Bolsheviks. And so Chudakova genuinely didn't know the answer to this question at that point. She also spoke very entertainingly about how long it took her even to get the 1976 article past the censors. For example, she needed to allude to the presence in the archive of the manuscript of

Bulgakov's wonderful satirical tale *The Heart of a Dog*, but that text had not yet been licensed for publication in the USSR (it had appeared in the West in 1968), and so she was not allowed to mention its title. In the kind of discreet game-playing so characteristic of the courageous scholarship of Soviet academics at that time, she simply decided to smuggle a description of this archival item into her article by inconspicuously starting to talk about it as 'Bulgakov's third tale' - and although on this occasion the censor did notice what she had been up to, he eventually conceded that this reference could stay in. The same schizophrenic attitudes were apparent when it came to providing specific references to catalogue numbers of the archive: Chudakova and others went to enormous lengths in a series of publications during those difficult years to smuggle in occasional specific mentions to catalogue references, so that other scholars could have some hope of tracking down the relevant item.

It was my privilege to benefit from this kind of generosity on the part of Chudakova and other Bulgakov scholars when I made two 4-month visits to the USSR in 1979 and 1980, as a very green postgraduate student who had seized upon the subject of the newly-rediscovered Mikhail Bulgakov as an ideal topic for the D.Phil. dissertation I was working on at Oxford University. My visit, like those of other British postgraduates in those years, was arranged under the terms of a cultural exchange agreement between the British and Soviet governments. British students, who had a tendency to want to pry into controversial subjects, were not entirely welcome, but had to be tolerated if the Soviet side was to be able to send its own students abroad. And so we were allowed to go there, and even to go to archives in some cases (though it took a full 13 years before I was finally allowed to use the Bulgakov archive in the Lenin Library). If you did get into an archive building, it turned out that there were various unwritten rules. First amongst these was that foreigners could not be granted access to catalogues. This meant that if you were to have any hope of doing any useful work, you had to be absolutely thoroughly prepared: you needed to have read every available publication on your subject, and thanks to the ingenuity of scholars like Chudakova, you could assemble a few crumbs of information from these, on which to base your archival requests. Another hindrance placed in our way by the Soviet authorities could emerge as you were leaving the country: there were several instances of western postgraduates having all their research materials simply confiscated at the border. This threat was alleviated by the staff of the Cultural Section at the British Embassy, who looked after us during our stay: they allowed us very kindly (and quite illegally) to use the diplomatic bag, and towards the end of our stay we were allowed to go along and stuff up to 2kg of papers and microfilms into a plastic carrier bag. After our return we then had to go along to King Charles Street in London, to the Foreign Office, to collect our research materials and take them back to our universities. Many Soviet scholars went out of their way to talk to us, entertained us in the evenings to meals and much vodka, educated us so that we should have a reasonable understanding of the world we were trying to describe, and on many occasions lent us their own notes taken from archives, or extracts from the catalogue, to try to fill the gaps with which we were struggling thanks to the Soviet authorities' obstructiveness. When I did finally complete my doctorate on Bulgakov in 1982, a significant proportion of the footnotes containing archival references had to be faked; and my examiners agreed that this was of course the only honourable option, given that spelling out just where I had got my information from could have compromised colleagues back in the Soviet Union, and caused them much unpleasantness.

It was with some trepidation that I approached Marietta Chudakova, as the leading expert on Bulgakov and someone who worked in the Lenin Library Manuscript Department (which was adamantly refusing to let me in), to ask her for a meeting. But in a pattern which was soon to become an established routine, she invited me home to her apartment, several floors up in a high-rise block of flats in a modern suburb of Moscow. I would be told at what time to arrive, usually mid-to-late evening, and I would turn up with a list of questions relevant to my topic, or arising from those materials I had been allowed to see in other archives. Marietta was a daunting person to meet, despite her small stature, and one always felt that her Tartar blood (her father, Omar Khan-Magomedov, was born in Dagestan) was what lent her a particular fierceness. She would fire questions at me or make scathing comments in her inimitable staccato delivery, straining my Russian to its limits. But over time, and as I prepared very conscientiously for each meeting, she came to treat me with great kindness, and was extraordinarily generous with explanations and materials. Nothing that I did subsequently, whether it was my doctorate (on the theme of the writer in Bulgakov's works), no the later books I wrote about Bulgakov, would have taken the shape they did had it not been for her wonderful instinct for pedagogy, and her determination that if I was serious about Bulgakov then it was important that I should understand him properly. And the evenings would always end over tea and snacks at the table, and conversation with Marietta and her charming husband Alexander Chudakov, himself a wonderful Chekhov scholar who died tragically in 2005 after being mugged in the entrance to their apartment block.

Chudakova's long devotion to the cause of Bulgakov (she is the author of numerous important studies of other early Soviet authors as well) was reflected in a whole series of articles which she published about him. But the culmination of her efforts came in 1988, when Mikhail Gorbachev's policy of *glasnost'* made it possible at last to publish long-banned texts in the USSR (many of which had been published earlier in Western émigré editions). At the same time, it became possible for important critical and biographical publications to appear. The present volume, Chudakova's *Zhizneopisaniye Mikhaila Bulgakova* (literally: *Description of the Life of Mikhail Bulgakov*), was first published in a 495-page edition, with a print-run of 50,000 copies. But things were moving so fast in those years, and the limitations on what it was permissible to say in public were shifting so swiftly, that in the very same year she published a second, extended edition of 671 pages, with a print run of 90,000 copies. This later edition included some rather more controversial material, such as evidence of a love-affair Bulgakov had had with a woman called Margarita, and the investigation of suggestions that Bulgakov's third wife Yelena had had close links to the NKVD (precursor of the KGB). She is also able to be less euphemistic about events such as the arrest of the poet Osip Mandelstam in 1934. It was certainly the first full biography of Bulgakov in Russian, although A. Colin Wright had in fact already published a biography in English, his *Mikhail Bulgakov. Life and Interpretations*, in Toronto in 1978.

When we pick up this book now, we can still admire the extraordinary range of knowledge and depth of investigation that it displays. Chudakova uses testimonials from contemporaries to provide us with the authentic flavour of the period, whether in relation to Bulgakov's schooling or to the circles of friends he began to move in when he became established in Moscow. Underpinning the writing is an extraordinarily detailed chronicle of his life, all assembled by hand on notes taken long before the advent of computers. The very title of the work is redolent of the pure chronicler's task, even though the work also succeeds in all the usual range of biographical goals: in capturing the writer's everyday life, his loves, and his professional tribulations, as well as the origins and gradual evolution of his literary works. It is a challenging read: it comes without an index, despite its length and the huge range of its subjects, and it demands the unwavering attention of the reader, as well as unquestioned devotion to the subject, to Bulgakov himself. If I look back at my 1988 edition, with its faded print on musty, yellowing pages, I remain enormously impressed by the extraordinary energy that went into its writing. This is even reflected in the way the words are crammed on to the page, 50 lines of text per page in a font size which doesn't make for entirely comfortable reading. Since 1988 there have been new publications of documents relating to Bulgakov's life, filling in details about his family and their lives, but also providing us with much more information about the literary policy of the Stalin régime, together with transcriptions of discussions at Politbiuro level which determined the very fate of writers and their works. Nothing can quite compare with Chudakova's study of Bulgakov, however, immersed directly as it is in the lives of people who knew Bulgakov, and produced from within the Soviet system which shaped his life. It is still both awe-inspiring and instructive to revisit one of the great monuments of Soviet-era scholarship, written in defiance of the censors, and championing one of the great free spirits of Russia in the twentieth century.

Professor J.A.E. Curtis,
Oxford

MIKHAIL BULGAKOV

THE LIFE AND TIMES

PREFACE

It was only in the mid-1960s, when the majority of Bulgakov's plays were published and a one-volume edition containing a considerable amount of his prose was released, that the author's name, which had been well-known prior to that chiefly among literary historians and those who had seen the play *The Days of the Turbins* (*Dni Turbinykh*), first began to appeal to an extremely broad readership in Russia. In late 1966 and early 1967, when his last novel, *The Master and Margarita* (*Master i Margarita*), was published and subsequently translated into numerous languages, Bulgakov's creative oeuvre achieved worldwide recognition, altering to a degree the perceived wisdom about Russian prose of the 1930s.

When the novel was published for the first time, the writer's widow, Y.S. Bulgakova, acquired from the state an archive of Bulgakov's writings, which she looked after for a quarter of a century after her husband's death, and happenstance dictated that it befell the author of this biography to sort through these archived documents and conduct a scientific study of them. The writer's creative output was revealed at that point in all its hitherto unknown glory, and in the process of sorting through and describing the manuscripts and other documents, many biographical and literary details came into circulation in the cultural sphere for the first time.

Of considerable importance in gaining an understanding of the writer's personality and biography were the conversations I had with Yelena Sergeyevna Bulgakova during my numerous meetings with her at her apartment in Moscow, in Suvorovsky Bulvar – a place considered to have great significance as a monument by students and admirers of Bulgakov's life and work.

As I strove to add to these archives and gain more of an insight into his biography, my knowledge of which contained gaping holes at the time, I attempted to track down his relatives and friends, gradually expanding the scope of my search. Thus it was that I ended up with hundreds of pages of notes from my conversations with the writer's contemporaries and those who had borne witness to his life and times.

Naturally, the recollections of his contemporaries, recorded during the chats we had, can often be rendered more complex by additional factors which, whether wittingly or unwittingly, distort information, including, for example, a degree of caution when expressing religious beliefs or other convictions, or when shedding light on certain events and how these events were perceived. This circumspection – so typical of older generations of Russians, and so easy to understand (yet no less sad because of that), even with regard to their views from a bygone era, which have changed as they have grown older – had an effect on how Bulgakov's character was portrayed in the book. Every single brush-stroke, moreover, in the portrait of a man as remarkable as our protagonist seems important: after all, only the sum total of these brush-strokes – living and breathing, in motion, and changing during the course of his life, with some qualities exaggerated and others suppressed – will enable me to provide a fully-rounded sense of the identity of the man who wrote *The Master and Margarita*. In so doing, I shall be following in the footsteps of a man who, back in the mid-19th century, devised a new approach to writing biographies that was ahead of its time then and is still a relevant and fruitful method today: Pavel Vasilievich Annenkov (an admirer of Bulgakov's work), who remains unsurpassed to this day as the best biographer not only of Pushkin but also of Gogol, Belinsky, Turgenev – of all those, indeed, about whom he left memoirs. "First and foremost, the author would appreciate it if the system whereby each and every detail of a person's life is given a separate explanation and a separate justification could be rejected permanently," he wrote, "and also the system of mourning and repentance for the protagonist to which the author resorts when, despite all his best efforts, he can no longer find the words with which to explain or justify certain phenomena." In other words, Annenkov warned against seeking to explain and justify certain actions and qualities in isolation, calling instead for the starting point to be the holistic nature of the creator and his creative output, and not replacing this with "an attempt to understand and portray a highly nuanced individual through a simple calculation of the extent to which this individual adhered to established ideas about proper and acceptable standards of behaviour, and the extent to which he departed from them. When this task is undertaken, it often happens that the author perceives a discrepancy between the norm and their subject when in fact there isn't one at all, and on occasion the author tries to make his protagonist fit into the rule without any need to do so at all, merely *because of the false notion that it is better for the protagonist to be given a place of honour than to be left in a vast, free place* [my italics – M.C.]. I tried, at any rate, not to make our hero fit into the rule, but to understand, as far as possible, his "living and breathing identity".

In this book I have drawn extensively on the unpublished memoirs, written down by me, of the writer's widow, Y.S. Bulgakova (1893-1970), his first wife Tatiana Nikolayevna Kiselgof (1889-1982), his sister Nadezhda Afanasievna Zemskaya (née Bulgakova; 1893-1971), his cousin Alexandra Andreyevna Tkachenko, and also material from numerous conversations with friends and acquaintances of the writer, from his schooldays to the final days of his life. Many facts about Bulgakov's life and creative oeuvre are being revealed here for the first time. It goes without saying that in the making of this biography, works by Soviet researchers and researchers from other countries were important and of use: over the course of twenty years, a sizeable number of such works have been consulted.

It is worth noting that this book is about a man who barely left any direct statements about subjects that are important to any biographer – from political ones to religious ones. Though he is not unique in this, it is nonetheless a fairly rare thing; it is something I would like my readers to bear in mind. For anything that would usually be referred to as a person's views, the biographer of Bulgakov is required to reconstruct these things on the basis of indirect evidence alone. In this regard, material related to his childhood and young manhood – the time when his personality was shaped – is particularly valuable. Even the most indirect evidence was important here – such as Yekaterina Petrovna Kudryavtseva's recollections of her father, Pyotr Pavlovich Kudryavtsev, which were sent to me in 1977; Kudryavtsev had taken charge of the history of philosophy department at the Kiev Spiritual Academy in 1897. She wrote in her letter that the memoirs "didn't even contain a single mention of the writer or his parents," but added, quite rightly, that what she had described in them was not so much "the everyday life of the professorship in those days (and the author grew up in the family of a professor from the Spiritual Academy, no less), as – first and foremost – the cultural, intellectual and moral situation which enabled, to the extent that is now known to us, the formation of his 'inner' identity. After all, Bulgakov was not only a great artist, but a writer of rare breadth, an 'emancipator of thought', if you will, and after all, all of this takes shape in a person – either consciously or unconsciously – during their childhood."

It has always seemed to me that anyone studying literature and society in our times must try to break through to the true picture, regardless of the pluses and minuses that are imposed retroactively, and that it is only by doing so that a biographer can express the tribute of his respect for a great writer, over whose life he takes it upon himself to think and ponder, then decides to share the results of this thought process with the reader.

Bulgakov loomed up before his readers a quarter of a century after his death, in the mid-sixties. He became part of the national culture at a time when society was on the crest of a wave, though this wave was already being transformed into some sort of convulsive spasm in those years; hence the sense of convulsion in the levels of knowledge about his biography and creative oeuvre back then, which can still be felt today. Bulgakov appeared to many to be a much coveted and long sought-after template, an object of faith and veneration. Various strata within society ascribed their own values to him, and it was these values – in his image – that they were really venerating.

Society needed a legend – and duly acquired or perhaps created one. The fact that there was no biography available – not even a first draft of one – and the properties of the works themselves, which were being read for the first time – the autobiographical nature of *A Theatrical Novel* (*Teatral'nyy Roman*), the space for direct and indirect biographical identification revealed by the author in his novel *The Master and Margarita* – were the things that prompted this to happen.

Ready-made evaluations came in from various sides. Over and above any faith or veneration by this time, and strictly for pragmatic reasons, they were formed and imposed upon people by the official institutions, among others, which were tasked with having a restraining influence: there was a need to pour cold water over the sentiment which was spreading like wildfire within society, the obvious preference for this "new" writer of the '20s and '30s, over those of his contemporaries whose authority had long been enshrined in law, with special efforts made to keep it going. People hastened to adopt Bulgakov posthumously, under the terms of a template or script that was already familiar to them; the story of his life was endowed with characteristics that could conveniently be put into circulation, and which bore little relation to the actual facts. Opposed to this in no small measure, in accordance with the structure of the social situation, was public opinion, including the literary and academic spheres. The writer's biography, before it had even taken shape, was immediately deconstructed: it was adapted to suit the needs of the publication of his legacy, to which readers were only able to get closer by going through great difficulties. A utilitarian approach to biographical fact took precedence. The words written about the writer took on the significance of some sort of lever, with the help of which certain matters which were only indirectly related to his life were set in motion.

This tendency in society to jump to conclusions about the writer's life and personality creates certain difficulties for his biographer even today. Those who read Bulgakov and love his work have grown accustomed not only to the notions about him that have gone into legend, but also to the indirect, ambiguous method of setting out the details of his life – entirely in keeping, incidentally, with the allusion-based method of storytelling about Russian history that has taken shape over the last quarter of a century. I therefore deem it necessary and, at the same time, possible for me to warn those reading this book that they should not look for any allusions in it, should not try to read between the lines. The author of this book has attempted to express in direct terms what she wanted to say to her reader.

The same goes for the testimony given by contemporaries about particular character traits or convictions that the writer had at various stages of his life – regardless of whether or not they appeal to the author of this book or its readers – and indeed to everything else in it. Wherever it was not possible to achieve the clarity required to make confident assertions about the writer's attitude to particular problems, this lack of clarity was left in place, rather than being artificially removed by the biographer.

There is no place in this book for invention, which carved out a large niche for itself in narratives about the writer's life long ago. The author of this book is of the opinion that narratives in the intermediary genre, constructed along the same lines as *The Lives of Remarkable People* (*Zhizn' Zamechatel'nykh Lyudey*), in a halfway-house between "belles-lettres" and science, have in no small measure exhausted their capabilities. I considered it necessary to construct this biography on facts alone, clearly setting out the boundary between fact and theory, and striving even then to avoid hiding from the reader how great or how little a basis there was for said boundary. One can't get by without a little bit of guesswork of course, and one shouldn't try to: what matters is to refrain from presenting pure speculation as something that has already been proven or is self-evident.

The hero of this book is a man who not only gave thought to his posthumous biography, but also talked about it with his friends and loved ones, pondered over it out loud, and even prepared it; a man who put a fair amount of thought into the relationship between myth, fiction and fact in the biographies of historical figures. Y.S. Bulgakova loved to repeat something he had once said, to the effect that myths are always created around each person of distinction, but that each of them had their own special myth, unlike any of the others. The existence of these legends is an essential part of our culture, and anyone who tried to get rid of them would end up looking absurd.

Anyone who sets about the task of writing a biography, however, is obliged to take steps to verify their sources, so as to separate the myth from the reality.

Over the last twenty years, we have all come to know Bulgakov's biography far better than we did in the year in which his most important novel was published; but what do we know about his personality?

What sort of man was he? Fun-loving. Artistic. Brilliant. His day-to-day life, his home life, was not akin, in its outward characteristics, to the life of a strict ascetic who shuts himself off from the world – it was the inner meaning of this life that was ascetic.

As he fooled around and played games, he transposed elements of his everyday reality into the artistic worlds that he created. "Following the lady into the room, with an unsteady gait and wearing a sailor's cap, there came a young chap, seven years of age, with an extraordinarily supercilious physiognomy, which was smeared with soya chocolate..." (from *Black Snow: A Theatrical Novel*). The family laughed at that: it was an accurate portrayal of Yelena Sergeyevna's youngest son. "The eldest, little Zhenya, felt offended," she told me during one of our meetings in November 1969, "by the fact that Serezhka was in one of Mikhail Afanasievich's books, and he wasn't. 'You know what, Zhenya, we could rectify that,' Bulgakov replied in a serious voice, 'but it'll cost you! If I were to write, for example: *As Margarita sat on the bench, she saw a young man walk past*, and I write about you, then that'll cost three roubles. If I write: *a handsome young man walked past*, then that'll cost five roubles. And if I write: *what a good-looking fellow! thought Margarita*, then that will cost ten roubles!'"

What sort of man was he? Withdrawn. Shut-off from other people. Intolerant of displays of familiarity. He placed a high value on the concept of maintaining a certain distance in all interaction, and knew how to do so himself. He opened up – and even then, it seems, not a massive amount – only to a small circle of extremely close friends.

"... At times wary in life's more trifling matters, and torn apart by contradictions, he did not lose, in serious things or in moments of crisis, his self-control or the vital forces with which he bristled," P.S. Popov wrote in a first draft – never published – of his biography of the writer. "His sense of irony was unfailingly combined with a great deal of feeling, his witticisms hit the mark, and were at times waspish and trenchant, but they never jarred. It wasn't that he despised people, he hated only human arrogance, narrow-mindedness, monotony, humdrum mundane matters, careerism, insincerity and deceit, howsoever they were expressed: in actions, obsequiousness, words, even gestures. He was bold and unrelentingly direct in his views. As far as he was concerned, falsehoods could never become truth. He followed his chosen path courageously and selflessly."

The author of this book is deeply grateful to the loved ones, relatives, friends and contemporaries of Bulgakov to whom I spoke; it was only through my conversations with them that I was able, to some small extent at least, to get a sense of the personality of this man, who might have been one of our contemporaries, yet who, it appears, was never recorded on a single roll of film.

This personality could only emerge in the book (if indeed it has emerged) at the intersection between various pieces of information about it – and this is made clear in the way the narrative is structured.

The life and work – it is a phrase which seems to state a problem rather than offer a solution.

The author of this book opted instead to write a comprehensive *biography* – Bulgakov's creative output is only mentioned to the extent that it proved possible to perceive it and trace its connections, manifested to a greater or lesser extent, to the facts of his biography.

CHAPTER ONE

The Kiev Years: the Family; Grammar School and University.

The War. Medicine.

Revolution.

1

Bulgakov's mother and father both hailed from the Oryol Governorate. "We were from a family of landowning clergymen," the writer's sister, Nadezhda Afanasievna Zemskaya, recalled, "our grandfathers on both sides were priests; one had had nine children, the other had had ten."

Their maternal grandfather, Mikhail Vasilievich Pokrovsky, the son of a deacon, was an archpriest, the abbot of a cathedral in the town of Karachev, in the Oryol Governorate. In a photograph taken in the 1880s, we see him turning a frank, open gaze to the camera. He has a youthful face, as does his wife Anfisa Ivanovna (née Turbina). In the photo she is seated, as is her husband, but even so one can see that she was an impressive woman, her hair tied back in a ponytail. All nine children are there in the photograph too: the eldest son Vasily, a student at the Military and Surgical Academy in St Petersburg, who died young; the eldest daughter Olga is seen standing, her arm on her brother's shoulder; Ivan and Zakhar, who were of secondary school age, are there. Also there is a boy aged nine – this is Nikolai Mikhailovich Pokrovsky, who went on to achieve fame as a doctor in Moscow; Bulgakov was close to this uncle for many years and later made him the hero of one of his stories… And beside him is Mikhail, younger still – he too went on to become a doctor, and his face appears in plenty of photographs of the Bulgakov family in Kiev; and little Mitrofan, who became a statistician. The nanny is there, holding Alexandra, whose married name in later life was Barkhatova, and beside her is a twelve-year-old girl with a very serious look on her face: this is Bulgakov's mother.

His paternal grandfather, Ivan Avraamovich Bulgakov, was a village priest for many years, and by the time his grandson Mikhail was born, he was the priest at the Sergiev Cemetery Church in Oryol. His wife, Olympiada Ferapontovna, became Mikhail Bulgakov's godmother.

The writer's father, Afanasy Ivanovich Bulgakov, was born on 17th April, 1859, and initially studied at the Oryol Spiritual Seminary, then at the Kiev Spiritual Academy (1881-1885); he then spent two years teaching – he taught Greek at the Novocherkassk spiritual college. In the autumn of 1887 he became the dean of the Kiev Spiritual Academy, initially in the department of ancient civil history, then, just over a year later, in the department of the history and study of Western teachings; from 1890 to 1892 he also taught at the Institute for Noble Maidens, and in the fall of 1893 he took up a position as an independent censor in Kiev: he censored books written in French, English and German. In 1890, A.I. Bulgakov married a young teacher from the progymnasium in Karachev, Varvara Mikhailovna Pokrovskaya. On 3rd May, 1891, their first child was born. At his christening, which took place on 18th May at the Kiev-Podol Church of the Exaltation of the Holy Cross – you can still see the church today if, as you descend the hill leading to Podol, you turn off into Vozdvizhenskaya Street – he was given the name Mikhail, probably in honour of the protector of the city of Kiev, the archangel Mikhail. Evidence for this is provided by the fact that the Bulgakovs celebrated his name day not on one of the saints' days nearer the start of May (such as May 7th (20th in the old style) – the birthday of Mikhail Ulumbysky), but on November 8th (21st in the old style), the day of the archangel Mikhail.

Mikhail did not have time to make his mark as an only child; instead, he immediately became an older brother: before he had turned three, he already had two sisters – Vera was born in 1892 and Nadezhda in 1893. In 1895, a third sister was born – Varya. Then, in October 1898, Nikolka appeared. And, in the year when Mikhail started attending pre-school classes (1900), Vanya was born.

That summer, his parents began building a dacha. Nadezhda Afanasievna Zemskaya told me a story passed down by her parents in 1969: "When my parents got married, they were unsure for a long time what to do with mother's dowry – whether to buy a house in Kiev (perhaps in Lukyanivka) or a dacha." In 1899 or 1900, two *desyatinas* of woodland were purchased – in Bucha, 29 versts from Kiev along the road leading to the South-West. They decided to build a house there – "renting for a family that size was both expensive and difficult…" In that first summer, in 1900, they travelled out to the dacha across Puscha-Vodytsia: they would get off at the last tram stop, then cover the rest of the ground on horseback or on foot. The following year, a railroad going in that direction was built; the next station after Bucha was Vorzel. The distance from the station to the dacha was about two versts… They built a single-storey house with 5 rooms, with a large store-room and two verandas. They had a lot of crockery, which they left there over the winter, opting not to take it back with them to the city. In the summer, the father of the household would arrive from the Academy, take off his tunic, put on a Russian-style caftan and a straw hat and go out to pull out stumps on the plot of land, which was marked out by a fence and an orchard – they only planted good varieties of apple trees, and plum trees; they did not plant many pear trees… There was a jetty on the lake, with a windmill beside it, and four Ukrainian brothers lived near them. They were millers. Their farmstead was duly known as *Melniki* (Millers); it was approximately one verst from Bucha. People used to go there to bathe – going on day-trips "to the Millers'…"

In Bulgakov's memories of his childhood – those memories which go all the way down to the root of a person's identity, and which are more than memories, and instead form some sort of indivisible nucleus of this identity – the roomy dacha in Bucha lived on, where they were never cramped, there was plenty of room for everyone, and where the prevailing atmosphere was one of familial and amicable unity and harmony; they also remembered the luxuriant Ukrainian forest, bathed in sunlight. (Might it not be on account of this that he was never able to love life at the dacha outside Moscow? The green spaces there probably seemed dusty by comparison, and all forms of housing felt cramped and unpleasant.)

On August 18th, 1900, the nine-year-old Mikhail was enrolled in the preparatory class at the Second grammar school; the singing teacher and choirmaster at this school was his father's younger (by 14 years) brother, Sergei Ivanovich Bulgakov, the godfather of Mikhail's younger brother Nikolai.

Eighty years later, in the fall of 1980, I had the good fortune of being able to get to know and chat to someone who was a fellow-pupil of Bulgakov's, Yevgeny Borisovich Bukreyev. (A cardiologist who treated several generations of Kiev citizens, his name is well-known in the city, as is that of his father, a professor of mathematics named Boris Yakovlevich Bukreyev, who lived to the age of 104 and was still giving lectures at the university when he was a hundred years old.) Short in stature and dressed with an old-fashioned attention to detail, and with the serious facial expression of a practising doctor, Yevgeny Borisovich began the conversation in some doubt.

"I don't know how I can be of use to you. I wasn't one of Bulgakov's friends – neither at the First grammar school, nor at university. We studied in the same department, but he gave up medicine, as you know," the elderly doctor said, with a barely detectable hint of disapproval.

"He practised for a while though…"

"Yes, he was a syphilologist, but I wasn't interested in that at all. He and I didn't have any contact with one another at all, either at university or later…"

My interlocutor's very manner of speaking was already restoring the link to that distant era, although he kept on repeating insistently: "To convey the atmosphere of that bygone age is impossible, really."

The only year in which Bulgakov and Bukreyev were close was in the preparatory class at the Second grammar school. The elderly doctor's memory of that time is a unique source, and as a result the merest trifles acquire a special value.

"Did we make friends? Yes, we were acquaintances – we would get up to mischief together. He used to tease me: *Bukreshka-tereshka-oreshka* he would call me… for some reason that's what he called me. He was an incredible tease, he came up with nicknames for everyone. In the preparatory class we had a teacher called Yaroslav Stepanovich, and we called him 'Viroslav' to his face. He had tuberculosis, that's right: he was tall and thin, and used to cough a lot. At the time no-one thought anything of it – they let him teach at the school even though he had open tuberculosis. The drawing teacher was Boris Yakovlevich. We called him Barbos Yakovlevich. Anyone who had ugly handwriting or was bad at drawing he would call Maralo Maralovich…!"

Thus, from out of the complete darkness in which that year, for us, is shrouded – the year in which little Misha Bulgakov, his backpack on his shoulders, ran off each morning to the Second grammar school ("Did anyone take him to school? Did you ever see his family, or a servant?" – "No, I never saw them. We all walked to school on our own,"), sounds of some kind start to make themselves heard, and particular phrases and little words gradually become discernable.

One of Bulgakov's peers, Ilya Ehrenburg, who was also born in Kiev, but who spent his childhood in Moscow, only visiting Kiev occasionally, recalled of the city: "There were some enormous gardens in Kiev, with chestnut trees growing in them; for a young boy from Moscow, they were as exotic as palm trees." For a little boy who had lived in Kiev ever since he was born, the chestnut trees were as familiar as poplar trees would have been to a boy from

Moscow; for Bulgakov, one can only imagine, their absence in the cities in which he was required to live must have felt like an empty space.

There was the Chernukha stationer's store on Khreshchatyk ("they used to sell school exercise books there, with brilliant, colourful covers; in books like that, even tough math questions used to look more fun"), and the Balabukha confectionery store, where you could get dried jam ("there was some candy that looked like a rose in a box, it smelled of perfume"). "The people walking past in the streets would be smiling. In the summer-time, people used to sit outside the cafes on Kreshchatyk," Ehrenburg recalled, "with their coffee or ice cream." The city looked like this right up until the outbreak of war, and perhaps even after it – it was described in very similar terms by Bulgakov's first wife, Tatiana Nikolayevna, in one of the conversations we had: "Kiev in those days was a happy city, with cafés outside in the streets, outdoor seating, with lots of people…"

… Bulgakov would later recall the happy, contented faces of the people of Kiev in the first decade of the century; he never could get used to the frowning, beleaguered crowds of Moscow in the twenties and early thirties, and, as he started work on his play about the future, *Bliss* (*Blazhenstvo*), he wanted to convey this feeling, in some lines written down for the play's heroine but not included in the final version of the text: "… Your eyes reassure me. I am struck by the look on the faces of the people here. They seem so serene. *Rodomanov.* Did the people really have a different look on their faces back then? *Maria.* Oh, but of course. They are so radically different from your people… The look in their eyes is horrible."

On August 22nd, 1901, Mikhail Bulgakov was enrolled in the first year at the First grammar school, housed in a beautiful building on Bibikovsky Boulevard, later described in *The White Guard* (*Belaya Gvardiya*) (the building still looks exactly as it did then today). The young Bulgakov's luck was in: as time passed, he was rewarded for the hard work he had put into his studies. As he looked back on this, Y.B. Bukreyev, who enrolled at the very same school in the same year, but in a different department (in today's parlance it might be described as a "parallel set"), wrote to me on November 4th, 1980: "Before I answer the questions you have put to me, allow me to paint a picture of some of the more general changes which took place in the life of a middle school in around 1900. In the nineties, the powers that be decided to make a host of changes in the Ministry of national enlightenment, and the man appointed as minister for this department was General Vannovsky, who proposed that the institutions responsible for education should act as a custodian and demonstrate a 'tender' attitude towards the schoolchildren, and also that they should increase the standard of education by recruiting teachers with better qualifications, such as university professors."

His memory of the 1900s was not letting him down. In the middle of the previous year, the minister of enlightenment, N.P. Bogolepov, had indeed died as a result of a wound inflicted on him on February 14th, 1901 by a student from Kiev named Karpovich. Bogolepov had brutally put down some student uprisings (shortly before he was assassinated, 183 Kiev students had been handed over to the soldiers).

Y.B. Bukreyev quite rightly recalled that "in Kiev, the First grammar school was selected for this kind of experiment, and from 1900 onwards, professors from the Kiev polytechnic institute and university were invited to teach there. Natural science, for example (an entirely new subject which had never been taught before at a middle school) was taught by Professor Dobrovlyansky, who had taught at the Polytechnic Institute. G.I. Chelpanov taught psychology and logic in the seventh and eighth grades [Chelpanov had been head of the department of psychology and logic at Kiev University from 1902 to 1906, and later founded the Moscow Psychological Institute, of which he became the director. – *M.C.*]. His place was later taken by an associate professor from the university, Selikhanovich..." Thus, the standard of teaching on offer was what one would expect to see at a university; it is hard to overstate just how significant this proved to be in the pupils' later lives.

Bulgakov was in the second department and Bukreyev was in the first, hence they had different teachers, but the singing teacher and class supervisor was the same for both groups: Platon Grigorievich Kozhich. "Kozhich, 'Platosha', was the choirmaster for the church choir," Bukreyev recalls; "a very dear and respectable man..." This man was at least the second choirmaster in young Misha's life (if we include his uncle, Sergei Ivanovich). One can imagine how the young boy would have heard the word being spoken at home and oft repeated, before it came to be personified first in the one man, then in the other – so that eventually, many years later, there would emerge, "moulding himself out of the greasy sultriness," the character who would say to Berlioz, at that fateful barrier: "'This way, please! Straight ahead, sir. Any chance of a small tip for showing you the way? ...I'm a church choirmaster out of work, you see...could do with a helping hand, sir...' – and, bending double, the bizarre character pulled off his jockey cap with a sweeping gesture."

Let's hear a little more from Yevgeny Bukreyev, though: "The Latin teacher was Suboch; we used to sing to him:

'Vladimir Faddevich, Let's have a drink, let's have a drink!'

This was because he always used to say to us all: 'Don't you ever touch the stuff!'

After the revolution, when Latin became surplus to requirements, he quickly retrained and taught arithmetic.

At the grammar schools there was the institution of class supervisors. These were people who were fully grown but of limited intelligence. One of them – he was approaching sixty and had a head like an egg… he was called Lukyan or Lukyanovich, something like that – was a good bloke, as we used to say: he never gave us timed assignments and was generally very liberal in his attitude towards us. For some reason Misha called him the Stallion." The man in question was no doubt Yakov Pavlovich Lukianov, who served as class supervisor from 1876 to 1910 (and perhaps later as well!); in a photo of the school's teaching staff taken in 1910, his "head, like an egg" can be seen.

Thus, the corridors of the First High School start to fill up for us with characters who, though they are phantoms, are nonetheless to some extent visible ("Selikhanovich spoke very badly, he had a lisp. He would always turn up for lessons wearing a crumpled, grubby tunic. His trousers were like bottles, and his hair was always tousled – carelessly combed…"), and elements of high school folklore start to make themselves heard, piece by piece.

"The most unpleasant of the lot at the school was the bulldog Maksim. One of the year-groups invited him out for a stroll and shoved him into the Dnieper. From that point onwards, they used to tease him all the time: 'Esteemed Maksim, how cold is it in the Dnieper?' adding an obsequious 's' after the last word – an old-fashioned way of showing respect in Russian. Maksim loved to add an 's' after his words. Bulgakov loved doing so too: *vinovat-s* (sorry), *blagodaryu-s* (thank you) [As we shall see later, incidentally, Maksim was to play a noble role in the life of one of Bulgakov's brothers… – M.C.]

There was also a Swiss named Vasily, of athletic build, like a real warrior. On public holidays he would stand at the door of the school dressed in blue woollen livery with gold trim, wearing a tricorn hat and holding a cane."

Twenty years later, the "vast, four-storey building" of the school will appear in *The White Guard* in a completely different period – the winter of 1918, and Aleksei Turbin, leaning over the banister, will see below him a "little white-headed figure" on "tottering, sickly legs". "Turbin was gripped by an empty melancholy. Right then and there, beside the cold banister, a memory came back to him with exceptional clarity.

… A crowd of schoolchildren of all ages was rushing down this same corridor, gleefully. Stocky Maksim, the old bulldog, was hurriedly chivvying along two small figures dressed in black, at the head of the remarkable procession.

"So be it, so be it, so be it," he was muttering, "so be it, on the occasion of the joyful visit of Mr Trustee, Mr Inspector shall be able to take an admiring look at Mr Turbin and Mr Myshlayevsky. What a great pleasure this will be for him. What a truly wonderful pleasure, indeed!"

One can only assume that those last words were uttered in a spirit of the bitterest sarcasm. Only to a man with perverse tastes could the contemplation of Messrs. Turbin and Myshlayevsky bring any degree of pleasure, particularly at such a joyful time as the visit of the school trustee.

Mr Myshlayevsky, who was tightly gripped in Maksim's left hand, had a deep cut in his upper lip, and his left shirt-sleeve was hanging by a thread. Mr Turbin, whom Maksim was pulling along with his right hand, had lost his belt, and all of his buttons had come off, not only on his shirt but also on the fly of his pants, such that, in an utterly improper manner, Mr Turbin's body and underpants were in full view for all to see.

"Let us go, there's a good chap Maksim, old thing," Turbin and Myshlayevsky begged him, turning their bruised and bloody faces towards him with looks that were designed to placate him.

"Hooray! Drag him along the floor, the Venerable Max!" the excited schoolchildren behind them were shouting. "There's no law saying you can terrorise second-years and get away with it!"

Good God, good God! Back then there was sunshine, noise and clamour. And Maksim wasn't like he is today – white-haired, sorrowful and hungry. Maksim had a thick head of black hair with just a few grey strands here and there; he had iron bars for arms, and a medal the size of a carriage wheel pinned to his breast..."

The schoolyard fights described here live on in the memory of another former pupil at the First grammar school, too. "*The infestation* – that's what they used to call the younger schoolchildren. On one occasion we beat up two brothers from year eight. There were eighty of us... Even so, when one of the brothers made a move on us, we rushed to get out of the way. It was Mikhail who encouraged us to get into that fight. But Paustovsky [he attended the same school but was two years below Bulgakov – M.C.] wrote in his memoirs: 'Wherever Bulgakov cropped up, his class would always win.' This was an exaggeration," Yevgeny Bukreyev observes, displaying the scientist's regard for accuracy. "He would take part in the fights, but he wasn't anything special. There was a boy named Ipat, for instance, we called him 'Patka'; he was quite short, but he was incredibly strong. Everyone used to call for him when a fight broke out, they would shout: 'Patka, Patka!' – and he really did win every fight in which he was involved… But Bulgakov was ever-present as a participant in these fights.

We used to fight in the schoolyard, often organising ourselves as cavalry: the weaker boys would get on the shoulders of the stronger ones. One of the sons of a professor from the Spiritual Academy, Golubev, was always the *kon* 'horse', and was consequently given the nickname 'koninchen', one that stuck…"

After the fourth year, though, all of that began to take a back seat.

"When we made the transition from the fourth year at school to the fifth, we had to start living more of a public-spirited life, you might say. In the fourth year, for instance (i.e. at the age of 13-14), we were required to read Bekel and Drepper. In the fifth year, we started attending a wide range of discussion groups, on economics, philosophy, religion and theology. Bulgakov never joined any of them," my fellow academic asserts. In the fifth year of school, we started interacting with the sixth, seventh and eighth years. The discussion groups were open to all these year groups. There would usually be 5-8 people in each group. These were all extramural activities – we would meet up at someone's house, never at school. The groups were always led by teachers from the school. In Selikhanovich's group, they talked about literary and philosophical matters – in the fifth year, you had to study Vindelband's philosophy textbook, for example. Bulgakov didn't join that group, he was inactive in that regard… When we reached the fifth year, it so happened that it was the year 1905, and all that that year brought with it. We used to smash the windows, of course, and spray ink from the inkwells; Bulgakov took part in this – in the same way that he took part in every collective activity… Naturally, we thought it a great lark to barricade ourselves up in the classroom and not let the teachers come in to teach us! We also used to elect a public council for the school, consisting of 1 or 2 people from each class. I remember the council meetings being held in some strange apartment, with kids lying about on beds and smoking…fiery speeches were made – but it never went any further than that… Bulgakov never once attended a single council meeting, protest or assembly. For three or four weeks there was complete lawlessness at the school, utter chaos, and then everything settled down again. Thanks to the head-teacher, Y.A. Bessmertny, none of the pupils came to any harm."

(This is quite an achievement, let us point out in parentheses. Few and far between are the academic institutions which, at this time or indeed at any other period in Russia's history, could boast of such behaviour on the part of their head-teacher in relation to the pupils – and this was in spite of pressure from the more powerful organisations above.)[1]

Bessmertny's predecessor was a man named Posadsky-Dukhovskoy – "he had an extremely oily smile, and oily little eyes," according to Y.B. Bukreyev; he was a mathematician, and also wrote books on hygiene at school, compiling the anthologies *In Memory of Pushkin* (*Pamyati Pushkina*, in three volumes; Kiev) and *In Memory of Gogol* (*Pamyati Gogolya*, Kiev, 1902). Bessmertny, who taught the languages of antiquity at the school, "was an extremely precise man. He loved to use the words 'bedlam' and 'superficiality' when speaking of the public unrest. After 1905 he was replaced by Nemolodyshev, who, by some strange coincidence, was also a maths teacher. He was a rather gloomy man, built like a bear: broad-shouldered and with crooked legs. Misha called him *The Wolfhound*, and the nickname stuck; he was quite a brutal man." The new head-teacher, who had written academic courses and workbooks on geometry, was almost ten years older than his predecessor, who was transferred to a school in Saratov in August 1907.

Let us hear more from Bulgakov's fellow pupil and peer, a man who was radically different from him at that time on account of his beliefs – albeit beliefs that were those of a child, not yet fully-formed.

"In 1905, in the fifth year, I was a firm believer in anarchy," Bukreyev recounts, "(and I still am today, by the way). I had the best collection of books on anarchy in all Kiev, it had all of Kropotkin's works in it. Back then, in Kreshchatyk, not far from the corner of Fundukleevskaya Street and Kreshchatyk, there was an apartment on the first floor that belonged to the dentist Lourier, and the dining room had been leased to the anarchists – there was anarchist literature on all the tables, and the door was open to anyone who wanted to come and read it."

---

[1] The author wishes to acknowledge with gratitude, however, a comment made on this subject and on my treatment of it by someone who read the text of this book in journal form, the doctor of physical and mathematical sciences P. I. Pimenov: "This is a bad example, although the idea itself is accurate. The strikes and demonstrations at the grammar schools were so insistent, and involved such large numbers of participants, that the authorities was often grateful when the disorder ended, and had no intention of taking repressive measures, for fear of provoking a continuation of the rowdy behaviour. Evidence for this was provided by the book *Strikes at St. Petersburg's secondary schools* (*Zabastovki v Srednikh Uchebnykh Zavedeniyakh SPb*), by Al. Pilenko, written in 1906, and even including lines from Pasternak's poem *Childhood*: 'While we to the Greek answer back in rude tones, push our desks 'gainst the wall, play at parliament during our lessons and wander in dreams in the Georgians' prohibited zone.'" (10th November 1987, Syktyvkar. 1900)

What was the young schoolboy Bulgakov like at that time? We already know: he was someone who took part in all the fights and did *not* take part in any social assemblies or gatherings.

"You must understand," adds Bukreyev – a man of sound mind and blessed with a very clear memory – is that Bulgakov, in his schooldays, was an utterly uncompromising monarchist – a 'kvass monarchist'. That's right, that's what they used to say back then – not only was there the term 'kvass patriots', people also spoke of 'kvass monarchists'. (One recalls how frankly the protagonist of *The White Guard*, of whom the author was so fond, speaks of his convictions in 1918: "Unfortunately," Turbin suddenly burst out, tugging at his cheek, "I'm not a socialist, I'm... a monarchist. And to be quite honest I'd go so far as to say I can't bear the word 'socialist'. And of all the socialists, the one I hate the most is Alexander Fyodorovich Kerensky." And when those who write about Bulgakov comment on these words by saying: "It is important to point out that the protagonists' monarchism is not autobiographical. None of this can be associated in any way with the Bulgakov family," they are not adopting the position of a biographer, but rather displaying the enthusiasm of an admirer who wishes to say as many good things as possible about their favourite writer.)

Even at this stage, in their schooldays – and not only in the senior classes, but before then too, under the influence of a multitude of factors – their families, the circle of people they would encounter at home, the presence or absence of someone whose authority might supercede, in a teenager's eyes, the authority of their parents – differences of opinion took shape within these peers and fellow-countrymen which were to determine their worldviews and social behaviour for a long time to come. So what sort of views predominated at the First School – the one at which Bulgakov studied and where (not by coincidence) the future protagonist of his first novel will study?

"Out of forty schoolchildren in each class, there were usually twelve to fifteen who were given financial support: there were all manner of stipends and bursaries – state ones and private ones," Bukreyev recalled. "The ones given financial support, of course, were more of a democratic group... Generally speaking, the moulding of a person's character takes place in unique circumstances. It is impossible to recreate the circumstances surrounding this process. There is a vast number of small details, which remain unknowable. Yet it is these trifles that are the very stuff of life. Recreating the spirit of that time, getting closer to the circumstances in effect at the time, is therefore impossible. Bulgakov, for instance, tried to avoid Jews during his school years, but in that regard, one needs to take into account the circumstances of his upbringing, the family background. It is a very difficult thing to understand when one is so far removed from it in time... In our department there were six Jews for every forty pupils. The priests had varying attitudes towards them, some were more sensible than others... When the duty teacher reported: "Father, Ginsberg stayed behind for the scripture class," one of the teachers said: "What of it, let him listen, Christ preached for those of other faiths too." [One cannot help but draw attention to the slight historical inaccuracy in this remark, or rather, its somewhat modernized stylization; one thinks, among other things, of the famous words of St. Paul's Epistle to the Romans about preaching the gospel, "for the Jew first, and also for the Greek," 1,16; the phrase "those of other faiths" as we understand it today is not entirely applicable to the situation in the first few centuries of Christianity. – M.C.] As a rule, converts tended to be held in less regard than Jews.

Bukreyev tries hard to define and evaluate Bulgakov's mindset, as a teenager and adolescent, at a specific time, in a specific setting: within the walls of the First Grammar School.

"As far as Bulgakov's family was concerned, professorial circles were not generally deemed to be very well-to-do. Most monarchists were children from very wealthy families, usually landowning ones, or from the very bottom of urban society – with a hint of the 'black hundreds' about them. Bulgakov certainly didn't have that vulgar hue about him, of course, but generally speaking our school was known for its more liberal stance by comparison with the other institutions, and therefore there weren't too many who shared his views... All in all, the First School was a place where diametrically opposed views were concentrated. Pyatakov studied there, for example – he was a good deal older than us..."

(Leonid Leonidovich Pyatakov – three years older than Bulgakov and Bukreyev – was, like his brother Georgy, one of the leaders of the Soviets' struggle for power in Kiev, and was killed by the Haidamakas early in 1918.)

"At that time the Lelyavskys were studying with us – they were the children of a very wealthy family of Kiev landowners, and there were also some children of important civil servants studying with us, and the two Golubev brothers – the sons of an incredibly 'black hundred-esque' professor from the Spiritual Academy. Bulgakov did not, of course, associate with such avid black hundredists. It's fair to say that he held right-wing views, but they were of a more moderate order."

As one could infer from my conversations with Bukreyev, this stance was expressed mainly in a passive manner: in his dislike of all kinds of assemblies, speeches, public declarations of his views and ideas. When Aleksei Turbin says of the Hetman, many years later: "If he had begun forming the officer corps back in April, we would have taken Moscow by now... It was the perfect time to strike: after all, the people are so starved in Moscow that they're eating cats, so they say. He would have saved Russia, the son of a bitch," – let us take note of the responses to this from his audience, who knew him well: "You... you... you know something, you ought to be the minister of defence, not a doctor," Karas chimed in. He was smiling sarcastically, but he had liked Turbin's speech, it had ignited something within him.

"At the demonstrations, Aleksei's irreplaceable, a real orator," said Nikolka.

"Nikolka, as I've told you twice now already, you're no great wit," his elder brother broke in. From the sarcastic banter that ensues among his listeners, one gathers that Turbin is no great orator, and this role is not one to which he is accustomed. It was an equally unfamiliar role, it would appear, for the young Bulgakov. My interlocutor, at least, insists that this was the case, returning to this theme several times: "I'll say it again, he was utterly apolitical... He would take part in the arguments at the School, then sit in the classroom for two or three hours after lessons finished – he was just finishing off his work, like everyone else. He steered well clear of all forms of community life, though..."

... So, he was "to the right" of what was generally speaking the liberal majority of the schoolchildren... A boy in whom, apparently, one could detect something homely and familial – a restrained attitude towards people of other faiths, a conservativism that was only natural in the family of a teacher at the Spiritual Academy – in other words a peaceful acceptance of the existing order, a reluctance to rock the boat. This reluctance proved to be such a firm, dependable quality that more than two decades later – decades which were extremely turbulent – and in a reality that was, in essence, completely different from the one in which he spent his young years, Bulgakov himself would stubbornly identify, in a letter to the government which played a decisive role in determining his fate, an important characteristic of his creative work: "deep scepticism with regard to the revolutionary process taking place in my country which lags behind so, and the contrasting of this with the beloved and Great Evolution..."

When considering how the views of Bulgakov the teenager and adolescent aligned themselves, one must keep in mind not only the selective way in which he formed ties of friendship, which, as one would expect for the family of a teacher at the Spiritual Academy, came into being mainly among a group of people who shared the same faith as him. One must also be aware of the specific situation pertaining in Kiev in the early 20th century: there were people of various nationalities living in and around the city at that time, who not only lived in communities that were closed to outsiders, but also bore grudges against one another which had their roots in the distant past or the not-so-distant past. To give you an example: in 1903, the well-known Kiev theatre critic N.I. Nikolayev published an article on the centenary of the Kiev Theatre – and its sole focus was on the ups and downs of the battle between the theatre's Polish and Russian management in the first half of the century that had just ended. Inter-ethnic tension was extremely high during Bulgakov's younger years in Kiev: it prompted the different nationalities to draw up boundaries around themselves, to identify strongly with a particular ethnic community, often taking this process to a level which was almost painfully acute. This trait made Bulgakov's native city very different from many of the other regions and cities of Russia at the time, in which the diversity of the local populace was, for the most part, merely a fact of life and not a cause of tension. In Kiev, a person's nationality (taken together with their religious affiliation) was often a matter that came to the fore – for example, when the need arose for any kind of group action to be taken in the politico-social sphere. Describing the situation in Kiev in 1906, when preparations were being made for the elections to the Second Duma, V.V. Shulgin, who hailed from the same city as Bulgakov, wrote in his final book, *The Years. Memoirs of a Former Member of the State Duma* (*Gody. Vospominaniya Byvshego Chlena Gosudarstvennoy Dumy*), published in Moscow in 1979: "The biggest group were the peasants… The second largest group in terms of numbers were the Polish landowners, and the third – the Russian landowners. The fourth largest group were the city-dwellers, who were almost all Jews. The fifth largest group were the priests, who were of Russian nationality. Finally, there was a sixth group – Czechs and Germans, colonialists." Shulgin indicates that they were liable to become unified in various ways, including on the basis of their social status ("there might be a bloc of all the landowners forming a particular class regardless of nationality, i.e. a union of Russians and Poles. If the Jews from the city opted to ally itself to this group, then this bloc would have a majority," – this was in terms of the number of seats they would have in the Duma). It so happened, though, that "landowners, priests and peasants all spoke together," i.e., as Shulgin says in his commentary on these events, "the idea of national unity, which was supported by the church, won the day." All of this (including Shulgin's comments) is very typical of the prevailing atmosphere in Kiev from 1900 to 1910. At the time of the elections, Bulgakov was still legally a minor, but he probably followed them with interest, and later took an interest in the activity of the Second Duma and then the Third Duma, which, it was hoped, would restore peace. Perhaps at this point it would be appropriate, skipping forward a little, to observe that Bulgakov was not only aware of the Turkic roots of his surname, but that he also considered it essential to highlight these origins in his bloodline. There are at least two facts which provide evidence of this. One relates to the year 1929, and we shall look at it later, and the other concerns the year 1936, when the novel *Notes of a Dead Man* (*Zapiski Pokoynika*) was being written. Bulgakov gives the protagonist of this novel, who is clearly based on the author, the surname Maksudov, which has an even more "Tatar" ring to it than his own surname – although it originated from an Arabic name. Perhaps the writer carried this surname in his memory through two decades, from the time when he saw it as a youngster in the newspaper reports about the assemblies of the III Duma. At one of these assemblies, in January 1909, V.V. Shulgin talked about the death penalty. The Russian people, he said, "have an instinctive disgust for the death penalty and for the brutalities of the justice system in general." This phenomenon "is our national pride and our national solace, and it provides strong support for our faith, when we say that the lord and master in this vast empire must be the Russian people, because we believe that only the Russian people will be a meek and merciful master. (A hand shoots up on the right: S.N. Maksudov says, from his seat: "Who do you mean by the Russian people though?") Commenting on this episode after the event, the man who had said these words explained: "Satretdin Nazmutdinovich Maksudov, a pure-blooded Tatar by descent, an educated man, who graduated from the Paris Faculty of Law in 1906." What he probably meant was that the Russian people incorporated a fairly large number of "non-natives", including Tatars. It is not beyond the bounds of possibility, incidentally, that Bulgakov may have seen this name in print at a later time, as well, in Moscow – in the year when the first draft of his future novel was being written: in episode 12 of the magazine *Pechat' i Revolyutsiya* (*Print and Revolution*), for 1929, it was reported that the Communist Academy discussion group on literature, art and language would be focusing, the following year, on a report by one Maksudov "On the state of Marxist criticism in Tatarstan…"

The nationality with which one identifies is not an equally straightforward and natural affair in all places and at all times. In the city in which Bulgakov spent his youth, matters of ethnicity were intertwined with the socio-political situation, and matters of history and traditions, and one's faith, were intertwined with the day-to-day interests of the various classes in society and other interests. V.V. Shulgin, for example, when describing the peasants who lived in the environs of Kiev at that time, defined them as follows: "In terms of their nationality they were Russian, or, as they used to be called in those days, *malorossiyane* ('little Russians'); Ukrainians, to use the modern terminology." For him, the only thing that is important and significant is their ancient shared past – Kievan Rus; the processes of nation-building that have taken place latterly are not even taken into consideration, as if they do not exist. Such a selective perspective on history, particularly risky for anyone involved in politics, was often seen in the pre-revolutionary years among Kiev's Russian intelligentsia. Traces of it can also be seen in several pages of *The White Guard*, and this helps us to reconstruct, to a certain extent, the view that the young Bulgakov was likely to have had on issues of nationality. It is worth noting, however, that even within the Bulgakov family, the attitude he had at the time was not shared by everyone. At one of the meetings we had in 1969, whilst showing us some family photos, Nadezhda Afanasievna Zemskaya, the writer's sister, said: "That's M.F. Knipovich, my fiancé at the time. He was a confirmed Ukrainian, as they used to say in those days, in other words he was extremely sure of his nationality; I, too, was in favour of Ukraine having her own language. Mikhail was against Ukrainization, but, of course, welcomed Knipovich into his home as a family friend..." (A few years later, Nadezhda Afanasievna married a philologist and Russophile, Andrei Mikhailovich Zemsky.) Also of significance to a biographer is the fact that among those close to the family – particularly whilst the head of the family was still alive – was M.A. Bulgakov's godfather, N.I. Petrov, a professor at the Spiritual Academy who had written works on the history of Ukrainian literature in the 18th and 19th centuries. In his unpublished memoirs (kindly made available to me in 1977 by Y.P. Kudryavtseva), M.Y. Starokadomsky, who attended lectures at the Academy (he was enrolled there in 1910), tells us that "at the Kiev academy there was an unofficial Ukrainian circle, inspired by the ideas put forward by the Ukrainian national movement. Its members were among the most active of all the student groups. They attended the Ukrainian club 'Prosvita', went to watch Ukrainian plays, and at their meetings they gave presentations on historical and literary subjects and sang melodious Ukrainian songs as a choir. Through this circle I found myself in the home of the professor of history N.I. Petrov, a great expert on the history of Ukraine. On certain days (known as *zhurfiksy*, from the French *jours fixes*), a progressive group of professors would assemble at Petrov's home: Kudryavtsev, Rybinsky, Ekzemplyarsky, Zavitnevich..."

In the 1900s, there were those among the professors of St. Petersburg who felt that "the Kiev Academy, in terms of its fresh and progressive approach, is now our leading institution," – this was directly linked to the fact that "it is in the hands of such a man as Kudryavtsev, who, though he is not a member of the Board, has the said Board in the palm of his hand. I took fright when I learned of this opinion, which was becoming increasingly widely held," K.M. Ageyev, a correspondent of Kudryavtsev's, wrote to the latter in 1906. "I recalled Golubev's attacks against you..." The movement from within at the Academy, the clash of opinions, had only increased since the start of the century, it seems, and it is fair to suppose that A.I. Bulgakov took up a moderate position, in the middle ground – perhaps a reconciliatory one. It was this position, it appears, that V.l. Rybinsky, with all the caution required by the conventional language of the obituary, later strove to outline: "When, some years ago, a circle of spiritual and secular individuals came together in Kiev, with the aim of discussing church-related issues and explaining the principles behind the pressing matter of the church reforms, Afanasy Ivanovich was one of the most committed members of this circle and showed great ardour when taking part in its disputes." And he goes to the trouble of explaining that "the respected professor was a long way from the superficial liberalism which everyone is so quick to criticize and deny; but at the same time he was also an opponent of the immoderate conservatism which is not able to distinguish between the eternal and the temporary, between the letter and the spirit, and leads to stagnation in the life of the church and in all the church's forms." This kind of spiritual make-up and intellectual behaviour, which the son looked upon as a source of authority whilst his father was alive, was perhaps something that he contemplated even more deeply in later life.

After the revisions brought about at the Academy in 1908 by Archbishop Antony of Volynsk (who, among other things, described P.P. Kudryavtsev as the "Russian Voltaire"), after the response to the outcome of the revision written by the Academy's progressive wing, "The truth about the Kiev Spiritual Academy", the introduction of the new charter and the split which was already taking shape within the academic world between those on the "left" and those on the "right", the progressive winds continued to blow through the teaching departments as well, and, to an even greater extent, it would appear, at the *jours fixes* discussions held at people's homes. In his younger years, Bulgakov always had a clear opportunity to become closer to these movements – through his familial ties to N.I. Petrov, V.I. Ekzemplyarsky and V.Z. Zavitnevich at least – but as yet, no facts have come to light, which might allow us to assert that he took this opportunity. The author asked Tatiana Nikolayevna (Bulgakov's first wife), for example, whether he attended court during the Beilis trial (which occurred in 1913, by which time Bulgakov was a student). No, she replied confidently, he was not present at the trial, they merely walked past the courthouse as they went about their business, and when the verdict was announced they saw people embracing and kissing one another. Yevgeny Bukreyev says the same thing: "I'm sure he didn't go into the courtroom." Let us compare with this evidence the recollections of his daughter, P.P. Kudryavtseva: "My father fought actively and ardently against the judeophobe tendencies in pre-revolutionary Kiev. I remember the Beilis case, which caused such a stir in 1913. I was in the 6th class at school at the time, so I would have been 15 or 16. Mama decided to hold a party one Sunday, and invite some of the young people, our peers. It so happened that this was on the eve of Beilis's trial, the commencement of which had been announced. I remember how anxious papa was when he found out about the plans for a party the next day: 'How can that be,' he said to mama, 'Beilis is to face trial tomorrow, and you're going to be dancing and making merry?' Needless to say, the party was cancelled."

The idea that the great writer, at any time in his life, held left-wing views, was dismissed as naïve long ago. The biographies of Bulgakov's illustrious predecessors, the Russian writers of the 19th century, reveal that on many occasions it was a very different story (it would be even more naïve, incidentally, to conclude from this that anyone who tended towards disreputable prejudices was immediately afforded protection by the powers that be). Yet Bulgakov, by contrast, still seems utterly unable to earn the right, in our collective consciousness, to have his own biography, as opposed to someone else's. His contemporaries often tried to make his record seem worse, whilst his admirers today strive to "improve" it.

It is probably particularly difficult for the modern reader to understand (and therefore hard to accept) that keeping to one side of socio-political activity by no means meant that one was immediately at some pole that was diametrically opposed to it, and that one would get stuck at a specific, pre-determined point. If one were side-lined in that way, the spectrum of possibilities open to one was fairly wide, and one of them was the life of a private individual, who guarded his independence and at the same time did not attempt in any way to contrast his way of life with other ways of life, or to impose it upon those who lived and acted differently. The desire to contrast it only manifested itself at times of crisis, when such a way of life needed protecting. In later years, providing this protection became an impossible task.

2

Biographers of the great and the good are usually keen to answer the following question: did their subjects distinguish themselves at all during their childhood? Did their teachers and classmates have particularly high hopes for them? As for what Bulgakov's schoolteachers thought of him, it is unlikely we will ever find out: teachers rarely live long enough to witness the fame of their protégés, and when this fame is so late in coming, their chances of living to see it are even slimmer.

The subject's status among his peers tells us a considerable amount – not about their talent, but about their personality type.

What was Bulgakov like – or rather, what was he reputed to be like – during his school-years? Bukreyev tells us: "In the first few years of the school he was the biggest prankster of all. Later he didn't stand out from the crowd. There were no indications at all that he was fully-formed. If you take the Kozhich boys, for instance – in the year above us – they were fully-formed whilst still at school…" He was referring to the sons of P. Kozhich, V.P. Kozhich and I.P. Kozhich, who went on to become film directors.

"Did his literary career come as a shock to his former classmates?"

"A total shock! No-one would ever have said of him: 'That one's going to make something of himself!' – you know, the way people usually talk about schoolchildren who are known for their literary talents or other aptitudes. He didn't demonstrate any particular aptitude for anything at all…"

(One recalls something that was said by one of Gogol's contemporaries, S.V. Skala, who once accompanied him on a trip to St. Petersburg when he was nineteen: "In those days we couldn't see anything special in him at all.")

The centre of his life was not at school, nor in any of the interest circles, but among his family and at the homes of his close friends. His school leaving certificate, issued on 8th June 1909, testifies to the fact that, "with his behaviour being outstanding", Bulgakov, the son of a state councillor, had acquired outstanding knowledge in only two subjects – divinity and geography; in all the other subjects his results were either good or satisfactory.

Mikhail Bulgakov's home life at the point when he finished school, however, was completely different from what it was when his schooling began.

In 1906, his father fell ill. "As early as in the spring of 1906," the author of his obituary would later write, "Afanasy Ivanovich began to feel a suspicious ailment of some kind. During the course of the year, the illness, to which the deceased initially attached no importance, grew stronger, and by the start of that academic year it was manifesting itself dramatically in the loss of his eyesight and a general intense weakening of his organism. Doctors' examinations soon established that Afanasy Ivanovich had suffered a severe chronic disease of the kidneys. An energetic course of treatment began. All the efforts of the doctors in Kiev, however, and later of the doctors in Moscow, to destroy the disease were fruitless. The illness progressed so rapidly that it was already plain for all to see that the sad end was nigh." Many years later, fate would force Bulgakov to relive every aspect of the rapid onset of his father's illness...

The last photos ever taken of Afanasy Ivanovich, that summer in Bucha, have survived to this day: they show him surrounded by all his children, and with the youngest of the lot – four-year-old Lyolya, the only one of the children who resembled their father, having inherited his dark hair colour and oval face.

Afanasy Ivanovich's last daughter was born in 1902, and she was delivered by the wife of his younger brother Sergei Ivanovich, who was a midwife by profession. That same year, Sergei Ivanovich passed away, aged just twenty-nine. This was evidently the first time that the eleven-year-old Mikhail had experienced the loss of a close relative. Afanasy Ivanovich considered himself duty-bound to invite the widow of Mikhail's brother, Irina Lukinichna, to live in his household. Throughout all the subsequent years, she lived in the Bulgakovs' house, spending most of her time looking after Lyolya, who was her special favourite.

In 1906, they rented the house at No. 13, Andreyevsky Hill, which was destined to become the family's refuge for many years and the model for the place where the action unfolds in the novel *The White Guard*.

Some difficult years began for the family in the autumn and winter of 1906-1907. Mikhail and his elder sisters, Vera and Nadya, knew that their father was dying. "They cured him of a disease of the eyes, but that had only been a consequence of his other illness," Nadezhda Afanasievna told me. "Father became very thin. When he could no longer read without help, I read him articles written in Czech, and he was unhappy with my pronunciation. He knew Latin, Greek, French and the West Slavic languages perfectly (he could also read German and English – he used to look through the books in these languages which had been 'sent to the censors', as they already used to say even then)…" It seems that Afanasy Ivanovich knew some of these languages rather well, and others less well, but this vivid example stayed in Bulgakov's memory forever, and was echoed many years later in a reply made by the Master to Ivan, which is imbued with the author's pride on behalf of his protagonist – almost childlike in its simplicity: "I speak five languages, in addition to my native tongue," the guest replied, "English, French, German, Latin and Greek. Oh, and I can read a little Italian, too," and even more so in Ivan's response: "'Well I never!' Ivan whispered enviously."

On 11th December 1906, Afanasy Ivanovich was awarded the degree of doctor of theology by the board of the Spiritual Academy. The board also launched a petition before the synod, as the obituary tells us, "to award Afanasy Ivanovich with the title of ordinal professor, with the allowance attached thereto. On 8th February 1907, the Holy synod upheld the petition. Afanasy Ivanovich had high hopes of being granted the traineeship."

Sure enough, A.I. Bulgakov's service at the Academy brought him 1200 roubles a year, and he made the same amount as a censor. The constant necessity to do additional work to supplement his salary, which clearly tormented him and, by a cruel twist of fate, only fell away in the final month of his life, seems to have lived long in Bulgakov's memory; this may have deepened his irritation with a similar necessity in his own life, which arose in the early twenties and did not go away until he died.

"On 9 March, Afanasy Ivanovich handed in his notice on account of his illness," the obituary went on. "On 11 March he took the last rites and, with great reverence, underwent the Sacrament of Extreme Unction. On 14 March, at around ten in the morning, Afanasy Ivanovich passed away… That same day, at 4 in the afternoon, a funeral service was held beside the coffin of the deceased, with professors and students from the Academy in attendance. On 15th March the coffin was moved to the Holy Spiritual Church of the Brotherhood monastery, and on 16th, the burial service took place at the great Brotherhood church. In his funeral address, one of A.I. Bulgakov's peers, D.I. Bogdashevsky, recalled the final days of his life: "You and I had a chat about various aspects of modern life. Your gaze was so clear, peaceful and at the same time so deep, as though you were testing me. 'How good it would be,' you said, 'if everything were at peace! How good it would be! Peace must be encouraged in every possible way.' And now, the Lord has sent absolute peace to you… 'Let me go,' – that was the last word you spoke before you died, to your wife, who loves you so ardently and who is so ardently loved by you.

'Let me go!' And you left this world! You could have said: 'Now lettest thou thy servant depart, O Lord, According to thy word, in peace' (Luke chapter II, verse 29)." A little over thirty years later, the dying man's last words would be echoed in the last chapter of his son's final novel: "'Let him go,' Margarita suddenly cried out in a piercing voice."

Thus, in March 1907, Mikhail, who had not yet turned sixteen, became the eldest son in a family that was now left without a father.

His grandmother Anfisa Ivanovna, who had been widowed long ago and used to travel from Karachev each summer to visit the Bulgakovs at their dacha, said to him: "Misha, you're a grown-up already, it's time you addressed your mother more formally." Thenceforward, he always used the formal form of the personal pronoun, *vy*, when speaking to his mother.

The Academy made sure that the biggest possible pension was secured – and the family received a stipend that was more than what Afanasy Ivanovich had been able to earn doing two jobs.

The family of the late professor was assisted by his former colleagues, including Vasily Ilyich Ekzemplyarsky, a professor of moral theology; along with A.I. Bulgakov, he was an active member of the Vladimir Soloviev Religious and philosophical society (the society's chairman was P.P. Kudryavtsev), and in 1916 became the founder of the journal *Khristianskaya Mysl'* (*Christian Thought*).

If you were to walk down the slope from the Bulgakovs' house towards the church of St. Nicholas the Good, which in those years stood intact, you would find a street called Borichev Tok on the left. On the right side of the street, in a building made in a rather unusual architectural style, with two and a half floors, the professor lived out the rest of his days. In the autumn of 1980, Father Alexander's wife, Tatiana Pavlovna Glagoleva, who was 75 at the time and was already fatally ill – once upon a time, before the revolution, she used to call on Ekzemplyarsky together with Lyolya Bulgakova, who was the same age as her, and lead him outside by the hand to go for walks – told me with a conviction I can't describe: "He was the most intelligent and most remarkable man I ever met in my life." And she showed me the vast collection he had accumulated, which I had heard about from some Kiev-based admirers of Bulgakov's work, N. Elshanskaya and M.L. Kondratieva, back in April 1975; they had heard about it from the priest Father Georgy, Ekzemplyarsky's pupil.

It was a collection of photographic reproductions of images of Christ. An accomplished photographer (all the best photos of the Bulgakov family were taken by him), V.I. Ekzemplyarsky took these photographs with a specific aim in mind. "He had set himself a goal: to write a work called 'The Face of Christ in representations'," Tatiana Pavlovna told me.

These photographs were mostly in the same format, with the majority brown in colour and stuck onto a grey mounting. On the reverse side, Ekzemplyarsky noted the name of the artist and the title of the painting or engraving with a blue pencil and gave each one a serial number. Judging by some of these numbers, the collection contained more than ten thousand works... Lyolya Bulgakov later helped the professor to sort the collection out, after he began to lose his eyesight, but her elder brother would doubtless have seen it too – far earlier and, one might imagine, on several occasions. The impressions left on him in his boyhood and adolescence by the sight of such an array of images depicting scenes from the gospels may well have stayed in the writer's visual memory and influenced some of his future plots – along with the paintings on the walls of the cathedrals in Kiev and the panorama of 'Golgotha' on the Saint Vladimir Hill.

In the summer, they went out to the dacha as usual. Nadezhda Afanasievna told us that the usual people turned up – Kornei Lukyanovich Streltsov, his wife Avdotya Ivanovna. (In 1923 Bulgakov recalls this surname, giving it to a character in the story *A Raid* [*Nalyot*]). In winter he worked as a stoker at the Religious and philosophical society, and in summer – as the caretaker at the Bulgakovs' dacha; his wife was their chef. Kornei set up a bathing hut in the garden, and water was transported there from the well. "Go and wash at once, boys, Vera wants to use the bathing hut," the sisters would shout. Their eldest sister was a real slowcoach.

The Bulgakovs would be joined on the journey to the dacha by Irina Lukinichna, an elderly woman who lived in their house – the servants called her 'the black countess': unlike Varvara Mikhailovna, she was a brunette. The children's grandmother Anfisa Ivanovna stayed at the dacha every summer. (She died in 1910, in Moscow, at the house of her son – the doctor Nikolai Pokrovsky.) According to Nadezhda Afanasievna, she was "not very literate, but curious, with a lively wit. She suddenly took up reading Dostoevsky and spent all her time reading. When I asked her about it, she said: "Nadechka, you must realise, I haven't much time left to live – I can't die without ever knowing such a writer!"

They would also be joined by Afanasy's nephews, Konstantin and Nikolai, the children of his brother Petr; Petr was a priest in the Russian mission in Japan (in Tokyo), and the nephews lived with the Bulgakovs permanently. When their only daughter died of meningitis in Tokyo in 1915, after a short bout of scarlet fever, Petr's wife, as Nadezhda Afanasievna tells it, came to visit and said to her mother: "Please give me Lyolochka! You've got seven, and we haven't got anyone now." This issue caused a great deal of anxiety. They didn't give away any of my brothers and sisters." In Bucha, just as in the city, the Bulgakovs also had Illariya living with them – Lilya – the daughter of Afanasy's brother Mikhail, who lived in the city of Kholm in the Lyublinsk governorate; he taught at the seminary there. In 1909, Varvara's youngest sister Alexandra Barkhatova (née Pokrovskaya) arrived from Karachev for the summer with seven-year-old Alexei and four-year-old Alexandra; they came again in 1912. More than half a century later, Alexandra Andreyevna Tkachenko (née Barkhatova), the writer's cousin, would recall this abundance of people before all else, along with the general sense of merriment and happy kindliness.

It stands to reason that the more all of this faded away irretrievably into the past, the more, through the contrast between it and his new life, it loomed large in the writer's memory in later years.

By 16 August in the old style – when lessons would begin again at the grammar school – the family would return to the city. The elder children would linger a little longer, travelling directly to the school by train.

Bulgakov's friends in his grammar school years were Platon and Sasha Gdeshinsky, the youngest of the five sons of Pyotr Gdeshinsky, an assistant librarian at the Spiritual Academy. This family was very close to the Bulgakovs and is therefore worthy of closer inspection. The eldest sons (from Pyotr's first marriage), Polikarp and Nikolai, had already been ordained by this time and worked as priests outside Kiev.

A Kiev citizen named S.A. Kasyanyuk passed on to me, on 15 October 1987, some accounts about Bulgakov in his boyhood that he had obtained from a relative, Nina Polikarpovna Gdeshinskaya, whose married name was Moshkovskaya (1900-1986). When an excerpt from *The Master and Margarita* was read aloud to her in the mid-'60s, she supposedly guessed that it was by Bulgakov, without having known beforehand. The eldest of the four daughters (Nina, Zina, Lida and Natalya) of Polikarp Petrovich (born in 1876), she and her sisters used to spend time at the Bulgakovs' house, it transpired, on Sunday afternoons: "Mishka loved playing with us. He would joke and play around. He would start off by saying: 'Let's go on an evac.' The plan for the evacuation would set everyone's imagination going. And then we start coming up with ideas about where we would go, and how we would get there.

He loved all kinds of silly nonsense. Spiritual séances, for example. He would tell all sorts of tall stories…" As my correspondent rightly wrote,

"Deep knowledge of 'nonsense' and the playing-out of it in the years 1910-1915 by M. Bulgakov, and the 'maturing' of this theme, thereafter, have long been known to have been key themes in the writer's biography.

His sister Sonya (born in 1898), whose memoirs I shall quote from, went on, according to Alexander Gdeshinsky's widow, to become "a most fearful atheist. When she taught in the village (from 1916 onwards), she would give lectures on atheism and say: 'Even if I couldn't convince them altogether, I felt it was important to plant a seed of doubt.' His sister Katya, who was a good deal older than her, was the same. And their elder brother Grisha suffered greatly from this and even came to visit his sisters from Odessa, where he worked as a priest, to try to change their minds. But Sonya said to me: 'Please tell him that I don't believe in these fairy-tales, and that I am to be left in peace.'"

Pyotr Gdeshinsky's younger sons, meanwhile, were studying at the spiritual seminary. They were not required to study there for long, however. "Misha often made fun of their calling at the seminary," one of the sisters, Sofya Petrushevskaya, recalled in a letter to Larisa Gdeshinskaya sent on 10th December 1971. "He once went to see them on his new bicycle. Sasha and Tonya started learning to ride the bike too, and when it transpired that they weren't very good, Misha got on the bicycle, did all sorts of crazy zigzagging movements and asserted that only seminary boys could ride like that." "He was an incredible tease," (Y. Bukreyev)... Even in his boyhood pranks – there was that passion for being a 'showman', for theatricality, which was to stay with him throughout his life and penetrate the atmosphere in their home (we will look at further episodes like this later), and his literature. And these zigzag movements on the bike would go on to be depicted in his novels on at least two occasions: "Patrikeyev perched himself on the contraption, [...] touched the pedals and rode hesitantly around the armchair, squinting with one eye at the prompt-box in fear of collapsing onto it, and with the other eye at the actress. [...] Patrikeyev set off again, this time squinting at the actress with both eyes, but was unable to turn around and had to ride off into the wings." (*A Theatrical Novel*). This was, so to speak, a recollection about "how seminary boys ride bicycles" – in stark contrast to the showy, virtuoso way in which he evidently strove to ride a bike himself as a boy, and it is in memory of his own efforts that, in *The Master and Margarita*, a little man rides out onto the Variety stage on an ordinary two-wheeled bicycle. "After a few rounds on the back wheel alone, the man stood on his head, unscrewed the front wheel and threw it into the wings. He then carried on with one wheel, turning the pedals with his hands..."

Their other sister, Katya, wrote to Larisa Gdeshinskaya on November 22, 1971: "Misha's influence on my brothers was seen above all in the fact that my brothers, who were studying at the seminary then, started preparing to enrol at the institute." Larisa Gdeshinskaya had heard this news from her husband: "Sasha said that it was thanks to Misha's influence that they took the secular route – the 'open house' evenings at the Bulgakovs' house, with much playing of music, had had quite an effect on them. He led them, so to speak, to the secular life – forced them to love all of that. And I think he used to try to persuade them to leave the seminary – although doing so was difficult, as you already had to pay to study at all the other universities by then." The brothers left the seminary, one after the other, in the fourth year – initially without telling their father, and, it appears, began working so that they could pay for their own education.

Lyubov Skabalanovich, the daughter of Professor Skabalanovich, told me on 10 October 1987: "My father was very far removed from politics. When an audit was held at the Academy, the archibishop said: 'They all ought to be banished, with the exception of Skabalanovich. He is devoted to religion, body and soul.' When my father was transferred from Mariupol to Kiev in 1906, he took charge of the department of theology. We lived in Podol, near the Academy, in an old, three-storey apartment block that was once a university building, in a huge apartment with nine rooms that had formerly housed the rector… Dr Ivan Pavlovich Voskresensky, who had treated A.I. Bulgakov that year, came by to see us. He arrived so late in the day that my mother had to wake me up so that he could examine me; he said to me: 'Forgive me, Lyubochka, for coming so late – I was at the Bulgakovs'.' The time soon came for me to join the preparatory class, at the famous German grammar school in Luteranskaya Street, next to the German Protestant church, and I saw the Bulgakov girls, whose time at the grammar school ended in the same year that I enrolled there. Lyolya, the youngest, came to see my sisters – that was how I got to know her, she used to come and visit. An assistant librarian from the Academy lived in our building. One of his daughters, Sonya, was two or three years older than me, but I wasn't really allowed to go and see her. My mother thought her to be very spoilt. An assistant librarian was considered to be unsuitable company." "How did she come to be seen as 'spoilt'?" I asked. "Well, she didn't listen to her parents, and was rude… After the revolution, her mother, a simple, kindly woman, said: 'I am old now, I shall die soon, I don't know where to go. I can't live with Sonya, for there I shall be given a dog's funeral, without any proper burial service.' The Gdeshinskys were not a very well-read family, of low intelligence. But the Bulgakov girls had read more widely. There was one time when I was at their place (I wasn't allowed to go outside very often). I was about 10 years old at the time. And their brother came out; he was 20. He hardly spoke to us – just a little bit, for the sake of civility, we were a lot younger than him after all. I recall him as someone who was utterly shut-off and withdrawn. He was fairly chubby, not particularly thin – the Gdeshinskys were pretty thin by comparison. He had a very ordinary face, one that was utterly unremarkable. I glanced at him – merely for the sake of doing so, without any real interest…"

On the floor above the Skabalanovich family there lived the family of professor Kudryavtsev. "The Academic fellowship lived a very shut-off life… There were two girls in the Kudryavtsev household too." One of them, Yekaterina Petrovna, passed on to me her memories of those years from so long ago (the daughters of the teachers at the Academy all studied at the same school, one that had been founded by a group of German colonials in Lipki – an aristocratic neighbourhood; its full name was the women's grammar school at the Kiev evangelical society of St. Yekaterina): "A typical scene greeted my eyes: Nadya Bulgakova was walking along the hallway with the elder Frankel, and they were talking about philosophical subjects. We later lived in Borichevy Tok in the same building as professor Ekzemplyarsky. And I was sitting in the dining room in our building, and the maid announced that someone had arrived. It was Mikhail Afanasievich; he had come to fetch Lyolya, who had been playing with us – she was 10 at the time. I remember that as she gathered her things, the young man chatted to my mother. I remember something he said: 'I got married, you know.' And it seemed to me that he also said, 'today'.

… In the summer of 1908, a love affair came into being in the life of Mikhail Bulgakov.

That summer, a schoolgirl from Saratov named Tatiana Lappa moved to Kiev. She was the daughter of the director of the treasury chamber. Her grandmother lived in Kiev, along with a paternal aunt – Sofya Nikolayevna, who was friends with Varvara Bulgakova (it seems they met whilst attending the Frebelev society for pre-school teachers, which was formed that year in Kiev).

Almost seventy years later, Tatiana Nikolayevna, née Lappa, told me: "My aunt said: 'I'm going to introduce you to a boy. He'll show you Kiev.'

We were introduced to one another; we walked around together almost all the time; we went to the Kiev-Pecherskaya monastery together. Then we started writing to one another. I was supposed to go and see him that year at Christmas, but my parents didn't let me go for some reason – they sent my brother Zhenya to Kiev and sent me to my grandmother's place in Moscow. And Misha's friend, Sasha Gdeshinsky, sent me a telegram: 'Send telegram by deception arrival Misha shooting self.' My father folded up the telegram and forwarded it in a letter to his sister: 'Pass on this telegram to your friend Vara…' Mikhail finished his studies at school, distracted in the extreme. The obstacles to their *rendez-vous* only served to intensify the love affair."

It is hard to say whether it was by his own will, or by bending to the will of his mother (the Gdeshinskys' sister is the only one who asserts this, in her memoirs) that he decided, in the summer of 1909, to become a doctor. Ivan Voskresensky, his mother's second husband, was a paediatrician. Some of his mother's brothers were also doctors. The young Mikhail's girlfriend, Tatiana Lappa, could remember how he hesitated over this decision.

In the same year in which he completed his time at the first grammar school, his younger brother Vanya was preparing to enrol in the preparatory class (he would later have the poet Nikolai Ushakov as a classmate), and his brother Nikolai was getting ready for the 1st year (along with Viktor Syngayevsky, who was a year younger). V.V. Kuze, who would go on to be a movie director, was two years away from enrolling at the school; fate would later bring him and Bulgakov together in Moscow. Boris Romashov, who would later become a playwright and share the same stairwell as Bulgakov, was about to join the third year; and Bulgakov's cousin and great friend, Kostya Bulgakov (who was three years younger than Mikhail) was about to start year six.

For Mikhail, however, the grammar school days were over. "O, those eight years of studies! How much there was in that time that was absurd, and sad, and desperate for a young boy's soul, but how much there was that was joyful. Grey days, grey days, grey days, *ut consecutivum*. Caius Julius Caesar, a stake through cosmography and eternal hatred of astronomy as a result. Yet there was also spring, spring and the thundering noise in the classrooms, the schoolgirls in their green pinafores in the boulevard, the chestnut trees and May, and, above all, the eternal beacon ahead of us: university, and what that entailed, a free life – do you realise what university means? Dusk on the Dnieper, free will, money, strength, glory.

And he had gone through all this…"

… No diary entries or letters by the eighteen-year-old Mikhail Bulgakov have survived. We have almost no reliable evidence about his thoughts, his hopes and fears, his life ambitions. The recollections of Alexei Turbin in *The White Guard* are pretty much the most convincing source we have to go on. And it is fair, I have no doubt, to describe this time in the life of the young

Bulgakov as a time of hope – hopes of acquiring confidence, strength, fame. What kind of fame, exactly? At that time, it appears, fame as a doctor. Many aspects of this profession were appealing to young Bulgakov. He would later confess to his biographer that the work of a doctor seemed "sparkling" to him. This is an important word, a significant and almost symbolic one. It is one that crops up repeatedly in his prose, in which the work of a doctor or an experimental biologist would always be depicted in a mysterious, attractive light, and the tools of his trade – sparkling in a literal sense – would play an important role. He used the word in a letter to his brother, who completed his medical training outside Russia, having split definitively from his mother, brother and sisters, saying: "Be sparkling in your research."

In the years 1909-1913, when Bulgakov began to master his chosen profession, his studies at university did not go smoothly, and were interrupted by student unrest. On 9 November 1910, the news of the death of Lev Tolstoy provoked a demonstration, and a number of students from the university were arrested due to their involvement in the disorder. It can be supposed that the death of Tolstoy left a deep, personal impression on Mikhail Bulgakov, and that he was not indifferent to whatever public demonstrations on the subject took place. No evidence of Bulgakov having taken part in the student unrest in 1910-1911 has yet been found (although attempts to find documents of this kind have certainly been made); on the contrary, there are grounds for supposing that he kept out of them, and that the fairly turbulent political life of Kiev's students in those years remained no more than the background to his own life. I would suggest, however, that a critical event in the life of a family friend, V.I. Ekzemplyarsky, which was linked to the name of Tolstoy, became a key part of his early student years. Early in the autumn of 1911, Ekzemplyarsky published a pamphlet entitled 'Count L.N. Tolstoy and St. John Chrysostom and their views on the vital significance of the teachings of Christ', in which he wrote: "Tolstoy is not a teacher of the church. That "part of the truth" which has passed through his consciousness, has been bound up right from the first centuries of Christianity in the creative works of the great church teachings, wrapped up in all their fullness… But Count L.N. Tolstoy – this living reproach to our Christian existence and rouser of the Christian conscience… Our conscience is lulled by this sham Christian life, and sweet is the awareness that one can consider oneself a follower of Christ, by making his Cross the adornment of one's life, but without bearing the burden of this Cross."

Ekzemplyarsky was fired from the Academy for publishing this pamphlet about the writer, who had been excommunicated from the church. This would of course have been talked about by Bulgakov's friends and loved ones. They probably also discussed the contents of the pamphlet, which, one must assume, Bulgakov read. And if this is so, then its author's thoughts may have served as one of the first things that prompted Bulgakov to start thinking about the writer's role in assessing the extent to which his life in the modern world corresponded to the teachings of Christianity, and about the vast potential scale of the broad instructive task that the writer assumes. It may be that the example set by Tolstoy, which was important to him in his literary life thereafter in a multiplicity of ways, became clear to him even then, when he read Ekzemplyarsky's pamphlet.

In January 1911, the Council of Ministers annulled the autonomy of the senior teaching institutions, banning student gatherings within the walls of the university. In response, a strike began on February 1, lasting until early April 1911. Classes at the university came to an almost complete stop. Fighting to prevent this was a group of students of an academic inclination; this group strove to keep the lessons going without interruption, and at its request, the professors were allowed to give lectures, even if there was only one student present in the auditorium. In all likelihood, Mikhail Bulgakov's sympathies lay on the side of this 'academic' group. These students were motivated by a desire to become qualified – to get their degrees as doctors and become free, as soon as possible…

"… After eight years at the grammar school, with not a swimming pool in sight, the corpses of the surgical theatre, the white wards, the glassy silence of the operating rooms…"

The year 1911 was one of constant unrest. In the spring, the trial of a student named Kryzhanovsky took place. In September, the chairman of the Council of Ministers, P.A. Stolypin, was murdered at the city's theatre, in full view of the packed theatre audience.

Shortly before this incident, which stirred up the city and the whole of Russia, in late July 1911, Tatiana Lappa had moved to Kiev, having completed her schooling in Saratov. She stayed with the Bulgakovs for a while – at their dacha. She wanted to stay in Kiev, with her grandmother and her aunt, but her father would not allow it: "Do some work in your first year – then you can go to Kiev!" and in early September she had to leave for Saratov (term was starting at the educational establishment where Tatiana had enrolled as a teaching assistant). There reigned over the Bulgakov's home that youthful liveliness which took root after their father's death; while he was alive, the atmosphere at home had been different, stricter – they had listened to readings from the gospel every Sunday.

In order to understand the ideas that were forming in Bulgakov's mind in his younger years, the biographer essentially has two main sources at his disposal: a general idea about the historico-cultural context of the 1900s, formed through a multitude of data, and the isolated accounts of his contemporaries. We must take particular care with regard to the latter. "It was apparently their father himself who read the gospel out loud," recalled Y.B. Bukreyev during our last meeting, on 8 September 1983. "They were a god-fearing family. But the children weren't religious at all. The atmosphere at their home after their father died was different… Varvara's admirers… She was very similar to Misha. She was no great beauty, but she was inordinately feminine. The students in those days were utterly indifferent towards religion. And what's more they were medics, you know. Medics don't take any interest in such things." The death of his father, the classes at the department of medicine, the new and powerful impressions that were left on him by his first introduction to Darwin's theory of evolution, the influence of his step-father, who was a doctor, and the influence of the times in which he lived, which were casting doubt over what had been irrefutable in the eyes of his father – all this had an effect on him. "We remember with veneration," one of A.I. Bulgakov's pupils from the Academy says beside his coffin, "that the deceased always pointed to his Christian calling – 'I am *a Christian first and foremost!*' – in his private life," and that "his highest religious interest, which combined within it both ecclesiasticism and his mood, was for him not just one of *many* interests in his life, but in a way the very essence of his life," that he believed – "even now, when everything around you seems to be objecting against you and your beliefs, that a naïve and pure, religiously complete Christian worldview *is possible…*" For Afanasy Ivanovich's eldest son, such a worldview was already an impossibility.

In March 1910, Bulgakov's sister Nadezhda Afanasievna writes in her diary that her older brother has left the rites of the church behind him (he did not wish to observe lent before Easter, did not fast) and decided to respond to religious matters by being an unbeliever.

Decades later, having lived through some of the fateful events of the 20th century, Bulgakov would once again return to these questions, to which he had found answers in his youth.

Let us return to the conversation I had with the daughter-in-law of the priest at the church of Nikolai the Benevolent, A.A. Glagolev, on whom Father Alexander in *The White Guard* is based. She was the wife of his eldest son, also a priest, Father Aleksei. Following the death of A.I. Bulgakov, Father Alexander asked Varvara Mikhailovna to teach his little son – "they used to take him to her place on a sleigh". His daughter Varvara, or Vava, would also go along, and another son. Did they befriend the young Bulgakovs when they grew up? "No," Tatiana Pavlovna replied straight away, adding: "The Bulgakovs were such free-thinking types, after all…" Let it be stressed, though, that this is the view of the wife and daughter-in-law of a priest. Anyone pondering over the biography and creativity of Bulgakov should keep this in mind: whatever happened to the eldest son of a doctor of theology during the first few years after the death of his father and in the subsequent decades – all this was built upon the foundations that were laid in his childhood: these foundations could no longer be taken out.

And so, in the house on the Andreyevsky Hill during Mikhail Bulgakov's university years, the mood was lively and fun. On "odd Saturdays", they would hold their *jours fixes*: young people would gather together, dancing and singing, with Kolya and Vanya playing the balalaika and the guitar… On these evenings, Sofya Gdeshinskaya recalls, her brothers would go to Andreyevsky Hill; Sasha would play the violin there, accompanied on the piano by Mikhail's sister Vara – like Sasha Gdeshinsky, she was studying at the conservatory, taking lessons on the grand piano; "Sasha played Vieuxtemps' First concerto, Järnefelt's 'Berceuse', Sarasate's 'Gypsy Airs', Haydn and Kreisler." Music is all around Bulgakov at this time, filling his life, awakening his private hopes already. The musical life of Kiev in those years and the role that these impressions played in his subsequent creativity is a special and important subject, one that has not yet been fully examined. He is constantly going to the opera, never misses a chance to see touring opera singers and very nearly starts to consider such a career for himself. This hobby faded away as time went on, but his particular love of opera singing never left him, nor did his passion for singing in general (this had begun in his childhood; it was triggered by his sister, who used to sing in a choir after school: "Vera's voice was quiet, but unbearable").

His first literary efforts also occurred in this period. The writer's sister N.A. Zemskaya wrote in a letter to Y.S. Bulgakova (dated 18th – 25th April 1964): "I remember that a long time ago (in 1912-1913), when Misha was still studying and I was a first-year student, he gave me his story *The Fiery Snake* (*Ognennyy Zmey*) to read – it was about an alcoholic who drank until he had white fever and died during a fit of the disease: he was strangled (or burnt) by a snake that had crawled into his room (a hallucination)…" At this stage, he was probably merely dreaming about being a writer (in the same way that he had dreamt of a career as an opera singer), and had not made a conscious and irrevocable decision.

At no. 13, meanwhile, the Bulgakovs now had some new "housemates" – an engineer named Vasily Pavlovich Listovnichy bought the house and moved into the ground floor with his wife, a Polish woman named Yadviga Viktorovna, and their little daughter Inna. "We bought the house together with the residents," his daughter Inna Vasilievna Konchakovskaya tells me. "Varvara Mikhailovna came to see my father and spoke to him in a way that showed great intelligence. 'I am a widow, I have seven children…' – generally, she managed to persuade him to leave them alone, promising that they were not troublesome folk." At that time, Mikhail already had his own room in the apartment – a corner room with a balcony. Listovnich's daughter tells of a dispute between Mikhail and her father over this room: Listovnich's mother, who was suffering from open-form tuberculosis, had been brought over from Chernigov, and Listovnich, fearing that his wife and daughter might be infected with the disease, asked Varvara Mikhailovna whether he could temporarily use Mikhail's room: "A separate entrance had been put in there, from the street, so my grandmother didn't interact with the Bulgakovs at all. In July, she moved to our house, and in October she died… Varvara Mikhailovna had given her consent, but Mishka had some harsh words to say about the matter" (from a note made by Y.B. Wolfson).

If the situation were to be described by a member of the Bulgakov family, it would probably have come across differently: downstairs, there were four people (and a maid) living in seven rooms, whilst upstairs, also living in seven rooms, it appears there were at least eleven people (including the two cousins and Irina Lukinichna, who shared Lyolya's room). Even the temporary loss of a room was no doubt a very sensitive matter.

Relations between the eldest of the Bulgakov children and Listovnich immediately became tense. The tension was only removed when Varvara Mikhailovna assumed full responsibility for all negotiations with the owner of the house.

Bulgakov spent around ten years living side by side with this man, and his life ought to find at least some small place in our tale (it goes without saying that a biographer cannot substitute for the character of Vasilisa in the *The White Guard*, the notion of a person from real life who may have prompted the novelist's work; such a practice has become customary, however, among admirers of Bulgakov, along with many other similar attempts to identify real-life prototypes for his characters).

V.P. Listovnichy was born in Kiev (in 1876), and was descended from merchants in the 1st guild; they "had an ironmonger's shop and a harnessry business in Podol," I learn from the daughter of I.V. Konchakovskaya, Irina

Pavlovna. "The Listovnichys then went bankrupt and, by the time Vasily was growing up, they were a very poor family [...] Vasily achieved material wealth all on his own, through his own efforts, and not through trade but through his work as an engineer." He studied at a non-classical secondary school in Kiev, then at the Institute of civil engineers in St. Petersburg; from 1911 onwards he worked as an architect in Kiev's academic district, building grammar schools and colleges. The memory of his family's bankruptcy, it appears, never left him. V.P. Listovnichy's grandson, a doctor named Valery Konchakovsky, relates the following story: "Mama once asked him: 'Papa, why do you work so much?' and my grandfather replied: 'Those who work a lot in their childhood and adolescence always have an inner fear of need; I want to bring up my grandsons in peace.' Clearly, the voice of his merchant forefathers was making itself heard in him too, even though he had already become a nobleman (and a distinguished citizen of Kiev): in his old age, he dreamed of opening a bookshop (he was very knowledgeable about books)." In the same letter, which was sent to the author of this book, my correspondent strives to identify the possible sources of irritation between the housemates: "My grandfather bought the house in 1909, by which time the Bulgakovs had been in residence there for a long time. Here was this young, 33-year-old new owner, full of energy and very active. He had a stable put up in the yard, and a shed for his carriage, and kept a couple of horses.

Before long he had dug up the yard, arranged for tens of cubic metres of soil to be carted off and had a brick building put up next to the yard. The work was done manually, with the soil taken away in dray carts, so no-one could get past very easily that summer. He generally set about putting his own stamp on the place.

He took part of the Bulgakovs' veranda for himself and put in an emergency staircase leading from the attic, and took away the corner room with the balcony for a whole year...!

He earned a lot of money, and had a maid, a cook, a porter and a coachman. The Bulgakovs lived modestly (though they too had servants), hence perhaps the unkind nickname of 'bourgeois' (this too is entirely understandable on a human level, and typical of so many of us).

During the war he was granted the use of a company car – a long, convertible Lincoln, which was forever looming up indistinctly outside the house. And in those days, throughout all of quiet, provincial Kiev, there were perhaps no more than a handful of such cars..."

"At Christmas," Tatiana Lappa recalls, "Mikhail came to Saratov: he brought my grandmother, Yelizaveta Lappa, with him from Kiev... We had a fir tree, and did some dancing, but we spent most of the time sitting and chatting…" Bulgakov met her parents, Nikolai and Evgenia. It was clear that Tatiana would soon leave for Kiev. Though she was still working as a teaching assistant at a girls' school, she felt awkward in this role. "The girls there were twice as big as me and twice as fat. The theology teacher once asked: 'Where's your class teaching assistant?' 'She's there,' came the reply. 'Well, just look at her! Ha ha ha!' … I would come home after the lessons barely able to speak…"

The family, with whom he became close that year, was completely different from his own.

Tatiana Lappa had been born in Ryazan, where her father worked as a tax inspector: then he had lived in Ekaterinoslav, doing the same thing, before being appointed as the director of the Treasury Chamber in Omsk; Tatiana went to school at the progymnasium there. "My father had built the building that housed the Treasury Chamber in Omsk; when he was transferred to Saratov, he built one there too." Congresses for tax inspectors took place in both Omsk and Saratov – and lunches were arranged at Nikolai's house: "The table was laid for 100 guests – it was a happy hunting ground for us children! In Omsk, two expensive Chinese vases were once brought by a guest for my father. At the next congress, there was a silver samovar, and then a silver dinner set for 12 people… When Mikhail and I met, my father had already reached the rank of a Councillor of State. My father had his own courier; at home we had a maid, a cook and a governess. It was a big family, too – six children, and I was the eldest. We didn't have a butler: the maid would serve the food at dinner. Appetisers were never served – father had a disease of the kidneys, so we loved to have preserves when we had guests…Mikhail liked the food at our house." He generally found everything to his liking at this house, which was affluent, but, it seems, not cold or snooty. Many years later, in the play *The Days of the Turbins*, the character Lariosik would say: "I gave speeches, on plenty of occasions… *in the company of my late father's servants*… in Zhitomir… There are *tax inspectors* there, you know…" By that time, Tatiana Nikolayevna was no longer with Bulgakov, and her father, who had welcomed Bulgakov to his dinner table, had been dead for several years, and yet, in accordance with that law whereby literature comes into being from absolutely everything, without exception, with which a writer comes into contact – with no restrictions whatsoever – his ghost was disquieted, and we can see, perhaps, the effect of that subtle humour with which Mikhail looked on Tatiana's stories about her father's servants, about the congresses with all their abundant food and about all the speechifying that took place…

The children in their families were brought up in different ways. Varvara Bulgakova, as Nadezhda said, "believed that children ought to be kept occupied at all times," and Mikhail once wrote some funny verses on this subject, describing how his mother would give everyone a job to do, first thing in the morning: "You go and fill a hole with sand, you go and dig it out again…"

This emphasis on democratic traditions in everyday family life, so typical of certain social classes within the Russian intelligentsia, and dictating a "working upbringing" for children and so on, were not present in the Lappa family. "I would come home from school, throw my dress onto the floor, and my mother would say: 'Don't pick it up, the maid will tidy it away; you never know how life might turn out, so as long as circumstances allow it – don't do anything!' We weren't given any preparation for anything… What did I think about my future? I lived in the present, and I gave no thought to the future at all!" The parents did not spoil the children in person, though. "Whenever father went away somewhere, he would bring back gifts and nice things only for our mother, there was never anything for us. We were given simple clothes to wear. But I was a bad daughter, a disobedient one! If papa didn't give me his permission to go to a concert or somewhere, I would still get out through the back door and go. The number of times he came after me to the skating rink… I studied music; father loved it when I played something: he would lie down on the divan and listen…"

The eldest, beloved, wilful daughter in a wealthy family, with the usual traditions of the hospitable Russian nobility of the provinces… Now, when he read the works of Saltykov-Shchedrin, a writer he loved – in his adolescence in particular – Bulgakov could now recognise in them the traits of the aristocracy, with which, it seemed, he was now coming into such close contact for the first time.

The 20-year-old Mikhail spent the late winter and spring of 1912 in a despondent state; his academic pursuits had been abandoned; he did not sit that semester's exams. His education would have to drag on for another year at least… (One can imagine the concern and consternation his mother must have felt.) And once again, in the summer of 1912, he travelled to Saratov. And in August, they went away to Kiev together. "I went away under the pretext of enrolling for History and philology courses…And I signed up for these courses, in the Romano-Germanic department, but didn't have any time to study – we spent all our time out on the town… I rented a room from a member of the *black hundred*… On Andreyevsky Hill, the Listovnichys had a dog in their yard, I was terribly frightened of it. And I said to Mikhail: 'What am I to do, I'm not going to come to you through the yard.' 'Well, in that case ring the bell, I'll come and open the door.' Everyone else went to his room via the yard, of course – the staircase from their flat to the main entrance was quite steep, you wouldn't want to keep going down it to open the door to everyone. They usually kept it locked up.' In this hallway, the Bulgakov brothers used to smoke, without their mother knowing…

In the autumn and winter of 1912 and 1913, Bulgakov and Tatiana Lappa were almost inseparable. "What did we do? We went to the theatre, we must have seen 'Faust' about ten times… Mikhail's mother called me in to see her: 'Don't marry him, it's too early for him.' But we nevertheless got married in April 1913.

Mikhail's mother ordered us to fast before the wedding.

The Bulgakovs always observed lent in the last week before Easter, and Mikhail and I would have lunch with them, then go to a restaurant…in my family (in Saratov), the religious rites weren't observed, and there was always a feast on the table at Easter, Father Alexander would come along and give us his blessing.

I didn't have a veil, of course, or a wedding dress – I hid away all the money that father had sent me. Mama arrived for the wedding and was horrified when she saw me. I had a linen skirt in the cupboard, and mama bought me a blouse. Father Alexander conducted the marriage service.

… For some reason there was an awful lot of laughter during the wedding. We rode home afterwards in a carriage. There weren't many guests at the reception. I remember there being lots of flowers, mostly narcissi…"

Documents in N.A. Zemskaya's archive show how painful Bulgakov's decision was for his mother. He faced the threat of being expelled from university for having failed to sit his exams; she may have guessed how far the relationship had gone (Tatiana told me that the money that her father had sent her was spent on an abortion); it was in these tense circumstances that the young couple were preparing for their wedding.

The best man and ushers – Boris Bogdanov, Konstantin Bulgakov, Platon and Alexander Gdeshinsky – were their closest circle of friends. "Boris would often visit, bringing me straw sticks from Balabukha's candy store (a type of candy that came in a box): 'Tasya, have some candy, Misha and I are going to play billiards.'" Konstantin Bulgakov, Mikhail's cousin, was very fond of billiards too.

"His true genius, though, the hobby that kept his gloomy laziness occupied all day, was carambola billiards at Shtifler's, and the praise of Granovsky or Pirogov never gave students of former times such a proud and shameful pleasure as the one afforded to today's student-dragoons by the approval of the ever-popular billiard scorekeeper Yakov: 'That ball there – you struck that one very cleanly.' His other hobby was the card game vint..." This description – an excerpt from a sketch by Kuprin called *The Student-Dragoon* (*Student-Dragun*), from his first book *Kiev Types* (*Kiyevskiye Tipy*) (Bulgakov doubtless read this in his childhood; like the rest of Kuprin's work, it is referenced in his prose many times) and, judging by critics' responses, had a huge impact, depicts the type of the aristocratic student with revolutionary views. Bulgakov was clearly quite distant from this circle (in terms of his level of wealth, if nothing else), but was a passionate billiard player.

Y.B. Bukreyev told me that in those student years, "an out-building was built… a Pole named Golombek opened a billiard hall. There were eight billiard tables. And next door there was a tavern – the students really liked going there. It was owned by a man named Fyodor Ivanovich… with a receding hairline and sleek temples, and an aquiline nose… Vint is a serious game that is played by dignitaries. But the students played it with bits of iron…" Bulgakov was to retain a love of billiards and vint (his father's friends, the older generation, played the latter) in his later life, too, though it was so different from his youth in Kiev.

After the wedding, however, Bulgakov did not neglect his lessons at the university. "He went to all the lectures, he didn't miss a single one," Tatiana Nikolayevna told me. "He used to go to the library – at the end of Kreshchatyk, a new public library had opened there, beside the merchant garden. It had a very good reading room. He was very fond of that library. He took me with him, and I would dip into a book while he did his studies. We never talked about literature in those days. He intended to be a doctor, and I think he would have been a good one. We talked about music and theatre a lot. Mikhail had been surprised by how much I knew about opera when we first met. I had been to see all the operas that were put on at the Ochkin theatre in Saratov – I was friends with Ochkin's stepdaughter, and she had an enclosed box there, so I could go to the theatre whenever I wanted to, without needing to get dressed up… In Kiev, we went to see *Carmen*, *Les Huguenots*, and *The Barber of Seville*, featuring some Italian singers. We went to all the orchestral concerts that were held at the Kreschaty Park. Mikhail loved the overture from *Ruslan and Lyudmila*, and he loved *Aida*; he used to sing 'Heavenly Aida, divine form'. The one he loved most was *Faust*, and he would usually sing 'Le veau d'or est toujours debout' and Valentin's aria, 'Avant de quitter ces lieux…'

… We used to go to the café on the corner of Fundukleevskaya, and to the restaurant 'Rotser'. His attitude to money was basically this: if you've got money, you must use it immediately. If you're down to your last rouble and there's a carriage waiting – then in you get, let's go! Or if one of them said 'I'd so love to go for a ride in a car!' the other would instantly reply: 'What's the problem then – let's go!' His mother used to scold him for being so frivolous. We went to have lunch with her, and she saw that I wasn't wearing my rings or my chain. 'So it's all at the pawnshop, then!' – 'But on the bright side, we don't owe anyone any money!' … There was a shop in Kiev called 'Lizel' – they sold frankfurters and smoked sausage there. You'd buy half a kilo of smoked sausage from Moscow and that was enough to fill you up.

What did we live on? Mikhail worked as a tutor… And my father sent me 50 roubles a month. The rent was 10-15 roubles a month, and as for the rest, we spent it straight away…"

The opera, concerts… In the homes of those close to the young Bulgakov, just as was the case on Andreyevsky Hill, the overriding tone was a 'childish' one, with lots of children of different ages; it was the tone of secure family fun. There were musical evenings, dances, plays produced and performed at home, such as 'the sea is restless' and 'the damaged telephone', the *jours fixes*, dinners, name-days, the sisters' admirers bringing bouquets of flowers on a daily basis (Nadezhda Bulgakova: "Misha once came back from Bucha, and after walking through the dacha, said: 'What's going on – there are bouquets standing around everywhere, like brooms!'" One can only speculate as to whether the memories of Bulgakov's loved ones were affected by the influence of his creative output, which had begun to be rolled out before them in a constant stream of works in the early 1920s, or whether he put his own comment from many years previously into his play, in which Nikolka says to Lariosik of his sister: "What misfortune! That's why everyone likes her – because she's a red-head. As soon as anyone clapped eyes on her, they would start dragging bouquets of flowers over here. So there were always bouquets standing around in our apartment, like birch-twig brooms.")

Billiards, cafés, the cinema…

"… They were legendary times, those days when, in the gardens of our motherland's most beautiful city, there lived a young generation that had never known sadness. At that time, a confidence took root in the hearts of that generation – the belief that their whole lives would unfold in a happy light, quietly, peacefully: dawns and dusks. The Dnieper, Kreshchatyk, the sunny streets in summer, and in winter – snowflakes that were not cold and brutal, but large and loving…

… And what happened was the exact opposite.

The legendary times came to an abrupt halt, and history intervened, suddenly and terribly."

A decade later, in his sketch *Kiev-city*, Bulgakov would accurately identify the "moment when it appeared" – "10 o'clock in the morning on March 2nd, 1917." The first signs of this appearance had been discovered, however, at least three years earlier.

In the summer of 1914, the Bulgakov family, as always, were in Bucha. One of the photographs they took depicts them bathed in sunlight and embellished by carefree merriment. In the photo, there are grown-ups – the uncles who were staying with their relatives, the doctors Nikolai Mikhailovich and Mikhail Mikhailovich, Ivan Pavlovich Voskresensky and Irina Lukinichna; and there are children who have already become grown-ups but who do not yet know it – Vera, Nadya, Varya, their friend Maria Lisyanskaya…

Mikhail and his wife travelled to Saratov that summer. Whilst they were there, a war broke out that was to develop into the First World War.

3

Yevgeniya Viktorovna Lappa, Tatiana's mother, set up a hospital at the Treasury Chamber. The wounded were brought back from the front line. "Mikhail started working at the hospital," Tatiana told me. "We stayed in Saratov until the start of the new term at university." A photograph of Bulgakov as a student medic surrounded by the hospital staff and the wounded soldiers is one of the very best photos from his youth.

"When we returned to Kiev in the autumn, my father suggested that we should take the silver with us (this was her dowry), but I said no – because of how heavy it was, no other considerations even occurred to me!" Their youth and financial security went on as before.

Bulgakov had two years left at university. Many of his comrades were already on the front line. Platon Gdeshinsky had gone off to fight, whilst Boris Bogdanov had become a volunteer.

Tatiana's sister, Sofya, set off for the front line as well. The Battle of Galicia was raging; the late autumn of 1914 proved a successful period for the Russian army, and the front line seemed a long way away. "My sister made the trip to Kiev," Tatiana recalls, "and brought us some 'Gala-Peter' chocolate, which tasted rather bitter, and some 'Kapleten' biscuits – round ones with salt and cumin."

The same life that they had had before the war continued.

In early 1915, Bulgakov suffered the second shocking experience to happen to him since his father's death; its traces would drag on for a long time.

Boris Bogdanov spent a lot of time at the Bulgakovs' house, just as he had done before; he had now been called up, but had not yet left for the front. He was courting Varya Bulgakova at that time, but she rejected him, and the following day he came to see them at home, having for some reason shaved off his moustache... Nadezhda Bulgakova told me: "I asked Boris: What did you do that for?! – And Misha spoke for him: 'La petite démonstration' (a little show of protest)."

We know what happened next thanks to Nadezhda and Tatiana's accounts, which agree with one another down to the smallest details.

Boris Bogdanov kept away from the Bulgakovs' house for a long time, then suddenly sent them a note in which he asked Mikhail to come and see him.

When Mikhail walked into his room, he was lying in bed – undressed, it would appear. Mikhail wanted to smoke. Boris said:

"You can take a thin cigar from my coat pocket."

Mikhail delved into the pockets of the overcoat, began searching for the cigars, and, as he uttered "All you've got left in here is one *tepeika*" (this seems to have been the slang word for a kopeck at the grammar school), he turned towards Boris. It was at that moment that the shot rang out.

The scene that met his eyes would rise to the surface of his memory many times thereafter. A description of it can be found in one of his short stories, *Morphine (Morfiy)*.

One can imagine how the student medic rushed about at the bedside of this man covered in blood, this man with whom he had shared a desk at school for several years, who had held the wreath above his head at his wedding, and who had courted his sister...

A note had been left on the cigar box: "No-one is to be blamed for my death." Mikhail was summoned to the investigator's office, since he was the only person who witnessed the suicide.

Tatiana recalls that she travelled around town with Varvara and Mikhail to deal with all the matters related to the funeral; it seems that they also went to the morgue. Varvara Mikhailovna found this death difficult to bear, as she had been very fond of Boris. He had not had a mother. Beside the grave, Boris's father thanked Varvara for having been like a mother to his sons.

As for the reasons for the suicide, various theories were put forward, as is always the case: Boris's father said that his son had not got on well with his bosses; his brother Pyotr said that it was because someone had called Boris a coward (it is possible that some thought he was taking too long to go off to war); and in the meantime a romantic theory spread around the city, which had it that the volunteer Bogdanov had ended his life because of Varya Bulgakova.

For Bulgakov, one can imagine that speculation about the reasons was a secondary concern, overshadowed by a thought that plagued him: the fact that his medical knowledge had proved insufficient to rescue his dying friend.

It may well be that the recurring theme of people killing themselves with a revolver (or a Browning) which we find in his prose had its origins in this biographical collision. (Let us note at this point that there was another suicide in those years that closely concerned the young Bulgakovs: on the eve of the war, Tatiana's younger brother, still a schoolboy, shot himself in Saratov, for reasons which were to remain a mystery).

... There was less than a year to go before the state exams.

In August, the situation on the South-Western front became catastrophic. The Germans had taken Lutsk, opening up a direct route to Kiev. The military chiefs were starting to contemplate surrendering Kiev and withdrawing the troops beyond the Dnieper.

Kiev was full of refugees, and in the meantime many people had evacuated their children from the city. Varvara Mikhailovna sent the three youngest children to her sister Alexandra Mikhailovna in Karachev; A.A. Tkachenko tells us that their relatives jokingly called them refugees.

On 24th August 1915, a twenty-year-old noblewoman, the granddaughter of Field Marshal Wittgenstein and daughter of a landowner with estates in the south of Russia, wrote in her diary: "Kiev is in the grip of panic. Everyone is packing up their things, getting ready to go, and fleeing. Everyone in the streets and on the trams is greatly troubled, and all talk is of where to go and how to get hold of tickets. And that last matter is a problematic one: there have been queues at the city station for almost three days now. On the other hand, the whole station is overflowing with refugees, from the platforms and all the waiting rooms and corridors to the steps outside the entranceways. It is overflowing in the true sense of the word, i.e. this great innumerable crowd of old men, children and women lying side by side on their luggage and simply on the floor. [...] On the day we arrived, there were about *10,000* people there! They were refugees from the region in which the army is engaged: from Rovno, Vladimir-Volynsky, Kamenets, Proskurov..." Bulgakov observed all this, too, little imagining, one supposes, that over the next few years he would see scenes far more fearful than this in his native city. "Influential people and soldiers," as the author of the diary writes, "are saying that it 'appears' that the whole of the *South-Western region and Kiev* will inevitably have to be surrendered. I think the only reason they add the word 'appears' is to soften the blow of such a terrible decision.

To surrender Kiev – the mother of all Russian cities, with all its holy sites, with the Pecherskaya Monastery, with all that is dear to the Russian heart, the first Russian city, sacred Kiev! [...] Let them destroy our estates, let them make us and thousands of people penniless, but let us defend Kiev! Can it really be that after such a blow, which would shake up all Russia, can it really be that one could have any faith in anything, still hold out any hope for anything?" The Bulgakovs didn't have any estates, but this attitude towards Kiev was no doubt very close to their own.

In the autumn of 1915, some of the departments at the university were evacuated to Saratov; the medical faculty stayed in Kiev: it was preparing doctors, to meet the needs out at the front. As early as late December 1914, several dozen doctors had been allowed to graduate early – they were from the group with which Bulgakov had enrolled in the first year (and included Y. Bukreyev – 'Bukreshka-reshka-oreshka' from the preparatory class at the Second grammar school), and he had fallen behind them because of his romantic entanglement with Tatiana Lappa. It was pretty clear that his own year-group would be allowed to graduate early, too.

Many of the students, not only in the fifth year but in the younger years, too, were already at the front line, in the hospital attendant brigades of the YuZOZO (South-West regional territorial organisations); back in 1915, Bulgakov had been declared "unfit for service in the field", but it was obvious that he was expected to go to one of the hospitals.

Usually, the state exams in medicine, which consisted of 22 separate subjects, dragged on (in addition to the time set aside in order to prepare for them) for four months – from June to September. In 1916, the tests were all squeezed into the months of February and March, and concluded on 6th April. Bulgakov's university days were over.

"Mikhail was never drunk, he didn't drink very much. There was only one occasion when I saw him drunk: he had been drinking with the other students after they had graduated. He came home and said: 'Do you know what, I'm drunk.' 'Go and have a lie down, then.' 'No, let's go out on the town.' We walked up Vladimirskaya street a short way, then went home again. Day was already dawning."

One can imagine how the young medical students felt that night, having become doctors ahead of time. Cracks were appearing in the front line that spring. The Lake Naroch Offensive launched on 5th March was not a success for the Russian army. The Minister of war, Sukhomlinov, was arrested, accused of inaction in violation of the law and other crimes, right up to betrayal of the state. The subsequent course of the war, the way it dragged on – all this was lost in the fog of an utterly uncertain future. Also permanently lost in the fog were all the things that had once been associated with university, in the dreams of a schoolboy – "free will, money, strength, glory…"

After completing his tests (but having not yet received his degree), Bulgakov, according to Tatiana, "signed up for the Red Cross" – i.e. voluntarily went off to work at the hospital in Kiev that was being managed by the Red

Cross. Before long, the hospital was relocated to Kamenets-Podolsk, closer to the theatre of war.

We may be helped in our attempts to imagine the kind of atmosphere in which the young doctor was working by the thoughts of one of the characters (holding a position of high office in the Red Cross) from V. Shulgin's book of memoirs, *The Years (Gody)*, referred to earlier: "In terms of its capabilities, the Red Cross is far weaker than the military institution. The military institution has far better equipment. There are lots of doctors, nurses, hospitals of all kinds. The resources they have for moving patients around, i.e. the hospital attendants' carts for taking out the wounded and diseased, cannot be compared with the resources at the Red Cross. [...] Yet the significance of the Red Cross has not at the same level as its material capabilities at all. Its significance is at a much higher level. And I assert this to them: 'Remember, you are the conscience of the military doctors!' Yes, the conscience, because, one must admit it, military doctors often have no conscience! [...] It is even hard to explain where this comes from. Is it a case of conventionalism? There is conventionalism running through the whole army, though. Yet soldiers have genuine heroism within their grasp. They not only kill; they are also killed. That's not the case with the doctors. Their duty, first and foremost, is to look after themselves. And this engenders some kind of different, baser psychology. I may be wrong when I say that, incidentally. But, in any case, the Red Cross maintains some kind of lofty tradition of humanity. And it can and must set an example for the doctors of the military institution, who have become so empty. Therein lies our significance!"

It is easy to imagine that the young doctor, let out of university early, was inspired by precisely such ideas whilst working at the hospitals of the Red Cross.

Preparations were being made for the attack by Russian forces which was later to become known as the Brusilov Offensive – after the general A. Brusilov, recently appointed commander-in-chief of the army of the South-Western front. Just a short time previously, in late March, he had been governor of Kamenets-Podolsk, visiting hospitals and handing out crosses.

On 22nd May, the attack began. Kamenets-Podolsk was no more than 50 kilometres from the front-line; from this moment on, the workload of the surgeons at the hospital was set to get bigger and bigger.

On 25th May, Lutsk was captured; the Austrians, panicking, retreated; in the first three days of the attack, the troops achieved a considerable level of success, of a kind long since forgotten on the Russian front.

At the start of June, the Russian troops forced their way through Prut and seized Chernovitsy. Since the attack was developing, the hospitals had to move closer to the front line. Bulgakov soon found himself in Chernovitsy, along with his hospital. By the start of July, the front line had moved no less than 80 km from Chernovitsy, thanks to the successful operations carried out by troops under Brusilov's command.

Fate dictated that Bulgakov was close to the theatre of military operations at the time of what can perhaps be described as the Russian army's biggest successes in the entire war.

"I went there too," Tatiana tells me. "It was suddenly announced that the wives must go away for 24 hours." (It seems that this was one of the dangerous moments during the attack, when there were fluctuations in the frontline.) "I departed, but barely had two weeks gone by when a telegram came from him. I went to see him again. Mikhail came to meet me in Orsh, in his car. The soldiers asked to see his permit; he handed them a prescription – they were illiterate. They let us through. Before Nadezhda (Bulgakov's sister) left – she was an activist at the time, often going to talk to the people – she had shoved some pamphlets into my hands, which I was to distribute, and I – fool that I was! – took them with me. I was terribly frightened afterwards that Mikhail would see them – he would have killed me! When we arrived, I threw them into the fireplace...

I worked as a nurse at the hospital in Chernovitsy, holding down the legs of the wounded whilst he amputated them. I felt unwell the first time, but after that I got used to it... He was a surgeon there, and spent all his time doing amputations... He would get very tired after a day at the hospital, he would come home and lie down, and read a book. He didn't take part in the fighting, and as far as I know he never drove out into the field of battle.

Suddenly, Mikhail was summoned to Moscow as a matter of urgency – to take up a new position. They set off, deciding not to go via Kiev; he travelled in his military uniform.

In Moscow, he was sent to Smolensk; we didn't even have time to go and see uncle (Nikolai Pokrovsky)..."

This took place, it appears, in the late summer of 1916. Bulgakov travelled to his new place of work before he had even received his doctor's diploma (the diploma is dated 31st October 1916).

The writer's sister, N. Zemskaya, later recalled (in a letter to Y.S. Bulgakova): "The entire year group, upon graduating, was awarded the rank of militia fighter of the 2nd class – the purpose of this being that they would not be called up to do military service, but would be used in the provinces: the experienced provincial doctors were taken to the front, to the field hospitals, whilst the young graduates replaced them in the rear, in the land hospitals… The graduates from Kiev were not allocated to the provinces straight away though, and Mikhail Bulgakov was able to spend the whole summer of 1916 working in the hospitals near the front line on the South-Western Front, where he had gone of his own free will, by joining the Red Cross."

Bulgakov's call-up for military service, placing him in the reserve for the ranks of the Moscow Regional Military and Sanitary Directorate, and more specifically – appointing him to a position in the Smolensk governorate – had come on 16th July.

The graduates from medical school in the year 1916 were called up for actual military service – but a large proportion of them were immediately assigned to the reserve units for a number of regional military and sanitary directorates. The young doctors were listed as being on military service and were considered to be on assignment in the provinces. This situation would later be described by the protagonist of the story *Morphine*, Dr Polyakov, in his diary: "My entire year-group, which was not subject to conscription for the war (the militia fighters of the 2nd class, who graduated in 1916) was stationed in the provinces."

Sixty years later, Tatiana told me that after spending the night in Smolensk, they set off on the train for Sychevka, a tiny provincial town; this was where the directorate for the provincial hospitals was located. It was September, but autumn was in full swing: it was cold and rainy. A typical landscape from the middle of Russia unfurled itself before the gaze of someone who had only recently said goodbye to the warmth, sunshine, richly diverse colours and fruits of Kiev in the late summer, with a frightening starkness.

"Doctor Bulgakov's period of service in the Sychevka district shall commence on 27th September," read the letter from the municipal council of the Governorate, which was apparently despatched just as the young doctor was making his way towards his designated place of work.

"Clearly, we set off to the municipal council… we were given a pair of horses and an open carriage – that was what they called it – it was fairly comfortable. The roads were filthy, and we travelled all day, covering 40 versts. We arrived in Nikolskoye late in the evening, and there was no-one there to meet us, of course. There was a two-storey building there; that was the doctors' building. It was locked; the physician's assistant came up to us with the keys, and said to us: 'That's your house…' The house had two halves, with separate doors: it was designed to house the two doctors that the hospital required. There was no second doctor, however.

Upstairs there was a bedroom and a study, downstairs there was a dining room and a kitchen. We moved into the two rooms and started to arrange things the way we wanted them. And on that first night, a woman who was about to go into labour was brought to us! I went to the hospital along with Mikhail. The woman was in the operating theatre; she was in terrible pain, of course; the baby wasn't facing the right way. I saw the woman, she had slipped into unconsciousness. I sat some distance away, busily searching for the right pages in the medical textbook, and Mikhail would step away from her, look at her and say to me: 'Find such-and-such a page!' And her husband had said, when he brought her in: 'If she dies, you won't get to live either – I'll kill you.' And he kept on making threats in the same vein afterwards.

Over the next few days, the sick began coming to the hospital, at first just a few, then up to a hundred people a day…"

Relations with the local peasantry were not idyllic.

The hospital had 24 beds in those days (plus another 8 for acute infections and two beds for women in labour), an operating room, a pharmacy, a library and a telephone… It had an outstanding set of tools, acquired through the efforts of Bulgakov's predecessor, Leopold Leopoldovich Smrchek, a Czech who had studied at Moscow University and worked in Nikolskoye for more than ten years. "I have had time to take a look around the hospital and it became perfectly clear to me that the place is equipped with medical instruments in abundance…" Bulgakov would later write in *A Young Doctor's Notebook* (*Zapiski Yunogo Vracha*). "'Hmm,' I uttered, very meaningfully, 'what a charming set of tools you have. Hmm.' 'Why of course, sir,' Demyan Lukich said sweetly, that's all thanks to the efforts of your predecessor, Leopold Leopoldovich. He used to operate from morning to night, after all.' At that point, I broke out into a cold sweat and gazed gloomily at the little cupboards, gleaming like mirrors." Downstairs, in the pharmacy, "bird's milk was just about the only thing they didn't have. There was a strong smell of herbs in the two rather dark rooms, and on the shelves there was everything one could wish for. There were even some patented foreign medicines, and I need hardly add that I had never heard of them before." And finally, in his study, the story's protagonist "gazed, transfixed, at the third accomplishment of the legendary Leopold: the bookcase was stuffed full of books. I must have counted around thirty surgeon's manuals alone, in both Russian and German…" (*The Towel with the Cockerel* [*Polotentse s Petukhom*]).

The hospital was located in a building that was once a landowner's house, and had been sold by its last owner to the district council. The façade of the white, two-storey building overlooked a lake: the lake had been formed when the little stream that ran alongside the hospital had been enclosed using a dam. The hospital was surrounded by a park full of larch trees (even today, there are some huge larch trees there, which the locals refer to as "German fir-trees"). On the opposite bank of the stream, which arced around the grounds of the hospital, there was a nature reserve. ("... One time, it was in the sunny days of April, I had set out all those English charms in a slanted, golden beam, and had just worked on my right cheek until it had a gleaming finish, when Yegorych suddenly burst in, dressed in torn leather boots and stamping his feet like a horse, and reported that there was a woman giving birth in the bushes in the Nature reserve, above the stream." – *The Missing Eye* [*Propavshiy Glaz*].)

The hospital was surrounded by woods on three sides, whilst on the fourth side the woods abruptly ended, and beyond the meadow, a verst away, one could see the village of Nikolskoye. On the other side, beyond the nature reserve, at a distance of one-and-a-half versts, was the estate of Muravishniky and the village of Muravishnikovo.

A descendant of the estate's owners, Alexander Rastorguyev, told me a few details which somewhat alter the perception of the lonely, isolated life led by the younger doctor at the 3rd Nikolsky point.

The owner of the estate, Vasily Gerasimov, who visited Bulgakov a number of times, often hosted a relative of his, the famous historian Nikolai Kareyev. The wife of the estate's owner, who died a few years ago, remembered Bulgakov well. In the summer, the artists Favorsky and Vereisky used to spend time at the estate, and as it transpires, Bulgakov may well have encountered them...

One of the landowner's sons, Mikhail Gerasimov, was in those days the chairman of the Sychevka district land association (Bulgakov doubtless met him in Sychevka, upon being given his posting to Nikolskoye), while his second son, a doctor named Vladimir, knew Bulgakov well.

"Opposite the hospital," Tatiana recalls, "there was a semi-dilapidated manor house. There was a female landowner who had lost all her money living there, a widow who was still fairly young. Mikhail courted her a little..."

A written source was also discovered which threw some light on the circumstances of Bulgakov's life at this time: the unpublished memoirs of N.I. Kareyev, written by him in July 1923. He remembers Muravishniky as the estate of his maternal grandfather, Osip Gerasimov: "I remember Muravishniky as it was when my grandfather was alive, and when his youngest son was in charge, the one to whom the estate was given, 'Uncle Vasya', and then when it was owned by his sons, Kolya, Misha and Volodya, who all died young, one after the other, in the early 20th century. Right here, before my eyes, in this "nest of nobility", three generations lived and then exited the stage…" It appears that Bulgakov visited the house up until the winter of 1916/17, as a guest of V.O. Gerasimov (who is described by Kareyev as "a good man, weak-natured and lazy", "a drunkard"), when, according to Kareyev, just a few days before the February revolution, "the house and all its contents burnt down, due to the carelessness of the guards." (It is possible that the memory of the fire, which Bulgakov, who lived one-and-a-half kilometres away, may well have seen, later influenced the description of a fire at a large country house in the tale *The Khan's Flame* [*Khanskiy Ogon'*]) Bulgakov met and spoke to its residents later, too, of course.

Tatiana told me the following:

"Around February of 1917, Mikhail was given some time off. We travelled to Saratov. We were there when news of the revolution broke: a servant said to us: 'I am now going to call you Tatiana Nikolayevna, and you will now call me Agafya Ivanovna.' We lived in my father's official quarters. My memory of that time is not good, I remember only that my father and Mikhail played chess the whole time… We returned home via Moscow. It must already have been March; outside Nikolskoye, we made our way across the lake on horseback – it had already thawed; there was no other way to get home." (N. Kareyev describes how, in almost the same year, whilst going to Sychevka "for Maslennitsa, we got stuck in the stream up to our chests.") In March 1917, Bulgakov travelled to Kiev. On his return, it appears that he attended some Emergency meetings of the municipal council in Sychevka. And he ardently discussed, of course, the events which had taken place and the possible future development thereof with the few people that life in Nikolskoye had given him to talk to. They, too, can to some extent be enumerated on the basis of Kareyev's memoirs. "The grandfather at Muravishniky had two grown-up sons: Pyotr and Vasily. Pyotr was a district police superintendent. His eldest son, Osya, who studied at the department of history and philology," who was not only Kareyev's cousin, but also his brother-in-law, was, in his words, "an outstanding teacher"; after the February revolution he once again became a comrade of the minister of people's enlightenment and soon came to the village "with a large number of observations and with some very definite predictions, which he began sharing with me. Gerasimov did not believe that a Founding assembly would form, and insisted on the possibility of a civil war and so on and so forth, although at that time he was sure, for some reason, that the peasants would remain calm;" "in the first four months after the revolution, which I spent in Petersburg, Gerasimov was probably the only person among all those that I met who knew what was going on in the country not just on the basis of the newspapers or the rumour mill." I would suggest that O.P. Gerasimov was one of the few people whose accounts and wise conclusions may have been eagerly listened to and pondered over by the 25-year-old Bulgakov, who, being in Nikolskoye, was so far removed from the events taking place mainly in the two capitals.

Let us return once again to the account provided by the woman who was sharing the days and toil of the young district doctor.

"In the summer of 1917, my mother stayed with us in Nikolskoye with my younger brothers, Kolya and Vova. At that time, after Kerensky's uprising, my eldest brother, Yevgeny (he was studying at the military college in Petersburg), had been sent to the front, and he was killed in his very first battle; an orderly brought home his things." (It is possible that this occurred during the attack on the South-Western front in July.) "Papa sent us a letter about this, and mama left at once, whilst my brothers stayed with us for another month or so…"

Whilst they were in Nikolskoye, the following incident occurred, Tatiana told me: whilst sucking out diphtheria membranes from the throat of a sick child using a pipe, Bulgakov accidentally infected himself and had to give himself an anti-diphtherial serum. Due to the injection he got a terrible itch, and then came out in a rash, and his face became swollen. He couldn't sleep because of the itching and the pain, and asked to be injected with morphine. He asked for it again on the second and third days, and asked his wife to call a nurse for him again, fearing another attack of itching and the insomnia that went hand-in-hand with it. The fact that the injections were repeated for several days in a row led to an effect that he had not foreseen due to the onerous physical condition he was in: he developed a tolerance… The disease developed; as he tried to fight it off, he lapsed into a feverish condition on numerous occasions: "I sobbed for whole days at a time," Tatiana recalled. She was pregnant again (the first time had been before the wedding); "my husband said: 'Have the baby if you want to, then you'll have to stay in this district.' 'Not for anything!' I replied, and then left for Moscow, to see my uncle… Of course, it was clear to me that you wouldn't get anywhere if you had a child at a time like that. But he didn't force me to do it, no. I didn't want to have it anyway… My father so wanted some grandsons… If Mikhail had wanted children – then of course I would have given birth to one! But though he didn't forbid it, he didn't want it either, that was as clear as day… And what's more, he was afraid that the child would be diseased…"

On 18th September 1917, Bulgakov managed to get a transfer to the hospital in the town of Vyazma.

That day, he was issued with a certificate by the Sychevka district municipal council which listed the operations he had performed that year, including one thigh amputation (one recalls the story from *The Towel with the Cockerel* – about the beautiful woman who fell into the decorticating machine). The certificate also states that there had been 211 in-patients that year, and 15,361 out-patients (i.e. an average of just over 40 people a day, taking all the public holidays into account).

On 20th September, the municipal council of the Smolensk governorate sent Bulgakov to take up his role under the authority of the Vyazma municipal council. In Vyazma they moved into Moskovskaya Street, living in three rooms next to the hospital. (In 1981, local historian A. Burmistrov published a letter written by Bulgakov: "Smolensk. Municipal council of the governorate. Dear Mr accountant. I most humbly request that my military allowance now be sent to me at the following address: "Vyazma. Town municipal hospital. With regards. Dr. Bulgakov. 10th October 1917.") The conditions here were completely different – for a population that was smaller than the one in Nikolskoye, there were three doctors! "A heavy burden slipped from my soul," the author of the story *Morphine* later wrote, doubtless recalling his feelings from that time. "No longer did I bear on *my own shoulders alone* that fateful responsibility for everything, whatever happened in the world. I was not to blame for constricted hernias and did not shudder when a sleigh arrived bearing a woman with shoulder presentation; I had nothing to do with purulent fluids, requiring an operation… For the first time, I felt like someone whose responsibilities were limited by some kind of framework."

Bulgakov was in charge of the departments for infectious and venereal diseases at the hospital.

It was in Vyazma, according to Tatiana, that he began to write in a more or less systematic way – in Nokolskoye he had only written in spasmodic bursts. "I once asked him: 'What are you writing?' – 'I don't want to read to you. You're very impressionable, you'll tell me I'm mad.' I knew only the title: *The Green Snake (Zelyonyy Zmiy)*", which, according to his sister's memoirs, had been commenced back in Kiev, and about some early drafts of what could later become *Morphine*.

The Bulgakov's were in Vyazma when the events of October occurred; they did not hear about them straight away. On 30th October, Tatiana wrote to Nadya Zemskaya: "Dear Nadyusha, write to me please, immediately, and tell me what is happening in Moscow. We are living in complete ignorance, we haven't heard any news from anywhere for four days now. We are very worried and it is an awful condition to be in."

We cannot presume to know what thoughts were going through the mind of the hero of our tale at this time, but a few years later, the mood which gripped Dr Bulgakov was to come up to the surface and find expression in his prose, refracted into the protagonist of *The White Guard*, Dr Turbin: "The eldest Turbin, clean-shaven, fair-haired, and gloomy ever since 25th October, 1917..." Bulgakov's acquaintances at the time reacted in a variety of different ways to what had happened. With regard to O.P. Gerasimov, for example, Kareyev recalls that "after the October coup, he began living on his own in the countryside and, when he came away from there to Moscow in early December, he managed to convince his wife and my daughter, who was staying with them, that 'nothing will come of it'. Then, though, it happened, and O.P. never returned to his estate, but instead died in one of the prison hospitals in Moscow..."; as for Kareyev himself, who lived in those areas in the summer of 1917 and 1918, "I did not decline the offer to give lectures, travelling for this purpose to the village of Voskresenskoye, four versts from Amosovo, where there was a spacious people's hall, built at my brother's initiative." He also gave lectures at the Zaitsevskaya School – for the peasants. Many people could sense that things were heading towards civil war. The documents that have survived from Bulgakov's life in the winter of 1917/1918 provide evidence that he had set himself the task, first and foremost, of liberating himself from military service – in order to get away from Vyazma and, it would appear, go back to Kiev. It is possible that he was also thinking about how to avoid getting caught up in the unpredictable mobilisation campaigns that were looming on the horizon. It was with this objective that he made the journey from Vyazma to Moscow in early December. Let us put forward a suggestion in connection with this trip.

It seems that it was still in Vyazma when he wrote the work entitled *The Ailment* (*Nedug*). In 1978, Tatiana, when telling me about the serious side-effects of the disease, which reached its peak in 1918, said: "*The Ailment* is about morphine, in my opinion..." (In 1973, prior to my conversation with her about this, I had put forward the view in print that the title *The Ailment* was more closely linked to the story *The Red Crown* (*Krasnaya Korona*, 1922), the subtitle of which was: "Historia morbi" (the history of a disease). Thus, the work that we know today as the long story *Morphine* was begun not shortly after what he had been through, but whilst he was still suffering from a disease that hit him very hard. Any claim that overlooks the fact that there was a definite autobiographical undercurrent to the story, therefore, is unlikely to be true; academics have known of this undercurrent for a long time: "The thing is, pathology never interested Bulgakov in and of itself," – in this case pathology interested him and was analysed by him with a medic's attention to detail. In the story *Morphine*, Dr Polyakov, whilst suffering from an addiction to morphine, voluntarily admits himself to a psychiatric clinic in Moscow in the autumn of 1917, in order to undergo a course of treatment. He registers the battles of October through the haze of the disease: "14th November 1917. So then, after the escape from Moscow, from the clinic of Dr … (the surname had been crossed out vigourously), I am at home again. The rain is falling in sheets and concealing the world from me. And let it continue to do so. I do not need it, in the same way that there is nobody in the world who needs me. I lived through the shooting and the coup whilst still at the clinic. But the thought of abandoning this therapy crept up on me like a thief even before the fighting broke out on the streets of Moscow. Thank you to the morphene for making me brave. No shooting can frighten me now. And in any case, what can possibly frighten a man who has one thing only on his mind: wondrous, divine crystals."

I would postulate that, first of all, Bulgakov may have left for Moscow without telling his family – earlier than on the date cited by him later – in order to attempt to spend some time in the clinic of one of his fellow doctors, or, at the very least, to have a consultation. It so happened that the events which turned Russian life upside down coincided with an extremely difficult personal collision-course. His condition in those days was, it seems, close to that of Dr Polyakov. Secondly, sharing L. Yanovskaya's perfectly justified view that *Morphine*, which had been printed in 1927, was a later edition of the novel that Bulgakov wrote a few years later, after Vyazma, "in outline", as he himself put it, *The Ailment*; however, I think the reason that "a couple of dozen pages" were torn out of Dr Polyakov's notebook in 1927 (*Morphine*) was not that "to the author of *Flight* (*Beg*), his early works about the civil war must have seemed naïve." They were a stinging record of how Dr Bulgakov felt at the time, shaken as he was by the fateful events of the day and by private catastrophe. It could not exist on pages printed in 1927: in 1921, the author wrote it freely, aware how clear it would be from what would happen next, and of the possibility of publication abroad.

After Moscow, he spent some time in Saratov; as N. Zemskaya later commented in letters to her brother, "he went further east, to his wife's hometown, to see her family and carry out her instructions with respect to her mother and father. The journey was extremely difficult: the transport links were destroyed, crowds of soldiers were pouring back from the front, and the trains were besieged by soldiers and passengers."

On 31st December 1917, Bulgakov wrote to his sister Nadya (she was in Tsarskoye Selo at the time) that in Moscow, he had "left with what he arrived in" (i.e. he hadn't managed to get an exemption from military service) and that "once again I'm at the grindstone in Vyazma." He wrote: "Recently, on the journey to Moscow and Saratov, I happened to see with my own eyes something that I never want to see again. I saw crowds smashing the windows of the trains, I saw people being beaten up. I saw buildings destroyed and burnt-out in Moscow. I saw hungry queues at the stalls, officers who looked hunted down and miserable... [...]

I live completely alone. Yet I have a large space for contemplation. And so I contemplate things. My only consolation is work and reading in the evening. I have been reading the old authors with great affection (whatever I can lay my hands on, since there aren't many books) and getting intoxicated by the pictures they paint of the olden days. Ah, why was I so late to come into the world! Why wasn't I born a hundred years ago. Yet it is impossible to rectify this of course! I am tortured by a longing to go away from here, to Moscow or Kiev, where life at least, although it is coming to a halt, is still continuing. I would particularly like to be in Kiev! In 2 hours, the New Year will be here. What will it bring me?"

He was anxious to know the fate of his younger brothers in circumstances which were becoming ever more complicated: he certainly already knew that in late October 1917, Nikolai had enrolled at the Junker school.

On 19th February 1918 (in the new style), his sister Varya sent a letter to Nadya from Moscow: "Misha is here with us. The commission exempted him from military service due to his illness. On 22nd February, the Vyazma municipal council issued him with a certificate confirming that Bulgakov, a doctor in the reserve, who had been assigned to the posting on 20th September 1917 by the Smolensk municipal council, had "performed his duties flawlessly" at the hospital in Vyazma.

His departure probably came not a moment too soon. Kareyev recalled that in the summer of 1918, an order was received from a provincial town calling for the arrest "of all former landowners, their managers or representatives, and other parasites as well." One could quite conceivably fall under the category of "other parasites" as a result of some misunderstanding on the part of the local authorities, or indeed on purpose, as part of some malevolent plan. Such was the tragic fate of Bulgakov's acquaintance M. V. Gerasimov, to whom I have already referred. According to Kareyev's memoirs, after graduating from the Derpt veterinary institute, Gerasimov "soon abandoned his profession and took up the position, which he then held for a long time, of chairman of the district council in Sychevka, where he was later elected to the city council." He died in 1918, "during the Yeremeyevskaya Night, as they called it there (it was some kind of personal vengeance, so they believe)."

And so two difficult years had come to an end. The world to which Bulgakov was returning from the back of beyond – as the Smolensk governorate was in those days – was completely different, however, from the one he had left two years previously.

The Founding assembly had just been dissolved, in early January, and thus a line had been drawn under *illusions* of any kind. In February, Germany put forward its ultimatum, simultaneously continuing its attack all the way along the front line.

None of this was of any help as Bulgakov sought to understand what sort of world he was now coming back to. Yet it was becoming increasingly clear: this world was changing, catastrophically and in a way that could not be stopped. Could the 26-year-old doctor, who had given up two years to backbreaking labour, have guessed that far greater hardships than those he had already been through were awaiting him?

His physical condition, like his spiritual one, was awful: he was still in the grip of a drug addiction. Episodes of intense spiritual depression kept recurring, when it seemed to him that he was losing his mind, and he entreated his wife: "You won't give me up to the hospital, will you?" Frightened and panicking at the thought that those around him would find out about his condition, and incapable of coping on his own, he forced his wife to go to the pharmacy for yet another dose, paying no heed to her admonishments. Worn out by all the circumstances of the last year, she too was dreaming of getting to Kiev as soon as possible.

"We travelled via Moscow. We left some of our things with my uncle, had lunch at *Prague* and left for the station straight away – the last train to Kiev from Moscow was just leaving, we wouldn't have been able to leave any later. That was another reason why we were going to Kiev, because there was no way out – there was nowhere to stay in Moscow…"

The heightened tension of the moment was caused by the fact that at this same time, the Treaty of Brest was being concluded; Ukraine had now genuinely become dependent on the German state. An equally significant and painful circumstance, as far as Bulgakov was concerned, was the fact that his native town, to which he was returning, was no longer part of Russia.

4

"… In Kiev, as I recall, no-one came to meet us. We hired a cab and drove to the Bulgakovs' house on Andreyevsky Hill. There were Germans all over the city." It was March 1918.

They now needed to find their feet and start making a living.

In the first few days after their return to Bulgakov's native town, after almost two years of being disengaged from life, they heard everything that their friends and loved ones could tell them about what they had seen and lived through. In March 1917, power in the city fell into the hands of the Executive Committee, elected by charitable organisations (one of the three "comrades of the chairman", representing the officer class, was L.S. Karum, who had recently become a relative of the Bulgakovs). In April, the Central Ukrainian Rada was elected, in opposition to which a committee was soon formed, as a body of power that expressed the will of the majority of the region's population.

… In November 1917, there was fierce fighting on the streets of Kiev. One of Bulgakov's brothers naturally found himself taking part in it – Nikolai, a young pupil at the military school. If we turn once again to the diary of the young noblewoman who was living in Ukraine at the time, in Bronnitsy, and whose view of the events in certain places must have been close to that of the Bulgakov family, then the unofficial account of these events looked like this: "In Kiev, the Cossack congress decided to establish order, but the Central Rada, it appears, wishes to declare itself to be on the side of the Bolsheviks. In the city […] there is artillery fire and machine-gun fire. Everything is being turned upside down and destroyed" (3rd November 1917); "In Kiev, Colonel Pavlenko (a Ukrainian) and comrade Pyatakov (a Bolshevik) are in charge of everything. They are both cut from the same cloth. The Rada has seized all power. Petlyura has declared himself the commander of all the armed forces in Ukraine…" (6th November), "… On 9th November, Ukraine declared itself a free democratic republic. The country's vulgar, bombastic 'Third Universal' [a directive issued by the Central Rada, headed by M.S. Grushevsky, in March 1917, together with the Ukrainian SR's – M.C.] had the desired effect on Ukrainian democracy, because it immediately gave the country what it wanted: land, an 8-hour working day, the abolition of the death penalty, an amnesty on all political crimes (would there be an amnesty for 'counter-revolutionaries', though?) [...] The 'Universal' abolished, of course, squireships, titles, medals and so forth. It adds that Ukraine will save Russia. Will it not be with the active assistance of Austria that our Grushevsky will save Russia? [Stealing a march on the negotiations in Brest by several months, Grushevsky had led separate talks between Ukraine and Austria. – M.C.]. The blood rushes to my heart when I think of the disgrace to which Russia has opened itself up before the face of all Europe, of all the world, due to the policy of comrade Trotsky-Bronstein! [...] Russian Russia will perish! It is disgraced, it cannot go on living! Yet let us die with it too, so that we do not see its disgrace, do not see the scorn of the whole world [...] Let all real Russians now go into hiding, somewhere far away, so that those allies who once respected their homeland, and now despise it, cannot hear their moans." Bulgakov's mood, one must suppose, was far removed from such feminine exaltation, but unless we appreciate the fact that nationalist and class-based feelings had reached boiling point in that fateful year, we will not be able to understand Bulgakov's worldview at the time, either, and it was this worldview that served as the gateway for his entry into literature.

On 12th December 1917, at the 1st All-Ukrainian Congress of Soviets in Kharkov, the Central Rada was declared illegitimate, and the Soviet People's Committee of Russia declared Ukraine's newly-formed Soviet government the only legitimate government, ordering that it must be given assistance immediately. Troops were sent into Ukraine. On the night of 16th January (29th in the old style), there was an uprising in Kiev, organised by the Bolsheviks. The Rada had a strong numerical advantage in terms of troops, however, and the Red soldiers did not make it into the city. As the authors of "The History of the Civil War in the USSR" tell us, "around one-and-a-half thousand workers were killed and tortured" beside the walls of the "Arsenal".

The uprising was doomed from the start and duly crushed, but before long the Ukrainian socialists in the Rada found themselves incapable of putting down an attack by the Red soldiers. On 26th January (8th February), the Reds took Kiev; in the following weeks, life in the city was chaotic; acts of looting became commonplace.

The newspapers in Petrograd reported: "Step by step, our troops knocked over the supporters of the Rada using artillery fire and bayonets, and eventually Kiev was taken. In a few places, groups of officers and soldiers are still clinging on, but the whole city is in the hands of the Soviet forces." (*The Voice of Labour*, 22ⁿᵈ January (10ᵗʰ February) 1918). On 30ᵗʰ January (12ᵗʰ February), the Soviet government arrived in Kiev (but in less than three weeks it was forced to abandon the city, under the terms of the Treaty of Brest). On 1ˢᵗ March, the Central Rada returned to Kiev – together with the Austrian and German troops who had joined it; on 29ᵗʰ April, the Rada was replaced with a German high-command: the Socialization of Ukraine was not part of its economic plans.

14ᵗʰ (1ˢᵗ) February was declared the first day of the new-style calendar in Russia.

On 15ᵗʰ February, the news came that General Kaledin had committed suicide.

On 20ᵗʰ February, Germany began its military operations; on 22ⁿᵈ February, Petrograd was declared to be under siege and the following slogan was put forward: "The Socialist fatherland is in danger".

Political life in Kiev over the previous year, as reconstructed by Bulgakov based on the newspapers and eyewitness accounts, was later echoed on the pages of *The White Guard*, in which, reading between the lines of a brief list of the main events of that year, that contains a large dose of sarcasm about Talberg and his flexibility as one coup followed another, one can attempt to identify – albeit with the caution required when adopting a "biographical" approach to an artistic text – the traits of the attitude of Bulgakov himself to what was taking place at the time. "In March 1917, Talberg was the first – the first, you must understand – to come along to the military school with a red armband, broad as a barn door, on his sleeve. This was in the first few days of the month, when all the officers in the City, on hearing the news from Petersburg, had been petrified and had gone off somewhere, into the dark corridors, so as not to hear any more. [...] By the end of that famous year, many wonderful and bizarre events had taken place in the City, and some strange people had been born in it, people who had no boots, but wore broad pantaloons beneath their grey, soldiers' overcoats, and these people declared that they would not leave the city for the front line under any circumstances, because there would be nothing for them to do at the front..." A later passage deals with the events which occurred in late January 1918 (the ones about which several inscriptions were left on the stove at the Turbins' house. "The men in pantaloons were driven out of the City at one stroke by grey, fragmented regiments, which had arrived from somewhere in the woods, from the plain leading to Moscow. Talberg said that those men, the ones in pantaloons, were adventurists, and that their roots lay in Moscow, although these roots were Bolshevik ones." This regarded the ceasing of the existence of the Central Rada, and the shift in power – before the signing of the Treaty of Brest, which changed the situation yet again: "But one day, in March, Germans came into the City in grey columns, and on their heads they wore red, metal helmets, which protected them from shrapnel, and their leaders rode on horseback wearing furry hats, and when Talberg caught sight of their horses, he knew where their roots lay. After a number of heavy strikes from the German guns outside the city, the Muscovites dashed off into the slate-grey woods somewhere to eat carrion, whilst the men in pantaloons hauled themselves back the other way, after the Germans."

In April, plans were being made in Kiev to elect a Hetman. Henceforward, the main source of power in the city fell into German hands. On 18th April (1st May in the new style), Vera Bulgakova wrote to her sister Varya in Moscow: "… only mother and Lyolya will travel to Bucha, and perhaps Vanya and Kolya as well, though I doubt it: they have various things to attend to in the city. Mother has let out half the dacha, the two rooms and the large veranda, to the Grobinskys, and has kept for herself and her guests the other 3 rooms and the small veranda. Misha, Tasya, Kostya and I are staying in the city. A group of teachers has asked me to take part in the opening of a private 'great Russian' grammar school, a mixed one, of the new style; this is very interesting, I am going to enjoy the work.

Spring is in full swing here, the lilac is budding, and will be blossoming at Easter."

There is a note in the letter for her uncle, Nikolai Pokrovsky: "I send you my best wishes on the day of your angel, I wish you all the best, and above all, that we may start living humanely once again as soon as possible. There is a feeling of exhaustion to the nth degree pervading the house at the moment. Mother has reached the nth degree of exhaustion both physically and nervously. The issue of finances has really made itself felt."

Bulgakov's younger brothers, and Bulgakov himself, were kept in the city, doubtless, by the political events, which were to determine the fate of Kiev and of the whole of Ukraine.

This was a relatively calm period for the peaceful citizens – after the siege of the city in late January, after the battles in the city in early March, order was restored to the streets; the difficulties people faced were chiefly to do with the concerns of day-to-day life, of the kind that one of Bulgakov's sisters writes about in a letter. On life in those months, on the life shared by all the young Bulgakovs, Tatiana Nikolayevna told me: "There was no maid in the house by that time. They cooked lunch themselves – taking turns to do so. After lunch there would be the clatter of the dishes being washed. When my turn to do the dishes arrived, Vanya put on an apron: 'Don't you worry Tasya, I'll do it. Only you have to come with me to the cinema afterwards, all right?' And so we went to the cinema, with Mikhail too – even under Petlyura and his men we still went! Since we had made up our minds to go, we would go, even if there were bullets whistling beneath our feet!" This was still a long way off, however. For the time being, young people once again gathered at the Bulgakovs' house eagerly, and things were fun and jovial once again.

It was essential, however, to start doing something, in order to keep his wife and himself fed. "Mikhail decided to start up a private practice. When we had left Saratov in the spring of 1917, my father had given me a silver dinner service – my dowry. We hadn't wanted to take it, to have to drag it around with us, but my father had insisted: 'it will come in useful'. Now, I decided to sell it. It was at that very time that I learned of my father's death – six months after he had died – in early 1918, in Moscow, on the very day when mother had arrived to see him… When I found out, I sent her 400 roubles immediately via the Red Cross, but unfortunately the money never reached her… With the rest of the money we bought all the things we needed in order to treat patients. I made 5000 roubles through the sale of the silver, but quickly spent it all.

Mikhail's office had a very convenient layout: the patients sat behind a curtain in the hall and couldn't see the people leaving the doctor's room; for patients suffering from venereal diseases, this was important.

The constant changes of government had a very strong impact on patient numbers: in the early days under each new government, there were hardly any people – they were probably too scared to come – but towards the end, there would be a lot of people. Most of the people who came, of course, were soldiers or the great unwashed – rich people didn't often contract those sorts of diseases. The money he made was therefore fairly small. I used to help Mikhail when he was receiving patients: I would hold the patient's hand when he was injecting him with neosalvarsan. I would boil the water. I removed the solder from all those damn samovars! I would get caught up in conversation and then find that the tap was already coming loose…"

The difficulties they had with their income were also related, one can suppose, to the special circumstances pertaining in Kiev in 1918-1919. The doctor Z.A. Ignatovich, in his unpublished memoirs, writes: "In Kiev, being as it was a large city and a hub, it so happened, utterly by chance, that a large number of doctors were located, who had returned from the Southern and South-Western fronts in 1918 and got stuck in Kiev, unable to get back to their permanent places of residence due to the civil war." This, of course, created a lot of competition.

G.N. Trubetskoy, in his memoirs, paints a picture of life in Kiev in those months which, in its details and even its emotional tone, is strongly reminiscent of some of the pages of *The White Guard*: "The aristocratic district of Lipka was... an awful ghost of the past. All Petersburg and Moscow would meet there, almost everyone knew one another. At every step you would encounter the typical faces of bureaucrats, bankers, landowners and their families. One could literally sense that there was a celebration taking place on the streets. It was down to this that the stories about some sort of Bacchanalia in the field of speculation and profiteering were spread. Anyone who had access to the institutions of government would earn his keep by obtaining all manner of permits for the exporting, sale and resale of various kinds of products. The landowners hastened to reimburse themselves for what they had lost, demanding that the peasants pay three times the normal price for what they had stolen. Those on the right, and the aristocrats, curried favour with the Germans. There were also those who openly decried the Germans whilst at the same time running to them through the back door, to try to wheedle something out of them! All those Russian circles, I must say, were far more disgusting than the Germans, who, against all expectation, behaved themselves in a way that did not raise eyebrows at all." There was thus a huge amount of material for anyone wishing to observe people's manners.

Who used to visit the young Bulgakovs' house at that time? Nikolai Gladyrevsky, a doctor and friend of the family, who helped Bulgakov in his practice for a while. His brother, Yury (Georgy) Gladyrevsky, also visited the house; he had a very pleasant baritone voice. "He used to sing 'Epitalama' and court Varya,' N.L. Gladyrevsky recalled in 1969, when I questioned him about those days. "He was a former officer then; he and Mikhail once went missing somewhere, they had some shared business, women-related, I think... But I didn't know anything about that, no-one knew anything... My brother was portrayed as Shervinsky in *The White Guard* and then in the play... And as for Lariosik – that was my cousin, Sudzilovsky. He was an officer during the war, then he was demobilized, and I think he tried to enrol at university. He came over from Zhitomir, he wanted to stay with us, but my mother knew he wasn't a particularly nice chap, and sent him off to the Bulgakovs. They rented out one of their rooms to him..." Tatiana Nikolayevna remembers Yury Leonidovich, too. "When Mikhail was receiving patients, he and I would often chat to one another in the room next door, and have a laugh. Mikhail would come in and say, giving us a suspicious look: 'What are you up to in here?' And we would laugh even more…" The vague contours of a *mise-en-scene* from *The Days of the Turbins*, which was to come into being a few years later – Yelena's laughter, Shervinsky's courtship of her – make themselves felt in these memoirs, faded as they are by the passing of time. "Did the young people still gather at our place then? Yes, they did…There was much singing, guitar-playing… Mikhail would play the accompaniment on the piano or be the conductor… In those days we had Sudzilovsky living with us – he was such a hoot! He was forever dropping things, and speaking out of turn. Lariosik is rather like him…" Pyotr Bogdanov arrived, the brother of the unfortunate suicide, a volunteer. Nikolai Syngayevsky was staying in the house as a private guest. Cousin Konstantin still lived in the house (Nikolai had already left Kiev). In one of the photographs from that year, showing a fairly large group of young people in the Bulgakovs' dining room – N.L. Gladyrevsky, N.N. Syngayevsky, and two admirers of the youngest sister Lyolya. The memoirs and photographs that have survived contain fragments of the reality – always chaotic – which was harmonized in strict order in the Turbins' household in *The White Guard*. As the years pass, however, the detailed nature of the correspondence between the two is becoming increasingly clear and increasingly striking. Tatiana recalls that even Karas from *The White Guard* had a prototype on which he was directly based: "There was definitely a Karas – everyone called him Karas or Karasik, I can't remember whether that was his nickname or his surname… He was just like Karas – short, fat, broad-shouldered… just like him. He had a round face… When Mikhail and I went to see the Syngayevskys, he was often there. Syngayevsky, by contrast, was tall, with long legs [one thinks of Myshlayevsky's 'legs like a pair of compasses' – M.C.], and generally had a nice figure…"

It is worth remembering that Bulgakov had arrived in Kiev in the early spring of 1918 in a very serious condition, after some unsuccessful attempts to cure himself (these were reflected in the story *Morphine*). His wife was the only person who saw all of this at first hand, witnessing all the details. "When we arrived – he lay there, flat out… And he kept asking me, beseeching me: He took to drinking opium straight from the bottle. He took valerium. When there was no morphine available, his eyes were all white, he looked pitiable. Whenever I wanted to go out, I would look at him and feel sorry for him…" He sent her to the pharmacy to get new portions – but she began stubbornly refusing to give him morphine; when she came home, she would say that they had refused to give her any. "I said to him one day: 'They've already put you on the blacklist'. At that point he got scared, but then he started sending me there again…" His fear of notoriety, his horror in the face of a hopeless future, which, as a doctor, he could see with great clarity – all of this helped him for a while, but then he would lose his cool. Once, Tatiana told me, he threw a lit primus stove at her; on another occasion he pointed a Browning at her. "Vanka and Kolya ran into the room and knocked the gun out of his hands… They didn't understand what was going on… Then they hid the Browning away somewhere. He wouldn't have shot me, of course, he was just threatening me… He felt very bad about it himself, he was tortured." It felt as though, as she narrated all this to me sixty years after the event, she pitied him just as she had done in those months. He had her to thank for the fact that he was cured of the disease, too. She began to trick him, injecting him with distilled water instead of morphine; she put up with his scolding and his bouts of depression. Little by little, something that happens only rarely began to occur: he lost his dependency. As a doctor, he was no doubt well aware that what had happened was almost a miracle.

That year, there was another married couple living at house No. 13 as well: Bulgakov's sister Varvara and her husband, Leonid Karum. According to Tatiana, relations between Bulgakov and his brother-in-law were strained; some of the character traits of Karum – a new person for Bulgakov in the house (his sister had got married in 1917) – would later prompt him to create the character of Talberg in *The White Guard*, although, of course, there is no point in trying to look for a biography or portrait of a real person in the novel. In terms of Bulgakov's biography, however, and of getting an idea about his circle of acquaintances in 1918-1919, there seems to be great value in some information that was kindly provided by Karum's daughter, Irina Karum. "My father was of German descent; his father was of purely German blood, but never lived in Germany; he was descended from Germans living in Riga; his brother and two sisters lived in Riga – Elsa and Anna, one of which was an elderly spinster, and the other was married to a school headmaster, at the school where my father studied. My paternal grandmother, Maria Fyodorovna Miotiyskaya, was Russian; she was the 16th child born to the owner of an estate near Bobruisk." My correspondent's grandfather, an officer in the Warsaw regiment, met his future wife when he went to stay with the owner of the estate. "The rules at that time, though, were that an officer from that regiment could only marry a young lady from a noble family. My grandfather had to leave the service and retire, and after doing so he married his beloved. My father was their first-born. Papa was an extremely hard-working, well-organised and orderly person; he loved order in all things; he wasn't miserly, but spent his money on things that he needed, distributed it in equal portions and *never in his life* (my correspondent's italics – M.C.) got into debt, a habit that he taught me as well. When he and mama lived as one family with the Bulgakovs in 1918, he couldn't see eye to eye with Uncle Misha and Auntie Tasya's way of life at all: they were liable to throw away money that they had only just earnt 'to the wind', as papa used to say. [...] Papa was utterly shocked by the fact that Mikhail Afanasievich was taking morphine, as well! Nowadays, when people openly describe the condition of people with an addition to morphine at that time, when they didn't have drug addicts, you can imagine what happened to Uncle Misha! [...] You can well imagine, though, the reaction this might have caused in a highly intelligent, tranquil, hard-working father, who loved my mother ardently and was trying hard to protect her from such scenes! He couldn't get his head around the fact that Mikhail's sisters and his were working, and he was living off them, leading a frivolous way of life! Of course, in that period, relations between my father and Mikhail were tense, but my father valued his brother-in-law's talent [...] He felt very sorry for Auntie Tasya, towards whom Mikhail was very arrogant, sarcastic all the time and treating her like a servant..."

In spite of the natural exaggeration that stems from familial devotion, one can make out, in these characteristics attributed by L.S. Karum to Bulgakov, some kind of basis in fact. Tatiana told me about that tension in their relations, which was engendered mainly by the difference in their characters, habits, family lifestyles. "I remember that we borrowed some money from Varvara, and we weren't able to pay it back straight away. One day I brought them some coffee, French rolls, butter and cheese. Karum said to Varvara: 'There they are eating and drinking, yet they haven't paid back what they owe us.' We all ate in the same dining room, you see – each person put out their food on the table and ate it..." Indeed, the married life of the Bulgakovs was already not nearly as lustrous as it had been in those pre-war years, which were on the face of it so recent, yet already seemed too remote, and L.S. Karum probably had good cause for considering the behaviour of his married brother-in-law to be "frivolous". Tatiana told me that at Easter one year, in either 1918 or 1919, her husband "arrived too late to attend matins. He hung around somewhere and came straight to Varvara's place" (the others had gathered at their mother's house opposite Andreyevskaya Church – she lived separately there with her husband – immediately after matins). "And he said to her: 'Well, God will punish me, so you don't have to.' He often repeated this line afterwards."

Many of the regulars at the house on Andreyevsky Hill, it transpires, were related to Bulgakov. "Kolya Sudzilvsky, who was often at the Bulgakovs' house, was a cousin of my father," I learned from Irina Karum in August 1987, "the son of the sister of my father's mother, Varvara Sudzilovskaya (née Miotiyskaya). They lived in Zhitomir. A. Gladyrevsky was a cousin of papa's, too, the son of Aunt Anya and her husband, Glayrevsky (a headteacher!), who moved from Riga to Moscow." And when, a few years later, Elena explains the arrival of Lariosik to the wounded Aleksei in *The White Guard* – "He is Sergei's nephew, from Zhitomir" – there would be a deliberate proximity in this, calculated for Bulgakov's relatives and loved ones, no doubt – to Karum's nephew, Nikolai Sudzilovsky.

I will quote an excerpt from an earlier letter I received from I.L. Karum on 20th August, 1981 (prompted by the first and only publication of the memoirs of T.N. Kiselgof during his lifetime, in which Tatiana pointed out that Karum was the prototype for Talberg). I.L. Karum wrote that as things stood in those days, her father "could have emigrated from Russia without any difficulty at all, as most of the former Tsarist officers like Talberg did. But my father went off to join the Red Army and went as far as the Crimea with it, under the command of Budyonny. He taught at the Feodosiyskaya infantry school (I was born in 1921 in Feodosia), then he was transferred to Sevastopol, then to Kiev, where he taught at the Kamenev military school for red commanders. He loved my mother, and they were never separated..." In 1933, Karum was arrested and exiled to Siberia. "We didn't know where he was, what had happened to him; we were driven out of the apartment, my mother got a job at the 'Bolshevik' factory, in the factory and plant training school, and we travelled to Bucha. The thing is that at the very spot where the Bulgakovs' dacha stood, they set up a pioneer camp for the 'Bolshevik' factory, also taking over the Lisyanskys' dacha, which was left untouched but was taken away from its owners. Mama managed to get me a place at that camp a couple of times, that was in 1933 and 1934, and, when she came to see me, on 'parent-teacher day' as they say now, we always went to the place where the dacha used to stand, and mama used to cry ever so much, I had great trouble persuading her to come away from there..."

... We know extremely little, however, about Bulgakov's life in those two years; about whether or not, for example, he made an attempt to establish any ties to the literary world. And the city certainly had a literary world, living a very diverse life. At Easter, at a meeting of the Kiev historical and literary circle, professor I.A. Linnichenko read a report on literary hoaxes (a subject in which Bulgakov later showed an interest). In May, a new kind of weekly journal began to be published: "Currents in art, literature, theatre and public life". In issue No. 3, which came out in June, a review by P. Pastukhov of S. Fedorchenko's book *A People at War* (*Narod na Voyne*) was printed. Sofya Fedorchenko, who had worked as a nurse at a military infirmary and written the book based on what she had seen and heard there, filling it with the soldiers' conversations, lived in Kiev at the time; in the twenties, Bulgakov befriended her and her husband in Moscow; it is possible that he first met her in Kiev.

Issue No. 7 of the journal contained an article entitled: "The artistic treasures of Kiev, damaged in 1918". It read: "With the departure of the Bolsheviks from Kiev, the troubles which came crashing down on Kiev have not yet come to an end. The terrifying explosion at Zverints, which occurred on June 5, provided a vivid reminder of what was suffered during the siege in January." The journal warned: "The Ministry of the Interior wants to destroy the monuments to Alexander, Kochubey and Iskra, and what is left of the monument to Stolypin…"

On 18th November 1918, the evening edition of the newspaper *Posledniye Novosti* (*The Latest News*) reported that on 19th November, an evening of literature and music would be taking place at the Kiev literature and arts club, at which Ilya Ehrenburg would deliver a lecture entitled "On contemporary poetry", and the writer Andrei Sobol would read an excerpt from his book, then Ehrenburg and L. Nikulin (referred to as a poet at the time, he later became a man of letters) would recite their poetry. On 30th November, the same newspaper printed a story about a report by N.N. Yevreinov (the famous director, playwright and expert on the theory of theatre from Petersburg), called "The Theatre and the Scaffold".

This period in Bulgakov's life remains the one that has been studied the least, but one thing is clear: many of his subsequent likes and dislikes, both literary and personal, had their origins in this time, when, in the exceptionally difficult circumstances created by the constant changes of government, many literary figures who later played a part in the cultural life of Moscow happened to be in Kiev.

Of the future professors in Moscow and Petrograd, N.K. Gudzy, V.F. Asmus and M.P. Alekseyev were all in Kiev at that time.

Among his future acquaintances in Moscow, Bulgakov may have met L. Nikulin in Kiev in this period; in September, in issue No. 8 of "Currents", Nikulin printed an article entitled "Books don't die", in which he wrote about recent publications (the full text of Pushkin's *Gavriiliada*, published for the first time; books by Blok and Yesenin, released by "The Ensign of Labour") and noted that among the futurists, "the curious gift of Mayakovsky" stood out; I. Ehrenburg also talked about Mayakovsky in his report "On contemporary poetry". A story by E. Zozul was printed in issue No. 9.

The well-known singer of ballads, Plevitskaya, was on tour in Kiev, and there were performances by the Moscow theatre "The Bat".

Kiev's academic and cultural life was in motion, and it is possible that it did not go altogether unnoticed by Bulgakov, but it was hardly his chief preoccupation. In the spring of 1918, i.e. soon after Bulgakov's arrival in Kiev, the remarkable Russian academic Vladimir Vernadsky also arrived in the city (Vernadsky's parents were from Kiev and he had spent his childhood in Ukraine) and began actively working to create a Ukrainian Academy of Sciences. "I set the condition then," he wrote in his memoirs in 1943, not long before his death, "that I was not going to be a citizen under a Ukrainian Hetmanship, I would take part in cultural work in Ukraine as an academic from the Russian Academy of Sciences." It was along the lines of this Academy that he organised his work, setting up a commission – for drawing up a charter for the Academy and so on. "The time was a revolutionary one, and they had to rescue the libraries at the estates near Kiev. A third commission was therefore formed, over which I presided." "We brought over from the surroundings of Kiev a host of libraries, many thousands of books." In October 1918, a list of members of the newly-formed Academy was published in the newspapers, as was its charter, and on 27th October the first general meeting of the Academy took place, at which the most senior member in terms of age was supposed to be the presiding officer, a professor from the Kiev Spiritual Academy, N.I. Petrov (M. Bulgakov's godfather), but for some reason the second eldest member presided over the meeting, professor O.I. Levitsky… V.I. Vernadsky was elected President of the Academy by a unanimous vote; on 9th November, he delivered a report on the significance of living matter in geochemistry, and in doing so published one of his most brilliant scientific concepts…

Although on the face of it, life in Kiev was progressing relatively calmly, some catastrophic events were already lurking beneath the surface. In April, Field-marshal Eichhorn issued an "Order on the spring planting", which provoked resentment among the peasants (it contained an order calling for the return of property owned by landowners).

In the summer, the tenseness of the situation became clear for all to see. On 9-10th July, news reached Kiev of the Leftist Socialist Revolutionary speech in Moscow and the killing of Mirbakh. In mid-July 1918 there was a strike by railway workers, across large swathes of Ukraine. Two trains that had departed Kiev were delayed mid-journey, and ten days later a train from Odessa was blown up outside Kiev. That same month, there were serious clashes with the German troops not far from Kiev, at Boyarka station. On 27th July, Simon Petlyura was arrested and put in prison. In early August there was an uprising in Kiev itself; it was badly organised and ended in bloodshed, with many fatalities. It was by now impossible to put a halt to the events that were unfolding, however. On 30th July, the commander-in-chief of the German army in Ukraine, Field-marshal Eichhorn, was killed - in broad daylight in the streets of Kiev, as Bulgakov would later write. On 10th August, the left SR who killed him, Boris Donskoi, was hanged in Lukyanovskaya Square.

On 20th June, the newspaper *Posledniye Novosti* (without doubt the model for the newspaper *Svobodnyye Vesti* (*Free News*) in *The White Guard*) reported, right at the bottom of the last page, in the section "Chronicle": "Information has been received in Kiev to the effect that a new 'volunteer army' is being formed in Odessa." On 16th July the congress of monarchists opened its doors in Kiev; on 23rd July, the same newspaper reported, in the characteristic tone of a newspaper that was not controlled by the party: "Kiev's monarchists decided that tomorrow, on the 9th anniversary of the death of Nik. Romanov, a funeral service will be held for a second time for the former tsar at a host of churches." On 13th September, a news story from Cologne was printed, restrained in its tone, which could not have appeared very seemly to Bulgakov and his circle: "His holiness the Hetman of All Ukraine, after inspecting Cologne, saw fit to depart for Hügel's villa..." The tenor of this story must have been about as reassuring as the ambiguous, vague reassurances in a report from Vienna: "... If even the states of the alliance are enmeshing the north of Russia with their bloodthirsty networks, as far as one can tell from the newspaper reports, at any rate, they are prepared to declare Ukraine's independence." The newspaper was trying to please everyone at the same time. On 7th November, S. Petlyura, was released from incarceration. On 8th November: "Kiev! Seize the day! The grand masquerade ball!"; 9th November: "Rumours of a renunciation by Emp. Wilhelm." "Plevitskaya on tour... Disorder on the railways..."; 11th November: "Ferment in the Austrian units"; "The charter of the Hetman of All Ukraine" – a call to remain completely calm at this dangerous time.

"Kiev and Ukraine felt strange and unusual at that time," V.I. Vernadsky recalls. "Kiev was full of German officers, wandering around Kreshchatyk, sitting in the coffee-houses. Some German newspapers arrived, which gave out inaccurate coverage of what was happening in our country and in Western Europe, but we didn't have any other news. In the south, in Podol, there were Austrian forces. Outwardly, everything seemed favourable in Kiev... yet we sensed that everything around us was merely decorum, and that the reality was something different. Eventually, the Hetman managed to send professor S.L. Frankfurt to Germany for economic negotiations of some sort. He was the first to bring some more specific news to Kiev to the effect that *everything we were seeing was just decorum* and that in reality, a peasant uprising had begun, and in Germany, a revolution; the country could not hold out much longer. At this time, foodstuffs were increasingly being bought up and exported to Germany. The peasantry began to defend itself. [...] Blatant propaganda began to be spread among the German troops and among the populace, new people emerged who had been in hiding before. One fine day, some German and Russian soldiers appeared (drunk and with their waistcoats unbuttoned), fraternizing with one another and singing revolutionary songs; discipline was shattered, the officers have gone into hiding, it's said that some have committed suicide. The German army has fallen apart. The process took place extremely quickly." This expressive account of what was taking place would serve as a good commentary for *The White Guard* (which conveys with such subtlety this sense of vibration, this alarming uncertainty, which penetrated, it seems, the very air in Kiev in the autumn of 1918), and it is useful material for a reconstruction of the most general traits of Bulgakov's life in those months.

On 13th November 1918, almost at the same time as the treaty of Brest was annulled, the news came through that a new government had been formed in Ukraine: the Directorate.

In order that the modern reader might be able to get a sense, in the broadest brush-strokes at least, of exactly what kind of choice Bulgakov and his brothers and friends were faced with in those weeks, of what the alternative courses of action were, let us explain some of the details of the specific situation in Kiev in the second half of 1918. In the fourth volume of *Sketches of the Russian Unrest (The Armed Forces in the South of Russia)* [*Ocherki Russkoy Smuty (Vooruzhennyye Sily Yuga Rossii)*], released in 1925 by the "Slovo" publishing house, A.I. Denikin described the situation at that time as follows: "The formation of the armed forces, for which the Hetman had been given permission by the German government whilst he was in Berlin, presented certain insurmountable difficulties. Universal conscription, on the introduction of which the minister of war, Ragoza, insisted, did not provide a promise of any success whatsoever, and, according to the people around the Hetman, could have resulted in a very sizeable Bolshevik component in the army. The formation of a class-based army – a 'free Cossackhood' of volunteers – grain farmers – had already been tried, with bitter consequences, in the form of the Serdyuk division, which had very nearly turned tail and fled. The plan drawn up by the general's staff to form a national guard adjoined to the Sich Division, using its instructors, was clearly intended to prepare armed forces not for the Hetman, but for the UNU [the Ukrainian National Union, created in August 1918 under the chairmanship of V.K. Vinnichenko; this body organised the Ukrainian Directorate. - M.C.] and Petlyura... All formations organised along national lines were met with furious, stormy protest among the Russian officers, who were in no way inclined to fight either for the Hetman, or for an independent Ukraine." It was in this interweaving of not two, but of multiple forces and movements battling one another, that Bulgakov's friends and loved ones had to determine where they stood. They faced a question that cannot be ignored for a man who consciously takes up arms: against whom, and in protection of whom, will they be used?

In mid-October, when the revolution in Germany began and it became clear that Germany would be required at any moment to leave Ukraine, and the semblance of equilibrium would collapse, the Hetman issued an order on the formation of a Special corps, directly subordinate to him – bypassing the government. The corps was intended "for the battle against anarchy"; internally, it was to be guided by "the regulation on the former Russian army, effective as of 1st March 1917"; the ranks of this corps were issued with "the uniform of the former Russian army". At the same time, it was announced that all officers would have to undergo registration and a warning was issued about the forthcoming mobilisation of officers and long-service unter-officers (under the age of 35), into either the Ukrainian forces or the Russian corps, at their discretion. "The first combination, in the eyes of the officers," as the author of *Sketches of the Russian Unrest* explains, "led to the assertion of Ukrainian independence inside the country" (this could in no way have been something that the eldest and the younger Bulgakovs had made allowance for), "and the second – was to leave for the front at once in order to protect it from incursions from the outside." A.I. Denikin confirms: "And the officers didn't go anywhere. Theoretically, out of conviction; not theoretically – out of self-interest. In both circles, a strong flow out of Ukraine had begun – some went to the areas where the Russian volunteers were, others – to the regions where there was not yet any forced conscription, where they could live peacefully, work in restaurants, earn some money 'playing the lottery' and engage in speculation." Bulgakov later portrays this disintegration of the officer class fleetingly in *The White Guard*, although the main period in which the novel is set is December 1918 – the height of the tension, when the officer class that remained in Kiev was more or less homogenous: everyone who wanted to flee and was able to flee had already done so ("The ones who are fleeing, they won't die," the author of *The White Guard* wrote, "- so who's going to die then?"). "Due to the complete collapse of the government organisation and the unsuccessful attempt at mobilization, there was a need to resort to a private organisation." The Minister of the interior "adopted the proposal that he had previously rejected: to enter into an agreement with the existing officers' self-assistance groups in Kiev and to give them resources and powers so that they could form 'brigades'; these units were intended first and foremost to keep the peace and maintain order in the capital. Thus it was that the brigades of colonels Sviatopolk-Mirsky, General Kirpichev, Rubanov, Golembkovsky and others came into being – some of them officers only, some mixed, with volunteers – predominantly from among the young people who were still studying, among whom the response to conscription was very mixed: some joined the officers' brigades, others sought 'more democratic groupings', others still – and there were quite a few like this – declared that they preferred Soviet power to Ukrainian independence, and laid low to see how events would unfold." (An echo of the latter "preferences" can be heard in the words spoken by Myshlayevsky in the last chapter of *The White Guard*, when he says that the Bolsheviks will arrive, "tax us to the heavens and use our money to cover their costs" – "but at least they'll do it in Russian"). Among the students who faced this choice was Bulgakov's brother Nikolai, who had enrolled at the faculty of medicine in the autumn of 1918.

On 14th November, a story appeared in the papers in Kiev about an order issued by General Denikin, which declared that all troops on Russian territory were subordinate to him and that all officers were to be mobilized. Denikin's representative in Kiev in all but name, general Lomnovsky, sent word to the head of Denikin's staff in connection with this: "I was invited just now to see the Hetman, who asked me to pass on this message: today, the commanders of brigades and local regiments came to see him and reported that they were switching over to your command. In the light of the complicated and alarming situation in Kiev, if this happens, it could result in disorder. It is essential to wait a few days, until the Entente troops get here. There are brigades patrolling the streets now, and an outpouring of officers could harm the situation. We are operating amid a tide of rumours, in which there is little to guide us." The chief of staff, general Romanovsky, denied that the commanders-in-chief had been given such an order: "An order was issued on the mobilization of officers only on the territory occupied by the Volunteer Army. It goes without saying that the troops on this territory are subordinate to the commander-in-chief." In summary, he said: "The order that appeared in Kiev's newspapers is the result of a misunderstanding of some sort." If this was indeed a "misunderstanding", then it was certainly one that had important consequences.

The Hetman, on learning that the brigades that had been formed were no longer to be subordinate to him and would now be "championing Russia-wide interests", published a new charter the very next day, which stated: "... after the great losses suffered by Russia, the terms for its future existence must, undoubtedly, be changed. On foundations of a different kind, on federative grounds, the former glory and might of the All-Russian state must be restored, and in this federation, Ukraine must take up one of the foremost places..." The Hetman was trying, without success, to satisfy the interests of different strata in society, in this case strata which were opposed to one another.

On 15th November, the morning edition of *Posledniye Novosti*, under the headline "Yesterday's day", reported: "On the streets, after midday, the mood was extremely lively – the public were seizing the evening papers with a rare level of curiosity, expecting to find out something about how things stood in Kiev from them. At that moment, the attention of those in the streets was drawn to an unusual to-ing and fro-ing of small brigades, the majority of which were officers from the volunteer units."

The general public's eagerness to read the newspapers was understandable: that very day, on 13th November, at an illegal meeting of representatives of political parties held at the premises of the ministry of communication lines, the Directorate had been elected, consisting of the writer and chairman of the Ukrainian National Union, V.K. Vinnichenko, S.V. Petlyura and others ("back in September, no-one in the city could have imagined the trouble that would be whipped up by three men who possessed a talent for appearing at the right time, even in such an insignificant setting as the White Church," the author of *The White Guard* later wrote); the first assembly of the German Council of military deputies took place, student gatherings and demonstrations were held. On 14th November, an order was issued by the Hetman to the effect that gatherings and protests were banned, institutions of higher education were to be closed and a curfew was to be introduced. On the same day, a student demonstration was organised at the university, protesting against these measures (the newspapers reported that 8 people were killed and 12 were injured – *Vidrodzhennya*, No. 188), and general Kirpichev announced that he was taking over command of the volunteer brigades, which were required to maintain "law and order" in Kiev (*Kiyevskaya Mysl'* [*Kiev Thought*], No. 215"). On 15th November, the Directorate's proclamation was stuck up around the city, calling for the overthrow of the Hetman. The Hetman and its ministers were offered the chance to leave without bloodshed, whilst the officers were informed that they could surrender their weapons and depart, to "wherever they saw fit to go". At that time, an uprising against the Hetman was already taking place, the driving force behind which were the Galician Sich units; the regiment of Bolbotun, who had switched from the Hetman's side to join Petlyura (Bolbotun was apparently the prototype for Balbachan in *The Days of the Turbins*) had already disarmed the brigades of officers in Kharkov and, without coming up against any impediments on the part of the German authorities (who were engaged in complex manoeuvring between the Hetman and the Directorate), declared that the Directorate was now in power.

Rather eloquent evidence of how the strategy of conscription to the Hetman's forces was going is provided by a short report in the morning edition of *Posledniye Novosti* from 15th November 1918: "According to information from the general staff, the conscription of officers is unfolding in all districts where the corps are present in an entirely normal and successful way." Translated from the language of this paper into the language of reality, this could only mean one thing: the officers were reluctant to join the Hetman's forces. For most of them, the actions of Denikin were particularly significant in this situation; Denikin himself would write, 7 years later: "The position I was in was pretty difficult. The armed force that was taking shape in Kiev decisively refused to march under the banner of the Hetman of an independent Ukraine. In order to maintain the upsurge of patriotism among the officer class and protect the region from invasion by the Bolsheviks before the allies were due to arrive, I decided to give the Kiev formations the flag of the Volunteer Army." On 17th November, Denikin sent a telegram to the Volunteer Army's representative in Kiev, Lomnovsky, ordering that he "unite control of all of Ukraine's Russian volunteer brigades, and his duties include ensuring that his actions are in harmony with the interests of the region, putting all efforts into the battle with the Bolsheviks and not interfering in the internal affairs of the region..." This program soon revealed itself to be impossible to implement. In the meantime, General Lomnovsky, on receiving this order, visited the Hetman on 18th November (the newspaper reported this immediately). That same day, another missive from the Hetman was published: "Due to the emergency situation, I hereby confer general command of all the armed forces operating on the territory of Ukraine on the general of the cavaliers, count Keller, in the capacity of commander-in-chief of the armies of the front… I declare that the entire territory of Ukraine is a theatre of military action, and for that reason all the civil powers in Ukraine are subordinate to general count Keller."

Thus, the voluntary Russian brigades were no longer directly subordinate to the Hetman; rather, they had indirectly been exempted from subordination to the high command of the Volunteer Army, although its flag symbolically flew over these brigades.

The menacing directive issued by the new commander-in-chief underlined the complexity of the function he had taken on: he was threatening court-martials to those who were "refusing to take part in crushing the current uprising, justifying this by saying that they consider themselves part of the volunteer army and only want to do battle with Bolsheviks, and not crush internal disorder within Ukraine." (morning edition of *Posledniye Novosti*, 21st November 1918).

A comment that is extremely typical of these times, by virtue of its non-committal style and the vague nature of its content, appeared in the evening edition of *Posledniye Novosti* on 19th November 1918: "Kiev, 19th November. Once again, the fog, the heavy, autumnal fog has descended upon us and bears down on us with all its weight. Of whence it came, and of which winds brought it to us, we shall say nothing, for nobody quite knows for sure" (in a word, nothing could "dispel the cloudy porridge that was cooking in people's minds" – as it was expressed in *The White Guard*). But the fog is here and we must live in it," ["… the fog was lifted and dispersed" – Bulgakov would later bring the first part of *The White Guard* to an end with these words, directly connected to the enveloping fog of those days – M.C.]. "We are surrounded by rumours and gossip on all sides. Provocative demonstrations start to come into being in the fog. Calls for demonstrations of all kinds reach our ears.

In such an atmosphere it is hard to remain calm, but remain calm we must."

It was indeed hard to remain calm.

On 27th November, General Keller resigned, having not been granted the absolute power he had demanded; in his farewell directive, he explained: "… I feel that without a united executive at this time, when an uprising is breaking out in all the governorates, establishing calm in the country is impossible…"

With increasing frequency, the name of Enno crops up in the papers from those days; he was the French consul "with special powers" appointed by the allied states to Kiev. After arriving in Odessa, he began sending telegrams from there from 20th November onwards to the German chiefs of staff in Kiev, and to the Hetman's government, on behalf of the Entente. By this time, of course, the allies were no longer at war with the Germans and were getting ready to replace them in Ukraine. Prior to this time, finding a solution to the matter of Ukraine's self-determination and national character had been postponed. The telegrams stated, among other things, that the Germans undertook to maintain order in Kiev and the whole region – until the arrival of the allies, and that "the states of the Entente will not, under any circumstances, allow an incursion by Petlyura's forces into Kiev…"

This was why people were awaiting the arrival of the allies with increasing tension with each passing day. In edition after edition, throughout November and early December, *Posledniye Novosti* publishes reports under a permanent newspaper heading, printed in a very bold font: "To the Allies' Arrival", interspersing them with run-of-the-mill information about literature and the theatre: "The second edition of the collected stories of G.N. Breitman, *The Repair of Love* (*Remont Lyubvi*), is on sale now"; "The 23rd edition of the satirical weekly magazine *Urod* (*An Ugly Person*) has come off the press"; "N.F. Baliev's *The Bat* (*Letuchaya Mysh'*), by the Moscow Theatre"; "The book by the priest and professor Sergei Bulgakov, *At the Feast of the Gods: A Contemporary Dialogue* (*Na Piru Bogov: Sovremennaya Dialogiya*), has come off the press and gone on sale".

19th November: "The allied fleet (from our own corr.). Odessa, 18. Rumour has it that the allied fleet is going to reach the Black Sea today." Then the next report, under a new headline: "The allied fleet is in the Black Sea": "… there are now reports that twelve military vessels have moved out of the Bosphorus, accompanying convoys carrying non-white troops, headed for Sevastopol." New paragraph: "The crew of the *Posadnik* ferry, which has arrived, had seen four minesweepers on the horizon."

On 26th November (a Tuesday), the newspaper "Evening" printed a report "Before the arrival of the French consul": "As it turned out, the French consul Enno, who was in Odessa, postponed his arrival in Kiev somewhat due to the statement made by representatives of the railway authorities to the effect that in 3 days' time, it would be possible for him to make the journey from Odessa to Kiev in extremely comfortable conditions, with a full guarantee that there would be no accidents of any kind. On Thursday, there will be a meeting for representatives of the allied consulates located in Kiev, at which the programme for the triumphal meeting that will be extended both to M. Enno, and to the allied soldiers arriving in Kiev."

And on the same page: "Victims of their duty. A new list has been published of those killed as they did battle against the Petlyura-ite officers. Today's list contains 33 killed…" Among them are colonels, lieutenant-colonels, the Yezersky brothers – warrant officers, a cadet named Yakobenko… "The remaining 18 bodies are so disfigured that there is no possibility of identifying them whatsoever. The corpses are completely naked, they have had their tongues cut out, their noses, ears, fingers and toes cut off and their whole bodies cut to pieces. Today, at 12 o'clock, the bodies of those killed were delivered to the surgery." It was against the backdrop of messages like this that the Bulgakov brothers were making ready to defend their city.

Incidentally, the reports about military actions on the same page of "Evening" sounded as optimistic as the ones in *Posledniye Novosti*: "Groups of bandits broken up by the state *varta* (the police under the Hetman's government)… On 25th November, a group of bandits, under cover of the morning mist, attacked a brigade of government troops, but was repelled, leaving 8 dead on the field of battle…On 25th November, a band of rebels moving towards Mirgorod was destroyed by government soldiers and the state *varta*".

The special correspondent of "Evening", twenty-year-old Mikhail Koltsov, who had recently graduated from Realschule in Kiev, also reported, optimistically: "The volunteer brigades are doing battle courageously. The French helmets, made of steel, on the heads of the volunteers, bear *upon them* traces of the true exercise of their duty as soldiers. The young Serdyuk division also demonstrated its energy and fearlessness. The same may be said of the Serdyuk artillery. Slowly but surely, the troops in Kiev are forcing Petlyura out of the capital." And after that the correspondent found himself in the rear of Petlyura's army, at an inn in the village of Yurovok: "The majority of those who have ensconced themselves at the inn are part of the brigade destroyed by the volunteers. What talk! What hatred!" He described a conversation between two people, in which one man's speech was pervaded with "a wild hatred of the 'perfidious inhabitants' of the Ukrainian capital, who were supporting the anti-Petlyura-ites through their sympathies, […] and was a mixture of Ukrainian, Polish and Galician jargon. The other man, a hard-drinking young man in a shabby coat, spoke Russian, clearly, and intelligibly, as far as I was concerned:

'They've got a nerve, they've really gone too far, those lizards in Kiev […] If I were in your shoes, comrade, I'd lay siege to 'em all, before doing anything else. Die of hunger, you sons of bitches! […]'

His eyes were sparkling, and his lips were twisted into a trembling, vengeful grimace.

'Another small glass for us both, comrade!'

The glasses clinked, bringing together – for the umpteenth time! – men who had recently been deadly enemies, a Bolshevik and a Petlyurite.

What was it that had so reconciled a shabby Communist who had strayed into Ukraine, and that furious, independent-minded Sich Rifleman? What platform united them?

Of the platform we shall say nothing… God forbid that the people of Kiev should ever see this platform come into being." Bulgakov, who was doubtless examining all the major newspapers carefully as he sought some sort of information about how things really stood, must have been amazed as he read these words, by a man who was printing an article against Petlyura and yet was sitting peacefully in an inn in his army's rear. (It was against the backdrop of these impressions picked up in Kiev that he would later interpret the leading role in publishing for the Communist party played by Mikhail Koltsova in Moscow). "… We have to see much that is tragic and absurd, sad and ridiculous in these terrible, merry days of ours," M. Koltsov concluded. Bulgakov was certainly in no mood for merriment. As I see it, he was most definitely devoid of any inclination for adventurism.

On 29th November, in a column of *Posledniye Novosti* headlined "The Situation in Ukraine", there are a large number of 'holes' created by the censors; it is impossible for the reader to work out what the "situation" is, and in the third column, two paragraphs under the heading "Stop press", two paragraphs have been completely deleted: the powers that be were clearly attempting to keep readers calm… On 30th November, the evening edition covered the negotiations between the German commanders and the consul, Enno; the arrival of Serbian forces in Odessa (in *The White Guard*, Shervinsky says: "Please send this important news: today, I saw, with my own eyes, some Serb billeting officers on Kreshchatyk." On the 2nd, a newspaper report read: "Tomorrow – flight… Yushkevich and Bunin passed through the city – they are emigrating. They read some of their stories out at the Intimate Theatre. A. Tolstoy was also expected to come, but he did not go through Kiev as it turned out," N. Ushakov recalled. The morning edition of *Posledniye Novosti* reported, on 3rd December: "As a result of a delay during his journey from Odessa to Kiev, the evening of prose and poetry with AL Tolstoy shall be postponed to a day in the very near future," but no new announcement followed this. The evening edition on 2nd December reported: "German cavalry units are ranged in front of our front line…the Fastov station was taken yesterday by the German forces. Petlyura's troops, after cleaning the station, went off, their destination unknown" (the author of *The*

White Guard quotes the newspaper *Svobodnyye Vesti*: "… departed, destination unknown, with his regiment and 4 vehicles"). This was the moment when Petlyura headed from the White Church through Fastov towards Kiev, but his attempt to seize the Fastov railway hub was paralysed by the evacuation of German troop trains which was already taking place, and caused a clash with the Germans; neither Petlyura, nor the handful of squadrons of militias led by Svyatopolk-Mirsky and the other forces who were rebelling against Petlyura, had enough men to tip the scales one way or the other. It was impossible to assess the actual situation on the ground, however: there wasn't enough information, and all that remained to do was wait and see how events would unfold.

On 2nd December: "In the coming days, it is expected that several large brigades of allied forces will arrive in Kiev." On 3rd December it was reported that officers had been killed at the hands of the insurgents, whilst on 5th December, no fewer than *four times* - in the reports from 2nd December to 5th December, the same report is repeated: "At the front outside Kiev and in the city, all is quiet!" There is also a report stating that the cruise ship "Mirabeau" has arrived at Odessa carrying French troops: "The first troop train has already set off for Kiev." (A few days later, a half-optimistic, half-desperate headline appeared: "The French are in Zhmerinok").

The more the dispatches sought to calm and reassure readers, the more the very air in Kiev's streets, it seems, was filled with anxiety; on 7th December, there was another story in the papers beneath a headline that had already been seen once before: "Mobilization in Kiev": "Pursuant to the law of 5th December 1918 on the conscription of those born on 1st January 1889 through 31st December 1898…" – and the address of the conscription centre was indicated. This law directly concerned two of Bulgakov's brothers – Mikhail and Nikolai. They probably did not hurry to enrol with the Hetman's army, though. Over the next few days, the press continued to hypnotize the citizens with the hope that the allies would soon arrive. On 11th December, the evening edition of *Posledniye Novosti* reported: "We know from reliable sources that the arrival of the first brigade of allies in Kiev is expected at the end of this week. Rooms have been prepared at the 'Continental' hotel for the French officers." And that very day, the news came through that some Senegalese soldiers would soon be arriving… The newspapers urged the people of Kiev to place special hope in these "non-white" soldiers, and this lent an additional shade of the fantastical to all that was taking place. An echo of this is found in the pages of *The White Guard*: "Our correspondent reports on the negotiations on the debarkation of two divisions of black colonial troops. Consul Enno is refusing to countenance the thought that Petlyura…" – Aleksei Turbin reads in the paper *Svobodnyye Vesti*, yet on the tiles of the stove at his house, there are messages "written by Nikolka in India ink and full of profound meaning and significance: 'If they tell you that the allies are hastening to come to our rescue, don't believe it, the allies are bastards.'"

"Where are the Senegalese squadrons?" the papers joked; "Where, oh where are they? Answer me, officer, answer me," Myshlayevsky says to Shervinsky – an adjutant to the Hetman. Shervinsky assures him, just like the papers: "The prince himself told me today that at the port of Odessa, the convoy vehicles are already being unloaded: some Greeks and two divisions of Senegalese have arrived…"

In order to recreate the atmosphere of the subsequent month – one of the most dramatic of Bulgakov's life in Kiev and in the lives of those close to him – let us turn to an eyewitness account. It is the diary of a military doctor, Alexander Yermolenko (1891-1958), who was in Kiev at the same time as Bulgakov. "24th November. For seven days now, the Hetman's guns and Petlyura's guns have been thundering outside Kiev itself. Petlyura, with his Austrian Sich Riflemen and the Bolsheviks added on (to them?) – on the one side, and the volunteer brigades consisting almost entirely of (former) officers on the other. Battle is raging alongside Post-Volynsk. It is so close to us that the volleys of artillery fire and machine-gun fire can be heard very distinctly. The German troops are not taking part in the battle." These are the very same events that are described to the Turbins by Myshlayevsky, after he has hauled himself into their house, half-frozen: "A whole day in the snow and the freezing cold… Good God! I thought… we would all perish! A hundred sagenes from one officer to the next – and they call that a chain? I was very nearly carved up like a chicken!" "Well, at dusk we made it through to Post. As for what's going on there – it's unfathomable. Along the way I counted four batteries, standing there undeployed; there were no shells, it turns out. […] And no-one knows a damn thing, of course. And the worst of it: there was nowhere to put the dead!" (*The White Guard*).

The author of the diary then writes: "On the 11th, I went to sign up. On the 9th, the mobilization of those born between 1889 and 1898 began. The doctors were called up on the same terms as everyone else, i.e. with a rifle. I was added to some sort of "protective brigade" and, being as I was over the age of 27, they let me go home, telling me that if the need arose, I would be called up to defend the city itself."

Was the exemption from military service that Bulgakov had received back in Moscow still valid now, in a different sovereign state? If not, then he would be in the same boat.

As a source for theorizing about Bulgakov's mindset in 1918, the speeches made by Turbin in *The White Guard* may be indirect (as is always the case when we are dealing with the statements made by a literary protagonist), but they are pretty much all we have to go on. "I would make sure that Hetman of yours," cried the elder Turbin, "for setting up this nice little Ukraine, I'd make him the first to be strung up! For 6 months he made fun of the Russian officers, made fun of all of us. Who terrorised the Russian populace with that hateful language, which doesn't even exist in the real world? The Hetman. Who unleashed that scum with the tails on their heads? The Hetman. Who banned the formation of a Russian army? The Hetman. And now, now that the cat's been laid over the stomach, they've started to form a Russian army? Look at it, just look at it!'

'You're spreading panic,' Karas said coolly."

On 13th December, the doctor – the author of the diary – writes: "Since midday today, the artillery has been at work all around Kiev. The streets are full of people, and the shooting isn't scaring anyone. On the contrary, most people are smiling, and the particularly loud blasts are met with witticisms. You get the impression that Petlyura doesn't scare anyone and that, if anything, the crowd is favourably disposed towards him, rather than hostile. There are no trains going anywhere now – for Petlyura is everywhere. The price of food has shot up: black bread costs as much as 5 roubles a pound, salo costs 24 roubles, a pound of firewood costs 8 roubles.

13th December. During the day, almost all the shops are closed. I had to work to the cracking of machine-gun fire and the volleys of gunfire.

Some said that Petlyura was already in Pechersk, others – that one of the Hetman's brigades had started an insurrection. A strange tension can be felt everywhere; everyone's nerves are shredded. Towards evening, the crowds started gathering in the streets, to see off the Hetman's brigades who were retreating from Kiev – with whistling and hooting. The crowds didn't show any mercy for the Red Cross, either. Some nurses who were travelling on a two-wheel coachbox were met with foul language worthy of the gutter. By evening, the news had reached us that Petlyura had entered Kiev from the Svyatoshin side, and that at the European bazaar there was a huge pile of bodies of volunteer brigades. There are machine-guns set up in many places."

On 13th December 1918, the morning edition of *Posledniye Novosti* reported: "Today, a draft law was introduced at the council of ministers, as a matter of urgency, on the conscription of new recruits born in 1900." This was an urgent conscription; Vanya Bulgakov, his younger brother, had been called up a year earlier though, ahead of time.

At this time, according to Tatiana's recollections, Bulgakov, like his younger brothers, went out to defend the city, not yet knowing that on 14th December the Hetman had fled the scene with the Germans. "Various people came to see him at that time; they conferred together and decided that they should defend the city. And he went off to do so. Varya and I were left alone, waiting for them. Then Mikhail came back on a cart and said that everything was ill-prepared and that all was lost – the Petlyurites had already entered the city. Meanwhile the boys – Kolya and Vanya – had stayed at the school. We were waiting for them, but they fell into a trap set up by the Petlyurites."

What was taking place at the school became the stuff of family legend and was written down fifty years later by Yelena Sergeyevna Bulgakova, on the basis of the account she heard from Nikolai Afanasievich's wife. The story even had a title: "How the caretaker Maksim rescued Nikolka": "When the Petlyurites arrived, they demanded that all the officers and junior officers gather together at the Pedagogical museum at the First grammar school (the museum at which the works of the grammar school students were archived). They all did so. The doors were locked. Kolya said: 'Good God, we need to get out of here, it's a trap.' No-one dared do anything.

Kolya went up to the second floor (he knew the building like the back of his hand) and got out into the yard through a window; there was snow in the yard, and he fell into the snow. This was the courtyard of their school, and Kolya made his way into the school, where he happened to chance upon Maksim (the caretaker). He had to get out of his cadet's uniform. Maksim took his things and gave him his suit to put on, and Kolya went out through a different door – in civvies – and made his way home. The others were all shot."

(One recalls a passage from *The White Guard*: the crowd of cadets and officers at the museum, which Turbin sees, and Malyshev's words: "I've just come from there, I was shouting, warning them, telling them to run away. There's nothing else I can do," and the description of Nikolka's escape through the courtyards: "As he fell from the second wall, he judged it quite well: he had landed in a bank of snow…" etc.)

That same day, 13th December, there was a story about a German commander in the evening paper. It said that "in accordance with the circumstances and facts, namely, that in most of Ukraine, power is in the hands of the Ukrainian directorate," "an agreement has been reached between the

German military command, the soldiers' council and the Ukrainian directorate, whereby the German troops will not put up any resistance whatsoever to the entry of the Directorate into Kiev." The poor Russian translation only served to intensify the intimidating effect of the document: "The preservation of order in the city is of the greatest importance.

In order to avoid acts of vengeance on the part of the Ukrainian troops, it is unconditionally necessary to put up impediments, so that, on the part of the voluntary brigades, before their departure, no terrorist acts whatsoever are undertaken against the Ukrainian troops. If this should happen, then the German authorities will not be held accountable for the consequences." A small note entitled "Special train" reported: "We have been told that between the highest German command and the Directorate, an agreement has been reached to let a special train through from Kiev to Switzerland." (Talberg would depart by this train in *The White Guard*...)

The operational dispatch from the staff of the high command of the Hetman's forces was, however, almost unperturbed, just as before: "At night, our units were engaged in a gun-fight with the enemy's reconnaissance teams on the Zhitomir highway.

In all the other sections of the enhanced positions in Kiev and in the city, the night was quiet..." Another headline in the same edition of the paper read: "A new production on tour!! At Bi-Ba-Bo all day..."

The next day, a Saturday, there was no new edition of the paper, and on the Sunday, having got to grips with the old and new style in accordance with the tastes of the new government – "2nd (15th) December", the same newspaper which, exactly three months earlier, had written about how his holiness had allowed himself the luxury of making off for his villa, published his renunciation and the proclamation of the Kiev city duma: "Citizens! The Hetman's regime, a reactionary and violent regime, has fallen. The soldiers of the Directorate of the People's Republic of Ukraine have entered the city..." The proclamation, among other things, raised the issue of the officers of the Volunteer Army: they were asked to retreat to Novorossisk with their weapons. There was an eloquently written first "Directive of the Directorate" signed by Vinnichenko, which read: "Those who are at present hindering the people from doing battle with the Hetman, the landowners and the capitalists, those who are hindering the assertion of the power of the people's republic, are criminals."

On the fourth page of the newspaper, a section entitled "Curiosities of mobilization" reported: "The conscription of young men continued right up until yesterday, and that is worth recording as a curious matter.

In spite of the booming of cannons, the acceptance commission continued to hold meetings and talk to the new recruits. Only the arrival of the forces of the Directorate put an end, at last, to the mobilization that had been declared. All those who had been recruited went off to their homes when the troops of the Directorate arrived. With this, the mobilization, if one can call it that, came to an end." Anyone reading these lines now will have no trouble imagining the impotent rage with which Bulgakov must have opened this paper, which described as a "curious matter" something that had very nearly cost his younger brothers their lives. Another paragraph, under the headline "Back to your homes", seems to be a direct commentary on Bulgakov's future novel and play: "On Friday, intense work went on all day to form a special corps of mobilized soldiers. When the duty officers heard of the reports in the evening newspapers, they said to the enlisted men: "Guys, you can all go back to your homes now."

Let us return to the diary of the eyewitness who chronicled life in Kiev over those few days: "*15th December*. Petlyura entered the city yesterday evening. The Hetman had renounced power in the morning." Today, the crack of machine-gun fire could be heard in various parts of the city, but there was not much of it, generally speaking. There are hardly any wounded. The Directorate has not yet arrived in Kiev.

19th December. The peal of bells could be heard at all the churches from the early morning. In the afternoon, the Directorate arrived: Vinnichenko, Petlyura, Shets, Andrievsky. Petlyura's marvellous troops (well-dressed, disciplined) filled the city centre. There are national flags everywhere, people everywhere. But like yesterday and the day before yesterday, no-one is speaking loudly, everyone is focused and taciturn. One hears Ukrainian being spoken, almost exclusively. Of the former officers, whom previously one could identify with just one look, there is no trace."

Mikhail Bulgakov hears and sees all this, and takes it away with him in his memory when he leaves Kiev – and then recreates it in the pages of his novel, thereby making life easier for his future biographers...

From some conservations I had with a woman from Kiev who had been a young girl in 1918-1919 and had spent her whole life on Andreyevsky Hill: "The bell-tower was opposite where the delicatessen store is today – that was where they took the officers who were killed. We went to look at them...

'To see if you could recognise anyone you knew?'

'No, not just to do that – we simply went along to have a look... Near Andreyevsky Hill there was a small church, there was a pile of dead bodies there, too... And there were bodies lying in the streets. I went there once – I saw one, lying there. He was so young, and handsome. The poor thing! But it was his own fault: they said to him, 'don't go!' – but he went anyway!"

A well-known historian, Z. (1904-1983) told me, in the 1970s, that he had been in the cadet corps in Kiev in 1918. He was 14; their division had not been sent to fight against the Petlyurites. The corps continued to exist under Petlyura's men, and under the Bolsheviks, although there were no training exercises. When they were taken outside to walk around the square after Petlyura had entered the city, they saw a dead officer – one with nothing on his feet. This made a powerful impression on him. The same witness told me that a few months later, in the spring of 1919, Denikin marched on Kiev; a troop train with Bolsheviks in it came out of the city. "My friend and I stood there – with our chevrons removed – not far from the roads. On the gangway of one carriage of the slowly moving train stood a red commander – a former officer, by the look of him. 'What's up, cadets – waiting for your lot, are you?' he asked, fairly amicably. We were sure at the time that Denikin would arrive at any moment. I was already 15 by then; to this day I can't understand why I didn't go to meet him, but instead waited calmly in the city. He turned back when he was 60 kilometres away. I've never cried so much as I did when he began retreating." As we consider the twists and turns in the subsequent fate of the Bulgakov brothers, let us not lose sight of the power of this emotion, which remained a vivid cause of concern for someone who witnessed the dramatic events of the day even half a century later.

The accounts of those who witnessed life in Kiev in those years resemble one another closely, right down to the details.

In January 1983, Lyubov Belozerskaya said to me: "I was in Kiev at the same time – in 1918-1919. Vasilevsky [her first husband – M.C.] was the editor of *Kiyevskoye Ekho* (*The Kiev Echo*). I didn't know him then – we got married later, in Odessa… The situation in Kiev was horrific. I once left my house one morning – there was a young man lying there with such an expression on his face… such suffering… He lay there in his student jacket, pulled halfway over his service coat – he had been hurrying to pull it over the coat, and they had shot him, he hadn't been quick enough!" And in response to a question from me, she added: "Of course, in *The White Guard*, it is all toned down! To a startling extent! After all, what took place was something awful! At that time I didn't fear anything – but *now* I remember what I saw – I sometimes have dreams about it nowadays, too – I recall it, and I am *gripped by fear*! Can you imagine what that's like?!"

Ehrenburg, who lived in Kiev from the autumn of 1918 until November 1919, writes about the same period, but one can see differences between his perspective on them and that of the author of *The White Guard*: "The troops of the Directorate came towards the city. Right up until the last moment, the white officers were emptying wine cellars, drinking, singing, fighting, weeping and shooting anyone who looked 'suspect'. [...] The Petlyurites walked across Kreshchatyk looking merry, they didn't lay a finger on anyone. Ladies from Moscow who hadn't managed to leave for Odessa on time exclaimed: 'How nice they are!' They rounded up the white officers and locked them in the Pedagogical museum (it seems this building was chosen due to its size, not because of anything related to teaching). I remember how frightened everyone was: there was a thunderous noise, and the windows were smashed in many of the buildings. The local people started putting water into their bath-tubs hurriedly – for perhaps the water would be turned off – and burning the Petlyurite newspapers. It turned out that someone had thrown a bomb into the Pedagogical museum."

One day, during that winter, an incident occurred at No. 13, Andreyevsky Hill, that remained engrained in Tatiana Nikolayevna's memory. "One day, some Blue-Coats came along. They had women's boots on their feet, but there were spurs on the boots. And they had all sprayed themselves with 'coeur-de-jeannette', a trendy perfume. 'Is there anyone hiding here?' They were looking for someone. They had a look and saw that there was no-one. Mikhail was just getting ready to go out, he had his coat on. They crawled under the table, under the bed, looked in all the corners, then said: 'Let's get out of here, they're poor, they haven't even got any rugs. There's another flat here – perhaps it's in a better state!' And they went downstairs, to see the architect, from whom they were renting the flat [Vasily Listovnichy – M.C.]. And there, they went their separate ways! We later found out about it – there was so much shouting – they asked us to go down to see them..." Listovnichy's daughter told us about this burglary as well: "There were so many groups of bandits around at that time – uncle Vlas, auntie Maruska – the whole of Podol had to put up with her... One of them burgled our house once, too.

... They didn't take any gold items – how could we hide them – they were on our persons! – they only took money..." Thus, the scene in which Vasilisa's place is robbed in *The White Guard*, like many others, was based on a real incident.

"Great, and frightening, was the year of our lord 1918, but 1919 was more frightening still," the narrator of *The White Guard* tells us. In what sort of atmosphere did Bulgakov prepare to see in this year?

The daughter of the man who owned the house told me in 1981: "The Bulgakovs once had some guests round upstairs; we were sitting there and suddenly we heard singing: 'God save the Tsar...' And it was forbidden to sing the Tsar's anthem! Papa went up to see them and said: 'Misha, you're grown up now, but why make the kids face the firing squad?' And Nikolka piped up at that point: 'We're all grown-ups here, we're all responsible for our actions!' Nikolai was generally the most tactful of them all...'

It is not clear when this episode is supposed to have happened, but it was probably in November – December 1918, the time when the corresponding scene in *The White Guard* and *The Days of the Turbins* is supposed to have happened – the anthem was outlawed under the Hetman, too.

... The eyewitness's diary: "**31 December**. The Directorate has not yet entered Kiev, the bunting has not yet had time to become tattered, yet already something heavy can be felt in the air. The allied consuls have already left Kiev, the trains have already stopped going to Odessa... All kinds of rumours, passed on by someone else in a whisper, are making everyone nervous. They say the Bolsheviks are approaching, they say the allied troops have already engaged Petlyura's soldiers in battle near Odessa.

All this is so believable. There is unrest in the city – isolated shots can be heard, now here, now there – around the clock. In the republican armies themselves, the level of organisation is not at all what it seems at first glance. Excesses with a lethal outcome between soldiers and the high command are not all that rare... Today I amputated the leg of one of Petlyura's soldiers."

On New Year's Eve, traffic on the streets of Kiev was permitted not until 10 o'clock, as had become customary, but until 2am.

In the first, New Year's Day edition of I. Vasilevsky's newspaper, *Kiyevskoye Ekho*, under the heading "The Bolshevik danger", it was reported that: "The attack by the Bolsheviks on the Kharkov governorate, undertaken by the Soviet forces, is causing general consternation in Ukrainian and non-Ukrainian democratic parties... Ukrainians have always (!) strived to live in peace with Soviet Russia, maintaining complete neutrality with respect to its internal position." Another report in the same edition asked the question: "Who is responsible for the shooting of the students?" Readers were reminded that on 15th November, "some bloody events unfolded: some students who had assembled were shot at by the Hetman's police and by Svyatopolk-Mirsky's brigade of officers"; the author assured his readers that the students had been demonstrating with red flags.

In the evening edition of *Posledniye Novosti* on 1st January 1919, there was a "New Year's satirical piece" by V. Stechkin:

"*– Wishing you new happiness in the New Year!*
I find that offensive!
… Was the old one any better?
… It'll probably be the same for fifty or seventy more years.
I agree.
It would be rather good, don't you know, to freeze oneself by anabiosis for roughly that number of years, and then thaw yourself out again.
Ah, it's the year 1969! Allow me to congratulate you.
You'd go outside and smoke a filtered cigarette that cost you six kopecks over a tenner.
You'd listen carefully to see what you could hear.
Is there no shooting going on?
There's no shooting!
Is no-one being robbed?
No-one's being robbed…Well, thank God for that.
Happy new year, gentlemen."

This must no doubt have chimed perfectly with the thoughts circling inside the mind of Dr Bulgakov – there was a good reason why, a few years down the line, the protagonist of his story *The Extraordinary Adventures of the Doctor* (*Neobyknovennyye Priklyucheniya Doktora*) would exclaim, in some notes dedicated to this very moment: "Why are you chasing me, fate?! Why was I not born a hundred years ago? Or better yet: in a hundred years' time. Or even better than that: if I'd never been born at all."

In any event, there certainly wasn't the faintest trace of any "new happiness".

On 20th January, in the third edition, there was an article entitled: "The funerals of the Sich Riflemen": "Yesterday, Kiev held funerals for the Cossacks who fell in the battle against the Hetman and his army." The service was held at the Vladimir cathedral; S. Petlyura gave a speech. A paragraph headed "The Unloading of Kiev" stated: "The word is that the first people to be exiled from Kiev will be the former volunteers and their families."

Bulgakov, who had long since become a politician by dint of circumstances and read the newspapers avidly ("… He bought a paper from the kiosk and opened it as he walked along… 'Here you, what are you elbowing people for? You should read those papers of yours at home…'" The behaviour of Aleksei Turbin on the streets of Kiev in the winter of 1918-1919 is surely taken from the author's own traits), and monitored, of course, how events were unfolding in revolutionary Germany, pondering over whether or not a worldwide revolution might be on the cards. He may well have studied with interest the bombastic satirical piece by Sergei Glagolin, "The Last Tango", in the *Utrenniy Byulleten' Vechernego Slova* (*Morning Report on the Evening Word*), trying to work out whether or not the Soviet authorities would succeed in establishing good relations with the new Germany: "The Soviet diplomatic mission travelled not to Germany, but to see Liebknecht, and it was trumpeted about everywhere that they were honoured guests, and that the German people had arranged the revolution specifically for the Russian Bolsheviks. Moscow was even planning to present revolutionary Germany with several hundred thousand arshins of muslin so that they could make red flags. In the end, though, there was nothing but embarrassment: 'The master of the house is not at home!'"

In this period, when, as Ehrenburg recalled, "nobody knew who was going to shoot whom the next day, which portraits should be hung up and which ones hidden away, which currency to accept and which one to try to offload to some muggins," rumours of the wildest kind were doing the rounds in Kiev. "Various refugees who were 'in the know' swore that the allies had ultra-violet rays with which they would be able to destroy both the 'reds' and the 'independent-ists' in a matter of hours… (*People, Years, Life* [*Lyudi, Gody, Zhizn'*]). A long time before this, in the 1920s, the poet Nikolai Ushakov also wrote in his memoirs: "Rumours went around about rays of ultra-violet light," and V. Shklovsky wrote about them as well.

This episode had also survived in the excellent memory of Yevgeny Borisovich Bukreyev, right up until the conversation we had in 1983: "I remember that when the Bolsheviks invaded, in 1918, a big sign was printed out and stuck up around the city, saying that to protect against the invasion, *rays of death would be used!* And at one end of Tsepny Bridge, there were some *projectors with blue glass lenses*. And when they were turned on, the soldiers who attacked from the other side of the Dnieper initially fell down flat on their faces… The effect created by these projectors, combined with the rumours, was very powerful…"

Sure enough, I came across that remarkable notice – in an edition of *Posledniye Novosti* dated 29th January 1919.

The Directive on Ultra-Violet Rays

The high command published the following announcement for the population of Chernigovshchina. I hereby inform the people of Chernigovshchina that, starting on 28th January of this year, against the Bolsheviks who are waging war on Ukraine, plundering and destroying the nation's property, violet rays which cause blindness are going to be used. These rays can blind a man even if he has his back to them. In order to avoid being blinded by these rays, I suggest that the people hide in cellars, mud huts and any building that the rays of light cannot penetrate. I am notifying you about this, citizens, so that we can avoid having any unnecessary fatalities.

In my view, it is entirely possible that both the red ray of light from the tale *The Fateful Eggs* (*Rokovyye Yaytsa*), and the rays of life used by Professor Yefrosimov in the play *Adam and Eve* (*Adam i Yeva*) were based on this legend that was going around in Kiev in the winter of 1918/19.

Let us return to the doctor's diary: "***4th January (1919).*** For two days now, work has been going on to clean and spruce up Kiev. The Directorate ordered that signs in Russian must be taken down, all over the city. Kreshchatyk looks very pitiful: the signs there are stuck up using fabric, others have been defaced with paint, and others simply look very tatty. Life here is exactly the same as how it was in Yuryev, under the Bolsheviks. Chaotic shooting going on, around the clock, growing stronger at night. Loads of drunks. In Yuryev, though, there were no organised groups of bandits, whereas here, half the papers are filled with descriptions of all kinds of attacks, murders and violence. Everyone is convinced that the reign of the Bolsheviks will soon be here.

20th January. I enlisted today. The mobilisation of doctors began on 18th. I can't say that things were organised in an exemplary way at the sanitary department, or even in a basic way, but things are nonetheless being done with great energy at the Directorate. Almost all the doctors ask to be sent out 'on commission' – no-one wants to go to where the military units are."

Bulgakov was soon mobilised, too – it is possible that, like Dr Yashvin from his story *I Killed* (*Ya Ubil*), he came upon, after his return home, "on the slit on an unpleasant-looking, government style envelope… A short message: 'Upon receipt hereof, you are to go to the sanitary department within two hours, to receive your posting…' So that's how it is: that brilliant army, leaving corpses in the street, father Petlyura, pogroms, and me with a red cross on my sleeve in such company…"

The eyewitness's diary: "***24th January.*** The Bolsheviks are already close. They have taken Nezhin. I have heard not a word about anything from home.

27th January. Well this, it seems, is the eve of Bolshevism. There is confusion in the city. In the morning, the state bank was evacuated, there are carts carrying military things, they're taking everything off somewhere. The republican soldiers are turning tail and fleeing wherever they can and however they can: in cars, in crowds and on carts. The sanitary council went away yesterday, leaving behind two doctors, who continued to assign jobs to the mobilised doctors... At Kreshchatyk, all you can hear is: I'm leaving, I've got a ticket, I couldn't get a ticket etc. The talk everywhere is of hitting the road. How terrible it feels on one's soul! My nerves are so shot to bits, and my soul is so full of political sensations of all kinds, that life has lost all value once again. It has become simply a source of indifference."

This specific mood – the loss of a sense of the value of life – can be felt in a story from 1922, *The Extraordinary Adventures of the Doctor*, to which we will return later, and in the story *I Killed*, in which the mood of the citizens in this period is painted by Bulgakov in hues that are very similar to the diary of this fellow doctor and peer whom he did not know (or perhaps he did know him, and had fleetingly made his acquaintance – who knows!): "The Bolsheviks attacked, from across the Dnieper and, rumour had it, in vast numbers, and, one must appreciate this, the whole city was waiting for them not only impatiently, but I would even go so far as to say – with admiration. For what the Petlyurite troops had brought about in Kiev in that last month of their time in the city is beyond comprehension. Pogroms broke out every minute, someone was killed every day, with the Jews the preferred victims, of course. Some things were requisitioned, and cars rushed around the city, carrying men with red woven badges on their sheepskin hats, and in the last few days, the cannons in the distance didn't stop firing even for an hour. Both day and night. Everyone was in some sort of gloom, they all had sharp and anxious eyes. Right under my windows, just yesterday, two dead bodies lay in the snow for half a day. [...] So in the end, I, too, started waiting for the Bolsheviks. And they kept getting closer and closer" (*I Killed*).

In the same edition of the paper as the one containing the "Directive on violet rays", a message from the Central information bureau under the Directorate was published, entitled "To the people of Kiev": "Over the last few days, enervating rumours have been spread throughout the city to the effect that the Bolsheviks have reached Kiev and that the Directorate and several Ministries are hastily being evacuated... These rumours have no basis in fact whatsoever. It can decisively be said that there is no direct danger facing Kiev..."

A report from the morning edition on Sunday, 2nd February, "In government circles": "... all civil institutions will be moving out of Kiev in the very near future..."

"*30*[th] ***January.*** The Bolsheviks have moved back a little. In a matter of days, it appears, work will start again at the ministries that were evacuated.

Everyone's hopes now rest only on the allies. If they do not intervene, it will be merely a matter of time.

3rd February. All the ministries that returned to Kiev were once again loaded into wagons yesterday morning and left for Vinnitsa. It has officially been announced that Kiev will be handed over to the Bolsheviks either tonight or tomorrow morning. There is almost the same amount of confusion everywhere as there was a week ago, but on the whole there is a little less panic. Tonight, the groups of bandits that have been formed tried to seize power in the city. The 3rd Black Sea regiment, which, as chance would have it, had been delayed in Kiev, fought them off. In all corners of the city, there have been mass attacks by looters – not just on individual apartments but on whole apartment buildings. The word 'bourgeois' is heard only rarely now; brother is simply stealing from brother, one man is stealing from his equal. I don't know how I am going to make a living. There is almost no money, food has started to go up in price again. If only the Bolsheviks would hurry up and take Kiev. Perhaps then I would be able to go home. There are no Germans in Kiev." (doctor's diary).

The morning edition of *Posledniye Novosti* on 4th February reported: "The sizeable forces of the republican troops have been stationed in Slobodka." Bulgakov was among them. All the evidence suggests that he was mobilised at precisely this time. On 29th January, there was a report about "the enlisting of new recruits" – "… from 1899 onwards and still under the age of 35…"

Tatiana Nikolayevna told me: "He was initially mobilized [unlike the very latest mobilisation – M.C.] by the Blue-Coats. I had gone out somewhere; I came home and found a note on the table: 'Come to such-and-such a place, bring this, bring that, they've taken me.' I turned up there and found him sitting on horseback. 'We're going over there, beyond the bridge – come out there tomorrow!' I did as he said, I took him something. Then back home I heard that the bluecoats were retreating. At one am, the doorbell rang. Varya and I ran to open the door: he was standing there, all pale… He ran inside like a madman, he was shaking. He told us what had happened: he had been taken out of the city along with everyone else, they had crossed over the bridge, there were some pillars or columns up ahead… He had slowed his pace and lagged behind, then he hid behind the column: and no-one noticed him… After that he fell sick, he couldn't get up. The doctor, Ivan Pavlovich Voskresensky, came round. He had a high temperature. It was probably something to do with his nerves. But he wasn't wounded, that's for sure."

A few years later, this episode was echoed in his prose twice in the course of a single year. "*On the night of 2-3* [...] I was mobilised yesterday. No, the day before yesterday. I spent a day on an icy bridge. It was -15 degrees (on the Réaumur) during the night, with the wind. The wind whistled all night long. There were lights burning on one bank of the river.

On the other, there are the outskirts of the town. We were in the middle. Then everyone ran into the city. I had never seen such a crush of people. Cavalrymen. Infantrymen. The cannons were on the move too, and the kitchen units. There was a nurse in one of them. I was told that I would be picked up in Galicia. It was only then that I worked out I ought to flee. All the blinds were closed, all the entrances to the buildings were boarded up. I ran to a church with chubby white columns. Shots were fired at me as I went in. But they missed me. I hid in the courtyard beneath an awning and sat there for two hours. When the moon had gone behind the clouds, I emerged. I ran home along streets that were deathly..." (*The Extraordinary Adventures of the Doctor*, 1922).

"At the white church with the colonnade, doctor Bakaleinikov suddenly detached himself from the black ribbon of men and, unable to feel his heart beating, walking on strange, unbending legs, moved away to the side, right outside the church. He stood near one of the columns. He moved closer to it." He flees; shots are fired at him. When he reaches home, his loved ones are horrified to see that he now has a tuft of grey hair. "Bakaleinikov wanted to say something else, but instead of speech coming out of his mouth, an unexpected thing occurred. He sniffled loudly. He sniffled again and started moaning like a woman, burying his head, with the tuft of grey hair, in his hands" (an early draft of *The White Guard*, 1922).

The shocking events he witnessed then – chiefly, it seems, the fact that he was forced to be present at killings he could do nothing to prevent, had an enormous impact on the substantive foundations of Bulgakov's artistic world.

Let us turn once again to the eyewitness accounts, so as to imagine what the hero of our tale saw on the streets of his native town following that "night of the 2nd to the 3rd" of February, which crops up in his creative oeuvre time and again.

The memoirs of the academic Vernadsky, which provide a social panorama of life in Kiev in 1918-1919, contain the lines: "… before long, everything changed again – the Directorate existed for just a handful of weeks – less than two months… The Directorate made several changes to the charter of the Ukrainian Academy of Sciences, including the introduction of a point that we protested against, namely that the Academy could print material in any language except Russian. Printing in Russian was not prohibited, as such, but you had to have a special justification for doing so.

Very soon after this, the government of the Directorate left for Kamenets-Podolsk and proposed that we all go with them. A large number of Ukrainians went with them. We stayed, though, and decided to regroup after the departure of the 'government'. Soviet troops were rumoured to be nearing Kiev.

Early in the morning on 5th February, when I went out of the house for a walk, Kiev was occupied by troops of some sort, apparently Russians, who wouldn't say who they were when people asked, but they weren't Petlyura's Ukrainians and they weren't Bolsheviks. They soon left, and everything seemed calm. On the morning of 5th February 1919, we held a general meeting of the Academy at the house where I lived in those days – at the former first grammar school on Shevchenkovsky (formerly Bibikovsky) Boulevard.

O.E. Krymsky, thanks to the Borotbists (Fighters) [a far-left Socialist Revolutionary party, who opposed both the Hetman and Petlyura's men – M.C.], was more *au fait* with what was happening than the rest of us. To us, it was clear that the Academy's fate was being decided. We came to the unanimous conclusion that after the meeting, we would send Krymsky, the secretary of the Academy, to meet the Bolshevik forces approaching Kiev on behalf of the Academy. We found out that the forces were led by Rakovsky and Manuilsky. Krmysky stayed in contact with the new government at all times. The Bolshevik soldiers' march into Kiev was a triumphal one. No major changes were made to the Academy's charter."

And the doctor's diary: "5th February. At 2pm, the Bolsheviks entered Kiev. They weren't regular troops, but participants in the uprising. They came in from the Slobodka side, across the Tsepnaya bridge. There were two men on horseback riding at the head of the brigade, with broad red ribbons wrapped around them. Each held a cocked revolver in his right hand and a bomb in his left. Behind them were three armed men on horseback. Next came an armoured car, behind which there was a marching band. They came out into Kreshchatyk to the accompaniment of the Internationale. Their audience shouted 'hooray!' and took off their hats. Their audience was the broad masses of the proletariat. Kreshchatyk was chock-full of them. All the 'insulted and humiliated' held their heads higher. In raised voices, people talked about the bourgeoisie. The beggars, who now constitute a dark mass in the city, started having fun too. I saw one of them walk up to a lady wearing inexpensive clothes and, when the lady passed by without a word, he spat in her direction and said in a loud voice: 'Yuck, what a parasite!' Petlyura's troops are nowhere to be seen. The Directorate has hopped it, according to the telegrams, to Stanislavov."

On 6th February 1919, the first edition of the "daily socialist newspaper", "Morning Kiev word", came out. A report headlined "Meeting of Soviet forces" describes the same thing that was recorded more fully by the eyewitness: "Yesterday, the commanders of the Soviet forces sent only a few small brigades to Kiev, with aims that were purely related to reconnaissance.

Regiments from the Soviet army are expected to arrive this morning..."

Everything took place as scheduled: at 11am, the troops entered Kiev; a demonstration was opened by the chairman of the executive committee, A.S. Bubnov (not long before this, he had been an underground Communist in Kiev; 10 years later, as the people's commissar for enlightenment, his fate would overlap with Bulgakov's). The first edition of the paper also contained a description of the recent events: "The Republican troops' departure from Kiev ended the day before yesterday. The only ones left in Kiev before the Soviet troops arrived were Sich Riflemen who were lagging behind their units. Only the Tsepnoi bridge remained guarded by a brigade of Sich Riflemen longer than all the others." The first nine decrees made by the temporary head of the Kiev garrison (and later mayor of the city) N. Shchors are all printed; one of them declared that the city was under siege; and a curfew was imposed after 7pm.

Let us examine a diary entry made by the doctor from Kiev on 5th February. Together with a description of the new government's entry into Kiev, he includes a comment on his private life: "As far as my own living resources are concerned, they have improved" – his more senior colleagues have given him a "practice in the city". It is with just such a practice that Dr Bulgakov is earning a living in the city at this time, too. And one can try to create a continuation of A.I. Yermolenko's diary using the diary of Bulgakov's protagonist in *The Extraordinary Adventures of the Doctor*, published four years later – if one bears in mind that at times, Bulgakov's path from his own life to his artistic work is incredibly short. At any rate, the story paints an image of what was happening to the author himself in those days, and after the handful of years that had passed, these events were given a comical hue. The chapter entitled "The Italian Harmonica" is dated "15th February": "Today, the cavalry regiment arrived, and occupied the whole district. In the evening, a man from the 2nd squadron came to see me (emphysema), and whilst he sat waiting in the waiting room, he played on a large Italian harmonica. This emphysema-addled chap plays magnificently ('On the Hills of Manchuria'), but the other patients were terribly perturbed, and it was simply impossible for them to listen to him. I let him jump the queue. He liked my apartment a lot. He wants to move in here, with his platoon. He asked me whether I had a gramophone... [...]

17th February.
I slept well tonight – the gramophone downstairs is broken.
I took out a piece of paper with 18 seals printed on it saying that I mustn't be sealed in, and stuck it up on the front door, on the door to the study and in the dining room.

21st February.
They have sealed me in...

22nd February.
... and enlisted me."

A.I. Yermolenko's diary:
"21st February. Mobilisation again. I enlisted today. It's possible I'll get exempted, like the assistant at the Clinical institute. [...] How I'd like to spit on the whole thing and live quietly at home in Syrovatka. But that's out of the question too, because it's going on there as well... mobilisation, and how absurd life seems! And this absurdity makes one feel terribly tired."

The life that was going on at Andreyevsky Hill in the winter of 1918/19 was the one that, in 3 or 4 years' time, would appear again, reworked and repackaged, in literary texts: first in the comedy *Self-defence* (*Samooborona*, 1920), which has not survived, then in a chapter in an early draft of *The White Guard*, in which "Kolka, as the secretary of the residents' committee, was in charge of the rota for the guarding of the building, and he couldn't resist the urge to put Vasilisa on duty at Easter, on the night of the 2nd, and to pair him off with the most incompetent and richest woman in the area: Avdotya Semenovna, the bootmaker's wife. The chart therefore stated: '2nd: from 8 till 10, Avdotya and Vasilisa.' And a lot of merriment ensured. Kolka spent the whole evening teaching Vasilisa how to use an Austrian carbine. Vasilisa was sitting on a bench by the wall, limp and with darkened eyes, and Kolka was throwing out bullets with the cartridge extractor, with a dry crack..." The Bulgakovs' neighbours on either side, who took turns, apparently, standing guard over the house (*Self-defence*), were the Moskvitinys (and shortly before them, a general named Komarnitsky), and Pyotr Grobinsky and his family (Vera Bulgakova mentions them in the letter cited earlier).

The early spring of Bulgakov's last year in Kiev arrived. On 8th March, our hero's fellow doctor in Kiev wrote in his diary: "On 5th, they celebrated the first anniversary of the revolution. My own affairs are going very badly [...]

I have no practice, and no money either. Yet life is getting more expensive by the day. Black bread already costs 4 r. for 50 pounds, and white bread costs 6 r. for 50 pounds, and so on. As for what lies ahead – there is nothing." "*8th April.* Well, life has really arrived now! And the worst of it is the hunger. Black bread costs 12-13 r. a pound. And there is no end to this in sight.

11th April. The day before yesterday, there was much chaos in the city. From the Kurenevka side, the rebelling peasants moved on the city, shouting slogans such as 'down with the commune' and 'beat the yids'. There are many breeding grounds for rebellion in Ukraine right now (a week ago they counted 50 of them), and all of them have roughly the same slogans. In Kurenevka, the attackers organised a pogrom against Jews. 15 people were killed. Before long the Soviet troops drove them out of town. Now a hush has descended, but one can feel the storm coming in the air." This is how N. Ravich recounts these events in his memoirs (*The Youth of the Century* [*Molodost' Veka*], M., 1967): "Back on 10th April, the Petlyurites organised an uprising in Kiev itself, in Kurenevka. Disguised as pilgrims on their way to church, and hiding their weapons under their coats, they seeped into Podol in small clusters. Eventually, after coming together to form a group of more than two hundred people, they charged at the Red Army teams. The surprise nature of the attack and the fact that some of the regiments included unreliable elements who had deserted Petlyura's army meant that this might easily have resulted in chaos in the city, but some of the group got involved in a pogrom against Jews, and the opportunity went begging…" It is worth noting that the rebels had moved on Kiev via Podol, setting fire to buildings and getting embroiled in gunfights; all this was thus happening not far from the Bulgakovs' house; the rebels reached the city centre, attacking the city bank and the telegraph office before the uprising was put down.

Let us return to the doctor's diary. "*29th April.* The day before yesterday, I received an order to go to the health department of the Military commissariat for the governorate. I went along and straight away I was ordered to go to Moscow. This is where I am to be appointed, under the mobilisation." The author of the diary is loath to "abandon everything and drive out into the hunger and the typhus. Moreover, they'll give me a different posting in Moscow, and then you're bound to end up at the front. And as for what that means, I heard all about that from a fellow classmate of mine who arrived from Moscow. I shan't leave Kiev so easily; I shan't give up what I've got without a fight. If one cannot live by acting directly in all things, then I shall try to go about things in an indirect manner." The next entry is dated

2nd May: "There is nothing for it: I'll have to go to Moscow. Today was a day of fighting. A commissar who owes a great deal to my boss weighed in to my affair. Yet I must nonetheless go to Moscow. I shall travel in the medical train. It is due to depart on 5th May." The diary entries end here, and we must part with the valuable historical document that its author created, knowing that there are grounds for believing that Bulgakov shared the same attitude towards the possibility of being enlisted and sent off to Moscow as the one expressed here by his fellow doctor and peer.

Evidently, he managed to avoid enlistment (one can only suppose that, like his colleagues, Bulgakov resorted to "indirect methods"), but he had to endure the burden of a rising cost of living, a meagre income and the other circumstances of life in Kiev for the rest of that year.

Let us turn to some excerpts from the diary of the female student in Kiev: "*6th February.* Today, the Bolsheviks entered the city. [...] Thank God we got through it without the battles we saw last year, [...] it's better to have one devil than several, just as long as it keeps its grip firm. If it's to be the Bolsheviks, then so be it. The endless shifts of government are enough to drive you mad. How many governments have we had now, since 1st January 1917? The Tsar's one, the temporary one, the rada, the Bolsheviks, the rada, the Hetman, the directorate, and now the Bolsheviks again. Most of the people I know have fled the city. I was against fleeing. What can they do to quiet, peaceful civilians, who aren't hurting anyone and who aren't getting involved in politics [...] *7th February.* The new government has set about its business zealously. It is setting aside the best apartments to use as its lodgings." People are telling "horror stories about Lipki [the aristocratic part of town. – M.C.]. They are chucking everyone out of the townhouses, not allowing them to take anything with them. They're using the private houses as barracks and institutions. *12th February.* [...] a series of arrests has begun. [...] *16th February.* 2 Red Army officers have moved in with us. They are peasants from the Kharkov governorate. [...] Our landlady's lodgers are behaving worse than before: at five in the morning the soldiers were playing on the grand piano and singing. [...] *10th March.* Private libraries are being destroyed. Private individuals aren't allowed to have any collections at all..."

"In March 1919," the poet Nikolai Ushakov recalled some years later, "the first Kiev underground poets' society, *Khlam* (*Junk*), was formed. [...] It moved into the basement at Nikolayevskaya. [...] From the basement, you could see the boots of the Red Army officers going past. [...] In Easter week, O. Mandelstam and Ryurik Ivnev came by. Zelyony was getting ready to take Kiev. In May, *Khlam* fell apart." Bulgakov does not take part, apparently, in any open forms of literary life; for him, this environment remains alien to him from an ideological point of view – it consists of those who work at the BUP: on Kreshchatyk, next to the Express cinema, is the Press and information bureau of the workers' and peasants' government of Ukraine. Every day, it hangs up reports about the situation at the front, and news about the revolutionary movement in Europe, on which high hopes are being placed. At this bureau are the people that Bulgakov will encounter in two or three years' time in literary circles in Moscow: Lev Nikulin (he was soon to write his poem *Kiev 1919*:

There is, in the Russian Revolution,
A troubling, non-Russian style:
The infantry, the golden dust,
The banner's Phrygian contribution,
And the armoured tanks in single file -
In old Sofiyskaya Square.

Mikhail Koltsov, the poet and translator Valentin Stenich (he was then living in the same room as Koltsov at the "Continental" hotel, as I learned from his widow L.D. Bolshintsova), who wrote of the government of the day: "O these men, as tough as rock, Aflame like warning beacons! They will be esteemed for centuries and centuries / And spoken of in the pages of books."

Let us return to the diary of the woman from Kiev once again. "*16th May.* What a frightening week it has been. More frightening than when the city was fired upon in 1918. [...] Grigoriev marched on Kiev. [...] There were mass arrests of Russian merchants and members of the Union of Russian people. Several dozen people were executed."

In June, Trotsky arrived in Kiev; he made speeches in which he threatened the intelligentsia and then left, after allegedly declaring that Ukraine was like a radish: white on the inside, red on the outside… Recording this, the student from Kiev notes (on 28th June 1919): "There have been a series of raids of people's homes in the city." On the night of 7th June, V.P. Listovnichy was arrested – as a hostage. Tatiana Nikolayevna recalled:

"One day, in the summer, we went off into the woods… I can't remember now who we were trying to get away from. We stayed with some acquaintance of ours along the Kiev-Kovelskaya road, in a shed in the garden. We made a fire in the yard and cooked our dinner on it. Two weeks passed… We slept in our clothes, in the straw. Varya, Kolya and Vanya, I think, were with us. Then we went back to Kiev on foot. The dacha in Bucha had been burnt to the ground by that summer – by the Petlyurites, I think; they lit a fire in the middle of the house and burned it down…"

The student's diary: "*25th July.* [...] On every corner there stands a stall or a kiosk that is filled to bursting with beautiful tomes. [...] It's painful to look at those books. They are almost all initialled, and many of them contain dedications. [...] *10th August.* Denikin's men are getting closer, and the Bolsheviks, without a doubt, are evacuating. The military people's commissariat is at Proreznaya, and at night you can hear them carrying something out of it. Even by day there are tram cars ranged alongside it, which they load up with things by the sack-full. But in the city, everything is at it was before; aside, perhaps, from the fact that the number of unsightly, futuristic billboards has gone up.

The squares and public spaces have been defaced with monstrous busts of Soviet figures. [...]. The names of the streets have been changed, such that the people who've lived here a long time can't find their way around at all, for the Bolsheviks are sticking strictly to the new names.

Stolypin street is now called Gershuny street.

The Marinsky garden has turned into a cemetery. In the summer of '18, the air throughout Lipki was infected thanks to this garden. Now, some of the graves have been tidied up. [...] Lipki is deserted. [...] No-one is very keen to walk along beside the Chek [the Ch.K. or 'Emergency Commission']. *24th August.* The other day, a new newspaper went on sale – the mouthpiece of the ministry of emergency affairs, "Red sword". It comes out on Sundays, clearly so as to sweeten the leisure time of the citizens of the RSFSR.

30th August. 7 in the evening. They're leaving! [...] The city has a frightful look to it. Everything is dead and boarded up; soldiers are running through the streets, firing shots into the air. [...] This morning was horrible: there was a list of people who had been shot last night in the newspaper. There are some names I know on it."

The Red Army left the city; so too did Mandelstam, and the impressions left on him by that final day were reflected, according to the poet's wife, in a poem he wrote in 1937:

> In the streets of Kiev, the Viy-demon,
> Some wife, I know not whose, seeks her husband.
> A smell of death pervades lordly Lipki.
> In the final available tram-car
> The Red Army's soldiers left the city;

A shout was heard from the sodden greatcoat:
"We'll be back one day – don't you forget it!"

On the morning of 31st, Petlyura's Galician units and the volunteers entered the city, and by evening Petlyura had conceded the city. "***31st August.*** [...] After 2 hours, demonstrations started to break out. A vast crowd moved through Kreshchatyk towards the Duma. [...] In Lipki, all the buildings of the Ministry of Emergency Situations were open. They were surrounded by huge crowds. There were women hanging onto the fences, peering through the cracks greedily. Indeed, they have been saying that it was awful inside the Chek. [...] The worst thing of all was in house No. 5 on the Sadovaya: there, the last 67 victims were shot and then buried immediately. The carriage shed or stable on this estate had been used as a torture chamber; they had even put a gutter in there, for the blood. The corpses of those who were killed lay there completely naked."

On the eve of the reds' departure, V.P. Listovnichy was taken out to be shot. In accordance with a family tradition, he was taken out to the wall three times. "For some reason they set up their firing squads a long way from the prison in Lukyanov – in Pechersk, on Sadovaya street, in the brick stables. People from Kiev went out there and saw blood and brains on the walls. But Vasily Listovnichy had been left alive for the time being, as a hostage, with a group of others who had been arrested; and for the last time they took him through the streets of Kiev from the Lykyanovskaya prison to the Dnieper, put him on a ferry and carried him off to the north. His daughter walked beside the column of prisoners from the prison to the Dnieper and cried all the way there." Her father's hair had turned grey in prison, and he had grown a long grey beard and moustache. He tried to flee from the ferry by night, "he crawled out of toilet window on one side, and an engineer named Nivin crawled out on the other side. They were shot at... The volunteers were already in Kiev, Nivin went to Yadviga Viktorovna's place and told them about the escape, and about how Listovnichy had been taken out to be executed three times. In one of the cells of the Lukyanovskaya prison, Inna Vasilievna found a message scratched into the wall: 'On the night of 31.VIII.19, without any accusation, trial or investigation, the civil engineer V.P. Listovnichy was shot.' This was the last trace of him on earth." It appears that he was shot dead whilst in the water.

On Wednesday, 21st August, V.V. Shulgin's newspaper *Kiyevlyanin* made its return. A year earlier, on 14th December 1918, he had lost his 19-year-old son in the fighting outside Kiev. His son had been a graduate of the First Grammar School, too, and had fought in the ranks of the so-called *Ordenskaya Druzhina* (*Militia of the Medal*), created by the Union of Holders of the St. George Cross. The militia refused to retreat: "We have not received orders," and, as *Kiyevlyanin* reported, in an article marking the centenary of the event, "all 25 young men died". This fact was undoubtedly known to Bulgakov and his brothers. Now, Shulgin's newspaper printed a portrait of A.I. Denikin's head and shoulders and an editorial entitled "They have returned".

"Yes, this region is Russian... We shall not surrender it – neither to the Ukrainian traitors, who have brought down disgrace upon it, nor to the Jewish executioners, who have spilt rivers of blood in it." In the political situation of those years, Bulgakov's line of thinking was similar to that of Shulgin as regards the actions of the Central Rada. In *The White Guard*, he makes a tongue-in-cheek reference to "the writer Vinnichenko".

Shulgin's words about "the Jewish executioners" were based on the lists compiled by the Kiev Ministry of Emergency Affairs, and, as always with this author, leave out any assessment of the actions of his fellow-countrymen – from within these same institutions, and others. Such a selective view was, by this time, alien to Bulgakov: "Little men, icon-bearing, Dostoevskyan" (*The White Guard*) have just as substantial a place in his acerbic reflections as those of other faiths and other nationalities. Had he shared the notion that was taking shape at the time (and has survived to our day), that revolution was the result of a foreign infection, for which the blame lay outside Russia, this could not have failed to have been reflected in the deeply political article which he was to publish in one of *The White Guard* newspapers just over two months later.

The editor of *Kiyevlyanin*, for his part, went on, with a grandiloquence that seemed fitting for the occasion: "In the row of majestic steps that lead to the temple of a united Russia, Kiev is the penultimate step. Above it, on the last step, stands Moscow – calling her, entreating her and marrying her.

The mother of Russian cities, the holy land of our ancestors, our Motherland, which has suffered so excessively – accept our filial greeting."

In an article entitled 'To the memory of the tormented', the newspaper assured its readers: "At present, the outcome of the battle between the Volunteer Army and the Bolsheviks has been decided: the Bolshevik force has been broken once and for all, Lenin and Trotsky's bandits are no longer capable of putting up any serious resistance against the Volunteer Army, and all that is left for the armies of Mai-Mayevsky, Sidorin and Baron Vrangel, led by A.I. Denikin, to do is overcome the distance and set up a rear and civil governance in the country." The imagination of the author and many of the paper's readers was filled with images of a not-to-distant future, "when Moscow and the Patriarch of All Russia will meet the saviours of Russia triumphantly on Red Square…How much joy there will be, how much ecstasy and affection."

On 13th September, the newspaper *Kiyevskoye Ekho* (Vasilevsky-Nebukva, never losing his presence of mind, continued to print it under the new government) proclaimed: "The registration of officers, civil servants and doctors is continuing at the Kiev Commandant's Office (45, Vladimirskaya)… Every day, at least a thousand people have been signing up…" and *Kiyevlyanin* began printing lists of those who had been shot in the last few months.

On 18th September, *Ob'yedineniye* (*Association*) reported that an image had been put up at the top of the Duma depicting the Archangel Michael – the city's keeper (his image adorns the crest of Kiev). Day after day, the newspaper reported on the trials that were taking place against figures from various Soviet institutions who had stayed in the city and been recognised by someone. The doctor Z. Ignatovich wrote: "Most of the temporary governments, when they arrived in Kiev, got involved in profiteering, speculation and stealing from the people. The Denikinites carried out brutal pogroms." City hospital number one was close "to Bessarabskaya Square, where there was a large Jewish population. Every night, cries of agony and weeping could be heard; something metallic was being struck, buckets or basins – it was a real Witches' Sabbath! In the mornings, the whole of Bessarabskaya Square was covered with dust, feathers, broken crockery and other paraphernalia from the monstrous fighting!"[2]

We do not know exactly when Bulgakov left Kiev. As soon as General Mai-Mayevsky's army entered the city, various city organisations began helping the Volunteer Army. On 17th September, *Ob'yedineniye* reported that the All-Russian union of cities had decreed that a sanitary brigade named after General Bredov must be formed, and also that the sanitary unit of the "reserve force for assisting the Motherland and the Front" was organising a three-day collection of tools and medicine in and around Kiev, to meet the needs of the Volunteer Army. One of the reports (about an assembly of "representatives of institutions and organisations providing services to the Russian volunteer army") contains a name that catches the eye, for it was later used in the novel *The White Guard*: "The Chairman of the 'Reserve of

---

[2] Military and medical museum of the Ministry of Defence of the USSR, Archives Department, OF–73662/7.

social forces", V.G. Talberg, and other representatives of other organisations, highlighted the need to bring all the organisations together under the flag of the Committee for assisting the Russian volunteer army" (*Ob'yedineniye*, 7(20) September 1919).

We find the following in the same edition of the newspaper: "Yesterday, on the occasion of the city festival of the miracle of the Archangel Michael, which this year coincided with the return of the statue of the archangel to the Duma building, a funeral service was held in the hall of the city duma." A story under the heading "Party life" read: "On 5th September, the city committee of the people's freedom party held an assembly, for the first time since the Bolsheviks' departure." On 8th October, General M.V. Alekseyev died in Yekaterinodar; he had formed the kernel of what later became the Volunteer Army and remained its most senior leader until he died; this news was like a lightning bolt, causing particular distress, it seems, among the younger participants in the struggle.

On 8th October, the newspapers announced that it was the last day of registration for those born in 1899 and 1900... It is unclear whether or not Bulgakov was still in Kiev when, on 13th October, as *Kiyevlyanin* reported a few days later, "the enemy, thanks to its considerable numerical advantage, broke through our lines and pushed rapidly towards Kiev. On the night of 30th September, its great powers reached Svyatoshin and went on the offensive. [...] By midday, a hasty evacuation had begun in the city. Some 50,000 people were evacuated. Among the refugees were women and children, without any possessions. Occasionally, Jews went missing," the paper notes, trying to show that it still had a conscience. "In the evening, the Bogunsk and Tarashchansk regiments occupied the site of the Jewish bazaar and part of the Bibikov Boulevard." There was some resistance in the city centre, then the Volunteer Army retreated to Pechersk. A day later, its counter-offensive began. "The crack of rifle-fire was heard on the slopes leading down to Podol," whilst machine-guns and grenades were also deployed. "The Bolsheviks were stubborn in the extreme, but their resilience was nonetheless broken. The fighting continued all night, then all day on 3rd October, when the artillery fire reached its apogee. [...] Finally, on 4th October, in the morning, the Bolsheviks, with massive losses, were pushed all the way back to the outskirts of the city, from whence they continued to fire their guns. At dawn on 5th October, our units fought off the last [...] brigades of red soldiers, then headed towards Svyatoshino, where by midday we had taken control." On Wednesday 9th (22nd) October, *Kiyevlyanin* reported: "Today, the funerals of those who fell for the sake of Kiev will take place." The paper told of the "heroic death of the headstrong" Dusya Zabello and Kotik Bimman; it had published two articles about the latter, a 16-year-old schoolboy, two days earlier: "Like many of Kiev's schoolboys, he switched his school blazer for a khaki uniform when the volunteers arrived in Kiev [...] and left the sanctuary of the old teaching institution to join the old Kirasirsky regiment"; after spending a night at the tomb of Askoldova, he had met his end in his very first battle, being in an advance unit; Kotik's last words were also quoted: "I am dying for a united, indivisible Russia…"

All of this provides clues as to the kind of atmosphere in which the younger Bulgakov brothers were living that autumn, as they made ready for the possibility of death. The youthful, pathos-filled tension they must have felt was conveyed three years later by a recurring line from the story *The Red Crown*: "Brother, I cannot abandon the squadron."

In October, the newspapers published order No. 35 dated 14th (27th) October 1919, by the "Most senior officer and commander of the troops", Major-General Dragomirov, on the call-up for military service "for the supplementing of the existing units." The part of this order that ought surely to interest us most is point 3: "… 3) medical and veterinary ranks:

a) military doctors on the staff, existing outside the staff, or doctors from the reserve, mobilized staff and white-ticket holders, and also ordinary doctors, aged 50 or under…" It is likely that Bulgakov was mobilized even earlier than this, though.

Tatiana Nikolayevna recalls: "He received a mobilization sheet, and a uniform, I seem to remember – a service jacket and a greatcoat. He was sent to Vladikavkaz, to a military hospital… I remember that when he was about to leave, a new café had just opened, a very trendy one, and I was very keen to go and have a look. And I asked one of my friends to take me there, and my friend laughed and said: 'What a frivolous woman! Her husband's leaving for the front, and all she can think about is some café!'

And I didn't even realise what it meant – whether he went to the front or not: I was, indeed, a fool…!

In Kiev, he was already dreaming of getting his work printed at this time. He had no intention whatsoever of going anywhere as a volunteer.

[…] His appointed destination was Vladikavkaz specifically, and he didn't go on the medical train, no… The reason I think that is that he stopped off in Rostov along the way. He went to play billiards – in other words, he was in control of his own actions. He lost a lot of money playing billiards there, and even lost my gold bracelet in a bet. My mother had given me that bracelet when I was a schoolgirl. Mikhail always asked me to give it to him 'for good luck', when he went to play. And that time, he had persuaded me to give it to him, to take with him on the journey – and he promptly lost it. He also bumped into his cousin Konstantin in Rostov (Konstantin had no connection with the army whatsoever, he had always been an engineer) and said to him: 'There's an 'I owe you' for you – go and buy back Tasya's bracelet!' And then he continued on his journey to Vladikavkaz!"

In Rostov, he of course read the local newspapers, paying particular attention to the reports about the situation in his native city; could it have crossed his mind then that he would never go back there?

In one of these reports, he might well have read the following: "The last week has seen fierce fighting along the river Irpen. The Reds, who got away from Petlyura, tried to break through to the north via Kiev, towards Chernigov. Their attempt failed miserably, after coming up against the durability and resilience of General Promtov's forces. The failure of the assault on Kiev forced the reds to retreat towards Radomysl, in the south-west. General Promtov's forces immediately went on the attack and are now chasing hot on the heels of the departing reds. [...] The continuing attack from the west by the Polish army is accelerating the course of events even more quickly, and accelerating the destruction of the Bolsheviks and of 'General' Petlyura's band of men in this region." (*V Moskvu!* [*To Moscow!*], 30th Sep. (13th Oct.) 1919).

Would he have believed that an attack from the west – whether by the Poles or anyone else, for that matter – "would accelerate even more quickly" the coming of peace and harmony to his homeland? It is more likely that he could see that the situation was becoming ever more complex, including his own situation, and all the more so – that of his younger brothers, who had stayed in Kiev.

"I lived without him in Kiev for a short time only, less than a month... I received a telegram from him, from Vladikavkaz, and that was followed immediately by a letter: 'I stopped in Rostov and played billiards.' I set off. People warned me: if the Makhnoites are in Yekaterinoslav, they'll lay waste to the train. I was afraid, of course I was..."

It is unclear whether or not Bulgakov was still in town when his brothers, Nikolai and Vanya, joined the Volunteer Army (by this time, one was 21 and the other 19). A photograph in which Vanya Bulgakov is seen beside some other cadets and headstrong youths, beside a machine-gun, was taken before late autumn arrived (there is grass growing, there are leaves on the trees and some of the cadets are dressed only in shirt-sleeves). Some memoirs written by Nikolai's wife, Kseniya Alexandrovna Bulgakova, in the late 1960's, have survived; they tell of how Nikolai "left college to go to the south, on the White Army's orders; he grew very sick, and his train was sent to Kiev with some other patients… The train was standing at Kiev-Tovarny station. His mother knew nothing about this whatsoever, but some maternal instinct drew her there, and when Nikolka opened his eyes in the railway coach, he saw his mother standing before him. This was a joyful moment for him, and for her too. It was the last time he ever saw his mother. After that, the train headed to the south. Once he was fit again, he found himself despatched to the Crimea, where he was very gravely wounded, only just surviving, and then the college was evacuated on the 'Rion' in 1920."

One can easily imagine the bitter regret that his mother must have felt about the fate of her two youngest sons, which doubtless intensified many times over after, over the course of a few months, as it became clear that the army they had joined was suffering a decisive defeat, and no news of them could be had. The circumstances of that last meeting between his mother and her very sick son became known, of course – either at the time or later – to Bulgakov, as did, perhaps, the news that his brother was later seriously wounded. This, along with the vicissitudes of the similar fate suffered by his younger brother, Vanya, laid the foundations for the plot of his 1922 story, *The Red Crown*, in which one of the scenes, at least, seems saturated with biographical motifs.

"My old mother said to me:

'I shan't live long. I can see what madness this is. You're the eldest, and I know you love him. Bring Kolya back. Bring him back. You're the eldest.'

I said nothing.

Then she put all her thirst and all her pain into her words.

'Find him. You're pretending that it needs to be like this. But I know you. You're intelligent, and you understood long ago that all this is madness. Bring him to me.'

I couldn't restrain myself any longer, and I said, turning my eyes away: 'All right.'"

And thereafter – about how his brother goes away to a war, from which he returns mortally wounded. (There are two clear clues in the tale which point to his younger brother Vanya being the prototype for this character: "He is 19 years old" and "I'm 10 years older than him.")

They didn't stay in Vladikavkaz for long: Bulgakov was sent to Grozny. "I went with him," Tatiana Nikolayevna recalls. "I travelled with him a few times to the surgical dressing unit – outside Grozny. We went to the unit on a cart, through a field of tall maize. The coachman, me, and Mikhail with a rifle on his lap – they had given it to us for the journey, the rifle had to be kept loaded at all times. There was a female doctor there, the director of this bandage unit, and she later said: 'no wives!' He started going there on his own. He would leave in the morning, then come home for the night. On one occasion, he was surrounded, but he somehow managed to break through and come home for the night anyway..."

"We later lived in Beslan – we didn't go all the way to Vladikavkaz. We were forever living in trains – in a heated compartment or private compartment. We didn't have any friends or acquaintances there. There was nothing there at all, besides watermelons. We spent entire days eating watermelons... Then we went back to Vladikavkaz – to the very same hospital from which he had been despatched. First of all, we lived with some Armenians – we rented a room from them; Mikhail had a batman. We made friends with a Cossack ataman – we used to go and visit him in the evening – and with General Gavrilov. Life in the city was fairly vibrant: there were the cafés, and you could hear music coming from them on the street... Then the general left, along with his regiment – there were rumours that the reds were attacking, and the hospital was disbanded – whilst the whites were still in charge, and the general's wife, Larisa Dmitriyevna, invited us to live with her – in her spare room. They were themselves renting a house from the ataman, I seem to recall. She had a son – a little boy, and a maid – a Finnish girl named Ayna. We probably saw in the New year, 1920, at their place..."

How else was Bulgakov spending his days in the autumn and winter of 1919/1920, besides his duties as a doctor?

Tatiana Nikolayevna recalled: "When I arrived in Vladikavkaz, he said to me: 'I'm going to have something published.' So I say to him: 'Well, congratulations – you've always wanted this.'"

These words, "I'm going to have something published," indicate that this was the beginning of his time as a published author; and therein lies the value of Tatiana Nikolayevna's testimony. There is other data, as we shall see, that confirms how accurate her memory was.

In later years, Bulgakov painstakingly encoded and disguised this initial moment in his career as an author. I would emphasize, indeed, that he did not attempt to hide it altogether, but to disguise it: he deemed it important to safeguard the very trace of his first ever publication, to leave a hint.

It was the newspaper feuilleton *Prospects for the Future* (*Gryadushchiye Perspektivy*), published on 26th November 1919 beneath the initials "M.B.".[3]

....

[3] *Groznyy*, 13th (26th) November 1919, No. 47.

The first thing that helps us attribute this article to Bulgakov is an indication left behind for us by the author himself: an album full of newspaper cuttings, which he kept whilst living in Moscow, begins with a fragment from a newspaper cutting – there is part of a headline: [G]roznyy – and the date. What else would Bulgakov place at the beginning of such an album, if not the first piece that he ever had in print? Having handled this part of the archive in 1971-1972 and come to this conclusion, the author of this book has encouraged researchers and fans ever since, at academic consultations and public speeches, to seek out this edition of the newspaper *Groznyy* (*Fearsome*), which used to come out when Denikin was in power.

Let us also cite the testimony of P.S. Popov. In 1940, in the foreword to an anthology of works by Bulgakov which was never published, he wrote: "His literary debut took place on 19th November 1919." One can put this down either to an error in reading the date (or a mistake in Bulgakov's oral account, written down by Popov), or to the existence of another publication by Bulgakov that has not yet been found – just a few days before *Prospects for the Future* appeared. In the autumn of 1969, when I asked Yelena Bulgakova where her husband had had something printed in November 1919, she told me, with the kind of circumspection that was common at the time, that she had made sure that anything that might have harmed Bulgakov's works was no longer part of his biography.

Within the last two years, copies of this newspaper have been unearthed.[4] The edition of the paper containing Bulgakov's article came out on just a single sheet. It transpired that in his album, the clue to the place and time of publication was not all that he left: on the reverse side of the fragment from the paper stuck into the album, there is also part of the text itself, with its author's initials... What ought to have been the most prominent part of his life had become, at a certain time, the flip-side, unseen, hidden from the eyes of strangers.

The article drew a line under what its author had experienced in the last two and half years and was embellished with gloomy forecasts. In it, *Prospects for the Future* were depicted in the most hopeless of tones. Two concepts dominated in this article, with whose help the author described the recent past, the present and the future: "madness" and "payment". The theme

---

[4] A complete edition of the newspaper can be found at the Academic library of the Central state archive. After reading the part of the serialized version of "Mikhail Bulgakov: The Life and Times" in which I made the suggestion about the writer's first publication ("Moscow", 1987, No. 7), staff at the Library kindly informed the author that they had this newspaper in their archives; I would like to take this opportunity to thank A.V. Sedyukhin, O.A. Grishina and L.D. Semenova.

of guilt and payback, guilt of the whole nation, which would later be closely bound in his work to that of personal guilt, originates, as we can now see, in Bulgakov's first ever printed piece. His story *The Red Crown*, published three years later, retains both of these concepts and themes, although they were later to undergo a transformation: both under the influence of what he had experienced in those years, and due to the new circumstances surrounding publication ("You're intelligent, it's long since been clear to you that all this is madness"; "Yes. The dusk is here. The important time of payback.").

The mood expressed in this article was not confined solely to its author. Two weeks before it was printed, Bulgakov could have read, on the opening pages of the weekly newspaper *V Moskvu! Organ Russkoy Natsional'noy Mysli (To Moscow! An Organ of Russian National Thought)*, which was published in Rostov-on-Don, an article by the paper's editor-in-chief, N. Izmailov, *A Black Anniversary* (*Chyornaya Godovshchina*), and found in it something that chimed with the thoughts he was having at the time; in the first few lines of the article, one sees a similar vocabulary being used: "For two years now, madness and betrayal have been wreaking their bloody treason against our poor Motherland...

For two years now, Russian blood has been shed in rivers in a fratricidal war.

For two years now, under a satanic plan [this train of thought is not one that we find in Bulgakov's thinking. – M.C.], the Russian people have been exterminated by hunger, cold, pestilence, torture and firing squads, deceived by their stupidly dreamy intelligentsia, and above all by its 'pride and glory' – the cadet contingent." The article's author maintained: "short-sighted and ignorant is he who believes that the Bolsheviks are the cause of all the ills that have descended upon Russia and are tearing her apart. Bolshevism is the inevitable consequence of the 'great revolution' [...] The emergence of this sickness can be traced back to the time when the so-called 'progressive bloc' was formed, which set as its goal the struggle against the Supreme power. [...] How did they dare – all those Milyukovs, Guchkovs, Maklakovs, Kerenskys [...] to start up that 'little fling' with the lady whose name was Revolution? It is not they, those Don Juans, that she has kissed with the plague-infected kiss of Almanzor, but Russia... [...] Enmity, violence and depravity have come into the world, hot on their heels..." Bulgakov too, it seems, blames those who, in his words, brought about "the madness of the March days", but he clearly does not see them, as Izmailov did, as "pawns in the hands of the Jewish masons." These are important differences.

The paper reported on successes at the front on the right bank of Ukraine, and on the willingness of Petlyura's Galician units to cross over to the Volunteer Army, and talked of the "difficult, bloody battle with the huge forces of reds attacking us, on our main operational line of communication towards Moscow." This alone would have looked pretty gloomy to the trained eye.

I shall quote Bulgakov's article in full, in light of its special biographical significance.

"Now, when our unhappy motherland finds itself at the very bottom of the pit of disgrace and disaster into which it has been cast by the 'Great Social Revolution', one and the same thought keeps occurring with increasing frequency to many of us.

It is a thought that refuses to go away.

It is dark and gloomy, it arises in our minds, and, imperiously, it demands a reply.

It is very simple thought: 'And what is going to happen to us now?'

It is only natural that this thought should arise.

We have analysed the events of our recent past. O, how carefully we have studied almost every moment from the last two years. There are many who have not only studied these moments, but also cursed them.

We see the present before our eyes. Its nature is such that one feels like closing one's eyes again.

So as not to see it!

What remains is the future. A mysterious, unknown future.

It is quite right to wonder: what is going to happen to us now?

Recently I happened to be flicking through a few copies of an illustrated British magazine.

I gazed at the marvellously taken photos in it for a long time, captivated.

And I thought long and hard about what I had seen afterwards…

Yes, the image is a clear one!

Colossal machines housed in colossal factories work feverishly, day after day, chewing on the stony coal, thundering, clanking, pouring out jets of molten metal, forgeing, fixing, constructing things…

They are fashioning the might of peace-time, replacing those machines which, not so very long ago, sowing death and destruction, were fashioning the might of victory.

In the West, the great war between great nations came to an end. Now, those nations are licking their wounds.

They will, of course, get back on their feet, and they will do so very quickly!

And, to all those who have finally seen reason, all those who do not believe the pitiful, delirious claims to the effect that our illness will spread to the West and infect it, it will become clear that there has been an almighty surge in the titanic work of peace-time, which is lifting up the Western countries to unprecedented heights of peace-time might.

And as for us?

We are late to the party...

We are so late that none of the latter-day prophets, I imagine, could possibly tell you when we will finally catch up with them, and whether we will, indeed, catch up with them at all.

For we are being punished.

We cannot begin to think about creating anything. We face the onerous task of having to win back, to recapture our own land.

The retribution has begun.

Volunteer heroes are tearing the Russian land from out of Trotsky's hands, inch by inch.

And absolutely everyone – the volunteers, going about their duty undaunted, and those who are lingering in the southern cities in the rear, imagining, in their bitter delusion, that the matter of rescuing the country will take care of itself, without their involvement – everyone longs passionately for the country to be liberated.

And it will be liberated.

For there is no country that does not have heroes, and it is a crime to suppose that the motherland has died.

There will be much fighting ahead, however, much blood will be spilt, because, for as long as the madmen that Trotsky has duped are still marching along behind that malevolent figure with guns in their hands, there will be no life; instead, there will be a deadly battle.

We must fight.

And whilst the machines of creation are clattering away in the West, over here, from one end of the country to the other, we will hear the clattering of machine-gun fire.

The madness of the last two years has pushed us onto a frightening path, and we cannot afford to stop or take a breather. We have begun to drink the cup of punishment and we shall drink every last drop.

Over there, in the West, innumerable electric lights will twinkle, pilots will pierce the air as it submits to them; the people will be building, studying, printing, learning ...

Whereas we, on the other hand... We will be fighting.

For there is no power whatsoever that is capable of altering this state of affairs.

We will be attempting to win back our own capitals.

And we shall win them back.

The British, remembering how we covered the fields with a bloody dew, crushed Germany, pushing the Germans away from Paris, and they will lend us some more greatcoats and boots, so that we can get to Moscow as soon as possible.

And we shall get there.

The miscreants and madmen will be hounded out, dispersed, destroyed.

And the war shall come to an end.

And then the country, bloodied and destroyed, shall begin to rise up... Slowly, with great difficulty, it shall rise up.

Those who complain of 'fatigue' will, alas, be disappointed. For they will have to get even more 'fatigued'...

We will have to pay for our past through backbreaking labour, through the harsh poverty of life. We will have to pay in both a metaphorical sense and a literal sense... for the insanity of the March days, for the insanity of the October days, for the uncontrollable traitors, for the corrupting of the workers, for Brest, for the insane use of machine-tools to print money... for everything!

And we will do so.

And only then, when it is already very late, will we begin to create a few things again, so as to become legitimate, so that we are allowed into the halls of Versailles once again.

Who will see the happy days I describe?

Will we see them?

Oh no! Our children might perhaps see them, or perhaps our grandchildren, for the scope of history is broad and sweeping, and it 'reads' entire decades just as easily as individual years.

And we, the representatives of an unsuccessful generation, dying whilst still ranked as a pitiful, bankrupt nation, will have to say to our children:

'Pay up, pay up in good faith, and remember the social revolution forever!'" The last line was the culmination of all the thinking he had done over the last few years.

Five years later, in October 1924, in a short autobiography that was intended for publication, Bulgakov would describe the moment when his life in print began – calculatingly obscuring the specifics and preserving elements of authenticity that were important to him: "One night, in 1919, as I travelled on a dilapidated train in deepest autumn, by the light of a candle placed on an empty kerosene bottle, I wrote my first little story. In the town to which the train dragged me, I took the story to the editorial offices of a newspaper. There, it was printed." The town in question, the name of the newspaper, and the contents of the story are all shrouded in a fog of uncertainty. Given that he refers to the work being printed in 1919, he is probably referring to the article *Prospects for the Future*; the short story genre would have seemed more harmless in 1924.

On the same day that Bulgakov's article appeared in the newspaper, which was published in the North Caucasus, *Kiyevlyanin* printed an article headed *Narrow, Weak Shoulders* (*Uzkiye i Slabyye Plechi*), in which one can perceive the bitterness of the approaching despair. "Yes, the stick is necessary for us," writes its author, who assures his readers that the need for a firm hand in charge of the country is something that not only the cadets, but also other groups have been asserting. "And when this happens, there will be no need for any artificial 'associations' of political and societal groups whatsoever, since there will only be one single party, with its power over a united Russia forged by means of history." In another issue, the paper's editor wrote, in a piece entitled "Two armies", that an army founded on looting would be "short-lived" (he would reveal his ideas about the moral death of the White Army in those months a few years later, in the book *The year 1920* [*1920-y God*]): "The worst ones will join the Bolsheviks, the mediocre ones will run off back to their houses, and the best ones will die." These deadly tones can be felt in Bulgakov's article as well; yet in his article, one has the sense not of an end that is nigh, but of a long and deadly journey; essentially, one finds in it something that foreshadows the future theme of *Flight*: "we cannot stop, we cannot take a breather... let us drain our cup to the end." (... "Let he who has finished his flight be at rest").

Extremely characteristic of Bulgakov's personality – that of a man interested in the natural world, a doctor, a university man, drawn towards positivism and creative action – was the bitterness with which the author of that article looked at the photos depicting the dynamic life of western civilization, in industry, science and elsewhere – Europe had already healed the wounds inflicted by the world war, whereas in his homeland, there was no end in sight to the destructive war that was raging. One could not look forward to building and studying, but only to more fighting... The author of *Prospects for the Future* has not lost faith in the idea that new days will come – but only in the vaguest and most ill-defined future.

Two days after Bulgakov's piece was published, *Groznyy* printed, just after an article by the well-known critic Sergei Krechetov, "In memory of the soldiers of glory" (which contained a theme that echoed Bulgakov's views – "the demons of madness are still flying over the Russian land"), an article by P. Golodolinsky was printed, entitled "Among the ruins of the social revolution (a response to the article by M.B.)". This response is of exceptional interest, helping as it does to shed light on the ideological context in which Bulgakov's political thinking was formed and manifested.

"It is shameful and painful to read the article by M.B., *Prospects for the Future*. It is as if it were not written by a Russian. Its lines are imbued with a gloomy pessimism and a pitiful humiliation of some sort.

Fortunately, however, there are not many people who think like that at the front. All the things the author talks about have already been thought about and pondered over, by my comrades in arms, in the quiet moments between the fighting. And there is one vivid thought that casts light on us, as we patiently bear our troubles and deprivations [...]

Bolshevism shall never be destined to take hold in Russia, because that would be tantamount to the death of our culture and a return to primordial times.

Our strength lies in the fact that that awful sickness – Bolshevism – visited our country first.

Its end will come soon and unexpectedly. The wrath of the people will descend upon those who pushed them into an international conflict. The Volunteer Army will seize the initiative, not through the conquering of Moscow, nor by a host of advantageous defeats, but purely as a result of its superior moral qualities.

Remember those epidemics which spread across Russia like lightning. The first of them was the contagious coup and the madness of the crowd, which tore onwards, unrestrainably, to the impossible ideals of socialism in waves of red banners.

The second was the soldiers' irrepressible cry, 'home!', and their flight from their positions. And the third epidemic, which is fading away now, were the slogans: 'beat the bourgeoisie, the officers and the intelligentsia'.

It is possible that a fourth one will come, just as quickly: 'We want peace! Give us a firm, legal government.' This last aspect is now a pressing matter, like a blister which has not yet chosen a place where it can break through. All around us, we hear: 'Give us peace as soon as possible, how good life was before.'"

The author delights in the allies' transition to a state of peace and exclaims: "'They are forging the might of the world,' but they have returned only to the old culture, whereas to get to the one to which we are to go to, they will also have to suffer greatly, just as our country is suffering. The new culture cannot be a continuation of the old one. There is the same colossal difference between them, as between the culture of Rome and the culture of the barbarians which replaced it, and which has achieved such power in our times. In this regard, we are not lagging behind, but have already overtaken other countries.

Having suffered a grave sickness, we are going to be guaranteed immunity from recurrences of it in the future.

The author can see no end to the country's poverty-stricken existence. But he forgets that we do not owe anybody anything. We shed blood doing battle with the central states – more so than any of our allies. The war brought us all the horrors of the revolution and we have not yet received recompense for all the hardships we suffered. The time of payback has not yet come for us.

If we are going to talk about payback, then we must ourselves present our invoices for payment, for reimbursement of the millions of lives lost on the battlefields of the European war.

We do not owe anyone anything, this must be clear to the allies, and it is difficult to believe that they could demand payment of all those inflated promissory notes which the usurpers of Russian state power signed off on.

The creation process is already taking place. It is calmly going about its work to the accompaniment of the howling of national passions. If anything, the Slavic states have become closer to us because of this war and because of the revolution in particular.

We have received quite a shakeup, and must acknowledge that it has aroused the people, who were sleeping. In the smoking ruins of the social revolution, we will build a new culture, to replace the old one, borrowed largely from foreign lands. The time of living work is still ahead of us, of striving for progress by all the people – the time of the glorious days of Russia."

The author of the response – the very first, perhaps, of the long line of critics that he was to have – was hurt by the gloomy coloration of *Prospects for the Future*. In its tragic tone, predicting as it did a long, "deadly battle", he detected an unpatriotic, "non-Russian" note (contrasting this with his confidence in a "speedy and unexpected" end to the war). The traits of Messianism, the stressing of Slavic communality – as a counterweight to the Western allied states, faith in the inevitability and creativity of a change to the old European culture – with a "new" one, "the culture of the barbarians" – this set of ideas, revealed in his adversary's article, originating in the previous century and strengthened by the war years, remained to a considerable degree alien to Bulgakov – therein lies the distinctness of his path. Also alien to him, as one can see by juxtaposing the two articles, was his adversary's belief in the inevitability of a global revolution (Bulgakov was sure that this was "pitiful nonsense"), combined, bizarrely, with conservative ambitions.

The pitting of Russia against the West (including the allies – "we don't owe anyone anything") in his adversary's article, in a manner tinged with regret and bitterness, makes the sobriety of the intellectual and socially-oriented position adopted by Bulgakov appear with even greater clarity. Even in this period, his patriotic feeling is fed not by groundless pride in the face of the West, but by the bitter realisation that Russia was lagging ever further behind the "titanic work of the world", the catastrophic fact that it was so late to the party – a lack of punctuality which made things very unpredictable ("none of the contemporary prophets" could say "when we finally catch up with them…" – the contemporary reader cannot help but be struck by the extent to which Bulgakov's thinking was ahead of the times).

Bulgakov's opponent seeks someone to blame on the outside – and easily finds one, in the form of the European governments. The guilty ones are those who unleashed the world war – it took away a million lives and brought the revolution. A payment must therefore be made not "by us", but "to us" (the idea of cancelling the Russian government's debts, which was later implemented, developed, as we can see, in a camp too, a long way from those who led the revolution). For the author of the response, the global conflict was evidence of the bankruptcy of the ruling class of the European states and indicative of the failure of the old culture (for Bulgakov, this was not the case). He calls for a breaking away from those in "foreign lands" and the construction of some kind of new world on the ruins of the collapsed "social revolution" (how interesting that his words seem to presage future slogans about social construction "in one, separate country", isolating itself from hostile countries around it). The constructor of this world would be the "people", who "were asleep" and have now been awoken (for Bulgakov, this notion did not exist at the time in such an unsegmented form; he was utterly alien to the kind of bowing down to the people, traditionally inherent to the Russian intelligentsia – and in this regard he differed from it).

And so, the words of the "Internationale", to which the residents of the Turbin household were to listen with tense, rapt attention in a few years' time – as the sounds of their unknowable future – on the stage of a theatre in the capital, were echoed in the late autumn of 1919 in the statements made by those who were still fighting against the new government, with weapons in their hands. This point is extremely important in terms of understanding the subsequent course of events and movement of ideas – and of Bulgakov's place in the flow of social life.

Bulgakov himself did not lay claim to a role as a prophet – nor indeed was he one (as I have already shown to some extent, he was irritated by the prophetic aspects of the Russian intellectual and writer at that time). Rather, his article contains a *commonplace* view, put forward without any embarrassment, without any accusations against this commonplaceness, with sincerely felt pathos. This pathos is simple and even, by the standards of those times, rather simple: in his eyes, the colossal amounts of destruction and the rivers of blood that had been shed were so significant, of such intrinsic value, that they needed no justification with any kind of grandiose objectives and could not be justified by them. His dislike of poetry, later attested to by many of his contemporaries, may have been in keeping with his dislike of all overly lofty objectives that people set for others, and of any high-powered game in which the life of another is at stake.

In later years, when this view of the structure of society, whereby it is seen through the prism of the interests of a person's private life, was losing more and more currency, and being pushed out by other approaches, Bulgakov was accused by his own circle of literary acquaintances of having a bourgeois view of things – justifiably so, to a degree.

An extremely important theme in the article is that of national guilt. There are no sweeping assertions about internal events having an external source; the author writes about "independent traitors", but not about infection by a different nation. He places all the responsibility, and the future payback, on his own people, harshly accusing it of having submitted to "stupefication", dreaming about a time when "we will start creating something once again." He is confident of the inevitability and rightfulness of the day of reckoning.

In the winter of 1919/1920, Bulgakov undoubtedly continues to get articles printed: on 1st February 1921, he writes to Konstantin Bulgakov: "I remember that *around a year ago* [my italics – M.C.] I wrote you that I had begun to get published. My *sketches* have been printed in many newspapers in the Caucasus" – this was certainly a reference to his *articles* (and not his satirical sketches; he wrote those, too, but that was later, in Soviet Vladikavkaz), published in the winter of 1919/1920. This is confirmed by an account given by Y. Slezkin: 12 years later, on 21st February, 1932, he writes with certainty in his diary, recalling his friendship with Bulgakov: "We met in Vladikavkaz, when the whites were in charge. He was a military doctor and *was working with the newspaper as a correspondent*."

In his letter, as one might well imagine, he continued to try to make sense of what was happening around him. He followed the news from Kiev with an understandable emotion. On 14th December 1919, the editor of *Kiyevlyanin*, with the kind of frank assessment of the situation that was typical of his newspaper, wrote: "It is no use trying to hide the fact that the situation in Kiev is serious, but it does not necessarily follow from this that it is hopeless." Civilians were being evacuated from the city. "… Many are saying: my wife won't make it without me, you see! … they will make it, and set up lives for themselves far better without us, than with us," V. Shulgin asserts; "… by defending the path for the retreat, we are turning ourselves from people in retreat to people on the offensive, and thereby reducing all our ills." Men "born between 1862 and 1870" are already being called upon to "take up arms", in a message "to the old men of the former, glorious Russian army"; people are already being called upon to follow the example set by the Bolsheviks, who managed to assemble several thousand communists rapidly in Petrograd, so as to defend the city (15th December), and taught "to be just towards the enemy, too": "If the Bolsheviks have managed to eke out temporary successes from fate of late, this has only occurred thanks to the colossal amount of energy, the colossal amount of tension of *all* the forces, both physical and mental, that they have been able to develop in themselves. If you like, this is a force of desperation, but it is still a force nonetheless," (Yaroslav G., Us and them – *Kiyevlyanin*, 16th December 1919 No. 83).

All of this is food for thought for Bulgakov in that winter, fodder for the changes in his worldview and in his very nature that we cannot see and that only manifested themselves some years later.

He published one of his stories in the first week of February 1920 (in the old style). A year later, he cut out several excerpts from this story from the newspaper (no copy of this paper has yet been found) and sent it to his relatives in Kiev, apparently reluctant, given the new circumstances, to entrust the entire text to the post. He accompanied it with subtle hints in the letter about the personal significance of this material, about its connection to certain events from that time that were well-known to the Bulgakov family: "I'm sending you three excerpts from a story with the subtitle: 'The gift of admiration'. They may only be tiny excerpts, but for some reason I can't help thinking that they may be of interest to you…" (a letter to Vera Bulgakova dated 26th April 1921). "That same evening, my mother told me what had happened while I was away, and told me about her son: 'The disorder broke out… Kolya went off to college three days ago and there's been no word of him since…', 'I suddenly see that something is hitting the wall in a number of places, and the tiles are sent flying all over the place.

'But Kolya… dear little Kolya…'

Mother's voice suddenly becomes tender and warm at that point, then she shudders, and she starts to sob. Then she wipes her eyes and continues:

'And Kolenka hugged me, and I could sense that he… he was sheltering me… sheltering me with his body.'"

There is no doubt that his thoughts about the fate of his younger brothers, which had remained unknown to him since the moment the Volunteer Army had left Kiev, influenced the plot of the story and were reflected in it.

The real inner meaning of the story becomes apparent when we look at a letter sent on 10th November (in the old style) 1917, by Varvara Bulgakova, in Kiev, to her daughter Nadya, in Tsarskoye Selo, where the Zemskys were living at that time: "I can understand that you went through a fair few anxious moments, since we have had to put up with a lot here, too. The worst thing of all was the position that poor Nikolaichik was in, as a cadet. He put up with the tribulations very well, and on the night of 29th to 30th I was with him: we were literally a hair's breadth from dying. On 25th October, military preparations had begun in Pechersk, and he was cut off from the rest of the city. Whilst the telephone at the Engineering College was still working, we spoke to Kolya on the telephone: but then the phone lines went down, too… My anxiety over Kolya increased, I decided to go and find him.

On 29th, after lunch, I reached him. I managed to make it to where he was; but from there, when Kolya and I tried to go out into the city beside the Konstantinovsky college at 7.30 pm (they had let him out for 15 minutes to see me off), the college came under fire, an incident that has been well-documented. We had just got past the stone wall in front of the Konstantinov college, when the first shots were fired. We threw ourselves backwards and hid behind a small section of the wall; but when the crossfire began – with shots fired at the College and from it – we found that we were in the firing line: bullets were flying into the wall where we were standing. Fortunately, among the random group of people with us (6 people), trying to take cover in this location, there was an officer: he ordered us all to lie down on the ground, as close to the wall as possible. We endured a terrible hour: there was the crackle of machine-gun fire and artillery fire, the bullets were smashing into the wall, and then the screeching of shells was added to all this… But evidently it was not yet our time, and Kolya and I remained alive (one woman was killed), but we will never forget that night… In a brief lull between the shooting, we managed (at that same officer's command) to run back over to the Engineering College. There, the flames had already been put out; the only thing still on fire was a projector; the cadets had got ready for battle; a command was issued by the officers: Kolya joined the ranks, and I didn't see him again… I sat on a chair in the hall, knowing that I would have to sit there all night, there was no sense in even thinking about going back home on that terrifying night, there were eight of us like that, caught there at the College by the outbreak of military action. When I recovered my senses after the shock I had been through, when the awful beating of my heart calmed down (I know not how my heart endured that dash across the open towards the Engineering College) – the bullets had started whistling past again – Kolya grabbed me in both arms, protecting me from the bullets and helping me to flee… The poor boy, how anxious he was about me, and I about him…

The minutes seemed like hours; I imagined what was going on at home, where they were waiting for me, and worried that Vanechka would come out to look for me and get caught in the crossfire… And my passive state became agony for me… Little by little, the people crawled out of the hall into the corridor, and then to the front door… There were two officers standing there, and a cadet from the artillery College, who had also become trapped there whilst heading elsewhere, and one of the officers said that he would accompany anyone who wanted to go with him across the field used for combat engineering to the slaughterhouse in Demievka: that district was outside the area that was under fire… Among those wishing to make the journey there were 6 men and two women (one of whom was me). And so we set off… But what a horrid and fantastical journey it was, in complete darkness, in the fog, across various ravines and gullys, through sticky, impenetrable mud… following one another in complete silence, with the men holding revolvers. Beside the Engineering College we were stopped by some patrols (the officer showed them his pass), and near the ravine that we were supposed to go down into, the figure of little Nikolai emerged from the darkness, carrying a rifle… He recognised me, grabbed me by the shoulders and whispered right into my ear: "Go back, don't do anything crazy. Where are you going? You'll be killed!" but I silently crossed him, kissed him ever so hard, the officer grabbed hold of my hand, and we started walking down into the ravine… In a word, I was at home by one in the morning (that kindly officer accompanied me all the way home). Can you imagine what awaited me? I was so tired, physically and mentally, that I collapsed into the nearest chair and broke out into sobs. But I was home, I could get undressed and get into bed, whereas poor Nikolaichik, who hadn't slept for two nights, had to endure two more terrible days and nights. And I was glad that I had been with him on that terrible night… Now, it is all over… The Engineering College suffered less than the other ones: four men were wounded and one went mad."

Speculation about what might have happened to his younger brothers, Nikolai and Ivan, seems to have been an endless source of agony from the end of 1919 (when the Volunteer Army left Kiev) until the first news about them arrived (at the beginning of 1922).

These thoughts were directly related to the need to take a decision regarding his own life. The events occurring on the front lines accelerated these decisions.

The winter of 1919/1920 was a critical period in the life of Bulgakov himself: as we shall see, it brought a change of profession and a decisive shift from one world to another, which would be concluded eighteen months later.

On Saturday, 15th (28th) February 1920, the newspaper *Kavkaz* (*The Caucasus*) first went on sale; its list of collaborators read as follows: Y. Slezkin, D. Tsenzor, Y. Vensky, V. Amfiteatrov (the son of A. Amfiteatrov) and M. Bulgakov.

The following coincidence is quite remarkable: many years later, whilst answering questions from his friend and biographer P.S. Popov, Bulgakov would say, judging by the notes made by his interlocutor, the following: "I underwent a spiritual crisis on 15th February 1920, when I abandoned medicine for good and dedicated myself to literature." For the sake of accuracy, let us stress that Y.S. Bulgakova was sceptical about this note, and when I asked her whether she remembered anything related to this date from her conversations with M.A. Bulgakov, she shrugged her shoulders and laughed: "No, I don't remember anything. And that doesn't sound like Misha's style at all – a 'spiritual crisis'! He never spoke like that."

I would suggest that those words about a "spiritual crisis" serve to encrypt (or rather, let us say, do not decode) the following external and internal events. It was on these very days (in the old style) that the first news about the catastrophe must have arrived: the attacks by the red soldiers, which pre-empted the white guard's planned mass offensive and ended in success. In the battle outside Yegorlykskaya, the whites' main force was defeated – the Cossack cavalry. The event directly affected Bulgakov's life. He now faced the terrible ghost of the future that awaited him around the corner. In this period, he turned away from medicine – an occupation, which, at the time, was directly associated with one or other government and its army – and took the decision, after much thought, to choose a free profession: that of literature.

At that very moment, a coincidence occurred which was to play a huge role in Bulgakov's later life.

"When the hospital was disbanded," Tatiana Nikolayevna recounts, "in the first few months of 1920, they paid out compensation – in 'ribbons'. That was what they called the money: it had a cream-coloured surface with a dark blue ribbon. No-one accepted this money, there was just one store that did – and there, I bought up all the fillets of *balyk*... [These were perhaps the very same, ever so slightly phantasmagorical fillets of *balyk* which would later be snapped up in *The Master and Margarita*, when Archibald Archibaldovich is the last to leave the restaurant after a fire has spread through it, 'with two logs of balyk fillet in his armpit,' whilst Koroviev manages to come out with 'a whole salmon with its skin still on, and its tail still attached'. – M.C.]. It was already clear that the whites would soon be leaving, but they had not packed their things. At that point, Mikhail sent me to Pyatigorsk – I can't remember what for. There were no trains, so I came back. But he wanted to get there at any cost. A day or so later, a train left for Pyatigorsk, and Mikhail made the journey – for a day. He came back and said: 'I seem to have fallen ill.' He took off his shirt and I saw it: an insect. The next day, he had a headache and a high temperature. A very good local doctor called on us, then the head doctor from the hospital came. He said that Mikhail had bilious typhoid: 'If we retreat, he mustn't make the journey.' One morning, I went out and saw that the town was empty. The head doctor had left, too. The local one had stayed. I ran to his house in the night, when Mikhail was at death's door and was rolling his eyes. At that time, in the struggle between the whites and Soviet power, there was looting in the city, and going out at night was scary; one time, an Ingush man grabbed me by the arm in a deserted street – I broke away and fled... During the illness, he didn't suffer any wild pain or loss of memory... He often reprimanded me afterwards: 'You're a weak woman, you couldn't get me out of here!' But when two doctors are telling me that he would die at the first stop-off along the way – how could I take him? That's what they were saying to me: 'What on earth do you intend to do – take him as far as Kazbek and then bury him there?'

When he recovered and grew a little stronger, he went to the police department. Yury Slezkin was already there." [On 6th April, *Izvestiya Vladikavkazskogo Revkoma* (*News of the Vladikavkaz Revkom*) published a directive: 'Comrade Yury Lvovich Slezkin is to be considered deputy of the sub-department of the arts in the Terskiy department of education as of 27th March.' – M.C.]. In *Cuff-notes* (*Zapiski na Manzhetakh*), three years later, Bulgakov would write the following description: "In a room on the fourth floor, there were two cupboards with their doors torn off their hinges, and with rickety legs. There were three ladies with purple lips, hammering away loudly on typewriters, or smoking.

A writer was sitting right in the middle of the room and sculpting a sub-department out of the chaos. Theor. fine arts. Grey, actorly faces were creeping towards him, asking for money.

After the typhoid, a lethal swell has come. It sends me staggering and makes me feel sick. But I am taking charge of it. Head of the Lit. Dept. I am finding my feet."

One of those "three ladies", Lyubov Ulukhanova, told me many years later, on 4th September 1980: "The room was very shabby: it was an institution that had had a second coming... There was someone called Margo working there – Slezkin was courting her, and Tamara Gasumyanits, with her two thick pigtails – she had just finished studying at the grammar school and came to work at Teo. Whenever I went into her office, Bulgakov was lying on her table: when he stood up, he would lean on the table or sit in front of her chair, resting his elbows on it... He had taken off his epaulettes, his cap was crumpled, and he wore leggings... As for what his profession was, nobody knew. He was a tease, he used to make up funny poems.

Everything that happened to him prior to February 1920 now had to be forgotten, since it could cost him his life. A year later, he warned his sister that his relatives must not have any 'treatment-related' conversations with an acquaintance of his, a woman from Vladikavkaz, who was visiting Moscow; conversations "which I myself have not had ever since I graduated from the university of natural sciences and have been engaged in journalism. Make sure Konstantin gets the message. He's remarkably prone to all manner of lapses" (a letter to N.A. Zemskaya dated 19th April 1921).

He joined his sister for walks in the park – the most beautiful part of the city. From the city park, where the orchestra played, they went down to the so-called track, strolling along the tree-lined walkways. "It was May; Mikhail was still walking with a stick, leaning on my arm. At that time, the Communists had just arrived, a commission of some sort, and they were searching for members of the white guard. And I heard someone say: 'That one had articles printed in white guard newspapers.' I said to Mikhail: 'Let's go, let's get away from here at once!' And we left immediately. I can't understand how he managed to stay alive that year: he might have been recognised ten times! They were difficult times. It emerged, for example, that the chief of police had been in the white guard underground movement... And at the house where we lived, there was the son of a Cossack ataman, Mitya; he often chopped wood for me, and even courted me a little. And one day he said to me: 'Join our group!' 'What group?' I replied. 'We're gathering together people and officers… Little by little, you can get your husband involved…' I said that I didn't feel any empathy for the whites at all, and that I didn't want to. And I later found out that he suggested the same thing to a nurse at the kindergarten, with whom he was romantically involved; and she informed on him, and he was shot. And people might easily have said of Mikhail, of course, that he had articles printed in a white guard newspaper. Even that Mitya could have given away his name!

A Russian theatre was organised at that point. Slezkin asked Mikhail to do the word of welcome before the performances. At the theatre, there was opera for three days (they had a very good baritone, Lyubchenko), then drama for three days. Slezkin was introduced to me one day: 'Where do you work?' 'At the CID department.' And he sorted me out with a job at the theatre, as an extra…

One day I was walking to the theatre, and I suddenly heard a voice: 'Hello, my lady!' I turned round, and it was Mikhail's former orderly, Baryshev; when I had gone to join him in Vladikavkaz, he had had an orderly, or servant… I always used to give him money so that he could go to the movies. 'I'm not 'my lady' to you any more!' I said. 'Where do you live?' he asked me. 'Here, in the city; and you?' 'I've crossed over to the Red Army!'

Initially, we carried on living at the general's wife's place and ate with her in the evenings for a while, but when I joined the theatre, I couldn't make it home in time for dinner after rehearsals, and the general's wife, Larisa Dmitriyevna, didn't leave me any food… Mikhail found out, and stopped eating the dinners she made.

The theatre didn't pay any money: they merely gave out Lenten butter and gherkins… The sub-department didn't pay him, either. They only paid him later, for the plays. We lived mainly on the proceeds from my gold chain: we broke it into pieces and sold them, one by one. It was twisted, like a rope, and only about as thick as my little finger. It was long – I used to wrap it twice around my neck, and it would still droop down; there was a jewel on the chest section, too. Ever since my parents had given it to me, I had always worn it, never taking it off, and in Kiev I would go down to open the door wearing it. And here's the thing I don't get: how come no-one every snatched it from me during all those changes of government? I mean it would have been so easy to pull it off my neck and run off… It was on that necklace that we made a living.

I started buying more and more liver at the market; I got hold of a meat-cleaver somewhere and used to make pies. We sometimes went down to the cellar – it was a long way from the theatre, and we would eat kebabs and drink arrack. I felt sick later – it smelled of smoke..."

In the local paper, Bulgakov was no longer being described as a writer; exactly one month later, however, a critic from that same newspaper, V. Voks, used this word in inverted commas, when publishing a report on a concert: "... The 'writer', Bulgakov, read out a word of welcome from a little notebook, which was a setting to music of books about the history of music and was essentially fairly lightweight..." (*Kommunist* [*The Communist*], 4th June 1920). This seems to have been the first ever piece of feedback, in print, about the writer Bulgakov... And in the very next edition, Bulgakov published a sharp-tongued "Response to the distinguished theatre critic", in which he parodies all his attacks and advises the editors "not to encourage Voks's boldness."

At the end of May, Bulgakov switches from being in charge of the literary group to the theatre group, and even starts to organise a National drama studio for stage art. In June, his play *Self-defence*, a humoresque in 1 act, is put on at the 1st Soviet Theatre, along with two 'miniature plays' – the drama *Flame* (*Plamya*) by Y. Slezkin and the lubok *The Red Army Officers* (*Krasnoarmeytsy*).

His switch to theatrical pursuits came not a moment too soon: his employment at the sub-department was already nearing its logical conclusion, so to speak. "On 15th April, there was a demonstration at the 'Gigant' cinema on the subject of: 'What is Soviet power?', where speeches were made by Comrades Kirov, Bonkvitser, Takayev, Naumov and others; as many as 2,000 people were present. [...] Comrade Kirov delivered a wonderful speech. He said he was very surprised by the mood that still prevailed among the locals. They had not learnt anything. They still thought that Soviet power was a temporary thing, that it would go away; they were still standing around whispering on all the corners and junctions, they were forgetting that Soviet power was an inevitability, it was history, and that there was nothing they could do to prevent it," (quotation from: *Teatr* [*Theatre*], 1987. No. 6. p. 137). Bulgakov, it seems, was becoming increasingly aware of this inevitability.

On 18th May, a review of the first Soviet theatre's production of *The Great Evening* (*Velikiy Vecher*) appeared in the paper *Kommunist*, beneath the pseudonym Minstrel. I am entirely in agreement with G. Faiman, who has suggested that the person behind this pseudonym was Bulgakov. Two excerpts from the review provide particularly persuasive evidence in support of this view: "As regards the other performers in the play, they can be divided into two groups: a small group, whose members, whilst preparing for the play, learned their parts, albeit badly; and another group, a very large one, whose members didn't get to grips with their parts at all. [...] As regards the staging of the play, one cannot pass over the hapless portrayal of the public demonstration, with shooting taking place off-stage. The crack of machine-gun fire, *as everyone knows* [this is typical of Bulgakov's style – M.C.], is not in any way akin to the patter of falling rain; it ought to sound far more commanding, and the singing by the small choir, who were constantly stamping their feet outside the window, was nothing like the fearsome chanting of protesters. All in all, the scene came across as very vapid, with the exception, of course, of the volleys of artillery fire. The theatre's director must pay attention both to certain of the cast, who do not want to learn their parts and force the audience to listen to the shrill, dampened wails of the prompt, from her booth, throughout the entire play; and also to how the mass-participation scenes are staged." (quotation from: *Teatr*, 1987 p. 141-142).

In late June and early July, at the summer theatre on the 'track', a public debate was held over the course of three evenings about Pushkin, which was described by Bulgakov in detail in *Cuff-notes*: "Dripping with sweat, in the stuffy air, I sat in the front row and listened to the speaker tearing into Pushkin with his white trousers." After preparing himself for two days, he delivered a speech of his own – in defence of culture, in defence of the great legacy of the classical writers – and the audience reacted ardently to his words. "The speaker was lying on both paws. In the eyes of the audience, I could perceive a silent, cheerful: 'Catch him! Catch him!'" Bulgakov's defensive speech in this debate, which took the form, popular at the time, of a trial against Pushkin, soon resulted in a response in print, too, in an article entitled "An attack made with unfit means": "The Russian bourgeoisie, which was unable to convince the workers using the language of weapons, has been forced to try to win them over using the weapon of language. Objectively speaking, we saw just such an attempt in the speeches made by Messrs. Bulgakov and Beme during the debate on Pushkin. One might think: what does the revolution have in common with the dead poet and with these gentlemen? Yet it was they who spoke, and it was Pushkin as a revolutionary that they set about defending. These speeches, which do not add anything to the poet's glory, merely reveal which class those who defend his revolutionary nature belong to... They reveal the counter-revolutionary nature of these men who defend the 'revolutionary' nature of Pushkin..." (*Kommunist*, 10th July 1920).

In addition to appearing in *Cuff-notes*, this debate is also described in another literary work: two years later, in the autumn of 1922, in Yury Slezkin's novel *The Stolovaya Mountain* (*Stolovaya Gora*) (its title takes its name from the mountain beneath which Vladikavkaz is located). The novel's protagonist is Aleksei Vasilievich Turbin – the name of the protagonist of the play *The Turbin Brothers* (*Bratia Turbiny*), which Bulgakov was to write in the summer of 1920. This play was destroyed a few years later by the author himself, and its plot remains unknown. A list of the characters survived: the Turbin family, including their mother, Anna Vladimirovna; Tatiana Nikolayevna recalled that the play was set beside the sea, and that the maid had an affair with one of the main characters (which led to one of the episodes in an early draft of the ending to *The White Guard*, in which Myshlayevsky impregnates the maid, Anyuta). The reviews in print indicate that the play was set in 1905.

Our focus currently lies elsewhere, however: it was no accident that Slezkin chose this name for his protagonist: the aim was undoubtedly to identify with Bulgakov, who, it is fair to suppose, put a great deal that was personal into his "first" Aleksei Turbin – the hero of his play from 1920. Thus, Slezkin's novel can serve as kind of source, which helps us to create an image of Bulgakov in the years 1920-1921.

The occupation of Slezkin's protagonist coincides with that of Bulgakov in the spring and summer of 1920. When he goes to see the actress Lanskaya, Aleksei comes out with a monologue. "I suppose I'm fairly tired," he says, "and I won't say no to a cup of tea. We've been working, we've built a new world. I've been dashing about all day like a squirrel in a wheel, and don't take that as sarcasm. In the morning I went to the Lito (the Literary Department): I wrote a report on the network of literary studios and a call for the Ingush and Osettians to preserve their memorials to the times of old." Then: "I shall become, by turns, a literary historian, a historian of the theatre, a 'special correspondent' on museum curating and archaeology, a cunning fellow in the revolutionary banners brigade – we'll get ready for Red Army week – and an arrack addict". He refers to "an amazing dive bar in the Caucasian style, where a fellow black as a demon serves hot arrack and *shashlik* in the booth right at the back" – the very same bar, apparently, that was filled with the smell of smoky arrack, which Tatiana Nikolayevna still remembered.

Yury Slezkin clearly listened to Bulgakov very attentively. Much later, he wrote in his diary: "The way he spoke was borrowed from me, in the form of the writer in *The Stolovaya Mountain*."

One can indeed see, in the pages of the novel, fragments of Bulgakov's way of speaking: if you reconstruct it on the basis of the accounts of eyewitnesses and some of the speaking habits of his own characters. "He does not hurry, for, in the back pocket of his trousers, among a dozen certificates and powers of attorney of all kinds, there lies a permit. The text on the lilac slip of paper reads: "entry permitted until two am". Yes, *rest assured of it – permitted*. There's nothing you can do about this. By all means, you can whistle as much as you want. This doesn't have anything to do with him. Not by *any account*"; "And you are still saying that I'm indifferent, and am not gripped by the wave of events? On the contrary: I am in their grip, one could even say I've been swallowed up by them." These lines differ from Slezkin's style through their finished phrases and energetic tone, indicating that they may be direct quotations of things that Bulgakov said. In some cases, we clearly have before us short stories that were told by Bulgakov himself and are being repeated: he was drawn to this genre throughout his entire life. These short stories are all in the same mould: they all serve to pull back ever so slightly the "mask" behind which the hero of the novel hides; this mask is a source of irritation not only for the other characters but also for the author himself. "Tell me, Aleksei Vasilievich, have you ever been sincere in your life?" Lanskaya asks him. "I look at you, and it seems to me that you're wearing a mask. It's as though you're always afraid of something, that you're hiding from something, or you want to cover something up, paper it over. When you talk, you look around you. I was afraid too, but I would always be thinking about how to strike out, and everyone could see that. But you're soft, you're a strange one, Aleksei!" It is not through literary devices, and rather with an everyday nakedness that character traits, seemingly of significance in Bulgakov's personality, are recorded: his lack of aggression, his reluctance to engage in any kind of conflict whatsoever (the conflict "over Pushkin" was an exception – and a typical one at that!), fear, related to his desire to move to the side – and only that. The author of *The Stolovaya Mountain* was certainly trying to portray this personality type, and some of the episodes from Bulgakov's life, with the resources available to him: dialogues, the hero's inner monologues, the stories he tells.

"No, the thing Aleksei couldn't tolerate, above all, was chattiness. Talking a little bit was fine – he himself wasn't against having a chat and telling a story about something or other – but chattering… laying yourself bare, in full, running naked in front of everyone… that was both shameless and foolish.

How many fools there are in the world…! No, just think how many stupid people there are, who are prepared to tell you all about themselves, to tell you their whole stupid story of their life and all their idiotic convictions – I think such and such about this, and such and such about that – and then they get offended when you don't lay yourself bare in turn, or if you tell them, with the same honesty that they have shown, that they are fools.

No, when all's said and done, it is both more becoming and safer to go about fully clothed.

Aleksei once had occasion to see... or rather, one of his friends had occasion to see such a naked person: he was not embarrassed by his nakedness at all. He in fact – naïvely – took pride in it. He simply came up and declared – I am such and such, and I do not wish to be different, and I won't put on a suit... Yes, he simply said it, with complete sincerity, from the heart. And just think: the people believed him. People took him to be who he really was, because he had no intention of appearing to be anything other than that... End of story. You don't believe that the story ended there? Just imagine it though – it did. Ever since then, no-one has seen him. Amen."

These pages from Slezkin's novel convey what he knew about Bulgakov's ideas about the forms of historico-social and 'worldly-wise' behaviour in critical periods, when a man's life itself has become dependent on the frankness with which he examines his own self.

At the same time, let us not shy away from describing things that were simple and, above all, comprehensible to all, in simple language: fear for one's life and the struggle to preserve it, in this period, were an extremely important, pretty much the most essential trait of Bulgakov's mood. And his sarcasm in relation to this fear (traces of which can be seen in the author's point of view in Slezkin's novel) sticks in Bulgakov's throat, seems out of place: life was a value too big for this. Moreover, he was surely gripped by the feeling that his true life, the one that depended on his talent rather than on the will of fate, had not yet begun.

D. Gireyev, who studied Bulgakov's life in the Caucasus, found in the archives a "Report by the commission investigating the activities of the sub-department of the arts" dated 28th October 1920. On the cover of this report there is a note: "Expelled: 1. Gatuev, 2. Slezkin, 3. Bulgakov (wh.), 4. Zilbermints." It is plausible that this note, "wh.", signified that Bulgakov's recent past had caught up with him (and in a fairly merciful form).

In October 1920, Bulgakov's play *The Turbin Brothers* was enjoying a run at the theatre (with the sub-title *The Hour Has Struck*) – "a four-act drama, written off the cuff, the devil knows how," as the author defined it in a letter to Konstantin. "My life, my suffering," he wrote in the letter, on 1st February 1921. "Ah, Kostya; you cannot imagine how I wish you were here, when *The Turbins* was put on for the first time. You cannot imagine what sadness there was in my soul, at the fact that this play was being staged in a godforsaken hole, and that I was 4 years late with what I ought to have started doing long ago – writing." (This lateness was indeed destined to play a fateful role in the years of Bulgakov's literary debut: its influence would be felt for another few years.) "At the theatre, the 'authors' shouted and clapped, they clapped... When I was called on stage after the 2nd act, I came out with an uneasy feeling... I looked uneasily at the made-up faces of the actors, at the audience as they applauded. And I thought: "This is my dream, it has come true... but in what monstrous fashion: instead of the Moscow stage, a stage in the provinces; instead of the drama about Alyosha Turbin, which I had cherished, a hastily written, undercooked piece. How fate mocks us."

This is the first documentary evidence of the long-held literary dreams of a man who, aged twenty-nine, found himself in the position of an emerging writer. The letter also contains important admissions about a work for which no outlet in print could be found (and which remains unknown: we can only suppose that a handful of finished works were taken to Moscow and printed in the very first year): "Then, *besides the stories which I can't get printed anywhere*, I wrote a comedie bouffe, *The Clay Bridegrooms* (*Glinyanyye Zhenikhi*). They didn't add it to the repertoire, of course, but they've said I can stage it on one of the days that are free. And here again: there is no such day, all the days are taken. Eventually, the other day, I took out of the typewriter *The Paris Communards* (*Parizhskiye Kommunary*), in 3 acts. The day after tomorrow, I am going to read it to the commission. Here it will make it through, I'm sure of it. But the thing is, I submitted it for an All-Russian competition, in Moscow. I'm sure it won't make it by the deadline, I'm sure it will fail. And again, it serves me right. I wrote it in 10 days. It's garbage, the lot of it: *The Turbins*, *The Bridegrooms*, and this play. I do everything in haste. There's a sadness in my soul.

But I am gritting my teeth and working, for whole days and nights at a time. Ah, if only I had somewhere where I could get published!" It seems that the fourth of the plays from the years 1920-1921 – *The Paris Communards* – was written in January 1921 and sent to Moscow for a competition whose motto was "To the free god of the arts".

In the same letter to Konstantin, he wrote a detailed account: "My God, what haven't I done: I've given and am still giving lectures on the history of literature (at the University of the people and the theatre studio), I'm reading out introductions to plays, and so on and so forth... Tasya has worked on stage as an extra. Their troupe has been disbanded now, so she's got nothing to do.

I live in an awful room on Sleptsovskaya Street, building 9, flat 2. I used to live in a nice one, I had a writing table; now I don't, and I write in the light of a kerosene lamp."

Tatiana Nikolayevna recalled: "The general's wife's house was turned into a kindergarten. She herself went away somewhere, together with her son. They gave us a bad room, near the theatre itself – on Sleptsovskaya. That's right, there was no writing desk there – and we couldn't afford to buy one! ... Sometimes we went to Milochka Beridze's place for lunch; her mother made us meals, in return for money..."

Together with Lyudmila Beridze, Slezkin and Khadzhi-Murat Muguyev, he was still giving talks in the summer of 1920 at the literary evenings at the Terekskiy department of ROST, inside the Summer Theatre. The whole motley, multi-ethnic literary and theatrical circle was transformed into the characters of Slezkin's novel, in which Aleksei Turbin instils a romantic sensibility in Milochka – a young woman striving to be in step with the times and condemning Turbin for his sceptical approach to modernity.

In 1921, Bulgakov writes his fifth and final play from the "Vladikavkaz" period. In his letters, there is no reference to this play, but unlike all the other plays, it – or rather, his work on it – is twice described in works by Bulgakov: *Cuff-notes* and the story *Bohemia* (*Bogema*). In these references, the play is given an exaggerated, yet nonetheless destructive self-assessment: "Seven days later, the three-act play was ready. When I read it through in my unheated room, at night, I must admit that I cried! In terms of a lack of talent, it really was something utterly special and astonishing. There was something dumb and impudent peering out of every line in that piece of collective creativity. I couldn't believe my eyes! What am I hoping to achieve, madman that I am, if I write like that?! Looking down at me from the green, damp walls and the black, fearsome windows was shame. I started to tear up the manuscript. But then I stopped. Because suddenly, with an unusual, miraculous clarity, I realised that they were right, those people who said: you can't destroy something once it's been written down! You can rip it up, or burn it... hide it from others. But hide it from yourself – never! Of course! It was indelible. That extraordinary piece was something I had written. Of course...!"

In 1923, in Moscow, Bulgakov destroyed his copies of all his plays. As though to confirm the writer's words, though – "you can't destroy something once it's been written down" – almost forty years after he wrote it (and twenty years after the author's death), a copy of this very play, the last one, was discovered: *The Sons of the Mullah* (*Synovia Mully*), which had been written "by the three of us: myself, my trusted Kumyk assistant [T. Peizulayev, a lawyer by training – M.C.] and hunger" (*Cuff-notes*).[5]

In April, he writes to his sister Nadya, in Moscow: "If I go a long way away and for a long time, please do the following: there are some manuscripts that I left behind in Kiev: *First Blossom* (*Pervyy Tsvet*), *The Green Snake*, and a draft of *The Ailment* that is particularly important to me. I asked mama in a letter to keep them. I suppose that you intend to settle down in Moscow permanently. Send those manuscripts out of Kiev, pick up all of them in your hands along with *Self-defence* and *The Turbins*, and throw them into the fireplace. I strongly request that you to do this." He also sent her some cuttings and programmes: "If I go away and we don't see one another, keep this in memory of me."

The first letter he sends in February to his cousin Konstantin contains the following lines: "What's next? I shall leave Vladikavkaz in the spring or summer. Where shall I go? It's unlikely, but possible, that I shall pass through Moscow in the summer. I wish to go a long way away..." He sent the recipient "one of countless" theatrical posters: "To remember me by, should we not meet again." In a letter dated 16th February, he returns to this subject: "In Vladikavkaz, I got stuck in a position of 'neither forwards, nor backwards'. My quest is a long way from being over. In the spring, I must go either to Moscow (perhaps very soon), or to the Black Sea, or somewhere..."

A letter to his sister Vera dated 26th April 1921 reveals Bulgakov's mood over the last year, one that was very difficult both psychologically and from a creative perspective. "I am very touched by your and Varya's wishes about my work," he wrote. "I cannot express how tortuous it is for me at times. I think you understand that for yourselves... I regret that I cannot send you my plays. First of all, it would be awkward, and secondly, they have not yet been printed, and are currently on the printers' lists, and thirdly, they are utter drivel. The thing is, my creative work is sharply divided into two parts: the authentic and the forced." He writes "authentic" prose, too, but the curtain is only drawn back over this in a letter to Konstantin Bulgakov dated 1st February 1921: "I am writing a *novel*, the only thing I have thought up

---

[5] In 1960, the only existing Prompt Book for the play was given to Y.S. Bulgakova by Tamara Soslanovna Goigova; on 20th December 1960, she wrote to the writer's widow: "I remember Mikhail Afanasievich well. We worked together at the dep[artment] of national education in Ordzhonikidze (i.e. Vladikavkaz – M.C.). Moreover, he had known my elder sister even before this, for she had been a nurse in the (1st imperialist) war, when he was a military medic" (Lenin State Library, arch. 562, 34.9).

in all this time. But I feel sadness again: after all, this is an individual piece of creativity, and what is going on now is something completely different."

It seems to me that some indirect information about this novel and his work on it can be extracted from Slezkin's novel: "The only thing he would like to write is a novel. And he will write one – rest assured of it. The novel won't get away from him. It will be written. Whatever happens.

All of these satirical articles and reviews – that's no more than a slice of bread. Even a matter as fruitful as being the director of Lito and teaching in studios… it is a matter of the utmost importance, he does not disagree with that – but the fact remains, the novel will be written."

The premiere of Bulgakov's last Vladikavkaz play, *The Sons of the Mullah*, written on the basis of local material (the civil war in the North Caucasus), a play in which it is practically impossible to recognise Bulgakov's style, took place on 15th May 1921. "In his native sub-department, the play created a furore," we read in *Cuff-notes*. "It was immediately bought for 200,000. And two weeks later, it was being put on." It was performed by amateur Ingush actors. A member of the cast, T. Malgasova, recalled: "There was a great mass of people, the audience nationally reacted stormily, and in a moment of particular pathos, a shot was fired by someone in the audience…" And this reaction on the part of the audience was also recorded in *Cuff-notes*: "The Chechens, the Cabardians, and the Ingush, after the heroic horsemen broke through and seized the sergeant-at-arms and the guards in the third act, shouted:

'Take that! The scoundrel! That's what he deserves!'

And they later joined in with the ladies from the sub-department as they called out: 'the author!', summoning him onto the stage."

Cuff-notes then describes a critical biographical turning point, the start of which occurs, it seems, over these very days, when, through short-lived but difficult work, accompanied even by a certain amount of psychological trauma, the required sum of money was earned. (In the story *Bohemia*: "One hundred to me, one hundred to Genzulayev. […] I ate up seven thousand in two days, and with the remaining 93 decided to get out of here. Onwards. To the sea. Across the sea and then across more of the sea, then to France – I'll dry off there – then to Paris!

The driving rain lashed against my face, and, hunching my shoulders, in my little overcoat, I ran down the side-streets one final time – homeward bound…

… You – the men of letters, the dramatists in Paris, in Berlin, have a go at it! Have a go, just for fun, at writing something worse! Even if you were as capable as Kuprin, Bunin or Gorky, you won't be able to do it. I broke the record!"

A grotesque description of what happened next can be found in the story *Bohemia*: "In 1924, they say, you could travel from Vladikavkaz to Tbilisi fairly easily: you hired a car in Vladikavkaz and travelled along the Voyenno-Gruzinskaya road, where it is extraordinarily beautiful. And it's only 210 versts. But in 1921, the very word "hire" sounded like a foreign word in Vladikavkaz. You had to make the journey like this: take a blanket and some kerosene to the station, and walk around the platforms there, peering at the endless sets of heated freight cars. Wiping the sweat off your brow, you would see, beside the open heated carriage on platform seven, a man wearing slippers... He would rinse the teapot and keep repeating the same filthy word, 'Baku'.

'Take me with you,' I asked."

Bulgakov did indeed travel to Tbilisi by a fairly circuitous route – via Baku. He departed on 26th May, and on 2nd June wrote from Tbilisi to Nadya and Konstantin, from the Palais Royal hotel, giving them his final instructions; on 11th June, Tatiana Nikolayevna forwards them this letter from Vladikavkaz to Moscow: "Dear Kostya and Nadya, I am summoning Tasya to come to me from Vladikavkaz, and with her I shall leave for Batum, as soon as she arrives and as soon as we are able. I may end up in the Crimea... I am reworking *The Turbins* into a big drama. That's why it must be thrown in the fireplace. As for *Parisian* [...] if they've already taken it for the production – marvellous, let it be put on as a triumphal play celebrating something or other, as a play it is hopeless. If they haven't accepted it – even better. Into the fire with it, of course. *It must serve its time as soon as possible.*" The letter ended with the following passage: "Don't be surprised by my roaming, there's nothing to be done. There's no other way. Well, that's fate for you! That's fate for you! I kiss you all, Mikhail." In the fourth year of the "extraordinary adventures of the doctor", the man himself was still hoping to change his destiny decisively.

The letter contains a post-script by Tatiana Nikolayevna: "In two hours, I am leaving to join Misha in Tbilisi;" the time is indicated: "3 am".

Many years later, she told me about this: "... the theatre had closed down, the actors had gone their separate ways, the arts sub-department had been disbanded, Slezkin had left Vladikavkaz. And there was nothing to be done. Mikhail left for Tbilisi, to put on a play, and to scout the place out a bit. Then I arrived. They refused to put on the play, and they didn't print it either. Nothing came of it... We sold our wedding rings – first he sold his, then I sold mine. The rings were unusual ones, very nice ones, he had ordered them from Marshak back in the day – that was the best jeweller's. They weren't rounded, but straight, and the inside of my ring was engraved: "Mikhail Bulgakov" and the date, of the wedding I suppose, and on his: "Tatiana Bulgakova…"

A faint trace of his literary meetings in Tbilisi is seen in the dedication left by Alexander Poroshin in the book *Departing ships. Poems* (*Korabli Ukhodyashchiye. Stikhotvoreniya*, Akhalkalaki, 1920): "To Mikhail Afanasievich Bulgakov. A. Poroshin. 11th June 1921. Tbilisi".[6]

"When we arrived in Batum, I waited at the station, whilst he went off to look for a room. He met some Greek woman, she showed him a room. We arrived, and I immediately bought a bouquet of magnolias – it was the first time I had seen any – and put them in the room. We lay down for a nap, and I woke up later with an insane headache. I put the light on, and cried out: the whole bed was covered with bedbugs… We lived there for two months, he tried writing things for the papers, but they didn't accept any of his work. He was very worried, he had no job and no decent room. There were lots of hovercrafts leaving for Constantinople. 'You know, maybe I'll be able to get away,' he said. He got into some negotiations with someone, he wanted me to go to Moscow and wait for news from him.

'If an opportunity arises, I'll follow suit.'

'Well, please do.'

'I'll summon you, like I've always done before.'

But I was sure it was the final farewell. I left for Moscow when the theatre group went on tour – as an actress, travelling with her wardrobe. We couldn't travel by rail, only by sea. We sold a leather bag at the market, my father had bought it when he was in Berlin, and I used that money for the journey. Mikhail sat me on the steamship that was headed for Odessa." In Odessa, whilst she was boarding a train to Kiev, her things were stolen from her. She arrived in Kiev and went to call on Bulgakov's mother – with no money, no possessions and no hope of seeing her husband again.

On 24th August, Nadezhda Afanasievna writes to her husband, from Kiev: "Some news: Tasya (Misha's wife) has arrived from Batum, she's on her way to Moscow… For the time being, he's in Batum…" One of the few accounts of his final weeks in the Caucasus is a description of a meeting between Bulgakov and Mandelstam at that time.

---

[6]   The inscription was preserved in M.S. Lesman's filing cabinet and handed to the author by R.D. Timenchik.

They may have met one another a year earlier, when Mandelstam spent a short period of time in Vladikavkaz: he is mentioned in *Cuff-notes*. The first account of their next meeting – in Batum, apparently – appears in the diary of Y.S. Bulgakova, who wrote, on 13th April 1935: "Misha went out this afternoon to call on Akhmatova, who is staying with Mandelstam [they lived in the same apartment building on Furmanov Street – M.C.]… Mandelstam's wife recalled that she had seen Misha in Batum 14 years ago, and that he had been walking along with a bag over his shoulder. This is from the period when he was poor and used to sell kerosene at the market." A second account of this possible meeting appears in a letter sent by N.Y. Mandelstam to Y.S. Bulgakova on 3rd July 1962 (I published the part quoted in 1980): "Do you know about the first meeting between O.M. and Mikhail? It took place in Batum in 1921. You can imagine how the three of us looked at the time. A young man walked up to us several times in the street and asked O.M. whether it would be worth his while to write a novel and send it to Moscow for a competition. O.M., who by that time knew literary life well, said that submitting something for a competition didn't mean anything, and that he should go to Moscow and get in touch with some publishers. They sometimes had long conversations about this 'practical' subject. O.M. told me that this young man, who was interested in the competition, had an outward appearance that inspired confidence ('There's something in him – I daresay he'll achieve something), and that he had probably accumulated material of a kind that meant it was no longer possible for him not to become a writer. Before long, we met up with Bulgakov in Moscow: by then he had had some short stories and *The White Guard* published. The tremendous success of *The Turbins* did not come as a surprise to us." (Let us observe, in parentheses, that Bulgakov seemed to Mandelstam and his wife to be a young man, whereas he and Mandelstam were in fact born in the same year: the poet, judging by the memoirs of contemporaries and a handful of photographs which survived, had aged quickly, whilst Bulgakov looked younger than he really was at this time). We will return to the intersections in the lives and creative work of Mandelstam and Bulgakov later; for now, let us stress the thing that seems significant: at the decisive moment when Bulgakov was determining his future destiny, the conversations he had with Mandelstam – one of the numerous factors, most of which remain unknown to us, which contributed to his decision to go to Moscow.

In early September, Tatiana Nikolayevna arrived in Moscow; N. Gladyrevsky had already been working here for a long time; he helped her get a job at hostel for medics on Bolshaya Pirogovskaya Street, where she shared a room with a cleaner. What she was supposed to do afterwards was utterly unclear. On 11th September, she wrote to Nadya, in Kiev: "With each passing day, my mood worsens, and I think in horror about what's coming next," i.e. about the approaching winter. On 18th September, she writes to Nadya again: "I am still living at the hostel, at Kolya's place [...]. I sent a telegram to Misha saying that I want to go back; I don't know what he will say. Kostya keeps nagging at me to go away."

Tatiana Nikolayevna didn't know that on 17th September, Bulgakov had already arrived in Kiev, having seen all his plans come to nothing in Batum and taken the decision to leave for Moscow.

A trace of what they went through in late August and early September can be found in *Cuff-notes*, at the end of the first section: "I am lying like a dead man on pebbles weathered by saltwater. I have lost all my strength as a result of hunger. My head aches from the early morning until late at night. And now here I am, at night, by the sea. I can't see it, I can only hear it, the rumble of it. It rushes in, then rushes back out. And the wave that arrives too late makes a whistling sound. And then suddenly, from the dark promontory, three tiers of lights come into view.

The 'Polatsky' is setting off for the Golden Horn."

This steamship, against whose sides Bulgakov's hopes were dashed, was mentioned in one of the Batum newspapers on 29th August: "On 20th August, two steamships arrived in the port of Batum: the 'Palatsky' (sic) and the 'Sheffield', taking with them a large quantity of freight and passengers.

"That's enough! Let the Golden Horn shine. I shall not make it there. There's a limit to my reserves of strength. They have run out. I'm hungry, I'm broken! There's no blood in my brain. I'm weak and fearful. But I will not stay here any longer. If that's how it's to be… then… then…" And then comes the last, shortest chapter, entitled "Home": "… I'll go home. Across the sea. Then in a heated railway carriage. If my money doesn't last – I'll go on foot. But I'll make it home. Life is fatal. I'll go home…! To Moscow! To Moscow!!

… To Moscow!!!

Farewell, Tsikhidziri. Farewell, Makhinjauri. Farewell, Cape Verde!"

CHAPTER TWO

The First Moscow Years

1

Between 20th and 29th September, 1921, Bulgakov travelled from the Bryansk station, with its famous glass dome, to Moscow.

It was a far cry from the entry that he had envisaged in the tragic days of November 1919.

If one considers certain pages of *Cuff-notes* to be a biographically accurate document, he arrived in the city in the dead of night. He was thus unable to go to the Tikhomirov hostel, where his wife was living at the time, and stayed the night, perhaps, with some people he did not know, as described in *Notes*. This is also confirmed by what Tatiana Nikolayevna said: she heard from someone that her husband was looking for her before they saw one another.

By that time, she had been living in Moscow for three weeks. "When I arrived, I realised that I would never see Misha again and that I should find my mother and sister. My mama, when my father had died in Moscow in 1918, had not wanted to go back to Saratov, and had moved to be with my sister in Petrograd. Two of my brothers had died by that time, and the third, who was studying at the military college, had gone out to the market one day and not come home: to this day, nothing is known about what happened to him…" She was unable to find her family: only much later did she manage to discover that her mother and sister were in Veliky Luky. "I don't know what I would have done, if it weren't for Kolya Gladyrevsky (he was courting Lyolya Bulgakova at the time, and wished to marry her). All that Varvara Mikhailovna gave me of her possessions was a pillow… Perhaps

Mikhail didn't find me at home the first time he came round, or perhaps it happened differently, but I remember that someone said to me: 'Bulgakov has arrived', and that he was looking for me. But I was so sure that he had left Batum and gone abroad and that we'd never see one another again, that I didn't believe it."

They stayed at the hostel for a few more days, in Anisya the maid's room. Tatiana Nikolayevna was still able to recall, for some reason, a little saying that Anisya used to repeat: "I live well enough, whilst waiting for something better…"

First and foremost, he had to decide what his profession was going to be, and then start thinking about the matter of housing. It appears that Bulgakov carried with him his certificate from the Vladikavkaz sub-department of the arts and some sort of letter of recommendation. He set off to track down the reciprocal organisation and discovered it on Sretenka, inside the huge building owned by the joint-stock company *Rossiya*, which is still there today, on the left-hand side if you stand facing Sretensky Boulevard. It is one of the very buildings whose threshold Bulgakov crossed in Moscow. "Essentially, I don't know why I went all the way across Moscow and set off for that colossal building. The piece of paper which I had carefully brought with me out of the mountain kingdom, might have had some connection to all of the six-storey buildings, but, more likely, had no connection with any of them" (*Cuff-notes*).

In this building, he found the Literary department (*Lito*) of *Glavpolitprosvet*, the part of *Narkompros* (the People's Commissariat of Education) responsible for political education. By then, names like these, to the sound of which the protagonist of *Cuff-notes* had listened in horror in March 1920 after coming to following a bout of typhoid, under the new government ("We're opening the Sub-department of the arts!" "Now… what might that be?" "What might what be?" "That… the super-partment? Ah, no. *Sub-department*! Sub? My goodness! Why 'sub'?"), were now very familiar to him.

He writes, in *Cuff-notes*: "That six-storey building was positively scary. It was full of corridors running all along its length, like an anthill, so that one could go from one end to another without having to go outside." The author of *Notes* finds two people at the Lito: "A tall, very young man, in a pince-nez. I was struck by his leggings. They were white, and in his hands he held a briefcase with a split in it and a bag. The other fellow, an old man with greyish hair and lively eyes that almost seemed to be laughing, was dressed in an astrakhan hat and a soldier's overcoat. There wasn't a single part of it that didn't have holes in it, and the pockets were hanging down in tatters. The leggings were grey and smooth; he wore bathroom slippers with bows on them.

'Could I see the director?'

The old man replied, affectionately: 'That would be me.' (This pattern of 'recognition', of course, is an undisguised reference to Chichikov's meeting with Plyushkin: 'Ah, but the landlord would be me, my good man!') 'The person he resembled the most was Emile Zola, minus the beard.'"

There is a written statement dated 30th September 1921: "I hereby request to be given the position of secretary of Lito. Mikhail Bulgakov."[7] It also contains a resolution: "The Art. Dept. I hereby request that you make him secretary of Lito, replacing comrade Goldebayev. Com. Goldebayev is to remain as a member of the Edit. Commission. Decl. Lito GPP A. Gotfried." The "old man" dressed in what, in Bulgakov's eyes, was such an unambiguous suit was the self-same A.P. Gotfried, a member of the Russian Communist Party (of Bolsheviks) since December 1918, the organiser of Counsels at stations outside Moscow. He was the deputy of A.S. Serafimovich, the director of Lito Narkompros – he was in charge of Lito at Glavpolitprosvet…

On the very same day, Bulgakov filled in his first questionnaire in Moscow – in a fairly carefully thought-through way, as we shall see: "… *Which parts of Russia do you know well, how many years did you spend there and have you ever been abroad.* – Moscow, Kiev, I haven't been abroad; *Did you take part in the wars of 1914 – 1917*" – struck through, '1917 – 1920' – struck through; *profession* – writer; *social status before 1917 and main occupation* – student." Everything that had to do with his father's family, with his diploma as a "medic, with distinction", with his involvement in both wars as a military doctor, had long been subject to a requirement to keep it hushed up.

In response to the question: "*Do you consider it necessary, at the present time, to engage in some form of shock labour, preferring it to more in-depth forms of work,*" he replied evasively: "In some cases", and in response to the question "*Did you take part in the revolutionary movement prior to 1917,*" he gave a very definite reply: "no".

Under a directive dated 1 October, he was appointed to the executive position of secretary of Lito, replacing Alexander Kondratievich Goldebayev; he may not have been aware that in doing so, by a quirk of fate, he had

....

[7] This document and subsequent ones were uncovered in f. 2306, f. 2313 and others at the Central State Archives of the RSFSR and prepared for printing by R. Yangirov, who kindly provided us with the opportunity to use these documents and the commentaries pertaining to them.

had a slight brush with the life of Chekhov, who had once edited a story by Goldebayev for *Russkaya Mysl'* (*Russian Thought*) ... "Having got into literature almost a quarter of a century later than Chekhov [though he was only three years younger than him – M.C.] and outlived him by twenty years," Goldebayev was thus able to relinquish his position to Buglakov, who was just making his first steps in Moscow's literary life...

The secretary's duties included "overall leadership of all the written work, sending of papers, maintaining of minutes of the Lito's board meetings, business correspondence with people and institutions, compiling of the 'Agenda' [note that this word had only just come into common parlance, and was therefore written in inverted commas – M.C.] for meetings of the board, implementing the directives of the board meetings, reporting to the director or his deputy about ongoing work and general supervision of the secretariat's work..."

The first minutes that Bulgakov drew up, on 2nd October 1921, contained the comment: "Start of meeting: 8 pm. End: 12 midnight."

A short time before he died, the writer Georgy Petrovich Shtorm, who was one of the first people to work with Bulgakov in Moscow, told me some details about this period, in a conversation we had in January 1978. Our conversation began in an unexpected way, when Georgy said, immediately after the introductions: "He kept his face, but I put on a mask."

Shtorm had a clear memory of the building in which they had met and where "the apartments were connected – through them ran that endless passage, which is described by Ilf and Petrov..." The man in charge, he recalled, was "a fellow named Bogatyrev". Shtorm himself had appeared at Lito soon after Bulgakov – and would soon find himself appearing in print in *Cuffnotes*: "At 11 in the morning, a young poet came in, who seemed to be feeling the cold. He said quietly: Shtorn.

'What can I do for you?'

'I would like to get a job at Lito.'"

The narrator of *Notes* then wrote down a resolution on his request.

"Then a curly-haired, rosy-cheeked poet arrived, full of the joys of spring, named Skartsov."

According to G. Shtorm, this man was Ivan Ivanovich Startsev (1896-1967), who later achieved fame as a bibliographer, but who was at that time a young imagist, who had arrived in the capital in 1921, soon became friends with Yesenin and wrote some memoirs about him five years later which contained candid details (censored from later editions) about the poet's everyday life, which many of his contemporaries had witnessed. Startsev became a regular at the café *Stoylo Pegasa* (*Pegasus's Stall*) (which Bulgakov frequented) and achieved fame of sorts in the literary Moscow of the day – one of the authors of memoirs about Yesenin wrote: "Vanya Startsev was a very young and happy guy, but he was notoriously slovenly. The poets therefore wrote a little poem about him and Yesenin: 'Vanya never takes a wash; Seryozha, though, is *chistenky* ('nice and clean'); Therefore, you'll find Seryozha sleeps quite often in Prechistenka.'" Isidora Duncan lived in Prechistenka; Yesenin made her acquaintance that autumn, at Yakulov's studio, which, as the memoirist put it, "gleamed with its glass room on the top of a tall building, somewhere near the 'Aquarium', on the Sadovaya"; it is thought that this occurred on 3rd October 1921 – i.e. at the very same time, it seems, that Bulgakov was moving into this building.

Ivan Startsev, who became a member of Lito, as has now been established, on 4th October, and had been fired by 1st November, was apparently one of the first characters to make a particularly strong impression on Bulgakov among the young literary circle in Moscow. He was one of the prototypes for Bulgakov's two future Ivans: the poets, Ivan Rusakov from *The White Guard*, and Ivan Bezdomny from *The Master and Margarita*.

"We went off to work at a most unreasonable hour," G.P. Shtorm told me, "after 2 o'clock… We had to write slogans for Pomgol [the Society for assisting the hungry in the Volga Region – M.C.]. A short distance away was Milyutinsky (now Markhlevsky) Avenue, opposite the church there were the windows of ROST, and in the basement there was a canteen. We used to have lunch together, we would eat potato soup (which he hated), potato cutlets (which I hated)…" (From *Notes*: "On Friday he ate soup and a potato cutlet in the canteen…").

… "Sad Shtorn," "quietly said" – how fascinating it is that there are merely two short phrases emphasized in the rapidly sketched portrait of one of the characters from *Notes*, and 60 years later they remained the most noticeable outward traits of the man on which he was based…

At a meeting on 10th October, the instructors, Shtorm and Startsev, were already present, and Bulgakov was told to "bring to life matters related to the supplying of all employees with the rations that they are due on the basis of their position." The question of rations was, needless to say, the dominant theme among all the issues facing the secretary of Lito at that time. At the same meeting, the employees were ordered to prepare, on an urgent basis, slogans for the battle against hunger. At the meetings on 11th and 12th October, the slogans were unveiled, with some of them accepted and paid for.

When one reads the slogans composed by Bulgakov and remaining intact in the archives:

You know, oh comrade, of the horror of hunger,
Does the flame in your honest breast burn strong,
And if you are honest, with whatever you're able,
Come help out the hungry, do come along,

one recalls a line from a letter he later wrote ("Ever since I was a child, I haven't been able to stand poetry…"), and a two-line poem from the newspaper *Svobodnyye Vesti* in the novel *The White Guard*: If you're not a wolf and you're honest and true, the Volunteer Army's the place for you."

On 20th October, Bulgakov writes the minutes for a meeting of the literary collegium of the Bureau (!) of artistic satirical articles (also held at Lito), where a report is read out by the Bureau's director "On the receipt of satirical articles and the procedure for reviewing them". At a meeting on 22nd October, for which he again writes up the minutes, satirical articles by writers who were famous back in the 1890s are read out: V. Tan-Bogoraz, whom Bulgakov would meet some years later on the pages of one of the Moscow journals, and V. Muizhel. 25th October is an important milestone in the chronicle of Bulgakov's literary life in Moscow – pretty much the very first one of all. On this day, at another meeting of the aforementioned Bureau, several satirical pieces were accepted and assessed, including one by M. Koltsov (three years earlier, Bulgakov had read it in the newspapers in Kiev, but back then, Koltsov's articles had had a very different tone) and one by M. Bulgakov himself: *The Muse of Vengeance* (*Muza Mesti*)".

Just over a month later, on 1st December 1921, Bulgakov wrote to his sister Nadya, who was still living in Kiev, and described his very first attempts to get into literary life in Moscow: "I wrote a satirical piece, *Yevgeny Onegin*, for *Ekran* (*Screen*, a journal about the theatre). It wasn't accepted. The subject of it was not suitable for a theatrical journal, but for a literary one. I wrote a literary satirical piece, *The Muse of Vengeance*. It was accepted by the Bureau of literary satirical articles under G.P.P., which should be released under Teo G. P. P. They paid 100 for it. They gave it to *Vestnik Iskusstv* (*The Herald of the Arts*)". I can tell you now that the journal won't come out, or that someone will find "Muse" not to be written in the right spirit at the last minute… etc. Chaos." This prediction proved accurate, and *The Muse of Vengeance* was never published.

I published that excerpt from the letter back in 1973,[8] but *The Muse of Vengeance (a small study)* was only discovered 10 years later, among some materials from the "Artistic department of Lito", in a folder containing "Poems and stories by various authors, dedicated to the struggle against hunger and the revolutionary struggle"; it was in the form of a typewritten copy, under a pseudonym that Bulgakov used during that first month in Moscow: M. Bull.[9]

"You are embellished by good deeds, Which for others are very distant…" – choosing the famous lines by Nekrasov for an epigraph, Bulgakov began his article with the words: "Thus did the poet mock, so caustically, the faceless representative of the class which, rather than with good deeds, had instead been embellished merely with a tunic with a red cap-band" (the tunic of the nobility). In the article, the author's various goals were merged together, and his various kinds of feelings were reflected, without being merged. Before us is a man who has already experienced and survived the bitterness of defeat, an incident which did not bind his destiny to the defeated, who has already been through the tempering of class-related literary struggles with the victors in Vladikavkaz. Now, he was supposed to carve out a niche for himself in the capital's literary life: adapt to a new life, without losing his identity, and put forward for publication the upshot of his torturous ruminations in recent years, without, however, ending up among those who merely tried to kowtow to the victors, unthinkingly.

In the piece about Nekrasov, one can constantly see original thoughts making themselves felt, amid the strata of phrases which were already becoming widely accepted; this independent thought is striving to express itself in collectively accepted verbal forms. The irrefutable need for "collectiveness" (in both the direct and figurative senses) in creative work had been taught to him with provincial directness in Vladikavkaz and Batum. Let us remember something he wrote in a letter to Konstantin Bulgakov on 1st February 1921, about his work on the novel: "… the only work in all this time that has been carefully thought through. But I feel sadness again: for this is individual creativity, and what is in fashion these days is something altogether different." The piece on Nekrasov was an attempt to write what was

---

[8] *Voprosy Literatury (Questions of Literature)*, 1973, No. 7, p. 252.

[9] Painstaking searches in the archive were conducted in parallel by G. Faiman and R. Yangirov; they both published the feuilleton (*Voprosy Literatury*, 1984, No. 11, p. 196-199; *Nedelya (The Week)*, 1984, No. 48, p. 14); unfortunately, both publishers felt it possible to agree to a number of cuts.

"in fashion" (with the anniversary of Nekrasov's birth around the corner), whilst also expressing something that had been deeply thought through. He described the poet laughing and feeling indignant about those who had "begot themselves"; "When he had approached his cross, in a creative agony (for he who creates cannot live without a cross), and on it mercilessly crucified, betraying his class, the noble muse, in the name of the residents of Zaplatov, Dyryavin and Neurozhaika."

To illustrate the collision, such powerful tools are chosen, that it seems as though the author is depicting his own current inner state. "Behind the poet, however brilliant he may have been, there always rose up, like a shadow, his class.

And from each line written by the brilliant Pushkin, it – his class – peers out, winking at us slyly. [Might this not be Bulgakov contemplating his own possible literary future? – M.C.]

A great sensibility, an aristocratic sensibility.

Pushkin pitied slaves, for a half-Godlike genius could not help but see wild Aristocracy for what it was.

Yet with the spirit of a genius, and the body of a noble, he only lightly touched, with his magic pen, those who, out of unbridled gentility, were moaning with a continuous moan.

He exclaimed:

Shall I ever see, my friends,
The people unoppressed.

And he went away from the slave, he locked himself away in the unattainable celestial spirits, whither his masterful genius led him." Nine years later, Bulgakov would write that he had made the same choice in a far more acute historical collision, and, without hesitating, would call this trait of his own creativity "a stubborn portrayal of the Russian intelligentsia, as the best stratum in our country" (a letter to the government of the USSR, 28th March 1930).

"All things come to an end. The same is true for the good life, too." For his description of this end, Bulgakov found words, which, precisely because of how deeply felt they were, perhaps, precisely because they were insufficiently rhetorical in nature, impeded the printing of the satirical article.

"…When the time came, the golden Breguet sounded, calling those who heard it from one pleasure to another.

And thus it went on until our times.

One day, though, it sounded with an unprecedented, alarming, funereal ringing, and gave the signal for the start of an unexpected ballet. [This was a reworking of some lines by Pushkin: '… the chiming of the Breguet lets them know that a new ballet has begun…' - M.C.].

From his spectacle, the tunics were lifted up, with red cap-bands on hair that stood on end. And many, very many, were deprived forever of a cap-band, and of their head at the same time." Frightening recent images had risen up before the consciousness of the writer, and he corrected them later with the necessary assessment of the situation: "For frightening was the rushing flow of wrath from the hordes of peasant warriors."

And, as in the article *Prospects for the Future*, he tried at the end of the piece to predict the distant future: "And more years will pass. Instead of the stormy fires, light will pour across the sky. The hordes of peasant warriors, made of steel, unrecognisable, are taking control of the land. And among them, there will be those who will start digging among the memories of the conquerors of the world and track down Nekrasov's finely-wrought verse, and, recalling their humiliated grandfathers, will say:

'He was our bard. Our oppressors, from whom he himself was engendered, he avenged with his stanzas, and expressed his sorrow over us.'

For his muse was the muse of vengeance and sadness."

The "conquerors of the world" – let us emphasize these words. For Bulgakov, "victory" and "defeat" were extremely important opposing concepts. In this period, they also define the structure of his social thinking, and several traits of his artistic worldview. His first satirical piece in Moscow is a word addressed to the victors, a word about them themselves and their poet.

Standing before the door of the Lito… for the first time, the hero of *Cuffnotes* painted in his imagination the following kinds of images of official literary life in the capital: "Here's the thing about the place: in the first room, there is a vast rug, a writing desk and cupboards full of books. There is a grandiose quietness. At the desk sits the secretary: his name is probably one of the ones familiar to me from the journals. Beyond that are some doors. The director's office. There is also a big, deep silence. Cupboards. Who was sitting in the armchair, of course? At Lito? In Moscow? Yes. Maksim Gorky. *The Lower Depths* (*Na Dne*). *Mother* (*Mat'*). Who else do you need… They talk about it… But what if it's Bryusov and Bely..?"

He pushed open the door: and his first collision with the literary world of the capital astonishes him: "I've come to the wrong place! Lito? An empty wooden desk. An open cupboard. A tiny little table with its legs sticking up in the air in the corner. And two men."

It was clear that literature was located somewhere outside the Literary department.

By the time Bulgakov was in the capital, literary Moscow was still continuing to experience and discuss two pieces of news: the death of Blok, which had occurred in Petrograd on 7th August 1921, and the shooting of Gumilyov on 24th August 1921. The news of the poet's death only spread across Moscow in early September; on 3rd September, an entry in Ivan Rozanov's diary read: "I heard from 'Commonwealth' about the shooting of Gumilyov. 'I thought,' he said, 'that Blok would be the Russian Andre Chenier, but as it turned out, this was the real Andre Chenier.'" In the same edition, in one of the famous Moscow circles – *Nikitinskiye subbotniki* (*Nikitinskiye Saturdays*), the first meeting was held after the summer break – it was dedicated to the memory of Blok. On 6th September, a rumour went around Moscow to the effect that "The Gumilyov who was shot was not *the* Gumilyov, but another one; Gumilyov was arrested due to the sale of some sort of manuscripts to Finland." And on 7th September, there was a diary entry written by the Moscow-based writer, reporting that V.M. Monina had said "that Veshnev had lied about Gumilyov: it was printed in the paper: the poet-nobleman," – there were still discussions about a report published on 1st September in the main newspapers. The same diary quotes the poet, Sergei Bobrov's wife, and another piece of "news" which had flown all round Moscow: "On 3rd, Anna Akhmatova died, and Polonsky asked Sergei Bobrov to redo his review of *Plantain* (*Podorozhnik*) as an obituary."

This atmosphere specific to Moscow, of rumours, each more fantastical than the next, surrounded Bulgakov, in the very first month of his life in the capital, and, one can imagine, struck him (although the rumours in Kiev, too, were well known to him). The citizens' passion for discussing tragic occurrences would later be echoed in a grotesque manner in the first edition (later destroyed) of *The Master and Margarita*, in which the poet Stepanida Afanasieva told all the writers she knew some "stunning details" about Bulgakov's death ("It turns out that Berlioz was having an affair with the doctor's wife, Katerina Trivolskaya; it was this unhappy liaison that took him to the tram.").

Memorial evenings took place throughout the whole of the end of 1921, for the two poets. There are some entries in I. Rozanov's diary: 2nd November – "… I'm at the *Literaturnyy Osobnyak* (*Literary Mansion*), where there were 3 talks about Gumilyov (the poet Olga Mochalova read out her memoirs about Gumilyov at various houses in Moscow over the next few months); 28th November: "In the evening, I was at the Union of Writers. There, Y. Eichenwald read out something about Gumilyov and Akhmatova."

Gumilyov's name was of course one that Bulgakov knew – not perhaps because of his poetry first and foremost (he was largely indifferent towards new poetry, although Tatiana Nikolayevna recalled that he had had some new *Apollo* books lying on the table in Kiev – he kept up to date with contemporary literature), but through his *Notes of a Cavalry Officer* (*Zapiski Kavalerista*), which had been printed from early 1915 to early 1916 in *Birzhevyye Vedomosti* (*News of the Stock Exchange*). This serialization had probably been read by the medical student, who knew that he was going to have to take part in this war but had already started to think seriously about literature. The wartime tales that this writer had produced must have caught his attention. The behaviour of the wounded officer, who "demanded that he be put in the ground, kissed and made the sign of the cross over the soldiers who had once served under him, and ordered them with conviction to run for their lives," may have stuck in his memory and been echoed later – when he himself started thinking about Russian officers as characters: Malyshev, Nay-Turs and Turbin. The feeling described by Gumilyov, however, experienced "only whilst out hunting for big game, leopards, buffalo," probably now seemed to him, as a doctor who had seen the horrors of war, somewhat alien and sickening. Also remembered, perhaps, amid all the talk about the circumstances of the poet's tragic death, and serving as food for thought, prompting debate or agreement, was the end of his *Notes*: "There are people who are born only for war, and in Russia there are as many such people as anywhere else. And, whilst they have nothing to do in the 'civil life of the northern state', they are irreplaceable 'in her military fate', and the poet knew that these were one and the same thing" (Gumilyov was quoting lines from Pushkin's *Poltava* here).

Returning to those lines from *Cuff-notes*, about whether Bryusov and Bely might not be having a conversation behind the imaginary door of the Literary department, we note that before long Bulgakov had the opportunity to see and hear the famous poet for himself: in early October, at the first meeting of the newly opened Moscow department of the Free philosophical association (of which N.A. Berdyayev, M.O. Gershenzon were members, along with G.G. Shlet, a Kievan 13 years older than Bulgakov, who had graduated from the same university as him and taught psychology at the girls' school in Fundukleyev Street, very near the First grammar school), Andrei Bely gave a lecture on Dostoevsky, whilst on Sunday, 16th October, at the Union of Writers, there was a get-together to see off Bely, who was leaving for Germany; he recited his new poem, *The First Meeting* (*Pervoye Svidaniye*), in which he sang of the "twisted alleyways of Moscow", alleyways which Bulgakov would soon come to know well.

Generally speaking, Moscow's writers were not to be found at the Literary department, where the new arrival in Moscow, Bulgakov, had hoped to encounter them, but at the cooperative bookshops, where they sold both their own books and other people's. Bryusov and Pasternak sold books at the stall on the Arbat, Y.I. Eichenwald and V.G. Lidin did so at the *Sodruzhestvo Pisateley* stall (*Commonwealth of Writers*) (Bulgakov soon got to know the latter), and N.S. Ashukin sold books at the *Zveno* stall (*Chain*). At the bookstalls operated by the publishing houses *Zadruga* (*Commune*) and *Kolos* (*Spica*), customers could browse through and buy Russian works printed abroad. In December 1921, many people read *Sovremennyye Zapiski* (*Contemporary Notes*), which printed A. Tolstoy's novel *Walking through Torments* (the possibility that the author might return to Russia had not yet been discussed at that point).

On 13 December 1921, I.N. Rozanov noted in his diary that someone had brought *Changing Landmarks* (*Smena Vekh*) along to *Zagruga* (the publishing house and bookshop). This tells us that the anthology was in circulation among the Moscow intelligentsia and that from this precise moment onwards, it could have fallen into Bulgakov's hands. It was soon republished in Tver, in the same binding ("... an anthology of articles, by S.S. Chakhotina and Y.N. Potekhina. July 1921. Prague"), with 10,000 copies printed; it was very widely read. It is fair to suppose that it was at precisely this time that Bulgakov first read that book, with whose title and contents the new authors argued – *Landmarks. An Anthology of Articles about the Russian Intelligentsia* (*Vekhi. Sbornik Statey o Russkoy Intelligentsii*).

In 1909, *Landmarks*, as is well-documented, having barely been released, became a sensation: there was a public renunciation by the culturally authoritative part of the intelligentsia of faith in the revolutionary methods of transforming society, and it was declared that there would be a shift to the religious and metaphysical tenets of a worldview. That same year, Bulgakov the young man had effected a departure from metaphysical tenets, from religion, but at the same time, in spite of the schema for public consciousness and behaviour that prevailed at the time, he was hardly coming closer to radicalism. If not at that time, then later, he might, perhaps, have shared the metaphysical component of the worldviews of the authors of the collection: in the parts where they talked about the "theoretical and practical superiority of spiritual life over the external forms of living, in the sense that the internal life of an individual is the only creative force of human existence…" At the same time, though, he perhaps remained indifferent to philosophizing about socialism and the future revolution. Now, metaphysics had become a reality; it was no longer possible for him not to think about it.

It is entirely plausible that in that first year in Moscow, he also read the second anthology by the same authors, only now, three years after its release, appearing in Moscow.[10]

As he read *Landmarks*, he must have felt an affinity above all with criticism of intellectual "love of the people" in its most extreme form – the kind that was so brutally refuted by the events of the revolutionary years. "The symbol of the faith of the Russian intellectual is the wellbeing of the people, the satisfying of the needs of the 'majority'. Serving this purpose is, for him, mankind's highest and, generally, only duty, and, what's more, *that* – from a crafty man," wrote S. Frank. "For precisely this reason, not only does he simply deny or not accept spiritual values: he is even openly afraid of them and hates them." This dogmatic duty on the part of each person to serve the common good, the 'national' good, directly, in circumstances when someone else is deciding, instead of you, what exactly that common good is, was probably something for which Bulgakov felt antipathy; he preferred to seek out his goals in life by himself. Judging by what we now know about his mood and mind-set during the first few years of the revolution, he may, together with P.B. Struve, have deemed the intelligentsia to be guilty of revolutionizing the masses, theorizing that this had been "not merely a political mistake, not merely a sin in terms of tactics. This had been a moral mistake. At the heart of this was the notion that the 'progress' of society could be not the fruit of the perfecting of man, but a stake which needed to be broken up in the historical game, by calling for a popular uprising."

There were a handful of assertions in articles by N.V. Ustryalov (collected under the title *Patriotic Material [Patriotika]*) which must surely have caught

---

[10] The anthology *From the Depths (Iz Glubiny)* "was completed and printed by the autumn of 1918. After the attempt on Lenin's life and the murder of Uritsky, however, the red terror began – it was decided that releasing the anthology under these circumstances would be impossible, and it was left lying in the printer's office [...]. Three years later, in 1921, apparently in connection with the mood created by the Kronstadt uprising, the typesetters at Kushnarev's printing office put it on sale without permission. Admittedly, it was not distributed any further afield than Moscow, and in Moscow, it would appear, it was passed from hand to hand, and wasn't sold in bookshops. Most of the copies were probably later confiscated. The handful of contributors to the anthology who still resided in Russia were saved, according to S.L. Frank, by the fact that the intended year of publication was still on the book's jacket – 1918. This anthology became an extremely great bibliographical rarity – scarcely more than two copies of it ever left the country." (S.L. Frank. A Miscellany. [Munich], p.54).

his eye, including this one: "The shudders of mass discontent and grumbling, truly, are running rampant throughout the unhappy, long-suffering motherland. [...] Let us agree to suppose that, when they have gained strength, they may turn into a new fit of epilepsy, a new revolution. What if that were to happen? I can say this much: it would be appropriate to refrain, decisively, from manifestations of any kind of joy whatsoever on this score – 'we've broken the Bolsheviks'. An end to Bolshevism of this kind would hide within it a great danger, and frivolous indeed are those who are already making ready to wolf down chestnuts roasted by peasant hands – these optimists will be lucky if they do not fall out of the fire and into the frying-pan [Bulgakov, too, it seems, was acutely aware of this risk – M.C.].

In the current circumstances, this will signify that the red power – as harsh and gloomy as the soul of St Petersburg – will be replaced by limitless anarchy, a new paroxysm of 'Russian rebellion', a new 'Razinovshchina', only this time on a scale never seen before. The granite of the banks of the Neva will melt into sand, will 'thaw' out to the end this time, the Russian state to its final depths..."

Fear of the "crowd" and the preference for the order which had taken root in Bulgakov during the war would perhaps play their role in his entire path through life thereafter.

Each evening, there were readings of new works – at the Writers' Union on Tverskoi Boulevard, at the meetings of the *Zveno* and *Literaturnyy Osobnyak* circles (chaired by Oleg Leonidovich, whose acquaintance Bulgakov soon made), the "Lyrical circle"... In the course of an evening, without going outside the Boulevard Ring, one could go to several such gatherings on foot. *Nikitinskiye subbotniki* prepared their first ever almanac. On 10th October, Lipskerov and Khodasevich read out works at the Writers' Union; Rozanov records this in his diary, writing on 9th November that he had been invited to a reading by P.P. Muratov of his comedy, and to another on 23rd November of the same author's *Magical Tales* (*Magicheskiye Rasskazy*). He observed, on the evening in question: "On the way home, shots were fired at the Nikitsky gates. A man carrying a revolver was dashing after another man." The new aspects of city life acquired during the revolution had not yet been blown out of the streets of Moscow.

On 20th November, Tolstoy's House at Khamovniky opened to the public. There was a general sense that Tolstoy was still present, still a part of life. His granddaughters lived in the same place, not far away – they were a part of literary Moscow: the wife of Sergey Yesenin (from 1925), Sofya Andreyevna – she lived in Prechistenka (and it appears that Bulgakov's uncle,

N.M. Pokrovsky, was her doctor), to which place Bulgakov himself was to move a few years later; and Anna Ilinichna – she married P.S. Popov in 1925 and befriended Bulgakov. In those days, she used to tell her friends happily: "I'm riding the tram, it's overcrowded, with lots of shoving going on, and I hear a woman say: 'Who does that one think she is, a countess?' And I say in response: 'I *am* a countess!' (the author was told this in 1987 by K.A. Martsishevskaya).

... This presence of Tolstoy in Moscow was attested to, in a way, by one detail of the city's appearance at the time: whilst strolling beside the Novodevichy Convent, down the avenues and paths of the square, 'which the Muscovites call Devichye pole, or just Devichka, [...] one might suddenly, to one's surprise, come across a person who had been taking a stroll just like you, an old man with his hair swept back and a long beard, his stone hands placed on his belt modestly and straightforwardly, for he himself was made of stone. Any passer-by would immediately recognise him as Lev Nikolayevich Tolstoy (the sculpture was made by S.D. Merkurev in 1911). The feeling created by this encounter, even for someone who knew about the effect it had, was always special.'

T.A. Kuzminskaya and Tolstoy's daughter, Alexandra Lvovna, lived at Yasnaya Polyana; members of the literary scene in Moscow would often go and visit them, and were met with a warm reception.

From June 1921 onwards, Tolstoy's house was known as a Museum-estate, and A.L. Tolstaya was appointed as its curator. The people of Moscow knew that she had been arrested several times in the past. One night, in the spring of 1920, she had heard "a thunderous noise in the room next door, like a body falling down. The supervisor ran up, there was a lot of fussing about, as they ran in, picked up the heavy object, and took it out. We jumped up and, by eavesdropping, tried to work out what was going on, on the other side of the door. What I didn't know at that stage was that in the next room, Gerasimov had died of a heart attack; he had once lived in our house, working as a tutor for my brothers. He had been a comrade of the minister of people's enlightenment under the Temporary government." This was the very same O.P. Gerasimov (the "marvellous pedagogue", as N.I. Kareyev described him), with whom, one supposes, Bulgakov used to meet up and chat during his time in the village of Nikolskoe and Vyazma.

Tolstoy's daughter was put on trial in the case of the so-called Tactical (National) Centre. The case was brought between 28th July and 3rd August. Before it, she, along with many others, was released, and she was then arrested again after the verdict had been delivered. The main individuals on trial were Professor N.N. Shchepkin, S.N. Trubetskoi, S.P. Melgunov and a handful of women. M.M. Osorgin wrote down this description in his memoirs: "The case was heard in auditorium No. 1 at the Polytechnical Museum, where Zhenya [Y.N. Trubetskoi – M.C.] had once given progressive, liberal lectures. It was a cruel irony: in the very place where once, subconsciously, the basic ideas which had led to the current chaos had once floated about, the trial was taking place of one of the people who wanted to restore order once again, or who slandered and condemned the absurdity of what was happening and were put on trial merely for wanting to restore the order that had been taken away, in criminal fashion, by society itself, by their fathers, or was being discussed in an ill-thought-through manner. The case was entitled 'On the national centre', but the main points in the allegations were: creating an alleged tactical centre for bringing together all the anti-Bolshevik organisations into one body, to fight against the existing order and as a practical resource – entering into an agreement with military organisations and permanent relations with the foreign forces doing battle against the Bolsheviks. Despite the serious nature of the accusation, all of the people on trial were free and not held prisoner, except for eight of them" – that too was a sign of the times – the judges relied on the consciences of the defendants and evinced a certain amount of respect for them. Osorgin gave an account, based on what he was told by his relatives, about how S. Trubetskoy spoke in court "utterly cold-bloodedly, arms slightly akimbo, as if he were at home; when asked about his lineage, he replied: 'Of noble birth and born a nobleman.' Krylenko answered all the questions directly and simply." One of the participants "objected to Krylenko, when he called the accused traitors: "At no time were they traitors, because they love Russia and, at any rate, did not betray her, like you, your honours (and he gestured towards the judges' stand with his hand) and like you, Mr Prosecutor, the former commander-in-chief (with a nod towards Krylenko), surrendering your position to the foe, fraternising with the enemy..."

Bulgakov must have been thinking along the same lines; he no doubt questioned people in Moscow about the details of the trial, the participants in which, as rumour had it, were discussing the possibility of altering the status quo. "Death hung above the heads of the people," A.L. Tolstaya recalled. "Our position was an awful one. There was no sense in denying our guilt, [...] but at the same time, we were scared of falling into the other extreme, starting to repent and ask for forgiveness." She also described how, in the courtroom, "unhurriedly, with a calm and confident gait, a man wearing a pince-nez, with shaggy black hair and a pointy beard, and fleshy, bulging ears, walked in. He started talking, quietly and eloquently, like a well-versed orator" – for some unknown reason, Trotsky had decided to speak in defence of one of the defendants, who, as a young academic, would be needed by the republic; this increased the chances of their lives being saved.

When the prosecutor asked A.L. Tolstaya: "Citizen Tolstaya, what was the nature of your involvement in the matter of the Tactical Centre?" she replied: "… I set a samovar to boil for the participants in the Tactical Centre…" "And served them some tea?" Krylenko concluded. "Yes, I served them tea." "And that was as far as your involvement went?" "Yes, it was." Before long, a satirical poem was doing the rounds in the city, composed by the writer A.M. Khiryakov: "From civil strife, my friends, recoil / Here, where a maiden bold and fearless / Is thrown in a prison, dark and cheerless / For setting a samovar to boil…" A.L. Tolstaya was sentenced to three years' imprisonment at a concentration camp at the Novospassky monastery; from there, she was taken off to do forced labour at the Commissariat of national foodstuffs, where, on the corner of Tverskaya and Gazetny, she used to type on her Underwood typewriter and go home for the night. "One time, forgetting that my status was that of a prisoner, I went to a Tolstoyan evening. The speaker was V.F. Bulgakov. As always, he spoke passionately and bravely about my father, about the violent acts committed by the Bolsheviks, about the death penalties, and suddenly, to everyone's surprise, he mentioned the fact that Tolstoy's daughter was right there in the room, and that she was under arrest and was currently doing forced labour." A few days later, she was taken back to the camp again: the prosecutor for the republic, Krylenko, on learning "that I had been present at the Tolstoyan evening, ordered that I must immediately be sent back to the camp and held there 'under the strictest supervision'"; many people intervened on her behalf, though, and before long she was released. She intervened herself on behalf of others, before A.S. Yenukidze, M.I. Kalinin, Menzhinsky; she describes how "a writer came to see me, I knew him because of his work at the front in the Land Union. He had just arrived from Siberia. He worked at the Kolchak, then went into hiding in Moscow. 'I want to make myself legal,' he said. 'Can you help me?'" After her visit to Menzhinsky, "the writer received papers, remained in Moscow and started getting involved in literature." Might this man perhaps have been one of the members of *Zelyonaya Lampa* (*Green Lamp*)…?

Some years later, Bulgakov became close to P.S. Popov and A.L. Tolstaya. The destinies, after the revolution, of the children of a writer for whom he felt himself to be the literary successor in this period would likely have been among the subjects of the amicable conversations at No. 10, Plotnikov side-street, and the facts cited above from A.L. Tolstaya's biography represent a possible route towards reconstructing these conversations, whose contents we cannot know.

On 19th January 1922, the eve of epiphany, Mayakovsky held a "purge of the poets" (it took place over the course of several evenings – ending on 17th March). At the literary gatherings, one could expect to encounter Khodasevich, Tsvetayeva and Mandelstam, whom Bulgakov had met the previous summer in the Caucasus.

Given that by the autumn of 1922, Bulgakov was already getting started on his bibliographical dictionary (!) of contemporary writers (an idea that he later abandoned), it is fair to assume that he must have been spending his time in the places where writers gathered together.

In the late autumn of 1921 and in the winter, though, he barely had any time left for this: all his time was taken up by the battle for existence, for a hunk of bread and a roof over his head.

During the first few days in Moscow, the situation as regards housing was hopeless. It was resolved when the husband of Bulgakov's sister Nadya, the philologist Andrei Zemsky, who had left for Kiev to visit his wife, agreed to let the Bulgakovs live in his room.

The room was at No. 10, Bolshaya Sadovaya street, a house which was destined to feature a number of times in Bulgakov's works: it was a five-storey commercial apartment building, built by the Muscovite millionaire Pigit in 1906. One of the residents of the building recalled: "Before the reconstruction of the Sadovoye Ring, before it was locked in position between huge stone buildings on either side, the building looked very appealing: it had elegant bay-windows, stucco balconies… There was a smart little palisade separating the building from the pavement. Above the cast iron railings, tight bunches of lilac, of unprecedented size, stuck out into the street… The apartments here were owned mostly by the intelligentsia: doctors, painters, lawyers, artistes" (V. Levshin, Sadovaya, 302a – *Teatr*, 1971, No. 11, p. 112 and others).

The fifth floor of the building belonged to the Higher Women's Courses, whose director was Maria Zemskaya; she had managed to allocate a room for the brother of her husband – Andrei Zemsky – and strengthen his rights to it in the first few years after the revolution, when, under a directive from the district Council, "elements who were alien by dint of their class were kicked out. In the place of the residents who disappeared there came new ones: workers from the nearby printing press. Some of them moved into the deserted apartments, others took up rooms in the apartments of the residents who remained. The ones who remained were intellectuals who had either accepted the revolution straight away or had gradually come to terms with it." Pigit's building was "becoming the first building in Moscow, and perhaps the first building in the country, to be used as a workers' commune. Management of it, and, to an extent, maintenance, were put into the hands of the public." (V. Levshin, Sadovaya, 302a). The upshot of this is described in one of the first stories Bulgakov wrote in Moscow, *No. 13. The Elpit-Workers' Commune House (№ 13. Dom El'pit-rabkommuna)* – in grotesque forms, of course, with a fire that destroys the whole building thrown in for good measure (V. Levshin notes, incidentally, that the fire was imaginary, too, albeit one that Bulgakov imagined "reaching catastrophic proportions"). Tatiana Nikolayevna recalled: "One morning, the roof caved in above the woman living in the room next to us – because of the snow that had accumulated on the roof: no-one had removed it. I heard a thunderous noise and a scream… By some miracle, she was rescued – she had been sitting in the opposite corner. Later, a baker moved into that room, with a pretty wife, Natalya. There were fights there all the time. How she shouted! And Mikhail couldn't bear to hear the sound of someone being beaten up… One time, he called the police – Natalya had been shouting: 'Help!' The police arrived, but the couple locked the door and didn't let them in. As a result, the police very nearly made Mikhail pay a fine for wasting police time… The building really became quite famous… To think of all the people that visited us there! On the side on which the windows overlooked the inner courtyard, it was like this: there was the baker, then us, then Dusya, a prostitute; people would occasionally knock on our door at night, saying: 'Dusya, let me in!' I used to say: 'Next door!' As it happens, she was a modest woman, she never made any noise; she had a husband living somewhere close by, as well… In the next flat there was a police chief and his wife, quite a jolly little lady… Her husband was often out of town, as part of his work; her little son would come running over to see us…" Tatiana Nikolayevna thought that this particular family closely resembled the characters in the story *The Psalm (Psalom)*. "On the other side of the corridor, in the middle, there was a kitchen. On either side of it, there lived a widow, Goryacheva, with her son Mishka – and boy, did she make him work hard – and some workers from the printing press, a husband and wife, they were bitter alcoholics – they used to drink homemade vodka. There was also a responsible labourer living there, with his wife. She was a simple woman, she used to go around washing the floors, and then he was sent to America, she went with him, and she came back wearing a fancy coat, with wavy hair, and she moved as though she couldn't feel her feet, and held her manicured hands out in front of her like this (gesturing). They were given a different apartment and moved away... The embittered drunkards were involved in the house management, they kept coming to see us, threatening to strike Andrei off the list, and they refused to register us, they clearly wanted money from us, but we didn't have any to give. They eventually registered us only when Mikhail wrote to Krupskaya. And she sent a note to our building, that read: 'Please register them'..."

Bulgakov's first typist in Moscow, Irina Raaben, recalled this incident as follows: "He lived with the help of some acquaintances, then decided to write a letter to Nadezhda Konstantinovna Krupskaya. He and I spent a long time composing this letter together. Once we had it printed it, he suddenly said to me: 'You know, I think it would be better if I wrote it out by hand.' And so he did. He sent the letter, and I remember him running in with a contented look on his face when Nadezhda Konstantinovna managed to secure him a big 18 square meter room somewhere in the Sadovaya district." This story seems reliable because of the details in it: much later, in the nineteen-thirties, Bulgakov would advise Anna Akhmatova, who had come to him to type out, on a typewriter, a letter to Stalin asking for the release of her loved ones: "Write it in your own hand – you're a poet, it will be better like that!" And so she did. Yet Bulgakov wrote down the story of his own letter in early 1924 somewhat differently, in the story *A Recollection* (*Vospominaniye*).

In a letter to his mother sent on 17th November 1921, Bulgakov writes about the closing down of institutions and the reduction of staff numbers, about the fact that "my institution too is falling victim to this and, apparently, living out its final days. So there shall soon be no position for me. But that is a mere trifle. I have already taken steps so as not to be late, and to make the transition into private service on time. You are probably already aware that it is only through that, or through trade, that one can exist in Moscow. And my official position, so to speak, was only good to the extent that I was able to receive around half a million in the last month. In the civil service, the pay is tight and comes late, and therefore I can no longer live through a position such as that alone. [...] Yesterday, I received an invitation, on terms that have not yet been made clear, to join an industrial newspaper that is opening. It is a genuinely commercial matter, and they are going to give me a trial. [...] The end of November and December will be difficult, the period of the transition to private firms. But I am counting on the vast number of my acquaintances and now, justifiably so, on the vast amount of energy which I have had to display, whether I wanted to or not. [...] In

Moscow, people count only in terms of hundreds of thousands or millions. Black bread costs 4,600 roubles a pound, white bread – 14,000. And the price keeps going up and up! The shops are full of goods, but what can you buy! The theatres are full, but yesterday, when I was walking past the Bolshoi as I went about my business (I can no longer imagine what it's like *not* to be going somewhere on business!), some ladies outside were selling tickets for 75,000, 100,000 or 150,000 roubles! Moscow has everything: shoes, fabrics, meat, caviar, preserves, delicacies – everything! There are cafes opening up, they're sprouting like mushrooms. There are hundreds of them on all sides! Hundreds!! A wave of speculation is building.

I dream of one thing only: getting through the winter, not getting torn apart by December, which, one must suppose, will be the most difficult month."

In this period, the plot of a play starts to take shape in his mind. In that same letter to his mother, he includes a question for sister Nadya: "I need all the material for a historical drama – everything that concerns Nikolai and Rasputin in the years 1916 and 1917 (the murder and the coup). Newspapers, a description of the palace, memoirs, and above all Purishkevich's *Diary* – I need it desperately!

A description of the costumes, portraits, recollections and so on. She'll know what I mean!

I cherish the thought of creating a grandiose drama in 5 acts, and of doing so by the end of 1922. I have already prepared a few sketches and plans. I am wildly attracted to this idea. The *Diary* cannot be had in Moscow. Ask Nadya to send it to me, at all costs! […] Of course, with the exhausting work that I'm doing, I shall never be able to write anything sensible, but the dream at least, and my work on it, are dear to me. If she should happen to get her hands on a copy of *Diary* temporarily, please copy out from it verbatim everything that has to do with the murder with the gramophone, the plot between Felix and Purishkevich, Purishkevich's reports to Nikolai, and the character of Nikolai Mikhailovich, and send it to me in letters (I think it would be okay? If you put them under the heading 'Material for a play'?). It may be awkward for you to burden her with this, but she will understand. There are no sets of newspapers from 1917 at the Rumyantsev Museum!! I strongly request your help."

This plot is fully compatible with the contents of the satirical article *The Muse of Vengeance*.

As he seeks, nervously and in fits and starts, to put his thoughts about the fateful turning point that he has lived through into some kind of order that is suitable for publication, he is striving to make inroads into literature as quickly as possible.

It is not clear what the contents of his second, unpublished satirical article, *Yevgeny Onegin*, was. It is possible (as R. Yangirov suggests) that it was a review of Tchaikovsky's opera *Yevgeny Onegin*, a new production of which had been put on at the Bolshoi Theatre. The premieres took place on 17th, 19th and 25th November and 1st December. One imagines that the specific atmosphere created by this event would not have escaped Bulgakov's attention. (It may have determined both the content of the article and the fact that it was not printed).

Back in November 1921, a debate had been held at the House of Printing: "Do we really need the Bolshoi Theatre?" Among the speakers was Meyerhold (*Pravda* [*Truth*], 10th November 1921). In December 1921, there was already talk of the Bolshoi Theatre's imminent closure – for both financial and ideological reasons. The Soviet People's Commissariat, at Lunacharsky's suggestion, unanimously decided to preserve the theatre. This decision provoked a furious letter from Lenin to the Politburo, in which he demanded that the Praesidium of the Executive Committee be ordered to cancel the directive of the SNK, and that Lunacharsky be summoned "for five minutes, for a hearing of the last word of the accused and to make it clear both to him, and to all the people's commissars, that the putting to a vote of directives such as the one currently being cancelled by the Central Committee, will, in future, lead to stricter measures being taken by the Central Committee." Thanks to the arguments set out by Lunacharsky, however, the attempt to save the Bolshoi Theatre was successful. Its fate was only decided once and for all in March 1922; on 14th March, the people's commissariat of enlightenment received an entry from the minutes for a meeting of the Politburo: "A report was read out... on the Bolshoi Theatre, and it was decreed: "To approve the petition of the Executive Committee of 6.02.22 (on the detrimental impact of closing the Bolshoi Theatre)." Lunacharsky later quoted something that Lenin had said about the Bolshoi Theatre in his memoirs (it was one of the two arguments he put forward in support of closing the theatre): "When all is said and done, it is a piece of culture that belongs purely to the upper classes, and this is something nobody can dispute." Lunacharsky explained: "What seemed specifically upper class to him was the whole pompous and courtly tone of the opera." For Bulgakov, the "pompous" tone of the opera was an integral part of his native culture, the culture with which he had been imbued since his childhood ("So long, so long, the red-gold Bolshoi Theatre, Moscow, the shop-fronts..." muses the narrator of *A Young Doctor's*

Notebook, when passing through Nikolskoye), with which he had no wish to part under any circumstances.

There is an episode in *Cuff-notes* which tells of the events of late November 1921: "a woman's face, encircled by a shawl, awoke and blurted out:

'Who've we got here then? Sign here.'

I signed my name.

The piece of paper said: 'From such-and-such a date, the Lito is being liquidated... Like a captain on his ship, I am the last to leave. I have ordered our affairs [...] to be wrapped up and handed over. I have extinguished the lamp with my own hand and come out. And immediately, snow fell from the sky. Then rain. Then neither snow nor rain, but something different, clung to my face, coming from all directions.

On the days of cutbacks and weather like this, Moscow is awful. For yes, indeed – this was a cutback."

On 23rd November 1921, the Lito was disbanded. In a directive of the same date, Bulgakov is declared "fired as of the 1/XII of this year, with his salary for two weeks in advance."

On 1 December, Bulgakov received notification that he had been fired from Lito "because of the disbandment". On the same day, he wrote to his sister Nadya: "I am in charge of the chronicle *Torgovo-Promyshlennyy Vestnik* (*The Trade and Industry Courier*), and if I go mad, it will be because of this. Do you have any idea what it means to launch a private newspaper." And, in the same letter: "I am literally tired to death. I have thrown my hands up at it all. I am not thinking about any writing at all. I am happy only when Taska serves me hot tea. She and I are eating immeasurably better now, than at the beginning." On 3rd December, he receives his employment booklet – an extremely important document in those days, without which it was almost impossible to get a job. In it, the former doctor Bulgakov records his new profession: "Writer", and in the column "education", he writes "secondary" (one recalls Maksudov's words in *A Theatrical Novel* about how he studied at the church-congregational school): it is worth reminding ourselves that since the spring of 1920, Bulgakov has been hiding the fact that he is a qualified doctor. His employment booklet states that he was registered on 22nd November, 1921 – the one-week period that elapsed from the moment he received it is fully in accordance with the proud arrogant claim made by the narrator in his satirical article from a few years later, "Moscow in the 1920's": "I, citizens, am a remarkable person, and I say this without any false modesty. I obtained an employment booklet in just three days, after waiting in line just three times, for six hours each time, and not for six months, like most dunderheads." And a later passage: "I have applied for a job five times, and overcome all obstacles…" His second job, then, was at the *Vestnik*, a Moscow-based "weekly newspaper, dedicated to the practical needs of medium-sized, small and cottage industries," a portent of the new economic policy which was around the corner. Its editorial offices were located in Tretyakovsky drive (building 11, room 9). The whole of December 1921 was filled with the tension of work that was a long way from literary pursuits: reporting work and journalism. The first page of the *Vestnik*, and parts of the second, third and fourth pages, were filled with advertisements, which provided the main source of funding for the newspaper. There was a permanent rubric, *The Trade and Industry Chronicle*, which Bulgakov was in charge of. It contained some extremely short notices: "The activity of the central trade exchange", "A review of the industry tax" and so on. This information, like the ads, had to be obtained from institutions and ministries all over Moscow. A description of these two months in Bulgakov's life – from late November 1921 to the middle of January 1922 – was written by him in a satirical sketch in 1924, "A tract on housing", the opening lines of which have gone into common parlance: "It was not from a marvellous distance that I studied the Moscow of 1921 to 1924. Oh no, I lived in it, I trod every corner of it, up and down. I walked up to almost every sixth floor in the city that housed an institution, such that I know every single one of them like the back of my hand. One might be travelling in a carriage along Zlatoustinsky side-street, for example, to visit Yury Nikolayevich, and recall:

"Goodness, what a huge house! Wait a moment, I've been inside it! I have, honest to God! And I can even recall when it happened. In January 1922. And what the hell was it that brought me there? If you please […] It was when I joined a private trade and industry paper and asked for an advance. The editor didn't give me an advance, but said: 'Go to Zlatoustinsky side-street, on the 6th floor, room no… - could it be 242? Or perhaps 180…? I forget. It's not important… In a word: 'Go and get a declaration at the Glavkhim'… or was it the Centrokhim? I forget. It's not important, anyhow… 'Go and get a declaration, and you'll get 25%.' If someone were to say to me: 'Go there, get a declaration,' I would reply: 'I shan't go.' I don't want to go around getting declarations. I don't like going to get declarations. It's not my specialty. But then… Oh, it was different then. I pulled my hat down over my head stubbornly, picked up that stupid declaration book and rushed out of the house like a lunatic. It was unbelievably cold, so cold that it might never be that cold again. I climbed up to the 6th floor and found that room, No. 200, and inside I found a red-haired man with a bald patch, who, after hearing me out, chose not to give me a declaration. [...] Were there any places that I didn't go to? I went to Myasnitskaya hundreds of times, to Varvarka – at the Business court, to the Old square – at the Central Union, I drove to Sokolniki; I dashed off to Devichye pole too. I was driven all over the vast, strange capital by a single desire: the desire to find a living for myself. And I found one – albeit a miserly, unreliable, shaky one. I found it in the most fantastical duties, as fast-flowing as a fever, obtaining it using strange, fragile methods, many of which seem absurd to me now, when life is easier. I wrote the trade and industry chronicle for the newspaper, and at night I wrote funny satirical pieces, which I personally found about as amusing as toothache..."

"I am overwhelmed with work at the *Vestnik*, he writes on 15th December to his sister Nadya in Kiev. "Taska and I are now eating rather well. If the *Vestnik* grows larger, I hope that we will continue to make a living from it. I get 3 million a month. It is horrid that there is no food allowance." These hours of relative wealth were already numbered, though.

They saw in the new year, 1922, with relatives – at the house of Boris Zemsky, the elder brother of Andrei Zemsky. In those days, he worked at a Science and technical committee attached to the N.E. Zhukovsky Military and aerial academy, which brought his household a certain degree of wealth. He lived in Vorotnikovsky side-street. "There was a kindergarten there, 'The Golden Fish,'" Tatiana Nikolayevna recalls. "The director of it was Maria Danilovna, Boris Zemsky's wife. It was a house designed like a mansion, with the kindergarten downstairs, and the Zemskys lived upstairs – Boris and his wife and children. His wife was short and plump, with dark hair... I remember, when we returned home, there was a flood in our room: the thaw had begun at night, and since no-one had cleared the snow off the roof, water had leaked through the ceiling. We spent the whole night carrying buckets of water around."

Bulgakov mentions this in a letter to his sister Nadya on 13th January 1922, in which he writes to her: "I have been dealt a blow, whose significance you will appreciate straight away [...] The editor told me that the *Vestnik* is ablaze under the burden of external circumstances. The editor said to me that there was still a chance, but I know for sure that he will survive the 7th edition. Finita! [...] Things will become clear in two days' time. [...] You will understand what I must be feeling today, as I fly off down the pipe together with the *Vestnik*.

In a word, I am crushed.

If I weren't, I would tell you all about how rain has been coming into my room, on the night before Christmas eve and on Christmas eve."

A few days later, the *Vestnik* was closed down – Bulgakov's second job in Moscow had gone up in flames, just as Lito had done before it.

At this exact moment, Bulgakov is weighing up the possibilities of making an income from literature – and he imagines himself in the role of an author of a satirical newspaper supplement about Moscow. He asks his sister Nadya – in the aforementioned letter dated 13th January – to put him forward for this role "at any of the newspapers in Kiev that are to your liking (preferably a big daily one)."

As an initial sample of his work, he proposes a piece that he wrote on the same night as the letter, entitled *The Renaissance in Trade (Moscow at the Start of the Year 1922)* [*Torgovyy Renessans (Moskva v Nachale 1922-go Goda)*]; he signs it with his pseudonym 'M. Bull', which would soon be used in print in reporters' comments. This is the first of the writer's handwritten creative texts that we know about; it is at once a literary and a biographical document: it enables us to see Moscow as it was in early 1922 and slightly before then through the eyes of Bulgakov himself. For that reason, we shall quote it here in full.

"To anyone who saw Moscow as it was just 6 months or so ago, the city is now unrecognisable, such is the radical change that has been brought about by the new economic policy (or NEP, an abbreviation which has already been given a right of citizenship among Muscovites).

The change was gradual at first... it happened bit by bit... Here and there, wooden hoardings started to be taken down, and from beneath them there emerged into the light of day, after a long interval, dim and dusty shopfronts. Lightbulbs were lit deep inside abandoned premises, and life began to stir by their light: crates and boxes of goods began to be hammered together, fastened with nails, repaired and unpacked. Newly-washed shop-windows began to gleam. One saw the flash of powerful, round lamps above the shop-signs, or narrow, blinding tubes of light around the window-frames.

It is hard to understand from what mysterious depths of destitution Moscow managed to extract its goods, but it did so, and with a generous hand, it dropped them behind reflective shop-windows and set them out on shelves.

Kuznetsky, Petrovka, Neglinny, Lybyanka, Myasnitskaya, Tverskaya and the Arbat all began to be filled with bustle. Shops began springing up like mushrooms, fortified by the life-giving rain of the NEP... State stores, cooperatives, artisanal stores, private ones... After the cake-shops, which were the first to crop up all over the place with their blazing lights, there came the fancy goods shops, the food stores, the stationary shops, the milliners', the hairdressers', the bookshops, the technical stores and, of course, the vast department stores.

On the bare walls, a colourful wave of signs began to appear, new ones every day, their dimensions growing bigger and bigger by the day. In some places they were done in improvised fashion, sometimes merely painted onto canvas, but beside them permanent ones appeared, featuring the new spellings, with bright letters, an arshin in length. And they were nailed on with huge, solid spike-nails. They are here to stay, in other words.

And the old, twisted and peeled iron sheets seem to close ranks and come to life among them, and the puny-looking hard signs look strangely out of place.

Everything is going further, getting bigger, growing wider...

Moscow is unrecognisable. Moscow is trading.

On Kuznetsky, the throng of pedestrians boils on the icy pavements all day long, the coachmen drive along in a chain, and the cars fly back and forth, their alarms wheezing.

Behind the windows, there is a riotous range of bright colours: toy figurines made by teams of handicraftsmen smile at passersby with their painted faces. Above them, from what used to be Shanks's shop, collections of ladies' hats, tights, boots and furs gaze out. This is one of the department stores of the Moscow Consumer Society. It has opened eight such stores all over Moscow. On Petrovka, in the twilight hours, a constant electric light pours out from the windows onto the pavements, blackened by the passing masses. The windows of the confectioners' shops gleam. Hundreds of vials containing the best foreign perfumes, made of cut-glass, milky-white, yellow, with manifold wonderful shapes and designs. Waves of fabrics, piles of ties, lace, rows of powder-boxes. And over there – the painted faces of the manequins shimmer languourously and lifelessly, priceless stoles, by today's standards, draped over their shoulders. The passages have come to life.

The vast edifice of Muir and Merrilees still stands there silently and emptily with its huge windows, but already, on the ground floor, the gigantic painted caricatures of Nulans and Po have vanished, and they are brushing away the rubbish from the doors. And Moscow already knows that in February, a Mostorg department store will be opened here, with 25 departments, and the former directors of Muir will be on its board.

There are cake-shops on every corner. And they are full of people all day long, right up until closing time. The shelves are brimful of white bread, cakes, French loaves. Pies are laid out on the shelves in countless rows. All of this at monstrous prices. It is a long time since the prices in Moscow put anyone off, however, and fantastical, astronomical figures, in the millions (this word doesn't even exist in Moscow, it has been displaced once and for all by the word 'lemon') are let through every day by the glittering, tirelessly clanking cash registers. At the former Filippov bakery on Tverskaya, there are piles up to the ceiling of white bread, cakes, pies, biscuits and arnicas, and the queues are endless.

The displays in the food shops are strikingly luxurious. They contain boxes of conserves piled high, black caviar, salmon, balyk, smoked fish, oranges. And there are always passers-by standing at the windows and staring at the fine produce, as though bewitched, unable to tear themselves away...

All 34 of the M.P.O.'s food stores, and the private ones, have already made it known, through advertisements, that they have Russian and foreign wine available, and the people of Moscow have been snapping up every last bottle.

In late November, *Izvestiya* (*Reports*) contained advertisements for the first time, and now they adorn the pages of all the newspapers and trade newsletters with their motley colours. The planes of the aviation group *Aerial fleet*, meanwhile, have already made their first attempt to drop flyers over Moscow, and they are now accepting advertisements categorized as 'from an aeroplane'. Each line of text in these ads costs 15 roubles, in the new currency.

The amount of traffic on the streets is growing with each passing day. There are trams in circulation on routes 3, 6, 7, 16, 17, A and B, and coachmen are picking up passengers each way you look, and haggling with them craftily:

'Be my guest, sir! A round *rublik*, not a kopeck more (100,000)! Off we go!'

At the Metropole, at the Voskresensky gates, at the Strastny monastery, the air rings at all the crossroads with the hubbub of countless people selling newspapers, thin cigarettes, fudge and bread rolls.

At the Ilyinsk gates, there are lines of women two rows deep hawking pies. On Ilinka Street, the sign 'Alpine council' has disappeared from the grey buildings with the columns, and been replaced by a different one that says, in huge letters, 'Stock Exchange', and inside it, meetings about exchange-listed stocks are being held, and transactions worth billions are being arranged with the help of stockbrokers.

Until late at night, the folk of Moscow are on the go, buying, selling, milling about in shops. Late in the evening, however, when the hands on the illuminated clocks on the streets are crawling inexorably towards midnight, and when all the shops have closed their doors, Tverskaya, that irrepressible street, still lives on.

And the air is rent by the cries of young boys selling cigarettes: 'Ira! Java! Mursal!' The windows of a plethora of cafés are lit up, and the shriek of violins emanates faintly from inside them. Until late at night, the people living in Kitai-Gorod, a place filled with the colours of trade in a way never seen before, bustles about, buying and selling, eating and drinking at the tables in the cafés."

In January, family ties were at last restored firstly with one of Bulgakov's younger brothers, who had departed with the Volunteer Army; on 16th January 1922, Nikolai, who by then was studying at Zagreb university, wrote to his mother: "My dear one, my dear mama, and all my brothers and sisters, so close to my heart! Yesterday, I experienced some unforgettable, treasured moments: unexpectedly, unforeseeably, your letter arrived, when I had just got home from the University. The tears rolled down my cheeks and my hands were shaking, when I opened this priceless letter. I sobbed, in the full sense of the word, such was the longing and anxiety that had built up in me: for so long I had not heard so much as half a word!

 Merciful God, can it really be true! Mother dearest, why do you not write me a single word about Verochka, where is she, what is she doing, is she well, does she ever write to you. How anxious I was about Misha and Tasya and my golden Varyushechka, after all it was only indirectly, from other people, that I learned that she was going to have a baby. Pass on Lenya's regards to her, and may she give birth to a lovely daughter – I so love Varyusha, how good and kind she is. How do Nadyusha and Andrei look, do they ever remember me? Give them big kisses from me. What you said in your letter about Lyolochka struck me deeply and made me anxious: she is a kind, golden girl. May she recall how she and I became friends in those final days and parted with touching ardour. May God grant her good health, happiness and prosperity – I have thought about her so many times, prayed about her, and told my acquaintances all about her. Olya Orlova, whom I see sometimes and who always enjoys talking about Kiev, sends her a big kiss. She is now a ballet dancer."

Nikolai then writes some deeply felt words for the attention of Ivan Pavlovich Voskresensky: "I associate with your person the very best, most vivid memories, as a person who brought our family solace and good ideas from a kind Russian heart, and examples of a flawless upbringing. I find it hard to express in words my deep gratitude for everything you did for mama in our difficult life, for our family and for me, at the dawn of my academic life. May God help you, dear, wonderful Ivan Pavlovich!" He reminded his cousin Kostya "about our life together when we were studying and working, and our meetings with Varyusha and Lena. Tell him that his relatives keep asking about him, they are sorry he doesn't write" (Konstantin soon left Kiev and travelled abroad). "Vanyusha doesn't reply to any of my letters, and I'm starting to get worried. [...] Now I'll tell you something about myself: I'm in good health, thank God, and I have probably changed horribly over the last few years: after all, I'm 24 now. I'm sending you one of my last cards..." He told them about his life as a poor student, filled with tense work, and mentioned that ever since he had seen his mother "that last time before leaving the country, I have not suffered any illnesses whatsoever..." (this indirectly confirms that he had been ill when his mother last saw him). He asked them to send a certificate from Kiev University stating his grades and "the cards of all my relatives, if possible".

This letter must have reached Kiev and then gradually made its way to Moscow.

It so happens that the second half of January and the first half of February 1922 – a difficult time in Bulgakov's life – are documented in a uniquely thorough manner.

It would be more accurate to say that at one stage, all of the first few years of his life in Moscow were thoroughly documented, but only a few tiny fragments of that extensive document have survived: between 1921 and 1925 (and probably in early 1926 too), Bulgakov kept a diary. This diary was confiscated from him during a search of his home on 7th May 1926, and was returned to him after a series of insistent requests in 1929. Y.S. Bulgakova told the author that when he received the diary, he destroyed it by his own hand, not wishing to keep such a deeply intimate document once it had been read by strangers. Yet before doing so, he cut out four excerpts from the text with a pair of scissors – as evidence of the diary's existence (gestures like this were typical of him, as we shall see. There is another theory too, though: that the diary was returned, and that those few pages are merely the part of it that happened to be left behind in the house, intact, after it was searched). Since the text of the diary was written on both sides of the page, some of the lines in these excerpts had the lower parts of the letters cut off, whilst others were missing the first few letters; the dates on the reverse-sides of the pages were also lost. The missing parts of the text have since been filled in with a sufficient level of accuracy. Below, we shall cite almost all of the excerpts from the diary entrieswhich remained intact (the lines, words and letters which were filled in later are in square brackets, and dotted lines are used in place of the lines that are missing altogether).

"A strong cold snap. The heating is working, but only weakly. And it's cold at night.

25th January (Tatiana's Day). I abandoned my diary. And that's a pity. [in] that time, many interesting things have happened. [I] am still without a position. My wife [and] I are eating badly. Because of this, I don't even [want] to write.

[Bl]ack bread is now 20 k. a pound, white [...] k.

[To] uncle Kolya [N.M. Pokrovsky – M.C.] by force, in his absence from Moscow, in spite of all decrees. ....

A couple have moved in..

[Here, the reader may detect the basis for the future story *The Heart of a Dog* (*Sobachie Serdtse*) – M.C.]

26th (?) January.

Joined a travelling troupe of actors: I am going to perform with them in the outlying districts. The pay is 125 per performance. A murderously low amount. Of course, due to these plays, I shan't have any time to write. A vicious cycle.

*

My wife and I are half-starved, such is our diet.

*

I hadn't noticed that Korolenko's death was greeted by an abundance of pieces in the newspapers. What tenderness.

*

I drank vodka today at N.G.'s place."

N.G., it appears, is Nikolai Leonidovich Gladyrevsky (according to T.N., he had a fondness for vodka, whereas Bulgakov preferred wine; she also said that Gladyrevsky rarely came to see them – there was not much love lost between he and T.N. – usually, Bulgakov would be the one who called on him. A few days later, he was unwittingly to play a fatal role in Bulgakov's life and the lives of his loved ones. The very next day, perhaps, N. Gladyrevsky left for Kiev. He told me what happened next in person in 1969. "In January 1922, I arrived in Kiev. I left my things with some people I knew and went round to the Bulgakovs'. I stayed the night there – the temperature was 40 degrees the next day. I came down with bilious typhoid. In the time that I was lying in bed at their place, their mother fell ill and died. She had gone out to the bathhouse (even though she had been advised against doing so) and fallen ill. And everyone said that I had infected her. But I couldn't have infected her – she had the dual form of typhoid, a completely different one from the one I had…"

Varvara Mikhailovna's death was not long in coming: she passed away on 1st February 1922. On 2nd February, Bulgakov received a telegram from Kiev: "Mama passed away. Nadya."

"On the day the telegram arrived," T.N. recalled, "he was supposed to be performing in a play with that travelling theatre company. He set off with a heavy heart – and immediately came back again. The show hadn't taken place – the theatre company had been disbanded."

On 9th February, Bulgakov writes in his diary: "This is the blackest period of my life. My wife and I are going hungry. We had to borrow a little flour, Lenten butter and potatoes from a chap I know. I've run all over town looking for work; there's none to be had.

My felt boots have fallen to bits."

This period was one that Tatiana Nikolayevna could well remember, too. When the following asked: "So you and Bulgakov survived Kiev in 1918-1919, then you were in all manner of circumstances in the Caucasus, then you found yourselves living in Moscow: which period do you remember as being the hardest of all?" she said: "That first year in Moscow was worse than any other place. It was not unknown, then, for us to go 3 whole days without eating anything, anything at all. We didn't have bread, we didn't have potatoes. And I no longer had anything left to sell. I just lay in bed and that was it. I had acute anemia. I even consulted a gynaecologist… But he said it was temporary… Then Mikhail managed to procure a sack of potatoes from the man…"

The excerpts which remained intact tell us much about the nature of the diary, about the author's efforts to record details of his day-to-day life, substantive details of it (right down to the prices of goods). Of interest is the fact that in the entry about the academic rations (one can understand why Bulgakov, who was starving and had neither rations nor handouts, was so acutely interested in this), Meyerhold's name appears: the very name that Bulgakov heard the first time he crossed the threshold of Lito: "I caught a glimpse of a room, full of women. Someone was hammering away on a typewriter. Then it fell silent. In a bass voice, someone said: 'Meyerhold.'" And he returns once again to this room, and this time "the bass had turned into a soprano: Meyerhold. October at the theatre." And Bulgakov repeats this a third time in *Cuff-notes*: "Meyerhold is phenomenally popular in this building, but he himself is not here." Shortly after Bulgakov arrived in Moscow, the theatre that was directed by Meyerhold was renamed in his honour – this must have struck Bulgakov, who was accustomed to the idea that the names of the living were only assigned to various institutions if the people in question were members of the ruling family.

15th February. "The weather has turned nasty. There is a cold snap today. I am walking around on what is left of my soles. My felt boots are no longer fit to wear. We are half-starved. We owe money left, right and centre. My 'job' at the military-editing council boils down to running errands, but I am thankful even for that." After a month of unemployment, an opportunity came up to get a job at the Scientific and technical committee – with Boris Mikhailovich Zemsky, the person on whom Bulgakov relied the most for support during the difficult winter months of 1921-1922. The same diary entry, after some lines which have been cut out, contains a speech about the state of the republic, which "as regards fire safety, is in a catastrophic position [this entry was perhaps made in connection with the fire referred to by V. Levshin at the Pi-git house – a fire that would be reflected several months later in the story about the Elpit Workers' Commune, about the complete lack of fire safety measures at that building, which resulted in disaster – M.C.]. And in what respect, indeed, is it not in a catastrophic position? If there is not going to be a conference in Genoa, one wonders what we are going to do. [...]"

The last entry that remains intact, or rather, the first few lines of it, are dated 16th February: "Don't believe in superstitions! I bumped into a funeral procession and... 1) there is *hope of sorts* at the newspaper *Rabochiy (The Worker)*..." As for what came next, as point two in the list of successes that day, there is no way of knowing.

Rabochiy, the Central Committee's daily newspaper, was first published on 1st March 1922, and Bulgakov apparently started working for it at the same time: his first piece, "When the machines are sleeping", appeared in issue No. 1 beneath the pseudonym "Mikhail Bull" (it was about the 2nd calico factory in Moscow).

A month later, N.L. Gladyrevsky, having arrived from Kiev, brings Bulgakov a letter from his sisters Nadya and Varya with a message about the fact that their younger brother, Vanya, is alive and well. (Prior to this, Nikolai Bulgakov, in the first letter he wrote to his relatives on 16th January 1922, had reported: "Vanyusha isn't replying to any of my letters, I'm already starting to get worried. [...] He hasn't even told me his address yet."). Bulgakov's reply to his letter to Nadya on 24th March 1922, provides a detailed and expressive idea about his life over the past month: "Dear Nadya, Kolya gave me the letter from you and Varya. I can't tell you how overjoyed I was to hear about

Vanya's good health." He then described his life, saying that he often spent time with Bob – Boris Mikhailovich. "He lives well. How cosy it seems at his place, particularly after that nightmare apartment at No. 50! The stove works properly. Vovka does headstands. Katya [B.M.'s younger sister – M.C.] boils the water, and he and I sit around and chat. He is a comrade of rare distinction and a charming person to talk to." It is very probable that one of the characters in *A Theatrical Novel* was based on the characteristics of B.M. Zemsky – the "friend" and "engineer" from whom Maksudov steals a revolver in order to shoot himself, and then gradually puts back in its place; according to Tatiana Nikolayevna, Zemsky always wore a military uniform, and he was probably the only one of Bulgakov's friends who carried a weapon around with him.

In the same letter, Bulgakov reported that he was now working in the Scientific and technical committee, as head of the publishing section (he tells his sister Varya that he "only recently found a job" in a letter sent on the same day). The chronicle of the events from the time that had elapsed, just as in the diary, also incorporated his relatives:

> Uncle Kolya, in spite of his protective certificates, was fired. Uncle Misha [Mikhail, the brother of Nikolai and Bulgakov's mother; he was a therapist who, according to T.N., had a permanent room in her brother's house, and used to visit quite often and stay for a long time; he suffered from some sort of mental disorder – M.C.] was put in the guest room, and a couple moved into his room, who have screwed in one 100 Watt lightbulb and one 50 Watt lightbulb and keep them turned on night and day; in terms of his diet, Uncle Kolya is living well.

*

> Besides N.T.K., I'm working as a staffer at a big new off[icial] newspaper. For the two jobs, I earn 197 rub. (under the Narkomfin's exchange rate for March that's around 40 million) a month, i.e. ½ of what I need for my life (if my existence over the last two years can possibly described as a life) with Tasya. She doesn't work anywhere, of course, and she does the cooking on a little iron stove. (In addition to my salary, I also have a plebeian ration. But I fear it is going to get more and more of a limp as time goes by.)
> ... Fortunately for me, the nightmare on the 5th floor, where I spent half a year fighting for life, is cheap (around 700,000 for the whole of March)... They stopped heating the place a week ago.

I am literally run down with work. I have no time to write and I am studying French, as I should be. I am collecting quite a library (the booksellers – the impudent, impolite bastards – sell books at higher prices than the shops).

Later that day, he wrote to his sister Vera: "I have a great many acquaintances in Moscow (from the worlds of journalism and art), but I rarely see anyone, for I am ablaze with work and I rush around Moscow solely in connection with newspaper matters." Indeed, between 1st March and 30th March, 8 pieces written by him appeared in the newspaper *Rabochiy*, beneath the pseudonym "Mikhail Bull", "M. Bull" or "Bull", or beneath his initials; each piece was about a visit to some enterprise or institution, as is clear from the headlines: "Injector systems. German ex-pats have them at an engineering factory," "We're creating something from nothing! (The 3rd state automobile repair plant)".

He continues to spend time with B. Zemsky in the evenings. On 9th April, Zemsky writes to his brother Andrei and his wife Nadya: "We have grown very fond of the Bulgakovs and see them almost every day. Misha fascinates me because of his energy, capacity for work, entrepreneurship and good spirits. He and I are great friends and we are inseparable in conversation [...] One can confidently state that he is catching his fate – it won't get away from him." Many years later, the author of the first biography of Bulgakov would recall these words.

On 18th April 1922, Bulgakov once again says that he has none of the free time that he needs for his work: "Sorry I didn't have time to send greetings on the Holy festival. I am leading such an administrative lifestyle that I literally don't have a minute. I took only two days off, for the holidays. And now my nightmare is starting again. [...] They stopped heating the place in March. All of the bookbindings are covered with mould. They will probably try to throw me out in a couple of days, but they'll meet with resistance on my side, on legitimate grounds (my job: I've been working as a senior engineer at Bob since March). I am making an effort to find a room. But it is all hopeless. They charge insane amounts to show you the room. [...] There are massive cutbacks in staff numbers everywhere. The rations for civilians have been done away with... Uncle Kolya is getting along wonderfully. He's been fired." In the interim period, he had added a third job to the two others: "A temporary role as a compere at a little theatre, [...] for April I should get only 130-140 million." A short time earlier, to judge by his letters, that amount would have sufficed for food at least, but prices are going up, and the rent for the room in April is already 1 ½ million. The room is damp.

The "Plebeian ration" at the Scientific and technical committee was a rather strange one, like all the rations at that time, but he was soon deprived of that too, as Tatiana Nikolayevna told me: "Bulgakov didn't work there for long, just over a month. He only got one ration – and it was reduced. I carried that ration – some cottonseed oil – in a bag, holding it by the handles with my arms stretched out, across the whole of Petrovsky Park to the Sadovaya – there were no trams in those days. But it wasn't winter – otherwise I wouldn't have taken it. They also gave him some flour – perhaps Mikhail brought it himself, I can't remember. Well, I brought the oil, fried up some pies, Stonov and Slezkin came over and ate the lot…"

There will be more about these literary acquaintances of Bulgakov's later. For now, let us merely say that in April 1922, Slezkin, whom Bulgakov had last seen in Vladikavkaz, was already in Moscow. He was living in Trekhprudny side-street, not far at all from No. 10, Bolshaya Sadovaya, and they met up frequently – both at the Bulgakovs' home and also, probably, at the homes of Bulgakov's new friends.

First, though, let us linger over another of his very first friends – one that wasn't a literary friend at all. Tatiana Nikolayevna said of him:

"Back in Batum, Mikhail had given me an address in Moscow – Vorotnikovsky side-street. Some relatives of Nadya supposedly lived there. I went there, to the kindergarten there, on the second day after I arrived in Moscow. But I didn't find any of the Zemskys there: Vera Kreshkova was the only person there. We got talking. She invited me round to her place; she and her husband, Ivan Pavlovich, lived in Malaya Bronnaya, house number 30, on the 5th floor." So, when Bulgakov arrived – in Moscow, besides Boris Zemsky's house, there was already another family, whom we could go and see in the evening, to have tea with them in true Muscovite style.

"Vera was the daughter of a priest, Ivan Pavlovich – the son of a civil servant from Vladikavkaz. He taught mathematics at the Military academy in Petrovsky park. She was quite a… well-built woman, and Bulgakov would go weak at the knees when he saw her – he loved plump women. And he kept saying to me: 'Invite Vera Fyodorovna round to see us, but don't invite Ivan.' And Ivan Pavlovich didn't like it when she said: 'I'm going round to see Tatiana Nikolayevna' – he was jealous.

They used to hold spiritual séances at their house, which Bulgakov liked to poke fun at. Tatiana Nikolayevna recalls that he once said to her: 'You know what, let's go and have a spiritual séance today at the Kreshkovs' place!'

They divided up the roles they would play: Bulgakov would kick her with his foot, and that would be the sign for her to knock on the little table. Apparently they had quite a few such mystical tricks up their sleeves. A full-blown row broke out with Ivan Pavlovich, however, following the publication of the story *The Séance* (*Spiriticheskiy Seans*) (*Rupor* [*Mouthpiece*], 1922, No. 4). Ivan could tell that the characters were based on himself, his wife and their maid... A remark made by the maid served as the key evidence. The story began like this:

"The idiot girl Ksyushka announced:

'There's some bloke out there to see you.'

Madame Luzina flared up:

'For one thing, how many times have I told you not to address me in the informal way! Who

is this bloke you're talking about?'

And she sailed off into the hallway.

In the hallway, Ksavery Antonovich Lisinevich was hanging a coat on a deer's horn and smiling acerbically. He had heard Ksyushkin announcing his arrival.

Madame Luzina flared up again."

And, after kissing her hand, Lisinevich was just "getting ready to cast a long and clingy glance in her direction, when her husband, Pavel Petrovich, crawled out from around the door. And extinguished the look.

'Y-e-e-s,' Pavel Petrovich began in his droning voice, 'some bloke'... hehe! Uncouth, they are! Uncouth, plain and simple. Here's what I think: about freedom... Communism. For pity's sake! How can one dream about communism, when there are little Ksyushas like that all over the place! Some bloke... Hee-hee! Do forgive me of course, for God's sake!"

When this story was read out loud to Tatiana Nikolayevna in 1978, she recalled that Vera Fyodorovna had retold it as a comic episode this precise phrase that her maid had come out with: "There's some bloke what's asking for you!" And it was precisely this line from the story that had perturbed Ivan Pavlovich – that *a bloke had come to see his wife*, and that such a thing had been put in print... Madame Luzina, according to Tatiana Nikolayevna, was "similar to Vera Fyodorovna outwardly, but not like her in terms of her behaviour, but Ksyushka was very similar to their maid." What happened with this story was effectively a repeat of the incident with *The Grasshopper* (*Poprygunia*): all that was needed was for one of the prototypes to feel offended, and to recognise some familiar situations in the story. "Napoleon, submitting to the hands of Ksavery Antonovich, who had cunningly managed to do two things at once – to tickle Madame Luzina's neck with his lips and to upturn the table – picked up a knife and plunged it into Pavel Petrovich's blister."

Ivan Pavlovich (who did not take part, Tatiana remembered, in the séances, but instead sat in the next room with his little daughter) thought it particularly shameless, apparently, that the man who was courting his wife was going about his courtship like this, in print!

Yet this was not the only cause of his consternation, it seems. One can well imagine that the monologues of the master of the household created a precise verbal portrait that was hurtful precisely because of how accurate it was:

"It's like I always say," Pavel Petrovich continued, embracing his guest around the waist, "Communism… There can be no argument: Lenin is a brilliant man, but… look, wouldn't you like one of these ration cigars… He-he! I got it today… But Communism is the kind of thing that, so to speak, by its very essence… Ah, torn, is it? Take another one, look – from the end… By its very essence it requires development, the kind we know well… Ah, damp, is it? Honestly, that's cigars for you…! How about this one, be my guest… By its content… Wait, the match has gone out… That's matches for you! They're rationed ones, too… Of well-known consciousness…" The recurring theme of these monologues – or rather, the tuning fork for them – is a solitary phrase that Tatiana remembered, and that she remembered precisely because it was repeated (compare this with the story: "he immediately began to drawl"): "He always greeted me with the same line: 'See what a mess this place is in?' or 'When on earth will this mess come to an end?' I replied: 'It will never end.'" Here, one sees the biographical significance of the story – i.e. its significance in terms of interpreting Bulgakov's mind-set during his first year in Moscow – a mind-set about which we have so few sources.

The story contains the following short scene: "You haven't got any strangers in the apartment, have you?" Boboritsky asked cautiously.

"No, no! You can speak freely!"

"Spirit of the Emperor, tell me, how much longer will the Bolsheviks be in power?"

"A-a-ah! Now that's interesting! Keep your voice down! Start counting!"

"That's it, that's it," Napoleon uttered, half-falling onto one knee.

"The-or… i… three… months!"

"Ah!!"

"Thank God!" the bride shouted out. "I hate them so much!"

This scene, perhaps one of Bulgakov's sharpest grotesque scenes, ends with the arrival at the apartment of the Cheka – the epilogue to the tale is as follows: "Boboritsky was put in jail for a week, the flatmate and Ksavery Antonovich were given 13 days, and Pavel Petrovich was given one and a half months." It is clear what sort of impression this epilogue must have made on someone who recognised himself in Pavel Petrovich.

Why were such "strong" literary resources chosen, when it would have been easy to guess what sort of effect they would have on these particular readers? This seems to be the first (but by no means last) example in Bulgakov's work of the creation of such a grotesque and at the same time fairly naked reproduction of a prototype.

He uses similar devices to portray human traits that he holds in contempt: the political disingenuousness of Talberg and Shpolyansky, related to the death of people. What was it specifically about the protagonists of the story *The Séance* that provoked such a powerful negative emotion in their prototypes (not hatred, but a destructive mockery?) There are almost no comments from Bulgakov from that time to go on about the social situation contemporaneous to him; it is through tangential sources that his mind-set is revealed – including through an analysis of his works and the context in which they came into being. It appears that the story in question confirms my theory about Bulgakov in 1921-1922 as a man for whom the lasting nature of the government that had taken power was a fact about which there was no room for any doubt, and which he had actively taken note of. Hence his mocking and scornful irritation against those "socially close" people, who continue to comfort themselves with unrealisable illusions, sapping one's energy and, at any rate, opposed to creativity. "… By night some expert, as he gets undressed, prays to an unknown God: 'What would it cost you? Let there be a downpour tomorrow. With hail. After all, in some places they get hailstones that weigh two pounds. You can manage one-and-a-half, can't you?' And he dreams:

'They'll go out, they'll take their placards out, and then there'll be a great gasp up above…'

And sure enough, the rain starts falling, and how! It gushes out of the rusty sewers. But it falls at an absurd time, a time when no-one needs it: at night. And in the morning, there's not a cloud to be seen in the sky!

And one old woman says to another, beside the gate:

'It seems whoever's up in the sky is on the Bolsheviks' side…'

'Seems you're right, dear…'

At 10 o'clock, a deafening march bowls its way along Tverskaya. Past the blinding shop-fronts, past the walls, covered with the faded stains of red flags, in new tunics with red, blue and orange epaulettes, in helmets, one after another, to the sound of the clattering of plates, the blare of trumpets, the red infantry marches past, regiment after regiment."

This is a sketch from the satirical piece *Red-stone Moscow* (*Moskva Krasnokamennaya*), dated July 1922. Exactly a year later, on 15th July 1923, Mandelstam publishes his sketch *The Cold Summer* (*Kholodnoye Leto*) in *Ogonyok* (*Little Flame*), in which there is a similar description, but here, Bulgakov's almost emotionless acceptance of the lasting nature of what has come into being has a corresponding emotion of joy, with which the author's interpretation of the material coagulation unfolding before the eyes of one of life's poets: "I am overjoyed by the sturdy shoes of the citizens (compare this with Bulgakov's description from a year earlier of how the Muscovites were dressed – 'On their feet, for the most part, is a *suspiciously crumpled rag* with steep heels. But the varnish is already succumbing. They are Soviet, reduced ladies in white slip-on shoes'), and the fact that the men's grey, English shirts and Red Army officer's chests shine through like an X-ray with raspberry-coloured ribs."

Let us go back to the ideas expressed or confirmed by the story *The Séance*. Let us remember the first document which provided evidence of Bulgakov's assessment of modern life: the letter to his mother dated 17th November 1921. As he tried to convey "what Moscow now amounts to, today," he writes: "Briefly, I can say that there is a wild struggle for existence taking place and a process of *adapting* to new terms of life." Even at this point, it seems, the new terms of life are seen as a given, from which there is probably no going back.

"I do not wish to be among the dead," he wrote in the same letter. In the first few months of his life in Moscow, he did not have the minimum conditions of existence: he had to try to obtain them on a daily basis. This made his way of life markedly different from the life of the Moscow houses that he frequented in the evenings to drink tea. There, these conditions existed; there was the possibility to wait passively for the time "when the Bolsheviks would go away", as the famous song *Fried Chicken* (*Tsyplyenok Zharenyy*) put it. Before Bulgakov, as he wrote just over two years later in the sketch *Forty Forties* (*Sorok Sorokov*), "clearly and simply [...] lay a lottery ticket with a word written on it: death. On seeing it, it was as if I woke up. I developed an unprecedented level of energy, a monstrous amount. I did not die, despite the fact that the blows came raining down on me like hail..."

It is clear that this difference of position was merely an additional hue, but this was the thing, perhaps, that lent such a disparaging character to the mocking description of the participants in a séance. There is no doubt that a belief in the permanence of the new government was something that Bulgakov already had in the Caucasus, and brought with him.

We know nothing about what sort of hopes he had for the initially successful actions of the Volunteer Army, or how he felt as he was driven to the Caucasus in the uniform of a military doctor. In any event, he came back from there having already seen the end of the white movement, one can assume, in its total defeat. His attitude towards his new friends in Moscow – lawyers and teachers who had sat out the entire war in their apartments in Moscow, there may also perhaps have been a little scorn, as a man who had been shot at and had seen with his own eyes exactly what was unfolding.

The fact that he had to hide from them the details of his life over the last few years probably lent a special kind of tension to his attitude towards them – a tension about which they probably had no inkling. It would reveal itself in unexpected ways – as it did in this story.

Bulgakov's mind-set in these years presents itself as the determining factor for an understanding of perhaps the most important thing in his later life, in his very destiny.

Let us cite an eye-witness account that relates to this time. In 1961, in a letter to N. Mandelstam, the biologist A.A. Lyubishchev, who was part of the generation that came before Bulgakov's, wrote:

"The old Russian intelligentsia, for a few years after the Civil War, lived under the illusion that Soviet power would not be long-lasting, and when this illusion came to an end, it transpired that there was a complete moral emptiness. They therefore went into a far bigger capitulation than those people for whom Soviet power had not been a phantom right from the very start. I clearly recall a meeting with an intelligent professor, V.M., in 1921. I had just got back from the Crimea to Petrograd, and I bumped into him in a corridor at the University. We were never particularly well acquainted with one another, but at that point he stopped, started talking and came out with this sentence: 'Well, what... our government will hand out some more food rations, and then be overthrown.' I turned to stone on hearing such nonsense from someone who was undoubtedly a very clever man, and could not even bring myself to say anything: this always happens to me when I hear something utterly unexpected, for which I'm not prepared at all. All this is undoubtedly a sign of 'ivory towers'; the contract with what I am expecting is so striking that when one comes up against reality, one loses not only physical resistance, but also spiritual resistance."

The circumstances of Bulgakov's childhood and adolescence meant that he was cut off, as we saw in the previous chapter, not only from the revolution, but also from the liberally minded intelligentsia; this determined a great deal in his attitude to the revolution, which was partially – although very frankly – expressed in his letter to the government in 1930. His spiritual baggage did not contain any illusions which might be caused to waver by day-to-day events. His personal experience of the revolutionary years had convinced Bulgakov of the irreversibility of what had happened (this is indeed recorded in one of the very first stories he wrote in Moscow). These two circumstances in the first instance conditioned, in my view, his energy, resilience, unwaveringness in the things which he deemed to be pertinent – qualities which surprised his contemporaries and later memoirists and their readers. Let us cite below an entry from a memoir which contradicts what has been said above:

"On 21st February 1932, Y.L. Slezkin, recalling the story of his relations with Bulgakov, writes the following: 'Misha lived in poverty then, in a dimly-lit, damp apartment in a large building on Sadovaya, with his first wife. There were old posters, newspaper cuttings and whimsical notices on the walls. Bulgakov was shy about his income, hunched over, he raised his eyes heavenwards, raised his hands and said: 'When will this end!', he stashed away his gold coins and recommended that I do likewise." The memoirist's attitude to Bulgakov, which changed over the years, but was always tense, is conditioned, here as in other cases, by a displacement of the real-life proportions. The "inherent" traits of all those who generally did not welcome the new government are shifted onto Bulgakov. The individual features of Bulgakov's attitude to what is happening, his energy in achieving the goal he has set himself and so on – the thing that B.M. Zemsky noticed – goes unnoticed by Slezkin, or else he fails to grasp it. The "gold coins" require an explanation: this referred to the golden 10-rouble "Nikolayevka" coin minted in 1899. From November 1921 onwards, paper money was printed – *Sovznaks* (Soviet notes), which fall sharply in value (Bulgakov writes expressively about this to his relatives during the first few months after this money went into circulation). A year later, banknotes started being printed – Soviet *chervontsi*, which were equal in value to the "gold coins", which had gradually become a hard currency. Holding onto gold coins in the light of these social and financial conditions began to be seen as a sign of illegitimacy, of unreliability: the thought crept in – perhaps this person was thinking about emigrating, or – worse still – restoration?

The situation recorded in *The Séance*, for Bulgakov in those years, was a compelling literary motif. Let us note the following scene in *Cuff-notes*:

"On Thursday, I had a magnificent lunch. At 2 o'clock, I went to see some friends. A maid in a white apron opened the door.

A strange feeling came over me. It was as if I had suddenly been taken back to ten years ago. At three o'clock I heard the maid starting to lay the table in the dining room. We are sitting down, talking (I had shaved in the morning). *They are cursing the Bolsheviks and talking about how they have exhausted themselves.* I can see that they are waiting for me to leave. I do not do so. Eventually, the landlady says to me:

'Perhaps you'd like to have lunch with us? Or perhaps not?'

'Thank you. I'd be glad to.'"

After a detailed list of the dishes that were served (a description provided as seen through the eyes of a hungry man), there is the following passage: "I wish to admit to an awful thing. When I left, I pictured what it would be like when their home was searched. The team would arrive. They'd all be digging around. They'd find the gold coins in the dungarees in the wardrobe. There was flour and ham in the larder. The man of the house would be taken away…

It is an obnoxious thing to think like that, but that's what I thought…"

That line, "The man of the house would be taken away", for the Bulgakov of those years, was some sort of scenario of revenge that he could envisage – revenge against those who possessed ten-rouble gold coins, and, accordingly, could enjoy a hearty lunch consisting of several courses each day. And this situation is recreated several times in his creative work: in the short story *The Séance*, in *The White Guard* and, later, in the novel *The Master and Margarita*.

*

There is no doubt, though, that Bulgakov began trying to acquire literary acquaintances as well, in the first few weeks after arriving in Moscow, and to carve a niche for himself among Moscow's writers.

Public literary life was mainly focused, as before, on the so-called *House of Hertzen* on Tverskoi Boulevard. In a letter to *Impressions of Moscow (Moskovskiye Vpechatleniya)* published in *Literaturnyye Zapiski* (*Literary Notes,* 1922, p. 7) from early 1922, Nadezhda Pavlovich wrote: "There is a Union of Writers which meets each Monday and serves as a refuge for literary societies – *The Zveno* and *Literaturnyy Osobnyak*, and there are Tuesday meetings of *Liricheskiy Krug* (*The Lyrical Circle*), an association whose members include Sergei Soloviev, Efros, Lidin, Lipskerov, Sofya Parnok, Globa and others." N.A. Berdyayev later recalled that in the poetry about the revolution, he "very quickly sensed the danger to which spiritual culture was now subjected. The revolution took no pity on the creators of spiritual culture; it was suspicious and hostile towards spiritual values. Interestingly, when the All-Russian Union of Writers needed to be registered, no sector of labour could be found, to which the work of a writer could be assigned. The Union of Writers was registered in the category of typographic workers, which was utterly absurd. The worldview beneath whose symbol the revolution had occurred not only did not acknowledge the existence of the spirit and of spiritual activity, but saw the spirit as an obstacle to bringing about the Communist system, like a counter-revolution. The Russian cultural renaissance of the early 20th century was something that the revolution ousted, interrupting its tradition. But there were still people left who were linked to the Russian spiritual culture. The idea took root in me that there was a need to bring together the remaining figures in spiritual culture and create a centre at which the life of the Russian spiritual culture would continue. This should not be a restoration of religious and philosophical societies.

The association had to be broader, incorporating people from various walks of life, but who all recognised the independence and value of spiritual culture. I was the initiator of the formation of the Voluntary Academy of Spiritual Culture (VADK), which existed for three years (1918-1922). I was its chairman and it was shut down when I left. This unique beginning stemmed from a conversation in our apartment building. The significance of the Voluntary Academy of Spiritual Culture was that, in those difficult years, it was the only place in which thought could flow freely and matters which were at the pinnacle of high-quality culture could be raised. We arranged lecture series, seminars, public meetings with debates. The VADK could not have a building of its own, of course, since it genuinely was a voluntary institution, not a state one. We arranged the public talks in the building of the Higher Women's Evening Classes, and the lectures and seminars in various places, at various institutions where we knew someone on the managerial staff. [...] I always spoke openly, not masking my thoughts at all. The debates that we had after the public speeches were just as free. The public talks in the final year were particularly successful. During three of them (one on Shpengler's book, one on magic and my one on theosophy) there was such an extraordinarily large number of people that there was a crowd standing on the street, the stairs were heaving, and I had trouble getting into the building and had to explain that I was the chairman. Once, as the chairman, I received a note from the administrators of the women's evening classes, during a speech, saying that the floor was at risk of collapsing due to the overly large numbers of people. It should be said, mind you, that we never put any ads in the newspapers, and people usually heard about the meetings by coming to the previous one, or via the writers' stall. There was a very large intellectual craving, a desire for free thought."

In the same year, 1922, Bulgakov could have become acquainted with the books of Florensky; one of them, *Fictions in Geometry* (*Mnimosti v Geometrii*, 1922), became his favourite.

Viktor Mozalevsky (whom Bulgakov met in 1922, if not before) writes, in his unpublished memoirs: "In 1921-1926, quite a large number of literary circles of all kinds sprang into being, and all manner of literary assemblies used to meet up: 'Okunev's Tuesdays' (they met at the home of the writer Okunev), 'The Poets' Store-room' [...], Sergei Gorodetsky was in charge there. They used to meet somewhere on Herzen Street." He also mentions the All-Russian Union of Writers at the Herzen House, where "evenings were organised – writers would read out stories, poets (more rarely) would recite poems." He mentions a talk by L.P. Grossman on Pushkin, and readings by I. Shmelev, Sergei Klychkov, Gerasimov, Kirillov, P. Romanov. "Some sort of scary story was read out by Pavel Muratov (the author of *Images of Italy* [*Obrazy Italii*]) and the novel *Egeriya* [*Egeriya*])." This was probably one of the *Magical Stories* (*Magicheskiye Rasskazy*) of P. Muratov, which were even mentioned in *Survey of Artistic Literature in Two Years* (1921-1922) [*Obzor Khudozhestvennoy Literatury za Dva Goda*] by I.N. Rozanov (*Literaturnyye Otkliki* [*Literary Reactions*]. M., 1923, p. 74).

P. Muratov, V. Mozalevsky, A. Chayanov: this was the interweaving of the fantastical and the everyday that was so tirelessly woven by the men of letters of the first few years after the revolution, against the backdrop of which Bulgakov's ideas came into being.

"I often heard stories there (or rather, excerpts from novels) that were recited by the author Boris Pilnyak. Many writers and ordinary members of the audience looked at the tall and jolly young man, Pilnyak, with admiration, who 'served up' his works for them theatrically and artfully. He was just starting to crystallize, in the opinion of many arbiters of that time, into a great writer, the writer of the epoch."

Bulgakov must surely have attended some of these readings, during the first few months of his time in Moscow, but there is no concrete evidence of this.

Getting to know the printing capabilities of that time was just as important to him, of course, as becoming acquainted with the literary milieu. Efforts to start up publishing houses were often linked to literary circles.

For example, *Nikitinskiye subbotniki* printed the 2nd and 3rd editions of *Svitok* (*The Scroll*), containing stories by A. Nasimovich, A. Yakovlev, N. Lyashko, B. Pilynak... Bulgakov was connected to *Nikitinskiye subbotniki*, but not perhaps in that first year.

Let us continue to list the Moscow almanacs which were published in 1922, and for which the preparations for publication and the compiling of subsequent editions under the same title were taking place before Bulgakov's very eyes.

Northern Days (*Severnyye Dni*), vol. 2, containing stories by B. Zaitsev, V. Lidin, A. Sobol; *Sovremennik* (*The Contemporary*), vol. 1 (with a tale by V.I. and N.I. Pozharsky, *The Fantastical Province* [*Fantasticheskaya Provintsiya*]); *Create* (*Tvori*), containing stories by M. Volkov, I. Zhiga and A. Krechetov-Volzhsky...

A Moscow publishing association published *The Shamrock* (*Trilistnik*, 1st almanac), with stories by S. Zayaitsky (*Wooden Houses* [*Derevyannyye Domiki*]), E. Zozula, Muizhel, B. Pilnyak, and with poetry by Mandelstam and Pasternak. The same collection contained a story by A. Frans, *Le Christ de l'océan* (*Khristos iz Okeana*). The anthologies on literature and art, *Shipovnik* (*Briar*), began to be published, edited by F. Stepun. The first volume contained stories by B. Zaitsev, N. Nikitin, L. Leonov, B. Pasternak (*Letters from Tula*, [*Pis'ma iz Tuly*]), P. Muratov; the almanac *Nashi Dni* (*Our Days*, No. 1) was released, edited by V. Veresayev, along with *Liricheskiy Krug. Stranitsy Poezii i Kritiki* (*Lyrical Circle. Pages of Poetry and Criticism*), issue No. 1 of which included poems by Akhmatova, Verkhovsky, Lipskerov, Mandelstam, Khodasevich, S. Shervinsky and A. Efros, and work by many of the same names in the prose section – Efros, Lipskerov, Khodasevich; there was also a story by V. Lidin. In the space of a single year, there were two editions of the almanac *Novaya Zhizn'* (*New Life*) (published by *Novaya Zhizn'*), with works by S. Klychkov, N. Teleshov, I. Rukavishnikov, D. Stonov (his story *Sagebrush* [*Polyn'*] was dedicated to the memory of V.G. Korolenko); and the second edition of the almanac *Peresvet*, with works by Pilnyak, Zamyatin, B. Zaitsev, P. Muratov; the prose writers I. Novikov and N. Ashukin composed poems for it.

There was also the *Moskovskiy Al'manakh* (*Moscow Almanac*) published by *Knigoizdatel'stvo Pisateley v Moskve* (*The Book Publishers of Writers in Moscow*) and containing works by B. Zaitsev, N. Teleshov, V. Veresayev, V. Shishkov and A. Bely.

As we can see, the circle of authors is fairly narrow, and the same names keep cropping up: they were all people who had to some extent made a literary name for themselves before the revolution, and this was in stark contrast to Bulgakov, who was just making his first steps in literature. He didn't manage to get anything published in any of the almanacs mentioned – neither in 1922, nor in 1923.

An account has survived of what seems to be one of his earliest attempts to get something printed in an almanac. T.N. said of this: "It was probably at the Union of Writers that he met one Nikolai Arkhipov; one day, he came home and said: 'I've just been at Arkhipov's place, I read my work to him (I don't remember now which work it was). He liked it a lot, he was laughing…' As far as I remember, nothing ever came of this, Arkhipov wasn't able to help him get it printed…"

The memoirs of Viktor Mozalevsky, together with other sources, may serve as a commentary on this account. "In 1921 (or 1922), I met the writer and publisher N.A. Arkhipov. He 'led' the publishing house *Kostry* (*Fires*) at that time, and published the *Feniks* (*Phoenix*) almanacs. […]"

Unfortunately, *Kostry* did not burn on for very long. In late 1923 or in 1924, they burned out altogether. […] N.A. Arkhipov was a business-like man, friendly and very favourably inclined towards writers; as a publisher, he paid them handsomely, by the standards of the time." As evidence of this, V. Mozalevsky mentions the fact that one of his stories was printed, but the second wasn't, yet the publishing house nonetheless paid him well.

The *Kostry* publishing house published the almanac *Phoenix* (only volume No. 1 was published) and the *Fires* almanacs. The author has a copy of *Phoenix* with an inscription by N.F. Belchikov to Y.G. Oksman ("as a keepsake about Moscow, 1st Aug. 1922", dated 27th Oct. 1922), which helps us to date the publication of the almanac roughly to between 1st August and 27th October 1922. On the reverse side of the contents page is a notice about the content of the first and second volumes of the *Fires* almanac: some prose by Leonid Andreyev, A. Globa, B. Zaitsev, I. Novikov, M. Prishvin, I. Ehrenburg, A. Yakovlev. The second book was never published.

Thus, the meeting with N. Arkhipov, which T.N. recalled, cannot have happened any later than in 1922 (or even at the end of 1921) – later, Arkhipov no longer had control of the publication. So which work did Bulgakov read to him? It was probably *Cuff-notes* – either the first part of it, which had not yet been included in *Nakanune* (*On the Eve*), or the second part. But it also could have been one of the stories printed in 1922 in *Rupor*: *The Séance* or *The Extraordinary Adventures of the Doctor* (which were essentially continued in *Cuff-notes*).

The works printed in these almanacs were immediately published by the publishing house *Fires* in separate books. It seems to have been out of a desire to get something printed in *Phoenix* or *Fires* – or, if he was lucky, as a separate book – that took Bulgakov, one day in 1922, to house no. 1 on Mokhovaya Street, where the publishing house was located and where, one must suppose, Arkhipov had his office.

N. Arkhipov himself had printed one of his own works in the first *Phoenix* book, *The Tale of a Man* (*Povest' o Cheloveke*), which the author had considered to be a major work on social issues, portraying the lives of society's outcasts with details that were a world away from Bulgakov's literary tastes and interests.

V. Mozalevsky's story, *Double Death* (*Dvoynaya Smert'*), however, which was also printed in *Phoenix*, may have been of interest to Bulgakov – both because of its direct representation of Pushkin, and because of its old-fashioned margins (which Bulgakov later made use of himself, in *The Theatrical Novel*), or rather, a part of the frame – an epilogue in the form of a letter, which read: "With sincere willingness I hasten to tell you all I know about the last minutes of the life of your nephew, Vikston…" One can even encounter lines in the story which find echoes in Bulgakov's prose, and which are not altogether alien to his story-telling techniques: "Meanwhile, history painted with vivid brushstrokes across the globe of his motherland. The Great Sower came forward ["An unknown, incomprehensible horseman came forward…" – in the finale of *The White Guard* – M.C.] and sowed sunshine around the globe. In the crystal ether, a row of suns hung, frightening the philistine bourgeoisie. The cities – and there were only a few of them on the globe – became scarlet, [compare with *The Master and Margarita*: "My globe is far more comfortable […] You see that piece of land, whose side is washed by the ocean? Look, see how fire is sweeping through it. A war has broken out there." – M.C.]. Some of the people started shouting: we're burning, burning, our hearts are turning to ashes, but we shall not arise from the ashes; others are shouting: we're burning, burning, we shall arise from the dark ashes. Which of them is right? The historian shall tell us which of them is right." Even this appellation to a future historian, the story's refrain, was also the refrain to *Cuff-notes* and some of Bulgakov's other early works.

Viktor Mozalevsky is one of the names which helped to recreate the literary and day-to-day backdrop against which Bulgakov's life was unfolding in his first year in Moscow.

At the end of 1921 and the beginning of 1922, there came together, from various corners of Russia, various writers who, in the 1910s, had formed the motley, 'multi-floored' literary milieu in the city. This milieu had fallen apart during the years of the revolution and the war and was now gathering together again – extremely diluted and now with new members – mainly from St. Petersburg and other cities. There were some among them who had known Bulgakov in the North Caucasus, from Y. Vensky to Slezkin.

"Y. Slezkin recently arrived here from Poltava," the young poet Yekaterina Galati (who had a book of poems published before the revolution) writes to B.A. Sadovsky on 25th April 1922. Bulgakov met her roughly six months later at a literary circle. "He too suffered a great deal and only just managed to avoid serious unpleasantness. Together with him and several others, we are publishing the almanac *Kol'tso* (*The Ring*) and the journal *Novaya Zhizn'*. It is the first book in the collection. B. Zaitsev, I. Novikov, I. Shmelev, Slezkin, Bely, Shengeli and I are taking part. We would like to ask for material from you – fiction, articles, memoirs – for the second almanac." The second almanac never saw the light of day. Apparently, Bulgakov was not invited to join these publications.

A year later, Bulgakov, in his sketch *Forty Forties*, recalled "his" April 1922 like this: "I walked up to the very highest point in the centre of Moscow, on a grey April day. It was the highest spot – the upper platform on the solid roof of the former home of Nirenzee, now the House of the Soviets, in Gnezdnikovsky Side-Street. Moscow lay beneath me, visible right to the very edges. Something that was a cross between smoke and mist was hanging over it, but peering through the smoke were countless rooftops, factory chimneys and the onion domes of the forty forties. The April wind blew onto the platform of the roof, it was empty up there, as it was empty in my soul. And yet this was now a warm wind that was blowing. And it seemed as though it was starting to blow down there, that the heat was rising from the womb of Moscow. It was not yet growling, like the wombs of big, lively cities growl, but down there, through the thin curtain of fog, a sound of some sort was nonetheless rising. It was unclear, weak, but all-encompassing. [...]

'Moscow has a sound, it seems,' I said uncertainly, leaning over the railings.

'That's the NEP,' my companion replied, holding onto his hat.

'Stop saying that damn word!' I replied, 'It's not the NEP at all, it's life itself. Moscow is starting to live.'

I felt both joyful and afraid in my soul. Moscow was starting to live, that was clear, but was I going to live? Ah, they were difficult times. You never knew how you would make it through the next day. Yet at least I, and those like me, had by now stopped eating groats and sweeteners [the previous chapter of the sketch had contained a description of people eating 'instructions of some sort, and yellow groats that had beautiful little stones, like amethysts, in it.' – M.C.]. There was meat for dinner; for the first time in three years, I did not 'receive boots', but 'bought' them, they weren't twice the size of my feet, just a couple of sizes too big. [...] That was April 1922."

On Sunday 26th March 1922, the first edition of the newspaper *Nakanune* was published. It was published in Berlin, but soon two of its editors arrived in Moscow: emigrants who had been involved with the anthology *Landmarks*, which had declared the need to come closer to the new Russia, as the fully-fledged successor of the Russia of old, and in July they opened an editorial office in Moscow. *Nakanune* was given all kinds of incentives by the official circles in the capital: it appealed to Russian readers abroad, who had to be made to believe in the new prospects. Bulgakov quickly formed a view on the opportunities that were opening up to him on the pages of this newspaper, which was "despised by everyone", as he later wrote in an unfinished autobiographical tale. He was interested, above all, in its typical reader: an intelligent, well-read individual, thirsting for literary news and news of daily life from Russia, with a good understanding of the traditions of the old-style Sunday newspaper supplement, in the spirit of Sytin's "Russian word". Bulgakov took it upon himself to resurrect and renew this tradition.

In March, the first edition of the newspaper *Novaya Rossiya* (*New Russia*) was published in Petrograd: it was similar to *Landmarks* in its tone, but was closed down after the second edition. A few months later, the paper was brought back in Moscow, under the title *Rossiya* (*Russia*), and before long, Bulgakov had a meeting with its editor, I. Lezhnev.

What events in that spring might have attracted his attention? On 27th March, the XI party congress began; the newspapers printed photographs of the congress, with Lenin, Trotsky, Zinoviev and Kamenev presiding over it. Bulgakov apparently discussed the NEP (New Economic Policy) program, proposed by the congress, with several friends – at any rate, he did so with party member Boris Zemsky. On the other hand, it is hard to imagine he took any interest in the investigation which began that spring, into a group of members of the Central Committee of the party of Socialist Revolutionaries, accused of counter-revolutionary activity – a trial which attracted a lot of attention from émigré Russians and various strata of society within the country, and about which Gorky had such strong feelings. There is no doubt that he took an interest in the personality and fate of Patriarch Tikhon.

Bulgakov's unceasing interest in matters of the church, which left no traces in any of his biographical documents, manifests itself in a diverse selection of his works: in *The White Guard*, in which Vsevyshny says to Zhilin: "I can't work out what I am to do with them, I mean with idiots such as that pope of yours, there are no others in the world. I'll let you into a secret, Zhilin, he's a disgrace, not popes," but "It's a pity, Zhilin, that's the thing."

There is a fairly passionate piece about the churches which were engaged in a dispute at that time – the "lively", autocephalous one and the old (i.e. patriarchal) one, in the sketch *Kiev-city* from the spring of 1923. Eventually, in 1928, the chapter from the first edition of *The Master and Margarita* is written, in which there is a bilious depiction of Father Arkady, who sells all the valuables at an auction held within the church…

Without question, the campaign to confiscate church valuables in order to help feed the hungry would have fallen within his purview in 1921-1922. Two key issues arose in connection with it that year: one of them was the issue of monitoring the spending by the Central Committee of Help the Hungry of the funds raised (back in the autumn of 1921, the foreign press had reported that "instead of spending the Russian people's money on the battle against hunger, the Bolsheviks are wasting it on maintaining a vast number of foreign-based spies, provocateurs and inciters of world revolution") – i.e. the question of openness in this matter of nationwide importance. The second issue was that of bringing the emergency measures in relation to church valuables into harmony with the needs of church services and church procedures. Patriarch Tikhon had written a piece for the newspaper *Pomoshch'* (*Help*, 1922, No. 2) on 22nd August 1921 with a message "For the praesidium of the All-Russian Committee for the provision of help for the hungry". The Patriarch wrote: "The Orthodox Church has never, under any circumstances, passed by with indifference the troubles which have beset the Russian people.

Today, also, as hunger moves over a significant part of Russia, the Church must make every effort, and is making every effort, to ease the fate of those parts of the population who are suffering from hunger.

I have already addressed, through representatives of the church, the peoples of all countries which the Lord has blessed with an abundant grain harvest, calling on them to come to the aid of the starving population of Russia. Now, I consider it my sacred duty to appeal to all the faithful progeny of the Russian Church – to the priests and the laity – calling on them, out of a sense of Christian charity, to take part broadly and actively in the provision of help to all those who have suffered and are suffering from hunger.

I am sure that every diocese, every congregation, every separate member of the Church, will consider it their Christian duty to make a considerable contribution to this great cause and will take part in the Church's work as it provides assistance to the hungry.

All of the church's work in this field will take place under my general leadership and supervision. For the leadership in the coming period of both the collection of contributions (monetary, material and foodstuffs) in Moscow and the provinces, and of the distribution thereof via the corresponding church organisations, newly formed for that purpose, I have created a Church Committee in Moscow, consisting of priests and lay persons.

To this I wish to add that the work of the Church in the matter of providing help to the hungry population may only be successful if it is performed in conditions which enable it to develop its activity unhindered, namely:

a) the Church Committee must have the right to collect the necessary monetary and material contributions by means of oral preaching in churches, by publishing applicable summonses, and by means of religious and moral readings, spiritual concerts and so on.

b) the Church Committee may, either independently or with the support of the All-Russian Committee, procure foodstuffs in Russia and receive monetary, material and food contributions from overseas.

c) the Church Committee may organise, in the places afflicted by hunger, via its special representatives or via local, newly formed church organisations, the broadest possible help for the hungry, without any distinction drawn between faiths, types, social classes or nationality, by means of public catering canteens, food warehouses and distribution points, and the opening of medical aid points etc., in full accord with the All-Russian Committee's plans.

d) All the monetary and material property of the Moscow Church Committee, and equally of the local Church Committees, shall not be subject either to confiscation, or to requisitioning.

e) The members of the Church Committee and its representatives, when they are performing their duties, shall enjoy a right to organise meetings periodically.

f) The activity of the Church Committee shall not be subject to supervision by the Workers and Peasants' Inspectorate. The Church Committee shall present reports on all its measures to the praesidium of the All-Russian Committee. The task of reviewing the monetary sums and materials shall be performed by the audit commission, appointed by me.

g) In order to establish good and rapid ties with the All-Russian Committee and its local bodies, the Church Committee is appointing special representatives.

Those are the main provisions which, I firmly believe, should lie at the heart of the Church Committee established by me in order for it to achieve its stated aims more precisely and quickly.

I am confident that the All-Russian Committee, for its part, will provide, within the limits of the rights afforded it, all kinds of support to the Church Committee, and equally to all its provincial bodies, in the matter of implementing its stated aims."

The message was dated 5th August 1921. In February 1922, the patriarch reminded people of how, back then, he had appealed with messages to individual Christian churches "calling on them, in the name of Christian love, to carry out collections of money and food and send them across the border to the people of the Volga territory, who were dying of hunger.

"At the same time," he wrote in a message dated 15th February 1922, "we founded the All-Russian Church Committee for assisting the hungry, and at all the temples and among separate groups of the faithful, people began collecting money which was intended to provide assistance to the hungry. But a church organisation of this kind was declared superfluous by the Soviet Government, and all the money collected by the Church had to be handed over and surrendered to the government Committee."

In his first few months in Moscow and particularly in his job at LITO, and his work on slogans for Help the Hungry, Bulgakov had no doubt heard plenty of stories from Muscovites about the vagaries of the travails of those in the community who had tried to help the hungry the previous summer. B.K. Zaitsev later recalled: "At that very time, in the summer of 1921, Russia suffered greatly from hunger. Following long-held maxims, the Russian intelligentsia, not pursuing any political objectives whatsoever, decided to come and help. A Committee for contributions was formed with some foreign benefactors (Hoover, Nansen and others). I was a member of that Committee, representing the writers. At first, the government allowed us to meet up and hold assemblies, presided over by Kamenev, but then suddenly everyone was arrested. The board of the Committee was exiled to the eastern provinces. I was let out two days later." N.A. Berdyayev remembered that, together with another member of the board of the Union of Writers, he had been at Kalinin's office, and had tried to bring about the release from prison of M. Osorgin, who was arrested in the same affair.

In December 1921, the government proposed that the church should donate money and food. "Desirous of strengthening the possible help for those dying of hunger in the Volga territory, we found a way," Patriarch Tikhon later explained, "of allowing the church and congregational Soviets and communities to donate, to meet the needs of the hungry, valuable church decorations and items which are not used during worship, and we made the Orthodox population aware of this on 6th February of this year in a special summons, which the Government authorised us to publish and which was distributed among the populace. Following this, however, after some ardent criticism in government newspapers in relation to the leaders of the Church, on 10th February the VTsIK for the provision of help to the hungry decreed that all valuable church objects were to be confiscated from the temples, including priests' goblets and other items used during worship," the patriarch wrote. "From the church's point of view, such an act is an act of sacrilege, and we deemed it to be our sacred duty to express the Church's view of this act, and also to inform the faithful priesthood about it." The patriarch explained that he could not approve of the confiscation of items from the churches, even in the form of a voluntary donation, of "sacred objects, the use of wish for purposes other than the worshiping of God is prohibited by the canons of the Universal church and punished by Her as sacrilege – for laymen, with excommunication from Her, and for the priesthood – with ejection from the order..."

On 16th March, 1922, *Pravda* printed a statement by Tikhon to the effect that there were not so very many valuable items in the churches, and that objects confiscated from the churches for the needs of the hungry, with an artistic and historic value, must not be sold to foreign countries. On 28th March, *Izvestiya* published a list of "enemies of the people", at the top of which was patriarch Tikhon, "with that whole church council of his", and there was a conversation between M.I. Kalinin and bishop Antonin, in which the chairman of the VTsIK stressed that there could be no talk of changes to the directive on church valuables, and bishop Antonin, after speaking in favour of confiscating church valuables, expressed a willingness to work on the Central Committee of Help for the Hungry.

It is fair to suppose that Bulgakov's destroyed diary there was a comment on the start of the trial of the priests, on 26th April 1922, and on the testimony given by patriarch Tikhon on 5th May in the building of the Polytechnical museum during the trial, and on the sentence (10 priests were sentenced to death by firing squad; 6 were later spared, but the other four were shot dead on the night of 12th – 13th August). Similar verdicts and executions took place in other cities, too. Bulgakov would have considered as a significant event the arrest of the patriarch in May 1922, and the transfer of spiritual power, that spring, to the "living church"; Bulgakov's attitude to this church was to be reflected a year later in his sketch about Kiev.

Naturally, Bulgakov followed the preparations for the Genoese conference (his interest in it was recorded, as we saw, in the fragments of the diary that remained intact for February of that year); he can hardly have been indifferent to the murder by a monarchist of the former minister V.D. Nabokov, which took place in Berlin on 29th March 1922, although we have no information for deciding what his train of thought was when reading the responses of the *smenovekhovtsy* (*landmarkers*) to this event (Vasilevsky-No-letter wrote, for example, in issue 5 of *Nakanune* – under the general heading "Under a first impression" with A. Tolstoy – that the monarchists never had any courage during the civil war, and that they hadn't had any when they had the chance to save the Tsar's family, after they were arrested, and that they had only found some in the sixth year after the revolution: enough for the shot that was intended for P.N. Milyukov but killed V.D. Nabokov). And he may, one supposes, have followed the articles by those who were laying the groundwork for a return to Russia with particularly strong interest – i.e. those who had managed to effect the departure that had eluded him, to Constantinople and onwards to Europe, only to grow disillusioned by their decision – *smenovekhovtsy*, whom he was soon to meet in Moscow.

On 25th April, *Izvestiya* reprinted the "Open letter from count A. Tolstoy to N.V. Chaikovsky", from *Nakanune* – and Moscow's writers learned of his decision to return to Russia.

In June 1922, Y.V. Klyuchnikov (one of the editors of *Nakanune*) and Y.N. Potekhin ("with whose extremely close involvement" the newspaper was published) printed several letters from Moscow, where they had arrived at the start of the month. In a satirical piece entitled *Prince NEP* (*Prints NEP*), Potekhin explained that "the current Moscow simply cannot be compared to the Moscow of 1918, when I left the place…" (*Nakanune*, No. 75). Of particular interest to us, however, for its sheer detail alone, is Klyuchnikov's sketch "Muscovites", which was printed in the same edition of *Nakanune* (No. 68), in whose literary supplement *Cuff-notes* was published.

Klyuchnikov had paid attention to the eyes of the inhabitants of the city, in many ways so new to him, in which he found himself – for now, temporarily. "In the eyes of the men and women of Moscow, unfailingly, there is some sort of secret. Something that is not suitable for saying out loud. Something that is for themselves alone. Something 'very deep'. […] If you are someone who likes eyes that are open as a mirror – and you've got some dollars to boot – go off to America." This trait of the physiognomy of the city's population in the early 1920s, which revealed itself to a fresh newcomer from the outside, was perhaps later picked up on by Bulgakov, too. He refers more than just a couple of times to the "anxious", "darting" and even "terrible" eyes of the residents of this city that gradually became his own.

The "secret" in the eyes, which was so perceptively spotted by Klyuchnikov, had a deep undercurrent. It reflected several layers of adapting to new circumstances, which had taken place during the five years since the revolution. Without a careful examination of those layers, any attempt to recreate Bulgakov's feelings during the first few years in Moscow, and their subsequent evolution, would probably be doomed to failure.

The philosopher and writer Fyodor A. Stepun, who would be forced to leave his homeland a few months later (two or three years later, Bulgakov's path was to cross that of his brother, Vladimir, so closely, that the banquet in honour of his first premiere in Moscow was held in his apartment), attempts, two years later, to provide a socio-psychological analysis of the environment in which Bulgakov now had to grow into a new life, and the position of which was in many ways analogous to his own, but in some way, as we shall see, were different from it. "The first idea which those of the intelligentsia who remained in Russia tried to use to resist the Soviet government," wrote Stepun, "was the idea of a 'boycott'. But the boycott could not last long. Besides the state, there wasn't a single employer in the country, and the country was being sucked deeper and deeper into need, with no way out. Thus, an unresolvable choice was created: either death, or working for the Soviets – and naturally, the choice was made in favour of work." In the spring of 1923, in one of the supplements in *Nakanune*, Bulgakov described the moment when he found himself in Moscow "in the midst of both groups" – sated "bourgeois" and heroes, "as naked as falcons". "And utterly clearly and simply there lay before me a lottery ticket, with a word written on it: death. On seeing it, it was as though I awoke from my slumbers. I developed an energy that was unprecedented, monstrous. I did not die [...] I adopted the protective techniques used in both camps. I covered myself with credentials, like a dog covers itself with fur." Stepun explained: "But for the government, there was always too little work; it also demanded a rejection of oneself and one's beliefs. By taking into the womb of its apparatus people who were consciously hostile towards it, it christened them, with a stubbornness worthy of the best application, "comrades", demanding that they call one another by this universal name of Socialist brotherhood. Nobody had either the strength or the opportunity to protest. [...] The word 'comrade' was, however, not merely a word in pre-NEP Russia, it was the style of Soviet life: covered by the worker's jacket, or coat with fur on the outside, a stamped felt boot, the cheap tobacco at the filthy Soviet institutions; herring soup and frozen potatoes in the canteens, the sledges and the rations. [Bulgakov went through all these aspects of pre-NEP existence in the most methodical of ways – starting in Vladikavkaz in 1920 and right up until the first year in Moscow – M.C.]. No matter how much the Soviet workers hated the Bolsheviks' "comrades", they slowly but surely began to fall under the yoke of Soviet service themselves, to become "comrades" in some extremely specific stylistic sense. This word which, all day long, never left their lips, yet filled their ears, penetrated, naturally, into the soul and, somehow or other, did something to that soul. Words are a terrible thing: they can be spoken in vain, but they can never be consumed for nothing. They are a kind of living energy, and therefore inescapably influence the souls of the people who utter them.

Thus, slowly but surely, the Soviet workers grew a resemblance to "comrades", and not only outwardly, to the extent that one's style of living is also its *essence* too, always. But, whilst stylistically turning into a "comrade", the Soviet worker nevertheless remained an irreconcilable enemy of the kind of government to which life forced him to bow down low. [...] Thus, beneath the layer of "comrades", the rank-and-file Soviet worker, like a civilian waistcoat underneath a service jacket, stroked within his soul the sacramental layer of a 'conspirator'..." It was this worker that became the hero of Bulgakov's *The Séance*. But this collision, on the whole, could not but affect Bulgakov himself, and all the more so – the circle of writers who were close to him in those years. It was a collision that was bound up in day-to-day life. "Whichever institution we went into, it was as though we were going into a psychoanalytical institution," F. Stepun recalled. The first step, on which everything depended, was the accuracy of the sociological diagnosis, the insight of the conspiratorial waistcoat beneath the communist jacket." This was not a reference to some real plot, of course, but to the most *socially close* of the workers of the day – to a certain "unspoken password". The clarification that follows is of particular importance, however. "Although there was nothing morally inadmissible in the use of this silent password, it nonetheless contained a certain something that was *shameful*," Stepun admits. "(After all, one felt ashamed during the war, too, to walk along bent-double along the trenches)... In the permission to call oneself a 'comrade' granted by genuine communists, in some sort of inner wink at any pseudo-comrade – 'give it a rest, a bird may be known by its song', in the efforts to save one's last bit of property and one's only – when all's said and done – life, in all this, one could constantly sense one's shameful, crooked back, bent-double before the *storm of life*. There was no hypocrisy in all this at the outset, but a certain habit of dissembling before life and before oneself was nevertheless formed, of course."

This "tendency towards dissembling" was formed in Bulgakov, too – primarily in 1920-1921. Prior to that, in Kiev in 1919, Bulgakov, judging by the accounts of his loved ones, did not work at any Soviet institutions. It was only in Vladikavkaz, in the spring of 1920, that he faced, to their full extent, the complex socio-psychological problems about which Stepun writes and which, with the degree of clarity possible in a work printed in Russia, were reflected in *Cuff-notes*. Stepun had imagined that things were "morally favourable" initially – "whilst the revolution was a storm, whilst the Russian man was rescuing only his naked life, whilst he knew distinctly, within him, what his truth was, and on what, ultimately, was the firm ground beneath his feet." This was the condition of the protagonist of *Cuff-notes*: "I am getting to grips with it all. – Zavpodisk. Narobraz. Litkollegiya. – Some man is walking around between the tables. In a grey jacket and monstrous breeches. He plunges into various groups, and they disperse. Whoever he looks at – they turn pale. They cast their eyes down, under the table. [...]

He came up to me. He bored into me with his eyes, pulled out my soul, put it on the palm of his hand and looked around attentively. But my soul was made of crystal! He put it back. He smiled benevolently."

To use Stepun's terminology, this is dissembling, but not hypocrisy. Without understanding the difference, we will not understand how Bulgakov, who at first shared this protective dissembling with very many writers, who were ridden roughshod over on various sides of the front before settling once and for all in Moscow in the early 1920s, later departs from hypocrisy – and above all from its penetration into his creativity. "By the time of the start of Denikin's manoeuvers, there was the sense, felt by a whole host of people," writes Stepun, having in mind those who, unlike Bulgakov, had found themselves up until then behind the lines of the Red Army, "that they had not just two faces, but a duplicitous face, i.e. a complete incapacity to work out which of their faces, the 'comradely' one or the 'conspiratorial' one, they actually felt to be their own.

By then, a large number of Soviet workers already, to some extent, had the mind-set that they were Bolsheviks, and for that reason sensed some kind of uncertainty in their presentiments about Denikin's arrival…"

With Bulgakov, the situation was different. By the time Denikin arrived in Kiev, he had apparently not yet felt that "uncertain presentiment" about which Stepun wrote; in the winter of 1919/20, he had lived through the invasion and retreat of the White Army, being on the same side of the front as this army. In Vladikavkaz, in 1920, he followed the events taking place in the Crimea (supposing, perhaps, that his younger brothers had ended up there) with feelings that were no doubt complex, and which we are hardly likely to recreate to any extent: in *Flight*, we will see only the late transformation of these feelings.

In the first years in Moscow, he was still plagued by the thought of the version of his fate which had not taken place, and which had been underlined in 1920-1921. Tatiana Nikolayevna recalled that he once met a nurse he knew, who had later been in Constantinople. "He invited her round for tea, she told us so many stories. He was always eager to listen to anyone who had spent time abroad, open-mouthed... She told us what everything was like over there – she had made it to Constantinople with the Whites, but had nevertheless come back... I said to him: 'Don't you go regretting anything...!'" His wife's well-meant advice can scarcely have had the desired effect; his feelings and ponderings about this painful subject were far too complicated.

In April and May, Bulgakov got intensely involved with *Nakanune*, and an important link in the chain of this relationship was the publication, in *Literaturnoye Prilozheniye* (*Literary Supplement*) No. 8 (published with *Nakanune* No. 68), on 18th June 1922, of the first part of *Cuff-notes*, which he had not managed to get printed anywhere else prior to that.

For a certain section of the Russian intelligentsia, both in Russia and overseas, the spring and summer of 1922 were a time of hope, and this group strove to cheer up those who had lost this hope, and to restore them to new life. On 25th June, there was a report in the literary supplement of *Nakanune* about the release of the first edition of the newspaper *Ekonomicheskoye Vozrozhdeniye* (*Economic Regeneration*) (published by *Pravo* [*Law*]); the editorial in its first edition said that among the mood of Russian society, "unrestrained black pessimism is prevailing, along with an irresponsible, fatal submissiveness to a brutal fate, and apocalyptic presentiments about the end being nigh." The editors felt, however, that however sad the position of Russia's national economy might be, hopeless pessimism ought to give way to a "will for life" and that after "real politics has taken the upper hand over outright utopianism" in Russia, the country's economic rebirth would be entirely possible.

The relationship between Bulgakov's worldview at that time and these hopes to some extent explain the lines in the sketch quoted above, *Forty Forties*: "Moscow is starting to live, that was clear. But am I going to live?"

Tatiana Nikolayevna remembered a little episode that is of great interest: Bulgakov and his wife's attempt, after they fell into a hopeless situation in the winter and early spring of 1922, to "take a risk" in a commerce that was just unfolding at that time... "We had this friend – Moiseyenko," Tatiana Nikolayevna relates. "We had met back in Vladikavkaz, under the reds, probably at the home of Zbrueva – an opera singer... She held parties, where much vodka was consumed... A lot of drinking went on. There was this wine from Kizlyar, a pale pink one, with a lovely taste, but when you drink a lot of it, you can't stand up properly. This Moiseyenko was there too. I can't remember what he did, but he was an interesting character. He often came over to see us, with his wife Olga. He used to say: 'Mishenka, I love you.' He genuinely did love Mikhail; he was older than him. And suddenly he appeared in Moscow. He came round to see us, he brought me some pies. I remember he used to say to me:

'Make some millet porridge with carrots – you'll have a risotto.'

It's an Italian dish – it's supposed to be rice with the carrots, of course, but, well, we made it with millet... I made it following his recipe several times...

And one day his wife brought us two icons with pearls around them:

'Hide these for us – they'll never come and search your place!'

We had those icons for a long time, locked away, then they came and collected them.

I think that Moiseyenko was involved in some shady business – commercial stuff... Then he just disappeared somewhere.

They bought some face-powder somewhere. And they said to us one day: 'Take this case if you like – you'll make some money out of it!' We took the case, containing goodness knows how many boxes of powder, and dragged it up to our flat on the fifth floor, but nothing came of it. We got in a fine mess with that powder – we sold it for not a single kopeck more than the price we paid for it... I was the one who sold it, of course – at the market..."

The summer of 1922 was approaching; Bulgakov spent it in Moscow, for the first time. "The weather in Moscow is marvellous right now," S. Auslender wrote to Slezkin on 23rd May 1922, "the first days of summer are here, there is tender greenery on the boulevards, yesterday there was a storm... everything has started to turn green... I have seen little of our mutual friends. Galati, in his desperation, is going off to spend the whole summer in Golitsyno. I saw Lidin, he is sulking, no-one is accepting his story *Chinas (Kitai)*..." – Y. Lezkin, S. Auslender, V. Lidin, Y. Galati – these were the writers with whom Bulgakov was to meet regularly.

Moscow had become deserted for the summer, but literary life there had not come to an end. The memoirs of Petr Zaitsev, secretary to the editorial board of the literary and arts newspaper *Moskovskiy Ponedel'nik* (*Moscow*

Monday) and then the *Nedra* (*The Depths*) almanacs and publishing house, help us to get an idea of the "cast" of literary Moscow in 1922. "In the summer of 1922," he wrote, "the following were in Moscow:

V.V. Veresayev, I.A. Novikov, B.K. Zaitsev, who had not yet left the country; there was G.I. Chulkov, and there were the young ones: A.S. Yakovlev, M.Y. Kozyrev; of the proletarian writers from *Kuznitsa* (*The Forge*), there was N. Lyashko, M. Volkov. There was V.G. Lidin, A. Sobol, A.I. Svirsky." Zaitsev goes on: "There was N.D. Teleshov and even the ancient Ignaty Nikolayevich Potapenko, who lived in one of the wings of the Herzen House. Outside Moscow, B. Pilnyak lived at his home in Kolomna; S.P. Podyachev was living in Obolyanov. [...] In 1922, a lot of homeless writers moved into two wings of the Herzen House, after returning to Moscow that year or arriving there for the first time [...] there was S.A. Klychkov and P.V. Oreshin with his wife, Olga, the daughter of the writer Mark Krinitsky (Mikh. Vl. Samygin). [...] I.S. Shmelev had returned from Koktebel, A.S. Neverov arrived from the Volga Territory. [...] M.M. Prishvin had already arrived in Moscow from a village in the suburbs..."

On 29th May, Khodasevich read some poems from the anthology *The Heavy Lyre* (*Tyazhelaya Lira*) at the Union of Writers – I.N. Rozanov made an entry about this in his diary. Judging by said diary, Khodasevich was still in Moscow in June (Rozanov met Berberova at his home on 18th June), and Pasternak was there until mid-August (before long, both poets were already in Berlin).

At the start of June, rumours were flying around the circles of Moscow's intelligentsia about arrests and raids.

On 2nd June, Rozanov, whom Bulgakov met umpteen times, whenever he went to the *Nikitinskiye subbotniki* at least, and who was an ever-present figure in literary Moscow at the time, and was indeed its chronicler, wrote in his diary: "At the museum [the historical museum, where he works – M.C.], all the talk is of yesterday's arrests"; [...] on 8th June, incidentally, the Historical Museum's director, N.M. Shchekotov made an announcement "on the return of comrades to their environment and the opening of an investigation against the individuals who let out false rumours." Pavel Popov would soon become a close acquaintance of Bulgakov.

On 7th July, there was a memorial service for Blok at the Union of Writers (one year on from his death); on 31st July, Rozanov comments on an evening hosted by the Serapions: Fedin, M. Slonimsky and V. Ivanov read from their works. On 28th August, he writes in his diary that, after going to a meeting at the Union of Writers that did not take place, "I walked around the courtyard with Mandelstam and Lipskerov. I met Parnakh" – the future hero of Mandelstam's *The Egyptian Stamp* (*Yegipetskaya Marka*).

By the summer of 1922, the Herzen House, which would later become such a stimulating place for Bulgakov's imagination and be transformed into the Griboyedov House, was put fully into the hands of the Union of Writers (in honour of the centenary of Herzen's death). The newly elected board planned to expand the library, opening a study room in it, "and, using the two houses in the courtyard, arrange a hostel, providing rooms for permanent residency, both for writers with disabilities, and for those members of the Union who, given the current housing crisis, cannot find a corner for themselves"; they dreamed of establishing supporting institutions, too: "As long as 'Rauspirt' is still at the Herzen House, there is no point even thinking about implementing the board's plans. The former excise board takes up a whole floor..." In this same note (under the title "The All-Russian Union of Writers"), the private journal *Rossiya* (*Russia*), which had only just appeared in Moscow, reported the names of the Union's newly elected board: "B.K. Zaitsev – the chairman, M.A. Osorgin and N.A. Berdyayev (comrades of the chairman), A.M. Efros – the secretary, N.S. Ashukin and A. Sobol (the secretary's comrades)... Y. Aikhenvald, V. Zhilkin, G.G. Shpet, I.A. Novikov – members of the board; candidates to replace them: V.G. Lidin, V.L. Lvov-Rogachevsky"; P.N. Zaitsev was on the Audit Commission.

Many years later, shortly before his death, B.K. Zaitsev wrote, recalling the years 1921-1922: "At that time, in Moscow, many of the old-style Russian intelligentsia remained. Our Charter stated that no communist could be a member of the Union. Is that a paradox? Of course it is, but back then, the government was still busy with the civil war, it had no time to concern itself with us.

Before the revolution, I had been personally acquainted with Kamenev and Lunacharsky. I was sometimes sent to see him with petitions calling for the release of members of the Union who had been arrested. Usually, both of them were sympathetic in their attitude."

The end of the civil war coincided with a strengthening in the government's attention on literary and public life. Preparations to exile philosophers and writers began in the spring of 1922, but nothing was known of these plans by those who were to be affected by them.

In the summer, B.K. Zaitsev left Moscow; he had been granted permission to travel abroad in the spring. He later recalled that, with help from Kamenev and Lunacharsky, he had been "let out with his family to go to Berlin, 'for treatment'. No, I did not think it would be forever. But my daughter, the ten-year-old Natasha, when the train crossed the border, threw a little flower down onto the Russian soil, lost in thought – to say goodbye. 'Papa, we're never going to come back to Russia.' But my wife and I thought it would just be a temporary absence."

Despite the geography, the distance between Moscow and Berlin was far closer in those days than it later became. There were journals in Berlin which had many Moscow writers working for them, including Bulgakov and Slezkin – *Novaya Russkaya Kniga* (*New Russian Book*), *Spolokhi* (*Flashes of Lightning*), and *Veretenysh* – an almanac by the *Vereteno* (*Spindle*) community of writers, artists and musicians, formed that spring, which, as one of the Berlin newspapers reported, "did not intend to restrict its activity to the émigré community, but established close ties with the creative forces related to it in Russia." In September, Klyuchnikov and Potekhin, on their return from Moscow, gave a talk on the subject "Russia today".

When you read the names of the writers who spoke at Berlin's House of arts that autumn, you see how similar this list is to a list that would have contained the names of the speakers at literary gatherings in Moscow, in 1922 or thereafter: V. Shklovsky, V. Khodasevich, A. Tolstoy, B. Pasternak, A. Bely, I. Ehrenburg, V. Mayakovsky, Y. Aikhenwald, V. Lidin… It was reported of Lidin that he had "arrived for a short time in Berlin, from Moscow," and his address in Moscow was added, too – Malaya Nikitskaya Street… Another writer of fiction arrived in Berlin at the same time as him – O. Savich. On 12th November, they spoke together before the members of the newly formed community *Vereteno*, but on 25th November 1922, in I.N. Rozanov's diary, there is this entry: "Savich has gone back." The author supposes that it was one of these two writers that took to Berlin, to be printed in *Novaya Russkaya Kniga* or the almanac *Veretenysh*, the following letter. "M.A. Bulgakov is working on compiling a full bibliographical dictionary of contemporary Russian writers with their literary silhouettes. The completeness of the dictionary depends to a considerable degree on the extent to which the writers themselves will respond to this work and provide some lively and valuable information. The author kindly asks all Russian writers in all the cities of Russia and in foreign climes to send autobiographical material to the following address: Mikhail Afanasievich Bulgakov, Apartment 50, 10, Bolshaya Sadovaya, Moscow.

We need the key chronological dates, first appearance in print, influence of the major old masters and literary schools and so on. Material containing vibrant, colourful dashes is preferable.

The request is particularly aimed at those who are just starting out, about whom there is no, or virtually no, critical or biographical material available.

Individuals possessing reviews of their work by critics are kindly asked to indicate who wrote them and where they were printed.

Please would all journals and newspapers reprint this message. Moscow. 6th October 1922."

The date on which the letter was sent to the editors of *Novaya Russkaya Kniga* may be no accident.

In September, there had been much talk in Moscow about the exile of cultural figures from both Petrograd and Moscow. On 26th September, Rozanov writes in his diary: "… (Zadruga). Conversations about those who are departing (today); 3rd October: "In the evening, at the last meeting of *Voice of the Past*, at S.P. Melgunov's place, Melgunov, Sivkov, Fedorov, Tsyavlovsky, Popov and I were there. My proposal about a photograph"; on 6th: "In the evening I was at the last meeting of the 'Zadruga' council"; and finally, on 8th October, a Sunday: "At 6, (the board) began seeing off Melgunov at 'Zadruga.'" On 6th October, at an emergency session of the All-Russian Union of Writers in Moscow, "in place of the departing B.K. Zaitsev and the exiled Y.A. Aikhenwald, N.A. Berdyayev and M.A. Osorgin, V.V. Veresayev, A.I. Okulov, B.A. Pilnyak and Y.V. Sobolev were elected."

That autumn, the following people left Moscow – in most cases because they were forced to do so: the philsophers Frank, Ilin and Vysheslavtsev, the writer and philosopher Stepun, the historians Kizewetter, Myakotin, economists, publishers, agronomists and so on. The results of these actions were not destined to make themselves felt to their full extent immediately. However, Bulgakov's idea about a bibliography may be put forward in connection with the impressions he picked up about the dissipating of Russian culture. It was specifically this autumn exile – a departure which to many, though not to all, seemed irreversible (as indeed it was) – may have prompted Bulgakov to make haste in collecting information about all contemporary Russian writers, regardless of where they lived. He was thus pretty much the first person to promote a task of vast cultural importance, which had not been resolved even to a modest extent hitherto.

We do not know how much progress Bulgakov made in collecting material; it seems he soon realised the true magnitude of his endeavour and decided not to see it through. Nonetheless, the very fact that this idea was born clearly indicates that the circle of his bibliographical and reading interests at that time was extremely broad. And the future comment made by the Master, when he guesses at the quality of the poems that Ivan does not read to him: "as if I've never ready any other poems?" had a deep autobiographical undercurrent beneath it: Bulgakov was very well-read in terms of the poetry and prose of the first few years after the revolution – in the same way that any bibliographer worth his salt needs to be well-read.

In the late autumn of 1922, a much-discussed subject among the Moscow intelligentsia was the fate of the publishing cooperative 'Zadruga', which had existed since 1911. Zadruga had its own bookstore: on 29th May, Rozanov notes that he met Pasternak at Zadruga. After the release of issue No. 1 of the *Bulletin of the Zadruga Bookstore* (*Byulleten' Knizhnogo Magazina 'Zadruga'*) by the Political department of the State publishers, the Zadruga collective was forbidden from printing any round-ups about literature, reviews and so on, and it was advised to confine itself exclusively to lists of the books available in its shop. As a result of this, the release of the second issue was halted." After the exile of members of the Zadruga cooperative (Kudryavtsev, Izyumov, Postnikov), Muscovites followed the course of events anxiously.

On 3rd November 1922, the literary historian N.M. Mendelson described in his diary a meeting of the Council of 'Zadruga' that he had attended the previous day: "Sivkov, the chairman of the board, gave a detailed report on how things stood. Kamenev had seen not A.L. Tolstaya, but V.N. Figner. It is hard to say how all this will end. There is a faint hope (on my part at least) that Zadruga will remain intact. From what Kamenev and [illeg.] Lebedev-Polyanski said, they concluded that it must be denied, in print and oversease, that the Board and Council of Zadruga had anything to do with the publishing of Korolenko's letters". [...]

12th November: "Zadruga is breathing its last – as a publishing house only, it appears: perhaps we will manage to preserve *Voice of the Past* (*Golos Minuvshego*) and the shop." Rozanov writes, on 2nd December: "An auction at Zadruga. I was late. Of 5 letters written by Blok, 4 were sold."

Voice of the Past, a journal about history and literary history, with which Bulgakov had been familiar since before the war (it came out in 1913 to 1917) and which was brought back in 1920, must have caught his attention. In Moscow, Bulgakov also used to buy *Russkaya Starina* (*Russia in Past Times*) and *Istoricheskiy Vestnik* (*The Historical Herald*) – journals like this interested him just as much as contemporary literature.

Tatiana Nikolayevna recalls that he often brought home new books, sometimes recommending them to her; "he used to chivvy me so that I read them faster – he had to give them back. Once, I remember, he brought a book called *Notes of a Miscreant* (*Zapiski Merzavtsa*), I can't remember who wrote it. "There, read that." It was a novel by A. Vetlugin, which was published in

April 1922 by the Berlin-based publishing house *Russkoye Tvorchestvo* (*Russian Creativity*) and drew attention from Russian critics abroad (Roman Gul wrote a damning review of it for *Novaya Russkaya Kniga*) and from those at home, who were more favourably inclined towards the author. The review by the journal *Pechat' i Revolyutsiya* (1923, No. 2) acknowledged that the book was significant as a "human document", "an attempt by a very adept person to paint a picture of the spiritual decay of an entire section of the 'green' youth, whom older figures from 'the other shore' are inclined to consider as the continuers of their doomed cause." Even earlier, V. Polonsky, referring in the same journal to Vetlugin's previous book *The Third Russia* (*Tretia Rossiya*), has asserted: "Now, Vetlugin is still trying to stay on the other side of the line which sets him apart from "that" Russia. But of the fact that he stands on the threshold of the editorial staff of *Nakanune* – of that there is no doubt." This was what made the situation in 1922-1923 so unique: attempts to draw closer together were taking place on both sides.

Bulgakov's interest in Vetlugin was not inconsiderable: we will see it later when one of the author's books, *Notes of a Miscreant*, helped him in his work on *Flight*.

The biography of this man must have interested Bulgakov too: the zigzagging destiny of a man who wrote under the pseudonym "A. Vetlugin", Vladimir Ilyich Ryndzyun, unfolded in 1917-1921, somewhere very close to the far less winding trajectory, which lacked the back-and-forth jerking motion but was still pretty odd in Bulgakov's eyes, of his own path in those same years. He naturally studied the cynical preaching of a man whom he could easily have met in Kiev, both in the novel and in the autobiography, published in the journal *Novaya Russkaya Kniga*, which Bulgakov had the opportunity to monitor. "In August 1918 I went to the Don," Vetlugin wrote in his autobiography, dated 26th March 1922, "and thence, avoiding mobilization in the Red Army, to Yekaterinoslav, Kharkov and Kiev. In Yekaterinoslav I learned how to play a high-stakes card game. From Kiev (where I lost everything), I went to Berlin, Munich, Vienna." After the revolution, in Austria, "I tried to get into Switzerland, disguised as a Ukrainian"; after being refused a visa, "I returned to Kiev. I started looking for a publisher for a poetry anthology. But Hetman Skoropadsky announced the universal mobilization. I fled to Kharkov, where I was mobilized as ataman Balbachan [similarly to how Bulgakov was mobilized as a Petlyurite soldier – and also fled – M.C.]. I fled back to the Don, to Rostov. Prior to February 1919, I was twiddling my thumbs, I used to go to coffee houses and write poems. In February, Denikin announced the conscription; in an attempt to save myself, I joined a white newspaper. I was suspected of Bolshevism, and signed my name "D. Denisov". In the summer I went to the Crimea, got very sad and dreamed of a distant voyage. In the autumn of 1919, I listened to "Silva", wrote articles about how "our victory is beyond doubt" [Bulgakov was already in a tragic mood in November 1919 – the author of "Future Prospects" gives his readers a call-to-arms, but already has a presentiment of defeat. – M.C.] and fought off typhus-bearing lice.

On 21st December 1919, he left Rostov on foot, in a snowstorm. I went through Armavir to Tuapse, and thence – "to Batum, which was held by the British in those days. I went hungry for three weeks in Batum and signed a contract with the foreign legion. Then I won my money back playing macao and opened a counting-house with two Georgians. We made some good money, darting around the Caucasus and the trans-Caspian. On 27th April 1920, Levandovsky took Baku [Bulgakov no doubt followed all these events tensely from Vladikavkaz – M.C.]: we lost two wagons of rice. I was evacuated from Batum with the British. On 3rd July 1920, I went to the Crimea on commercial business; I lost my last money and my last faith in the white movement. I fled to Constantinople. I was hungry"; in the autumn of 1920, he made it to Paris; "Here, for the first time, I saw the light, gave up my recklessness and started working. For money, I worked for the newspapers; for my soul, throughout 1921, I wrote two books [...] I continued to play cards and go to the races. In the breaks, I studied Paris by night, read Pascal, got drunk and went on trips to Ocean. In one-and-a-half years, I ate my way around Russian Paris till I felt sick, reaching out so as to be closer to Russia"; early in 1922, he arrived in Berlin, sold two more books to "Russian creativity" "and returned to Paris. And it was back to the card-games and the beastly hurt of being awoken during the day"; in March, he was back in Berlin, where he sold two more books; "I live quietly, I get up late, I wander down the Kurfürstendamm and veer noticeably to the left!" "I was at the medical and the historical-philological faculty," Vetlugin recalled. I graduated from the legal one. I intended to "stay on" and study "the history of the philosophy of law..." But, as the short fellow Sergei Auslender used to say: '... When that chanter stops singing, I'll write a novel'..." What were Bulgakov's feelings on reading about the twists and turns of what was essentially a version of his own fate – the one that never happened? Did he feel any regrets? Did he dream of a quiet life (the unfulfilled wish of the inhabitant of flat No. 50), like his former colleague at the medical faculty, and of "veering to the left", whilst wandering down the Kurfürstendamm, rather than along Bolshaya Sadovaya Street? The chanter, at any rate, stopped singing, and he himself decided to set about writing a novel. And he was due to meet Sergei Auslender any day now, in Moscow.

In Moscow that summer, people were reading and discussing A. Sobol's book, *Oblomki* (*Fragments*), and particularly his story *The Dining-Car* (*Salon-Vagon*); O. Savich's story *The Foreigner from No. 17* (*Inostranets iz 17 №*) did not escape Bulgakov's notice either, it seems. To get a sense of what he was reading that year – knowing, as we have seen, that he even had special goals in his reading – we ought to look at the critical reviews from that time, which recorded what was making the news in literary life.

"In 1920 and 1921, the imagists were causing a stir in Moscow. The main ones were Yesenin, Marienhof, Kusikov and Shershenevich. In 1922, there was nothing left of them," Rozanov wrote in his "Review of fiction over the last two years", dated November 1922. "Kusikov and Yesenin had left the country. Shershenevich was devoting himself to the theatre. Marienhof had simply fallen silent. "The imagists got fed up with themselves," others commented. Yet their adversaries, the futurists, grew stronger: Kruchenykh and the centrifugist Aseyev arrived in Moscow. The former immediately began publishing one book after another in a highbrow language, as if nothing had changed since 1914. Aseyev almost achieved widespread recognition with his book *The Steel Nightingale* (*Stal'noy Solovey*). S. Tretyakov's book *Yasnysh* attracted far less attention. But the hero of the season was the third centrifugist, B. Pasternak, who released his third book of verse, *My Sister, Life* (*Sestra Moya Zhizn'*). An interesting detail: the book had become known to literary Moscow in its manuscript form back in the summer of 1921 and had quickly gained popularity. Its publication in book form probably added little to the reputation he had already acquired. The same can be said for Vasily Kazin's book *Working May* (*Rabochiy May*) [...] Only in 1922 was a collection of his poems published which had long since been known to all his admirers, who followed him in the newspapers. Other proletarian poets have somehow started to lose their gloss latterly." The round-up identified, as the most significant phenomena in prose in those two years, Korolenko's *The Story of My Contemporary* (*Istoriya Moyego Sovremennika*), A. Bely's novel *Letaev's Cat* (*Kotik Letayev*) and I. Shmelev's story *The Bottomless Cup* (*Neupivayemaya Chasha*); it also comments on stories by B. Zaitsev, B. Sadovsky, P. Muratov, and mentions V. Lidin and Andrei Sobol – who had set about the task of "portraying the revolution, but as onlookers, without a revolutionary spirit." Pilnyak is singled out as the one who "in the current year" was "in fashion" – alongside the *Serapionovy Brothers*; "he is considered the best writer about everyday life in the revolution", writes Rozanov. "Alexander Yakovlev has made a real name for himself in the last two years," "Of the other prose writers, the following have attracted attention": Grigoriev, Kozyrev, Semenov, Shishkov, Volkov, Neverov, Lyashko, Pasternak, Leonov, Bibik, Bobrov and others. "It is too early to talk about a blossoming of fiction: all of this represents merely the first swallows arriving. The level of technical mastery is still higher in the poetry," the critic concludes. This synchronized cross-sectioning of a two-year period in literary life as it was in autumn 1922 is done fairly accurately: the fiction scene in Moscow is presented just as it appeared to an observer at that very moment. Along with many authors who were not cited by Rozanov from those listed earlier in the almanacs of 1921-1922, this is almost the whole of Moscow's literary milieu in the summer of 1922, the people who were getting together in various circles to read their works, who were meeting each other at the editorial offices of the almanacs, or in bookshops. The writers themselves assessed their day-to-day lives and its atmosphere at a fairly low level. Typical of the feelings of the average writer is the second letter from Y. Galati to B. Sadovsky, sent on 25th July 1922: "... I am sorry that I shan't see you in Moscow, but I fully understand your decision not to leave Nizhny. Here, you would not have been able to tolerate the stuffiness and the hustle and bustle over nothing. Literary Moscow is like a muddy, foul-smelling pond, in which not only are there no big pike or carp, but there's no sign of any perch either.

Agile mosquitoes dance on the water, stupid bugs and tadpoles jostle one another, and the poor fisherman has nothing to hope for. It may be that my pessimism is making me inclined towards hyperbole. But now, alas! It is shared by all those who once swam in pure, free-flowing waters. [...] Besides Slezkin, I do not meet up with anyone. I cannot read "new works" without shuddering and feeling bewildered. All these new individuals are collapsing into a single, wild form of some kind, and I am turning away from it."

Before long, Bulgakov found himself in the same literary circle as the author of this letter and V. Mozalevsky, who left several images of life in this circle in his memoirs: "In 1922-1923, beneath the welcoming 'Green (lampshade!) lamp', of the journalist Lidiya Kiryakova (she died in 1943), several writers gathered together, at her invitation, for a literary 'tea'.

Yury Slezkin read his story *The Stolovaya Mountain*. Listening to him that evening was Bulgakov, along with Auslender, Stonov, the bibliophile Shamurin, myself, someone else, I forget who, and, obviously, the 'hostess of the salon', Lidiya Vasilievna. After a reading over 'tea', there was a discussion of the story and perorations on literary and theatrical subjects of the day – Meyerhold, Tairov, *The Empress's Plot* (*Zagovor Imperatritsy*) [a play by A. Tolstoy and P.

Shchegolev – M.C.], the Theatre of the Revolution – *Lake Lyul* (*Ozero Lyul'*) [a play by A. Faiko – M.C.]. At that point, the hope was expressed that some new writers would create some new chef d'oeuvres, and people sceptically said thinks like 'there's nothing original or noteworthy yet'; then we reverently looked 'back', we looked at Pushkin, at L.N. Tolstoy: M.A. Bulgakov was awaiting the appearance of a new *War and Peace* [...] At a certain point, all those involved in the discussion under *Zelyonaya Lampa* decided to meet again two weeks later. This was how *Zelyonaya Lampa* was lit..."

Since Slezkin wrote his novel *The Stolovaya Mountain* (it was published as *The Girl from the Mountains*, M., 1925) between May and September 1922, the first meeting of *Zelyonaya Lampa* took place roughly in September-October 1922. Also in the circle was B. Gornung, who told the author in 1975 that the name came from a circle which had been formed by the poet G. Maslov in Tsarskoe Selo in the pre-revolutionary years, and had been resurrected by him in the first years of the revolution in Omsk. "We arrived from Omsk – Lidiya Kiryakova (the life and soul of the salon), Auslender, Venediktov, Shamurin, Aseyev, Tretyakov… in Moscow – at Malaya Dmitrovka, at Kiryakova's flat… The others were Mozalevsky, Galati, Bulgakov. I remember that late in 1922, we met several times." The accounts of these two memoirists, therefore, do not contradict one another: the circle was clearly formed in the autumn of 1922. "The 'Lamp' had no literary platform at the outset, of course," Mozalevsky continues. "We read our works, discussed them. Slezkin read *The Stolovaya Mountain*, *The Chess Move*, Bulgakov read his stories and his tale about the Turbins, based on which the play *The Days of the Turbins* was later written; Stonov and Shestakov read their stories, and an essay on Tsarskoe Selo, Venediktov read something, Galati read her poems. The writer Gusyatinsky read some endlessly long fantastical story about the insane building manager, Shlepkin, over the course of several evenings. [...].

The meetings of *Zelyonaya Lampa* used to last until "long after midnight". Then we would go home – myself, Shestakov, Auslender, B.P. Denike, Slezkin, and others, on foot, of course. We would take a breather beside the Pushkin memorial and the disputes which had flared up and died down again back there, at the *Zelyonaya Lampa* salon, would sometimes break out again…Occasionally, after someone had read out a story at one of the meetings, the members of the circle would not begin discussing it straight away, but would maintain a heavy, lengthy silence. And at such times, Denike would say, comfortingly: 'Well, all right, we'll talk about that beside the Pushkin memorial.' [...] We loved the Russian writers – Pushkin, Gogol, Lev

Tolstoy, Dostoevsky. Most of us had read Blok and held him in high esteem (the long poem *Retribution* [*Vozmezdiye*] was read out).

We were cautious about novels which we thought had been written "to order". Literary society back then, and readers, considered the works of Pilnyak to be new, significant, honest. There were arguments about him at *Zelyonaya Lampa*, but we were cautious about Pilnyak, on the whole.

I remember how we applauded Shestakov, when he read out his poems about Simbirsk (Ulyanovsk), about Karamzin, about the "Simberian geese" flying over the city…

We loved listening to Bulgakov's stories (he was an outstanding reader) and particularly his novel (or story) about the Turbins.

In 1924, someone, I think it was Denike, brought Marcel Proust's novel to *Zelyonaya Lampa*. […] Not all those who attended *Zelyonaya Lampa* were fascinated by Proust. But many got into it deeply, admiring this new form of writing, whereby the "lost time" alternately was resurrected, like a phoenix, and then flew off into the astral spaces."

Certain traits of the atmosphere within the circle can be divined through the cursory, fragmentary memoirs of this participant in *Zelyonaya Lampa*. These traits – being orientated primarily towards the Russian classics and to phenomena from contemporary literature that were closely related to them (Blok's *Recompense*), indifference towards Western literature, distrust of modern Russian works (Pilnyak) and a certain opposition of their tastes, in this regard, to "the literary community of the day".

The lines about how they "reverently looked 'back'" (at L.N. Tolstoy) and about how "Bulgakov was awaiting the emergence of a new *War and Peace*" are not insignificant, and are reinforced by other accounts. E. Mindlin recalls Bulgakov's entry into one of the circles: "Even the most modest Russian writer is already bound, by the fact alone that in Russia there was 'the appearance of Lev Tolstoy to Russian readers…' Someone shouted out from their seat: 'The appearance of Christ before the people…!'"

"Bulgakov replied that for him, the appearance of Tolstoy in Russian literature meant the same thing that the Evangelical tale about the appearance of Christ before the people meant to a believer in Christianity.

'After Tolstoy, one cannot live and work in literature in the way one would have done, had Tolstoy never existed at all.'"

Seven to eight years later, in what was perhaps his most distinctive bit of self-characterization, Bulgakov would speak directly about the Tolstoyan tradition, asserting that he had made it his task, "specifically, to portray an intellectual family from the nobility, which, through the will of an ineluctable fate was thrown into the camp of the white guard during the civil war, in the traditions of *War and Peace*. Such a depiction would be entirely natural for a writer who was bound by ties of blood to the intelligentsia."

The key figure in the circle was Y. Slezkin, with the reading of whose novel *Zelyonaya Lampa* had begun. All of the people who formed Bulgakov's literary company in the first years in Moscow (the 'pre-Gudok' years) acknowledged the seniority of Slezkin, and almost all of them had him to thank at the time of their literary debut: he had been a famous writer of fiction back in the 1910s. Viktor Mozalevsky recalled: "In 1915, I met Slezkin at the literary society *Mednyy Vsadnik* (*The Bronze Horseman*). Outwardly, he was a fine-looking man, with dark hair and a fine figure, and he dressed with a Wildean elegance. He was cheerful, witty and friendly; he gave off the sense, admittedly, of being an 'acclaimed writer', but he was friendly to young people. I was in Petersburg for a few days once, and he took me around, at his own initiative, showing me all kinds of literary sites, and arranged an evening 'for me', i.e. a reading of my story." Slezkin doubtless enjoyed playing the role of the host, the benefactor to these young talents, and those closest to him were keen to support this style of relations. In 1926, D. Stonov writes to him in a tone full of feeling: "My dear friend! Your letter both gladdened and saddened me. It gladdened me because, in spite of all the nonsense, in spite of all those needless, transitory moods, you still think of me as your good old friend. There is no higher thing in life than a good memory of some sort, and particularly one that dates right back to when we were young. *You are the first 'living' writer that I have seen, that I recognised, you are the first to get acquainted with my helpless lines.* I shall thus remember, for the rest of my life, Poltava, the start of the year 1921, and you, you, Yury."

Slezkin, recalling his first years in Moscow, also mentions *Zelyonaya Lampa*: "In those days we had a literary circle that used to meet, *Zelyonaya Lampa*, organised by Auslender and myself. Auslender had just returned from Siberia. I took Bulgakov along there, too."

"Bulgakov used to mention *Zelyonaya Lampa*, I remember that," Tatiana said, in response to a question from the author; "I remember one time when it had been agreed that he would read something there, and we drove a long way – it can't have been to Bolshaya Dmitrovka, that was close to our place, and we rode in a carriage. There, he read the first few chapters of *The White Guard*... Stonov was there, and Slezkin; Slezkin embraced him, then kissed him, and then Mikhail found out that he had been complaining about him behind his back. Mikhail told me that himself." This reading did not take place straight away, though. In 1922, the novel's plot was probably not yet fully-formed. For the time being, Bulgakov was still listening to the other writers when he attended *Zelyonaya Lampa*.

Most of the writers in the circle were united by a shared desire: to forget their recent past or, rather, the desire that others might not recall it. Two of them found had been in Omsk in February 1919, under Kolchak: Sergei Auslender (1886-1943) had travelled there from Moscow, and N.Y. Shestakov (1890-1974) – from Simbirsk (his native town). In 1927, the Siberian writer V. Zazubrin wrote in his sketch, "Siberian literature of 1917-1926": "Under the Kolchak government in Omsk, a group of poets 'with an agenda' emerged. The group sung the praises of the white movement. It was led by the poets Y. Sopov, G. Maslov, Shestakov and others," and half a century later (and a quarter of a century after his death), researchers into the literature of Siberia, with a somewhat belated fury, remembered that Auslender had been "a constant 'embellishment' in the admiral's court entourage at all triumphal ceremonies and banquets attended by dignitaries" and had had much work printed under Kolchak.

A.I. Venediktov (1896-1970) apparently had a very similar fate: he had been in Irkutsk, and took part in a literary circle there, known as the *Poet's Barge* (*Barka Poetov*), but also spent time in the Far East of Russia: the long poem *Mary from Vladivostok* (*Meri iz Vladivostoka*) (with an epigraph by G. Maslov, who had retreated from Omsk with the White Army and died in Krasnoyarsk of typhus in March 1920) has the dates: "Vladivostok. Autumn 1918. Irkutsk. Spring 1921." Venediktov printed this poem in 1923 in the almanac *Literaturnaya Mysl'* (No. 2) and apparently read it prior to that at *Zelyonaya Lampa*.

Professor Y.G. Oksman recalled in one of his letters (2nd June 1963) that in July 1921 – shortly before his death – "Gumilyov hosted the poet A.I. Venediktov at the House of arts, who had been an officer under Kolchak, having been released from prison before that, and an active participant in literary life in Omsk in 1919. A.I. Venediktov handed Gumilyov, as the editor of the "Poetry" section of the almanac *Literat. Mysl'* (*Literary Thought*), his poem *Mary from Vladivostok*. (In the early 1920s, we all regarded it very highly!) Gumilyov liked the poem a lot, and he recommended it for publication. The manuscript of the poem, with a note of recommendation from Gumilyov, was confiscated from Gumilyov when he was arrested and returned to all his relatives along with all the others after he was shot."

The members of the *Zelyonaya Lampa* had quite a lot to reminisce about and talk about – with a cautious glance over their shoulders, but clearly with an adequate degree of openness…

In February 1922, *Novaya Russkaya Kniga* printed the following biographical information about Auslander: "... in 1918-19 he lived in Omsk. He was one of the leaders of the newspaper *Sibirskaya Rech'* (*Siberian Speech*), and took part in literary evenings and discussions. He wrote the pamphlet *Admiral Kolchak* and the novel *Visions of Life* (*Videniya Zhizni*); part of the novel was printed in the supplements of *Sibirskaya Rech'*. Prior to the surrender of Omsk to the Soviet forces, he made off on horseback – his fate thereafter is not known." Auslender, having arrived in Moscow, can hardly have been pleased to learn that this information had been published.

In short, all the members of *Zelyonaya Lampa* had something to conceal in relation to their lives in recent years.

As he moved from place to place in those years, all trace of the man was lost for a while, and even in the autumn of 1922, when Auslender was already sitting down to discuss literary matters at *Zelyonaya Lampa*, the almanac *Kameny* (*Stones*), published in Chita, was reporting that he had died "during the evacuation in Siberia, in the winter of 1919/20." This evacuation was depicted, incidentally, in a grotesque and tragic manner, embellished with a kind of dark humour, in N. Shestakov's story *The Evacuation* (*Evakuatsiya*), printed in his first collection of stories in 1926, but probably written earlier and, perhaps, read out beneath *Zelyonaya Lampa*. In his memoirs, Mozalevsky writes of some "fun tales" which were read out by Shestakov. Besides *The Evacuation*, these were probably *Stronger than Copper* (*Prochneye Medi*), published in the same collection, a unique cycle of funny stories and semi-parodic poems, united by a character invented by the author – one Polikarp Ivanovich Zaglushkin. In the foreword, the "real" author explained that his hero "had been born on 20th January 1876 in Kurmysh", and that during the revolution, "under the influence of the opium of religious prejudices, on the one hand, and as the result of shady parents, on the other, Zaglushkin had even raised up arms against the revolutionary proletariat and fled with some Czech bandits to Siberia. But there, on seeing with his own eyes all the skulduggery of the brutalized gold-diggers, the alert writer had soon realised that he didn't belong with them... In November 1919, Zaglushkin, on the orders of the military authorities, had been evacuated from Omsk to Nizhny Novgorod. But the days of Kolchak's rule were already numbered. Under the influence of events, and also due to his own convictions, the poet gradually shifted over to the platform of the Soviet government and even became a member of the party." Thus, in the biography of this made-up character, certain facts from the author's own biography were played upon and made to disappear, having been drastically altered: after this, and until the end of his days, N. Shestakov only spoke in public as the author of plays for children – as a rule, plays with a socio-political undercurrent.

Thus, almost all the members of *Zelyonaya Lampa* had behind them at least two layers of literary work. Firstly, a "pre-revolutionary" layer, one like the collection of *Fantastic Tales* (*Fantasticheskiye Rasskazy*) by V. Mozalevsky, which contained French marquises, and Cupids who suddenly struck the hearts of a sister and brother – Eolina and Makarei, and so on; or *The Heart of a Warrior* (*Serdtse Voina*) – a collection of stories by S. Auslender from 1916, containing honour suicides, and varied salon-based situations (one recalls Bulgakov's embittered lines from 1921 about the failure of one of his Vladikavkaz plays: *It's a Salon Work! A Salon Work!* [*Salonnaya! Salonnaya*]), or Slezkin's tales, which continued the old tradition of the secular story. Secondly, the layer of what was written and printed in 1919-1920 – in the south of Russia, in Siberia or somewhere else, in a short period in those years. The first layer had to be overturned, bringing to the surface new material from life – mostly accumulated during the years of the revolution and the war. Bulgakov did not have this pre-revolutionary layer: with the exception of the manuscripts which were left in his writing desk in Kiev and were partially created, perhaps, back in 1916-1917. As for the second layer, which in Bulgakov consisted of the articles and stories, still largely unknown, printed in the newspapers in the Caucasus in the late autumn of 1919 and the winter of 1919-1920, it simply had to be laid to rest. As the hero of Slezkin's tale *Phantasmagoria* (1923) puts it, "My advice is to forget the past as quickly as possible, if you wish to build a present and secure a future… *The past does not exist*."

As we saw in Shestakov's tales, these people, who had behind them a past which weighed down their first literary steps in their new situation, also chose, as a method of breaking away from this past, a tongue-in-cheek depiction of biographies similar to their own (Zaglushkin, in Sherstakov's case). For Bulgakov, by contrast with Sherstakov, his attitude to *The Extraordinary Adventures of the Doctor* was neither tongue-in-cheek nor designed to brush the past aside, but was openly empathetic. This is extremely interesting: whilst painstakingly concealing, during those first years in Moscow, his recent past, leaving out or "jumping ahead" of these years in his autobiographies ("Travelling in 1919-1920 around the North Caucasus…" he writes in one of them), Bulgakov discloses generous amounts of them in his fictional works – this past is the only thing he writes about, recreating it time and again! His inner literary strivings prove to be more powerful than any notions about sensible ways to behave.

And so, as they gathered together under *Zelyonaya Lampa* at one of the houses in Moscow, they really were taking leave – with a smile – of their past. They imagined their literary future in very different ways, however. This eventually led, among other things, to Bulgakov swiftly – in just a few years – parting ways with his literary circle from that time.

Slezkin's *The Stolovaya Mountain* was read out, it seems, in November 1922, and by 1st December 1922 a review by Y. Sobolev of the novel had appeared in the journal *Ekho* (*Echo*); the novel had not yet been printed, but it was known in manuscript form.

I used material from the novel to reconstruct certain features of Bulgakov's behaviour in Vladikavkaz in 1920; now, the novel is important to us in other respects: firstly, it helps us to understand through what eyes a man like Slezkin was looking at Bulgakov in Moscow in 1922, and secondly, we know for a fact that Bulgakov read the novel himself in the autumn of 1922, since he "recognised himself" in it (*A Theatrical Novel*).

On 5th November 1922, an excerpt from the novel had been published in *Literaturnoye Prilozheniye* (No. 25) that came with *Nakanune* from a novel that was entitled *Walking Allowed* (*Razreshayetsya Khozhdeniye*) and was entirely dedicated to its protagonist – Aleksei Vasilievich Turbin. Certain details which did not make it into the version of the novel published in Russia tied the hero to the prototype for him, apparently very directly, almost unequivocally, right down to the props of his day-to-day existence in Vladikavkaz: "Aleksei is in his room. A lamp is lit beneath a pillow-case, a manuscript lies on the table – it is a set of lectures about Russian theatre in the pre-Petrine period," "They are afraid about their diplomas as doctors, as though they are a shameful stain – to have fallen to such an extent. Just as long as there can be no blood, no fighting. Just think: three years. Three years of nothing but leapfrogging. One group is conscripted, another lot is conscripted, they cripple each other and force each other to have to patch themselves up. What kind of people are these, what kind of people!", "He walks up to the portrait of Karl Marx, takes out the manuscript of the novel from behind it, thrusts it under the table and smooths downs the crumpled pages with his thumb…" (p. 4).

Yury Slezkin was observing his new friend with fixed attention even back in Vladikavkaz; he was interested by Bulgakov's character and by the complex life situation in which he found himself, and with which he was coping using slightly different means from those used by Slezkin himself. This difference must have grown starker in Moscow. Slezkin's attitude to the proposed rules of the game was such that he could not help but be irritated by a man who had not declared his true thoughts on the existing problems, yet did not say or write anything that he did not think; doubtless he was not hastening to effect the "restructuring" to which, reflecting vociferously, all the others around him were transitioning, somehow or other. It was this difference that really irritated the soul of the author of *The Stolovaya Mountain*, and it was by this irritation that most of the pages about Aleksei Turbin were inspired: this protagonist and his situation occupy the author's thoughts more than the plot of the novel.

Slezkin supposed that Bulgakov's "manner of speaking" had been "captured" in the novel. The observation of this manner, begun in Vladikavkaz, no doubt continued during his work on the novel in Moscow.

Bulgakov's speech was never recorded (at least, no recordings of it were ever found); we know of a stenograph of only one of his performances, which probably gives us even less material than comments quoted by memoirists. The repeating turns of phrase in Slezkin's novel – "if you please", "if I'm not mistaken", "so, so", "I suppose" – capture, perhaps, not so much specific aspects of that manner, as much as its general trend. The text of the novel no doubt conceals some quotations which can no longer be recognised with any certainty from things that Bulgakov himself said, excerpts from certain oral stories that he told, significant stories from everyday life, interpreted for him verbatim, such as, for example, the story of one deserter: "Here is a man who is deprived of common sense. He saw that there was nothing he could do, threw away his weapon and went home. Simply, modestly and wisely, he made way. Do me a favour, be so kind… But he was probably too sure about the rectitude of his actions. More so than caution required. Yes, yes – slightly more, and he was sent back. That's the point."

In the autumn of 1922, Bulgakov writes an article about Slezkin's work (without mentioning his new novel). The sub-heading – *Yury Slezkin (Silhouette)* – ties it to the idea of the biographical dictionary (it was published in December in issue 12 of the journal *Spolokhi*). The article clearly reflected Bulgakov's restraint in his attitude to Slezkin's prose and his desire to analyse it as accurately as possible, outlining where he could its strengths – so as not to harm their personal relations. Thus, this "literary-critical study" (in the article's sub-heading) is not only the only example we know of a literary and analytical study by Bulgakov, but also a kind of mirror reflecting some biographical situation.

The happy fate of Slezkin the fiction writer during the first years of having his work printed, a period which began ten years before Bulgakov's literary debut (admittedly, Slezkin was 6 years his senior), the picture that his rapid success clearly painted before the author of the article, having carefully studied the reviews and, one can suppose, given Bulgakov fodder for a comparison with his own fate, later served, perhaps, even to prompt him to carry out that enumeration of "scornful" reviews which was later set out in his letter to the government (1930). "The Plague of Egypt for all Russian writers – the innumerable criticisms and reviews – has reared its head about Y. Slezkin several times, both on the pages of journals, and on the greying, now hopelessly yellowing pages of the newspapers," Bulgakov wrote in an article. "Slezkin got lucky with them. The little comments and slightly bigger reviews have some sort of shared tone and taste. And if you cast aside all that is dark, vague and curiously contradictory, with which our newspaper and journal criticism is so rich, one can say that they looked on Y. Slezkin, almost without exception, brightly and favourably. They immediately took an interest in him; many immediately took a liking to him. Starting with *The Cardboard King* (*Kartonnyy Korol'*) – the first book of novellas, the word 'talent' fleetingly appeared in the reviews, and in *Apollon* (*Apollo*), M. Kuzmin wrote of his 'undoubted gift'. Others seized up on this word. Living water was sprinkled onto the pale-green shoots of his writing. The shoot shot upwards. In 1911, *Landowner Galdin* (*Pomeshchik Galdin*) was printed in *Russkaya Mysl'*. From small novellas, from the mannered *Maya* and *The Lady* (*Gospozha*), Slezkin moved on to a fairly large canvas. On the basis of this canvas, it is convenient to study Y. Slezkin, since on it he had already manifested himself, revealed a host of features, based on which a writer can be judged." Bulgakov, who was already approaching thirty, methodically describes the story of a darling of fate: a figure so different from him, and moves on to look at Slezkin's creativity. That summer, Slezkin himself published this notice in a lengthy biographical work: "A collection of works in 10 volumes is ready for publication" (*Novaya Russkaya Kniga*, 1922, No. 6).

Bulgakov clearly derives pleasure from quoting a scene in which cavalry captain Galdin transports, in his carriage, a dead man disguised as someone who was alive:

"The horses began moving. The dead body rocked forward, falling onto Georgy Petrovich's shoulder. He pushed it away from him and adjusted his hat on his head. 'It's nothing, nothing – we'll be there soon,' the cavalry captain said, gazing forlornly at the forlorn face of his already deceased neighbour." After this short retelling, Bulgakov provides another quotation: "The dead man once again fell in his direction, nuzzled close to Galdin and, his head hanging low, kept a silent watch over the living one, as he slept.

The storm gradually faded away. From behind the clouds, the quiet moon floated out. 'How enthralling,' thinks the reader, imagining the face of the handsome Galdin sleeping in the moonlight, and the dead face with bulging eyes leaning over him."

In the choice of quotations made by the author, and in the way he cannot hold back from giving us the same picture twice over, it is clearly visible that some strictly Bulgakovan motifs have been highlighted – one recalls the future Nai-Turs, who "became significantly more cheery (…) in his coffin", and in particular – the striking image in the first draft of *The Master and Margarita*, when Ivanushka, having escaped from the psychiatric clinic, and after pushing the hearse containing Berlioz's coffin away from him, starts flogging the horses: "At a bend in the road, the carriage tilted to one side, and the deceased slipped out of the coffin. Ivanushka, forgetting that he was driving the carriage, looked on, with a wild-eyed stare, as Berlioz, with dead eyes and dressed in a black suit, jumped into the coffin rakishly, like a little boy, delighting in the effect his actions produced."

One suspects, on reading Bulgakov's article about Slezkin, that the image that made such an impression on Bulgakov when he read Slezkin's work had some influence on this scene.

In his quest to identify Slezkin's strengths, Bulgakov juxtaposes him with the literary backdrop against which he appeared, and here, perhaps, is the most pertinent part of the article: some assertions behind which one can divine Bulgakov's own literary agenda for the year 1922. "Y. Slezkin is unfailingly miserly and constricted, and on his pages one can find everything except water. And this, of course, is not only not a bad thing, but is decidedly a good thing. Slezkin sheds descriptions in miserly fashion, Slezkin does not bother with tedious pages. […] The abundant happenings do not crawl after one another, getting embroiled in a boggy mire of Russian verbosity, but run along in a well-structured line, switching places and sparkling. […] One of Slezkin's critics once said that invention is an unpleasant guest; that is not true. In the period when Slezkin came out into the arena, invention truly became a welcome guest in fiction writing. After all, it had become positively terrible how Russian writers were able to create sadness. Whatever they set about doing, everything turned into a tedious grey picket fence in their hands, behind which there lay drunken deacons and unusually stupid and melancholic men. Even in the best cases, life, in their works, resembled the well-known dream:

Snow, and on the snow there lies a splinter.

In the worst cases, it became so dusky that even the plausibility disappeared, and a kind of invention was the upshot, but one that was unquestionably dreadful.

There was a large amount of literature like that. A fantasist, on the grey background of the heavy-minded pages of Russian literature, was positively essential." The fable, and invention as traits that were essential in modern prose – this is emphasized and expressed, no doubt, as his own literary task, too, which must be embodied in his stories over the next two and a bit years (one can surmise that the plot for *The Diaboliad* (*Dyavoliada*) had already been conceived in his mind at this time; the story was finished by the summer of 1923).

The next point from Bulgakov's own literary program, as it can be perceived in the article, relates to language. "It seems there is not a single person among Y. Slezkin's critics who would not agree that the language he uses is outstanding.

As sad as this may be, this is probably the case. Y. Slezkin writes in a fine language, one that is correct, pure, almost academic, stylishly separating each and every page.

… Like rosy cheeks without a smile… The rosy cheeks of the fiction writer Y. Slezkin never smile. His outward appearance is irreproachable.

… Without grammatical mistakes… There is style in his hand, he writes like a meticulous painter. He writes until everything has been rounded off and ironed out. To anyone who knows Y. Slezkin well, it is clear that he cannot write in any other way. He would stop being Y. Slezkin by one third, if anything different, anything shaggy and impetuous, noisy and dishevelled, were to come pouring out of his pen." The whole chapter about language leaves an impression on the reader that is extremely ambiguous; one can imagine the subject of these lines himself grasping at what appeared to be an unconditionally positive trait, only to slip up on the very next sentence, losing his balance.

"Y. Slezkin's style binds itself harmoniously to the essence and content of his works. His smooth style is at times maddeningly boring (O, those rosy cheeks without a smile!), but one cannot deny it." Why? "For otherwise, one would have to deny the whole of Slezkin, too…"

This attack against a smooth style shows that Bulgakov was already fully conscious of his own particular speech-oriented style, which was so different from this sleek and rounded one. There are echoes here of the quarrels about language which took place in this group – between Bulgakov, Slezkin, Stonov, Auslender and others – quarrels founded on the difference in attitudes to language, which was later expressed in the circle's assessment of *The White Guard* at the first readings by the author and reflected in *A Theatrical Novel*.

At the end of the article, Bulgakov poses the question: "Well, and what if we were to try to uncover his intimate characteristic, that hidden and characteristic something which defines the writer altogether…?" – and an answer is revealed to us by the extent of Bulgakov's awareness of his own characteristic and defining traits: "Y. Slezkin stands to one side. He is always on the side-lines. He knows the souls of his protagonists, but never puts his soul into them. His soul is closeted away, it is always on the side. He does not teach his protagonists anything, never preaches and never shows them the way. […] It is because of this that Slezkin looks at his protagonists from the side. He writes them lightly and sweepingly, and Pan Yatskovsky comes out vividly, but Y. Slezkin does not live or breathe this Yankovsky. […] Y. Slezkin has the talent of seeing life just as it is, but he does not love it and, when he needs to write it, he colours it the way he wishes." One can't help recalling Maksudov's moral teachings here, from *A Theatrical Novel*: "One must love one's heroes…" For Bulgakov, this is both a lever for writing itself, and an ever-present hue in the protagonists he has already created.

The end of the article deals with what has already been said in connection with *The Séance* – Bulgakov's position in life in his first years in Moscow, which he expressed several times in sketches for *Nakanune*.

"What can we learn from this marquis, who is late by a whole century and finds himself in the midst of a vulgar, coarse century and its zealous advocates? Nothing that will bring any pleasure, of course. He who dreams of an exquisite life and *creates, recalling leather tomes*, always has a sadness about what has been lost in his soul.

His heroes are not warriors, nor are they the creators of that 'tomorrow' about which sober teachers speak so hotly in thick journals. They are therefore not fit for life and they always bear the shadow of death or the hallmark of impending doom."

Bulgakov himself would like to "teach" something, and although he does not try to paint the "creators of that 'tomorrow'…" either, protagonists who are not adapted for life are clearly abhorrent to him. He does not agree to see himself as doomed and, glancing back, obtains there not an awareness of being doomed, but – an unusual image for the literature surrounding him – a support for fitness for life in today's world. "I do not wish to be among the number of the dead" – these words from a letter to his mother dated 17th November 1921, are not only his personal catchphrase, but also a tuning fork for his literary intentions in those years. And although he would soon set about portraying exactly that, a dead person – the hero of *Diaboliad* – this hero was portrayed, essentially, as his opposite: a "little person", deprived of inner support. (As we shall see, incidentally, a protagonist of altogether different kind was to die in his next tale – Professor Persikov).

One way or another, Bulgakov calls on us to look into the face of a "coarse, rough century", not giving way either to dreams of "a refined life", nor to recollections about something that has been lost forever. One cannot create, whilst "recalling leather tomes" – this is a fleeting reference to his attitude to the literature of the past, which cannot be fully ascertained from this article and can only gradually be reconstructed.

It is probably fair to say that Slezkin's novel about Bulgakov and Bulgakov's article about Slezkin, in the late autumn of 1922, were at the centre of Bulgakov's literary and day-to-day interactions with the circle closest to him.

… Tatiana Nikolayevna's future husband, David Kiselgof, who had applied to join the College of defenders in the summer of 1922, once invited several friends to visit him, as well as some Moscow-based writers that he didn't know – without their wives, as Tatiana recalled, underlining the literary nature of the evening. "Davy was very fond of writers," she said. "He had a wonderful room with beautiful armchairs, he invited writers to see him and once invited Stonov, Slezkin, Bulgakov and his friend, the lawyer Vladimir Komorsky, whom Bulgakov got to know there." Komorsky recalled that Boris Zemsky had introduced them to one another. Whichever version is true, Bulgakov began eagerly spending time at Komorsky's home at Apartment 12, No. 12 Maly Kozikhinsky Side-street – not far at all from his own house on B. Sadovaya.

In 1922, Bulgakov often took refuge in this lawyerly environment, which had retained a sense of affluence and sustainable forms of existence, when he was worn down by life at flat No. 50 and by the daily pursuit of money. This fact is recorded with good taste in some of his articles from those years: "'Step this way then, gentlemen, if you please,' said the host genially, indicating the table with a sweeping gesture.

We didn't wait to be asked twice, took our places and unfolded the starched napkins, which were standing on end.

There were four of us around the table: the host – a former attorney at law, his cousin – also a former attorney at law…" (*Four Portraits* [*Chetyre Portreta*]).

He eagerly began courting the lady of the house, and Komorsky later described this to Tatiana Nikolayevna in comic fashion: Bulgakov would arrange a rendez-vous with Zinaida Vasilievna, Komorsky would help her into her felt boots and see her off; they would wander around, then Zinaida would get cold, and she would say to Bulgakov: "Let's go and have tea at our place!" They walked up the stairs, Komorsky was coming the other way, and Bulgakov explained: "Zinaida Vasilievna and I just bumped into one another by chance, you know…" This half-secret, half-obvious flirtation was, for Bulgakov, part of what he found attractive about the atmosphere at the house. According to T.N., he didn't introduce her to the Komorskys for some time; whenever he fixed rendez-vous with Zinaida, he would warn her: "Bear in mind that if you should meet me in the street with a lady, I shall pretend I don't know you!"

"He usually came to see us on his own," Komorsky recounts, "and brought two bottles of dry wine… Cutlets were prepared for him; Bulgakov liked the food at our place." This circle of residents of Kozikhinsky, Trekhprudny and other nearby side-streets recognised both Zinaida and the Komorskys' apartment in a satirical piece entitled "On the good life" (from the cycle "Moscow in the '20s): "How about this, for example?" the author asked, talking about the excruciating feeling of seeing 'the uneven distribution of apartment benefits'. "After all, Zina had set things up for herself quite miraculously. Somehow, in the dense heart of Moscow, she had not so much a little flat, as a three-room candy-box. Complete with bath, telephone and husband. Manyushka, the maid, cooked the cutlets on a gas oven, and Manyushka has a separate little room of her own, too. I pressed Zina, holding a knife to her throat, demanding an explanation as to how they had managed to secure these three rooms?

After all, it is supernatural!!

Four rooms – and three people. And no random strangers at all.

And Zina said that one day, a man had arrived in a truck and brought a slip of paper that said: 'sling your hook'.

And she had taken it and…not slung her hook.

Ah, Zina, Zina! Were you not already married, I would have married you. I would have married you, as sure as God is holy, and I would have married you for the little telephone and the screws on the gas oven, and wild horses wouldn't have been able to drag me out of that apartment. Zina, you are an eagle, not a woman!"

It was the kind of literary periphrasis of domestic situations that was so typical of Bulgakov.

The owner of this home that was so open to writers, loved literature and loved the arguments which broke out around his table; he was fairly good-humoured, benevolent and patient, but he was at times perturbed by his guests' modern way of speaking. "Slezkin once said: 'I can even drink with the devil!'" Tatiana Nikolayevna recalls. "Komorsky was very disappointed..." At his table, she recalled, there were lots of arguments, it was noisy. "We were once discussing Lidin's tales, and Stonov shouted out: 'There's no smell, no smell!' And of Pilnyak, he always used to say: 'There's a smell, a smell!' He always came together with Slezkin: 'the old man' – *he* called Bulgakov that..."

This whole atmosphere, both at the "evenings at Kozikh" (Bulgakov would later write those words to Komorsky in his first collection – "in memory of the evenings at Kozikh"), and at the *Zelyonaya Lampa* – circles where Stonov and Slezkin played the main roles – is echoed fifteen years later in scenes from *A Theatrical Novel*, in which a discussion of Maksudov is taking place during a noisy dinner: " 'Language!' one of the writers was shouting (the one who had turned out to be a bastard), 'language, above all! The language never looks good enough... A metaphor is not some dog, please take note of that! Things are bare without it! Bare! Bare! Remember that, old man!

The words 'old man' clearly related to me. I felt a cold shiver run down my spine." (As Bulgakov writes elsewhere: "Ever since my childhood, I have been unable to tolerate familiarity, and ever since my childhood I have been forced to suffer from it.")

1922, the first 'full' year of Bulgakov's Moscow life, was coming to an end. For him, December was marked by some small yet nonetheless significant literary events. The newspaper *Nakanune* and its *Literaturnoye Prilozheniye* printed several of his writings in a row: on 10th December – *On the Night of the 3rd* (from the novel *The Scarlet Stroke (Aly Makh)*, on 21st – *The Capital in a Notepad (Stolitsa v Bloknote*, chapters 1 and 2), and on 31st – the story *The Cup of Life (Chasha Zhizni)*. On 29 December, the newspaper's editor-in-chief, E. Krichevskaya, wrote to him: "P. Sadyker came to see me and said that he had seen you and Katayev and reached an agreement with you about a permanent job, securing a regular income for you. I could only welcome such a decision.

What are you writing. How have you arranged things with your *Notes*. I spoke to Sadyker about them and advised him to take them to Berlin for publication, if you have not yet made arrangements. I await a letter from you."

December also saw his story *No. 13 – The Elpit-Workers' Commune* (1922, No. 2) published in the *Krasny Zhurnal Dlya Vsekh (Red Journal for All)*, whilst the journal *Rossiya*, in its 4th booklet, declared that Bulgakov was one of its authors, for the first time.

Thus, the results of the year from a publishing perspective were the strong ties that Bulgakov had established with the newspaper *Nakanune*, which promised a regular income, albeit a modest one, and also the relations that he had started to form with the journal *Rossiya*.

No documents have yet been found that shine any light on the story of how Bulgakov met the editor of the journal, Isai Lezhnev, and of how the second part of *Cuff-notes* was printed. All we can do is turn to the literary reflection of this fact: the manuscript for *To a Secret Friend (Taynomu Drugu)*, created seven years later, in 1929:

"You see: in the Moscow of the pre-historical times (the years 1921-1925), there lived one remarkable man. There were as many freckles on him as there were stars in the sky (on his face and his arms), and he was known for his great intelligence. His profession was as follows: he was an editor of pure blood and divine mercy and he contrived to publish (in the years 1922-1925!!) a thick, private journal! The most monstrous thing of all was that he had not a single kopeck to his name. But he had an indescribable iron will, and, working out of an agreeable, dirty apartment on the outskirts of Moscow, he published things.

As you will see later, this publishing led both him, and a host of other individuals, whose inexorable destiny set them on a collision course with this newspaper, to some remarkable consequences.

When a man has no money, and meanwhile his painful imagination is as hungry as ever, he has to flee somewhere. Sure enough, my editor fled to a certain person.

And he spoke to him.

And the upshot was that the other man took the publishing house under his control. Some paper appeared from somewhere, and some books, at first slim ones, then big thick ones too, and they started being published. [...]

And meanwhile some frosts set in. The whole of Moscow had turned pale, and one evening, wearing my cloth coat, I arrived at *Sochelnik* (*Eve*) and saw Rudolph there. Rudolph was sitting in a diaconal fur coat, with wet eyelashes. We got talking.

'Aren't you writing anything?' Rudolph asked.

I told him about the piece I had written. Everyone knew that Rudolph loved to print only those people who had already made a name for themselves, he was very clever in the way he ran his journal (it was still a slim one in those days).

With a condescending smile, Rudolph said to me:

'Show it to me, why don't you.'

I immediately took out the manuscript from my pocket (I even slept with it). Rudolph, after reading all four sheets then and there, in his fur coat, said:

'Do you know what? I shall publish an excerpt from it.'

I tried everything I could think of not to reveal the delight I felt to Rudolph, but, of course, I couldn't help but do so. To have something printed by Rudolph was very nice for me – me, a man dressed in a cloth coat in winter. [...] I remember he paid me something for the excerpt, and I saw it put in print very soon afterwards. That gave me enormous pleasure. And I derived just as much pleasure from the fact that I was included on the cover, in the list of contributors to the journal" (this was in the journal's 4th booklet, for December).

... On the eve of the New Year, 1923, Valentin Katayev came round and invited Bulgakov to see in the new year together. Tatiana recalls that Bulgakov said that he had been invited to the Komorskys. Katayev turned to Tatiana and said: "Well if he's been invited – why don't you join us and our group!" "... Mikhail didn't like that, either: 'What foolishness, you going round there!' But at that point, Zinaida Komorskaya sent a special message saying that he must bring his wife at New Year's... it was Tatiana's first visit to Kozikhinsky. I went in my solitary black dress – made of crepe de Chine, with panne velvet: I had fashioned it out of an even older summer dress and skirt. Davy Kiselgof was there, with his wife. Davy and Volodya started making overtures to me, and Mikhail didn't like that. We laughed a great deal, Davy grabbed me by the ankle at one point. And when we were walking home, Mikhail kept reprimanding me: 'You don't know how to behave...' Only he was allowed to behave however he liked, whereas I was supposed to behave quietly..." Trifles, insignificant details. These are tiny dashes at best, with the breadth of a hair, and had almost been wiped away altogether by the half-century that divided my conversations with Tatiana from those years.

At this point, things have the same level of significance that he himself attributed to the corporality of everyday life; which makes one all the more convinced of the need for small details in order to build his biography. Bulgakov's words in a letter to his mother about his obsessive efforts "to restore the norm in three years: an apartment, clothes and books" – compel us to pay close attention to each of the components of this norm that he identifies.

It is not a matter of indifference, to the biographer, how he was dressed in his first year in Moscow and how his wardrobe later changed – this is of interest, not least because, when reproducing his conversation with Rudolph, it is not for nothing that the author informs his reader, within the short space of the episode, that he was wearing "a cloth coat", that Rudolph was dressed "in a diaconal fur coat" and, finally, emphasizes that Rudolph had agreed to publish him – "a man dressed in a cloth coat in winter!"

At any rate, all the descriptions of his first winter in Moscow include a cold coat, unsuitable for winter, which was either a re-stitched version of the overcoat or had replaced it (this may have been done to avoid unwanted questions). On 17th November 1921, he writes to his mother: "We are both rushing around Moscow in our little coats. I therefore walk with a sort of sideways gait (the left side seems to be particularly draughty)."

The autumn and winter of 1921 appear to have been described with a pretty strong degree of closeness to biographical reality in the sketch *Forty Forties*, in which Moscow appears to the hero "for the first time – in the tearful autumn mist, and on subsequent days – in a burning frost. White days and a cloth coat. Oh, that damn sack-cloth! I can't describe how cold I got. I froze and ran around. I ran around and froze." And then another reference: "…in that hessian sack-cloth".

N.L. Gladyrevsky, already gravely ill, told this author on 19th December 1969: "Misha used to get very cold, and I gave him my Romanov-style semi-fur coat. 'They don't let me go into the editorial offices in it,' – that's what he used to say to me, instead of any words of gratitude… But in exchange for that, he gave me the coat he had arrived in, a black one – like the one the German prisoners of war used to wear. I got hold of that half-coat in 1915: a comrade and I – we were in hospital at the time, with the Red Cross – we went to the Officer's economic society and bought ourselves some semi-fur coats… A comrade of mine then sent them to Moscow, and I gave it to Misha, and he gave me a coat that had been damaged by the wind. You know, when I wore that coat in winter, I had the impression I wasn't wearing a coat at all."

Yet here is description of an altogether different garment, left by a witness of Bulgakov's life in those first few years in Moscow – in *Gudok* (*The Hooter*): "Bulgakov works in the room next door, but for some reason always puts his sheepskin coat on our coat-stand each morning. *It is a sheepskin like no other: it has no buttons and no belt.* You shove your arms into its sleeves and can consider yourself dressed.

Mikhail Afanasievich himself gives the following account of the sheepskin:

'It is a Russian *okhaben* cloak. They were in fashion in the late 17th century. It is first mentioned in the chronicles in the year 1377. Nowadays, in Meyerhold's work, pensive boyars fall from second-floor windows wearing such coats." (I. Ovchinnikov).

Tatiana couldn't remember the Romanov-style semi-fur coat but had a clear memory of the *okhaben* – "It was a fur-coat shaped like a rotunda, of the kind that old priests might wear. It was made of racoon fur, and the collar was folded down with fur on the outside, like the way priests wear them. It was long and had no buttons – that's right, and it started to smell and had to go. It was probably his father's coat. Perhaps his mother had sent it to him from Kiev with someone, or perhaps he'd brought it himself in 1923..."

Many people recalled this coat, each of them describing it in their own special way. V. Katayev writes that Bulgakov once turned up at the editorial offices of *Nakanune* wearing the fur coat over his pyjamas – and then notes that Bulgakov himself vehemently denied this episode ever took place; Tatiana denied the episode could even have been possible. It bears the hallmarks of a legend about a provincial sort who was out of place in the life of the capital.

In a photograph published in *Rupor*, Bulgakov is wearing a blouse with a turn-down collar – a smock.

"He was dressed, of course, horridly, with that ghastly little military hat, with no insignia, of course, and that *pokhaben* (*sic*). Back in Vladikavkaz, he had had a smock sewn for him made of coarse linen fabric – with built-in pockets and a belt. At home, he had some pyjamas – Kostya had given him some foreign ones – his parents often sent parcels to him from Japan. The pyjamas were brown, with a medium-sized check pattern, blue and red I think – like Scottish kilts often are. And he always walked around in those pyjamas at home, and then one man he knew – Leonid Sayansky – even drew a caricature of him on the pyjamas..." Memoirists later ascribed a special significance to these pyjamas. "Blue-eyes had a proper writing desk, as any proper Russian writer ought to, piled high with manuscripts, newspapers, newspaper cuttings and books with bits of paper sticking out of them.

Blue-eyes was to a small extent playing the role of a famous Russian writer, even, perhaps, a classic author, and went around in striped, baize pyjamas at home, fastened at the back with a rubber band, which did not conceal his handsome figure, and, of course, in well-worn open-toed slippers.

There were various curios from the colour journals stuck on the wall above the desk, reviews full of furious criticism, and also the frontispiece of the newspaper *Nakanune* with some of the letters replaced, so that it wasn't "Nakanune" but "Nunenaka" (V. Katayev, *My Diamond Wreath* [*Almaznyy Moy Venets*]).

What was the furniture like in the room at the time the Bulgakovs moved in, and in the subsequent eighteen months?

"There was already some furniture in the room: two small wardrobes, a hazel writing desk, a divan, a large mirror... There was even some crockery – there was a white soup-bowl. We used to eat on the white kitchen cupboard, initially. Then one day I was walking around Moscow and I heard someone say: 'Tasenka, hi!' It was the wife of the treasurer from Saratov. She invited me round to her place: 'Let's go – I've got your parents' furniture there, after all.' It turned out that she brought some furniture from Saratov, including my parents' desk. It was an oval-shaped, hazel desk with curved legs [the desk stood in T.N.'s apartment whilst she was still alive, but it had been somewhat defaced by a neighbor, who had sawn off two of its legs in a fit of rage – M.C.]. Mikhail and I went round there, he liked the desk a lot, and we took it back with us and also took our collected works of Danilevsky, in a nice binding... The desk had belonged to my paternal grandmother, and she had got it from one of her ancestors... Then we bought a long bookshelf – the bookends were two sphynxes – and hung it over the writing desk."

On 30th December, 1922, Bulgakov went to a meeting of *Nikitinskiye subbotniki* – to read his *Cuff-notes*. No more than about twenty-five people had assembled to listen to him – the usual members of the circle: V. Veresayev, V. Dynnik, V. Zayagintseva, K. Lipskerov; among the writers of fiction who had already made a name for themselves, Andrei Sobol, M.Y. Kozyrev and A.Y. Yakovlev were there; the venerable Vasily Cheshikhin-Vetrinsky was also there, the author of some famous sketches about Russian writers and critics – the 40th anniversary of the start of his literary activity had been celebrated by the group at the previous meeting, on 23rd December, at which it had been announced that Bulgakov would be in the program for the next meeting. Ivan Rozanov, a permanent member of the *Nikitinskiye subbotniki*, was there too. A sheet for signatures was passed around, and Bulgakov signed his name on it in large letters, larger than all the others. "Mikhail Afanasievich indicates in his introductory word," read the minutes, "that in these notes, which consist of 3 parts, there is a portrayal of the life of a poet somewhere in the south, laid bare. The writer arrived in Moscow with the fixed intention of making a literary career for himself. Mikhail Afanasievich reads out chapters from the 3rd part of the book." From this brief record it becomes clear that this reading of *Cuff-notes* began at the end. It was only continued the following year. We do not know whether this continuation was planned in advance, or whether the audience requested it; at any rate, there was no discussion of *Cuff-notes* at all on this occasion – after it, Ilya Selvinsky started reading his long poem *Lynx* (*Rys'*), and it was this work that the audience discussed. In the diary of one of those present at the meeting, in a brief entry about the meeting, Bulgakov's name is misspelt: "30th Dec. Nikit. Saturday. Readings from *Cuff-notes* by Mik. Yak. Bulgakov, *Lynx* – a long poem by Selvinsky…" Although this error is understandable – the person who made it was probably thinking of a name that had long been known to all the group's members, that of the "Saturdays" secretary, Mikhail Yakovlevich Kozyrev – it is nonetheless telling: Bulgakov was not yet known in Moscow.

2

It was now January 1923 and Bulgakov was in the middle of his second winter in Moscow. He was having difficulty adjusting to the northern climate; he would later recall his first impressions here in his sketch *Moscow in the '20s*, writing: "There was an absolutely incredible cold-snap, of the kind that one never even sees."

How did the Moscow of that time look to a man from Kiev, albeit one who had left Kiev several years ago? Not how it looked to a native Muscovite, at any rate. To get a sense of Bulgakov's early impressions of the city, let us look at the capital through the eyes of a certain woman from Kiev. She arrived in Moscow on 1st December 1922 – from the same station that Bulgakov had come from one year earlier. "I took a carriage from the station," she told this author over sixty years later, in December 1986, "down some narrow little street, between the banks of snow. The low buildings were drowning in snow. I asked the coachman: 'Will we be in Moscow soon?' He turned around and said angrily: 'You wanted a different Moscow, did you? We're riding down the Arbat!' And I had thought we were in some village!"

After the imposing four and five-storey buildings on the spacious streets of Kiev, the appearance of the little streets and side-streets of Moscow, piled high with snow, with their low-rise houses, was not that of a city, of a capital. A city under a mountain of snow, bad clothes, cold snaps, and memories of the other city, where 'in winter, the snow is not cold, not brutal, but big and affectionate…"

… In one of those Moscow side-streets, people were thinking about Bulgakov during those first few days of the New Year. At the latest meeting of *Nikitinskiye subbotniki*, celebrating Christmas Eve, a playful list of those who were absent was drawn up, including "Lidin – the foreigner", "Bulgakov, the man without cuffs". Lidin, a short time before this, on 2nd December, had read a report at one of the meetings called "Foreign impressions". He spent much time travelling to Europe, to organise his publishing affairs. "… At present, he is printing two volumes of stories at the Berlin publishers, *Little Flames* …", *Novaya Russkaya Kniga* announced in September 1922, reporting on Lidin's arrival in Berlin, "and he has a book coming out with *Helikon*... his latest story is being translated into English for a publisher in New York." Bulgakov's literary life was proving far more difficult to fashion.

On 7th January, there was a procession through the streets of Moscow, marking an innovation: the "Komsomol Christmas". Placards were carried; one of them depicted a woman with a happy new-born baby and a caricatured priest. The sign read, in big white letters: "Prior to 1922, Mary gave birth to Jesus, but in 1923 she gave birth to a Komsomol member". They walked along wearing disguises; Komsomol members in long caps carried five-point stars on poles, depicting the Magi learning of the birth of Christ. Bulgakov had never before seen anti-religious actions in such shocking and large-scale forms.

On 14th January, the first day of the new year under the old calendar, around forty people gathered for the latest Nikitinskiy Saturday meeting. The literary historian N.K. Gudzy was there, with the folklore expert Yury Sokolov; the writers Sobol, Lidin and Savich were there. The poet and translator K. Lipskerov was there, as was I. Selvinsky. P. Antokolsky came along, perhaps to listen to Andrei Globa, with whose reading of his three-act drama, *Hugo's Wedding* (*Svad'ba Khiuga*), the meeting began. (Many years later, in 1936, his literary path was to cross Bulgakov's again – on a Pushkin-related matter. Antokolsky was soon to play a role in the fate of Bulgakov's first plays).

On the agenda for this literary meeting and tea-drinking session (the members always sat around a table where they were served tea and sandwiches, which was not an insignificant factor in attracting admirers of contemporary literature in that time...), the second point was: "Mikhail Bulgakov. *Cuff-notes. Part I and II*. And immediately after this, another entry: "There were no discussions on what was read out, due to the 2nd section: 1) The Christmas tree, 2) Improvisation, in which the following are to take part..." – and then there were several names and "a number who wished to remain nameless". Might not Mikhail Bulgakov, the man who signed his name first on the list of those present – and did so not in pen, like the others, but the way he loved to do so, with a coloured pencil (red on this occasion)?

On the sheet that everyone signed, his signature – just as at the first reading – looks rather demonstrative. He was announcing himself to literary Moscow, where he was not yet very well known.

There were some Kievans at the Saturday meeting who had only arrived fairly recently in Moscow, incidentally: not just Gudzy, but also Valentina Dynnik, famous in those days as a translator of poetry; she had graduated from Kiev university in 1920. There is a short entry about the evening in Rozanov's diary: "Globa's play. Bulgakov's *Cuff-notes*. Konst. Mik. Stakhovsky. Gifts and jokes. Poems about Gudzy's trip to Kiev (*chercher la femme*: Gudzy is courting Lado Rustaveli) and about Yury Sokolov and Dynnik…"

On 14th January, an editor at the newspaper *Trud* (*Labour*), Avgust Yavich, offers Bulgakov (in a letter) a "sketch on daily life, 3 times a week", for the page on "Production, Domestic Life and Labour". In the same month, edition No. 5 of *Rossiya* printed the second part of *Cuff-notes*.

The events of his Moscow life which had begun the previous summer and given him little cause for optimism, meanwhile, came to their conclusion. "*Zadruga* is closing down once and for all," N.M. Mendelson writes in his diary on 9th January 1923. "The shop is already known as *Sredi Knig* (*Among Books*)." The same subject crops up in Rozanov's diary: on 25th January, he writes that the shop *Zadruga* has "been closed down once and for all" and says that it "may be confiscated". On 5th February: "In place of the shop *Zadruga* and *Sredi Knig*, *Kolos* has opened, but without a sign."

"Yesterday morning, on Tverskaya, I saw a boy," he wrote in a mock-triumphal tone, at the start of the next chapter of the satirical piece *The Capital in a Notepad*, which was being printed in instalments by *Nakanune*. Passengers from tram No. 6, which was coming towards me, were hanging out of the tram and pointing their fingers at the boy. It was only after I had wiped my eyes that I realised what was going on.

The boy did not have a tray around his neck filled with butterscotch, and the boy was not shouting out in a wild voice:

Ambassadors cigarettes! *Java*!! *Mursal*!!! Get your paper – crowdmangledbycar!

The boy was not pulling candies out of another boy's mouth and stamping on them. The boy did not have a thin cigar between his lips. The boy was not indulging in foul language. […] No, citizens, this solitary boy, whom I was encountering for the very first time, was walking along, swaying moderately and moving unhurriedly, wearing a delightful, comfortable hat with ear-flaps, and etched into his face were all the virtues that one could possibly hope to see in a boy of 11 or 12 years of age." The triumphal tone of the piece becomes more and more exaggerated. "No, this was no boy. This was a cherub, plain and simple, in warm gloves and felt boots. And on the cherub's back was a w-o-u-n-d, poking out of which was the corner of a dirty math exercise book.

The boy was walking to a school of the 1st rank to s-t-u-d-y. That's all. End of story."

These words, which brought the piece to an end, took on a special weight when written with the pen of the man who, just over three years ago, in his first article, amid the smoking ruins of his homeland, had written with the most acute bitterness about how over the coming years, there, in Europe, "they are going to be building, teaching, publishing, learning… And we… we are going to be fighting…" There now glimmered within him the hope, it seems, that he would one day see the rebirth of the country. "From out of the chaos, order is gradually being born," he wrote, striving to reassure his foreign reader and, probably, himself. After putting these words at the start of chapter 8 – "The cost one pays for smoking", printed on 1st March 1923 and singing the praises of the fines imposed for the cigarette-ends tossed onto the floor of the train, or for smoking at the theatre, he ecstatically tells of how, over the shoulder of the person being fined, "the policeman appeared out of thin air". And finally, he rises up to the heights of comic, but by no means mocking or sarcastic inspiration: "the guardian-angel, who, instead of wings, had a small, graceful rifle slung over his shoulders."

In September 1922, the author of the sketch *Chichikov's Shenanigans* (*Pokhozhdeniya Chichikova*) dreams, in a powerless fury, of putting an end to his Gogolesque protagonists – Petrushka, Selifan, the hoarder Proshka and Neuvazhai-Koryto – who had been given new positions in the new Russia, for the performance of which they were not in the least bit ready.

At the start of 1923, he is hoping for something better.

"And the stormy, bloody rains came. Great tremblings occurred, the whole earth was shaken. Those who managed to keep their red cap-bands, having managed to slip away from under the head of the axe to attic rooms and lofts overseas, sat gazing at the sky, lit by the shimmer of bloody sheet lightning, and, shaken, whispered to one another:

'My goodness, how they set it all alight, those grey-pawed devils.'

And, like cowards, they thought:

'Let's hope they don't come over here.'

It is worth remembering that in this, the first of Bulgakov's sketches about Moscow (*The Muse of Vengeance*, October 1921), the author is clearly striving to rise to the surface of literary life. As he tries to measure himself up, to adjust himself to the conditions of the capital's publishing industry, with which he is not yet familiar, he uses generous amounts of retouching. For all that, the very presence of those foreign 'penthouses' with their 'cowardly' inhabitants is not a matter of indifference when it comes to understanding his future work.

The sketches in *Nakanune* were, first of all, not artistic in the pure sense, but rather journalism, and secondly, they were directly aimed at Russian readers abroad. Let us listen carefully to the words with which he starts one of the chapters of *The Capital in a Notepad*: 'The Friedrichstrasse-ian belief that Russia is finished is not one that I share, and I would go further: as I observe the kaleidoscope of Moscow, the presentiment forms within me that "everything is taking shape", and we can still live a fairly wonderful life.' For all the apparent simplicity of these comments, there is a far from straightforward undercurrent behind them. Here, it is fitting to turn once again to the account by Stepun, who analysed the precise moment of the birth of this new intellectual self-consciousness, as it divided into two and three, and which transformed into something different a few years later. 'At the very high point of Denikin's advance, when rumours were going round Moscow to the effect that Ryazan and Kashir had already been taken, my wife and I were once at the house of an officer from the old regime. It was warm and cosy in the beautiful, requisitioned apartment. The table was embellished with an enormous pie, cognac and liqueurs.' There were a handful of red military specialists among the guests. That was my first and only meeting with the revamped Russian officer class. The impression of them that stayed with me, in spite of the idyllic name-day setting, was extremely unpleasant.

All the generals had the red lining of their jackets, a sign of their rank, showing, but the linings were padded with a mourning band. They could all sense this 'blackish-red' colour in one another, but, in spite of the old friendship that united all of them, they nonetheless hid it from one another. [...] The talk, of course, was of Denikin and his invasion. One of those present had developed a real smart-aleck theory about how it was possible that Mamontov might seize Moscow, on the basis that he was both a Cossack and a regular cavalry officer at one and the same time. [...]" They talked about his invasion, "as if they were talking about the war between the British and the Boers." Outwardly, the red 'specialists' were listening and raising objections in that kind of objective-strategic style, but in their eyes, and behind their eyes, some strange, fiery and feverish questions were running, in which everything chimed with and winked at everything else: fierce hatred of the Bolsheviks, with an intense jealousy of the volunteers who attacked, because of their successes; a desire to see their own officer group, which had remained in Russia, achieve victory over Denikin's officers, with a clear disgust at the thought that the victory of their group would also be a victory for a Red Army that was far from being theirs; fear of the denouement, with a firm belief that nothing was going to happen, that when all was said and done, the people attacking were *our lot*.

In all the conversations that evening, everything was constantly doubled up, ambiguously: everyone looked at both parts penetratingly, everyone heated up one another with a swivel-eyed stare, faces eddied and swirled like disguises, and the disguises floated away into "nothingness".

The atmosphere was horrid and ghostly, provocative, provocateur-like."

In 1923, there is no longer any talk of an attack by *our* group, but the idea of one's own victory, for the group remaining in Russia, was undoubtedly present in Bulgakov's consciousness.

On 13th January 1923, in the second edition of *Literaturnyy Yezhenedel'nik* (*Literary Weekly*), there was a story saying that "the publishing house *Novaya Moskva* (*New Moscow*) was preparing to print the literary-artistic collections *Nedra* (*The Depths*), edited by N.S. Angarsky," that "it was proposed that they would be published every 2-3 months" and that the first collection would go out of print in January of the following year." The experienced and energetic editor dealt with the task of organising this new matter far sooner in fact, and this had a direct effect on Bulgakov's literary fate.

L.L. Fialkova has convincingly made the case that Bulgakov must have paid attention to S. M. Chevkin's play *Yeshua Ha-Notsri. An Impartial Revelation of the Truth* (*Iyeshua Ganotsri. Bespristrastnoye Otkrytiye Istiny*), which came out in 1922; his attention may have been drawn to the play by a scathing review by Sergei Gorodetsky in *Krasnaya Niva* ([*The Red Cornfield*], 1923, No. 12): "Clearly attracted by the personality of Christ, the author turns his life into the story of a neurotic doctor, rather than a stage in the struggle of the slaves against the masters...Admittedly, the miracles from the Gospel are debunked in the play, but this is too modest a contribution by comparison with the modern tasks of revolutionary propaganda... The author must rewrite the play and make the masses the main character."

We will only add that, that same spring, Bulgakov may have come across the name of Chevkin's play in a "List of books and journals received by the editors for reviews" printed by the journal *Pechat' i Revolyutsiya*; he may also have noticed a review of the play in *Byulleten' Knigi* ([*Bulletin of the Book*], 1922, No. 7-8).

Be that as it may, phrases used by the reviewer from *Krasnaya Niva* are almost transposed – many years later – in a novel for the plot of which Bulgakov drew generously on literary and societal life in Moscow in 1923: "Bezdomny had drawn the chief figure in his poem, Jesus, in very black colours, yet in the editor's opinion, the whole poem had to be written again."

Bulgakov must have been more and more exercised by the kind of writer whom Zamyatin would soon characterise with one splenetic epithet: "In my (heretic) point of view, a stubborn enemy who refuses to surrender is far more deserving of respect than a man who turns into a Communist all of a sudden – a man like Sergei Gorodetsky, let's say."

The borders between Russia and foreign lands in the literary process taking place at the time were flexible, just as they had been before. On 6th January 1923, a new Petrograd journal appeared, *Literaturnyy Yezhenedel'nik*, one of the articles in which stated: "It is typical – even the foreign 'landmark-ness' has so far been poured into the mould of journalism alone, leaving in literature only the faint light of the works of A. Vetlugin, I. Ehrenburg and others, of rather dubious artistic value."

On 20th January, it was announced in the *Literaturnoye Prilozheniye* to *Nakanune* that 13 writers were "writing a collective novel. 12 chapters have been written. There is a portrayal of the Soviet forces with the haidamaks, the whites' retreat and so on." The following writers were named: "N. Ashukin, M. Bulgakov, Efim Zozulya, M. Kozyrev, V. Lidin, K. Levin, Boris Pilnyak, A. Sobol, Y. Sobolev, Yury Slezkin, D. Stonov, A. Yakovlev and A. Ephros." The two-weekly *Korabl'* (*Ship*) journal was published in Kaluga in January, with a report saying: "Mikhail Bulgakov has written the book *Cuff-notes* (about the revolution, life, a writer's fate and more). Excerpts from this book have been printed in the *Literaturnoye Prilozheniye* to *Nakanune*.

There is also the following story in the journal: *Collective Novel: The Circle of Thirteen* (*Kollektivnyy Roman: 'Kruzhok Trinadtsati'*) – this is the name of the collective of writers in Moscow who are currently engaged in working on a collective novel, the duty of which is to portray the revolutionary era; the same authors were listed; "To date, thirteen chapters have been written, but the novel is still far from finished." And the following notice appears entitled *The Government Inspector* in the same edition: "A group of fiction writers have launched a petition to secure approval for the satirical journal *Revizor* (*The Government Inspector*). According to the project, the journal will not have anything in common with the humorous publications and tabloids sold on the streets. The journal will be edited by M. Bulgakov."

Yury Sobolev wrote a long piece about the proposed novel for the journal *Echo* (No. 6, dated 1st February, 1923), saying: "The 13 are writing tirelessly. Six of them got through a drawing of lots… The novel is dynamic, the mystery in it is engaging, modernity and the revolution are reflected in it vividly and deeply. The main protagonists have already taken shape, and the action has already moved from Ukraine to Moscow. Images of the civil war in the south have already been dealt with, and now the Moscow of 1920 is rising up before us…"

Might not the chapter from the novel *The Scarlet Stroke*, when it was printed in December 1922, have been intended by the author as a small part of the tale which had already altered its contours? And for that reason, did he not perhaps surrender it, indeed, to the shared booking office of a collective plot…?

The title, *The Scarlet Stroke*, may have been a provisional one. It may also have been the title of a 'collective novel' that Bulgakov suggested to his fellow writers. However that may be, the name does not refer to the movement of scarlet banners, but, apparently, to the movement of the red cavalry.

This short word, conveying motion, would become the prototype for the future title of a play about the same period: *Flight* (*Beg*).

The attention of all of Moscow's fiction writers of a certain ilk (those, let us say, who were far from being preoccupied by the prose encouraged by "Proletkult" – the organisation "Proletarian Culture") was focused, that year, on Ukraine in the time of the civil war as pretty much its main subject. Many of them had personal impressions common to the others (often hidden in their autobiographies), and they processed their material in a similar way – and in this sense, their works really can be likened to a "collective novel".

Y. Slezkin wrote his tale *Phantasmagoria* about the same place and time, clearly striving to overtake Bulgakov, who had already printed, in December 1922, the chapter about doctor Bakaleinikov from his novel about "the haidamaks" (as this subject was described in the jargon of the writers of the day).

In 1923, when Bulgakov replaced the name of Bakaleinikov with his preferred name for his hero (one recalls the words from his letter to K. Bulgakov in February 1921 about "a drama about Alyosha Turbin"), it may have been partly out of spite against Slezkin. The latter, as we saw, had already used this name, "his" name, in the autumn of 1922, in his novel *The Stolovaya Mountain* – giving his protagonist some of Bulgakov's own traits, seen from a certain angle. This may have come as a surprise to Bulgakov; it certainly annoyed him. Bulgakov now wanted to exact revenge, perhaps, by showing the "real" Alexei Vasilievich Turbin.

The material that had been written and printed on this subject must have both sharpened Bulgakov's memories of what he had lived through, and lit his literary and polemical fuse.

In the novel about the civil war in Ukraine that he had begun in 1923, the surnames of the heroes were not made up, but real, time-honoured Kievan names or military names. Besides V.G. Talberg, whom we have already mentioned, one can cite Nikolai Germanovich Talberg (his brother, apparently), who was descended from nobles from the Kiev governorate, and who lived in Kiev from 1886 until his death (in 1910) and had his work published in newspapers in Kiev. Zakhary Myshlayevsky, who had graduated from the Kiev spiritual seminary in the first half of the 19th century, appeared on the "List of civil servants and teachers from the Kiev military district" in 1859 (Kiev, 1859, p. 237). The historian A. Petrovsky told this author on 9th October 1980, in Kiev: "This is a military name. There was an aide to the Chief of Staff of the Caucasian military district, in Tbilisi – Alexander Zakharovich Myshlayevsky; he had a son… Among all the military ranks listed, there is one man with that name." There was indeed an A.Z. Myshlayevsky, at any rate, who was chief of the General Staff in the 1900s, a military historian and theoretician. Petrovsky went on: "When *The Days of the Turbins* was performed here in Kiev, I spoke to Pavel Pototsky about the play, and I asked him: 'What do you think, why did Bulgakov give his hero that name – 'Turbin'?'

And he said:

'It's very easy to see why. There was a commander of the Imperial Guard in the Volynsk regiment, Major-General Alexander Fyodorovich Turbin – I think he came to Kiev before the First World War and gave lectures at the headquarters of the Kiev Military District. And Bulgakov used his surname.'" (A.F. Turbin, born in 1858, wrote several works about the art of warfare, and died in the years after the revolution).

Thus, the surname of the main protagonist of the novel and the play, chosen at a very early stage (one recalls a line from the letter: "instead of the drama about Alyosha Turbin, which I have been cherishing" – that was written at the start of 1921!), meant something different to each group: Bulgakov's friends and loved ones recognised in it a surname that was connected to them by ties of blood; people in the military saw it as a military name; and V. Katayev and his circle were irritated by it, seeing it as a 'made-up' name.

Let us highlight another surname which is perhaps reflected in another character in the novel, also loved by the author: the "General list of officer ranks" of the Russian Empire (St. P., 1908) contains one lieutenant in the Imperial Guard of the hussars' regiment, Nai-Pum…

That same month, news arrived from Kiev: Vera, the eldest of the Bulgakov sisters, sent a telegram announcing her arrival in her native city. On 23rd January, Bulgakov wrote her a letter, playing the role of the older brother, after the death of their mother. She had been the head of a family which, although it had disbanded, still maintained, in his eyes, some kind of family unity. "Dear Vera, thank you all for the greetings you sent by telegram. I was overjoyed to hear you were in Kiev. Regrettably, it's not clear from the telegram whether you've returned for good or only temporarily? My dream is for all of us to settle down, at last, in lasting nests in Moscow and Kiev. [...] I was so happy when I read your words about a 'family in harmony'. That is the main thing, for all of us. True enough, with a little bit of goodwill, you'd have got along famously. I'm judging by myself: after those years of difficult tests, I value peace more than anything! I would so like to be among my own. There's nothing to be done. Here in Moscow, in conditions that are immeasurably more difficult than the ones you face, I am still thinking of getting my life going – in a normal channel.

In Kiev, then, there is hope for you, Varya and Lyolya. I have spoken to Lyolya a great deal about this. What we experienced has taken its toll on her, as it has on everyone, and just like me, she wants peace and harmony in Kiev.

My great request for you is this: live amicably, in memory of mama.

I am working very hard and suffering from deadly fatigue. I may be able to come to Kiev for a long visit in the spring."

In this letter, one can see a reflection of the plot that was taking shape for the new draft of *The White Guard* – in the call to "live amicably, in memory of mama", in the ideas about calmness, peace and harmony as a key value. The proposed trip to Kiev is also a link in the work that was under way on the novel.

"I shall not write to you about how I managed to exist in the period between 1921 and 1923. For one thing, you wouldn't believe me, and secondly, it has nothing to do with the task in hand.

But by 1923 I managed to find a way to live.

In one of my absolutely fantastical jobs, an agreeable journalist by the name of Abram befriended me.

Abram took me by the sleeve in the street one day and led me into the editorial offices of a certain big newspaper, where he worked. At his prompting, I offered my services as a processor. That was the name they gave at the office to the people who transformed poorly written material into material that was fit for printing." (*To the Secret Friend* [*Taynomu Drugu*], 1929). The earliest documentary evidence of Bulgakov's job at *Gudok* (the name means "The Hooter") is a membership card for the All-Russian professional union of education workers (division for workers in the press, place of work – editorial offices of *Gudok*, processor), issued to Bulgakov on 19th February 1923. This "way to live" was still fairly limited, however: this is indicated by the fact that Bulgakov also worked as an author for another publication. 23rd April 1922 saw the publication of the first issue of *Weekly of the Central*

House of Workers in Education and Art (*Yezhenedel'nik Tsentral'nogo Doma Rabotnikov Prosveshcheniya i Iskusstva*); in August 1922 it was rebranded as *Golos Rabotnikov Prosveshcheniya* (*Voice of the Workers of Education*), whose task was "to cover, in its pages, principle and practical matters of professional work among workers in education in the Moscow governorate". I. Lezhnev was on the journal's editorial board; he was the man who recruited Bulgakov, it seems. By February 1923, Bulgakov had written two pieces: *Kaenpe and Kape* and *At a School in the Town of the III Internationale* (*V Shkole Gorodka III Internatsionala*), which were printed in issue No. 4 of the journal, published on 15th March.

In one chapter of the article *The Capital in a Notepad*, printed in March 1923, Bulgakov mentions the two journals, as having a bearing on his literary biography, which had been proving difficult to fashion in recent months. Among the "monstrous" contrasts that he presents for the Russian reader living abroad, Bulgakov especially highlights this one: "There are posters up bearing world-famous names… and yet at the kiosk on Red Square, where they sell magazines, the shopkeeper had popped out and his temporary stand-in was an illiterate old woman! I swear – she was illiterate!

I went up to the kiosk myself. I asked for *Rossiya*, and she gave me *Korabl'* (the font is similar!). It wasn't what I wanted. The old woman fumbled about in the kiosk. She gave me something else. It wasn't what I wanted.

'What's wrong with you, can't you read?!' (I asked her that sarcastically).

But down with sarcasm and long live despair! For sure enough, the old woman couldn't read."

The Seliphanas and Petrushkas floating to the surface of the societal process are increasingly driving him to despair, as he prepares the plot for a "monstrous story" about a dog who is given a job at a Soviet institution and acquires extensive social opportunities.

In the 7th edition of the booklet *Russias* (*Rossii*) in *Literaturnaya Khronika* (*Literary Chronicle*), Bulgakov is mentioned among famous writers whose work the journal is following, and in this hierarchical, non-alphabetical list, he was put in eleventh place – between L. Nikulin and M. Shkapskaya. The article read: "Mikh. Bulgakov is finishing his novel *The White Guard*, which covers the era of the struggle with the whites in the south (1919-1920). His other book – *Cuff-notes*, portraying in grotesque form the adventures of a writer during the revolutionary years, part of which was printed in *Rossiya*, will be partially printed in the 2nd edition of the almanac *Vozrozhdeniye* (*Rebirth*)."

"After that, I got stuck," writes the author of the manuscript for *To a Secret Friend*. "However much I ran around Moscow with the aim of selling someone a chunk of my work, I didn't achieve anything. The chunk didn't appeal to anyone, nor did the work as a whole. At one place, the editor told me that he thought what I had written to be counter-revolutionary, and insistently advised me not to write anything else in the same vein. Some dark forebodings took hold of me, but soon passed. *Sochelnik* came to my aid. One of the big-wigs from that particular publication, who was over from Berlin – a man with a yellow briefcase made of leather from some tropical beast, after reading what I had written, expressed the desire to print my work in full.

A department of *Sochelnik*, taking advantage of my poverty and the sludge of autumn, offered 8 dollars a page (16 roubles). I recall that, by turns feeling ashamed on their behalf, and languishing in a powerless rage, I received a heap of multi-coloured, Soviet notes, whose value was plummeting."

The man with the yellow briefcase was Pavel Abramovich Sadyker, one of the editors at *Nakanune*, who had arrived in Moscow "for some reconnaissance", as E. Mindlin writes in his memoirs about this newspaper. On 21st February 1923, he writes to Bulgakov from Berlin on headed paper from the *Nakanune* publishing house: "At present, after the release of our first books, it has become clear that we will soon be able to publish some new ones. When I was in Moscow, you suggested that I should publish your *Cuff-notes*, but I could not decide anything then, since I did not know how things stood at our publishing house. Please grant me the publishing rights. Unfortunately, we cannot provide a royalty of the kind you would get in Moscow. The maximum we can pay is 7-8 dollars per printed page. The money will be paid when the manuscript is submitted. The money will be paid to you by our Moscow office. If your desire to publish *Cuff-notes* with us has not yet gone away, do not delay in sending us the manuscript as a matter of urgency via Semyon Kalmens. We will publish the book quickly and elegantly."

In the final months of winter, which were almost entirely filled with newspaper work, Bulgakov spoke out sharply in an article called *The Biomechanical Chapter* (*Biomekhanicheskaya Glava*) against Meyerhold's theatre; he wrote in comical, grotesque tones, emphasizing old-fashioned traits in the author of the piece himself, and a demonstrative conservatism in his tastes: "… Judge for yourselves: at this shabby, run-down, draughty theatre, instead of a stage, there is a hole (there is not so much as a trace of a curtain, of course). At the back of the stage, there is a bare, brick wall with two windows…" And thereafter, in the Tolstoyan tradition of the distancing description of the opera through the eyes of Natasha Rostova in *War and*

Peace, there came a description of the famous play *The Magnanimous Cuckold* (*Velikodushnyy Rogonosets*)." It is worth remembering that in 1920-1921, Meyerhold had led the theatrical department of the People's Commissariat of Education, bringing to life the program he had put forward at the end of 1920, *Teatral'nyy Oktyabr'* (*Theatrical October*) – a politicization of the theatre, which Bulgakov did not like.

On 15th April, *Voice of the Workers of Education* prints his piece *The 1st Children's Commune* (*1-ya Detskaya Kommuna*), and on the same day, *Forty Forties*, one of Bulgakov's best articles from that period, was published in *Nakanune*. The piece was dated March 1923; in its final section, it shows the Moscow of that month, seen through Bulgakov's eyes. This is essentially a page of autobiographical text: we see the streets he walked down; his observations and impressions, his regrets and his hopes.

"Moscow now goes to bed at night without putting out its fiery eyes.

From the early morning, it flares up with a honking of horns and a ringing of bells, and hurls waves of pedestrians along the sidewalks. The trucks crawl across the rutted, crumbling, reddish snow. On clear days, aeroplanes fly off from Khodynka with their bass drone. At Lubyanka, the trams move around, just as before, tumbling out from Myasnitskaya and Bolshaya Lubyanka. They trundle on, one by one, down the slope, past the printing pioneer Fedorov, beneath the old castellated wall, towards the Metropole." He is painting a picture, recording the visible, external changes, striving to create the "effect of presence" for foreign readers. "The dark windows on the ground floor of the Metropole have been lit up, as though they have had a cataract removed, and revealed rows of colourful book covers. At night, a sphere is lit up above the entranceway like a gemstone: Goskino (State Cinema) II.

On the opposite side, across the square, Testov suddenly got up and pushed a sign out into the entryway: 'Peasant soup.'"

Bulgakov "physically" takes his reader on a tour of Moscow, describing what he sees step by step. "In Okhotny Ryad, the signs are so huge that they oppress the little shops. But Paraskeva-Pyatnitsa looks sad and wan. They say she's going to be taken down. That's a pity. How many times I have seen this narrow passage between the windows and the meat carcasses and the flower-stalls and the white side of the church, standing in the very middle of the street.

The bell-tower that had stood in the little square, where Tverskaya crosses Okhotny Ryad and Mokhovaya, has already been taken down.

The rows of trading stalls on Red Square [where the GUM shopping centre now stands – M.C.], which for several years were a remarkable example of nastiness, of desolation, are full of shops [...] Inns are growing and being resurrected as quickly as an epidemic. On Tsvetnoy Boulevard, in the smoke, the clanging of a "natural" polka can be heard amid the din:

Let's go, let's go, dear angel, Let's go and dance the polka, I h-e-e-e-e-ear, h-e-e-e-e-ear... ... The sounds of an unearthly polka!!! [Eighteen months later, he had an article called 'The sounds of an unearthly polka' printed in *Gudok*, repeating these 'sounds', which had become an earworm for him, in the epigraph. – M.C.]. The coachmen are now turning around in their seats, striking up conversations, complaining that times are hard, that there are so many of them but the public prefer to travel by tram.

The wind blows the film posters displayed all the way down the street into coils. The fences have disappeared under millions of multi-coloured posters. They summon people to see new foreign films; they announce 'The trial of the prostitute Zaborova, who infected a Red Army soldier with syphilis', and dozens of debates, lectures, concerts. There will be a discussion of *Sanin* [a novel by M.P. Artsybashev – M.C.], of Kuprin's *The Pit* (*Yama*), of *Father Sergius* (*Otets Sergiy*); Wagner will be played without a conductor; *Land on End* (*Zemlya Dybom*) will be performed [a play by S. Tretyakov – M.C.] with military projectors and vehicles, there will be concerts on the radio, the tailors are making tunics for the marksmen, they'll add gleaming stars to the sleeves and epaulettes full of diamonds. The kiosks are piled high with magazines and dozens of newspapers...

"And then the March sunshine spattered out, the snow melted. The trucks started honking with an even deeper, more furious and merry voice. A branch line has already been laid down towards Vorobyevy Gory; there, holes are being dug, boards are being carried about, and there is the screech of wheelbarrows; they are getting ready for the all-Russian exhibition." (Work was taking place between Neskuchny Garden and Sparrow Hills at this time: the All-Russian Agricultural Trade Show was due to open there in the summer). "And, as I sit there on the 5th floor, in a room piled high with second-hand books, I dream of going up to Sparrow Hills in the summer, from whence Napoleon once gazed, and I will see the forty forties burning on the seven hills, and Moscow breathing and sparkling, mother-Moscow."

In April, the question of the publishing of *Cuff-notes* arose again. The evidence of this is a draft agreement that survived in M.A. Bulgakov's archive "between the joint-stock company *Nakanune*, as represented by the Company's managing director, P.A. Sadyker, on the one hand, and Mikhail Afanasievich Bulgakov on the other..."; "The size of the work is approximately 4 ¼ (four and a quarter) printed pages." The royalty is set at 8 dollars per page; clause 10 of the contract read as follows: "In the event that any reductions in the length of the book are required at the request of the censors, then Bulgakov will not object to them, and JSC *Nakanune* is entitled to effect said reductions"; clause 12 read: "Bulgakov has received the royalty for the first edition, to the tune of 34 (thirty-four) dollars, in full". The draft contract is dated 19th April; the next day, on 20th April, Bulgakov writes a note to Pavel Abramovich (i.e. Sadyker), in which, after thinking the draft agreement over, he says: "I cannot agree to reductions being made without any discussion. That cl. 10 must be removed or rewritten together. In all other respects, the agreement is fully acceptable to me" (a copy or draft of the note survived in the collection of the well-known Moscow book-dealer E. Zippelzon; it may have been kept in one of the books in the writer's library, a substantial portion of which came into Zippelzon's possession after the war). The book was due to be published very soon – in a month's time: in his autobiography in 1924, Bulgakov would write: "The Berlin-based publishers *Nakanune* bought that book from me, promising to publish it in May 1923."

On 26th March, the trial of the Catholic priests came to an end (the case of the concealing of church valuables); archbishop Tseplyak had his sentence of execution commuted to a prison sentence, whilst the prelate Butkevich was shot on the night of 1st April (Easter-Eve for the Catholics). The Komsomol staged a play in which the Pope was put on trial and given the death sentence. On 3rd May, the church of the renovation, to the horror of the faithful, lost the "office and title of patriarch" of patriarch Tikhon, who had been arrested and was awaiting trial.

In the first half of May or at the end of April, Bulgakov leaves for Kiev. Among the reasons was this one: "Varya had written to him: 'I've got Tasya's bracelet, I'm not going to send it, come and get it if you want.' And he did," Tatiana said, in one of our conversations. Whilst there, he sees his family and a few of his childhood friends who were still around (most of them had left the country by then), including Sasha Gdeshinsky. On 8th May, he writes something on his writing desk at home, for them to remember him by: "Due to a lack of shirt-cuffs, I wrote this on the desk. MB. May. 1923." At Gdeshinsky's house, they talk about the past, the present and the future; a year later, recalling this meeting, A. Gdeshinsky would write to Bulgakov: "You can't stop life – you can't stop life – you said that yourself." One can hear the same note being sounded in the sketch *Kiev-city*, too.

On his return to Moscow, Bulgakov immediately sets about writing the article *Lord Curzon's Benefit* (*Benefis Lorda Kerzona*), which is printed on

19th May by *Nakanune*. Its start – intentionally, perhaps – referenced the start of the second part of *Cuff-notes* and the piece *Forty Forties*, with a description of the autumn of 1921, and Bulgakov's arrival in Moscow, after travelling from Kiev, at the same station: "At exactly six in the morning, the train ran beneath the dome of the Bryansk station. Moscow. Its high-rise buildings again. After the caricatured provinces, with no newspapers, no books, with wild rumours – Moscow, the vast city, the only city, the state, only here could one live. […] And there were the buildings. And I shall never leave Moscow for any other place again. At ten, the sheet of *Izvestiya* – I haven't held it in my hands for a month. On the very first page: 'The murder of Vorovsky!' […] At two in the afternoon, there was no way of cutting across Tverskaya. A ribbon of people rolled slowly down it, as far as the eye could see, in an uninterrupted flow, and above it was a forest of placards and banners. A mass of old, familiar ones, from October and May, but among them new ones could be glimpsed, manufactured with remarkable speed, bearing very grandiose inscriptions. A black mourning placard floated past: 'The murder of Vorovsky is the death knell for Europe's bourgeoisie'…"

The article is of interest in that, pretty much for the first and last time in Bulgakov's oeuvre, it contains a portrait of Mayakovsky. "… On a little balcony, beneath the obelisk of Freedom [Sovetskaya square, opposite Mossovet; the obelisk of Freedom, erected there in 1919, was taken down in 1941 and replaced in 1954 with a memorial to Yury Dolgoruky, which had been created in 1947 to mark the 800th anniversary of the founding of Moscow – M.C.]. Mayakovsky, opening wide his monstrous, square mouth, blurted out over the crowd, in a trembling bass:

> Baring the teeth of his crown,
> let
> the lion of Britain whine,[11] gale-heft.
> The Commune can never go down.
> LEFT!
> LEFT!
> LEFT![12]

---

[11] Written at the time when British and thirteen other interventionist armies were attacking the young Soviet State (Herbert Marshall).

[12] *Left March* (*Levyy Marsh*), translated by Herbert Marshall in *Mayakovsky*. London: Dennis Dobson, 1965, p. 129.

'Left! Left!' the crowd shouted, in response. A new ribbon of people rolled out from Stoleshnikov, bending towards the obelisk.

The crowd was calling for Mayakovsky. He came out again onto the balcony and thundered:

'You have heard, comrades, the ringing of bells, but do not know who Lord Curzon is!'

And he began explaining:

'From beneath the mask of a polite Lord, a face with long fangs gazes out!! […]

'Curzon must resign!!'"

Here, Bulgakov is describing a man who is utterly alien to him, his polar opposite. It is an objective, almost impartial description. For Bulgakov himself, a passionate attitude about Curzon's ultimatum is impossible, but he faithfully reproduces what happened that day on the streets of Moscow, wishing to convey to the overseas reader an idea of the content and the scale of the demonstrations, and their mass character: "At Okhotny, the endless rows went across the entire width, and it was clear that Theatre Square was packed full of people. […] Brass trumpets were playing marches. Here, an effigy of Curzon was being carried along on a spit, whilst a worker ran up from behind and beating him across the head with a shovel. The head, in a scrunched-up top-hat, shook from side to side helplessly. Behind Curzon, a gentleman emerged from a passage with a placard attached to his chest: 'Note', followed by a gigantic cardboard puppet with a notice saying: 'And here's our 'answer' […]. At Theatre Square, there was a sea of people. I have never seen the like of it in Moscow, not even during the October days" (i.e. on the only anniversary of the revolution that he had spent in Moscow, to date – the fifth anniversary).

Descriptive articles such as this could not have existed at *Gudok*, and Bulgakov therefore stays fully within the parameters of the satirical article decrying elements of everyday life. Six years later, in the manuscript for *To a Secret Friend*, he looks back with humour on the tricky situations which arose from time to time, when one of the editors would say to him: "I hope you get infected by an article about the French minister.

I felt a dizziness come over me.

I shall explain what I mean, my friend, and you'll understand me: is it sensible to write a good article about the French minister, if hitherto you haven't had anything to do with that minister? The conclusion is predetermined, don't forget: you must present the minister in a funny and disrespectful light, and you must certainly pour scorn on him. Where is this minister, what is this minister? A political sketch can only be written well if the author genuinely hates the minister."

In the spring, Aleksei Tolstoy arrived in Moscow for a short visit, prior to moving back to his native land permanently.

On 30th May, the literary circle that met at Slezkin and Komorsky's homes arranged an evening reception at Komorsky's flat in honour of Tolstoy's arrival. Komorsky says: "Zinaida was ill, she was lying in bed in her room. Tatiana Nikolayevna had taken over her responsibilities; she was wearing a white dress. A table was laid in the little dining room, and we danced in the living room. I struggle to remember who was there. Slezkin and Bulgakov were there of course; there were lots of writers there…" Komorsky and Tatiana both recall that Bulgakov had a burning interest in A. Tolstoy at the time, and that he was "eating him up with his eyes" at this gathering. This interest was later reappraised, retrospectively; real details from the evening formed the basis for that "party, organized by a group of writers to mark a most important event: the safe arrival from overseas of the acclaimed writer, Izmail Alexandrovich Bondarevsky" – a party to which the protagonist of *A Theatrical Novel* sets off "in great excitement".

"The critic Konkin", at whose apartment the party takes place, has a surname whose first syllable resembles that of the name "Komolsky", and this appears to be no accident; "Likospastov was as quiet as a mouse, and I somehow got the sense that he was probably one place below all the others" (a reflection of the reappraisal of Slezkin's standing when taken out of his comfort zone in *Zelyonaya Lampa*). "From the next room there was the sound of a piano being played, someone was quietly playing foxtrot… I remember that we danced on a carpet in that room, which made it uncomfortable" – all these tiny details are transmuted 'live' from Komorsky's flat. Izmail Alexandrovich himself was painted in destructive colours.

In June 1923, Bulgakov sat in the public gallery at the criminal courts, during an unusual trial. He printed his first article about this case in *Nakanune* on 16th June, under the pseudonym of F. Iks: "Roll-Royce, or Doberman-pincher", describing the rules of police raids competently. On 20th June, *Nakanune* printed his article *The Komarov Case* (*Komarovskoye Delo*), which makes clear how powerfully affected he was by the case that he saw in court. "Starting in the spring of 1922, people began disappearing in Moscow. For some reason, this happened most often to horse-dealers from the city or peasants from the suburbs who had gone into the city to buy horses. Not only were these men failing to buy horses, but – to add insult to injury – they were themselves disappearing.

Meanwhile, by night, some strange and unpleasant things were turning up: in the deserted spaces beyond the Moscow River, in the ramshackle houses, at abandoned, unfinished bathhouses at Shabalovka, some stinking, grey bags were found. They contained the naked corpses of men.

After several such finds, an acute sense of anxiety began to be felt at the Moscow criminal investigation bureau. The thing was that the bags containing the dead men all bore the same fingerprints – they were the work of one and the same man. [...] The bags had all been tied up in the same way: the way people who are familiar with show-jumping tie knots. Perhaps the killer was a coachman?"

As he sits and observes the trial, Bulgakov strives to understand "the most frightening thing of all in all this" – the murderer himself: "I have no wish to write an article on crime, let me assure the reader, but there is no possibility of doing anything else, because today, I have had the desire in my head all day long to understand this Komarov, and it is a desire that refuses to go away.

It turns out that he had some special canvas mats, and he let the blood drain out of the bodies onto these mats (so as to avoid soiling the bags and the sledge); when he had sufficient funds to do so, he also bought a galvanized steel vat for the same purpose. He killed his victims carefully and in an extraordinarily economical way. [...] Cattle are killed using the same method. With no mercy, but with no clumsiness either.

... Reporters, sketch writers and locals have been bandying about the word 'man-beast' for two weeks. It is a vapid word, lacking content and explaining nothing. And the meaty, businesslike manner of the killings was revealed to such an extent, that for me personally it immediately killed off all of those non-existent 'monsters', and another phrase was confirmed within me: 'Not a beast, but by no means a man, either.'"

One cannot, under any circumstances, describe Komarov as a man, just as one cannot describe as a clock an empty chamber that has had its mechanism taken out of it. (The hero of his story *The Heart of a Dog* would soon say that being able to talk "doesn't necessarily mean you're a person.")

At the end of his article on crime, Bulgakov talks about the sentence in interesting terms: "The sentence? *What sense* is there in holding forth about that? Komarov was first given his sentence when the police brought him in," – and he then talks about how the murderer had only just been saved from the lynch mob. The matter of the author's opinion of the *highest measure* is put to one side. He says the following, however: "Some old women in the building where I live passed sentence, too: 'boil him alive'. 'He's a monster. A butcher. How many children did he leave orphaned, by killing those thirty-five men, the son of a bitch.'"

This article is interesting above all in that it contains what is pretty much the only psychological analysis conducted by Bulgakov in a non-literary piece of writing. Importantly, it also represents a continuation of Bulgakov's thoughts on the psychological mechanism of violence being done against a human life – either through murder or the death penalty. Without doubt, some of the results of these thoughts were used in *Flight* a few years later – in his work on Khludov ("Monster – Serafima shouts at him"). Khludov's 'sacks' are easy to recognise as a culture-specific term, but in their proliferation of these 'sacks' in the play, one can perceive a nod to the sacks containing the victims of the coachman Komarov, which captured his imagination so vividly.

Bulgakov spent the cold, rainy summer of 1923 in Moscow, working intensively for *Nakanune* (but working on two major works at the same time, as we shall see later). On 26th July, his story *Samogonnoye Ozero (The Samogon Lake)* was published in *Literaturnoye Prilozheniye* to *Nakanune*, apparently, it reflected the kind of life that was being led at flat No. 50, where he still lived, to the letter. At the same time, the almanac *Vozrozhdeniye* came out, with the first part of *Cuff-notes* – with a host of passages that had been cut out by *Nakanune* restored to the text. On 2nd August, he writes the article *Chanson d'été*, which began with a description of the summer that was now nearing its end: "The summer of 1923 in Moscow was very rainy. The word 'very' requires some decoding. It does not mean that it rained often – every other day, or even every day, let's say – no, it rained three times a day, and there were days when it didn't stop raining all day. Moreover, it also rained at night three times a week. Downpours would suddenly start, without warning. Heavy downpours lasting one-and-a-half hours, with green lightning and hailstones the size of dove's eggs."

This rain was the primary impression made on the people of Moscow, and Bulgakov's article is echoed by a letter from S. Auslender to Y. Slezkin (who was then living in the Chernigov governorate): "The main thing here is this disgusting summer, with nothing but rain and cold [...] this continually grey colour scheme in the sky, the sleet and the cold, make one lose one's patience. There were several rainstorms that led to part of Moscow being flooded, and the trams weren't even running. [...] Of the writers, I have been seeing Lidin more often than the others, and somehow feel closer to him. The other day, I was asked to organise a literary evening at the centre for teachers' evening classes on the Yaroslavskaya road. I drove there with Lidin and Bulgakov. We felt sorry that you weren't there. For some reason, it turned out to be a very agreeable and jolly trip. We were given a very grand reception. Bulgakov gave an off-the-cuff introductory speech, I even felt ashamed, for the audience were writing things down in their notebooks, and he was talking such a load of rubbish…"

At about this time, Bulgakov received a letter from Kiev from Gdeshinsky (dated 6th August 1923), in which the tone was rather different; his friend informed him that Bulgakov's sister, Vera, had given him "your recollections of Kiev, to read; once again, I couldn't help but marvel at your talent" – Gdeshinsky was referring to the sketch *Kiev-city*, which Bulgakov had sent to his sister after it was published by *Nakanune* on 6th July.

On 27th August, Slezkin, apparently influenced by the letter he had recently received from Auslender mentioning Bulgakov, writes to him (only two letters from Slezkin survived in Bulgakov's archive): "Dear Mikhail. I am writing to you from the blessed, one-horse town of Krolevets, whither I have come from Chernigov to spend the summer. One finds the authentic countryside here, with an innumerable quantity of gardens, vegetable gardens, denes, dusty hawthorns and charming, brightly painted little houses. […] I don't even feel any urge to go to Moscow, but it's time I did so… I shall set off in the first few days of the month. What is happening at *Nakanune* nowadays? What of Semyon Nikolayevich, the great Valesha, the excellent proletarian and the charming Bellochka? [S.N. Kalmens, V. Katayev, A. Tolstoy and, it seems, the wife of M. Levidov, who worked in the editorial offices – M.C.]. What news is there of our Berlin books? When will they finally be published? What is new in literature, more generally?

In Chernikov and Krolevets, I gave lectures on Moscow, in which I mentioned you and Katayev as the most talented of the young writers working at *Nakanune*.

What of your novel? I have high hopes for it. Have you finished *Diaboliad*. I will enjoy listening to it, when I arrive. Though you always squint at me with suspicion, I love you pure-heartedly and I believe in you as a writer. [This entire sentence speaks volumes for the tension in Slezkin's attitude to Bulgakov, to which reference was made above. – M.C.] I myself am writing an unlikely composition set against the backdrop of contemporary life in the provinces. I have heard such things and seen such things here that – mmm! You'll be licking your lips." This was the kind of predatory literary attitude to daily life that appalled Bulgakov and that was reflected in *A Theatrical Novel* (let us quote some lines by B. Pilnyak: in a letter to his friends in Berlin (April 1922), he described how he sat at his table at his house in Kolomna, "and the sun came out and people came out onto the streets and did so much in their lives that, devil knows it, one would need to let loose a hundred writers on Kolomna alone, and even that wouldn't be enough," – Rus. Berlin. Paris, 1983, p. 192).

... Dear, if our books have already arrived from Berlin – be so kind, send me one copy of each, one of yours, one of mine. They'll be read here in one sitting!

Are there any new prospects, from a publishing perspective?

Write to me, dear friend, don't forget. [...] I kiss you. Your Yury Slezkin.

"Dear Yury," wrote Bulgakov on 31 August, "I am hastening to reply to you, so that my letter reaches you while you are still in Krolevets. I envy you. I have utterly worn myself out in Moscow.

At *Nakanune*, there are masses of new people from Berlin, although some of them are here only temporarily: Nebukva, Bobrishchev-Pushkin, Klyuchnikov and Tolstoy. These four gave a lecture at Zimin's [i.e. at Zimin's Theatre – M.C.]. The lecture was remarkable in all respects (though more on that later).

The hard-working count feels good, portly and affluent. He is going to spend the winter in Petersburg, where they are already setting aside an apartment for him, but for the time being he is living outside Moscow, in his dacha." The character of Tolstoy, his position in life, is continuing to provoke intense interest in him (albeit interest that is coloured with a dash of irony): according to an account by Katayev, Bulgakov travelled with him to Tolstoy's dacha in Ivanovka.

Bulgakov's telling line about the lecture is a clear indication of the serious thinking he had done about the position of writers from *Nakanune* and about what made them closer to him and what divided them from him.

"The printing of our books is causing irritation in me: there is still no sign of them," Bulgakov continues, in his letter to Slezkin. "At last, Potekhin has informed me that they are expected in a couple of days. Rumour has it that they are ready (yours and mine will be the first to be published). It will be interesting to see whether or not they publish them. For my book, I am really very worried.

They didn't even think to send me a copy of the corrections, of course." Bulgakov has not yet lost hope in the idea that a book containing the full text of *Cuff-notes* will be published, but his anxiety soon proved to be well-founded. In the manuscript for *To a Secret Friend*, he wrote: "For three months I awaited the publication of the manuscript and I realised that it was not going to be published. The reason became known to me, a sign of disapproval from the censors had been hung above the story. The censors had long been having whispered conversations with someone in Moscow and Berlin." Three months – i.e. June, July and August, which had all past since the time when the book's publication had been promised. It appears that the aforementioned reason became known to Bulgakov in September. The last reference to the failure of the plan for a Bulgakov's first separate book came a year later, in the autobiography referred to previously, in which he writes that the *Nakanune* publishing house promised to publish the book in May 1923 "and didn't publish it at all. At first this upset me greatly, but later I became indifferent to the matter."

The letter to Slezkin contains important evidence about two major plans which came to fruition that year: "I have finished *Diaboliad*, but I doubt it will be accepted anywhere. Lezhnev refused to take it.

I have finished the novel, but it has not yet been redrafted, it is lying in a huge mass over which I am thinking a great deal. I shall change a few things here and there."

Generally speaking, the summer of 1923 was, for Bulgakov, a time of hope, more than anything. "Lezhnev is starting work on a thick monthly journal, *Rossiya*, with our writers and foreign writers involved," Bulgakov wrote to Slezkin. "He is currently in Berlin, in talks. It appears that Lezhnev has a huge future in publishing and editing ahead of him. *Rossiya* is going to be printed in Berlin.

… It is hard, in a brief, hurriedly written letter, to tell you much that is new. In any case, things are clearly moving towards a livening up, rather than a depression, in the literary and publishing world.

Come over! We shall have many interesting things to talk about. […] I kiss you. Your M. Bulgakov."

The journal *Rossiya* was at the centre of Bulgakov's attention in 1922 to 1923. It was not for nothing that in *A Theatrical Novel*, he gave the journal that was based on *Rossiya* the name *Rodina (Motherland)*: like many others, he perceived this word, which was of inestimable importance to him, in the journal's title, so unusual for the press in those days. A powerful impression was clearly made on Bulgakov by the fact that, after some sharp criticism in the mainstream press, not only was the journal not closed down, but it was transformed into a "thick" journal: someone was supporting the editor, Lezhnev. "The journal is being turned into a 'thick' two-monthly (20 printed sheets)," Lezhnev wrote to Ustryalov on 12th August 1923. "The editing and censoring of the material will remain in Moscow, as before, but we will print it in Berlin. Some of the copies will stay on site for distribution overseas.

[...] But we will take care of the publication itself using private funding, of course. We will provide reptilian [i.e. dependent – M.C.] methods of working, from a material and ideological point of view, to the amateurs from *Nakanune*. [...] An intellectual connection between Russia and the West has still not been created yet." Lezhnev intended "to give broad circles of the émigré community an objective idea about contemporary Russia – in a host of fictional works, sketches portraying daily life, and articles on business." As he completed *The White Guard*, Bulgakov was not only dreaming of having it published in *Rossiya*, but was also to some extent trying to align the novel with the direction that the journal was taking. "Culture and life are constructed in accordance with the law of succession," wrote the editor of *Rossiya*. "After the revolutionary disruption to this thread of succession, there occurs either a rapid movement away towards the past, or an insuperable and insistent binding together of the chains, a cicatrizing of the fabric, there is a mixing of the blood of the two epochs, the two cultures. The idea of the concrescence, the synthesis of two cultures is a most pertinent and modern idea…" (*Rossiya*, No. 7, March 1923, p. 10).

In the autumn of 1923, a second meeting that was important for the next few years of Bulgakov's literary life took place: his meeting with the editor-in-chief of the journal *Nedra*, N.S. Angarsky.

3

The circumstances of how the two men met are not known: P.N. Zaitsev recalled his meeting with Bulgakov in the summer of 1924 as the first one; in fact, it must have taken at least a year earlier, for on 11th March 1924, the 4th booklet of *Nedra* was released, containing *Diaboliad*.

Between November 1922 and October 1923, Angarsky lived in Berlin, managing the publication of the anthologies for *Nedra* from there. His letters to P.N. Zaitsev reveal that Angarsky definitely read all the material that was sent to the editors, and not only set out his opinion on whether or not to print them in detail, but also monitored the extent to which the authors took his comments into account, giving Zaitsev instructions as to which writers he was to maintain relations with, and so on. In what was apparently his last Berlin letter, from 2nd October 1923 (a reply to P.N. Zaitsev's letter from 18 September), there is not a word about Bulgakov, nor is there anything about him in the previous letters. It seems that Bulgakov had not approached *Nedra* prior to the second half of September 1923. One can confidently suppose that Bulgakov did not meet Angarsky any earlier than the middle of October, 1923 (in one of the letters, Angarsky tells Zaitsev: *"I shall leave Berlin for Moscow on 11-13th/X"*); they may have met in late autumn – the 4th *Nedra* anthology had not yet been compiled in mid-November: Serafimovich only sent the manuscript for *The Iron Flood* (*Zheleznyy Potok*) on 17th November, 1923.

Angarsky himself, an old Bolshevik who had spent time in a hard labour camp for political prisoners, was a remarkable figure in literary life and publishing policy in the 1920s. He was an editor who loved his job and held it dear; he did not fear personal responsibility, on the contrary, he valued it highly, refusing to accept half-hearted measures in maintaining one's own specific line. "Comrade Frich and I differ too much in our literary tastes, and therefore cannot work together," he wrote on 10th February 1923 from Berlin in response to some proposals about the editorial staff. "No, I stand firmly in favour of one-man command, and shall not switch to having a collegiate system." After listening to what V. Veresayev had to say about the material submitted for inclusion in *Nedra*, he nonetheless made sure he had the final say, and specially wrote to Zaitsev: "I repeat once again: there is no such thing as a deputy editor in nature." When the publisher of *Nedra*, Drauden, started exerting too many rights in the management of the almanac's affairs, Angarsky, as always, expressed his position very clearly in a letter to Zaitsev (dated 14th February 1923). "He thinks that literature is something akin to a Latvian battalion, where he can issue orders with the kind of aplomb that comes naturally to him. [...] I must have done with D. I am going to push for a complete breaking of relations, and I shall not make any concessions at all. Literature is an area in which I have never made concessions to anyone, and I shall not allow an impolite person to do as he pleases."

The literary orientation of the editor of *Nedra*, which remained firm and unambiguously expressed at all times, was nevertheless fairly broad and could not be put into just one line; it cannot be defined so much in one or two sentences, as much as it can be explained on the basis of diverse assessments of it, taken together, which help us gain a better understanding of the literary circumstances in which Bulgakov grew closer to *Nedra* in 1923.

The excerpts from Angarsky's letters help us to understand just how discouraging for Bulgakov those initial conversations with this key figure in Moscow publishing must have been.

The first story (the author himself gave it a very strange name in the sub-heading: 'A tale about how two twins brought about the downfall of a chief clerk') by Mikhail Bulgakov, who was still very little known in the literary and publishing world and had been published mainly in *Nakanune*, satisfied, one must assume, Angarsky's editorial and publishing requirements. Clear evidence of this is provided by the fact that *Diaboliad* was immediately accepted for publication and included in the upcoming 4th edition of *Nedra*.

... The exhibition had opened at Neskuchny in August, and Bulgakov goes there – on assignment for the editors of *Nakanune*.

A lengthy article with 13 chapters, *The Golden City* (*Zolotistyy Gorod*), is dated September – October 1923. Among the accurate descriptions of the objects at the exhibition, the article contains the telling figure of a "professor and agriculturalist", who "said in his speech that the tractor was not what we needed right now, and that in our poverty-stricken state, it would lie like a heavy burden on the peasantry. 50 people signed up to object to the sceptic or defend him, despite the fact that the dispute has already been going on for a long time." A speaker, "in a soldier's little overcoat and tunic," declares: "... our professor is asleep. He wants to turn us back to the old ways, but we don't want the old stuff. Naked and barefoot as we were, we defeated our enemies, and now, when we want to build something, the academics tell us that we mustn't? What are we supposed to do, dig up the earth with a shovel? That is not going to happen, comrades." The professor says that he is only against fantasies, and calls for record-keeping, for good sense, for strict calculations, he demands foreign credit. [...] A "short-coat" arrives and advises the professor that if he doesn't like being in Russia, which wants to have tractors, he should go to some other place, such as Paris for example." At the end of the sketch, some old Russian songs are whistled out on wooden pipes: "And in my soul I feel a cross between sadness brought about by these pipes, and a vague hope of some sort."

The professor and the "short-coat" are the prototype for the pair of "Professor Persikov and Rokk, which would appear just a year later in the story *The Fateful Eggs*, and also for Preobrazhensky and Sharikov in *The Heart of a Dog*.

Bulgakov frequented literary cafés, too, which still existed in those days. Tatiana recalled that they once went into *Stoylo Pegasa*, where they saw Yesenin for the first time. "He had only just arrived from America. We went into the café. We sat down and had something to drink... We probably commented on something. The way things stood with us, we never had a kopeck to spare, so that we could comment on something... And then we saw Yesenin walking by. He was wearing a top-hat and carrying a bag, and he had a switch of birch twigs in his hands. He walked into *Stoylo Pegasa* and went over to some lady. He got down on his knees, held the switch up to her, and she kissed it... Then he went out onto the stage outside and started reciting verses – I can't remember which ones."

Bulgakov may also have seen Yesenin during his first few months in Moscow – on 19th February 1922, for example, when Yesenin spoke at the House of printing at a literary auction to raise money for the victims of the famine in the Volga region. During those months, despite his extreme poverty, Bulgakov tirelessly frequented all literary gatherings; when he went to meet Veresayev, incidentally, he may well have ignored Yesenin's recitation altogether; Yesenin's outward behaviour must have been just as alien to him as the mannerisms of Mayakovsky. On 11th May 1922, the newspaper *Rabochiy*, where Bulgakov worked at the time, reported, as did other newspapers, on Yesenin's departure with Isidora Duncan the previous day to Konigsberg, and on 14th May, *Nakanune* printed some responses to the poet's time abroad. Yesenin's foreign journey lasted more than a year; he returned to Moscow – without Duncan now – on 3rd August 1923 and gave recitals at *Stoylo Pegasa* several times before the year was out; it appears that Bulgakov saw him there during the first months after his arrival. Both Yesenin himself, and the young poets from his immediate circle in Moscow over the next few years – Ivan Startsev and Ivan Pribludny – became, in this author's view, building material for "the two Ivans" – first Ivan Rusakov in *The White Guard*, and then Ivan Bezdomny in *The Master and Margarita*.

There is an undated note in Bulgakov's archive to his sister which this author believes was written in the autumn of 1923: "Dear Nadya! I have sold the story *Diaboliad* to *Nedra*, and the doctors have discovered that both of my knee joints are infected; in addition to that, I've bought a rather nice set of silk furniture.

As for what is going to happen next, I don't know – my illness (rheumatism) is oppressing me greatly. But if I do not die like a dog – I would be very much against the idea of dying just at the moment – I shall buy a rug, as well. [...]

Your deceased brother Mikhail."

As for these purchases – such a rare thing during those first few years in Moscow – Tatiana recalled: "A Jewish man once brought some working furniture to one of the residents in our building. And either there was no-one at home, or they refused to take it – and the man came and knocked on our door: 'You don't need some furniture, do you?' I wasn't at home at the time, I'd probably gone to see my sister. Bulgakov had a look at the furniture, and he liked it. And they were selling it cheaply, too, and he'd just received some money for something. It was boudoir-type furniture, in the French style – bright-green upholstery with little red flowers. A little sofa, an armchair, two soft chairs, a dressing table with frilly edges... Two soft pouffets. This furniture wasn't suitable for our room at all – it was too miniature for what was a fairly big room (25 m^2 or more). But Mikhail just wanted everything to be comfortable in the room..."

Here, we can begin to see that light touch of tastelessness that has been emphasized by many memoirists – most of whom did not look favourably on Bulgakov, admittedly. Muscovites are eager to see provincialism in this (interestingly, this is particularly true among Muscovites who had themselves arrived from the provinces at the same time as Bulgakov). Rather, this was that indifference to taste that was characteristic of many middle-class intellectuals in the 1910s; at home, on Andreyevsky Hill, there probably wasn't a distinct style, as such – there were just objects which didn't cause any aesthetic irritation, things he had been used to since his childhood. Now, after several years of making his home in rooms that belonged to other people, he wanted to have something that was his, something that might, through an unseen characteristic, divide his life from the 'samogon life' on the other side of the wall.

When the note to his sister was written, Bulgakov already knew, it seems, that one of the Kreshkov brothers (there were three of them: Ivan, Alexander and Vladimir), Vladimir Ivanovich, had brought some rugs over from the Caucasus, and was offering to sell them at a good price. And Bulgakov bought one – "he paid somewhere between 200 and 150 roubles for it. It had been my rug, from when I was aged ten. Between 1918 and 1921, it had laid at my uncle's place, in a basket. All the things disappeared – they got damp and come apart at the seams, but the rug had remained intact – it so happens that I had scattered some shag over it, and it had been preserved. It hung over the sofa in our flat, and we put a new one over the bed. We also had a camp-bed – a folding one, made of canvas…" (T.N.)

It is worth noting that this same furniture, purchased in the autumn of 1923, also cropped up ten years later in a diary entry by Y.L. Slezkin – the one we have already quoted from, containing the description of the room on B. Sadovaya: "… Bulgakov has started drinking red plonk, he's bought some *boudoir-style furniture*, and for some reason he ordered some trousers with a silk lining… He has told everyone about this, not without a degree of pride."

… And here again, the details of what was in his rooms, the details about his toilet, may cause the reader to object – "why focus on such trifles? Isn't this akin to trying to work out whether or not a great man had a cold on a given day?" And once again I say that there is indeed a need to recreate all these trifles, in respect of Bulgakov, specifically – due to the extremely great significance that the objects from which everyday life takes shape held for him. For Bulgakov, they were Things with a capital letter, and they could easily be transformed into a literary thing. They were part of the norm without which life was unimaginable, the absence of which was an obstacle to creativity. It was not for nothing that, even after more than ten years had passed, when Bulgakov had already lived in a fairly nice three-room apartment for nearly a year, his wife Yelena would write in her diary: "For M.A., the word 'apartment' is a magic word. There is nothing in the world he envies so much as a nice apartment! It is some sort of foible of his" (23rd August 1934, diary of Y.S. Bulgakova). A lightbulb that is glowing only dimly (or that is switched off) is for him a sign, a symbol of a person's unsettled state, of defeat, almost of death: "O, only he who has himself suffered a defeat knows what that word truly looks like! It is like an evening in a house in which the electric lighting is defective. [...] In a word, it is like death." (*The White Guard*).

"… To restore the norm – an apartment, clothes and books." It is no coincidence that all the memoirists, mixing accuracy with exaggerations, refer somehow or other to the way in which Bulgakov dressed, to his outward appearance: the significance of what he wore to Bulgakov himself made his clothes significant to those around him. "Later, when 'blue-eyes' became famous and got rich for a while, our suppositions about his provincialism were confirmed: he wore a bow-tie, a colourful dinner jacket, button-up boots with prunella uppers and even – and this seemed utterly incredible – he put a monocle in his eye…" (V. Katayev, *My Diamond Wreath*). V. Katayev had mentioned this monocle earlier, too – in one of our conversations in July 1976 in Peredelkino, even before he thought up and began the story: "He became completely different! Altogether different! The monocle appeared, and the boots with prunella uppers"; then – in November 1977: "So I say to him: 'What's all this Misha? Have you lost your mind?!' And he says: what? A monocle is a wonderful thing!'" The stamp on the receipt for the monocle, which was written out on 8th September 1926 by a clinic on Gagarin side-street, testifies that the monocle was bought on 13th September – i.e. on the day of the premiere of *The Days of the Turbins*. This monocle, which everyone remembered (and which was recorded for posterity in a photograph), an object that was so striking in the 1920s, the monocle that Bulgakov *insists* on wearing (just as he insisted on wearing the trousers with the silk lining), completes, in my view, the image of Bulgakov's attitude towards clothes. In those years, suits were, for him, a reminder first and foremost of his lost social status (see the story *Four Portraits*: "I, a former… you know what, that has no relevance… am now a person of no fixed profession"); it was imbued with sense, intended to be *read* – and in difficult circumstances, Bulgakov put it together piece by piece, telling his friends about the details: hence those trousers with a silk-lining that Slezkin had remembered. This may have been the first suit that he bought in Moscow: Tatiana recalls that this suit – a dark-brown one – was made for him that autumn by the tailor.

This in itself was quite an occurrence. "We were provincial types," V. Katayev recounted. "We appeared in Moscow from Kiev, from Odessa, where the civil war had only just ended, and where power had kept changing hands in the cities. Here, though, the revolution had only lasted a few days; here, life had been going on peacefully for ages! I remember that on the first night after I arrived, I stayed on the tenth floor of the Nirensee building. I was then taken to see Andrei Globe… And after talking to us for a while, he suddenly said:

'Please excuse me, I have to go and see the tailor.'

The tailor – I ask you! We couldn't imagine that at all!" (22nd July 1976).

Bulgakov had doubtless been waiting for that visit to the tailor ever since he arrived in Moscow – as a sign of his "restoration of the norm".

Let us compare this with another of V. Katayev's recollections: "I once won 6 gold ten-rouble coins... I spent two on food, and with the other 4 bought a beautiful English suit at GUM. When I say beautiful, I mean it... It was greyish-black in colour... But I had no shirt, no tie, no boots. (Laughs). But I didn't let that stop me – I wore a sweater under it! We didn't ascribe much importance to this... But for him, all that was important. The difference in our attitudes to this reflected a difference in our mentalities, one that was age-related..." (22nd July 1976); "He was older than the rest of us in that group, and that means something when you're that age – the fact that when the war started, he had been a student in the fourth year, whereas I had been a volunteer with barely even a secondary education, so he was seen as the eldest..." (30th November 1977, Peredelkino).

That autumn, his official responsibilities at *Gudok* changed, too: he went from being a processor to a sketch writer. One of his first sketches was printed on 17th October 1923: *The Troubled Journey. A Monologue by the Boss (Not a Fairy-tale, but a True Story)* [*Bespokoynaya Poyezdka. Monolog Nachal'stva (ne Skazka, a Byl')*] and signed as follows: "The monologue was written down by Gerasim Petrovich Ukhov". The next one appeared two weeks later, on 1st November (*Secrets of the Madrid Court* [*Tayny Madridskogo Dvora*]) and concluded as follows: "The conversation was overheard by G.P. Ukhov", and then another, on 22nd November (*How Buzygin Came a Cropper* [*Kak Razbilsya Buzygin*]), which was signed: "The documents were assembled by G.P. Ukhov."

It was at that point that someone finally decided to take a closer look at the sketch-writer's signature. As I.S. Ovchinnikov, who held a senior position at *Gudok*, recalled in his memoirs about Bulgakov: "There was quite a hoo-ha in the editorial offices, when, in an edition that had already been printed and distributed, they suddenly discovered Bulgakov's brand new pseudonym: Gepeukhov."

That autumn, Bulgakov, for the second time, was in Moscow for the festivities marking the anniversary of October. On 9th November, his sketch, *November, the 7th day (How Moscow Celebrated)* [*Noyabrya 7-go Dnya (Kak Moskva Prazdnovala)*], signed with the initials 'M.B.', appeared in *Gudok*: "In the two days before the holiday, the windows in many shops had already started to be filled with red light. Rows of lights and garlands were hung up in them, ribbons were hung up, and portraits of the leaders of the revolution were put on display.

By evening, when the labourers and office workers of Moscow were scurrying back to their homes, these warm, red niches were already shining among the pale lights of the shops, as a reminder of the fact that the anniversary was approaching.

And on the square in front of the building of the Moscow Soviet, workmen fussed about all day long, until late in the evening, and roasting pans were ablaze.

The workmen built a portal and some new, white walls, and removed the flowerbeds and *parterres*. [...]

A mother was carrying her two-year-old child in her arms in the crowd, and he looked to either side and babbled something, waving his arms. And when the orchestras suddenly started playing and the singing began, he couldn't contain himself any longer, and he started jumping up and down in her arms and shouting.

On that anniversary, not only did finely-chiselled and soldered columns of workers take to the streets with their placards, but beside them there was a continuous procession – formed of groups, clusters and individuals – of men and women, who held their children by the hand and said:

'When you grow up, you'll march with them, too.'

But for the fact that the initials 'M.B.' were repeated later in *Gudok* beneath articles that were undoubtedly by Bulgakov, it would have been hard to conclude that this sketch was written by him: his unique writerly style hardly left any imprint in it. There is nothing that indicates it was not written by him, by the way; the narrative style is dispassionate, perfunctory, but even this perfunctory aspect is clearly something that the author finds difficult to achieve. A few years later, recalling, perhaps, the story of how this sketch came into being, Bulgakov records his dialogues with the editor and his spiritual condition in such situations:

Whenever there was a public holiday of some sort related to the revolution, Navzikat used to say:

'I hope that by the time of the public holiday in two days' time, you will be infected with some heroic story.'

I turned pale, blushed, and wavered.

'I don't know how to write heroic revolutionary stories,' I said to Navzikat.

Navzikat couldn't understand this. His view of journalists and writers was rather strange, as I had long since realised. He imagined that journalists could write anything at all and feel indifferent about their work, whatever they wrote. And yet, for some reason, there was something that I wasn't able to explain to Navzikat: for example, that in order to get 'infected' with a good story about the revolution, one would need, first and foremost, to be a revolutionary and to be pleased when a celebration of the revolution comes along. In contrary cases, a story written by someone who comes up with it out of financial considerations or some other reason is bound to be a bad one…"

This spontaneous feeling, which stayed with Bulgakov, became more and more unique in later years.

For now, he was sufficiently assimilated into the literary milieu in Moscow. This milieu was continuing to expand.

On 7th November 1923, G. Alekseyev returned to Moscow; shortly before doing so, he had earned himself a review from an officious publicist, one of the directors of the state publishing concern, N. Meshcheryakov. The reviewer quoted his book *Dead Flight. A Tale about Foreign Years* (*Mertvyy Beg. Povest' Zarubezhnykh Let*), which described the life of former white guard officers in camps near Berlin. Citing the descriptions in it with satisfaction (they were written in the Gorky-esque style of the fiction of the 1910s, which Bulgakov managed to overcome with his prose), the reviewer concluded his review with the following image: "The portrait is painted in a talented fashion and by a man who knows what he is about. The author loves the characters he portrays; he is at pains to seek out the human traits in them. This only serves, however, to make the portrait even more murderous." Such a review certainly called for a response.

The name of G. Alekseyev was not new to Bulgakov: he had been an assistant to the editor of News of the Day and the editor of the literary newspaper *Nash Ponedel'nik* (*Our Monday*), and then editor of *Svobodnaya Rech'* (*Freedom of Speech*) in Rostov-on-Don, a newspaper that Bulgakov would certainly have read in late 1919 and early 1920.

On 22nd December 1923, for the third time in a year (counting from 30th December 1922), Bulgakov comes to *Nikitinskiye subbotniki*, to listen to Ovady Savich reading his story *The Pension von Offenberg* (*Pansion fon Offenberg*). On the same day, a regular of these Saturday meetings, the artist Alexander Kurennoi (1865-1944), painted his portrait, putting his signature and the date on it. In the painting, Bulgakov looks remarkably young: he looks like a young student, his hair cut very short, almost as a soldier would wear it, and with a tranquil, slightly mocking look on his face.

Also at the gathering were A. Neverov, Vera Inber, I.N. Rozanov, Ada Vladimirova and A. Antonovskaya. Neverov and Rozanov took the floor, commenting on the merits of the language of the story. Bulgakov says nothing.

In a brief entry in Rozanov's diary about the meeting and the speeches, Bulgakov does not feature; in the list of signatures of the attendees, his signature is to the right of everyone else's. He was not at home in this literary environment in Moscow. "In the interval," writes Rozanov, "Vadya [O. Savich – M.C.] took us into the other room. There, six of us (me, Vadya, Zarkhi, Neverov, Kirillov, Sobol) got through two bottles of port." After the break, N. Berendhof read his poems. 3 days later, Rozanov writes that on Christmas day, news spread like wildfire around literary Moscow of the sudden death of A. Neverov; the funeral was held on 29th December.

In his new role as a full-time sketch-writer for Gudok, Bulgakov offered the newspaper the long story *A Raid (In a Magic Lantern)* [*Nalyot (V Volshebnom Fonare)*], telling of a period of time during the Civil War: it was about the things that had occupied the writer's mind most during the year in question. The story was printed on 25th December 1923. From that month onwards, Bulgakov's sketches were printed regularly, but particularly frequently – 4 or 5 a month – from the summer of 1924 onwards.

He had spent the whole of the past year writing about the recent past, but his own past was standing at his back, refusing to go away.

Y. F. Nikitina left an oral account of the following episode. At one of the Nikitina Saturdays, Bulgakov, spotting someone among those present, rushed over to embrace him, in full view of everyone. After embracing one another, they stood in silence for what seemed like an age. Nobody knew what this was about. Nikitina later found out from the man in question, B.Y. Etinhof, what it was that connected him to Bulgakov. Apparently, at the moment when the Red forces broke through the Southern front, a large group of officers was taken prisoner; there were doctors among them. Etinhof had been a commissar in these units. He said to the doctors: "Gentlemen, we are losing men due to typhus. Will you look after us?"

This suggestion was made at a time when all of the prisoners were due to be executed by firing squad. And Bulgakov allegedly said in response that he was in a position in which he could see no way out, and that he was a doctor first and foremost, and an officer only on a secondary level…

The man had stayed alive, whilst the others were executed. It was the memory of this that caused them, on meeting several years later in Moscow, to embrace one another in silence; this silence seems to hold up from a psychological perspective. Y.F. Nikitina recounted all this to the journalist V.M. Zakharov in the early 1960s, and he, in turn, passed it on to me on 25th October 1987.

What stood behind this meeting at the Nikitina Saturdays, if it really did take place, and was not the fruit of a memoirist's over-active imagination? The possibility of there being some genuine basis behind Nikitina's story is confirmed by an entry about B.Y. Etinhof, described as "an old friend from back in the Vladikavkaz days", made in Y.L. Slezkin's diary on 29th December 1932: "He is a Communist, somewhat of a poet, a little bit of a musician, he's smart, cultured, an aesthete… and cunning. He is now married to Yevdokiya Fyodorovna Nikitina [...] Boris Yevgenevich is my former boss (he was director of popular education in the Vladikavkaz District, when I was struggling away there as head of the sub-department for the arts").

Tatiana Nikolayevna never said anything about Bulgakov having been taken prisoner by the Reds; it is hard to pick out a moment when this could have happened – in the autumn of 1919, Bulgakov ought to have been successfully making his way to his designated posting, since the whole of the south of Russia was in the hands of the Volunteer Army, and at the time when the Reds' attack was unfolding, he was mainly in Vladikavkaz. He did however leave the city in February 1920, before he came down with typhoid, and could have been caught up in the crossfire somewhere. The real story behind the excitable encounter in Moscow may have been – and this is more likely – some sort of critical situation during the first few months after the arrival of the Reds in Vladikavkaz, when Etinhof may have shown Bulgakov a munificence that was so dear in those years. It is worth reiterating, though, that the end of 1919 and the start of 1920 is a period in Bulgakov's life that is known only very approximately, and it is entirely possible that some unexpected discoveries may be made in this regard.[13]

I shall mention another person whom Bulgakov met that year – the journalist Leonid Sayansky (Leonid Viktorovich Popov). He was just two years older than Bulgakov, but his work had been published since the 1910s – in *Solntse Rossii* (*The Sun of Russia*), *Novyy Zhurnal dlya Vsekh* (*New Journal for All*), and so on, and had had a book published, *Notes of a Cossack Officer* (*Zapiski Kazachiego Ofitsera*), in 1915; in the mid-1920s he had become a humourist, writing little booklets for various publishers, including *Gudok*. "… Bulgakov first met him at *Gudok*, I think. Then his

---

[13] A key to verifying this episode may be the attentive analysis of these months in the biography by B.Y. Etinhof; the author wishes to draw the attention of all those with a taste for investigating to this task.

wife arrived from somewhere. They started coming to see us regularly, and they always brought a bottle of champagne. We rarely went out anywhere in those days; they came to see us almost every evening.

The Yulia in question was an actress, but didn't have a job anywhere; she later *fled* from Sayansky. She flirted with Bulgakov at every opportunity. And he always said to me: 'You've got nothing to worry about – I'll never leave you.'

One time, Sayansky came to see us, and we were just getting ready to go to the Komorskys. He knew them. Mikhail says: 'Come with us – I'll tell them you're an Englishman!' Sayansky had a remarkable parting in his hair. I later noticed in *A Theatrical Novel* the part where the editor asks: 'How do you manage to have such a remarkable parting?' – and that was of course a reference to Sayansky's parting! Mikhail never had a parting like that.' One can see this 'remarkable parting', by getting hold of a copy of the 1915 edition of *Notes of a Cossack Officer*. That evening, the three of them really did go over to the Komorskys' house, and Sayansky kept quiet all evening, as they had agreed he would, fearing only lest someone might start talking to him in English; for in addition to the Komorskys, Nadya was also there, Komorsky's niece, and she had studied English… but Nadya was even more afraid than he was, fearing that this Englishman would turn to her and come out with some long peroration in English… This was the kind of high-jinx that was so typical of Bulgakov.

"At New Year's, the Komorskys were invited somewhere else, and we set off for the Sayanskys. We saw in 1924 with them and their parents. Sayansky's father was retired, he was a former military man I think…his wife was there, at the table, she was elderly…There were no other writers there, besides Sayansky and Bulgakov…" – this is how Tatiana recalls the last New Year that they were to spend together. "On Tatiana Day, 25th January, Bulgakov wanted to celebrate my name-day and invite the Komorskys round, but days of mourning had been declared [due to the death of Lenin] and there was no wine to be had anywhere, so we didn't invite them. And then he went out and bought me that carved wooden casket. And from that day forth I always carried it with me wherever I went.

Prior to that, on 24th January, we had spent the whole night standing outside the House of Unions, but hadn't been able to get in, and went home numb with cold. Bulgakov then went there on his own, and got it."

On 27th January, Bulgakov's report, *Hours of Life and Death (From Nature)* [*Chasy Zhizni i Smerti (S Natury)*] was printed in *Gudok*. It contained lively dialogues featuring people who were in a desperate rush to bid goodbye to V.I. Lenin:

"Dearies, don't let anyone jump the queue now, will you? Keep order, citizens!

We'll all die one day…

Use your brain before you open your mouth. If you died, for example, what difference would it make? What difference – come on, tell me, citizen?

Don't insult me!

I'm not insulting you, I just want to make my point. A great man has died, so keep quiet. Keep quiet just for a moment, and let it sink in."

The report also contains a sketch describing the first impressions of what the author saw: "In a coffin, on a red plinth, there lies a man. He is yellow, with a waxy yellowness, and the bumps on the forehead of his bald head are steep. He is silent, but his face is wise, important and tranquil. He is dead. There is a grey jacket on him, and on the greyness is a red stain – the medal of the banner. The banners on the walls of the white room are in a check pattern: black, red, black, red. There is a gigantic medal – a gleaming ring of candles in a flickering fire, and at its heart there lies, on a plinth, a man, doomed by death to eternal silence.

Just as, with his words, he prompted countless helmets of sentries to words and actions, so, now, he has killed, with his silence, the sentries and the flow of people coming to say a final farewell."

4

In the first few weeks of 1924, an evening was organised to greet the returning *smenovekhovtsy*. Bulgakov already knew some of them. "Potekhin lived somewhere on Myasnitskaya, in Zlatoustinsk side-street," Tatiana recalled. "His wife was very beautiful, she was of merchant stock, and he used to call her 'merchant-woman' for that reason. Klyuchnikov's wife was the pianist Dolenga, and Bulgakov often escorted her to concerts, as her page... He used to visit both men at their homes. Potekhin organised parties at home, where there was much dancing and a little drinking..."

Tatiana recalled that Bulgakov went to the party on Denezhny side-street with D. Stonov and Y. Slezkin. At that point, he was only known to the audience who had gathered for his sketches in the Berlin-based newspaper *Nakanune*. "Before me," Belozerskaya recalled, "there stood a man aged 30-32; he had fair hair, combed smoothly into a side-parting. He had blue eyes, his features were not quite correct, his nostrils were cut out deeply; when he speaks, he wrinkles his brow. [...] I agonised for ages before finally working out who it was that Bulgakov resembled. And suddenly it dawned on me: he looked like Chaliapin!" As we shall see, the friendship between the two that began at Denezhny Side-street was soon to change Bulgakov's private life.

In February or early March, 1924, in the fourth edition of *Nedra*, *Diaboliad* was published. Yevgeny Zamyatin was among the first to comment on the story, writing a lengthy review of it. With his usual strictness, even harshness of assessment, but with an understanding of the possibilities open to the young author: "The only bit of modern material in *Nedra* is Bulgakov's *Diaboliad*. This author's instincts are undoubtedly sure when it comes to selecting the compositional setting: elements of fantasy that are rooted in everyday life, a changing of images that is as rapid as at the movies – one of those (few) formal frames into which one can put our yesterday – the years 1919 and 1920. [...] The absolute value of this piece by Bulgakov – which really does not seem to have had much thought put into it – is not great, but it seems fair to say that one can expect good things of this author." It appears that the two writers struck up a friendship the following year, when

Zamyatin came to Moscow for the premiere of *Levsha* (*The Left-Handed Craftsman*).

Bulgakov gave the very first prints of *Diaboliad* to his first typist in Moscow, who had typed for him on the promise of being paid later at the end of 1921 and in 1922 (11th March 1924 – "To Irina Raaben, in honour of our painstaking, collaborative work on the typewriter), and to the Komorskys, who had given him such warm welcomes on those winter evenings in 1922-1923 at their home in Maly Kozikhinsk (12th March – "To Zina and Volodya Komorsky, in memory of our evenings at Kozikha"). But Bulgakov's life in this part of Moscow, which he had got to know so well over the course of just over two years – Bolshaya Sadovaya, Trekhprudny and Maly Kozikhinsky, Patriarch's Ponds – the very places which would soon crop up in the topography of *The Master and Margarita*, was already coming to an end. In subsequent years, he was required to live in places which, for people born and bred in Moscow, had traditionally been associated with a notion of "old" Moscow – the area around Starokonyushenny Pereulok: Prechistenka, Ostozhenka…

The house on Bolshaya Sadovaya was associated with need, with the fraught search for ways of earning money in the first years in Moscow, 1921-1922, with the hopeless attempts to win money at the nearby casino. V. Katayev recalls these attempts in his tale *My Diamond Wreath*, and Tatiana told me about them too:

"He would wake up at one a.m.: 'We're going to the casino – I've got a feeling I can't fail to win now!'

'I'm not going anywhere, I need some sleep!'

'No, we're going, come on!'

And we would lose everything, of course. In the morning I gathered together everything we had in the house and took it to the Smolensk market."

1923, the year in which, as Bulgakov wrote some time later, "I found a way of living", was a year in which he worked predominantly on his novel – and it was extremely intense, arduous work.

Let us listen to Tatiana again. I recorded many of my conversations with her not only on paper, but also on a tape-recorder, with her permission. It is hard to convey in writing the intonation of her speech, which was not a monologue but was always merely a part of the conversation. "… He wrote *The White Guard* by night and loved to have me sitting close by, doing some sewing. His hands and feet would get cold, and he would say to me: 'Some hot water, right away'; I heated the water on the kerosin stove, and he put his hands in a tub of hot water…

'What was causing that? Problems with his heart?'

'No, apparently it was a problem with his nerves; he used to get very tired…'"

When and where did the author's first readings of his novel take place – those readings of a freshly completed work, among a handful of friends, writers that he knew or half-knew, which were a common phenomenon in Moscow life in the 1920s? On 9th March, 1924, Yury Slezkin told *Nakanune* about a reading of the novel *The White Guard*, over the course of four evenings in the circle *Zelyonaya Lampa*… One of the members of this circle, which met in the early 1920s at the house of Lidiya Kiryakova on Bolshaya Dmitrovka – beneath a green lamp, sure enough! – was the linguist Boris Gornung; shortly before he died, Gornung told me, in October 1975, that he had been present at these readings. "The last time I saw Bulgakov was in January 1924 – so those readings must have taken place before January. I recall that Bulgakov's first wife, Tatiana Nikolayevna, was present at all the readings."

He read at other places, too. The artist Natalya Ushakova told me that the writer Sergei Zayaitsky had said to her, early in the spring of 1924: "Come and see me – a young writer who has come over from Kiev is going to read something." This reading at Zayaitsky's house was the start of Bulgakov's friendship with a new circle of friends – people who described themselves as "children of the old Moscow". This was how he came to know Natalya Ushakova and her husband, Nikolai Lyamin, who worked for the State Academy of the Artistic Sciences. They lived in one of the side-streets off Ostozhenka, the apartment which, as anyone interested in the topography of *The Master and Margarita* might surmise, Ivanushka ran into, after following Woland, and saw a naked woman in the bath… Whether or not this is the case, we know for sure that one of the first readings of the novel took place in this very apartment, in either 1928 or 1929, when its working title was still *The Engineer's Hoof (Kopyto Inzhenera)*…

"The day after his reading of *The White Guard*," Natalya Ushakova continues, "I met Bulgakov in Okhotny Ryad. We greeted one another, he walked on, and I got a strange feeling from him – it seemed to me that a student was walking past: he somehow held himself shyly, he was awkward somehow…"

Among these representatives of "old Moscow", he did not immediately feel at home, and was not recognised as "one of us" straight away. All these people – art historians, philology experts, artists, writers – had known one another since they were children; they had had the same home doctors when they were young, and their parents had encouraged them to become friends with each other. To them, even in 1924, he was still "a writer who has come over from Kiev" – this was a far cry from how things stood at Gudok, in his literary circle in the first years in Moscow, where they had all been new to the city: Katayev, Olesha, Ilf, and Yevgeny Petrov, and they had all come from the south, and all had memories of the times of the civil war that were shared by the others to a greater or lesser extent.

Here, in the "Prechistenka" circle, he seemed like a provincial type ("One couldn't describe him as elegant," Natalya Ushakova told me), and for that very reason, it seems, he initially felt shy and was like an awkward student: many recall that although he was into his early thirties by then, he looked considerably younger.

In the first months of 1924, some important events in Bulgakov's life took place: he began to have an affair with Lyubov Belozerskaya, who had arrived together with the *smenovekhovtsy*. A step towards the future changes was his divorce from Tatiana Nikolayevna. "We got divorced in April 1924," Tatiana Nikolayevna told me, "but he said to me: 'You know, it's just convenient for me – to say that I'm a bachelor. But don't you worry – everything will stay as it was. We're just getting divorced formally.' 'So I'll be a 'Lappa' again?' I asked. 'Yes, and I'll be Bulgakov.' But we carried on living together on Bolshaya Sadovaya…

He introduced me to Lyubov Yevgenievna Belozerskaya. She had previously lived in Kiev, with a journalist named Fink, then she left with Vasilevsky-Nebukva. Then Vasilevsky brought her to Moscow, and there was some man who was expected to propose to her. But the proposal never came; Vasilevsky abandoned her, and she had nowhere to live. She started spending time at Potekhin's house, and we invited her to stay with us. She taught me to dance the foxtrot. She once said to me:

'All that is left for me to do now is poison myself…'

I told Bulgakov what she had said, of course… Well, in a literary sense, she was competent, of course. All I did was sell things at the market; I did all the housework too, and I got so tired that I couldn't do anything else… Komorsky encouraged me to get a qualification in hat-making, and I got a diploma and wanted to earn some money somehow. One day I hired someone, but Mikhail said:

'How can you hire someone – I need to work!'

'All right, I'll cancel it.'

So nothing ever came of my work – all I did was make hats for myself. I held my own against him. But he always said to me, whenever I scolded him for flirting with someone: 'You've got nothing to worry about – I'll never leave you.' He would go out all over town, whilst I sat at home... Washing and cooking..."

A trace of the affair that he had begun with Lyubov Yevgenievna Belozerskaya is left by Bulgakov in one of the sketches printed by *Nakanune* on 26th May 1924, *The Housing Question* (*Vopros o Zhilishche*), which is entirely dedicated to the housing crisis in Moscow, which had become even more acute for Bulgakov: he now saw it through the prism of the poverty-stricken position of this woman, his new love. One of the characters in the sketch mentions that he is moving out of his impossible room behind a partition and leaving for Orekhovo-Zuevo. "He's off to Orekhovo-Zuevo, whilst his friend L.Y. [Lyubov Yevgenievna, no doubt – M.C.] is leaving for Italy. Alas, she doesn't have a place at all – not even one behind a partition. And this most beautiful of women, who could have embellished Moscow, can't wait to go to lousy old Rome. And Vasily Ivanovich [the same one who drinks home-made vodka and indulges in debauchery right beside the author of the article, in apartment No. 50 – M.C.] will stay, but she will leave!"

The whirl of feelings which took hold of Bulgakov that spring, and which were caused in large part by the impossibility of finding a new roof over his head, which had become absolutely essential, was reflected in something that Tatiana remembers him saying: "He said to me:

'Lyuba can live with us, can't she?'

'How would that work? In the same room?'

'But she's got nowhere to live!'"

Bulgakov's publishing affairs were going well that spring. *Diaboliad* was published in *Nedra*, and on 10th April 1924, he signed an agreement with the editor of the journal *Rossiya*, I.G. Lezhnev, for the printing of the novel *The White Guard* in the journal.

The author reserved the right to provide excerpts from the novel to the *Nedra* anthologies and to the newspapers *Nakanune* and *Posledniye Novosti* (Petrograd). The royalties that were provided were very small, however. His determination to change his life and the lack of the material conditions needed to do so clearly caused him to experience despair that spring on several occasions.

On 12th April 1924, Bulgakov attended a meeting of the Nikitina Saturdays. A lot of people had gathered this time – around fifty. Bulgakov's name was the twelfth name on the attendance sheet.

During the meeting, he "read excerpts from a novel that does not yet have a name". Judging by the accounts of those present, one can surmise that this work was either *The Way One Lives* (*Zhitie-bytie*), or *The Story of the Town of Tarabarsk* (*Istoriya Goroda Tarabarska*).

Let us quote the minutes of the meeting, since this was a talk that Bulgakov listened to:

"*A. M. Peshkovsky* – the merchant's prayer is not objective enough. He might have thought like that, but he couldn't have prayed like that.

N.A. Stepnoi. Does Dorokhov's form suit the times? A peaceful, smooth scope. This is the vast saga of a behemoth of a time. Now, one cannot approach this issue the way Dorokhov approaches it. It is a simple reference guide about an epoch which we no longer need."

Dorokhov may have appealed to Bulgakov, who by then had already completed his novel about the civil war, first and foremost as the author of *Kolchakovshchina* – a work written about the same events but seen from the other side of the front line, shining a light on the gory details of the whites' behaviour with a perfunctory tone.

After the discussion of Dorokhov, K. Zelensky read out his observations, *Vera Inber and surroundings*, and Inber herself read her long poem "on the boy with freckles".

It is possible that Bulgakov stayed behind to listen to the third part of the evening: "L. N. Seifullina," the minutes report, "read a story by the Siberian writer Zazubrin – *A Dormitory* (*Obshchezhitiye*).

This was another writer who may have interested Bulgakov, as the author of a novel about the civil war, *Two Worlds* (*Dva Mira*), containing those same frightening details that one does not find in later descriptions of these events. It may well have been the perfunctory style adopted by both writers in describing them that tempted Bulgakov to go to the meeting – although Zazubrin's story described life in times of peace. This material was also of interest to Bulgakov in these years – as one can see from the story *Diaboliad*.

In May, Bulgakov attempts to get the full text of *Cuff-notes* printed in *Nedra*. He wrote to the secretary of *Nedra*:

"I would be very pleased if *Cuff-notes* were thought suitable. Personally, I like this work very much. […] I desire nothing for myself other than death. How well my affairs are going!"

He planned to get himself a job as a secretary at an editorial office at around this time, but on 31st May came down with appendicitis; he wrote to Zaitsev about this, saying: "I shall not take up a job, I shall move to the south as soon as I get some money." But the money never materialised, it seems (*Cuff-notes* was not accepted by *Nedra*), and he wasn't able to go to the south that summer.

Bulgakov visited a number of literary circles that year, and two of them met at P.N. Zaitsev's house. One of them was a circle of poets (which later formed the Uzel publishing house). L.V. Gornung told me in September 1981: 'They met at Zaitsev's place, in house No. 5 on Starokonyushenny Side-street, in the famous house of Korovin, in the cellar – there was a heated cellar there... Bely used to go there, albeit only rarely, and Sofya Parnok; Pasternak read his *Aerial paths* there, and Maximilian Voloshin read some poems there in March." Bulgakov was indifferent about the latest poetry and it is unlikely he went to these meetings, but P.N. Zaitseva recalls that he read *The Fateful Eggs* at the poets' request, whilst B.V. Gornung asserted in my conversation with him that early in 1925, Bulgakov read *The Heart of a Dog* to the same circle. We know a few things about the second circle thanks to Zaitsev's memoirs: "Alongside the circle of poets... I made an attempt to organise a small circle of writers and visionaries, 'fantastical' writers. M. Bulgakov, S.S. Zayaitsky, M.Y. Kozyrev, L.M. Leonov and Viktor Mozalevsky were supposed to form the main group, with plans for an expansion of the circle later. My plan did not come to fruition though. While organising the circle, I did not properly think through its goals, did not confine it to people who were like-minded in their creative work.

... We held meetings, though: sometimes at my place, sometimes at Leonov or Kozyrev's place, once or twice at S.S. Zayaitsky's home...

At first, they were all interested in the task of organising a circle. The idea of bringing together writers based on the specifics of their creative gifts and mastery seemed appealing and somehow likely to succeed.

But cracks started appearing soon after the first two meetings. A host of issues came up, which had hitherto been passed over in silence, due to how sensitive they were: why did we have three ladies, for our five writers? After all, this wasn't supposed to be a literary salon, was it? Why had the circle been organised by me, a prose writer, and not by a poet?

On one occasion, we were at S. Zayaitsky's place. The artist N.A. Ushakova and her husband, N.N. Lyamin, came along as guests... We started talking about the circle, and someone, very probably Bulgakov, uttered the word 'order', i.e. that our circle ought to take the form of a kind of literary order. At first, everyone was overjoyed by this idea, but a minute later a dangerous thought occurred to all of us at the same time: what if there was someone with a 'loose tongue' amongst us? The suggestion had had more of a jokey, decorative character, but... how can I put it! One could sense something else in it...!

And at one of the meetings, Bulgakov made a brief announcement to the effect that he had been summoned by the authorities, and that they had said that the circle was attracting attention, and told him that the circle had to be closed down…

Tatiana recalls that in the summer, she and Bulgakov moved out of flat No. 50 and into flat No. 34 in the same building, No. 10; the new flat was opposite their old one, across the courtyard. "In this flat," Tatiana said, "there lived a millionaire, Artur Manasevich. He gave money to the building management committee for the upkeep of the building… His windows were right opposite ours – he could see everything that went on in our lives… When his brother died, he had to find someone new to move in, and he said: 'The quietest people are the Bulgakovs.' The room was worse than our first one, of course – that one had been sunny, whereas here, the Venetian window looked directly onto the wall of a studio. He stuck up wallpaper all over the room, and told us there was a telephone and everything… We decided to move." Tatiana later learned that Bulgakov, as he prepared for the changes in his life that had been ripening over the course of that year, had wanted to leave her not among the 'samogon' lifestyle of flat No. 50, so often described in his sketches, but in a far quieter flat, in which a certain family lived – a husband, wife and son, who son got married and left home, and another female neighbour.

In the summer of 1924, judging by the memoirs of P.N. Zaitsev, Bulgakov had another meeting at *Nedra*: Zaitsev had come up with the idea of buying *The White Guard* back from Lezhnev – "for the conditions for the novel were one-sided, and at our *Nedra* Bulgakov could earn incomparably more.

The novel made a strong impression on us [Zaitsev and Veresayev]. Without pausing for thought, I spoke in favour of it being published in *Nedra*, but Veresayev was more experienced and more sober than me. In the letter he wrote setting out his feedback, V.V. Veresayev commented on the merits of the novel, the mastery, objectivity and honesty of the author in showing the events and cast of characters, the white officers, but wrote that the novel was utterly unacceptable for *Nedra*. The letter was fairly long and was like a negative review in style. Veresayev did not dispute the author's talent, but stated that the orientation of the novel, in his opinion, was not suitable for us for ideological reasons. Perhaps Veresayev had recalled how his own novel, *Dead-End* (*V Tupike*), had recently been received.

Bulgakov was embittered by this review. His hopes of straightening out his material difficulties came crashing down. He was eking out a living at that time writing short articles, stories and sketches for *Gudok* and for medical journals. I tried to reassure him as best I could, saying that Veresayev's review was of course significant, but that the last word would be had by the editor-in-chief of *Nedra*, N.S. Klestov-Angarsky, whose return from Berlin I was awaiting.

In the summer, V.V. Veresayev left for the Crimea. In August, I too went to Oreanda, spent some time in Gaspre and saw Veresayev there. He reiterated to me that *Nedra* could not publish Bulgakov's novel either in an almanac or in book form. [...] On the road to Koktebel, I spoke to Angarsky about Bulgakov and his novel. Angarsky had read the manuscript, but he too was inclined to think they couldn't publish it, although he was still wavering. He, too, considered *The White Guard* to be a work of talent, the novel had made a powerful impression on him with its realistic portrayal of real events, its vivid and juicy descriptions of people, of their characters, but Angarsky was concerned by the portrayal of the white guardsmen, the recent enemies of the Soviet government, who might elicit feelings of sympathy in readers.

And, after hesitating for a while, Angarsky decided to support Veresayev: the novel could not be published for ideological reasons.

The problem was not that editors in those days were vengeful people; the problem had more to do with the general circumstances of those years. It was in precisely this period that Soviet literature was just starting to take shape. There were only a few Communist writers; the number of writers who acknowledged the Soviet government unreservedly and collaborated with it was also small. There was a need to select and recruit writers carefully. Both Angarsky's *Nedra* and A. Voronsky's *Krug* had to do this job.

Angarsky and Veresayev were both sold on Bulgakov's talent and his realistic portrayal of life, but they decided not to publish the novel. With this unhappy news for Bulgakov, I returned to Moscow early in September.

Later that month, Bulgakov came to our offices at *Nedra*, and I told him what the editorial board's response had been. Our rejection of *The White Guard* cut him like a knife. He had grown thin since I last saw him. As before, he was getting by on incidental income from the little journals published by the Palace of Labour at Solyanka, and he was greatly in need of money.

He sat down at the table next to me and became lost in thought: mechanically, he began drawing the outline of something on a sheet of paper that was lying there.

And suddenly it dawned on me.

'Mikhail Afanasievich, haven't you perhaps got something else ready, that we might be able to publish in *Nedra*?'

After a moment's thought, he said: 'I have a story that's almost finished… with elements of fantasy…' I pushed a clean sheet of paper towards him.

'Write out a request asking to be issued with an advance of one hundred roubles, for your forthcoming story. When can you bring it to us?'

'You shall have it within a week, or a week and a half,' he replied.

I did the official paperwork for his request, writing on it: 'Pay one hundred roubles', and Bulgakov dashed off to the accounting department of *Mospoligraph*. After ten to fifteen minutes he came back with the money and shook me firmly by the hand.

A week later, he brought to our offices the manuscript of his new story – *The Fateful Eggs*…" (the publishing house *Mospoligraph*, so important to Bulgakov in the years 1924-1925, would soon be referenced in the full name of Sharikov – Poligraph Poligraphovich…).

P.N. Zaitsev's archive contained a sheet of paper covered in writing, with an explanatory note on the reverse side that was written in his own hand in the 1960s: "M.A. Bulgakov, whilst waiting for me and for his royalty fee in the editorial offices of *Nedra* in 1924, poured out his sadness in drawings and aphorisms." The sheet contains notes written in Bulgakov's hand: "Veresayev's tel. number? [each letter has been written over many times, ponderously – M.C.]. 2-60-28." And then to the side of that: "But his phone number won't help me…" Above and to the right of this: "Fog… fog…" And below: "Is there life beyond the grave? Tomorrow, perhaps, they'll hand over some money…" Even lower down is a drawing drawn with the same pen: a self-portrait with eyes full of despair. To the right are three dancing stick-figures, like the ones from Conan Doyle's *The Adventure of the Dancing Men*. It seems safe to assume that this sheet of paper genuinely was filled in, semi-mechanically, by Bulgakov at the very moment when P. Zaitsev was doing the paperwork for his request for an advance. When exactly did this happen? It may have been at the end of August; for on September 4th, Zaitsev sends Bulgakov a letter in which, on Angarsky's behalf, he chivvies him along with the story: "So then, we are expecting the manuscript tomorrow or the day after tomorrow!"

There is another memoirist, too, who remembers the period when Bulgakov was finishing his story (the plot of which he may well have thought up only after Nedra rejected *The White Guard*). Many years later, Vladimir Manasevich – by then known as Vladimir Arturovich Levshin, the mathematician and writer, would describe details of the life that Bulgakov lived in the apartment owned by his parents. Among other things, he reproduces an interesting telephone conversation involving Bulgakov that he claims to have overheard: "He is calling the *Nedra* publishing house; he asks them (for the very last time, no matter what!) an advance for his story *The Fateful Eggs*. It becomes clear that they are refusing to agree to do so.

'But listen to me,' he says, trying to convince them, 'the story is finished. It just needs to be reprinted… You don't believe me? Fine! I shall now read the ending out to you…'

He fell silent for a short while (he was 'fetching the manuscript'), then began to improvise an ending to the story. He spoke so fluently, in such smooth, distinct passages, that it was as if he really was reading from a painstakingly crafted manuscript. […] A minute later, he was rushing off to collect the money. […] Incidentally, the ending that Bulgakov made up on the spot was very different from the ending that was eventually published. In the 'telephone' version, the tale ended with a picture of the evacuation of Moscow, which is brought about by the arrival of hordes of giant boa constrictors. In the final version, the boa constrictors are killed off by the freezing temperatures before they reach the capital…"

This episode is remarkable in two respects. Firstly, the recollection of the improvisation itself seems to hold water: Bulgakov's manuscripts clearly indicate that he was writing down a text that had already been composed in his mind, and that "writer's block", those long periods of contemplation with the pen held above the piece of paper, was not something he suffered from: once the plot had been thought through, the words that formed the fabric of the story issued forth easily and quickly (though this did not preclude the writing of draft after draft, sometimes starting the text again from the beginning). Secondly, it is of no little interest that Gorky, who was not familiar with this version, wrote to Mikhail Slonimsky on 8th May 1925: "I like Bulgakov very much, very much indeed, but he wrote the ending of the story badly. He refrains from using an attack on Moscow by reptiles – and just think what a monstrously interesting image that would have been!"

"The story was suitable for our anthology first and foremost because of its size," P.N. Zaitsev later recalled, "there were four printed sheets in it… After reading the story, I passed on the manuscript to V.V. Veresayev (Angarsky had flown to Berlin on business). Veresayev was ecstatic when he read it. Overlooking the rules of our agreement with N. Angarsky, whereby Angarsky was supposed to have the final word, Veresayev accepted the story for the next almanac, and he and I immediately agreed to include it in the collection. […] When he got back to Moscow and read the proofs, Angarsky scolded us for taking the law into our own hands, but deep down he was happy…

… The poets, the members of the circle which used to meet at my home, asked me to try to persuade Bulgakov to read his story at one of our meetings. They were all very keen to hear it. I passed on their request to Mikhail Afanasievich, and at the very first meeting he read *The Fateful Eggs*. Bulgakov was a good reader, and all those listening to him had high praise for the author's gift: his ability to combine real life with fantasy. Among the poets assembled there was Andrei Bely. He liked the tale very much. It seems to me that for all the differences in their creative individualities, they both had something in common, and that was Gogol. A. Bely thought that Bulgakov had a rare talent. A year later, in 1925, Bely wrote the first volume of his novel *Moscow*, which also contained a brilliant inventor as its protagonist, Professor Korobkin; just like Persikov in Bulgakov's story, Korobkin is also setting out new paths in science: in *The Fateful Eggs*, a 'ray of life' is discovered, whilst in *Moscow*, Korobkin releases the super-energy of the atom for the good and benefit of humanity.

Strangely, though, whilst A. Bely was interested in Bulgakov and thought him an interesting, original writer, Bulgakov did not see anything in Bely.

I recall that sometime later, I mentioned Bely's name during a conversation with Mikhail Afanasievich.

'Ah, what a liar he is, what a great liar…' Bulgakov exclaimed. 'Take his last book for instance [the novel *Moscow* – M.C.]. For every ten words in it, you'll struggle to find two words of truth! And what an actor he is!'

[It may be that he had noticed the correlation between Korobkin and Persikov– M.C.].

The Fateful Eggs caused an argument between me and A.K. Voronsky, the editor of *Krasnaya Nov'* (*Red Soil*). […] He couldn't forgive me for having pinched a good story from right under his nose. […] S.N. Tsensky said to me: *The Fateful Eggs* is the only work in our *Nedra* that isn't boring to read…' (one recalls Zamyatin's review of *Diaboliad* from a year earlier).

The recitations are also mentioned in a letter from P.N. Zaitsev to Voloshin dated 7th December 1924: "We meet on Wednesdays. The following read their works: A. Bely – his new novel, M. Bulgakov – the story *The Fateful Eggs*."

Bulgakov may have met Bely for the first time at his recital. Among the few books from Bulgakov's personal collection that survived in the archives is A. Bely's *The Eccentric of Moscow* (*Moskovskiy Chudak*), with an inscription by the author: "To the deeply respected Mikhail Afanasievich Bulgakov, from a genuine admirer, Andrei Bely (B. Bugayev). Kuchino. 20th Sept. '26." Bulgakov, in turn, gave a copy of his collection *Diaboliad* to Bely – evidence of this comes in the shape of a note from Zaitsev dated 7th October and discovered in Bely's archived letters: "I leave you: 1) Bulgakov's book *Diaboliad* – a gift from the author, who was very touched by the attention you bestowed on him..." (the note probably dates from 1926).

R.V. Ivanov-Razumnik comments on *The Fateful Eggs* too, and on 10th November 1926 he writes to A. Bely: "This tale by the young (and not untalented) Bulgakov tells of Meyerhold being killed during a performance of *Boris Godunov* in 1927, during the scene in the council of boyars, when he is crushed to death by some naked boyars who fall off the trapeze. It is not as improbable as it sounds."

Y.S. Bulgakova told a number of people what Bulgakov had told her about his first meeting with Veresayev (who played an active role in his fate that autumn). One of those who heard her account published it in a book, and I shall quote from this book below, since the writer's widow, though somewhat perturbed by the very fact that it had been published, did not question the accuracy of the outline of her story, as reproduced in the book (see A. Less. *Unread Pages* [*Neprochitannyye Stranitsy*]. M., 1966). "One rainy autumnal evening, Bulgakov rang the bell at Veresayev's apartment. The writer himself opened the door.

'Bulgakov,' he said shyly, as he came in.

And, on account of his nervousness, for some reason he took off his galoshes.

'What can I do for you?' Veresayev asked.

'Nothing, really, Vikenty Vikentievich,' Bulgakov mumbled guiltily... 'I just wanted to shake you by the hand... I liked your book, *A Doctor's Notebook*, very much.'

Veresayev said nothing.

'Well then, goodbye,' said Bulgakov after a minute's silence, and then he started putting his galoshes back on.

'Wait a moment, tell me what your surname is again?' asked Veresayev, cupping his hand to his ear.

'Mikhail Afanasievich Bulgakov.'

'So it's you – you're the author of *Cuff-notes*!'

'I am indeed.'

'My dear man,' Veresayev exclaimed, 'why on earth didn't you tell me earlier?...Take your coat off and please come in, you shall be my guest!'

The consolidation of his ties with *Nedra* is an important part of Bulgakov's literary life in 1924-1925. His name crops up in a 'Note' written by the editor of *Nedra* to the party institutions, dated October 1924. This document is fairly important in terms of understanding both Angarsky's position with regard to literature and publishing, and what it was that may have caused him and Bulgakov to be ill-disposed towards one another. "With regard to the publishing plan, I can tell you that this can be provided for a period of no more than three months; the publishing house cannot provide a plan for a longer period due to the lack of suitable literary material.

Plans are easy to draw up in other sectors of the publishing industry, but not in the field of modern literary fiction; here, one has to base things on the dimensions of the writers' creative output, and these dimensions are terribly small. In the last two to three years, only a handful of literary works have appeared which the *Nedra* publishing house could have published.

The prospects for literary creativity are even more unappealing. How can one talk about creativity, if the writers don't have the basic conditions for creativity, they don't have a room to work in. Here are some examples: Vsevolod Ivanov sleeps in strangers' apartments and can't work. The talented novelist Bibik has been exiled from Rostov-on-Don merely because he was once a Menshevik many years ago – he has been kicked out of his house at the very moment when he had begun writing again and was sending us some fairly good things. What's curious about it is that we have stepped up our efforts to recommend his novels to the workers.

The talented writer of fiction, Bulgakov, doesn't have the money to pay his rent."

Angarsky did not mince his words when describing the contemporary literary situation: "Of course, as far as literary garbage is concerned, there's absolutely masses of it: rejected manuscripts can be bought up at the editorial offices by the pound, and graphomania is growing more quickly than state industry.

The other difficulty about drawing up a lengthy plan is the fact that many very literary works are not suitable for *Nedra*: some due to the fact that they are too modern and slavishly derivative (Vl. Lidin), others due to their form and content: A. Bely, A. Remizov, B. Pilnyak, I. Ehrenburg. *Nedra* sets itself the task of presenting realism in art, a realism that is healthy, strong, understandable to millions of people, and for that reason, works written in flowery, brittle, purposefully confused language (almost in a style designed to resemble Dostoevsky) are not accepted at *Nedra*. We have rejected all those 'so complex' intellectual concerns, all those 'chasms' and 'lapses of the soul' that one finds in A. Bely, Ehrenburg & Co. Our point of view is that if an author has something to say, if he is in the grip of an idea and the need to express that idea, then the form appears in and of itself and will be just as clear and simple as the idea, and accord with it fully.

If, however, a writer has no idea whatsoever, if he picks up his pen not so as to uncover that idea during the process of writing, if he, as people tend to say nowadays, is in a "process of tortuous searching", then it is clear that the form, for that writer, will be just as confused as the content."

Two editors as different from one another as I. Lezhnev and N. Angarsky saw, in Bulgakov, one and the same quality, one that was essential to them: an outward "liberation" from those "tortuous searches", a willingness to show the reader not the search, but the end result. And in many ways, it was this property of his prose that compelled certain subtle and penetrating critics of it to overlook it: Eichenbaum and Tynyanov, the latter of whom wrote in an article published in the summer of 1924: "In this interim period, 'successes' and 'finished things' are not valuable to us. We don't know what to do with good things, in the same way that children don't know what to do with good toys. We need a way out. It is acceptable for 'things' to be 'failures', what matters is that they bring the possibility of 'successes' closer (*The Interim*). Shklovsky's position was more complex, more dependent on personal and biographical circumstances.

It is not a case of the blindness of some and the far-sightedness of others (let's not forget that Angarsky elected not to print *The White Guard*); rather it is about the movement of the literary process, whereby, all too often, the "very best" artistic quality goes unrecognised by a writer's contemporaries, and then becomes visible, identifiable, in some other branch of the literary movement.

Angarsky also defined another set of writers whom he found unacceptable: "The Nedra publishing house does not print, either, 'gold-leaf', the 'transformed people' one finds in Remizov and his school, the people one finds in Nesterov and Vasnetsov, such a people does not exist and all attempts by the 'people's poets' – Klychkov, Klyuyev, Yesenin – to portray the people by means of stylizing them as they were in the old days, with some churchiness added for extra flavour, suggests only that these authors are trying to move away from life and reality towards "splendid isolation", to distant, ancient Rus and its simple peasants, and are covering with gold-leaf that which ought to be called by its own name, straightforwardly…" Bulgakov may have been able to agree to some extent even with these harsh ideological assessments: the civil war had strengthened his scepticism about the deification of the ordinary peasant; at this time, he had probably already written the scene in

The White Guard in which Myshlayevsky shouts out: "... it's the local peasant men – bloody Dostoevskyan icon-bearing bastards!" I.S. Ovchinnikov, from the staff of *Gudok*, describes in his memoirs "a conversation I had with him long ago. The countryside was already seething. The peasants were all set either to torch the landowners' estates or wreak a terrible vengeance on the landowners themselves.

Bulgakov jokes:

"Rejoice and be glad! This is your icon-bearing populace! These are your Platon Karatayevs!"

In his "Note", Angarsky had posed the question: "What is our attitude towards proletarian writers?" His answer was as follows: "When we talk about 'proletarian' writers, we mean those intellectual-writers who, if not entirely, then to a considerable degree, stand on the viewpoint of the proletariat." This man, who himself, undoubtedly, stood "on the viewpoint of the proletariat", believed that there was no literature to be had outside the intellectual world; otherwise, one would get that very same "imaginary proletarian writer" that Mikhail Zoshchenko created and parodied ("... I am parodying, with my works, that imaginary but authentic proletarian writer who *would exist* in today's living conditions and in today's environment," wrote Zoshchenko in 1928. "*Of course, such a writer cannot exist, not now, at any rate*. But when he does exist, his society, his environment will be boosted significantly in all respects." [My italics – M.C.].

Angarsky gave some examples of the 'proletarian' poets and writers of fiction whose work he published (Tikhonov, Serafimovich, Bakhmetev etc.). "But we rejected the anthology by the 'Create' collective, led by Krechetov-Volzhsky, as overly self-conscious writing, devoid of talent. (Double-barrelled surnames in literature are fatally dull: why should some Sidorov or other suddenly become Krechetov-Volzhsky, or Lara-Persky?) Choosing a nice name is easy, writing something good is rather more difficult." As one reads these lines, one gets the feeling that Bulgakov must have been impressed by Angarsky's temperament alone. And the sarcasm seen in his views chimes perfectly with the surnames that Bulgakov would later give to the hack writers in one of his plays: Ponchik-Nepobeda and Marin-Roshchin (*Adam and Eve*, 1931).

The subsequent pages of *Notes* (*Zapiski*), important in many respects, can also be seen as pretty much a direct explanation of his interest in Bulgakov's creative work – and particularly his third story, which the author would soon start working on. "Proletarian writers fall under a bad influence at every turn," wrote Angarsky. "We look into the distance and we see not what is really there, but the ideal that we have written. Derivative doggerel, mostly imitating Surikov and Koltsov, more rarely Blok, is viewed by us entirely from the point of view of the author's social background. We play along, reassess their work and waste paper on mediocre exercises instead of simply saying: give it up, stop writing, or else you'll contract an incurable disease worse than syphilis. One must know the past of Russian literature, understand and have a feel for the classics. The very idea of surpassing bourgeois literature is impossible if one is not acquainted with it. Are the proletarian writers familiar with this literature? Do the young people get to know it? No. And if this is how things stand, then we are not destined to see any lower workers' literature." Yet there was a boundary, beyond which the similarities between Angarsky and Bulgakov, if they did not end altogether, then at least became more complex: "One can feel hatred for the types and the characters found in Tolstoy, Turgenev, Dostoevsky. But one cannot help but feel admiration for their beauty, the mastery with which they are portrayed. I altogether admit worldviews and attitudes to the world which are not connected to the past at all. I admit a completely new set of sensations, but one cannot reveal these sensations and concerns, one cannot put them into an artistic form without an up-to-date preparation, without an artistic education." The idea of "literary studies" had come to the fore. "The editors of *Nedra* are actively seeking new authors from the lower social strata. We are willing to correct manuscripts patiently, provide advice, discussion and support, but as yet we do not know of a single talent of any note.

But we believe it, we feel it: he will come.

If we do not publish the 'stylizers' of the Russian language (Klychkov, Klyuyev), we don't publish its detractors either, we don't publish Babel because of his scornful and thuggish attitude to the Russian people – the attitude of a rural chief of police."

Here, their tastes differed: Bulgakov seems to have liked Bunin and was irritated by Babel. One must take into account the fact that the words spoken by Babel's characters about the Russians, against the social backdrop of the time, proved, for Bulgakov, to be unjustifiably indistinguishable from the position of the author himself, and shocked Bulgakov. Also at play was the fact that Babel was at the height of his fame at that time. "Babel lived opposite us," Belozerskaya recalled. "Babel was *very* famous. Babel's renown was very great. He was talked about, written about…"

Let us return to Angarsky's *Note* again. Having listed the writers who, for one reason or another, were not suitable for *Nedra*, he wrote: "What remains are the *poputchiky* (fellow travellers) from various trends and ideologies.

They have now taken up a central place in literature. They are fellow travellers because life itself drags them along after us: they are 'fellow travellers' whether they like it or not. Yet it would be too absurd to expect them to sing the praises of our reality and rehabilitate it, to accept it fully. They are generally talented and take life as it is, tearing off, of course, the labels that we hang on things and phenomena. We think we are looking at some sort of opposite world, but in actual fact they are showing us reality as it really is, the one which, amid the noise of day-to-day events, we fail to see, and from which we hide away behind labels, notices, tags.

Such an artistic portrayal of life is not something we are scared of, for chaos and stupidity, vulgarity, are present in our lives in abundance. [...] And in the writings of the 'fellow travellers', we are trying to trim off the most important thing of all: their attitude to the revolution and the new life. That is why we have rejected plenty of works that were infused with a bourgeois attitude to the revolution as a whole. But if we had displayed even a small degree of attention to the 'fellow travellers', and had not criticized them as 'absconders', had not considered them as people 'of free profession' [who were subject to high taxes, unlike the 'labourers' – M.C.], and had not ejected them from their apartments, we would have achieved a great deal: they would proably have *followed* us, as opposed to being dragged after us, as they are now."

Regardless of what Bulgakov thought about this 'trimming' operation and about how Angarsky had done it in his work, when defining his attitude towards the subjects that were most pressing in the eyes of the editor – he did not want to turn down *a certain degree of attention*. It was in the expectation of procuring some of that attention and understanding that he intended to offer his new story to Angarsky.

5

The writers from *Gudok* continued to visit the house on Bolshaya Sadovaya. Olesha was among them; Tatiana did not like him (she claimed that he used to get drunk very quickly and had no self-restraint). Interestingly, the novel *The White Guard*, which was well received in the 'old Moscow' circle, made no mark whatsoever here. Evidence for this comes in the shape of the recollections of Katayev (when I spoke to him in July 1976).

"Back then, we saw him as being at the level of the sketch-writers of the pre-Revolutionary school – the ones from *Russian word*, such as Amphitheatrov... Doroshevich," V. Katayev recalled. "But Doroshevich was at least seeking a new form, whereas he wasn't. We were critical of those sketch-writers, but for him, they were the gold standard. When I once uttered a disparaging remark about Yablonsky, he said, insistently:

'Valyun, one mustn't talk like that about the writers from *Russian word*!

For my part, I was an admirer of Bunin. And it came as a surprise to me when Bulgakov suddenly recited, by heart, the ending of *The Gentleman from San Francisco*. The likes of Blok and Bunin – as I saw it, they oughtn't to have existed as far as he was concerned! His literary tastes ought to have ended at some earlier stage..."

In *The White Guard*, Yelena recites the ending of *The Gentleman from San Francisco* (*Gospodin iz San-Frantsisko*): "... Darkness, the ocean, a blizzard." The story as a whole served, in my view, as the impulse behind one of the plot lines in Bulgakov's second novel, concerning Berlioz; the sudden death of a man who is certain of his power over life, an important sign (and one that could be decoded later) given to those around him.

"To us, he was a sketch-writer," Katayev repeated, "and when we found out that he was writing a novel, we saw it as some sort of eccentricity on his part... Satirical articles were his stock in trade... I remember him reciting part of *The White Guard* to us – it didn't make any impression on us at all... To me, it seemed to be on a par with Potapenka. And what kind of made-up surnames were those – the Turbins! [Katayev didn't know that this was the surname of Bulgakov's maternal grandmother – M.C.]. [...] It basically seemed of secondary importance, traditional."

What seemed of primary importance then – Pilnyak?

"Well, no! But I re-read his work recently, you know, and realised that he was a great writer."

What did you consider to be great literature *back then*?

"Bely's *Petersburg* – we used to pray for him. Sologub... Aleksei Tolstoy... Bulgakov never praised anyone... He didn't acknowledge them... We were forever getting terribly carried away about something – we suddenly took a great liking for Voltaire, for instance. He had very inflexible tastes. He wasn't excited about anything. [...] The NEP came in back then, you see? We were against the NEP – Olesha, myself, Bagritsky. But he might well have been in favour of it. He might have been. [...] Basically, he didn't want to make those strings quiver (Olesha used to say that: 'One mustn't make the global strings quiver') – he didn't acknowledge Voltaire. [...] To look at, he was similar to Chekhov..."

"He wasn't excited about anything" – this is nothing other than the coldness towards contemporary literature, finely observed by Katayev's "penetrating gaze" (as he himself defined his gaze in our final conversation on 30th December 1985), a marked refusal to be engaged in the literary disputes of the day. The only thing that existed was the Russian literature of the previous century, which had neither been multiplied nor diminished, and which was not subject, in his opinion, to the fluctuations of differing assessments. Let us remember once again what he said about the "appearance of Lev Tolstoy before Russian readers".

"But there were occasionally flaws in Lev Nikolayevich Tolstoy's work," Serafimovich suddenly said; "Mikhail Afanasievich is wrong to think that there is not a single flawed line in Lev Tolstoy!" "There isn't a single one!" Bulgakov said passionately, with conviction. "I am utterly convinced that every line written by Lev Nikolayevich is a genuine miracle. Let another fifty, one hundred, five hundred years go by, and people will still be thinking of Lev Tolstoy as a miracle!"

"Was Olesha on friendly terms with Bulgakov?" I asked Olesha's widow, Olga Suok, on 21st May 1971.

"Yes, very much so. In the twenties, they used to call each other almost every day. 'Hello, Yura.' 'Misha, I'm unwell.' 'What's the matter, Yurochka?' Then they would start to have a professional conversation. Bulgakov gave him advice in a serious voice: 'Don't drink... Drink tea.' The way they talked about women was hilarious. It's hard to convey it, it was all about the shades of meaning, the intonation..."

The friendship between the two writers from *Gudok* was at its high point when he was living in the house on Bolshaya Sadovaya. L.Y. Belozerskaya said that Olesha used to visit him later, as well, though – "Bulgakov used to call him 'Boy'."

A trace of these relations and disputes about contemporary literature is found in an inscription made by Y. Olesha on 30th July 1924 in a collection of his sketches in verse, published in *Gudok* under the pseudonym 'Zubilo': "Mishenka, I shall never write any abstract lyrical poems. That is no use to anyone. A poet ought to write sketches, so that his poems are of some use to people who are on a salary of 7 roubles.

Don't get angry, Mishunchik, *you are a good comic writer* (Mark Twain is a comic writer too). In a year, I shall give you another work by 'Zubilo'. I kiss you. Your Olesha" [my italics – M.C.].

For Olesha, then, and for the other writers at *Gudok*, Bulgakov was above all a comic writer, the author of satirical articles, funny stories, of *Diaboliad*, packed full of comic adventures, which influenced, we should note, the authors of *The Twelve Chairs*.

On 29th September 1924, the proofs for the first part of *The White Guard* arrive, but this section was only published as a newspaper supplement early in 1925 (*Rossiya*, 1925, No. 4).

In the late autumn of 1924, some significant changes took place in his non-literary life.

Tatiana Nikolayevna said to me: "One day at the end of November, Misha was drinking his tea in the morning, and he said: 'If I can find a pretext, I shall leave you today.' Then he came back after a few hours: 'I have come back with a pretext, I want to collect my things.' 'You're leaving?' 'Yes, I'm leaving forever. Help me pack up my books.' I helped him. I gave him everything that he wanted to take with him. We hardly had anything at all at the time anyway.

… Then on top of that, Madame Manasevich, the landlady of our apartment, said to me: 'How could you let him go like that? And you didn't even cry!' For a long time, the people in our building didn't believe we had split up – we had never had any rows, so how could it be true? But things were very tough for me for a long time, of course. I remember I used to lie in bed all day long, something strange happened to me: I felt as though my forehead was swollen, and was going off somewhere far, far away…

Anyway, the next evening Katayev arrived with a bottle of champagne: Mikhail's sister Lyolya was supposed to be coming over that day, and he had been courting her. The bell rang. I thought it was Lyolya; but in came Mikhail, with Yulia Sayanskaya. We all sat there together. I can't remember whether we drank the champagne or not." Tatiana was not only left on her own, she had no profession whatsoever and she had no booklet from a professional union, which meant that her financial situation was soon very precarious – even with the occasional support she got from Bulgakov.

Whilst Bulgakov was looking for a new place to call home (a far from straightforward task), *Nedra* signed a contract with him on 27th November 1924 for a collection of stories on 8-10 sheets (i.e. 200-250 typewritten pages).

Thus he was awaiting the release of the first book in his life, and the novel on which he had placed his main hopes for several years was being printed in the journal *Rossiya*; they were the hopes of a writer who had had a long apprenticeship, but who was still considered a beginner in the field of literary life. The novel was one that he had dreamed about, and these dreams can be seen if one reads between the lines of a story from 1923, *The Samogon Lake*, which was deep within the impossible daily life of apartment No. 50:

"… […]'s wife said:

'I can't take it any more. Do what you want, but we have to get out of here.'

'Kid,' I replied in despair, 'What can I do? I can't get a room. A room costs 20 billion, I only get paid four. Until I finish the novel, there is no other hope for us. Just have patience.'

'I'm not complaining for my own sake,' his wife replied. 'But you'll never finish the novel. Never. Life is hopeless. I'm going to take some morphine.'

When these words were uttered, I sensed that I seemed to be made of steel. I answered her, and my voice was full of metal:

'You shall not take any morphine, because I do not allow you to do so. And I shall finish the novel, and I don't mind telling you that it will be such a novel that it will make the sky turn hot.'"

With the New Year around the corner, he was awaiting the release of his first novel, about which he had just written in his autobiography (Oct. 1924): "I love this novel more than all my other works." The New Year brought promises of literary fame, of the kind of wealth that he had not been able to achieve in just over three years of living in Moscow. An apartment (which was part, we recall, of his task of "restoring the norm in three years") remained one of his most impossible dreams.

Bulgakov moved in with L.Y. Belozerskaya initially at the school where Bulgakov's sister, N.A. Zemskaya, worked as a teacher – in the mezzanine (similar to a choir-loft) of the former grammar school on Nikitskaya, and before long was renting a room on the second floor of a wing of house No. 9, Obukhov (Chisty) Side-street.

P.N. Zaitsev describes in his memoirs how Bulgakov saw in the New Year: "I remember meeting up with Bulgakov just before 1925 began. I had been invited to see in the New Year with a particular group of friends, on the condition that I came along dressed in a masquerade costume. I agreed, and, in an attempt to find a suitable costume that wouldn't look too out of place, decided to pop round to see the Bulgakovs. It turned out that Lyubov Yevgenievna had a number of costumes, which I started to try on, and at the same time I suggested to the Bulgakovs that we could go together. His wife said no, but he, to my surprise, agreed.

On the way there, Mikhail Afanasievich suggested that we should devise a little comedy for our hosts:

'You know everyone in this house, Pyotr Nikolayevich, but nobody knows me there, so let's play a trick on them. Introduce me as a foreigner…'

When we arrived at the house and began walking up the stairs, M.A. put on a small black mask. And that was how we appeared. I played the role of the interpreter (we said who we were in French, which Bulgakov spoke better than me), and he made himself out to be a rich gentleman who had come to Moscow to get to know Russian customs a little better. We were treated to tea and cakes, and for an hour we played out our harmless vaudeville, but then it struck midnight, and, as we said 'happy new year' to one another, we took off our masks. That was how we saw in the year 1925!" [K. Paustovsky recalls another practical joke like this in a story about Bulgakov in his memoirs, so we know there were at least three such incidents.] Thus, the arrival of the "foreigner" who was soon to appear at Patriarchs Ponds was rehearsed.

In this year, Bulgakov developed stronger ties with the circle he found himself in at Zayaitsky's house, and then at the home of the Lyamins – in a room that contained a remarkably beautiful fireplace; in the cold Moscow winter, when the apartments were poorly heated and it was always cold, it was at the Lyamins' that this circle would meet for literary readings, and other events. There would be sometimes be as many as thirty guests, the radiators were turned on, and in the room, with its very high ceiling, it was always warm and cosy. The furniture was very stylish.

Bulgakov quickly became firm friends with Nikolai Lyamin, a philologist descended from a wealthy family of tradesmen; he used to call on him for games of chess. Lyamin's wife, the artist Ushakova, would take up her knitting at such times, and Bulgakov would get angry: this was not, apparently, something that was included in his vision of the "norm" of how the lady of the house ought to behave. "He couldn't stand it when I did my knitting," N. Ushakova recalled.

In this circle of people born and bred in Moscow, he also met some old friends: "He knew Natalya Bekhteeva (the wife of the artist) from Kiev, their dachas had been next door to one another."

In the mid-1920s, this circle was bound "professionally" mainly with the State Academy of Artistic Sciences, which opened its doors in 1922 in Maly Levshinsky side-street (Bulgakov soon moved to this side-street). The Academy was housed on two floors; on the ground floor lived the art historian Boris Shaposhnikov, who also worked for the Academy – a handsome man with well-chiselled features and graceful movements. Bulgakov formed a friendship with him and his wife, the unattractive but intelligent Natalya Kazimirovna, that was warm but not particularly close.

N.A. Severtsova left some vivid memoirs about this circle, which initially included the artists Falk and Kandinsky, and the philologists F.A. and M.A. Petrovsky, who were brothers. "They would come to see us, and have very intelligent conversations, disputes, working out who should do what, and what to read." The philosopher G.G. Shpet used to come, and "the more one put pressure on him in any dispute, the more unwordly the look on his face became, it became predatory like that of a cat, and he would answer questions in such a way that everyone started laughing and no-one could say anything in response, and he would look ecstatic in his victory"; "More and more people joined the group, feeding off one another's reasoning, even though their opinions were often contradictory and irreconcilable; in the disputes, everyone was able to explain their own opinion. In the evenings, we would go to someone's house, and drink vodka, then visit some of the basement establishments on the Arbat and drink beer; we didn't eat very much, we had a lot of fun and no-one complained about life. We went about our business, and two weeks later we would be sitting without a kopeck until payday." The "Gabriches" lived in the apartment of Professor A.N. Severtsov (he taught at Kiev University until 1911) – in the zoological museum on Nikitskaya Street (now Gertsen Street). This building was destined to become the main setting for the story *The Fateful Eggs*. The pages in N.A. Severtsova's memoirs about her father make one think that the impression left by the original character of this remarkable academic (it is entirely possible that Bulgakov still remembered him from the university), by his outward appearance and way of life, were reflected in Professor Persikov. "Love of animals," Severtsov's daughter recalls, "was something that everyone in our home shared. There wasn't a single living creature that we thought unpleasant or abhorrent. Vipers are poisonous and cannot be tamed. Tarantulas are poisonous, particularly in spring, and so on; but frogs are wonderful, especially the big ones – so green, and how they croak."

Her father "was not a believer, and only went to church when strictly necessary"; "he was *taller than average*, broad-shouldered, *slightly stooped*, with long arms... I always used to marvel at how he picked up thin glass slides from the table, taking them right by the edge, and they would never fall out of his hand, and he would invariably lay them down in exactly the right place at the first time of asking. Yet at the same time, he was constantly knocking his shoulder against things, his pockets would collide with door handles, and he would also bump into any objects or walls that were in his path. All you could ever hear was him bumping into things, and the eternal refrain: 'Ah, devil take it!' He said 'devil' all the time. 'Devil take it', 'What the devil', 'Devil take him' – the devil was always there, in all cases and all intonations."

The professor's daughter does not mention Bulgakov's story, and this only serves to make the parallels to the real-life behaviour she describes more expressive. Let us quote some excerpts from *The Fateful Eggs*, concerning Professor Persikov: "he was tall and slightly stooped"; "This could lead to devil knows what!"; "To the devil's mother with him" – Persikov said, in a monotone..."; "Well, of course, if you were to take half a pound of frog-spawn...then certainly...devil take it, well approximately that amount..."; "Together with that devilry that you're writing..." "Well, to the devil with them, all of them!" Persikov shouted melancholically..."; "I am not going to drink any tea...and devil take the lot of them..."; "Devil knows," muttered Persikov. "Well, his physiognomy is abhorrent. He's a degenerate."

"Does he have a glass eye by any chance?" the little man asked, in a husky voice.

"The devil only knows. No, he doesn't, he doesn't have a glass eye, but his eyes are always darting about," and so on. In May 1928, Persikov is "exactly 58 years old" – the same age as Severtsov was in the autumn of 1924, when the story was being written; in the work of Bulgakov, who was so fond of inserting *precise* details about the prototypes for his characters into his texts, such a subtle coincidence may well indicate that my suggestion is correct.

Professor Persikov's assistant is called Pyotr Stepanovich Ivanov, whilst Severtsov's pupil is called Boris Stepanovich Matveyev; and let us note some of the other characters from the Zoological Museum present in N.A. Severtsova's description: "The lab assistants of the department of comparative anatomy and of the zoological museum lived downstairs. The senior lab assistant and anatomist, Felix, lived there with his wife and daughter. Two of Felix's nieces and his brother also lived there, looking after the frogs in their tank, and the rats and other animals used in the experiments. Felix was old, he was sixty, he was an esteemed old man, everyone respected him. He was very thin, quite short, with a grey beard and sticky-up grey hair; he was a little hunched, but very nimble and obliging. He carried out his instructions to the letter. Aleksei Nikolayevich couldn't live without Felix. 'Natashka, run downstairs and call Felix.'"

In *The Fateful Eggs*, there is a reference to "the institute's ever-present caretaker, old Vlas." The man who takes his place is Pancrate, and the protagonist can't live without him; whenever he is in difficulty, the first thing he does is to shout out: "Pancrate!"

Professor Severtsov lived, like Persikov, under the Zoological Museum; his office was located on the building's second floor, right behind the museum. In the 1920s, the young Gabrichevskys lived in this apartment too, and we know that Bulgakov visited them on 31st December 1925, to see in the New Year. It is likely he had been there earlier as well, and that the impression left on him by Severtsov, that remarkable academic and original character, were turned into a short story.

We mustn't forget that the milieu in which he now found himself, after moving to the side-streets of the Prechistenka district, was very different from the heterogeneous groups at *Zelyonaya Lampa* or *Gudok*, which had consisted of people from various cities all over Russia, who had come to Moscow and who were united only by their interest in literature.

These people whom he met in the mid-1920s – upbeat and vivacious, well-educated, and for the most part affluent – formed a certain group, into which they accepted Bulgakov, some eagerly, others with more restraint, with a certain snobbery inherent to those from the capital's wealthy set. It seems fair to suppose that the complexity of his attitude to this set in the future was related to these initial impressions from his interaction with it, although the main reasons for his gradual departure from it were rooted in something deeper.

"He was a pro-vin-cial!" one of my interviewees told me, pronouncing each syllable separately, as he recalled his impressions from half a century earlier. "That's all there is to it! And when he saw people *like that*, when he had already become an adult, he felt jealous and sometimes *retreated* – on account of this inferiority complex of his, as Freud might put it…! Three years ago, I was on a coach tour around Kiev. We passed by a certain building, and the tour guide announced: 'The great Russian writer Bulgakov lived in that building.' And I thought: 'Yes, he was great – in Kiev!'

… The other thing is that Bulgakov was uncouth. I once saw him sitting at a table, with Zayaitsky. And Bulgakov's seat – it might as well have been empty! I'm not talking about his intelligence, you see, but about his knowledge of how to conduct himself in society… He didn't know how to behave with people. To put it simply, he was uncouth! Alexandra Lyamina told me that one time, when he thought no-one could see him, he took a handkerchief from his pocket and used it to wipe his boots…! And there's a big problem with that, namely, that in art, that sort of thing is considered second-rate. There's a machine you can get for making thin cigars; it has written on it 'Ideal for second-rate'. I don't mean to say that Bulgakov was second-rate, but something similar to that." Bulgakov cannot have failed to notice even small doses of this kind of attitude.

In this environment, people loved one another; they loved 'their own kind'. S.V. Shervinsky described Alexandra Lyamina to me as follows: "Very intelligent, tactical. Her father was a numismatist, who had moved away from commercial matters. She carved out a wonderful position for herself in NEP-era Moscow very early on: she was a dressmaker for the government, a real artist… She had a very solid position indeed." Let us add that her studio was in the home of the Toplennikovs; the dressmaking profession played quite an important role in this world – Lyubov Yevgenievna still had a rebus picture puzzle, which she decoded for me as follows: "Lyubochka Bulgakova is a good seamstress."

Some anonymous memoirs by an author who knew this group well reveal that the lines spoken by the "lady" in *The Heart of a Dog* ("I swear, professor," the lady muttered, undoing some sort of buttons on her belt with trembling fingers, "this Moritz… […] This is my final passion!") "are related to the fact that the charming Alexandra Lyamina, N.N. Lyamin's first wife, had at one time fallen head over heels in love with V.E. Moritz, left her husband and taken up with Moritz. Moritz, who had lived with his wife and daughter at 7, Ostozhenka, annulled his first marriage, and in 1922 N.N. Lyamin married N.A. Ushakova. Mikhail Afanasievich had moved to Moscow after all these unsettling events, but they were still the talk of the town, and Moritz was widely spoken of as a seducer and lady killer." S.V. Shervinsky recalls: "V.E. Moritz's mother, Zinaida, nee Yakunchikova, encouraged an aptitude for business in her son at an early age, he managed her affairs when he was just a young man; then he abandoned all that and enrolled at Moscow University… He was in charge of the Soviet pavilion at the international exhibition in Paris.

We usually had dinner at the Lyamins' house. Why? First of all, Lyamin was an intelligent and remarkable man, and secondly, he had a charming wife, and thirdly, they were rich, and that was quite important! Lyamin had been brought up by the lawyer Gorenshtein – and inherited money from him (Lyamin had been an orphan)."

N.A. Ushakova's great-grandfather had been a peasant in the Tambov governorate; "He sent his son to stay with relatives in St. Petersburg; they grew fruit, they used to supply the whole city with it; my grandfather was a capable man too, like my great-grandfather; he married the owner's daughter, and made a living for himself; he bought the estate and gave it to his son, a biologist – my father, Abram Abramovich Ushakov, who studied at the natural science department of Petersburg University. In 1917, my father himself gave the estate away to some peasants, there was a garden and a wood there… From the time before 1917, all I miss is the estate – it was a real oasis in the steppes…".

As an artist herself, she writes: "Bulgakov wasn't interested in artists at all – not in painting, not in anything. Like how some people don't have an ear for music. I'm not saying that he wasn't interested, let's say, in the Louis XVI furniture that we had at our place. At the time when he often came to see us in the afternoons, the table stood in front of the divan, and above the divan, hanging on the wall, was a Sapunov, a tableau from *Le Bourgeois Gentilhomme*. And he usually sat opposite it; one would think, given his interest in Molière, that that ought to have interested him. But all he ever did was tease me: "What an awful painting you've got there!" The only thing that might sometimes interest him was who was portrayed in a painting…"

S.V. Shervinsky told me, recalling the younger days of the inhabitants of Prechistenka and Ostozhenka: "You can't imagine how much strength, how much energy was consumed by doing nothing. That's what we used to say: "Nothing much – just killing time". Nowadays we're far more used to hearing about time killing us, no? Yes, killing time… we used to turn it into an art form."

One of the writers that Bulgakov found most interesting to talk to in those years, though, was S.S. Zayaitsky. Zayaitsky had suffered from tuberculosis of the bones since his childhood (it took him to an early grave in 1930, at the age of 37), and had a hunched back; according to all who knew him, he was the most fun to be around in the entire group.

In his younger years, Zayaitsky had studied at the famous Polivanovskaya grammar school and he was the bard of the Prechistenka whose topography and history Bulgakov was now getting to grips with, after moving to this remarkable district in Moscow. Zayaitsky had even written a poem when he was a boy, in 1914, called *Prechistenka*, which began with the lines: "*Prechistenka, may you be blessed. You coddled us, like a mother in a cradle*", and in 1917 he had written the long poem *The Neurotic*, in which he lovingly described the very same side-streets in Prechistenka and the

Arbat, which were soon to become the setting for one of Bulgakov's stories. In 1924, when they met, Zayaitsky had already achieved fame as a writer of prose, as a master of the adventure and satirical genres.

In one of the side-streets in Prechistenka, there was a house containing several families with whom Bulgakov was close friends. This house was known to all Moscow, for it belonged to the professor and medic Vasily Shervinsky, who had treated Turgenev back in the day; Shervinsky had been given the house for life in 1918, and he leased apartments in it to Y. L. Leontiev, the children's writer V.N. Dolgorukov, a descendant of the Dolgorukys. A well-known figure in publishing lived here too: Gorky's peer Alexander Tikhonov, along with Andrei Arendt and his wife. This social circle in Prechistenka became Bulgakov's circle of friends, a circle that was already ready to listen to his new works right up until the end of the 1930s; Bulgakov remained friends with the Arendts, indeed, until the end of his life. With Sergei Shervinsky, however, he was unable to form a strong friendship: for reasons that were both literary and domestic. Shervinsky told me about this: "When he read *The White Guard* to us, I said to him: 'You know, you've got a character there who's got my father's surname. Please change at least one letter in it for me.' But he refused to do so." They fell out over the matter...

... The man from Kiev, who had long ago shaken off the dust of Kiev's streets in the sun-baked foothills of the North Caucasus, on the streets of Vladikavkaz and Tbilisi, in the docks of Batum – in Moscow, to begin with, he must have felt like a man from Kiev all over again: for that was how people saw him and wished to see him. And he began to cave in under the curving motion of Moscow, deciding to become even more of a Muscovite than the ones who had been born there, to become the bard of Moscow, of its high-rise buildings, streets and side-streets.

CHAPTER THREE

A Theatrical Five Years (1925-1929)

1

The most "theatrical" period in Bulgakov's life began on 19th January 1925, when he "started sketching the bare bones", as he wrote in his diary, for the play version of *The White Guard*.

Issue No. 4 of *Rossiya* came out in the first few months of the new year, containing the start of the novel *The White Guard*, and meanwhile the next issue of the journal, containing the next part of the novel, was being proofread. In February, the sixth *Nedra* almanac came out, with the story *The Fateful Eggs* (it was printed almost simultaneously – initially with the title *The Red Beam* (*Krasnyy Luch*) – in the weekly journal *Krasnaya Panorama* (*Red Panorama*). Bulgakov, however, had stopped working on the play and was wholly engaged in a new story, which he was writing for *Nedra*. The manuscript for this one contains the dates "January – March 1925". On 14th February, a new member of staff at *Nedra*, B.L. Leontiev, sends him a greetings card, informing him that N.S. Angarsky would like to see him "on Sunday, 15th February at 7 in the evening for a literary recitation. Please bring with you the manuscript for *The Heart of a Dog* and read from it. N.S. is looking forward to seeing you and your wife there." Just a few days after this recitation, during which Angarsky clearly took a liking to the story, to judge by his subsequent behaviour, Leontiev sends Bulgakov another card: "Dear M.A. Hurry up, work as fast as you can to provide us with your story *The Heart of a Dog*. N.S. may go abroad in 2-3 weeks and we won't have time to get the thing through Glavlit. And without them, we're unlikely to get anywhere. If you don't want to see the work perish until the autumn – hurry, hurry!"

Bulgakov had apparently read from a rough draft to Angarsky and was now hurriedly finishing it off (perhaps taking into account some ideas put forward by Angarsky and others who had heard the story) and preparing it for re-printing.

On 7th March, Bulgakov read the first part of the story at a "Nikitinska Saturday" meeting. He went to the recitation with Lyubov Yevgenievna. Among the 45 people present were M. Kozyrev and Ada Vladimirovna, Sofiya Parnok, V. Lidin and Vera Inber; on 21st March, he read the second part. On this occasion, one of the listeners, M.Y. Schneider, made a rather important point: "This is the first literary work that dares simply to be itself. The time has come for the 'making real' of our attitude to what is happening." Commenting on the "perfectly pure and precise Russian language", the speaker talked of the "strength of the author", who is "higher than his task".

Y.N. Potekhin talked about Bulgakov's place in the literary process, about the explanatory force of the story: "The fantasy in Mikhail Afanasievich's work merges organically with an acute portrayal of the grotesque in everyday life. The elements of fantasy operate with extraordinary force and are extremely convincing. Many people sense the presence of Sharikov in everyday life." Potekhin, who had arrived in Moscow from Berlin in August 1923, criticized the Moscow-based writers for having failed to notice a writer like this for several years, and they, feeling hurt, defended themselves.

"It is a work of great talent," I.N. Rozanov said during the discussion. Soon after this, it seems, he filled in a card on Bulgakov for his *Guide to Modern Literature* (*Putevoditel' po Sovremennoy Literature*): "Bulgakov, Mikh. Afanas. Cont. writer of fiction, with a lively gift for satire. In *Cuff-notes*, he portrayed the lives of Russian writers during their hungry years in humorous fashion. Among his other stories, *The White Guard*, *The Fateful Eggs* and *The Heart of a Dog* are being published. In the last two, he turns to fantasy, in the style of Swift." He also marked on the card how many lines he intended to set aside for the writer in his *Guide*: "5 lines". As we shall see, though, Bulgakov was destined never to see these lines in print: the card remained in I.N. Rozanov's archive. It is of interest, as a snapshot of how Bulgakov's work was received by an authoritative literary expert in the spring of 1925.

The author himself, and a number of his listeners, sensed that the story *The Heart of a Dog* was the precursor for some far broader plots for stories about contemporary life. The implementation of these, through force of circumstances, would soon have to be put on the back burner for several years.

The reviews were coming in, meanwhile, for his so significant publications from the start of the year. "Thank you for the 6th book of *Nedra* and for your publications," M. Voloshin wrote to Angarsky on 25th March 1925. "I received them over a month ago. […] I was very sorry that you decided not to publish *The White Guard* in the end, especially after I read an excerpt from it in *Rossiya*. In print, one sees things more clearly than in manuscript form… And on a second reading, that work seemed to me to be a very original and substantial work; as a literary debut, one can compare it only to the debuts of Tolstoy and Dostoevsky."

Angarsky wrote back, on 20th April: "Bulgakov read your review of his work and was *very* flattered. I do not agree with you in your assessment of his novel: the novel is weak, whereas the satirical stories are good, but getting them past the censors is very difficult. I'm not sure his new story, *The Heart of a Dog*, will get through. The way things stand in literature is generally bad. The censors have not fully understood the party line." And sure enough, on 2nd May, Bulgakov receives a letter from Leontiev, through which Angarsky informs him that the story cannot be printed in the spring, since the collection *Diaboliad* is due to come out in May, and he offers Bulgakov a choice: either postpone the collection until the autumn, or publish *The Heart of a Dog* in the 8th book of *Nedra* (and not in the 7th one, which had been submitted to the printers); "the censors are still delaying the manuscript", wrote Leontiev. On the same day, N.S. Angarsky went abroad on a business trip, and on 21st May Leontiev wrote a despairing letter to Bulgakov: "Dear Mikhail Afanasievich, I am sending you *Cuff-notes* [the full text of which they had not succeeded, in three years, in publishing – M.C.] and *The Heart of a Dog*. Do whatever you want with them. Sarychev at Glavlit declared that it is not worth cleaning up *The Heart of a Dog*. 'The thing as a whole is inadmissible', or something along those lines."

Angarsky had a fixed opinion of the story, though, and had no intention of giving up as yet. On receiving a message about Sarychev's verdict from the editorial office, he decided to take some new steps to rescue the work. And Leontiev soon (the letter is not dated) writes to Bulgakov: "Dear and respected Mikhail Afanasievich, Nikolai Semonovich sent me a letter in which he asks you to do the following. Send a corrected version of *The Heart of a Dog*, immediately, to L.B. Kamenev at Borzhom. He will read it while he is on holiday. In 2 weeks' time, he will be in Moscow, and at that time he will no longer be involved in this work. You must send an accompanying letter, too – one from the author, one that will bring a tear to the eye, explaining all the ordeals you've been through to date [so there had already been a fair few ordeals that were not reflected in Leontiev's letters – M.C.], etc. etc.

This must be done through us... And hurry up about it!" The letter clearly upset Bulgakov considerably – he highlights the words 'from the author' using two coloured lines, and puts four more lines under the words 'tear to the eye', adding two exclamation marks. Bulgakov clearly couldn't see why the letter had to come from the author, and not from the editors, who supported the story, and he certainly couldn't imagine himself as the author of a letter that would "bring a tear to the eye".

He opted not to send the manuscript to Borzhom, and instead waited for Angarsky's return. Bulgakov himself set off for Koktebel at some point between June 10th and June 19th.

In a letter that I believe was written on 29th March 1925, I. Lezhnev wrote to Bulgakov: "Dear Mikhail Afanasievich! I am sending you the proofread version of the third part of the novel. I strongly request that you select some small but arresting excerpt from anything you have written at any time, to be read out at an evening celebrating the third anniversary of the journal. Today, at 7 o'clock sharp, several authors will gather at Polyanka, who will read out some excerpts set aside for the evening. We strongly request that Lyubov Yevgenievna and you come over in the evening for a preliminary read-through and bring with you the excerpt that you have in mind. Bear in mind that the theme for the evening is: Russia and *Rossiya*. It would be good if the excerpt were at least indirectly related to that theme.

If you manage to read through the corrected text I am sending you today, then bring that with you too. Say hello to L.Y. from me. We look forward to seeing you both. Yours, I. Lezhnev."

On 4th April, *Vechernyaya Moskva* (*Evening Moscow*) reported: "On Monday, 6th April, at the Column Hall of the House of Unions, there will be an evening celebrating the third anniversary of the journal *Rossiya*.

Speeches will be given by the following: Andrei Bely, I. Lezhnev, V. Bogoraz (Tan), M. Stolyarov. There will be prose and poetry read by Kachalov, Luzhsky, Moskvin, Chekhov, Diky, Zavadsky and the authors: Andrei Bely, P. Antokolsky, M. Bulgakov, B. Pasternak, D. Petrovsky and O. Forsh."

A few days later, the newspaper reported on the event in a restrained, tongue-in-cheek style: *Rossiya* on Russia (An evening at the Column Hall, celebrating the third anniversary of the journal *Rossiya*).

"It is hard even to believe that in the course of some three hours, one could manage to repeat the word 'Russia' so many times in a row. Any attempt to find, in this 'Russian' flow, any inverted commas, bringing clarity, would be doomed to failure from the start. Clearly, 'Russians' alone know (if they know at all, that is) where their *'Rossiya'* in inverted commas ends, and where the un-inverted-comma'd Russia begins.

For Tan-Bogoraz, things are in a comparatively advantageous position. 'Our journal,' he says, 'is a small affair; it is not a journal, but a mini-journal, and indeed, three years is not a particularly long period of time, but in the conditions in which it, as they say, was forced to develop, every month should count as a year.' [...]

'History trickles through us,' says Lezhnev, 'and yet we are only people.'

We, it transpires, have 'grown tired', have 'drained the bitter cup to the end' (frozen potatoes and so on). And therein lies 'our' undoubted 'tragedy'.

Lezhnev does not despair, however. Ahead, there are some wide-ranging prospects. 'We' are not only 'conquering' new paths, but also 'laying down' new paths. The current mechanical association of humanity must be replaced, in Lezhnev's opinion, with an organic one, and in Lezhnev's opinion, Russia, in this 'organic association', will play the role not of some finger or ear, but (think a little higher up!) of the 'nervous system'. Russia (it is not clear whether he meant the one in inverted commas, or the one without them) must perform the function of a 'worldwide intelligentsia'. No more, no less.

Who, though, will lead Russia to this glorious future, Lezhnev asks; 'the Communists, or us, my fellow travellers?' (aha!) and he straight away gives us the answer to this: 'Both them, and us.'

In Russia, they say, there are 130 million people, and if one of those millions embellishes all the others, the reverse process is happening at the same time (all this is true; only who told Lezhnev that his 'we' is equal to all the other millions).

Andrei Bely starts to quote people. In good faith. The opinions of Dostoevsky, Pushkin, Nekrasov and Blok with regard to, and about, Russia – he knows them like the back of his hand. The overall effect is: 'you are both wretched and abundantly wealthy, you are both powerful and powerless, dear mother Rus.'

For his own part, Bely tells us that in the syllable 'rrrusss' itself, 'one hears strength and light'. In 'rrr', you see, there is strength, whilst in 'sss' there is light. Thought-provoking.

The last of the 'Russians' to speak, Stolyarov, 'understands' today's Russia as something of a duality, and it turns out that one half of it – 'Asian, politically and economically poverty-stricken' – has become a 'hillock' over the other, apparently far nicer, 'half', preventing the latter from moving forward. The task of *'Rossiya'*, it turns out, is to facilitate in every possible way the merging of these two halves (apparently, in order to do this, the 'bad' half will have to stop sticking out like a hillock in front of the 'good' half). And for this to happen, in Stolyarov's opinion, it is essential to fight 'against all that is narrow, formalistic and utopian.'

Among all these extremely engaging talks, certain quotations that are referred to in them are particularly memorable, for example: "where are you bounding off to, proud steed, and where will you set down your hooves?" or: "what is it you want, Rus?" Bulgakov's name is not mentioned in the speech.

A speech that was printed in *Vechernyaya Moskva* under the title *Russia*, also began on a comic note: there is now a multiplicity of "Russia"s, seen and unseen", but ended on a threatening note: 'Citizen Lezhnev, do not rely on the agility of your hands! That, from every point of view, is a risky trick!'

One day near the end of winter, he brought back to the house on Bolshaya Sadovaya, for Tatiana Nikolayevna, the journal *Rossiya*, containing the start of his novel. On the first page, she read: "Dedicated to Lyubov Yevgenievna Belozerskaya." "I find that very surprising," she said to him, "for it feels as though we lived through all this together... I sat beside you all that time, while you were writing, and heated up water for you. I waited for you in the evenings…" And he said: "She asked me to do that. I can't say no to someone who isn't mine; but to someone who is mine – I can…" "Well then, take your book away with you." Not usually one for dramatic gestures, she was unable to restrain herself, and she hurled the journal at his feet.

On 3rd April, Bulgakov receives a mysterious-sounding note written on headed paper from the the Art Theatre studio: "Deeply esteemed Mikhail Afanasievich! I would be extremely glad to get to know you and to discuss a number of matters which interest me and may pique your curiosity too" – and a proposal to meet. At the meeting, it transpired that the first part of the novel *The White Guard*, in the journal *Rossiya*, had sparked strong interest in one of the directors at the Art Theatre – as suitable material for a play.

On 25th April, the editor of *Rossiya* asks him in a letter to come and see him on the 29th to discuss a number of matters, including: "2) by that time, I hope, I shall have the first copies of No. 5; 3) I need the end of the novel, for the subsequent work on it, 4) we need to talk about the questionnaire that we are sending out to our writers, and that we will print in No. 6. As you will understand for yourself, all these matters require you to be present in person. I urge you not to let us down and to be prompt, once again."

On the same day, Y.N. Potekhin writes to him as well, "to remind him about the lamp", ending his letter with the words: "Greetings. I await you."

This, one supposes, was about the latest meeting of *Zelyonaya Lampa*, whose light was still burning – the next meeting was to take place at Potekhin's house.

On 30th April, Bulgakov registers his marriage to L.Y. Belozerskaya; he makes a note to that effect in his working booklet (it survived in the archive). They had a lot of fun together; his wife's talented story-telling about Constantinople and Paris aroused his imagination; together, they wrote a comedy – "based on French life" – *White Clay* (L. Belozerskaya).

On 2nd May, Valentin Katayev, with whom he has maintained a friendship, gives him his book of stories, *Edward the Idler* (*Bezdel'nik Eduard*), inscribed: "To dear Mikhail Afanasievich Bulgakov, with unfailing friendship, from the prolific Valyun." Bulgakov, who would celebrate his 34th birthday on the 15th of the month, had not yet had a single book printed, but his collection *Diaboliad* was due to be released any day now.

On 10th May, Bulgakov writes to Voloshin: "Much-respected Maximilian Alexandrovich, N.S. Angarsky passed on to me your invitation to Koktebel. I am extremely grateful to you, could you be so good as to write a few lines, to say whether and I might be able to get a separate room at the dacha in July / August. It would be very nice to call in on you. My greetings to you. *M. Bulgakov.*" He is still living in Obukhov Side-street at this time (bldg. 9, flat 4).

A postcard arrives from M. Voloshin on 1st June, in which he agrees to host Bulgakov and his wife at the dacha in Koktebel, and they start to get ready for the trip. On 7th June, I. Lezhnev writes him a letter written in an affectionate, mock-angry tone: "Dear Mikhail Afanasievich! You have forgotten about *Rossiya* altogether. It is high time you were submitting material for No. 6, we must collect the ending to *The White Guard*, and you still haven't brought us the manuscripts. I entreat you not to postpone this matter any longer. […] How do you feel, after the operation?" There is indirect data confirming that Bulgakov submitted the manuscript for the final part of *The White Guard* that very day, and he left for Koktebel soon afterwards.

It was there that he met Voloshin – the man who had probably thought more highly than anyone else of Bulgakov's debut.

The other guests that summer were the writer Sofya Fedorchenko and her husband, and the Gabrichevskys, a married couple. N.A. Gabrichevskaya recalled that Alexander Gabrichevsky and Bulgakov "made friends, saw a lot of one another and spent time talking on the beach."

They played charades, with Bulgakov usually the one to organise the games.

A. Ostroumova-Lebedeva painted Bulgakov's portrait (it shows him dictating *The White Guard* to his wife) – he has a reddish tan in the painting, and has a bandage tied around his head.

The Bulgakovs did not spend long there – just over three weeks. Before their departure, on 5th July, Max Voloshin gave Bulgakov one of his numerous watercolours, with the inscription: "Dear Mikhail Afanasievich, to the first man to record the soul of the Russian species, with profound love."

On 7th July, Lyubov Yevgenievna wrote a postcard at the Lozova station (outside Kharkov): "We went on a magnificent walk, without any particular adventures. We spent a day in Yalta and went to Checkhov's house. We went to Sevastopol by car. The Leonovs were too afraid to go into the sea at the last minute." Bulgakov added a short note: "The stations are all mangy. My greetings to everyone."

Awaiting Bulgakov in Moscow was the collection *Diaboliad*, which had already been published, it seems – the copies given as gifts to N.A. Ushakova and N.N. Lyamin are dated 18th July.

In late July or early August, he submits a story to the editors of the Moscow newspaper *Zarya Vostoka* (*Dawn of the East*) – probably *The Cockroach* (*Tarakan*) (the story was printed on 25th August 1925).

On 15th August, the first story from *A Young Doctor's Notebook* is published in *Krasnaya Panorama* – *The Steel Throat* (*Stal'noye Gorlo*), and over the next few days, his cycle of articles describing life and customs, *A Journey around the Crimea* (*Puteshestviye po Krymu*), is published in *Krasnaya Gazeta* (*The Red Newspaper*); on 24th August, the director of the publishing house *Zemlya i Fabrika* (*Land and Factory*), Vladimir Narbut, concludes a contract with him to publish *Crimson Island* (*Bagrovyy Ostrov*), a short parody of an adventure novel, and *Nedra* signs a deal with him to publish *The Fateful Eggs* as a separate book.

Most importantly of all, though – the play *The White Guard* was completed in August: on 31st August, the director I. Sudakov announced that a recitation from the play would take place, with Stanislavsky among those present.

In this note, Sudakov calls Bulgakov "Mikhail Leontievich", which reminds one of the conversation between Maksudov and Ivan Vasilievich in *A Theatrical Novel*.

At this moment in time, the attempt to get *The Heart of a Dog* published comes to an end; the episode prefigures future failures in getting his prose published, and signals his transition towards writing for the stage over the next few years.

In an undated letter (apparently from the end of the summer), B. Leontiev wrote to Bulgakov: "Greatly respected Mikhail Afanasievich, Nikolai Semyonovich has returned to Moscow. Please send us your manuscript for *The Heart of a Dog* as soon as possible. We will get it through. Only hurry. Yours, Bor. Leontiev. P.S. If anything should happen to the work, tell me at once." (i.e. he has heard nothing from Bulgakov for some time about his publishing affairs).

And so, Angarsky, on returning from overseas at the end of the summer, immediately concerned himself with the fate of the manuscript, deciding to appeal for help from the same person, who had also, apparently, returned to Moscow; one can see from the correspondence that he was hopeful of success.

On 11th September 1925, Leontiev tells Bulgakov: "Your story, *The Heart of a Dog*, was returned to us by L.B. Kamenev. At Angarsky's request, he read it and gave us his opinion: 'it is an acerbic political pamphlet on modernity, under no circumstances can it be published.'

One shouldn't, of course, place too much significance on the two or three most acerbic pages; they could scarcely have altered much in the opinion of a man such as Kamenev. And yet, it seems to me that your refusal to give us the corrected text earlier played a sad role here."

Although the editors are trying, as we can see, to lay the blame for this failure on the author, there is no doubt that both Angarsky and Leontiev genuinely felt bitter about the outcome of this matter. They fall quiet about the issue of the publishing of the story for many months.

Difficulties had begun to rear their head at the Art Theatre, too. Let us note first, however, that in early September, Bulgakov had struck up a relationship with a second theatre, an off-shoot of the Art Theatre studio: the Vakhtangov Theatre. On 16th September, V. Kuza, one of the theatre's leading actors and a member of the board, sends Bulgakov an advance and tells him that he wishes to see him at the theatre once his health is better, to sign a contract for the play *Zoya's Apartment* (*Zoykina Kvartira*).

As for the play *The White Guard*, opinions differed. On the one hand, I.Y. Sudakov sent a note to Bulgakov that read: "A.V. Lunacharsky, after reading 3 acts, told V.V. Luzhsky that he thinks the play outstanding and sees no reason as to why it should not be put on". On 12th October 1925, Lunacharsky, having read the play, wrote to the theatre, saying that he did not find "anything obstacles in it to the play being produced", but added his own "personal opinion": "I consider Bulgakov to be a very talented man, but this play is distinctly mediocre…" Attitudes to the play, not only inside the theatre but also further afield, were clearly complicated. One of the numerous pieces of evidence for this is the ultimatum sent by Bulgakov to V.V. Luzhsky on 15th October 1925, in which he sets out his terms for the theatre – he is clearly already exhausted by the effort of trying to get his play through the labyrinth of a theatre with two directors, and with cliques that were opposed to one another both in the administration, and among the actors – in short, through the complex structure of the theatre's mechanism, which would be depicted in such a grotesque and vivid fashion ten years later in *A Theatrical Novel*.

Bulgakov's terms were as follows:
"1. Performances on the Large stage only
2. This season (March 1926)
3. Changes, but no fundamental destruction of the essence of the play.

If these conditions are unacceptable for the Theatre, I request permission to consider a negative answer as an indication that the play *The White Guard* is free."

That autumn, complications arose with the journal *Rossiya*, in the sixth edition of which the novel *The White Guard* was due to be printed. Apparently, in mid-October, the journal went completely bankrupt, and the publisher Kagansky left the country, without having paid the author any money, and Lezhnev refused to return the text of the novel's ending to Bulgakov. Evidence of this is seen in the following declaration made by Bulgakov to the 'conflict commission' at the All-Russian Union of Writers: "The editor of the journal *Rossiya*, Isai Lezhnev, after the Rossiya publishing house closed down, withheld, without having any right to do so, the end of my novel *The White Guard*, and has not given it back to me." We know that Bulgakov was invited to the commission on 4th November "to testify on the matter that you have raised."

One can imagine the ardour with which Bulgakov must have read a letter that arrived from an official named D. Umansky, who had taken his story *The Fateful Eggs* abroad in order to help get it translated: "When I arrived in Vienna, I read your story again: its content may be interpreted in a way that is unfavourable for the USSR, and I have *changed my mind* (!): in my view, it ought not to be published outside the USSR in a foreign language! Satire demands the most cautious of approaches! *Does it not?*" [my italics – M.C.]. Worthy of note here is the blindness displayed by the author of the letter in respect of the author's feelings and thoughts: he is calling on Bulgakov to support his actions, whilst expressing an opinion like that about his satire! As we shall see later, life was to bring Bulgakov into collisions with people like this, who spoke a different kind of language altogether, on a number of occasions.

Veresayev offered his assistance to Bulgakov in a warm letter sent on 28th September 1925: "… I am not doing this for you personally, you must understand, but out of a desire to safeguard at least a little of that powerful artistic strength that you are now the bearer of… In light of the harassment that is currently occurring against you, you will be pleased to learn that Gorky has taken great note of you, and values you highly." On 10th October, Bulgakov receives a letter from the publishers *Krug*, asking him to call on A.N. Tikhonov: evidently, Tikhonov, who had strong ties to Gorky, had had the idea of publishing Bulgakov's prose.

At around this time, Bulgakov receives a letter that was sent out to the members of the All-Russian Union of Writers: "The Moscow Department of the Board of the All-Russian Union of Writers has ordered that, in order to mark the grand opening of the House of Herzen on 1st November, a literary exhibition should be organised, reflecting the writing work being done by the Moscow members of the Union in the years since the revolution. The exhibition committee requests that you submit, by 20th October at the latest, a portrait of yourself, your signature and your works, published in 1917-1925 (all of them, if possible)."

Bulgakov's reply, written on 18th October 1925, is interesting. "Dear comrades, in response to your invitation to the literary exhibition, I am sending you *Diaboliad*.

As regards my portrait:

Given that I have not made much of a name for myself either in the field of Russian literature, or in any other fields, I consider that presenting my portrait for public view would be premature.

Moreover, I do not have one.

Yours respectfully, M. Bulgakov."

In September, October and November, Bulgakov works intensively, reworking and shortening the play whilst at the same time tirelessly trying to sort out the increasingly complex relations with the theatre: this was something that was new to him, and it clearly consumed a great deal of nervous energy. When he is invited by the prose writer Sofya Fedorchenko to a reading that she is to give of one of her works, he includes a few words about himself in his reply: "I am entombed beneath a play with a grand-sounding name. All that is left of me is a shadow, which it will be possible to show to the public in the form of an appendix to the said play."

In my view, he is referring to *The White Guard*, but, remarkably, he also manages to write a second play by the end of the year: *Zoya's Apartment*. The writer Lev Slavin recalled in his memoirs that the play's author had said to him: "I didn't write *Zoya's Apartment* myself: what happened was that Kuza dipped me into the inkwell and wrote it, with me as the pen."

The directors from the Vakhtangov Theatre, A.D. Popov and V.V. Kuza, call on Bulgakov on 15th December: the negotiations on the future production are actively taking place.

Natalya Ushakova recalled in her memoirs that Bulgakov saw in the New Year in their company, "at the Gabrichevskys, I believe." There were drawings hanging from the fir tree: miniature portraits of the guests. Among N. Ushakova's archived documents was a little ink and watercolour drawing with a thread attached to it (for hanging it on the tree) – a caricature of Bulgakov, with an inscription underneath it: "Maka remembers the Koktebel set". "He hadn't liked it at all in Koktebel," N. Ushakova recalled, with a laugh, as she explained the story behind the drawing. With a little help from Lyubov Yevgenievna, the nickname 'Maka' had really caught on among the 'Prechistenka' set.

On 1st January 1926, the Vakhtangov Theatre enters into an agreement for the play *Zoya's Apartment*, and on 11th, Bulgakov performs a reading of it at the theatre; V.V. Kuza writes him a congratulatory note: "I congratulate and thank you on behalf of the entire studio. The play was accepted unanimously."

In the play's female protagonist (the numerous attempts to publish it in Russia succeeded only in 1982 – *Sovremennaya Dramaturgiya* (*Contemporary Drama*), No. 2, published by V. Gudkkova), people later saw all manner of possible inspirations from their own time. L.Y. Belozerskaya mentioned Zoya Buyalskaya; others cited Zoya Petrovna Shatova, described by Marienhof in his memoirs *A Novel without Lies* (*Roman bez Vrania*, M., 1927). V. Levshin, Bulgakov's young neighbour at apartment No. 34, sought prototypes of an altogether different kind: he wrote of Zoya's similarity to the wife of the artist Yakulov (his studio was located in the same building on Bolshaya Sadovaya), Natalya Shiff – "who had a figure of rare beauty, a ridged nose and an asymmetrical face, a face that was generally far from agreeable to look at" (in *A Theatrical Novel*, Maksudov, who has thought up the plot for a second play, catches a glimpse of "a woman with an asymmetrical face"). The literary historian R.D. Timenchik passed on to me something he had heard from the daughter of the man who created the St. Petersburg literary and artistic cabaret, B.K. Pronin, that the accepted wisdom in their family was that *Zoya's Apartment* portrayed Pronin's 'Mansard' in Moscow, on Bolshaya Molchanokvka Street (the artistic club where there was also a Chinaman, due to whom Pronin was exiled in 1926...).

At exactly this time, another thread that bound Bulgakov to the period when he hoped to achieve fame as a prose writer breaks apart: the *Nedra* publishing house informs him on January 4th that the story *The Fateful Eggs* is "free": the separate edition of it that had been in the pipeline has come to nothing. The recent situation involving *Diaboliad*, which had been confiscated soon after its release, no doubt played a role in this. Life was stubbornly pushing Bulgakov towards the path of being a playwright. For the time being, this path was one that appeared bright and rosy. The reworked version of the play *The White Guard* had satisfied the directors of the Art Theatre. Rehearsals began on 24th February.

And, at last, the Kamerny Theatre signs a contract with Bulgakov for the play *The Crimson Island*, which he undertakes to provide to them by 15th June; if the play cannot be put on, Bulgakov is to provide a play based on the story *The Fateful Eggs*.

Thus, over the course of 1925, Bulgakov went from being a writer of fiction, known to a narrow circle of admirers, to a playwright who was well-known, if not to the public, as yet, then certainly to the theatres of Moscow – the directors and actors, and the theatre critics. He is already receiving letters from the theatres of Leningrad, too, along with requests to put on both plays.

He was invited to attend a debate at the Colonnade Hall at the Kremlin, entitled 'Literary Russia', and duly attended it; in a report about the event describing the speeches made by Shklovsky, F. Berezovsky and A. Voronsky, he appears in the list of speakers between O. Brik and V. Kirshon.

His fame as a writer of prose is maintained, too – in part by the readings he gives before large audiences. In the first few months of 1926, he read from his works in public on three occasions.

Yet he only ever reads from a single one of his works, evidently one of his favourites. On 21st February, he attends an evening of literary humour at the Polytechnical Museum, where members of the public read excerpts from works by Zoshchenko and Babel, whilst he and Vera Inber read their own works. "Bulgakov read *Chichikov* – under Soviet conditions" (*Vechernyaya Moskva*, 22nd February). And on 1st March, L.V. Gornung writes in his diary: "An arts and literature evening was arranged today at GAKhN, as a fund-raiser, with the aim of helping the poet M. Voloshin, whose poetry is not being printed at the moment. M. Bulgakov read from the manuscript for *Chichikov's Shenanigans*, a sort of sequel to *Dead Souls*. The writer Y. Slezkin, whose fame came mostly before 1917, read his story *The Bandit*. B. Pasternak read two excerpts from the long poem *1905*. [...] The money raised went towards much-needed repairs to Voloshin's home. He sent watercolours to Fedorchenko [the evening had been arranged by the writer Sofya Fedorchenko – M.C.], Bulgakov and Pasternak".

As for his fiction, on 3rd March he is informed that Nedra has been granted permission to publish a new edition of *Diaboliad* (to replace the one that was confiscated); and on 25th March, *Krug* announces that it is preparing to publish the book *The White Guard*.

Relations with the Art Theatre were going well: Bulgakov had become a much-loved author, and on 2nd March a contract was signed for a second play, *The Heart of a Dog*, with the author promising to submit it no later than 1st September. The plan seemed to be that whilst one play was having its run, the other one would be going through rehearsals, for the second half of the following season...

On 26th March, Bulgakov watches a rehearsal of the first two acts of *The White Guard*, in the company of Stanislavsky and other senior figures from the theatre. An entry in the *Rehearsal Diary* states: "K.S., after watching two acts of the play, said that the play was on the right track: he had really liked 'The Grammar School' and the 'Petlyura scene'. He praised some of the cast and said he considered the work they had done important, successful and necessary. [...] K.S. encouraged everyone to continue working at a quick, upbeat tempo along the same track." Yet three days later, V. Kuza sends a nervous message to Bulgakov about the play *Zoya's Apartment*: "What are you playing at? Aleksei Dmitriyevich is waiting for the extra scenes in act 4, and I have had to cancel the rehearsals. Remember, Wednesday 31st/III is the final deadline." And on 10th April, the Bolshoy Drama Theatre in Leningrad signs agreements for both of the finished plays.

At the end of April, the Art Theatre's editorial and artistic collegium decides to change the name of the play *The White Guard*, and Stanislavsky agrees to the change.

The second edition of the collection *Diaboliad* is published; he receives his complimentary copies on 26th April. If we add to this two slim collections of satirical articles and short stories that were published in the same year – collections to which the author attached no significance at all, by contrast with his attitude to *Diaboliad* – then this was how the writer's life in print concluded: Bulgakov would never have the chance to see his work in print again.

One day that spring, Angarsky and Leontiev both called on Bulgakov at home, one after the other, only to find that he was not in. A note left by

Leontiev tells us that they had come to ask him for the manuscripts for the story *The Heart of a Dog* – "not to print or publish them, any longer", but merely "for temporary use", as a "big, big favour". The editors urged him to remember that "relations between us were not so very bad, we did not cause you unpleasantness alone." The words that come next are important in terms of understanding this period in Bulgakov's life: "Do not reject us at the time of the cessation of your printing activities and your transition to the theatre: let us part amicably."

It should be said, in fairness, that there was nothing in the circumstances of the last year to prevent Bulgakov from parting on good terms with the publishing house to which, in the first half of the 1920s, he owed more than he did to any other one: according to the memoirs of those close to him, Bulgakov always felt respect and devotion to Angarsky, seeing him as a man who was genuinely dedicated to literature and who had managed, with a rare stubbornness and firmness, to protect the interests of an author he had once believed to be talented, and about whom his opinion had not changed.

On 7th May 1926, there was a search of his home. L.Y. Belozerskaya wrote in her memoirs that the men who conducted the search were detective Slavkin and his assistant, along with the landlord of the building, as a witness. During the search, they started to "turn the chairs upside down and poke holes in them with a long needle. And at that moment something unexpected happened. M.A. said:

'Well, Lyubasha, if they shoot your armchairs to bits, I shan't be held responsible.' (I had bought the chairs at a second-hand furniture shop for 3 roubles and 50 kopecks a piece.) And we both started laughing. Perhaps it was nervous laughter."

In 1970, L.Y. Belozerskaya found out from me, for the first time, that during the search at which she had been present, they had taken not only the story but also the diaries. By then, she had already handed her memoirs to the Manuscripts department of the V.I. Lenin Library, after agreeing with the arguments we put to her in favour of doing so (the author of this biography took part in the negotiations, as an academic expert at the Manuscripts Department, having undertaken to conduct negotiations with anyone who might be able to add to the Bulgakov Fund that had been set up within the Archives Department). The only thing mentioned in the memoirs was the manuscript for *The Heart of a Dog*. Meanwhile, in the section of the archive that was assembled latterly by Y.S. Bulgakova herself, there was a copy of the relevant application by the writer, which he sent to the Chairman of the Soviet of people's commissars on 24th June 1926: "On 7th May, representatives of the OGPU conducted a search of my home, (order 2287, case 45), during which the following manuscripts, which are of immense, intimate value to me, were taken away:

The story *The Heart of a Dog*, 2 copies thereof, and *My Diary* (3 exercise books).

I entreat you to return them to me."

L.Y. Belozerskaya said, incidentally: "I don't remember him keeping a diary at all!" He probably never showed it to his wife.

It is hard to underestimate the impact of this event on Bulgakov. The idea that his intimate diary entries, which were not known about even by his nearest and dearest, were being read by strangers, undoubtedly tormented him for many years; all the more so given that he was a reserved person, who suffered when anyone was overly familiar with him, a man who was shut off from almost everyone, and deeply sensitive. Also of significance is the fact that his diaries recorded, with a considerable degree of frankness (as can be seen from the surviving excerpts), his view of day-to-day events, of the situation in the country. From this moment on, a new phase of his relations with the government commenced. On the one hand, he had nothing to hide now; on the other – pressure could be brought to bear on him, forcing him to express remorse, or to make assurances that he his views had changed.

It appears that he was aware of both of these factors.

The incident itself, I would say, had a greater impact on the editor of *Rossiya* than it did on Bulgakov: his home was searched the next day, the publishing house's warehouse and bookshop were sealed off, and Lezhnev was detained and, before long, sentenced to three years' overseas exile. He would return several years later, to a country that had changed dramatically, and as a completely different person from the one on whose "staying power" Bulgakov had so counted in the summer of 1923.

2

Bulgakov, almost the very next day after the event that had drawn such a gloomy line under his fate as a writer of fiction, was due to set off for Leningrad. The notice advertising the evening event that he was due to attend, scheduled for 10th May 1926, had already been printed: "The Large auditorium of the concert hall (on Lassal). The All-Russian Union of Writers is organising a big literary and artistic evening." Among those listed as taking part, beneath the name of A.A. Akhmatova, was: "Mik. Bulgakov (the author of the collection *Diaboliad* and the novel *The White Guard*, who has arrived from Moscow)" – and then L. Borisov, Zamyatin, M. Zoschenko, M. Kuzmin, V. Kaverin, B. Lavrenev, N. Nikitin, F. Sologub, N. Tikhonov, A. Tolstoy, K. Fedin… Bulgakov now had a chance to see everyone who was anyone in the literary Leningrad of the mid-1920s.

Krasnaya Gazeta entitled its report on the evening, published in its evening edition on 13th May 1926, "The trooping of the literature". The very first paragraph must have offended Bulgakov's tastes somewhat: "… All the divisions of the literary army, the prose writers, playwrights and poets, passed before the eyes of his majesty the reader, and earned the approval of the monarch."

The report makes it clear that the evening lasted until after midnight, and therefore the journalist restricted himself to commenting "only on the works which were read out last night for the first time." Fedin read a chapter from his new story *The Transvaal*, whilst Zamyatin read a few scenes from his play *The Tragedy of Atilla* (*Tragediya ob Atille*), which he had just finished. "We see before us the frightening figure of the leader of the Huns, nicknamed 'God's scourge'…"

Immediately after that, the newspaper presented a Muscovite: "A guest from Moscow M. Bulgakov yesterday read *Chichikov's Shenanigans*, an amusing tale about modernity, which inspired much mirth among the audience. Gogolesque characters, forever vivid, were once again put before that audience, wearing the make-up of our day-to-day lives on their faces." The occasion would have been particularly amusing, one suspects, for the author himself.

It is possible that this was the evening when he was first introduced to Akhmatova. Zamyatin, whom Bulgakov already knew, was, at any rate, a suitable interlocutor for a story about day-to-day living in Moscow.

"And one feels inclined to add," A. Selivanov, the author of the report, concluded merrily, "that whenever our writers step out from their closed circle of 'private evenings' into the big arena, they are invariably met with great artistic and material success."

Two days later, in its Saturday edition, the newspaper printed a sketch by Bulgakov, *Akathist to Our Quality* (*Akafist Nashemu Kachestvu*).

As early as on 7th May, a rumour had spread like wildfire around Moscow's literary circles to the effect that the belletrist Andrei Sobol had committed suicide by shooting himself with a revolver on a bench on Tverskoi Boulevard, opposite the statue of Timiryazev, i.e. not far from the building that housed the All-Russian Union of Writers (a union that Timiryazev had been chairman of for several years). Bulgakov cannot have been unmoved, surely, by this news of the death of a man who, albeit far removed from him in a literary sense and a psychological sense, had nonetheless been in the circle of his first literary acquaintances in Moscow and had published the first of his Moscow stories in the journal *Rupor*. The laws of creative writing are harsh, and to my mind it has always been possible to perceive some sort of genetic link between the tragic event at the end of Tverskoi Boulevard and the memorial to the made-up poet Zhitomirsky, which, in the first draft of *The Master and Margarita*, is positioned opposite the 'House of Griboedov' – the House of Herzen, the home of the Union of Writers, that I mentioned earlier.

On 13 May, the day of the rehearsal for *The White Guard*, Bulgakov, according to oral accounts by several contemporaries, was allegedly summoned by the investigating officer to give testimony. In order to do this, incidentally, he had to make sure he got back in time from Leningrad. If one takes into account that his contract with *Smekhach* (*The Laugher*) for a brochure (a small collection of articles), which was preserved in his archive, is dated 10th May, then the time available for the journey was no more than 1-2 days.

At the theatre, another delicate situation had arisen: the artistic board of the Art Theatre was proposing a new name for the play: *Before the End* (*Pered Kontsom*), whilst Bulgakov was coming back to them with some alternatives of his own: *White December* (*Belyy Dekabr'*), *1918*, *The Taking of the City* (*Vzyatiye Goroda*), *The White Blizzard* (*Belyy Buran*). K.S. Stanislavsky writes, that day: "I can't say I was very fond of the name *Before the End*... But I do not know of a better name, if this play is not to be prohibited. With all four of the suggested titles [proposed by the author – M.C.], the play will, undoubtedly, be banned. I would avoid the word 'white' altogether. It will only be taken in a phrase of some sort, such as *The End of the Whites* (*Konets Belykh*). But a title like that is inadmissible. Unless a better one is found, I recommend calling it *Before the End*. I think this will force people to look at the people somewhat differently, from the very first act."

On 14th May, V. Veresayev gives Bulgakov his translations of *The Homeric Hymns*, which have just been published, with the inscription: "To Mikhail Afanasievich Bulgakov, with huge hopes for him."

So then, in May 1926, the journal *Rossiya* closed down once and for all; incidentally, the author had lost hope of finishing the publication of the novel *The White Guard* a good deal earlier. Many years later, describing his hero Maksudov in *A Theatrical Novel*, Bulgakov undoubtedly recreated, to some extent, his own mood in 1925-1926. "Incidentally, about the novel," he wrote. "Let us look at a few home truths. No-one had read it. No-one could read it, for Rudolphi had disappeared, having clearly not had the time to distribute the book." Yet the novel had garnered attention, and not just from the theatres; Gorky found out about it in Italy, and on 8th July 1926, he wrote a letter to Sergei Grigoriev, a writer of prose who was well-known at the time, asking: "Do you know Bulgakov by any chance? What is he doing now? Has *The White Guard* gone on sale yet?"

Bulgakov happened to be negotiating with the director of one of the biggest publishing houses of the day (and a talented poet), Vladimir Narbut – about a separate edition of the novel *The White Guard* (and concluding – for starters – a contract for the publication of the sketch *Chichikov's Shenanigans*). Thus, not one, but two fairly major publishers are expressing the wish to print the novel, with its so unhappily formed fate. For Bulgakov, the desire to print it was all the more acute, given that the unprinted part had been taken overseas and was in someone else's hands.

At the end of May, Tairov goes to great lengths to persuade him to visit the Kamerny Theatre, for negotiations about *The Crimson Island*.

On 30th May, an article by V. Shklovsky appears in *Nasha Gazeta* (*Our Newspaper*), entitled *The Closing of the Season. Mikhail Bulgakov* (*Zakrytiye Sezona. Mikhail Bulgakov*). With the season about to begin, when two plays by Bulgakov the playwright were due to appear on the stage, Shklovsky was effectively bringing down the curtain on Bulgakov the fiction writer, providing a harsh assessment of his prose using the story *The Fateful Eggs* as an example.

The article was not a first blow on the part of the critic, though, as it might appear, but rather a counter-blow, and this was clear to both men, at least.

In order to understand this, one must go back to roughly three years earlier, to the story of the novel *The White Guard*.

In January 1923, V. Shklovsky had published his biographical book *A Sentimental Journey* (*Sentimental'noye Puteshestviye*).

In it, he described Kiev in the winter of 1918/19, where his lot had cast him.

Interestingly, his descriptions are very similar to certain pages of *The White Guard*, which had not yet been written, in terms of the details selected and the composition, although, naturally, there are stark differences in terms of style and in the way the events described are covered.

"Kiev was packed full of people. The bourgeoisie and the intelligentsia were wintering in the city.

At Kreshchatik, there was the constant gleam of Vladimirs and Georgys [the orders of St. Vladimir and St. Georgy, medals awarded in the Russian army – M.C.].

A noisy bustle filled the city, there were many restaurants…

The following forces were in Ukraine: in Kiev, Skoropadsky, backed by the officers' divisions; the officers did not even know themselves why they backed him, but such had been Enno's orders [the representative of the allied troops – M.C.]. Around Kiev was Petlyura, with an entire army.

In Kiev there were also the Germans, who had been ordered by the French to support Skoropadsky. […] And further away – the hungry Bolsheviks."

The author recounts how the 4th Tank Division conducted itself.

"I was given a good welcome and assigned the task of repairing vehicles.

Several officers joined the division at the same time as me, with the same objective as the one I had.

Petlyura's men had already surrounded the city. *One could hear the rumble of the cannonade* and at night one could see the lights of the gunfire.

It was winter, *there were children sliding down all the slopes on toboggans.*" A single, tiny detail in *The White Guard* indicates, in my view, that Bulgakov had read *A Sentimental Journey* very attentively, and had been influenced – subconsciously, no doubt – by details of the description of Kiev in the novel: "When Nikolka arrived [after the death of Nai-Turs, at the time when Petlyura's men were already entering the outskirts of the city – M.C.] at the start of his street, the steep Alekseyevsky Hill, and began walking up it, he saw at the gate of house No. 7 the following scene: a couple of little squirts in little grey knitted jackets and hats *had just come sliding down the slope on a toboggan*. […] *The shooting had grown louder.* […] "How peaceful they look, riding down like that," Nikolka thought to himself in surprise," and the children explain to him: "They're settling a few scores with the officers. That lot had it coming. There are eight hundred of them for the whole city, and they were playing the idiot. Petlyura's arrived, and he's got a million-strong force."

There are other descriptions that show powerful similarities, too: "Petlyura's men entered the city in formation.

They had the artillery with them. […] The people met them in crowds and said to one another, loudly, so that everyone around them could hear:

'To think, the Hetman's men said they were just armed mobs, coming here – but these aren't mobs! They're proper soldiers.' This was uttered in Russian, and out of loyalty" (V. Shklovsky, *A Sentimental Journey*). In Bulgakov's book, Petlyura's entry into the city is described with a great many details, indicating that the troops were indeed proper soldiers; even the lines spoken by the onlookers are similar: "Oh my… so much for 'fifteen thousand'… What lies they told us. Fifteen thousand… mobs… disintegration… God, there are too many of them to count. Another battery… and another, and another…" (*The White Guard*).

Of far greater importance however, in my view, in the creative history of *The White Guard*, are the following authorial confessions in *A Sentimental Journey*, dedicated to the author's activity in a tank division: "They took the armoured vehicles off us and sent them to the front, initially far away, to Korosten, then just outside the city and even to the city, to Podol.

I 'sugared up' the Hetman's vehicles.

Let me describe how this is done: you throw the sugar – as grain or in lumps – into the petrol tank, from whence, as it melts, it slides into the discharge nozzle together with the petrol…

As a result of the cold produced during evaporation, the sugar freezes and blocks up the orifice.

You can blow air through the nozzle using a tyre pump. But it will just get blocked up again.

But the vehicles nonetheless moved out, and they were soon positioned outside our area of work, in the Lukyanov barracks. […]

And around the city, at night, one saw the gleaming flashes of gunfire.

The officers and the students were mobilized.

At the university, they shot and killed the students for some reason." And after Petlyura's departure, "the volunteers were held at the Pedagogical Museum; then someone threw a bomb, and it turned out that there was some dynamite stored there, there was a terrible explosion, many people were killed and all the glass in the buildings was sent flying everywhere."

Bulgakov, it seems, had read this book as soon as it had become available in Moscow; such was the vital importance to him of the material that it covered – from Kamenets-Podolsk and Chernovits in the time of the world war to Kiev in 1918. Now, he was able to find out more details about the things he had probably heard about in Kiev.

In *A Sentimental Journey*, Bulgakov was presented with the view of a person looking on from the outside at what the Bulgakov brothers had experienced from within, when they found themselves among those "students" and "volunteers", whose death is described with a large dose of cold-bloodedness and detachment by the memoirist.

The author of *A Sentimental Journey* reflected, on arriving in Kiev in the late autumn of 1918: "The Germans had reached the end of the road. They had been crushed by the allies, one could sense that.

And that meant that Skoropadsky's regime was at death's door too, *and even from this point of view something had to be done.*

Petlyura's men moved out of Ukraine" [my italics – M.C.]. These thoughts are also seen in *The White Guard* by the character Shpolyansky, as he reasons, in front of his comrades-in-arms: "'You know, my friends, when it comes down to it, one has to ask oneself whether we're doing the right thing by protecting this Hetman.

... Who knows, maybe a clash between Petlyura and the Hetman is something that is preordained by history, and from this clash a third historic force is destined to arise – the only correct one, perhaps.'

The men listening to Mikhail Semyonych idolized him for exactly the same reason that he was idolized at the *Prakh* club: for his exceptional eloquence."

It is after this interlude that the decision to 'sugar up' the vehicles is taken; the results of this are described in the text in a way that is similar to how Shklovsky's professional described it: "Some kind of filthy mess had got stuck in the discharge nozzles, and however hard they tried to pump air through the nozzles using tyre pumps, nothing they did was any help" (*The White Guard*).

"The Hetman's City perished three hours earlier than it ought to have done," states the author of *The White Guard*, "and the reason for that is that Mikhail Semyonovich, on the evening of 2nd December 1918, said the [...] following:

'They're all bastards. The Hetman and Petlyura alike. But Petlyura, on top of that, is a pogrom-monger. *The most important thing, though, isn't that. I'm bored, because I haven't chucked a bomb for so long.*" The words that I have put in italics also seem to paraphrase an excerpt from *A Sentimental Journey*, the author of which, who until recently had planted bombs, writes: "And the guns were already firing. I love the thunder of guns in the city and the clatter of the fragments of shells on the tarmac. *It's good when there are cannons.*" [My italics – M.C.] To the author of *The White Guard*, who had been a doctor until recently, love of these phenomena was, of course, something that was alien to him, incomprehensible, hostile. And for him, the extra three hours of life in the City signified the rescuing of many lives, perhaps including the lives of people he knew.

On 12th December 1967, V.B. Shklovsky told me: "I knew him a little bit in Kiev. I was in command of the armoured tank division: I went to see the general, who was forming a detachment to join up with Denikin. I asked him: 'What are you counting on?' He replied: 'I am a Russian. My national hero is Lenin. It is Stenka Razin, the Russian bravado and so on. And he will undoubtedly tear me apart. But I do not want to join him, because I am not in agreement.' Now that was a conversation that really cut to the chase." That day, and on a number of later occasions, I spoke to Shklovsky about *The White Guard*. He did not deny the link between his own life and the figure of Shpolyansky. An article I wrote to mark the 90th anniversary of his birth (*Sovetskaya Kul'tura* [*Soviet Culture*], 22nd January 1983), it was suggested for the first time that he had been the person upon whom the character from Bulgakov's novel was based. Viktor Shklovsky read the article and responded favourably to it. In the last few months of his life, we discussed a number of times the time when the two men knew one another in Kiev. He could vividly remember him sitting at a café – it was probably "at the café Crooked Jimmy", he told me shortly before he died, "that was where the Union for the rebirth of Russia used to congregate…" And when I asked him: "In connection with literary matters?" "No." In connection with the Union?" "Yes. He was a member of the Union, though a fairly insignificant one.

"And, I suppose, someone shall have to die" – that is what bothers the author of *The White Guard* the most in the situation that had arisen. "The ones who run – they won't die… so just who, exactly, is going to die?!!" Shklovsky, who was willing to risk both his own life and the lives of others that year, would certainly have had some objections to put to Bulgakov – objections which, in their own way, were convincing – had he felt a desire to have more than a fleeting conversation with him in December 1918.

In June, Bulgakov and his wife move to a new home – flat 1, building 4, Maly Levshinsky side-street. This is the address given in an application dated 24th June – the day of an advance preview of *The White Guard*; after this preview, the Glavrepertkom held a meeting with representatives of the Art Theatre-1, where some expressed the view that the play "is nothing but an apologia for the white guards." One of the numerous demands made was that the scene involving the grammar school must come across not as a demonstration of the heroism of the white guards, but as a way of discrediting the entire white guard movement."

In June, a tiny booklet of his "Stories" came out in "Smekhach's Library"; in connection with this, the journal *Smekhach* (*The Laugher*) offered its readers a medicine called "Cherry raspberry", "which has the blessing of eight to ten thousand grateful patients"; the prescription included 4 issues of *Smekhach*, the 15th book from the Library – "The Stories of Mikh. Bulgakov – 1 copy", the 16th book – "The Stories of Ostap Vishnya – 1 copy. All for just 80 kopecks. To be taken throughout the entire month of May." There was a short clarification: "Cherry and raspberry were included in the dose so as to vary the flavour a little. Cherry, you see, is a southern thing: Ostap Vishnya [Vishnya is the Russian word for cherry]. A popular Ukrainian comic writer, of the male gender. And for raspberry, we have Mikh. Bulgakov. Also of the male gender and also a comic writer. And he, too, could equally have been Ukrainian, although he writes well in Russian too. So all is well on that score (No. 21, p. 11).

This occurs shortly before the time when the reputation of the "comic writer", which had been consolidated throughout 1922 – 1924 (the previous summer, Olesha signed a book for Bulgakov: "You are a good comic writer...") is displaced, for a long time this time, with his reputation as an extremely popular dramatist.

On 26th June, the latest theatre season at the Art Theatre came to an end, and the authors, actors and directors all went off on holiday.

Bulgakov and his wife spent July outside Moscow, in Kryukov, where, at the Lyamins' recommendation, they moved into "the dacha of some old Muscovites, the Ponsovys", as L. Y. Belozerskaya recalls.

Later that month, he entered into a correspondence with the director A.D. Popov, who wished to secure some changes to *Zoya's Apartment*. In a letter dated 16th July, for example, he requested that the third act of the play be dispensed with altogether; Bulgakov received this letter in Kryukov on 25th July, and on 26th he wrote back to Popov from Moscow. His short summer break had finished; on 30th July, he sends back to *Rabochaya Gazeta* (*Workers' Newspaper*) 50 roubles, thereby cancelling out an advance given to him at some stage for the abstract of the novel *The Victorious Planet*. No trace of the plot for this novel survives. It may well have been an attempt to write a novel similar to *Iprit*, the one by Shklovsky and Ivanov, and contained a description of a war between Soviet Russia and a European coalition. We will see later that Bulgakov makes use of a similar plot in 1931, in his play *Adam and Eve*. The surviving financial document may well be the last echo of the time when Bulgakov was striving to achieve success as a writer of fiction – as a famous author whose work is read by many and sells well.

On 3rd August, A.D. Popov writes to him: "I greatly regret that your utter exhaustion, your nerves, and above all, your distrust of the theatre to which you gave your play, is impeding a business matter and our productive work."

On 11th August, Bulgakov sent a reply to the director Popov, and on the same day, he received an excerpt from the minutes of a meeting of the Artistic Policy Council regarding the repertoire of the Vakhtangov Theatre for the forthcoming season (*Zoya's Apartment* was included in it): "Propose to the Glavrepertkom that it conduct a special check and examination of the play *Zoya's Apartment*."

Evidence of organisational measures of a kind is found in an inscription in the collection *Diaboliad*, made on 12th August, to Vladimir Petrovich Nemeshayev – an employee of the Society for the protection of authors' rights, under the Moscow society of playwrights and composers (MOD-PIK), which was located at 25, Tverskoy Bulvar – in the same building as the All-Russian Union of Writers. This building was destined to play an important role, in a few years' time, in one of Bulgakov's new and most voluminous prose works. It was perhaps his memories of that stuffy Moscow summer of 1926, of tedious hours spent in the cramped rooms of the House of Herzen, that came to life when the idea for this work was formed.

… He had long since come to feel at home in Moscow; at the bookstores of Kuznetsky Most, the booksellers of the day knew him well. Many years later, on 12th July 1987, Klavdia Mirkina (nee Barmina) told me: "The shop of the *Novaya Moskva* publishing house was in the building of the former American store, at 7, Kuznetsky Most. My department was on the left-hand side as you went in: fiction, children's books, poetry and literary criticism. Novikov-Priboi used to come in, and Mayakovsky… He once said to me: 'Give me your criminal poetry!' This was Yezhov and Shamurin's anthology. It turned out that they hadn't paid the poets. Mayakovsky counted how many of his poems were there and walked out. Bulgakov used to drop in, too. I remember him saying: 'Could you find me some literature about the civil war.' And I did so.

Was there anything that made him different in any way from the other writers?

Yes. He was intelligent. The other writers used to reprimand me, asking why I hadn't displayed their novels more prominently. But he never even mentioned that! It was his intelligence that made him so different from the others. We had his collection of stories – *Diaboliad*. It used to sell out quickly. The way it worked was like this: you would order 20, 30 or 50 copies; then when they'd sold out, you would order a new batch. Sometimes we would get the response: 'they're sold out'. And at that point we would say to the customers: the work is sold out. Usually, the writers asked: 'How's my work getting on?' But he never asked.

Who did he usually come to the shop with?

He came alone, alone. He mostly came on his own. Mayakovsky was different – he usually came in with some friends in tow.

What did he tend to buy most often – poetry, prose?

Bulgakov didn't buy poetry. He bought stories about the civil war, specifically. There used to be these tiny little books that he would get. And he bought journals too."

The mid-1920s was the start of a turning point.

Certain phenomena had developed that were not immediately noticeable to an onlooker, but which were increasingly altering the life of society and colouring its prospects in very murky hues. One such phenomenon was the increasing size of the gulf between Russian and Europe.

In 1925, the journal published by Gorky, *Beseda* (*Conversation*) was closed down. The writer had intended it precisely as a way of unifying foreign and Russian literature. Conceived of by Shklovsky and managed by V. Khodasevich, the journal was published with his direct participation. As Khodasevich wrote to one of his correspondents on 3rd June 1925, *Beseda* had come to an end, "for the émigrés did not read it, and nor did anyone else, and it was subject to a ban on being imported into Russia." In his letter, Khodasevich wrote that in March of that year, his request to have his Soviet passport extended had been refused.

A curtain slowly but surely descended between the two Russian writers between 1925 and 1927. N.N. Berberova recalls, as a milestone, one fact from the summer of 1927: "Olga Dmitriyevna Forsh, whom I had known from Petersburg in 1922, when she had been one of Khodasevich's closest friends, arrived in Paris from the Soviet Union that year. She came to call on us immediately after her arrival. She was delighted to see Khodasevich, the conversations they had were neverending… […] For both of them, this reunion after five years apart was quite an event." Forsh "talked about the changes in literature, about the party's policy with respect to literature, at times cautiously, at times sincerely, ardently. […] She said that everyone over there had one hope alone.

'And what are they hoping for?' Khodasevich asked.

'For a global revolution.' Khodasevich was stunned.

'But that's not going to happen.'

Forsh fell silent for a moment. Her face, which was rather heavy at the best of times, became gloomy, the corners of her mouth turned down, the light in her eyes went out.

'Then we're done for,' she said.

'Who's done for?'

'All of us. The end will come for us.'

Two days went by, and there was no sign of her, and then we went to see her one evening to find out whether she might perhaps be unwell. She was staying on the rive gauche, with her daughter, an artist named Nadya, who had emigrated. […] She said to us that she had been at "our" embassy the previous morning and been handed an official ban on meeting up with Khodasevich. She was allowed to see Berdyayev and Remizov every so often, but she was not allowed to see Khodasevich. 'You ought to go now,' she said, 'You're not allowed to stay here.'

We stood there in the middle of the room, as though utterly lost.

She managed to utter the words: 'Vladya, forgive me,' through force of effort.

… We stood at the gateway in silence for a while and then wandered home. It had now become uncontrovertibly clear to us: they had cut us off, and it was to last thirty or forty years, forever…"

On 21st August, Stanislavsky returned to Moscow from his holidays, and for Bulgakov that meant a return to his work with the theatre on *The White Guard*. He wrote to A.D. Popov that day: "I am, indeed, exhausted. In May, there were all kinds of surprises, not linked to the theatre [undoubtedly a reference to the search of the apartment – M.C.], also in May there was the race to put on *The Guard* at the Art Theatre 1 (and the viewing by the government!), and in June endless odds and ends of work, because not a single one of the plays is bringing in any income, and in July the corrections for *Zoya*. And as for August, everything is happening at once."

On 24th August, Stanislavsky holds a meeting about *The White Guard* with Bulgakov and others. "We drew up the whole plan for the play, and recorded all the additions and amendments to the text," an assistant to the director wrote in his "Rehearsal diary". "Konstantin Sergeyevich explains the whole [play] in terms of the actor and the director." And an entry in the same diary on 26th August reads: "M.A. Bulgakov has written a new text for the school [i.e. the scene in the school, which was the subject of the key complaints when the preview took place – M.C.], in line with the plan approved by Konstantin Sergeyevich" (let us note a very small, yet telling detail: in the handwritten exercise book used for this *Diary*, the authors initials are misspelled: 'M.V.' – the theatre was still having trouble remembering his name; he would later riff on this error to powerful effect in *A Theatrical Novel*).

On 17th September, a rehearsal was scheduled to take place for employees of Glavrepertkom. Tense preparations for it were under way. Stanislavsky made the following request to the entire workforce at the Art Theatre: "Given that the early-stage dress rehearsal for *The Days of the Turbins* is going to be shown in a very rough and ready form, and that it is nonetheless important, both for the actors involved in the production and for the members of Glavrepertkom and Politprosvet, for us to have a full house, Konstantin Sergeyevich urges you to give your complimentary tickets only to your very closest relatives, and under no circumstances to give them to actors from other theatres, or to individuals who are involved in art or the press." A note made a few days later by an assistant director read as follows: "At the end – a general meeting of Glavrepertkom with the board of directors. Glavrepertkom considers that the play, in its current form, cannot be staged. The matter of approval remains open."

"His face pale, S. came backstage to see the cast; they had already heard the rumour that the play was going to be banned," writes M.I. Prudkin, who played the role of Shervinsky, in his memoirs. "If they do not allow this production to take place, I shall leave the theatre," said S. "I can see for myself certain miscalculations in the play, of an ideological nature, which can be overcome…"

On 18th September, though, another rehearsal takes place: "Everyone involved was present. Complaints about the whole of the play." The next entry in the 'Rehearsal diary' reads: "The public dress rehearsal scheduled to take place on 19th September has been cancelled due to the lack of clarity as to whether or not it has been given permission."

Behind these brief diary entries is the theatre's struggle – invisible to us today – to keep the play; the struggle was taking place on these decisive days. An entry on 22nd September reads: "Photo-shoot. Everyone in make-up and costumes." This photograph survives today: Bulgakov is seated in the middle, surrounded by the cast of the production.

Entries in the *Diary* comment on the final re-workings of the text: "The scene with the Jew is cancelled", "The 'Internationale' has been re-done – rather than getting quieter, it now gets louder", and his words unwittingly evoke a comparison with the situation on board a military ship: "Serious circumstances compel me to introduce a categorical ban on all performers and staff of the theatre, not involved in the play *The Days of the Turbins*, from being among the general public in the auditorium, foyer and corridors, both during the play and during the intervals."

The actors of the Art Theatre-2, Stanislavsky's pupils, send him a letter on 23rd September: "Today, on a day that is difficult for you and for the theatre – all of us, as one, wish to convey to you and to the whole theatre – our excitement and our heartfelt devotion to the theatre's work."

An entry is made in the *Diary*: "Full dress rehearsal with an audience… Seen by representatives of the [government] of the Union of SSRs, the press, representatives of Glavrepertkom, Konstantin Sergeyevich, the Supreme Soviet and the Directorate of theatre directors.

During today's performance, it will be decided whether or not the play is to go ahead.

The play is to be performed with the latest crossings out and without the 'Jew' scene.

The reaction to the play was very dry at first (the first half of the 1st scene), but then the auditorium was won over, the cast became more assured, bolder, the audience reacted wonderfully.

When it was over, A.V. Lunacharsky expressed his own personal view, namely that the play might very well make it through."

On 25th September, *Nasha Gazeta* reported: "A public preview, by invitation only, was held on 23rd September. The play is currently approved for staging at the Art Theatre, subject to a number of alterations."

On 27th September, at a debate on the prospects for the theatre season at the House of printing, the first strongly-worded attacks to be made against the play were aired for the first time: the theatre critic Orlinsky, according to the person who wrote a report on the debate, "is troubled as to why it is that all the parades, the singing of the Internationale and so on, takes place at the back of the stage… The 'fear of crowds of extras' at the Art Theatre, Orlinsky says, has reached the point where in *The White Guard*, for example, there isn't a single servant or orderly, not even so much as a scullery maid. And this, against the backdrop of all this *Bulgakovitis*, is telling."

In this atmosphere of heightened tension, on the morning of 2nd October, the public dress rehearsal of the play took place. The appearance of the officers on the stage was greeted with whistling from some of the younger members of the audience. Most of the audience greeted the play with excitement and with empathy. That evening, before the premiere, the play was discussed at a debate entitled 'The theatre policy of the Soviet government', at the Communist Academy. Lunacharsky spoke about the play *The Days of the Turbins*: "The arrival of this play on the stage of the Art Theatre is a thorny subject, of course," he says, "but material resources and creative energy have gone into it, and thus, if we were to take it off the stage, we would be radically undermining the theatre's position." According to A.V., the dubious ideology of this play holds no danger for us, for, in his opinion, 'our stomachs have grown sufficiently strong that they can even digest this spicy food'... "The author of the play, Bulgakov, gently tickles the man in the street by the right heel." Bulgakov sobs over the death of an officer, whereas, according to A.V., "an officer ought to have a death befitting of the officer class…" Comrade Orlinsky then took the floor, with objections against what Lunacharsky had said. In his opinion, it would be "inadmissible to put on *The White Guard*… *The White Guard* is a political demonstration, in which Bulgakov is exchanging winks with what remains of *The White Guard* movement." A report of the speech given by Mayakovsky, printed over thirty years later, enables us to examine the first ever public response on his part to Bulgakov's work – the first step in what was to be the complex history of the intertwining of their literary fates. Mayakovsky backed what Lunacharsky had said, stating far more bluntly and harshly the viewpoint of one who very definitely did not approve of the play, but who considered it entirely acceptable and permissible for it to be shown to the public. He insisted that it should not be seen as "an incidental part of the Art Theatre's repertoire. I think that it is the correct logical conclusion: they started off with Aunt Manya and Uncle Vanya, and ended up with *The White Guard* (Laughter). I consider it a hundred times nicer for this to come bursting onto the scene, than for it to be covered up as apolitical art. [...] As regards the policy of banning plays, I consider it to be an extremely damaging thing."

On 5th October 1926, the premiere of *The Days of the Turbins* took place. According to the recollections of those who attended the first few performances, the atmosphere inside the theatre was remarkable, and unlike anything they had experienced at any other premiere ("I can remember seeing plays at which "God save the Tsar" was sung on the stage," recalled one of the people I spoke to, K.S. Rodionov, on 2nd April 1981. Rodionov was almost the same age as Bulgakov would have been. "How did people react to the play in the theatre?" "Well, they all fell under its spell!"). There were instances of audience members fainting during the performance, and an ambulance had to be on call outside the entrance to the theatre. And this is understandable if one remembers that only five or six years had passed since the end of the civil war, and that many of those sitting in the audience had had husbands, brothers, fathers who had served as officers, and who had been killed, or gone missing in action, who had gone away and had to part forever with their nearest and dearest, who had been exiled, who were waiting for their past to catch up with them with each passing day. Let us quote from an "Open letter to the Moscow Artistic Academic Theatre (the Art Theatre I)", which appeared in *Komsomolskaya Pravda* on 14th October 1926 beneath the signature of the poet Alexander Bezymensky. He wrote that his brother, Benedikt Ilyich Bezymensky, had been killed "in Lukyanov prison, in Kiev, in 1918, when power was in the hands of Hetman Skoropadsky, the Germans and… all the Aleksei Turbins. I did not see any respect to the memory of my brother in the play that you are putting on. […] I cannot stress this enough: *I am not saying anything against the author of the play, Bulgakov, who shall remain exactly what he has been: a nouveau-bourgeois brat, spitting out poisonous, but powerless spit on the working class and his communist ideals.* But you, the Art Theatre, you are another matter." The writer of the letter asserted that the theatre had, "on behalf of the class truth of the Turbins", given "a slap in the face to the memory of my brother." The polarized interpretations of the play were thus set out. Bulgakov painstakingly collected cuttings from the newspaper reviews. He underlined the sections in Bezymensky's letter with his own hand; it is easy to imagine the feelings that took hold of him as he read about the very characteristics for which he had received acclaim. Some years later, Bulgakov enclosed an excerpt from the underlined section in a letter to the government – as an illustration of the critical assessments of his work; he also added some words from the speech by Lunacharsky, mentioned earlier, which was soon published in full in the "Programme of the state academic theatres" (No. 55), in which the author of the play said the following: "He likes the dubious witticisms that are exchanged by his drinking mates, the atmosphere of a dog's wedding surrounding some red-headed wife of an acquaintance…" Above all, it was the tone of this kind of journalism that Bulgakov could not bring himself to accept. He had his own methods of defence – shortly before the premiere, he had his photo taken *with a monocle in his eye* and started giving the photo to his friends and acquaintances.

A celebratory banquet with a large number of guests was held at the flat of V.A. Stepun, an actor from the Art Theatre, due to the lack of space at Bulgakov's tiny apartment.

In October, *The Days of the Turbins* was performed 13 times, before being performed 14 times in November and 14 times in December.

On 28th October 1926, meanwhile, the premiere of *Zoya's Apartment* takes place at the Vakhtangov Theatre. On 10th November, at a meeting of the Presidium of the collegium of the People's Commissariat for Education, Bulgakov's request to have permission granted for the staging of his play *Zoya's Apartment* in the provinces is rejected.

On 16th November, Bulgakov receives a summons to appear before the investigating officer on 18th; we do not know the reason for the summons; on 17th, V.V. Kuza sends him a message: "On this occasion, our torments, and yours, have ended, it seems; the Repertkom welcomed the play, and called it interesting and socially valuable. Only 2 corrections have been made – I shall tell you about them tomorrow when I see you."

Bulgakov sees in the new year, 1927, in the glow of literary fame – for the very first time. He is the author of two plays that are being performed to packed audiences at famous theatres in Moscow. He has left an extremely tense and difficult year behind him, one that was marked not only by the extremely complicated twists and turns of getting the play through all the obstacles, but also by the alarming events that had affected his private life in May, and perhaps caused some concerns about the future.

The critics are sharp-tongued in their reviews of the play; nonetheless, Bulgakov's fame is at its highest point. People are in raptures over his work; for the first time, his literary acquaintances from the first few years in Moscow envy him (it is no accident that the theme of jealousy about an artist later crops up, with such force, in *The Master and Margarita*, in the play about Pushkin, and in *A Theatrical Novel*).

Bulgakov experienced the impact of this frightening feeling, which gnawed away at the envious writers themselves, in its full extent. Back on 7th February 1926, D. Stonov had written to Slezkin: "In our times, a diabolical degree of tempering is essential. The soul must remain at one remove from all the troubles of everyday life. [...] My personal view is that a writer has to be an awful hermit – alone with his soul, with no-one else." Behind these lines, one can discern the draining feeling of expectation about the premiere at the Art Theatre of a play from someone who only yesterday was the inexperienced, unsuccessful author of a solitary, unpublished novel. On 8th October, Stonov writes to the same person: "I think *Moskovskiye Novosti* will be of interest to you, permit me to tear you away from your work for a few minutes. At the centre of events is Bulgakov's play, *The Days of the Turbins*. It was only granted permission to be shown at the Arts [Theatre], only in Moscow, and even then – word has it – it will be soon be taken off the repertoire. The press are criticising it (Lunacharsky and others), but the public aren't praising it either. You were right, right I say: Bull [this nickname seems to have come from the first pseudonym he used in Moscow – "M.Bull" – M.C.] is a representative of the petty bourgeoisie, and it was in this spirit that he approached events. Yekaterina Galati [a member of *Zelyonaya Lampa* – M.C.] was at the premiere. She doesn't like the play – it was better at the recital."

A lukewarm attitude towards the play was also seen in those who felt no personal enmity, but sincerely sensed the foreignness of the author's message. On 27th October 1926, the Moscow critic A. Derman wrote to the critic A. Gornfeld, based in Leningrad: "Due to a lack of money, I do not go to the theatre or to concerts. The only thing I have seen lately is Bulgakov's *The Days of the Turbins*, an unimportant play (and one that is spoilt by the censors' deletions, and, worse still, their excretions), which is performed with extraordinary talent by the young cast of the Art Theatre."

In print, all of this looked far more acerbic. The official attitude to a play in which there were people dressed in officers' epaulettes that could serve only as a target and nothing else, and who were portrayed with a warm, familial feeling, took shape quickly.

Documentary evidence survived in the writer's archive, however, about the attitude towards the author of *The Days of the Turbins* among that part of the audience which did not have the ability to express their feelings in print. According to Y.S. Bulgakova, one day, in 1926 or 1927, a man refusing to give his name turned up at the Art Theatre and asked the staff to pass on a letter to the playwright. Y.S. Bulgakova herself told me, during one of our conversations in 1968-1969, that Bulgakov held this letter very dear and carefully looked after it. Here is the text of the letter:

"Dear Mr. Author,

Remembering your sympathetic attitude towards me and knowing that at one time you took an interest in my fate, I am hastening to inform you about my subsequent adventures after you and I went our separate ways. After waiting for the arrival of the reds in Kiev, I was mobilized and began serving the new government not out of fear, but because of my conscience, and I fought the Poles with enthusiasm, even. It seemed to me then that only the Bolsheviks were a genuine power, strong through the people's faith in it, that will bring Russia happiness and prosperity, that will turn its inhabitants and roguish icon-bearers into strong, honest, straightforward citizens. Everything about the Bolsheviks seemed so good, so intelligent, so smooth; in a word, I saw everything through rose-tinted lenses, until I myself turned a little red and very nearly became a communist; and it was my past that saved me – the nobility and the officer class. Yet now, the honeymoon period of the revolution is over. The NEP, the Kronstadt rebellion. For me, as for many others, the intoxication is going away and the rose-tinted glasses are starting to take on darker shades...

General meetings held under the watchful, inquisitorial gaze of the district committee. Resolutions and demonstrations drawn up under duress. Barely literate bosses with the appearance of little Udmurt idols, who lust after every typist. No understanding of what they are doing, and instead a spur of the moment approach to everything. A Komsomol that enjoys spying on people for no particular reason. Working delegations – knowledgable foreigners, reminisicent of Chekhovian generals at a wedding. And lies, the endless lies... And the leaders? They are either small men, who are holding onto a power and comfort of the kind they have never seen before, or wild fanatics, who think they can crash through brick walls with their foreheads. And the idea itself! All right, it's not such a bad idea on paper, it is fairly coherent, but it absolutely cannot be implemented in real life, much like the teachings of Christ, although Christianity is more comprehensible and more beautiful.

So here's the thing. I am now on the bottom rung of the ladder. Not in a financial sense. Oh no. Even in these times, I am doing fine in terms of my work, I get by. But it is rotten to live without believining in anything. For after all, not believing in anything and not loving anything – that will be the privilege of the generation that comes after us.

Lately, either out of a passionate desire to fill the spiritual vacuum, or perhaps it really is the case, but I sometimes hear barely perceptible note from some kind of new life, a real one, a truly beautiful one, one that has nothing in common with either the Tsar's Russia, or with Soviet Russia.

I am appealing to you with a great request on behalf of me and on behalf, I think, of many others like me, who are feeling an emptiness in their souls. Tell me, whether it's from the stage, from the pages of a journal, whether directly or in the language of Aesop, however you want, just let me know whether you can hear these scarcely audible notes, and what is the noise they are making about?

Or is all this self-deception and the current Soviet emptiness (material, moral and intellectual) a permanent phenomenon?

Caesar, morituri te salutant. Viktor Viktorovich Myshlayevsky."

On 14th January 1927, the 50th performance of *The Days of the Turbins* at the Art Theatre took place (the author himself writes a note about this in an album that he starts keeping several years later, dedicated to the story of *The Days of the Turbins*). *Zoya's Apartment* was being performed with success in several cities around the country.

On 7th February 1927, there was another dispute at the Meyerhold Theatre – this time over the production of *The Days of the Turbins* at the Art Theatre and K. Trenyov's play *Lyubov' Yarovaya* at the Maly Theatre. Bulgakov addressed the general public, unable to stay quiet this time in the face of his constant opponent over the last year – the critic A. Orlinsky. The stenograph survived and, after being ironed out by Y.S. Bulgakova, was published in 1969 in the journal *Ogonyok*; it is one of very few surviving records of how Bulgakov actually spoke when addressing an audience. E. Mindlin was struck by his restraint: "At last I have seen Orlinsky in the flesh and been introduced to him. I am satisfied…" S. Yermolinsky, who did not yet know Bulgakov at that time, remembered him being far more nervous.

He was particularly bothered, as the stenograph indicates, by this line by Orlinsky: "… panicking, the author and the theatre changed the name of the play". Everything that hinted at surrender, at retreat, everything that attacked his personal honour, always hurt him more acutely than anything else. "… I can say firmly and assuredly that the author of *The Turbins* did not, and does not, feel any panic whatsoever, least of all from the appearance of comrade Orlinsky on the stage. I did not change the name of the play in a panic. I know the author of *The Turbins* rather well."

Orlinsky had complained that the play contained no orderlies, no servants, no workers, and Bulgakov explained this, to much laughter and applause: "I… who saw the white guardsmen in Kiev from inside my home, behind some cream-coloured curtains, hereby assert that in Kiev, at that time, i.e. when the events in my play were taking place, orderlies were not to be had, for love nor money."

P.Y. Zabludovsky, who graduated from the medical faculty of Kiev University in 1919, describes, in a letter to me that was written on 29th November 1987, his memories of this discussion, at which he was present. "The chairman of the social court was A.V. Lunacharsky, which lent the court a great deal of authority, even a sort of official character. There was standing room only in the theatre. A fellow named Orlinsky laid into Bulgakov; he introduced himself as follows before his speech: 'I shall not hide the fact that I was in the political department of the division which fought against the Whites, whose uniform Bulgakov wore.'" As for the dialogue about the servants, Zabludovsky said: "Bulgakov replied that under the circumstances at that time, no-one had any servants, and his former servant had left, to go back to her home village. Orlovsky: 'You couldn't get them for gold?' Bulgakov: 'I never heard of anyone paying their servants in gold.' Orlovsky: 'Well, whoever had gold may have paid their servants with it. The Turbins, I suspect, probably did have some.' This was the kind of level at which this "accusation" was being made. Bulgakov was asked, incidentally, who he had wanted to portray in Aleksei Turbin, and how he related to him personally; he replied that in Aleksei Turbin "I showed a person whom I love and who merits profound respect." At the end, Lunacharsky drew up the prosecution's public sentence, albeit one that was couched in very polite terms."

The argument about the orderly is significant. Judging by the stenograph, Bulgakov went on to add, penetratingly: "... even if I had introduced this orderly, I assure you, and I know this for a fact, I would not have satisfied the critic Orlinsky (laughter, applause). [...] Allow me to present very briefly two scenes featuring the orderly: one written by me, and the other – by Orlinsky. My version would be as follows: 'Vasily, put the samovar on' – that is Aleksei Turbin speaking. The orderly replies: 'Certainly,' and then he is never seen again throughout the rest of the play. Orlinsky would have needed a different orderly…here comes the definition: being a good sort of fellow, Aleksei Turbin would never have flogged his orderly, or given him a thick ear – that is what is of interest to Orlinsky." Lastly, Bulgkov parodied Orlinsky's complaints that there were no workers, Bolsheviks etc. in the play. He talked about the artistic categories of taste and background, defending them, protesting against the rigid schemes of a proper portrayal, defending his right to convey the epoch using his own artistic means.

He was nigh on the only person who had freely moved away from the standard format of having "Red" and "White" brothers, which Shklovsky highlighted as having reigned supreme over the literature of the 1920s, in witty fashion: "It is a bad thing when Lavrenev's *Enemies* and Slonimsky's *Lavrovs* and Fedin's *Brothers* are based on red, white and pink brothers. The plot of Olesha's novel [*Envy*, 1927 – M.C.] is structured around two brothers – a red one and a white one" (he might well have added Aleksei Tolstoy's brothers-in-law to the list). In Bulgakov's works, the critics did not find any 'red' brothers in the places that had already become customary for them.

On 10th March, Gorky writes to A.N. Tikhonov: "What of Bulgakov? Couldn't I have a chance to look at his play?" And on 25th March, Tikhonov replies: "Bulgakov is attempting to stage his play *The Crimson Island*, but so far unsuccessfully. I shall try to send you a copy of the play. He is working on the novel *The White Guard* – he is rewriting it almost entirely."

In the same month, it is announced in print (in the *Programmes of the State Academic Theatres* [*Programmy Gosudarstvennykh Akademicheskikh Teatrov*]) that Bulgakov is writing a play for the Art Theatre, "depicting episodes from the battle for Perekop." In April, a contract was signed with the Art Theatre for the play *Seraphima's Knight* (*Rytsar' Serafimy*), which Bulgakov promised to submit to the theatre "no later than 20th August 1927". Apparently, the rumours spreading around Moscow about this play compelled Meyerhold to send Bulgakov the following letter, on 26th May: "Unfortunately, I do not know your first name and patronymic. Please give me your play for the forthcoming season. Smyshlyayev [Valentin Smyshlyayev, a performer from the Art Theatre II whom the Bulgakovs had known for a short while – M.C.] told me that you already have a new play and that you would not object if this play were to be put on at the theatre that I direct." On 21 June, Meyerhold thanked him for his reply (since lost) and wrote, regretfully: "Ah, how annoying that you do not have the play! Oh well, what can one do?!" And he then asked Bulgakov to promise to call him in the autumn, to arrange a meeting.

Of course, in June, the play *Flight* can scarcely have been finished, not even in draft form. For me, though, there is no doubt that Bulgakov did not wish to give it to Meyerhold at all – after all, there was nothing stopping him from taking up the conversation again in the autumn. There was much about Meyerhold that put him off: starting with the manner adopted in his letters, whereby he thought nothing of writing to somebody without knowing their first name and patronymic!

On 1st August 1927, Adolf Frantsevich Stui, "hereinafter referred to as the 'Supervisor'" (the architect and developer, who was entitled to operate the residential building) and Bulgakov, "hereinafter referred to as the 'Lessor'", signed an agreement: Bulgakov had secured, on a lease, an apartment consisting of three small rooms, a kitchen and a bathroom – the first separate apartment of his life in Moscow. He moved in on the ground floor of house No. 35a on Bolshaya Pirogovskaya. "When you walk out of our building and glance to the left," Lyubov writes in her memoirs, "you see an elegant, six-tiered belltower and the outlines of a monastery [the Novodevichy Convent – M.C.]. It was an extraordinarily beautiful place. Probably one of the best places in Moscow." They moved in at the end of August; on 5th September, Bulgakov invited his sister Nadya to visit them at their new flat.

The moving-in day coincided with the news that *The Days of the Turbins* had been taken off the repertoire at the Art Theatre.

Vechernyaya Moskva reported on 17th September that *The Days of the Turbins* had been excluded from the repertoire, but by then steps had been taken that were destined to bear fruit. In Bulgakov's album, mentioned earlier, there is a note in his hand: "12th October 1927 – on Wednesday a cable arrived at the Theatre with the permission, and on 13th the play was added to the repertoire." On 13th, Lunacharsky wrote to Stanislavsky: "You already know, of course, that for this year at least, you are allowed to stage *The Turbins*."

On 20th October, *The Days of the Turbins* was performed at the Art Theatre, for the first time in the new season. That day, Stanislavsky writes a letter to K.Y. Voroshilov, in which he thanks him "for his responsiveness" to the theatre's affairs and, among other things, for his help "in the matter of securing permission for the play *The Days of the Turbins*," and on 25th October, Vladimir Blyum (pseudonym: Sadko), a fervent opponent of Bulgakov at all times, who had actively helped to secure the removal of the play from the repertoire, was prompted by this new development to write an article in Zhizn' Iskusstva (*The Life of Art*) entitled *The Beginning of the End for the Art Theatre* (*Nachalo Kontsa MKHATa*).

On Bulgakov's attitude towards the critics from those years, who accompanied his every step across the boards of the theatres, there is the following story that was passed on orally by Y.S. Bulgakova. Whilst standing in line one day to collect a royalty, Bulgakov had a man pointed out to him, and was told that the man was the famous critic and author of satirical sketches, who wrote using the pseudonym Sadko. Bulgakov went up to the man and said: "Are you Bloom? Allow me to shake your hand: *you write with conviction*." This may or may not have actually happened, but the point is that it might well have done: there is a good reason why the future protagonist of *The Master and Margarita*, whilst reading furious articles aimed at his novel about Pilate, keeps getting the sense "that the authors of these articles are not saying what they really want to say, and that this is the very thing that is causing their fury." On the other hand, it was whilst made up to look like Bloom, an employee of Glavrepertkom, whom the entire audience could recognise, that Savva Lukich, a malevolent character from *The Crimson Island*, appeared on stage at the Kamerny Theatre. In the epilogue to the play, after the preview of the show has ended, "Savva Lukich is alone, motionless, sitting on his throne above the crowd. He looks deep in thought and grim-faced. All eyes are on him." The director of the theatre asks: "Hm... Well, what does it please you to say with regard to the play, Savva Lukich?"

A deathly silence ensues.

Savva: It shall be banned.

A groan can be heard from the entire theatre company. The faces of the stunned musicians can be seen poking out from the orchestra pit. The prompt sticks his head out his booth in amazement." Later, in a letter to the government, Bulgakov would write openly that the play was aimed at the Glavrepertkom, which had killed "creative thought" and wrecked Soviet drama, and would say, with an artist's pride: "I did not express these thoughts in a whisper, in the corner of the room. I put them into a dramaturgical pamphlet and staged that pamphlet at the theatre."

There was still a long way to go before this letter was written, though. For the time being, he was finishing off the fourth play in this three-year period – *Flight*.

In this play, a number of motifs that were extremely important to Bulgakov, related to material about the civil war, were brought to life; they had been outlined back in 1922 but he had not found a way to use them in the novel *The White Guard*. Remember how the protagonist of the story *The Red Crown*, after losing his mind because of all he has been through, recalls: "I went away, so as not to see a man being hanged, but the fear went away along with me, in my trembling legs."

That same year, the behaviour of Dr. Bakaleinikov, after seeing "the first murder in his life", is described in similar terms: "Bakaleinikov sniffled in a most bizarre fashion, as though he were croaking, and then set off, wobbling drunkenly, forwards and to the side, away from the bridge, towards the white building." The description of the murder of the Jew on the bridge, seen by the protagonist of early drafts of a novel about the civil war, is reproduced almost word-for-word in *The White Guard*. Here, though, it takes place outside the field of vision of the novel's protagonists – and thus outside the field of their *personal* responsibility.

In a similar way, this theme (of personal participation: albeit by being present during a murder and not intervening – and, consequently, of personal guilt) is shifted to one side in the scene-by-scene draft of the play *The Days of the Turbins* – the brutal interrogation scenes are kept separate from the scenes featuring the Turbins (it is also significant that they do not end tragically). In the first draft of the play (perhaps closer to the early drafts of the novel, which have not survived), the interrogation of the deserter and the murder of the Jew unfold directly before Alexei's eyes – in a dream. This dream, and Alexei's cry upon waking: "Come quickly, come quickly! You have to help him. He may still be alive…" are no doubt brought about by what was an important plot impulse for all of Bulgakov's creative oeuvre: the protagonist's efforts to relive events from the past and alter their course. Only once is this fateful, irreversible collision between the past and the present removed, and a situation is recreated, so that the protagonist can intervene in the course of events: in the story *I Killed* (printed in 1926 in *Meditsinskiy Rabotnik* [*Medical Worker*]), Dr Yashvin, having been forcibly mobilized by Petlyura's men, shoots dead a colonel who is guilty of murder.

Something similar happens in *Flight*: two of the characters, Seraphima Korzukhina and the page, Krapilin (the former is sick and cannot remember who she is, whilst the other, suddenly coming to, shouts out 'I was in oblivion!') hurl frightening accusations at Khludov which prove to be deadly for them themselves.

Khludov later denounces Korzukhina to the counter-espionage services, and she manages to stay alive by some miracle, and orders that Krapilin be hung.

Thus, six or seven years after the end of the war, Bulgakov is still attentively investigating that psychological situation, the unsolvable nature of which led to the protagonist of *The Red Crown* losing his mind – the opportunities and consequences of a direct collision between man and a deadly force. "Then, of course, there was nothing I could do," the hero of *The Red Crown* realises, "but now [i.e. whilst going through all the pangs of conscience and after losing his reason – M.C.] *I* would boldly say: "Mr. General, you are a monster! Don't you dare hang people!" This "Mr. General", who is only described in outline in the story, prefigures Khludov, with the madness that has overtaken him. The poor, mentally sick man tells the general about how his brother, who was killed in battle (after he, the elder of the two, could not convince him to leave the field of a senseless battle), appears before him at night: "Mr. General, he stood there in silence and would not go away. Then I became bitter as a result of this agony and with all my willpower I wished that he would appear before you, just once… I assure you: you would be finished, just as I am. At one stroke. And by the way, perhaps you, too, are not alone during the hours of night? Who knows, perhaps that dirty man, covered in soot, from the lamplight in Berdyansk, comes to see you? If he does, then it is right that we are suffering. I sent Kolya to help you with the hanging [the chain of shared responsibility – M.C.], but you were the one who hanged him. On the basis of an oral command, with no official number." In *Flight*, too, Khludov is forever having visions of the people he has hanged. The link between the theme of madness, which is central for this figure, and the story of the disease suffered by the protagonist of *The Red Crown*, and also the disease affecting Petlyuran colonel Leshchenko from the story *I Killed*, is obvious: Petlyura's men are shown to be equal to the volunteers; a murder, by dint of what it is, displaces, for the author, the divisions between the slogans beneath which it is committed.

An excerpt that survives from an early draft of the novel (1922) sets out the two most critical aspects of the plot, its two centres – a personal loss of one's home, of peace, of tranquillity ("My God! O peace! O serene repose!" the author exclaims, together with Dr Bakaleinikov, as he is mobilized against his will) and that of personal guilt: "Mobs! But I... I am the filth of the intelligentsia!" the same character exclaims, as he turns his back on a murder that is taking place before his very eyes. In *The White Guard*, ultimately, one of these two themes is chosen: the former; the heroes of the novel, as they gather together at the Turbins' house, are individuals who have suffered in the true sense of the word (unlike Shpolyansky, the Hetman and others). Only once, whilst praying for her brother's life, does Yelena say, in prayer: "We are all guilty in our blood, but do not punish us."

"Will anyone pay for this blood?" the author asks at the end of the novel, and then he replies: "No. Nobody." This reply is not definitive, however – it is not for nothing that an epigraph was left in the printed text of the novel, which does not relate to *this* particular novel in essence, but which then presents the end of it: "And the dead were judged, as is written in the books, in accordance with their deeds..."

The protagonist of the story *The Red Crown* is prepared to answer *personally* and he does so – with his madness. And Khludov pays in the same way for the immeasurably greater blame that he must bear in the other play, which Bulgakov finished at the end of 1927.

It seems to me that even before strongly-worded accusations were made against the author of the play *The Days of the Turbins* and the novel *The White Guard* appeared in print due to his overly sympathetic portrayal of the protagonists, the writer himself was already thinking about a play which was to contain a second motif, one that was just as important to him: "it is right that we are suffering", *Flight* is not a continuation of *The Days of the Turbins*, but the second side, the flip-side, of the self-same problems, which even in this play are not exhausted, and which retained all their pertinence in Bulgakov's later work: for the events of that fateful year, everyone is responsible.

The play not only gave rise to and developed themes which had been examined previously; in it, with hindsight, one discovers some sort of remainder: that which remains undeveloped in this play, but which will be developed in later texts.

Immortality is a tranquil, light-filled shore;
Our path is the struggle to reach it.
May he rest, he who runs no more…!

This epigraph to the play *Flight*, taken from the works of Zhukovsky ("a bard in the mould of the Russian warriors") back in 1927, is the programme for a line adopted by *The Master*, which embodied most fully the theme that runs through the whole of Bulgakov's oeuvre (the peacefulness of immortality as the ultimate goal of living, one that embellishes it substantially) – and this despite the fact that the plot of this particular line in the novel, about which the author was surely already thinking, probably did not exist yet.

Also of importance in terms of the play's plot coming into being was the fate of the newly returned *smenovekhovtsy*, which was still a happy one in those years.

Among the things that helped to shape the plot of *Flight* and the character of Khludov as nigh on its main protagonist, there were many printed sources, in addition to the obvious one that is always cited – Slashchov's book *Crimea in 1920* (M., 1924). Among them, no doubt, was V.V. Shulgin's book of memoirs, *The Year 1920*, with its detailed analysis of what happened to the "White idea" in 1919-1920 (this analysis may have been reflected in Khludov's utterances: "No-one loves us, no-one… What's needed is love, and without love you won't achieve anything in a war! *(Scoldingly, to Tikhy)* I am not loved"; the final pages, filled with feeling, of Shulgin's book about the fate of White thought and the White movement may to some extent have influenced the decision to call the novel *The White Guard*.

Let us also mention A. Averchenko and the book by A. Vetlugin, *Heroes and Imaginary Portraits* (*Geroi i Voobrazhayemyye Portrety*), published in 1922 in Berlin (like Shklovsky's *A Sentimental Journey*). The description of General Slashchov that it contains may not only have provided Bulgakov with details for his portrayal of Khludov (the cocaine-like paleness of his face – "white as a bone", for example), but also served to set the tone for his work on this character. In the years 1924-1927, a large number of memoirs about the civil war were published, including memoirs written by people who fought on the other side of the front line: ten years later, whislt working on the libretto for an opera about Perekop, Bulgakov would compile a list of these sources.

The birth of the plot of Flight and its implementation is explained in the broad creative context of Bulgakov's work in 1926-1928, first and foremost – alongside the creative story of the novel *The White Guard*, which was finished in these years.

A host of biographical facts must also be taken into account. The end of 1926 was the time of the triumph of *The Days of the Turbins* at the Art Theatre, of *Zoya's Apartment* at the Yevgeny Vakhtangov Theatre, of success with the general public over and above the scathing reviews of the plays in the press. Bulgakov had suddenly become an extremely famous playwright; his dream had finally come true – the one that he had written to his cousin about from Vladikavkaz, after the premiere of the play *The Turbin Brothers*: "This is my dream coming true… but in what a monstrous fashion: rather than the Moscow stage, a stage out in the provinces," and so on. Now, he really had conquered the Moscow stage – and he had done so at one of the most respected theatres in the city. The stage was now eagerly awaiting new works by him. In the light of these successes and his optimistic expectations, the fate of those who were roaming about in Constantinople or Paris during this period, and about whom he heard from his new literary comrades who were returning to Russia, presented itself to him in that year as something that required an immediate and unequivocal assessment. He began thinking about the plot for a new play, this time directly addressing the root problems of modernity, and, apparently, he believed that by shining a light on one side of the historic struggle, he would be able to expand the scope to cover the whole of it.

The idea of *Flight* as a movement, alien to someone from a nonmigratory culture, who is bound to his birthplace, his home, had occurred to him far earlier, of course, than his thoughts about the people who fled to Constantinople and Paris. As early as in his first printed work, he would write about the madness of "the last two years", which "have pushed us onto a frightening path, and we cannot stop, we cannot pause to catch our breath." This was, indeed, his understanding of *flight*, something akin to Zweig's *Amok* – hasty, disjointed movement, guided by someone else's will – without a plan or goal, without any productive outcome.

The plot of *Flight* came into being and developed against the backdrop of several important phenomena from the public life of the day. One of these was the 'return' movement, hard to analyse for a number of reasons even today, which developed among a fairly wide range of social classes among the émigré community.

Khodasevich asserted that "the influence of Moscow spheres on those who spearheaded the return movement had the aim not of actually getting them to return to Russia, but merely to cause confusion in the hearts and minds of the émigrés." On 10th July 1926, Khodasevich wrote his personal analysis of the situation in a letter to Mikhail Karpovich, giving us an idea of how the changes that had taken place in the country were seen not from within, but from without. "I am talking about *present-day* Russia. I left that place 4 years ago, but knowing what happened, and reading the newspapers and magazines from there, I can work out what it is like. The RSFSR of 1922 and the era of "military communism" was an extremely liberal country compared to the USSR of 1926. You, who did know, *did not see* the former, are psychologically right when you imagine its traits as less scary than they are made out to be, and I understand if you (like the foreigners) do not entirely believe us émigrés. [...] You say: I would return, "if there were the slightest possibility of living there, without becoming a scoundrel." In that little 'if' lies the most sacred simplicity." Khodasevich asserted: "You will become a scoundrel on the day when you go to the Soviet consulate and fill in their questionnaire, in which you will renounce everything, even yourself. (If you are not prepared to do so, you may as well not go there). And as for the scoundrel that you shall become once you step onto the soil of the USSR... one could write a whole book about that. For, once you sit down in the railway car, you will strike up the following conversation with the person seated next to you: *Your neighbour*: Where are you travelling from, may I ask? *You*: From New York. *Your neighbour*: Were you there long? *You*: Since 1916. *Your neighbour*: What did you do there? *You*: I worked out there. *Your neighbour*: Did you feel remorse at having gone against the workers' and peasants' rule? Are you ashamed of your heinous deeds? (thereafter, there are two possible scenarios):

I. *You*: Yes, I am very ashamed. I acted wickedly and associated with scoundrels. And I kept up a correspondence with them, too.
The Devil: (whispering into your ear): What a scoundrel you are, Mikhail Mikhailovich. I'm very glad.
Your neighbour: Here's 20 kopecks for your work.
II. *You*: No, I'm not ashamed, it's just that I missed Russia and want to live and work there, without fighting against the workers' and peasants' rule.
III. *The Devil*: (whispering into your ear): Bravo! What evasiveness!

Your neighbour: You're not ashamed? I see... (takes out an arrest warrant). Allow me to escort you to the local division of the GPU; on the following grounds: etc.

I assure you that there can be no third way. The only possible difference is that the conversation might take place not at the first station, but the third, or even in Moscow." Khodasevich brought this passage to an end by stating that he was certain that Karpovich's 'returnism' would "lead to nothing beyond sadness (of an entirely natural and esteemed kind)". Bulgakov began writing a play about 'returnism' that went all the way to the end.

How would he have felt about Khodasevich's harsh and poisonous diagnosis, if it had become known to him? We shall not attempt to answer this question. He was thinking this in the very same year in which he wrote the letter about the same thing – about those who "missed Russia" and wanted "to live and work there, without having to struggle against the worker-and-peasant government."

Did he have a third version prepared for these people? And if he also thought that there could be no third version – what was it that moved his plot, the plot for a play about a flight over there and a flight back again?

Flight contained some idea on the part of the author that was expressed in the epigraph selected by the author and was aimed far into the distance, above and beyond the specific historical situation.

In the final scene, Golubkov and Seraphima "run out of the bedroom", having decided to "go home" to go towards, one must suppose, hope. A possible alternative – that of showing them moving towards uncertainty and, perhaps, eternal rest, that will arrive after torments that are not yet known to them, remained unused by the playwright – although, retrospectively, students and directors may read this into the play today, perhaps justifiably to some extent.

Bulgakov's name had already achieved a certain degree of fame in Europe – mainly among Russian spectators and readers. On 13th October 1927, the Paris-based newspaper *Days* reported: "The production in Riga by a Russian drama group of the play *The Turbin Family*, acclaimed in Russia [...] had tremendous success." In Riga, a separate version of the novel *The White Guard* appeared, in which the end of the novel, which was not printed in *Rossiya*, was written by someone else on the author's behalf – based on the final act of *The Days of the Turbins*: the final scene perhaps reflected the personal recollections of the unknown writer about Kiev at the time when the Bolsheviks invaded early in 1919.

Bulgakov was no doubt tormented by these 29 printed pages of someone else's text, included beneath a cover with his name on it.

Barely a month had gone past since the updating of *The Days of the Turbins* on the stage of the Art Theatre, when *Zoya's Apartment* was removed from the repertoire of the Vakhtangov theatre. This served to intensify interest in Bulgakov's works among the Russian émigré community. In the same month, on 26th November 1927, the newspaper *Days* reported: "The directors of the Russian drama in Riga have managed to get, from Russia, another play by Bulgakov, the author of *The Days of the Turbins* – *Zoya's Apartment*. It will be performed by a studio from the Moscow Art Theatre, and this play by Bulgakov was soon taken off the repertoire, because the government did not take kindly to it. *Zoya's Apartment* will be performed in Riga in a production by Ungern."

Eventually, on 8th December 1927, a report appeared in *Days* beneath the headline *Bulgakov at GPU?* It read: "The author of *The Days of the Turbins* and the play *Zoya's Apartment*, Bulgakov, was summoned to the GPU and subjected to an interrogation, and it is for this reason that his works are published overseas, and his plays are performed on foreign stages. The GPU were particularly interested in knowing whether or not Bulgakov received a royalty. Bulgakov was interrogated for more than 3 hours."

If this report can be relied upon, then it is possible that these circumstances served as the main impulse that prompted Bulgakov to take steps to publish his letter about the actions of the former publisher of *Rossiya*, Z. Kagansky, who had declared himself to be the writer's authorised representative (the first letter is dated 28 November).

Kagansky, alas, had a legal justification for doing this, which did not become clear to Bulgakov straight away. Certain phrases in the letter from 15th December, submitted via a member of staff from the agency for the protection of authors' rights, V.L. Binshtok, to the foreign newspapers, were clearly calculated not so much to be read outside the country, as much as inside it. He asserted that "neither Kagansky, nor other individuals, in spite of the assurances they gave, received copies of my plays *The Days of the Turbins* and *Zoya's Apartment*, from me. If such copies are in their possession, then they may be ones that they copied out by hand, or copies that they received without permission and without the author's knowledge, and taken overseas in the same way. It seems highly likely that they are drafts or sketches for the novel *The White Guard*, which were not published in the USSR, i.e. material received by illegal means."

The essence of the problem was that, given the lack of a convention between the USSR and the other countries (not until 1973 was one drawn up), the rights of Soviet authors, whenever their works were published abroad (or their plays were put on), were not protected. They could rely only on the goodwill of the publishers; the personal influence of an author who had already made a name for himself might, ultimately, play a decisive role in how the situation developed.

In mid-February, he submits an application for a two-month overseas journey. In an additional note included with the application, entitled 'The aim of the foreign travel' and dated 21st February, he explained that he wished to travel to Berlin, "to ensure Kagansky is held accountable", and to Paris, to hold negotiations with the theatres that wanted to stage *The Days of the Turbins*, and with the Society of authors and dramatists, which he had joined a short time earlier. Thereafter, Bulgakov wrote: "In Paris, I intend to study the city and think through the plan for putting on the play *Flight*, which has now been accepted by the Moscow Art Theatre (act IV of *Flight* is set in Paris).

The trip ought not to take more than 2 months in any event, after which I shall have to be in Moscow (in order to put on *Flight*).

I hope that I will be granted permission to make the journey, for the sake of the important matters set out here in good faith." And he added, in a post-script: "P.S. A refusal to grant permission to make the trip will make the circumstances extremely difficult for my future work as a dramatist." He was counting on his request being supported by Gorky.

On 1st March, the Art Theatre enters into an agreement with Bulgakov for *Flight*, whereby the author would return his advance if the play was banned.

8th March 1928 is the date contained on "Certificate No. 8-664", which Bulgakov held onto: "The Adminstrative department of Mossovet hereby announces that the granting of the right to travel overseas is refused you."

... Early in 1928, the talk in Moscow was still of the strange and tragic event that had taken place a week before New Year. On 26th December, the newspapers published articles entitled "The illness and death of Bekhterev". They reported on how the extremely famous academic and doctor had arrived in Moscow from Leningrad for a congress of psychiatrists and brain surgeons; he was elected honorary chairman of the congress, and gave a speech; on 23rd December he attended the play *Lyubov' Yarovaya* and felt unwell later that evening; his condition worsened over the course of the next day, and no diagnosis could be found for it (and this despite the fact that the brightest and best of the country's medical experts all happened to be in Moscow). By the evening, it had been determined that he was suffering from an "acute gastric illness"; his heart began to grow weak, and at around 12 midnight, Bekhterev died. It was decided that his brain should be put on display at the Institute of the Brain, which he himself had founded, and since he had been the one who came up with the idea of having a pantheon for the brains of great people, this prompted the People's Commissar of Health, Semashko, to talk of a "cruel irony of fate" (*Krasnaya Gazeta*, evening edition, 26th December 1927). Over the next few days, the newspapers reported all kinds of phantasmagorical details about the transportation of the urn containing his ashes, and the brain, to Leningrad: both of them are put on display at one of the stations, in the stationmaster's office; an honorary guard is formed outside. Then "the urn and brain were put on board the train, in two adjacent compartments" (*Krasnaya Gazeta*, evening edition, 28th December 1927).

Bulgakov, bound as he was by ties of friendship and familial ties to Moscow's doctors, could not, in my view, have failed to hear about the hypothesis that was soon being discussed about Bekhterev meeting Stalin, about the diagnosis that the psychiatrist frivolously shared with his colleagues (paranoia), and about the connection that his rapid death seemed to have with his loose tongue.

... The birth and development of the plot of *The Master and Margarita*, and our very perception of such important elements of its plot as the head of Berlioz, lopped off, stolen and then turned into a chalice, the murders, the series of evil deeds which are described at the hangman's ball at Woland's place – all of this looks different against the backdrop of what we know about the evil deeds that were part of the reality of that epoch.

On 16th March, Bulgakov submits two copies of *Flight* to the Art Theatre.

In April, Bulgakov decided to leave for Tbilisi and Batum – to have a look at the places that he left in the bitter days, almost bereft of hope, of 1921. As he travelled through Gudermers on 22nd April, he wrote a quick postcard to Y.I. Zamyatin, in which he wrote, among other things: "I am travelling to Tbilisi, though I am very unwell indeed."

L.Y. Belozerskaya wrote in her memoirs: "We were met at the station by someone M.A. had known from his time in Vladikavkaz – Olga Turkul, a petite, rosy-cheeked, modest woman. She gave us a room for the first night. The next day, we moved to the Oriant hotel on Prospekt Rustaveli... It was nice and warm. We sleep with the windows open... We go bathing in the sunshine. We go bathing in sulphur baths. We walked down the Verisky Hill into the old town, to Zakurie. [...] Olga Turkul took us to a cake shop in one of the side-streets and introduced us to the French lady who ran it, and also to her granddaughter, Marika Chimishkian, a half-French, half-Armenian, young and very pretty girl, who was later connected with our family for many years…"

In November 1969, Marika Chimishkian told me: "Olga was a milliner, a friend of Tatiana Nikolayevna, Bulgakov's first wife, in Vladikavkaz… She was Polish and died in 1937. That spring, she said to me: 'I want to introduce you to my friends.' The Bulgakovs wanted to visit the Botanical Garden, but I said to them: 'I can't come – I've just come back from there, I'm tired.' Bulgakov said: 'Ah! Well in that case I'll go and hail a cab.' So off we went for a drive along the Kodzhorskoye Highway. We laughed a great deal. Then Bulgakov said: 'No, we mustn't part company today!' And it so happened that the Maly Theatre was on tour at the time, at the Opera Theatre in Tbilisi – and that very night, *The Government Inspector* was going to be performed, with Stepan Kuznetsov in the lead role. Bulgakov ran off to get the tickets."

"A short distance away from us, in a box," Lyubov Yevgenievna recalled, "there was an elderly Georgian lady in national dress: a low hat pushed forward onto her forehead, and curls hanging down at the sides… Everyone in Tbilisi knew that woman: she was Stalin's mother.

I watched the first act and started to get bored.

'Here's the thing, chaps,' I said to Maka and Marika, 'after seeing Meyerhold's version, it's a little boring to watch a production like this one. You stay here, I'm going to head off'" – and she went to take a stroll around the town. As for Bulgakov, according to her recollections, he was with her at the dress rehearsal for *The Government Inspector* (at the start of the winter of 1926/1927) at Meyerhold's theatre, and he attempted to demonstrate to his wife (on the coach journey home) "that such a wilful incursion into a work distorts the author's idea and shows a lack of respect for him. I seem to recall that we were shouting so loud, as we argued, that all Moscow could hear us."

From Tbilisi, they travelled via Batum to Zelyonyy Mys. … Our coach was the first one to get across the mountain pass. Nothing scary happened." Thus, Bulgakov had completed – in the opposite direction – the journey that his illness had prevented him from making back in February 1920.

"Our train to Moscow left at 11pm. We went for a walk around the city. M.A. didn't think it had changed much in the 6-7 years that had elapsed since he his time as a journeyman. […] To kill some time, we bought tickets for a show at the dwarves' theatre. They were performing the operetta *Bayadera*. The auditorium was packed to the rafters. I had never seen such a funny show: it was like watching children playing the roles of adults. We were particularly captivated by the protagonist, the lover. He was wearing a helmet made of cork and was waving his hands about, whilst trying to convey passion with his voice. The applause was thunderous. The audience showered him with lilac.

Later, at home in Moscow, Maka took off the dwarf actors with a comical, stony physiognomy and a funny walk on unbending legs, and he held his head in a funny way as well."

On 9th May, when Bulgakov was still in the Caucasus, a meeting of the Repertkom was held, at which the decision was taken to ban the production of *Flight*. This news awaited him on his return to Moscow.

The text of the decision taken at the meeting and submitted to the Art Theatre on 18th May stated that even the final scene of the play – the protagonists' decision to return to Russia – was needed by the author not to underline the historical righteousness of the fact that these lands had been conquered, but in order to lift up his protagonists to an even higher degree of intellectual superiority; and also that the author introduced a whole group of military leaders of the white movement into the play, who were extremely imposing and noble in their actions and convictions. The play became caught in a dead-end.

On 18th May, Bulgakov submits a statement to the OGPU, in which he says that he asked Gorky "to petition the OGPU for the return to me of my manuscripts, containing a reflection of my mood in recent years (1921-1926) that is extremely valuable to me"; "Alexei Maksimovich informed me that his petition had been successful and that I would receive the manuscripts. But the matter of the return of the diaries dragged on, for some reason"; Bulgakov asked him to "get my application going and return my diaries to me." Gorky, meanwhile, was still in Sorrento, and Bulgakov appealed to him, apparently via Y.P. Peshkova, relying on the letters of recommendation that Gorky had enclosed in letters to various writers. On 28th May, Gorky arrived in Moscow, and this must have given Bulgakov increased hope of securing his help, in the diverse forms it could take. The possibility that Gorky might actually get involved in his literary affairs had now arisen. Y.I. Zamyatin immediately came over from Leningrad to arrange for a production of his play *Atilla*, and on 8th June he wrote to his wife: "Yesterday I had lunch at Bulgakov's (he had come back early from the Caucasus due to the banning of his play)." It is fair to suppose that when Zamyatin sees Bulgakov over the next few days, their conversations touched on both men's literary affairs and, perhaps, it was these conversations that prompted Bulgakov to appeal to Gorky.

Gorky spent the whole of June in Moscow, trying to make sense of the changes that had taken place in the last 6 years; on 25th June, his son wrote to his wife: "Yesterday was a remarkable day. Duka [that was what Gorky was called within the family – M.C.] – and Kryuchkov [Gorky's secretary – M.C.] walked around Moscow in their costumes and with their faces painted. Duka had a beard, and Kryuchkov had a moustache and a little beard. They went to several tea-houses and pubs, spoke to various members of the public and had lunch at the station." Moscow, as it was seen through Gorky's eyes on those few days, can be seen in his sketch *Letters to Friends* (*Pis'ma Druziam*), published on 3rd July in *Izvestiya*.

On 9th June, *Vechernyaya Moskva* quoted the chairman of the newly organised Artistic and political council at Glavrepertkom, F.F. Raskolnikov: "Permission is granted for *Zoya's Apartment* to be struck off the repertoire." And on 30th June, *Izvestiya* reported that the Board of the People's Commissariat of Education had approved the decision of the Glavrepertkom to remove from the repertoire of the Art Theatre the play by Bulgakov accepted for production, entitled *Flight*, whilst the play *The Days of the Turbins* was to remain in the repertoire until "the first new play" appeared.

Bulgakov now found himself in a very unnatural position, whereby he must have been awaiting with horror the putting on of plays by his fellow dramatists. On 12th June, V. Katayev wrote an inscription in a copy of *Squaring the Circle* (*Kvadratura Kruga*): "In memory of our theatrical adventures, to Mishuk from Valyun".

M.A. Chimishkian recounts: "That summer, after meeting Bulgakov, I went to Leningrad and wrote to him about this: I gave my uncle's address. When I arrived, my uncle said to me: 'A young man just came looking for you, with an interesting lady.' It was the Bulgakovs. We met up, they introduced me to the Zamyatins. I remember that we were all together at the People's House for the operetta *Rosemary*; in the theatre's summer building, the fleas started biting us… I remember that we set off to have a ride on a rollercoaster, it was tremendous fun."

Back in July, Bulgakov had filled in a form at the Drama Union in the name of Y.P. Peshkova, in an attempt to procure his manuscripts from the GPU – the ones taken in May 1926. "Mikhail Anasievich! It is not 'conscionable' at all to disturb me,' Yekaterina Pavlovna wrote on 14th August; she was always willing to provide active assistance to the many who needed her. "I haven't forgotten about your manuscripts, and twice a week I pester those it may concern with questions about them. But the individual who gave the order is not in Moscow. Apparently this is why the matter has dragged on so long. As soon as I receive them, I shall notify you. I squeeze your hand. *Yek. Peshkova*."

In mid-August, Bulgakov left for Odessa: the Kiev state Russian theatre in Odessa had expressed its intention, on 9th July, of staging *Flight* – in spite of the Repertkom's ban. He writes to his room on 19th August, after taking a room at the Imperial hotel. On 22nd August, the *Evening news* in Odessa reports that Bulgakov read *Flight* to the board of the artistic council of Russian Drama; "After the recitation, an exchange of views took place. The impression made by *Flight* was a powerful one, a vivid one. The overall assessment is that the play is not only strong in a literary and scenic sense, but that it is also acceptable from an ideological perspective. It has been decided that *Flight* will be included in Russian Drama's repertoire for the upcoming season." On 24th August, Bulgakov enters into an agreement with the Kiev Russian Theatre in Odessa on the staging of *Flight* and leaves for Moscow.

M.A. Chimishkian told me (in 1969 and 1982) that she travelled from Leningrad to Moscow on 8th September, and was met at the station by Mayakovsky, who knew her well from his time in Tbilisi (she had been on good terms with Kira Andronikova, who later married Pilnyak, and her sister Nato Vachnadze; all of them knew Mayakovsky), and the Bulgakovs. "Bulgakov and Mayakovsky had moved to one aside, and were talking quietly about something, and Mayakovsky took my ticket from me (I had a free railway ticket) – he said that we would resolve the matter later, when I arrived in Tbilisi! – and wrote down Bulgakov's telephone number, and Bulgakov picked up my suitcase and took me to the car – it was already waiting [this was how the parties in high positions divided up their fields of influence, it would seem – M.C.]. Lyubov Yevgenievna said to me, while we were in the car:

'You are invited to a name-day today! People knew you were arriving today.'

And at Natalya Ushakova's name-day, I met all of their friends."

During those few days, Bulgakov was once again revived by fresh hopes. On 28th August, P.A. Markov informed Stanislavsky, who was in Kislovodsk: "Gorky told me, through Nikolai Teleshov, that *Flight* has been given the go-ahead – the news has not yet been confirmed, but it gives me reason to hope that *Flight* will be included in the repertoire.

On 11th September, *The Days of the Turbins* was staged at the Art Theatre for the 200th time. Bulgakov receives a letter from N. Khmelev, P. Markov, I. Sudakov and others containing warm words about the play, "which brought the theatre so much joy, anxiety and alarm." On 15th September, a letter arrives from Zamyatin, from Leningrad – "Happy *The Crimson Island* Day to you! My dear old thing, allow me to remind you of your promise to give us *Premiere* for the Drama Union's almanac."

On 27th September, Bulgakov wrote back: "On top of the love I feel for you, following the congratulations you sent, there has now been added a sense of horror (reverential horror, that is). You gave me your congratulations fully two weeks before *The Crimson Island* was granted permission.

You must, therefore, be a prophet.

As regards this permission, I don't know what to say.

Flight was written. It was shown. And *The Crimson Island* was given the go-ahead…

It is a mystery.

How? What? Why? To what end?

The impenetrable fog clouds one's brain.

I hope that you will not deprive me of your prayers?"

There was indeed good reason for pondering other things, for trying to seek out mystical explanations: at this very time, permission was suddenly granted (it was published in *Izvestiya* on 26th September) for the production of *The Crimson Island* that had been submitted to the Reperktom in early March, 1927, i.e. one-and-a-half years ago! (And on 6th October, the Kamerny Theatre signed a new contract with Bulgakov). As far as *Flight* was concerned, there were still rumours flying around, and it was not for nothing that Nemirovich-Danchenko, in a cable to Stanislavsky in Badenweiler, opts for the unusual *present* tense form of the participle: "Whilst continuing with *The Siege* [*Blokada*, a play by Vs. Ivanov – M.C.], we wish to set to work immediately on rehearsals for *The Fruits of Enlightenment* (*Plody Prosveshcheniya*) and the *allowed* [my italics – M.C.] *Flight*.

Let us return for a short while to Bulgakov's letter to Zamyatin. By that time, the two of them had enjoyed close, amicable relations for some years; it was the kind of literary friendship that Bulgakov had felt the absence of in Moscow, where most of those close to him were mainly involved in the academic world and the world of actors. In his letter, Bulgakov wrote about the fate of the article that Zamyatin had been waiting impatiently for: "In the last two weeks, I have added another 13 pages to the seven pages of *Premiere* that were lying motionless in the right-hand drawer. And yesterday I burnt all 20 pages, after first correcting the mistakes in them, in the stove beside which you have sat many a time at my place. And it is a good thing I came to my senses on time. Before the real, living people around me, there can be no talk of submitting such an opus to be printed.

It is a good thing I didn't send it.

Forgive me for not keeping my promise, I am sure that they would never have printed it anyway, not under any circumstances.

There will be no *Premiere*.

My exercises in the field of refined verbosity, it appears, are over." And he ended this entire passage with the gloomy conclusion: "A man has been destroyed." It is easy to reconstruct the mood that had taken hold of him on those days: *Flight* had still not received permission, *The Days of the Turbins* was doomed (it was due to be replaced by Vs. Ivanov's play), and Bulgakov can scarcely have had any faith in the idea that the future production of *The Crimson Island* would last very long, given the attitude that Repertkom now had about his plays (let us not forget, moreover, that Repertkom was the main target of his play).

The letter also contains some words that require an explanation: "The little old man stayed with us. We reminisced about the trip to the coast.

Ah, Leningrad, you wondrous city!"

An entry in L.Y. Belozerskaya's diary helps us to decode these lines: "Marika Chimishkian came to see us, from Tbilisi. I wasn't at home. Marusya ran a bath for her. Meanwhile Pavel Markov came to call on us, at Pirogovskaya; M.A. said to him: 'We have a guest visiting us, a little old man, he's good at telling jokes! He's having a bath just now; he'll finish up and come and join us soon…

One can only imagine Pavel Alexandrovich's surprise when, instead of an old man, Marika walked into the dining room! I have already mentioned that she was an extremely pretty girl. Markov started laughing. […] Maka was content. He was always happy when his jokes came off – and they almost always did."

It is natural to suppose that the article was dedicated to the relationship between contemporary critics and the theatre and the playwright. The experience of the two premieres had given Bulgakov a vast amount of material for analysis and conclusions, and it was that that gave the article the sharpness which, in the eyes of the author himself, made it unsuitable for publication.

On 30th September, Gorky watches *The Days of the Turbins* with his family at the Art Theatre. "Aleksei Maximovich was full of praise for the production, the acting, the author," P.A. Markov writes, later that day, to Stanislavsky.

In order to give a full picture of Bulgakov's changing moods in connection with *Flight* over the course of September, let us quote from the correspondence between his friends: on 1st September, N.N. Lyamin writes to P.S. Popov, from Moscow: "Mikh. Af. is in Moscow, in a good mood, for there is reliable data that suggests that *Flight* has been granted permission."

On 9th October, Gorky gives his support to *Flight* at a discussion held by the artistic council of the Art Theatre and members of Glavreperkom; the play also received ardent backing from the authoritative interpreter V. Polonsky ("The play we have read is one of the most talented plays of recent times. It is more powerful than *The Turbins* and far more powerful, of course, than *Zoya's Apartment*), and also the head of Glaviskusstvo, Al. Iv. Svidersky, who said, during the discussion of *Flight*: "If the play is artistic, then we, as Marxists, must consider it to be Soviet. The terms 'Soviet' and 'anti-Soviet' must be forgotten. One must not have a negative attitude towards an artistic play, even if it were to have some flaw, because it provokes discussion. [...] We have already reached a point where we can put on plays which provoke discussion and an analysis of events. Plays such as *Flight* encourage thinking, they encourage criticism, they engage the masses in an analysis and a discussion, such plays are better than archi-Soviet plays. This play must be allowed to go ahead, indeed it must be shown on the stage as soon as possible. Corrections to the play must be made by the director and the artistic council."

Y.S. Ganetsky, an activist in the Russian and international revolutionary movement, took part in the discussion; he said: "I found nothing with which I could find fault from an ideological perspective."

Later that day, Glavrepertkom decides to grant permission for *Flight* to be put on, and a report to this effect is published in *Pravda* on 11th October.

On 10th October, rehearsals commence at the Art Theatre, and on the 12th, the Leningrad Bolshoi Dramatic Theatre signs an agreement for the staging of *Flight*.

The middle of October, 1928, is the apex of the ephemeral success in Bulgakov's theatrical destiny. The theatres are asking for *The Crimson Island* and *Flight*; Bulgakov himself is in Tbilisi and is smoothing over relations with the theatres in Leningrad, via cables, in connection with these plays. On 16th October, he receives cables congratulating him on the success of *Flight*. Over the next few days, however, fresh complications arise, and on 24th October, *Pravda* reports that *Flight* has been banned by Glavrepertkom because it contains an apologia for the white movement. The speeches made by L. Averbakh and V. Kirshon at the meeting of Glavrepertkom – "Why we are against M. Bulgakov's *Flight*" – are soon published (*Na Literaturnom Postu* [*In the Literary Post*], No. 20-21), and they showed that the determination of the enemies of Bulgakov's play is unbreakable. On 5th November, material appears in *Rabochaya Moskva* (*Working Moscow*) related to *Flight*, under the heading: "We shall strike out against the *Bulgakovshchina*! The spineless policy of the Glaviskusstvo. We shall disarm the class enemy at the theatre, the cinema and in literature" (the "policy of the Glaviskusstvo" is the position adopted by A. Svidersky, who supported Bulgakov). On 25th November, *Komsomolskaya Pravda* publishes a speech by F. Raskolnikov, calling for "the campaign against *Flight* to be rolled out more broadly!" the Art Theatre does not call a halt to rehearsals, meanwhile, hoping that there will be a change for the better.

On 9th December, a private viewing of *The Crimson Island* took place, and the premiere was held on the 11th. After this, the artistic council of the Kamerny Theatre, considering the decision to grant permission to have been a mistake on the part of Glavrepertkom, adopts a directive, a draft version of which read as follows: "The play *The Crimson Island*, if it can indeed be described as belonging to the genre of satire, has its blade pointed at Soviet society as a whole, but not against the elements of time-serving and bureaucracy, as the directors of this play seem to imagine…"

The year 1928 ended with a guessing game that gave little cause for optimism.

3

We do not know when exactly in 1928 it was that Bulgakov turned back to writing fiction, which he had abandoned several years beforehand.

All we can really say with any certainty is that it was in this year that work on the novel which was later to become *The Master and Margarita* commenced. Bulgakov himself put the year 1928 as the date when the novel was started on the title page of later drafts of the manuscript.

... Eight years later, in *A Theatrical Novel*, the doubts and soul-searching of a writer who has finished his first novel are described as follows: "Well come on then, sit down and write a second novel, since you've made up your mind to do so... but there was the very crux of the problem, the fact that I well and truly did not know what this second novel ought to be about? What was I to tell humanity...? First of all, I set off for the bookshops and bought some works by my contemporaries. I wanted to find out what they were writing about, how they wrote, what was the magic secret of this trade. When buying books, I spared no expense, buying all the very best that there was on the market." As he reads the works of the best authors (one can easily identify the prototypes behind them: A. Tolstoy, L. Leonov, B. Pilnyak and others; they are all named in a list of prototypes for *A Theatrical Novel* compiled after Bulgakov's death at the behest of his family) and strives in good faith to get the hang of literary modernity, to find something he can relate to in its material and forms, the protagonist becomes aware of the horrifying truth that he "gleaned nothing from the books by the very best writers, discovered no paths, so to speak, saw no guiding lights ahead, and I found it all repellent." It appears that Bulgakov felt something akin to this when *The White Guard* was published, and these difficulties served, among other things, as an incentive for his switch towards the theatre in later years. The "paths" that opened up in the prose of his contemporaries proved to be unenticing to him, and he could not yet see anything with which he felt a kinship.

What was it that was preventing this writer, with his extremely active imagination, from coming up with the plot for a new novel? In one of his stories from the first half of the 1920s, he writes: "I swear to you all, there's something that always happens to me – each time I sit down to write about Moscow, the damn image of Vasily Ivanovich stands before me, in the corner. [...] I stand with my head leaning against the stone wall, and Vasily Ivanovich is above me, like the lid of a coffin." "Vasily Ivanovich" is the trope of the resident of "apartment No. 50", the prototypes for whom were the workers from the printing press, the drunkards and debauched revellers, with whom Bulgakov somehow managed to live as a neighbour in his first years in Moscow.

For Bulgakov, "writing about Moscow" in these years meant writing about modernity, about today. The existence of the figure of "Vasily Ivanovich" (which is also "a wall", "the lid of a coffin", the hostile force of people and circumstances) cuts off, for the author, the possibility of writing about modern life, without taking this figure into account, without demonstrating, on the one hand, its oppressive force, and on the other – without seeking some means of coping with it in the same place, within the space of an artistic text.

In Bulgakov's tale *The Heart of a Dog*, which was written after *The White Guard*, essentially "instead" of a second novel, the protagonist – an eccentric doctor – defeated those who performed the role of "Vasily Ivanovich" in the story, with fantastic ease, in one fell swoop, as though in a lucid dream. All three stories showed in painstaking detail that it was impossible for the author to approach the subject of modernity without making use of the grotesque. The might of the protagonist of the last of the stories was depicted as a condition that was absolutely essential for Bulgakov's artistic vision of modernity. Thus, by the particularities of Bulgakov's artistic thinking, the groundwork had been prepared for a novel in which the characters inhabiting present-day Moscow would be confronted with an individual of whose might they would soon have reason to be convinced.

An exercise book has survived that contains excerpts from the first draft of the novel; it contains some pages headed "Material", which show that right from the start of the development of the plot, there were two central figures, who are compared and contrasted in obvious fashion: they are given their own special sheets in the pages of "Material", headed "About God" and "About the Devil". In this sense, the novel he had in mind really was markedly different from the fiction of the mid-1920s, in whose surroundings its plot took shape.

The atheist propaganda of Moscow in the early 1920s, which took on such expressive forms as the "Komsomol Christmas" of 1923 or the "New Testament without the imperfection of the evangelist Demyan", and at the same time, the activation of the "living" church, his attitude towards which, as one can see in his sketch from 1923, *Kiev-city*, was extremely negative – all of this compelled Bulgakov to address once again something that, in his youth, after a certain critical juncture, had ceased to be an issue.

Something that had been demoted, back then, to the field of that which was decided, which was no longer relevant (neither to him nor to his wife, who was from the same generation as him), once again became, in those first years in Moscow, relevant – i.e. a matter up for discussion.

Even earlier than that, though, the tragic experience of 1917–1920, which he had lived through in full, had led him to seek an answer to the fundamental questions of existence.

Aleksei Turbin's dream in *The White Guard* is the worldview of an altogether different person from the student in Kiev completing his first courses at the department of medicine, and it is a worldview which, in my opinion, is coherent.

As to whether this critical juncture found expression in the external side of his life, whether it was noticeable from the outside – that is another matter. The testimony provided by his first wife, which is not subordinated to any predetermined trend, and is at times heterogeneous, calls for particular attention here. I believe it is necessary, in this context, to quote in full her answer to my question about whether or not Bulgakov wore a cross on his body: "No, he never wore one, I know that for a fact. And I didn't wear one either. My cross was probably at my mother's house. As for his, I've no idea where it was. He never took it with him anywhere." As far as the area of thought for one of the subjects of the new novel was concerned, it was, first of all, to a considerable extent closed off from his first wife, and secondly, the new direction taken by his thoughts may have appeared under the influence of his impressions from later years and taken shape after he split from Tatiana Nikolayevna.

Let us quote a brief episode that Tatiana Nikolayevna recalled, relating to the time when Bulgakov was working on his first novel: "He was writing *The White Guard* in Moscow…One day, he read part of it to me, about that… prayer uttered by Yelena, after which Nikolka or someone [she was layering onto this memory her memories of the play, in which Nikolka gets wounded – M.C.] recovers… And I said to him: 'What did you write that for?' He got very angry, and said: 'You're just a fool, you don't understand anything!'"

Why did you ask him that question?

"Well, I thought to myself: 'After all, these people [she meant, of course, the Bulgakov family – the sisters and brothers and their friends, whom she recognised in the protagonists of the novel – M.C.] weren't so dim as to believe that he would get better because of that…'"

Let us also note that for Tatiana Nikolayevna, who had already lived with Bulgakov for eleven years, it is clearly something new for the author to be writing about this episode in a novel, and that she does not, apparently, believe that the author shares his heroine's feelings.

One can imagine that he found this distrust particularly irksome. He had changed, and his wife could remember him as he used to be. She knew a great deal about his former years, and this knowledge was perhaps oppressing him already.

As for the appearance of the devil in the very first scene of a novel, this would have been far less surprising for the literature of 1928 than for the period ten years later – when he was working on the final draft. This scene grew out of his ongoing fiction writing and entered into a polemic with it. "On 26th March 1913, I was sitting, as always, on the Boulevard Montparnasse…" – thus began Ehrenburg's novel *The Extraordinary Adventures of Julio Jurenito and His Pupils* (*Neobychaynyye Pokhozhdeniya Khulio Khurenito i Yego Uchenikov*), which quickly became famous after it was published in 1922. On the next page, we read: "The door to the café opened and a rather ordinary-looking man walked in, unhurriedly, dressed in a bowler hat and a grey waterproof coat." The protagonist immediately realises that the man standing before him is Satan, and he offers him his body and his soul. Thereafter, a conversation begins which is sort of inversely reflected in Bulgakov's novel: "I know who you think I am. *But he doesn't exist.*" And the protagonist manages to get the following answer out of Satan: "All right, let's suppose he doesn't exist, but is there something that exists…?" "No"; "*But there must be something that's keeping all this together? Someone who's controlling this Spaniard? Is there any meaning in him?*" These fruitless invocations uttered by Ehrenburg's protagonist and narrator make one think of what seems to be a *counter*-question asked by the "foreigner" in the first chapter of Bulgakov's novel: "Who is in charge of all this?" (from the draft written in 1928) and the dispute that follows it. I am of the opinion that the first scene of Bulgakov's novel contains a hidden or direct polemic with the position adopted by the protagonist and narrator of Ehrenburg's novel, which is deliberately brought closer to the position of the author (needless to say, both scenes reference Fyodor Karamazov's conversation with his sons about God and the devil).

The sense one gets of a literary polemic taking place is also strengthened by the fact that an excerpt from Ehrenburg's novel was printed in the same issue of *Rupor* as *The Séance* – No. 4. *The Séance* was one of the very first stories Bulgakov wrote in Moscow; this issue of the journal also contained a portrait of the author, perhaps the first portrait of Bulgakov to appear in print. It is quite conceivable that the writer studied this issue of the journal from cover to cover. Thereafter, Ehrenburg soon attracted Bulgakov's not overly friendly attention: in 1927, just before Bulgakov began working on a new plot for a novel, two new editions of Ehrenburg's book were released.

1927 also saw the publication, in an "almanac of adventures" called *A War Fought in Gold* (*Voyna Zolotom*), of a story by Alexander Grin (whom Bulgakov had met in Koktebel) called *Fandango*. This fable centres around the arrival in Petrograd, in the cold and frosty winter of 1921, beside the House of academics, of a group of exotically dressed foreigners. "Right next to the gates, among the carriages and automobiles, there appeared before my eyes a group to which I would have paid more attention had it been a little warmer. The central figure in this group was *a tall man wearing a black beret with a white ostrich feather in it, with a gold chain around his neck over a black velvet overcoat, padded with ermine*. He had a pointy face, a ginger moustache that diverged in an ironic arrow, a golden beard that looked like a narrow screw, and smooth, powerful gestures…" Three men "in coats thrown over their shoulders across the lower lip," form his entourage and call him "Senor Professor". These "mysterious foreigners", as the narrator refers to them, turn out to be Spaniards: they are a delegation that has brought gifts to the House of academics.

This eye-catching spectacle – some exotic foreigners in the centre of a city that is going about its mundane life – used by Grin to set up the story, could not have failed, it seems to me, to have caught Bulgakov's attention.

One finds similarities between many details from the storyline about Woland and the story *Fandango*: for example, the description of the group assembling at the House of academics, where the visitors show an audience of academics the gifts that they have brought, is strongly reminiscent of Woland's séance at the Variety, which Moscow audiences found so striking in later editions of the novel: "The audience was an ordinary, *ration-receiving* audience: doctors, engineers, lawyers, professors, journalists and a large number of women. As I later learned, they had gathered here in drips and drabs, drawn by the eccentric delegates." The head of the delegation "sat up straight, leaning back slightly on the hard back of the chair, and cast his gaze around those assembled. His right hand lay in front of him on the table, on top of some pieces of paper, and with his left hand he toyed with the gold chain around his neck… His dark-green eyes, with their sharp and steely pupils, moved towards me" and so on. (*Fandango*). Bulgakov, judging by his friends' memoirs, did not like Grin's prose, but that did not preclude the possibility that one writer influenced the other.

The figure of the "foreigner" as the protagonist emerged in the prose written by the very same literary circle in Moscow that Bulgakov joined in 1922-1923, the very years when a new literature was taking shape. A hero appears in whom the traits of restraint, imperturbability, an elegant dress sense, are underlined; a hero who is "clean-shaven, well-mannered and always looking fresh" (A. Sobol, *Love on the Arbat* [*Lyubov' na Arbate*]). He is a foreigner, or a quasi-foreigner (an émigré who has been sent on an espionage assignment, perhaps, dressed to look like a foreigner). Devilish traits may also be hinted at in the description of him.

Let us examine a couple of scenes from two stories from the period. "The next day, there was no wind. All day long, people's breath remained close to their mouths, covering their faces with heat. As he strolled through the city park beside the house itself, Fomin sat down on a bench, because the overwhelming day-time circles, blinding him and floating before his eyes, and the sultry din of the little hammers at his temples, had made him feel dizzy. And when James Best floated up before him on the path, which gleamed brightly with every grain of sand, he seemed to Fomin to be only a fantastical figure in the baking hot, blinding circle. [...] As he passed by Fomin, he doffed his cap politely:

'Good day.'

In response, the startled Fomin began to wobble and fidget on the bench. And he started thinking about Best. Who was he, where had he come from and what was he doing here" [O. Savich. *The Foreigner* from issue No. 17, 1922; my italics – M.C.]. And another scene.

In A. Sobol's 1923 story *Fragments* (*Oblomki*), a random group of "men of the past" is eking out an existence in the Crimea – a duchess, a poet and others. They exclaim: "I shall leave this place – even if it's with a demon, even if it's with the devil"; "The devil! The demons! They've all run off too. They've forgotten we even exist. If we could just get our hands on one of them... the devil with it!

And, peeking through his fingers as he holds them over his eyes, the poet sees a cloven hoof, some mocking lips above a thin, narrow beard, and a thin hand with a carbuncle on its dark little finger." "And in the morning, a new resident appears in Patatuev's garden, all of a sudden, as if he fell down from the mountains; he didn't come in a horse and carriage, but it doesn't look as though he came on foot either: there isn't a single spot of dust on him, there is not a stain on his thin, polished shoes, the fold on his trousers makes them look as if they have just been ironed, there are no wrinkles on his gloves and his tight, white shirt-front is immaculate." The circumstances surrounding the sudden appearance of this new protagonist, just as in O. Savich's tale, seem to prefigure the arrival of the "foreigner" in the first scene of Bulgakov's novel, the plot of which came into being deep within the bowels of the literary process taking place in the early 1920s. "He is swarthy, his eyes are green, dry, with no sparkle, but they suddenly light up from time to time, as though some multi-coloured lights have come on behind his pupils, and the whites of his eyes are filled with dots of light – and at such times, his entire physiognomy changes: his lips rise up at the corners of his mouth, his chin becomes narrower and bends at the end into the shape of a hook, and his eyebrows stand on end…" this portrait could almost be a preliminary sketch for the portrait of the "foreigner" in Bulgakov's book. Its subject is Viktor Yuryevich Trech, who says of himself: "I know everything, and I can do anything" and, objecting to the question "You're… damn it, you're the Devil. Who are you?" he says: "The Russian devil is small and unsuccessful, whereas I am broad-shouldered and my luck is always in." He takes the woman with him to Konstantinople, and the corpse of the man is found the next day beside the sea.

The idea that "foreign" is a synonym for "devilish" is one that is deep-seated in Russian history, but which was given new life, powerfully and dramatically, right at the start of the 1920s. The foreigner who appears at Patriarch's Ponds in Bulgakov's novel in 1928 certainly doesn't do so out of a clear blue sky, as one might suppose; rather, he is the latest in a long line of cosmopolitan foreigners in literature – characters with elements of devilry about them (Trech, as we find out in the middle of the story – the reader finds this out, but the protagonists do not – "can wiggle his thick, grey ears beneath his smoothly combed locks of hair"; his name, written backwards, spells *Chyort* ('devil').

Lastly, let us cite Alexander Chayanov's book *Venediktov, or Memorable Events from my Life* (*Venediktov, ili Dostopamyatnyye Sobytiya Zhizni Moyey*, M., 1921), which N.A. Ushakova gave to Bulgakov as a gift (she had done the illustrations) in the mid-1920s. Bulgakov loved this book. For starters, the fact that the narrator, Bulgakov, shared his name, must have pleased him; he was very sensitive to what Pushkin described as "strange coincidences" (one recalls Venediktov's exclamation at the end of one of the chapters: "Your soul is in it, Bulgakov!"). The hero of Chayanov's tale senses "the indisputable, terrible and significant presence of someone" in the city, and, eventually, whilst he is watching an opera, he scans the rows of seats and his gaze comes to rest on one particular man. "There was no mistaking him. It was him! [...] There were no tongues of flame around him, no smell of dampness, everything about him was mundane and ordinary, but that diabolical mundaneness was saturated with something significant and commanding." The atmosphere of devilry and mysticism which filled the streets of Moscow, in which the action unfolds, the supernatural dependency of some people on the will of others, the image of disgusting debauchery, the theatre where important events take place – all of this influenced, I think, the formation of the plot for Bulgakov's novel.

In 1928, the plot of the novel began in the middle of June, "at the time when wicker baskets are on sale, filled to the brim with soft, mouldy strawberries, and clouds of flies buzz above them..." "I swear," the narrator said, "that horror overtakes me the moment I reach out for my pen, in order to describe these monstrous goings-on. All that concerns me is that, not being a writer, I shall not be able to convey these events in any cohesive way...".

"At the hour of sunset, there appeared on the last bench at Patriarch's Ponds" (just as in the final version of the novel) two men – Vladimir Mironovich Berlioz and Antosha (later changed to Ivanushka) Bezrodny; a description of their conversation ensued. Berlioz was explaining to Ivanushka what sort of caption in verse he ought to compose for a sketch that had already been drawn for the journal *Bogoborets* (*The Theomachist*, "of which Vladimir Mironovich was the editor" – a caricature of Christ and a capitalist. Whilst listening to him, Ivanushka draws in the sand a "hopeless, mournful face of Christ in the sand, with a stick... Beside him, the capitalist's mug appeared, looking like that of a bandit..." "Is that how it's drawn?' Ivanushka asked. 'Yes, like that,' said Berlioz." "At that very moment a citizen emerged from Yermolayevsky Side-Street..." After an extremely detailed description of this "citizen", containing many clarifications and comparisons of alternative descriptions of his appearance, "the citizen of the kind identified" interferes in Berlioz and Ivanushka's conversation, asking one of the most famous questions in the novel, among its readers: "If I heard you correctly, you do not choose to believe in God?" asked the German, and as he did so, he opened his eyes very wide; there was both curiosity and friendliness in them. 'We do not,' replied Ivanushka." The stranger's gaze then falls on Ivanushka's drawing. 'Bah!' he exclaimed, 'Who do I see before me? But that's Jesus! And you've drawn him fairly well. But tell me, what's that on his eyes?' 'A pince-nez', Antosha-Ivanushka chimes in. After a couple more sentences, Ivanushka tries to wipe away the drawing, whereupon the "foreigner", looking frightened, stops him.

'What if you provoke his wrath? Or don't you believe he ever feels any wrath anyway?'

'That's not the point – whether he feels wrath or doesn't – the point is, he has never existed anyway!'

'What makes you say such things!' the stranger exclaimed.

[…] 'After all, it was he who stood at dusk on the roof of the temple. […]'

'He flapped his palms as though they were wings and shouted: the dusk is burning out! Swallows are circling somewhere far away! And as he stands there, he is so tempted to jump down, as he listens to those who whisper in his ear: …Jump from the roof-tops! There's no risk at all, because, just a couple of steps away, there are already some […] angels, standing there waiting to grab hold of the bold experimenter [i.e. this is a description of one of the three temptations of Christ by the devil, who invited him to jump down, so as to prove his ability to work miracles and thereby force people to believe in him – M.C.].

'Are you quite certain he didn't exist?' the odd stranger asked.

'Quite certain,' said Berlioz.

'Swear it on your honour,' his interlocutor asked.

Berlioz and Ivanushka shrugged their shoulders in response, looking bewildered.

'… I've got you there, haven't I, you naughty so-and-sos, you ought to be ashamed,' he laughed, 'in the depths of your souls you believe in him, but for reasons which I cannot comprehend, you are afraid to admit it.'

After that, in the second chapter (*Woland's Gospel*, then *The Gospel According to Woland*, then *A Gospel from the Devil*), Woland talked about the day of the crucifixion as if he had witnessed it with his own eyes, addressing the other men on the bench at certain points during the story: 'After all, nobody really wants to die on a cross, esteemed Vladlimir Mironovich – not even if it is all done in triumphant fashion, nobody really wants to." The entire story was contained within the second chapter, and in the third chapter, *The Engineer's Evidence*, "Vladimir Mironovich was the first to come to his senses, and he stole a furtive glance at the man as he was speaking." And Ivanushka promptly calls him to one side "for a few words" and whispers in his ear: "You know, Volodka, it would be good to find out what sort of character this chap is."

This, to be blunt, was a stupid proposal. Why, after chatting to someone about everything under the sun, why must one, after all this, ask one's interlocutor who he is?

Berlioz's eyes immediately took on an unpleasant look, however, and a dark thought flickered over his [...] face." "He's peddling all sorts of gibberish, perhaps he's from *The White Guard*? Why don't you ask him who he is?" Ivanushka continues, but, beating the two acquaintances to it, the stranger stretches out to them his visiting card, recommending him as a specialist "in white magic" and a juggler – "I have come to Moscow to perform at the Music Hall." Then, turning to Ivanushka, Veliar Veliarovich Woland (for this was the name that the stranger gave) says: "greatly esteemed Ivan Sidorovich, as I guessed from the conversation, you believe firmly in God"; "It is essential to be thorough… prove your lack of belief to me," Woland said in wheedling tones, "step on this portrait, this depiction of Christ."

"This is simply very strange," said Berlioz.

"I don't want to!" Ivanushka protested.

"You're afraid," Woland said bluntly.

"Not a bit of it."

"You're afraid."

Ivanushka, looking confused, glanced at Berlioz, expecting, as was always the case in all the difficult situations in his life, to be given some help.

"He does not believe in God," said Berlioz, "but it would be childishly absurd to prove one's unbelief in such a way!"

"Well, if that's the way it is," Woland uttered sternly, "allow me to inform you, comrade Bezrodny, that you are a lying swine. And you've no call, no call to gawp at me like that!"

Woland's tone had become impudent so suddenly that Ivanushka was taken aback. In theory, he ought to have given this fellow a thick ear at that point, but Russian men, as is generally accepted, are not only rather impudent, but also rather cowardly.

"No, no, it's no use gawping at me," Woland went on, "and there was no sense in me jabbering on like that either! An atheist to boot, would you believe it! A theomachist, too – he fights against God! A member of the intelligentsia – and that's how he behaves!"

Ivanushka could not tolerate this last insult.

"Me – a member of the intelligentsia?!" he wheezed, "me… an intellectual…" he yelped, with a look on his face that suggested Woland had called him a son of a bitch, at the very least…

Ivanushka moved towards the drawing decisively and raised a rapidly moving boot over it.

"Wait!" [...] the stranger cried out in a strangled voice. Ivanushka froze. "Stop him!" added the engineer, turning towards Vladimir Mironovich.

"I am against all of this," said Berlioz, "and I shall certainly not get involved in encouraging him or stopping him."

"Just think for a moment, [...] most idolized Vladimir Mironovich!"

"I'm sick and tired of your stupid jokes," Berlioz replied.

And at that moment, the boot whizzed through the air, a stamping of feet was heard, and Christ flew apart in the wind, in a cloud of dust. And then the clock struck six o'clock.

"Ah," Woland exclaimed, covering his eyes with his palm coquettishly, and then he added suavely: "well there you are, Vladimir Mironovich, everything is in order and the daughter of the night, Moira, has finished weaving her thread."

"Goodbye, doctor," said Vladimir Mironovich, "it is time I was leaving."

"All the very best to you, citizen Berlioz," Woland replied, bowing politely. "Pay homage over there!" he gave a vague wave of his hand. "Your respected mother lives in the White Church, if I'm not mistaken?"

"That's strange... that's rather odd," Vladimir Mironovich thought, "how does he know that... He isn't a spy after all, is he? Devil take it... What a fanciful conversation."

"Perhaps I could give her a telegram from you? I could run over to the post office on Sadovaya right now..." Woland suggested.

Vladimir Mironovich merely gave a wave of his hand and, turning towards Ivanushka as he walked, said to him:

"Well, that's all then, Ivan! Mind you don't arrive late for the meeting...!"

"OK," Ivanushka replied, "I'll run home first, as well."

Berlioz gave a wave of his hand and set off. There was a wind blowing, bringing with it clouds of dust. At Patriarchs' Ponds, the evening had already unfurled its sails sweetly, with their golden wings... and the crows were bathing in the blue haze above the lime trees. "Not even the Gods are able to rescue a person they hold dear, when his hour of death has come." With these lines from *The Iliad*, that make no sense to Ivanushka, Woland watched Berlioz go, and thereafter, the depiction of Berlioz's death followed. After a shout of: "A man's been run over!" there was the sound of "a policeman's nightingale-like whistle. But, in essence, there was no real point in whistling now: for Vladimir Mironovich was already a long way away from us. His head was lying there, just a couple of steps from the tram, with the tongue for some reason sticking out." When he started the second draft of the novel, Bulgakov puts the following snatch of dialogue into the first scene: Woland suggests that Berlioz has "an atheist boss, and it stands to reason that everyone does the same thing as their boss, so as not to go hungry." "These words hurt Berlioz. A disdainful smile flickered over his lips, and a haughty look appeared in his eyes. 'For one thing, I do not have any kind of boss whatosever,' he said with dignity and very reasonably: Vladimir Mironovich had reached a time of life where nobody could order him around, just as nobody could put pressure on his conscience – he had no superiors above him whatsoever."

It is fair to suppose that the figure of an editor with such powers appeared as a character in the novel at precisely the time when Bulgakov was working on the article describing the relations between a playwright and a critic. The author would have been thinking at the time about Vadlimir (!) Ivanovich Blyum, the editor of the journals *Vestnik Teatra* (*Theatre Herald*) and *Novy Zritel'* (*New Theatre-goer*), and also L. Averbakh and Mikhail Koltsov, the editors of *Ogonyok* and *Chudak (The Eccentric)*, and A. Lunacharsky, with whom Bulgakov's theatrical destiny had already crossed paths several times, and who, in his eyes, was unquestionably in a position whereby "no-one could order him around".

The "disdainful smile" on Berlioz's lips and the haughtiness in his eyes were characteristic of a whole class of people that had certainly taken shape by that time. Bulgakov's observant gaze picked up all signs of people's sense of their own social class – a feeling that he certainly felt scorn for. This was that same sense of his own special status that had prompted F.F. Raskolnikov, back in 1923, so write the following lines in a letter to his wife, Larisa Reisner: "There can be no talk of control over me. I know for certain that the party has boundless trust in me,"[14] and, in the autumn of 1929, caused him to start talking in such a patronizing tone to those who had come along to discuss his play, that it sent Bulgakov into a fit of rage – we shall come back to this later.

For now, let us suggest that the idea of a clash between an all-powerful editor and a "truly" all-powerful being, and about the portraying, in the novel, of an image of terrifying revenge, appeared at the very moment when the article was destroyed – as a form of compensation for the impossibility of having his said on this subject in a published article.

Let us return, though, to our speculation about the text of the first draft.

Shaken by what he has seen, Ivanushka makes an unsuccessful attempt to catch Woland, and then eventually appears at a restaurant which, in the

---

[14] For the sake of accuracy let us add that this letter from Afghanistan, dated 26th August 1923, goes on to say: "Meanwhile almost the letters from mother reach me with clear traces of having been crudely, ineptly opened and resealed" (Lenin State Library, f. 245).

draft written in 1928, bore "the wild name of Griboyedov's Hovel." The reconstruction of the chapter *The Episode at Griboyedov's Hovel* enabled us to see that this chapter was a key moment, a cornerstone of the novel's plot: it took shape straight away and changed little in all of the later versions.

"'Shush, comrades,' Ivanushka said in a mysterious whisper, 'we need some dark wax'.

The hush that descended on the restaurant after these words was such that you could have heard a pin drop. For a moment it was disturbed only by the cat-like steps of the pirate, in his bath slippers. Displaying a considerable lack of interest in the important message which Ivanushka intended to give him, he moved quickly, penetrating deeper into the restaurant;" "'He just appeared out of nowhere!' Ivanushka declared, and his eyes took on an utterly manic look." He tries to persuade someone to run and fetch "Aleksei Ivanich. Tell him from me that he is to send some riflemen on a motorcycle, to catch the engineer. Or else they've got no chance of catching him!'" "'Just make sure you warn him that they should attach little icons to their chests, they must wear icons, and if by any chance they haven't got enough icons, they should put little crosses on themselves… like so…' […]

The colour drained from his pale face altogether, and he lay down on the asphalt.

It was only then that the crowd decided the best course of action might be to throw themselves on Ivanushka… The combative Ivanushka tried to beat them off with his arms.

'You anti-semite!' someone shouted hysterically.

'What are you talking about,' someone else objected, 'can't you see what condition the man's in? He's no anti-semite! He's lost his marbles!'

'Call the psychiatric clinic right away!' people shouted from all sides."

That night, the duty nurse at the hospital to which Ivanushka is taken catches sight of a bulldog of vast proportions in the garden, and it later emerges that Ivanushka escaped from the hospital that night (apparently with the help of Woland, who visited him during the night). The bulldog is clearly intended to remind the reader of the bulldog from Goethe's *Faust*, in the guise of which Mephistopholes enters Faust's study; when Faust tries to chase him away, the dog starts to grow before his very eyes.

As the funeral procession moves from Griboyedov House (which was based on Herzen House on Tverskoi Boulevard, the home of the All-Russian Union of Writers and a host of professional literary organisations) towards the Novodevichy cemetery, appearing all of a sudden "in a filthy torn white shirt and covered in soot from head to toe," […]

"At a bend in the road, the carriage tilted to one side, and the deceased slipped out of the coffin. Ivanushka, forgetting that he was driving the carriage, looked on, with a wild-eyed stare, as Berlioz, with dead eyes and dressed in a black suit, jumped into the coffin rakishly, like a little boy, delighting in the effect his actions produced." On reading these pages, it is hard to escape the feeling that the author's pen was guided by a very specific wish: not having had the opportunity to do battle against any of those eloquent editors during his lifetime, he refuses to grant Berlioz, who embodies this type that was so hateful to him, a pleasant funeral, seeing this as a fitting way to punish him.

Eventually, the carriage goes careening off into the river, coffin and all (as one can surmise by piecing together the fragments of text), "and nothing remained of it – not even the bubbles – the spring rain took care of them." Thus, no trace is left of the eloquent editor; it was not for nothing that Woland warned him that he would end up in the water after his death ("Am I going to drown?" Berlioz asked. "No," Woland replied laconically). As for Ivanushka, he is taken back to the hospital.

In one of the chapters, Garasya Pedulayev (Stepa Likhodeyev in later drafts), after being literally thrown out of Moscow by some unknown force, flies above the roof of his own home on Bolshaya Sadovaya and sees an endless and extremely beautiful garden, and beyond it "a vast mountain, piled high into the sky, with a summit as flat as a table-top." Instead of the street in which he lives, which he keeps trying to catch sight of, he sees some sort of "avenue, along which a little tram was merrily dinging its bell. Then, turning back in the vague hope of seeing his home on Sadovaya there, Garasya realised that there was no way he could possibly do so: not only was his home no longer there, but the whole of the Sadovaya had disappeared." "Garasya started sobbing like a child and sat down on a bollard in the street; around him, he could hear the even noise of a garden. A dwarf in a black jacket and a dusty top-hat emerged from the garden.

His girlish, hairless face wrinkled up in surprise when he caught sight of the weeping man.

'What's up, citizen?' he asked Garasya, gawping at him.

The Director did not say anything in reply to the dwarf.

He merely asked, 'What garden is this?'

'It's the Track,' the dwarf replied in surprise.

'And who are you?'

'I'm Pulse,' the little fellow squeaked.

"And what's that mountain over there?" Garasya enquired.

'Table-top Mountain.'

'Which city am I in?'

An angry expression appeared on the native fellow's tiny face.

'What's your game, citizen, having a laugh, are you? I thought you were being serious!' And he walks away from Garasya, looking upset; at that point, Garasya calls out: 'Little man! Stop, have pity on me…! I… I've forgotten everything, I can't remember anything, tell me where I am, which city I'm in.'

'Vladikavkaz,' the dwarf replied.

At that, Garasya slipped off his bollard, bumped his head on the ground, and fell silent, his arms spread wide apart.

The little man tore the top-hat from his head, threw it as far away as he could and shouted, in a soft voice:

'Policeman! Policeman!'"

Thus, the impressions left by Bulgakov's summer trip to the Caucasus – and specifically his trip to the dwarf theatre in Vladikavkaz – were included in the novel, allowing us to date his work on chapter eight to the end of the summer of 1928, at the earliest.

In the first draft, Woland oversees the evening at the Variety alone, with no assistants, personally "twisting the head" of the master of ceremonies, Pyotr Alexeyevich Blagovest, and pulling it off his neck "like a cork from a bottle…"

There was a character in the novel who later disappeared from it altogether. The chapter *What is Erudition* began with a description of Fesya's childhood and the wonderful education he had received; he had demonstrated "extraordinary aptitudes for history"; whilst studying history and philology at Moscow University, Fesya sent one of the professors "into a state of ecstasy" by giving him his work *Categories of Causation and the Causal Link*.

After the revolution, Fesya gives lectures four times a week – at Khumat (an acronym for *Khudozhestvenniye masterskiye* [Arts studios]), in the barracks of some military division, and at the Academy of Fine Arts… Ten years went by in this fashion (i.e. the episode described in the novel was supposed to have taken place in 1927 or 1928), and Fesya was planning to go back to his research into the "causal link", when all of a sudden, in a "military newspaper, an article appeared…there is no need to say who wrote it, incidentally. It said that a certain Truver Reryukovich, a former landowner, used to deride the peasants on his estate outside Moscow, and when the revolution took his estate away from him, he fled to Khumat to escape the thunder of righteous wrath…" And at that point, for the first time, the quiet, softly-spoken Fesya "banged his fist on the table and said (and I... forgot to warn you that he spoke Russian very badly), mixing up his 'r's and his 'l's:

'That scoundrel probably wants me dead!' and added that not only had he never derided his peasants, but that he hadn't even seen them – not a single 'specimen'. And Fesya was speaking the truth. He really and truly had never seen a single peasant man in his vicinity. He had spent his winters in his study in Moscow, and in the summertime he had left the country, and he never saw his estate outside Moscow." On one occasion he nearly went there, but, after deciding first of all to get to know the Russian people through a solid source, he read Pushkin's *History of the Pugachev Rebellion* (*Istoriya Pugachevskogo Bunta*), after which he rejected the idea of making the trip altogether, demonstrating a firmness of resolve that was surprising in him. One day, however, after returning home, he proudly asserted that he had seen a real Russian peasant: "He was buying cabbages at Okhotny Ryad. He was wearing a fur hat with a flap. But he didn't come across as a beast, in my eyes."

A short time later, Fesya was flicking through an illustrated journal and came across the peasant he had seen, albeit without his fur hat. The caption beneath the little old man read: "Count Lev Nikolayevich Tolstoy."

Fesya was stunned.

"I swear to the Madonna," he said, "Russia is an extraordinary country! Its counts are the spitting image of its peasants!"

Thus it was that Fesya was not telling porkies."

The chapter ended here, half-way down the page; one can see what important material it contained in terms of understanding the original plot of the novel. The theme of the intelligentsia and the people in pre-Revolutionary Russia can definitely be seen here; as for the ratio between "seriousness" and grotesque with which it was to be put in the novel, that remained unknown. We can only speculate as to the role that had been prepared for Fesya in the plot of the novel; the author doubtless planned to use him, in his capacity as an expert on demonology, in the storyline about "devilry". A meeting between him and Woland was envisaged (by contrast with Berlioz, whose erudition was only superficial).

At this stage of the novel's plot development, neither the Master nor Margarita featured; this can be confidently asserted, in spite of the fact that the novel had only been written up to chapter 15 and that at least half of it still had to be written.

The novel was entitled *The Engineer's Hoof*. In that year, the word "engineer" would have sounded both significant and multivalent. It was associated with the word "spets" – i.e. a "bourgeois specialist", a phrase used to describe journeyman engineers, industrialists and other qualified experts who found work in people's commissariats and head offices. They agreed to collaborate with the Soviet government, without sharing its ideas, goals, methods of implementing them, etc; "Engineers" was also used to refer to foreign experts from various countries contracted to work at construction sites, industrial firms and so on. Thus, it is in keeping with the spirit of the times that the words "bourgeois" and "foreigner" crop up in Ivanushka and Berlioz's conversation alongside the word "engineer". Furthermore, in the summer of 1928, i.e. at the time when I would suggest that Bulgakov started writing the first few chapters of the novel, an investigation was taking place into the so-called "Shakhtinsk Affair", wherein a number of engineers were accused of sabotage and espionage; one cannot fully understand the atmosphere of the scene at Patriarch's Ponds without taking these circumstances into account, for it surely contained a nod to those events – and the same goes for Ivanushka's entreaties at the psychiatric clinic: "Listen…" he said to the doctor, "call him and say: an engineer has appeared, and he is killing people at Patriarch's."

In the figure of the Master, who would go on to play a central role in the chapters of the novel set in Moscow, one could see a direct link to Yeshua from the chapters set in the New Testament. With tremendous artistic daring and boldness of outlook, the author of the novel was giving the reader the opportunity for that kind of interpretation of his new hero, as well: as a modern incarnation, and yet one that was not recognised by his contemporaries, of the man who had been "recognised" with utter certainty in his own novel.

A few years were to pass before this transformation of the plot occurred, however.

CHAPTER FOUR

The Crisis Years (1929-1931)

1

Early in 1929, the ban on *Flight* became a *fait accompli*: a rehearsal took place at the Art Theatre on 25th January, and it soon became clear that it was to be the last.

In this theatre season, which was to become Bulgakov's last for a long time, his literary destiny began to intersect and interact with that of Mayakovsky: prior to this point, the two had been no more than well-mannered adversaries in games of billiards and well-mannered literary adversaries (for Mayakovsky's words about *The Days of the Turbins* at the discussion in 1926 sounded very polite when considered in the light of his usual literary polemics).

In those final days of 1928, when Bulgakov, looking hard at the year ahead, sees in it, with unmistakable clarity, the death of pretty much all his plays, Mayakovsky reads, at the Vs. Meyerhold theatre (on 28th December 1928) his new play, *The Bedbug* ([*Klop*], a satirical comedy – just like *The Crimson Island!*). On 30th December, he reads it at an extended meeting of the theatre's Artistic and political council; in a resolution adopted at the meeting, the play was "a significant phenomenon in Soviet drama from both an ideological and an artistic perspective" and the "inclusion of it in the theatre's repertoire" was welcomed.

Thus, Mayakovsky, in Bulgakov's eyes, entered into the field of dramaturgy, at the very moment when the theatrical stanchions beneath Bulgakov's feet were wobbling more than ever.

On 2nd February, Stalin writes a reply to a letter from the dramatist Bill-Belotserkovsky, in which he provides the following assessment of the play *Flight*: "*Flight* is a manifestation of an attempt to evoke pity, if not sympathy, in respect of some sections of the anti-Soviet émigré community; thus, an attempt to justify or half-justify *The White Guard* cause. *Flight*, in the form it is in now, is an anti-Soviet phenomenon."

Incidentally, I would have nothing against a production of *Flight* taking place, if Bulgakov were to add to his eight dreams another one or two dreams which depict the inner social springs of the civil war in the USSR, so that the audience member can understand that all these Seraphimas – 'honest' in their own special way – and all these freelance university lecturers found themselves kicked out of Russia not because of a caprice on the part of the Bolsheviks, but because they were sitting on the necks of the people (in spite of their "honesty"), that the Bolsheviks, when chasing away these "honest" supporters of exploitation, were putting into effect the will of the workers and peasants and therefore acted utterly correctly." The replies tell us much about the nature of the questions – thus, the answer to the third question, it seems, repeated it, either in part or in full: "Why are Bulgakov's plays performed so often? Because, one must assume, there are not enough of *our own* plays that are suitable for performance. When there are no fish biting, even *The Days of the Turbins* is a fish" (let us not forget that Stalin himself watched the play at least 15 times). An assessment of Bulgakov's other plays was provoked by the questions posed, too – "… One recalls *The Crimson Island* […] and the garbage like it, which for some reason was eagerly let through for the Kamerny Theatre, which truly is bourgeois." With that, *The Crimson Island* was effectively destroyed; the play *The Days of the Turbins* is characterised, among other things, as "a demonstration of the all-destroying power of bolshevism", and moreover the author of the play was "blameless" with regard to the play's success – this combination of assessments had to be puzzled over and deciphered. The fate of the play *Flight* was now directly dependent on whether its author agreed to alter it.

Word of the letter immediately got out, of course, among literary and theatrical circles. Out of devotion to the Art Theatre, Bulgakov refused to rewrite *Flight* or to add anything to it – indirect evidence of this is seen in the lack of any documentary traces whatsoever of attempts to rewrite it in his archive.

I would suggest that, besides purely creative reasons, there were other factors at play too: Bulgakov, due to his personality and stereotypical types of behaviour, could not force himself to react to the demands that were being made about his play, as expressed in a letter addressed not to him himself and not to the theatre's directors, but to a private individual who had no kinship with him whatsoever.

There is no doubt that the letter had a powerful effect first and foremost on the directors of the Art Theatre. *Flight* was now all over, *The Days of the Turbins* was dragging on for a few final weeks: the premiere of Vs. Ivanov's *The Siege*, which had taken place on 26th February, had provided a basis for them to be removed: here was a play that was 'ours'.

Rehearsals began for Mayakovsky's play, meanwhile, immediately after it was granted approval by the Theatre's Board (on 30th December), and on 13th February 1929 the premiere took place – such a short period between the first rehearsal and the premiere would have been unthinkable for a play by Bulgakov! Documentary evidence survives which suggests that Bulgakov was present at one of the first performances. *The Bedbug* was performed almost every day until the end of the season; in the autumn, the play was put on by a branch of GBDT in Leningrad (a place where Bulgakov had not managed, in the last two-and-a-bit seasons, to get a single one of his plays put on). In both productions, Bulgakov's name was uttered on stage in every performance, for the play's author had included it in a "dictionary of dead words" ("Bureaucracy, *bublik* bagels, bohemia, Bulgakov..."), which may have seemed particularly accurate that spring.

On 6th March 1929, *Vechernyaya Moskva* publishes a story entitled "Theatres to be liberated from Bulgakov's plays". *The Crimson Island* was to continue until the summer, but at the end of the season, it too would be taken off the programme – like the other two plays.

That winter, Bulgakov went to play his favourite card game – vint – at the home of the accountant of the Art Theatre, Vanda Fyodorovna, and her husband. They lived on Pushkin Square, not far from the Art Theatre. The bets placed were never more than a griven, but there was always much laughter and joking.

That spring, after returning on 2nd May from another journey abroad, Mayakovsky starts work on his second play – *The Bathhouse* (*Banya*).

By the summer, it has become clear that Bulgakov's position is utterly hopeless.

It is possible that in these months, he even makes an attempt to try out a genre that is utterly alien to him: that of the sketch on a topical subject. In those years, this was a form of making some easy income that was very popular among a certain literary circle. One of Bulgakov's acquaintances from that time, a man who was quite distant from him, however, told me on 8th September 1980: "I do not have many good things to say to you about

Bulgakov. He was haughty, arrogant. He had a poor opinion of Mayakovsky, and for me, Mayakovsky was everything.

On 28th August, Bulgakov sends a letter to his brother Nikolai (the brothers had resumed their correspondence a short while earlier; on 25th April of that year, Bulgakov wrote to him: "Our terrible and lengthy separation has changed nothing: I have not forgotten, and shall not forget, you and Vanya").

The letter was surprisingly frank, characterising the situation in plain, direct language: "I now wish to inform you, my brother: my position is not good.

All my plays have been banned from being shown in the USSR and not a single line of my prose is being printed. In 1929, my destruction as a writer took place. I made one last effort and submitted an application to the Government of the USSR, in which I asked them to let my wife and I go overseas for whatever period of time is possible

There is no hope in my heart. There was a bad omen: Lyubov Yevgenievna was not allowed to leave the country on her own, despite the fact that I had stayed behind. (This was a few months ago!)

There is a dark rumour already crawling around me, to the effect that I am doomed in every sense.

Should my application be rejected, one can safely assume that the game is over, the decking packed away, the candles blown out...

I shall have to sit around in Moscow and not do any writing, because people cannot look with indifference upon my writings, or even upon my name.

I wish to inform you without any pusillanimity, my brother, that my demise is merely a matter of time, unless, of course, some miracle occurs. But miracles seldom do occur.

I strongly urge you write to me and tell me whether my letter makes sense to you, but do not under any circumstances write me *any words of comfort or sympathy at all*, lest my wife might become agitated.

... What is not good is that this spring I felt tired, and indifference crept in. There is a limit, after all.

I am glad you have found a job and I believe you will make a career for yourself in academia. Write to Ivan that I remember him. Let him write to me, just a few lines at least. Your letters are a great comfort to me and I imagine that, after reading this letter, you will write to me often.

... Well then, I kiss you, Nikol,

your M. Bulgakov.

P.S. Please reply to this letter as a matter of the utmost urgency."

The application mentioned in the letter was addressed to several individuals: Stalin, Kalinin, Svidersky, Gorky. It was submitted via A. I. Svidersky. Bulgakov wrote: "This year marks 10 years since I began doing literary work in the USSR." He reminded the recipients that he had submitted "requests for the return of manuscripts to me" on a number of occasions, and that he had "received refusals or received no response to the applications at all" (this is how we know that by the summer of 1929, Y.P. Peshkova had not been able to get hold of the manuscript using the power of attorney he gave her).

"By the end of the tenth year, my strength has been broken; I am not capable of existing any longer, being poisoned, knowing that I cannot have my work published, or performed, any longer inside the USSR, and being in a state of nervous breakdown, I am appealing to you and I ask for you to petition the Government of the USSR to exile me from the USSR, along with my wife L.Y. Bulgakova, who is also signing up to this request."

On 3rd September, Bulgakov wrote to Gorky: "Greatly respected Aleksei Maximovich! I hav submitted a request to the Government of the USSR asking for me and my wife to be given permission to leave the USSR for whatever period of time is assigned to me.

I ask you, Aleksei Maximovich, to support my petition. I wanted to set out in detail, in a separate letter to you, everything that is happening to me, but my exhaustion and despair are immeasurable. I cannot write anything."

Reminding them that all of his plays had been banned, Bulgakov asked: "Why hold a writer in a country where his works cannot exist? I am asking for a humane resolution: let me go."

In conclusion, Bulgakov asked Gorky to let him know when he received the letter.

That same day, he sends a letter to his secretary of the Central Electoral Commission of the USSR, A.Y. Yenukidze: "In light of the fact that the absolute unacceptability of my works for Soviet society is obvious, in light of the fact that the complete ban on my works in the USSR condemns me to death, in light of the fact that the destruction of me as a writer has already led to a material catastrophe" (the author of the letter gave assurances that he could provide documentary evidence of the "impossibility of living, starting from next month" – he was referring, among other things, to the need to pay tax on income from his plays, that had been received during the last season, and, apparently, had already been largely spent), "given the immeasurable exhaustion, and the fruitlessness of all and any attempts, I am appealing to the supreme body of the Union – the Central executive committee of the USSR, and I request that you allow me and my wife Lyubov Belozerskaya to leave the country for whichever period the Government of the Union deems it necessary to assign to me.

Mikhail Afanasievich Bulgakov (the author of the plays *The Days of the Turbins, Flight* and others).

I am quoting this letter from a draft that was preserved in the writer's archive; it may be that certain phrases were softened by the author in the final text, but all the same, three documents from the late summer and early autumn of 1929 show signs of a condition that is close to temporary insanity – the condition of a man who is at the end of his tether and is prepared to take desperate measures.

One can get a sense of the state that Bulgakov was in by looking at the press from those days. On 15th September, in an article entitled 'Before the curtain is raised' in *Izvestiya*, the critic R. Pikel wrote with satisfaction: "This season, the audience will not see Bulgakov's plays. *Zoya's Apartment* has been closed down, *The Days of the Turbins* have ended, *The Crimson Island* has disappeared. We do not wish to say, by writing this, that the name of Bulgakov has been erased from the list of Soviet dramatists. His talent is as obvious as the fact that his output is socially reactionary. We are referring only to his past works for the stage. That kind of Bulgakov is of no use to Soviet theatre."

Whilst drawing a line under all of Bulgakov's "past" plays, the article did not shut the door on him altogether, leaving some small chink for the prospect of future work. In the first half of September, however, he can hardly have been in a fit state to perceive that chink.

On 28th September, Bulgakov writes to Gorky again: "Yevgeny Zamyatin informed me that you received my letter, but that you would prefer to have a copy of it." It turned out that Bulgakov did not have a copy, and he reproduced it content "approximately", and wrote near the end: "I would now like to add the following to this letter: all of my plays have been banned, not a single line of my work is being published anywhere, I have no work ready at all, not a kopeck in royalties is coming in from anywhere, not a single institution, not a single individual responds to my applications, in a word – everything I have written in the last 10 years of working in the USSR has been destroyed. All that remains to be done now is destroy the last thing that is left: me myself. I request that you make a humane decision: release me. Yours respectfully, M. Bulgakov."

His name was already being used in the plural at that time, and people were already expressing surprise that he was still a member of the All-Russian Union of Writers: "The Bulgakovs and the Zamyatins lived peacefully side by side in the union alongside genuine Soviet artists of the word," wrote *Zhizn' Iskusstva* in a piece headed *The Lessons of Pilnyak-dom* (*Uroki Pil'nyakovshchiny*); B. Pilnyak was being subjected to strong criticism at this time, after publishing his novel *The Red Tree* (*Krasnoye Derevo*) overseas, in No. 39 on 29th September.

On 2nd October, Bulgakov receives a letter of convocation: he is summoned to appear on the 3rd before the Politupravleniye (PUR) to give evidence – I would posit that this summons was related to the decision to return his manuscripts to him: according to Yelena Sergeyevna's account, they were returned to him in 1929; meanwhile, on the days when he sends out his applications, the manuscripts, as is clear from the text of these applications, have not yet been returned to him. No other reaction to the applications, made in such a despairing tone, was forthcoming. This circumstance is significant in terms of understanding the events which were to play out over the course of the next year.

On 3rd October, he is informed that the organising of a Residents' co-operative commonwealth is continuing for members of the Dramatic Union living in Moscow, and that a general meeting of the members of the Residential and construction cooperative "House of the Dramatist and Composer" will take place on 16th October. Each letter of summons of this kind that he received that autumn only served to make the uncertainty of the future even more self-evident to him. He had joined this particular cooperative eighteen months earlier, when he had indeed been a practising dramatist.

In the letter to Gorky dated 28th September, the line "I do not have any work ready" is crossed out – perhaps because he had remembered the novel that he had left unfinished, or the fact that he was now writing some work – albeit one that also remained unfinished that year.

Let us return once again to the winter of 1929. On 28th February, at Maslenitsa, the Bulgakovs met Yelena Sergeyevna Shilovskaya in Moscow, the wife of a bigwig in the military, Y.A. Shilovsky. She began spending time at their home and became friendly with Lyubov Yevgenievna. Soon Bulgakov began having a secret affair. In October 1968, Yelena Sergeyevna told me: "In the summer of 1929, I went away to take a course of treatment in Essentuki. Mikhail Afanasievich wrote me some wonderful letters while I was there, and sent me bunches of red roses; but I then had to destroy all those letters, I couldn't keep them. In one of the letters, he wrote: 'I have prepared a gift for you that is worthy of you…' When I returned to Moscow, he handed me this exercise book…"

This slender exercise book, which was filled with text almost to the end, remained intact among the writer's archived documents. There is a date at the top of the first page: "September 1929", and then: *To a Secret Friend*, written in large, elegant letters. Beneath this are several alternative subheadings, as is usually the case in Bulgakov's manuscripts: "The Dionysian masters. Dionysus's Altar. Scenes. "Tragedy waves a tawdry cloak."

These attempts to hit upon the right title for the chapters alone show that the work was to have something to do with the theatre. The exercise book began with the words: "My invaluable friend! And so, you insist that I should tell you, in the year of the catastrophe, how I became a playwright? [...] The author of the manuscript divided his life in Moscow into two periods: the second one was, apparently, the theatrical period: a historic time, a time of literary fame, which had once broken off but had recommenced.

"Now I shall jump on ahead: several years have passed, and, as you have already guessed, Rvatsky has been found abroad. And there, he got hold of my novel and play. As for how he managed to smuggle out of the country a novel that was as heavy as a tombstone, I have no idea.

I once met an extremely intelligent man. I told him everything. And he said, with a snigger:

'You know what, that Rudolph of yours was taken away by an unclean force, and so was Rvatsky.'

It dawned on me that this was true.

'And it is very simple. After all, you said yourself that Rudolph sold his soul to the devil?'

'Yes, he did.'

'Well, naturally, his time is up, so the devil appears and says, please...'

'Oh Heavens! Where is he now?'

Instead of replying, he pointed at the ground, and I was afraid."

So the author had intended to tell of how he had "become a playwright", but stopped after describing how this playwright wrote a novel and began to get it printed in a journal. The last chapter was called *The Novel is Published*. As the author's friends make their first objections – "What a sub-standard novel, Mishui, you…" – the story broke off. That last sentence is on the last line of the page. There is something strange about the fact that the text breaks off, mid-word – even though no pages have been ripped out of it, and there are still two clean sheets in it.

There is no sense in trying to guess why and at which particular moment his work was interrupted. This may have occurred in September or October.

This period: the end of September and the first half of October, gives us a basis for certain speculation regarding the emergence of some of the writer's other plots.

On 23rd September 1929, Mayakovsky reads excerpts from *The Bathhouse* at an assembly of the Artistic and Political Soviet of the Meyerhold Theatre, and Meyerhold, speaking during the discussion, says that Mayakovsky's play "is the most significant event in the history of Russian theatre," and that "if we recall Russian dramatists, then we must recall Pushkin, and Gogol, despite the fact that Mayakovsky's techniques are very different from Gogol's, and his approach is different", that "Mayakovsky is starting a new epoch, and we must welcome the extremely strong dramatist that we are obtaining in the shape of him."

The comparison with Pushkin and Gogol must have sounded shocking to Bulgakov. Equally powerful was another parallel that was drawn in the same speech: "The lightness with which this play is written was accessible, in the history of the theatre, to only one playwright: Molière. Yesterday, when I heard the play for the first time, I remembered Molière, and comrade Katayev – the author of *Squaring the Circle*, who came here today for the recitation, also looks back on Molière. I am expressing this idea not only on my own behalf, but also on behalf of comrade Olesha…"

V. Katayev, who was present at the recitation, remembered this comparison being made: "After the reading, the debates began; thanks to someone's sleight of hand, they all boiled down to the idea that thank God, a new Molière had now appeared among us." Katayev also recalled that P.A. Markov and other figures from the Art Theatre were at the reading, including P.A. Markov: "He had secretly been keen on Mayakovsky for a long time, desirous of making him write a play for the Art Theatre. Mayakovsky – on the stage of the Art Theatre! Now that would be something! […] Markov had recently used all his cunning to drag Mayakovsky along to a performance of Bulgakov's *The Days of the Turbins* at the Art Theatre. Mayakovsky had slipped out after the third act."

Bulgakov found out about all this, of course, and also found out about the presence of the Art Theatre people at the reading on 27th September and what they thought about it. L. Brik wrote about them in his diary and added the following comments in his memoirs: "The only thing that was written down about the discussions after the reading, was: 'Markov said that in order to put on Mayakovsky, he, Mayakovsky, needed a theatre of his own.' Regardless of whether or not *The Bathhouse* could have been put on at the Art Theatre, this was impossible anyway, because the play had been given to Meyerhold."

In order to provide further evidence of my theory about what happened next, let us remember that on 3rd September, Bulgakov writes to Gorky "I cannot write anything", and in a letter to A.S. Yenukidze from the same day, he talks of being "exhausted beyond measure" and of the "fruitlessness of all and any efforts". There are no references in any of the documents we know about to any new ideas for dramas, and the manuscript addressed *To a Secret Friend* also suggests that he was finished with writing plays, and drawing a line under it. And yet a manuscript survives in the writer's archive, in which, beneath the date 'October 1929', a new play was commenced.

I would suggest that the idea for a play about Molière was brought to life first and foremost by the impression made on him by the reaction of the literary and theatrical world to Mayakovsky's new play.

Bulgakov hears Mayakovsky being compared to Molière not only by Meyerhold, who is as far removed from him as Mayakovsky himself, but also from his own recent friends – Katayev and Olesha; he must also have been interested in the attitude towards him of the young actors at the Art Theatre. "Molière? … I shall show you what sort of man Molière really was, and who can really be compared to him today…" this, or something to that effect, may have been, in my view, the irritated creative thought process that played out, leading to the decision to write a play about Molière. The decision was certainly taken suddenly: Y.S. Bulgakova recalls that Bulgakov told her conspiratorially in the autumn of 1929 "that he had had the idea of writing a play": "At some point in the autumn of 1929, M.A. called me on the telephone very insistently – urging me to go and see him at Pirogovskaya. I did so. He carefully closed all the doors, and said to me, in a whisper, that there was some extremely important news, that he would now tell me. I was used to his pranks, tricks and funny games, but even I couldn't work out at that point whether he was joking or being serious.

He made me swear a thousand times not to tell anyone, then at last told me that he had decided to write a play.

'Well, how about that! Is it a contemporary one?'

'If I tell you the first few words of it, you know, if I tell you the first line of the play, you'll know straight away when it's set and who it's about…

'Go on then…'

'Wait…' Once again he started checking all the doors, whispering incantations and looking about him.

After all manner of refusals, and, above all, assurances that the first line would explain everything, he said, in a whisper:

'Ragueneau, a glass of water!' and he looked at me triumphantly. 'Well, have you got it?'

'What a disgrace I am – I haven't got it at all – neither the setting, nor the subject of the play.'

'Ha, you're just pretending. You've got it.'

I had to confess my complete ignorance.

'Well, goodness me… It's all clear, Ragueneau was Molière's servant, the play is about Molière! He runs off-stage to his bathroom and shouts: 'Ragueneau, a glass of water!', and wipes his brow with a towel. Careful, mind: not a word to an-y-one!'"

There is one circumstance that strongly supports my theory about the play's origins: Bulgakov could never stomach Mayakovsky's work, but it didn't provoke him as long as it remained under the banner of futurism, modernism, or any kind of innovation. When he moved into assessments of literary and theatrical work of a different order – that of the classics, of Pushkin, Gogol and Molière, it prompted a strong reaction from Bulgakov: this was an expansion into the area that he considered his own, one which, by contrast with the innovative trends, he undertook to assess. It transpires that the play *Molière* was a way of engaging in literary polemics – not with the text of Mayakovsky's play, but with his interpretation – i.e. with the 'texts' of Meyerhold and the others who were the first to see *The Bathhouse*.

It is noteworthy that the second play too, begun and abandoned (perhaps after being pushed to one side by his work on the play about Molière) that year – what later became *Bliss* – was thought up not without the influence of Mayakovsky's plays *The Bathhouse* and *The Bedbug*.

Thus, in the autumn of 1929, when Bulgakov, having given up all his attempts to write plays, had made up his mind to alter his life dramatically and was writing one application after another, Mayakovsky's literary fate suddenly crossed paths with his own, by prompting the birth of one play and planting the seed for another one that would appear much later.

Biographical details about October 1929, when work on *Molière* was begun, are scarce. Zamyatin was still in Moscow, and frequently visited Gorky in connection with his affairs. On 24th October, he informed his wife that he had been "at Mikhail Afanasievich's place" the previous evening. "He had some kind of problems with his heart, and was taking valerian, and lying in bed," and that the next day the two of them were planning to call on R. Simonov (an actor from the Vakhtangov Theatre).

2

That summer and autumn, the group from the Prechistenka district began to unravel.

In the summer of 1929, N.K. Shaposhnikova told me, B.V. Shaposhnikov and S.S. Zayaitsky were living with their families outside Poltava. A friend arrived from Moscow and warned them that Boris Shaposhnikov's office had been sealed off. He decided to travel to Moscow alone; they agreed that if everything was all right, he would notify his wife; if he did not return, Tata Ushakova would send a cable, informing Natalya Shaposhnikova that she needed to come to the capital. Zayaitsky said: "In my opinion, you'll receive a cable with good news". Sure enough, the cable read: "I'm alive and well, I'll be held up here for two weeks." During those two weeks, Shaposhnikov was warned: "You'll have to move out, all the same." In the late autumn, three of the Prechistenka set were forced to leave their homes, which were located within a few minutes' walk of one another, simultaneously: B.V. Shaposhnikov, F.A. Petrovsky and S.S. Topleninov. Such was the nature of life that autumn.

Topleninov's wife, M.G. Nesterenko, recounted that they had been dancing at the home of some friends that evening. "We had taken with us V.E. Moritz's gramophone, so that no-one would have to sit at the grand piano. And when we got there, we realised that Seryozha had left it on the coach: it had been behind him... We got home from the party late, between 2 and 3 am, and they were already waiting for Seryozha, upstairs in his mother's room.

In the morning, Natalya runs in:
'They've taken Borya!'
'They took Seryozha too!'
'And to think – I ran over to you seeking consolation!'

Shaposhnikov was exiled to Veliky Ustyug, and the others were also taken to cities in the European part of Russia. After a year or two they came back, but the Topleninov family broke apart – Sergei came back with a different woman; Maria Nesterenko moved to Leningrad, and he moved back into his half-basement.

A few months after the autumn arrests, V.E. Moritz was arrested too, while he was on his way to work at GAKhN; the smashing of the State Academy of Artistic Sciences was thus completed within six months.

"When they closed the Academy in the autumn of 1929, in early 1930 there was a purge of the Board of GAKhN," the linguist Apollinaria Solovieva wrote in her memoirs over thirty years later; "I was present at the purge. Pyotr Kogan, who was the president of GAKhN and was himself a victim of the purge, spoke some stern words to G.G. Shpet. Natalya Ignatova reprimanded Kogan for this; he was a good, delicate man at heart. But 1) the "stern" words were called for by the circumstances, and 2), in Shpet's worldview," wrote the author of the memoirs, who had completed a course lasting many years of social re-education, "there really were moments of veneration of Western European culture, which impeded him from penetrating into the precise meaning of the October Revolution. The friendship between Kogan and Shpet remained unchanged until Kogan's death. On 4th May 1932, the day of Kogan's funeral, Shpet led Kogan's wife by the hand from the house where he had lived to the gates of the Novodevichy Cemetery." This group played a considerable role in Bulgakov's life. Boris Yarkho was a celebrated wit, and a prolific writer of epigrams.

He had come up with some risky witticisms, too: "No, nothing will come of electrification: for every 'Ilyich's lightbulb', a 'Vissarionich's off-switch' will be found!"

When they saw in the New Year, 1928, at the home of the Petrovsky brothers (at 2, Granovsky Street), where the entire GAKhN set had assembled, he proposed a toast:

> May he, to whom with a heavy heart
> We've whispered these last ten years:
> "Depart, depart, depart",[15]
> This New Year's wish fulfill
> And shout out, for us all to hear:
> "I will, I will, I will!"

There were some tragic stories: Morozov's wife, the renowned beauty Turkestanova, was sent straight to a psychiatric clinic upon her release from prison, and never emerged from it. As for Morozov himself, an incident occurred that was "monstrous", to use the word chosen by N.A. Ushakova and M.V.

---

[15] The Russian line is уйди-уйди-уйди; a tin whistle known as the *uidi-uidi* ('go away, go away') was sold in stalls at all the crossroads in Moscow. – M.C.

Vakhtereva, who told me about it. In front of numerous assembled guests, he struck Natalya Gabrichevskaya across the face. A.G. Gabrichevsky and N.N. Lyamin set upon him, throwing him out of the apartment and pushing him down the stairs. He never showed his face at their homes again. Many years later, on meeting N.A. Gabrichevskaya in Koktebel, he asked her: "Can it really be that you didn't grasp why I did that…?" And he explained that he had needed to be seen to be banished from polite society in public. "And among the guests," he added, "there was someone who would be able to confirm that this incident happened, should it ever prove necessary…"

Let us return to literary matters, though (although what I have just recounted was to have a bearing on literature as time went on).

A not insignificant role in Bulgakov's fate that year was played by F.F. Raskolnikov, whose weight in society had increased dramatically: he had replaced Voronsky as editor of *Krasnaya Nov'*, a journal that was so important in literary life, and in one of the first interviews he gave, to *Vechernyaya Moskva*, he promised to print a withering article about Bulgakov in one of the upcoming issues. On top of this, he had been given a position of considerable responsibility at Glavrepertkom.

What made things worse was that Raskolnikov had high hopes of becoming a playwright in his own right. It seems fair to suggest that the acclaim enjoyed by Bulgakov's plays somehow became woven into the motives (perhaps concealed even to him) for the decisions to ban those plays, which were taken with his involvement.

The Art Theatre was preparing a production of L. Tolstoy's *Resurrection*, based on an adaptation for the stage written by Raskolnikov. The production designer was I. Sudakov; in a letter dated 25th September 1930, he gave the adaptation an acerbic, condescending assessment. The author was performing readings of his play *Robespierre*. There is a remarkable incident related to one of these readings. Y.S. Bulgakova wrote a diary entry about a story Bulgakov told concerning the reading – at one of the Nikitinsk Saturdays. When reading it, one must bear in mind the grotesque nature of the stories Bulgakov told orally, which were similar to the grotesque pages of his prose. I would therefore invite readers to free up the episode itself from the exaggerations lent to it both by the wonderful story-teller and by the temperamental memoirist.

"There was an unusually large audience, and there were several artistic directors there, such as Bersenev, Tairov and various others – I forget who. There were actors there, too – some of the sycophantic ones.

Misha was sitting at the end of the fourth row, next to the passage, as far as he could remember.

Raskolnikov finished his reading and said, after a lengthy ovation:

"Will there be a discussion now? Well, come along then, comrades, let's get started…"

He said this is a bossy, condescending way. And Misha decided on the spur of the moment to speak, and to maintain the same tone when doing so. He raised his hand.

The man chairing the meeting listed the names and wrote them down: "Bersenev, Ivan Nikolayevich; Alexander Yakovlevich Tairov… Bulgakov… (the man said this with a certain trepidation)… (then he listed the others who had put up their hands).

Bersenev got things going.

"Well then, comrades… we have just heard a remarkable work by our dear Fyodor Fyodorovich! (A handful of sycophants seized the moment to start another round of applause). I shall be brief and I'll get right to the point. I have heard many astonishing plays in my lifetime, but never have I heard one that has affected me with such unusual force, one that has… I would say, turned me upside down, my soul, my consciousness… no, such a play as that I have never heard! I sat in my seat as though bewitched, I could not come to my senses throughout it… I find it hard to speak, such is my excitement! What an event this is, comrades! We are present at a real event. My feelings prevent me from… prevent me speaking! What can I say? Thank you, I bow down low to you, Fyodor Fyodorovich!" (And Bersenev bowed down low to Raskolnikov, to the sound of stormy applause from the audience).

(Raskolnikov, meanwhile, saying: "all right, all right, comrades…" came down from the stage and sat down in the third row, right in front of Misha).

"Next please, comrades!" said the presiding officer. "Ah! Esteemed Alexander Yakovlevich."

And Tairov began, stuttering slightly:

"Yes, comrades, it is no easy task to give a speech appraising such a work as the one we have just heard now! During my lifetime, I have been present at many discussions of the plays of Shakespeare, Molière, the ancients, Sophocles, Euripedes… But comrades, these plays, for all their magnificence of course, are nonetheless distant from us! (A shout came from the auditorium: "this play isn't a modern one, either!") Comrades!! Yes! This play is not a modern one, BUT! What our dear Fyodor Fyodorovich has so brilliantly done is that, taking a subject that is not modern, he resolves it in such an unexpected way that it becomes incredibly close to us, it is as though we are living in the time of Robespierre, in the time of the French Revolution! (Things are shouted out from the auditorium but the words can't be made out). Comrades! Comrades!! The play by our beloved Fyodor Fyodorovich is the kind of play that it would be a great joy for any theatre to put on, for any director! (And Tairov, crossing his arms over his chest, and then moving them apart helplessly, went back to his seat, accompanied by an even louder ovation from the sycophants).

"Whose turn is it now?" said the presiding officer. "Ah yes, comrade Bulgakov! Please proceed."

Misha got to his feet, but he did not leave his place: instead, he started speaking from where he was, gazing at the neck of Raskolnikov, who, as I mentioned, was now sitting in front of him.

"Y-e-ess... I listened carefully to what the previous speakers had to say... very carefully... (Raskolnikov shuddered). Ivan Bersenev said that not a single play in his life had excited him as much as the play by comrade Raskolnikov. That's as may be, that's as may be... I shall only say that I am genuinely sorry for Ivan Nikolayevich, since he has been working at the theatre as an actor, director, and an artistic director, for many years now. And, as it now transpires, he has had to work on material that has left him cold. And only today... what a pity, what a pity... In the same way, I did not quite understand what Alexander Tairov said. He compared comrade Raskolnikov's play to Shakespeare and Molière. I am a great admirer of Molière. I love him not only for the subjects he chooses for his plays, for the characters of his protagonists, but also for his remarkably powerful technique as a playwright. Each appearance by a member of the cast in a play by Molière is essential, is justified; the intrigue is crafted in such a way that every single link in the chain must be kept in place. Here, by contrast, in comrade Raskolnikov's play (at this point Raskolnikov's neck turned red), one cannot understand anything about what goes with what, about why one character appears on stage at any given moment, rather than another. And why is that character now going away? The first act can simply be dispensed with, the 2nd needs to be rewritten... It is like seeing an amateur play, at a dacha in the summertime!

As for the language that is used, I simply feel insulted on behalf of the orator who spoke earlier, over the fact that he has never heard a better language than the one used in comrade Raskolnikov's play. He spoke to us about the uniqueness of this language. Yes, it is certainly a unique language... if you'll allow me, I noted down a few phrases which I found particularly striking, for instance... "he had sucked in this revolutionary ardour with his mother's milk".

Yes... well, these things happen. It was not a success.

After this, Misha told me, what took place was the kind of thing that happens at the bazaar, when someone is the first to throw a brick against the wall. It was utter bedlam. Some of the subsequent speakers really did propose that certain scenes and characters should be deleted altogether.

The meeting came to an end. Raskolnikov's neck had now turned dark-blue; Misha got to his feet and headed for the exit. Sensing a chill run down his back, he turned around and saw Raskolnikov's eyes looking at him, full of hatred. His hand was reaching for his pocket. Misha turned back towards the door. "Was he going to shoot me in the back?"

On 6th December, the first (hand-written) draft of the play about Molière, entitled *A Cabal of Hypocrites* (*Kabala Svyatosh*), was completed. According Yelena's memoirs, Bulgkov "asked me to bring my Underwood typewriter to Pirogovskaya. He started dictating the play to me..." It appears that this first introduction to the play for her was marked by an inscription in the Paris edition of *The White Guard*, made on 7th December: "To dear Yelena Sergeyevna. A refined and generous reviewer. Mikhail Bulgakov." On the same day, the Drama Union gives Bulgakov an official note "for presentation to the Financial Inspectorate to the effect that his plays: 1. *The Days of the Turbins*, 2. *Zoya's Apartment*, 3. *The Crimson Island*, 4. *Flight* are banned from all public performance"; the note referred to the Repertoire number indicated by the Chief Committee for Monitoring of the Repertoire for 1929; it was signed by a member of the board, Y. Potekhin (an old friend). At this moment in time, the author is pinning all his hopes on his new play.

On 28th December, he writes the following postscript in a letter to his brother: "My position is warisome," giving us an idea of the mood the playwright was in with the New Year around the corner, after he had made a decisive attempt to return to the theatre.

On 16th January 1930, Bulgakov writes to his brother: "Let me tell you about myself: all my literary works have died, as have their plots. I am doomed to silence and, very possibly, to complete starvation. In indescribably difficult circumstances, in the second half of 1929, I wrote a play about Molière. The best specialists in Moscow acclaimed it as one of the strongest of my five plays. But all the indications are that it will not be granted permission to be shown on stage. My torments with it have gone on for one-and-a-half months now, despite the fact that it is about Molière, the 17th century, despite the fact that I didn't touch upon the modern day in it at all.

If this play should die, there will be no way to save me: I am already *suffering a disaster* now. I have nothing to protect me and nothing that can help me. I am informing you, utterly soberly: my ship is sinking, the water is nearly at the level of the bridge.

I must drown with manful courage. I ask that you relate to my message with great attention."

The frankness of the phrases used in his letters to his brother, from the summer onwards, seems to be of cardinal importance to him: he is assuming that there is the possibility that his letters are being opened and read by the censors.

The news about the play *A Cabal of Hypocrites* reached Stanislavsky, as well; he was holidaying in Nice that winter. "Bulgakov's play is very interesting," he writes on 10th February to L.M. Leonidov, and he adds, with concern: "Might he not give it to someone else? That would be a pity."

On 11th February, Zamyatin, who had arrived in Moscow on 19th January, writes to his wife in Leningrad: "In the evening, I am due to be at the Drama Union, where Mikhail Afanasievich will be reading his new play."

The tone of Bulgakov's letters to his brother, which have become the key sources documenting his life in the winter of 1929-1930, remains the same as before, however: on 21st February, he wirtes the following summary of the situation: "In circumstances of unutterable hardship, I have tried to perform my task as a writer in the way I ought. Now, my work has ceased. I am like a complicated (I suppose) machine, the products made by which are of no use to the USSR. This has been made all too clear to me, and is being made clear to me now regarding my play about Molière. At night, I rack my brains torturously, trying to think up ways of saving myself.

I can see nothing, though. To whom, I think to myself, would I write an application, in any case?" These letters play the role of brief confessions, and declarations – simultaneously.

As one can see in them, Bulgakov has not lost his energy or hope, has not stopped looking for effective methods of fighting back against his adversaries in literature and at the theatre.

18th March 1930 turned out to be the day which brought Bulgakov face-to-face with the search for these methods.

3

Ten days later, in a letter that became a fairly important act, Bulgakov recalls the article by the critic Pikel, published 6 months earlier, which had "expressed a liberal idea: 'We do not wish to say, by writing this, that Bulgakov's name has been crossed off the list of Soviet dramatists" and "reassured a writer whose work had been banned" by saying that "this was about his past works for the theatre".

"However," Bulgakov adds, "life, in the shape of the Glavrepertkom, has shown that R. Pikel's liberalism is not founded on anything.

On 18th March 1930, I received a slip of paper from the Glavrepertkom, informing me laconically that not my past play, but my new one, *A Cabal of Hypocrites (Molière)*, had not been granted permission to be performed. [The last few words in the letter were written in bold for extra emphasis. – M.C.].

I shall put it briefly: beneath two stacks of official paper they are buried – my work at the book depository, my imagination, a play which earned countless positive reviews from theatre experts – a fantastic play.

R. Pikel has got it wrong. It is not only my past plays that have perished, but also my current ones, and all my future ones. And I, personally, with my own hands, threw the draft of my novel about the devil into the stove, along with a draft of a comedy and the start of my second novel, *The Theatre*.

There is no hope left for any of my works."

... At around this time, Raskolnikov writes to Gorky from Revel: "I am sending you heartfelt greetings from Estonia, where I am staying for only two weeks. I am very glad to have left Glaviskusstvo, because, to tell the truth, I did not get any satisfaction out of this administrative work. It is a very pleasant thing to enjoy art, but it is not peasant to be in charge of it. I feel far more drawn to political work in the field of international politics and creativity, literature..." (22nd March 1930).

The changes of personnel at that decisive time – the years 1929 and 1930 – were part of a big political game, but in no way weakened the pressure that was being exerted on literature; on the contrary, this pressure was steadily increasing; it would be naïve in the extreme to associate this pressure with the ill will of this or that critic or party bureaucrat.

Let us return to Bulgakov's letter.

What kind of letter was it?

Many years later, in January 1956, Y.S. Bulgakova told the story of a letter she sent to her eldest son, Major Y.Y. Shilovsky, and after his departure she wrote down what she had told him in her diary. "When I met them (on 28th February 1929), they were pretty hard up. To say nothing of the awful state of mind that M.A. was in: all his works had been banned… no-one wanted to take him on, not only as a reporter, but even as a worker at the printing press. When he raised this matter at the Art Theatre, they refused to listen. In a word, there was only one way out: to bring his life to an end.

It was then that he wrote a letter to the Government. As far as I recall, we handed them out (they were printed out [i.e. lots of copies of the same letter. – M.C.] by me, despite fierce resistance from Shilovsky) to seven recipients. I think the seven were: Stalin, Molotov, Kaganovich, Kalinin, Yagoda, Bubnov (the People's Commissar for Education at the time) and F. Kon. The final draft of the letter was written on 28th March, and we handed it out on 31st and on 1st April…

On 3rd April, when I was with M.A. in Pirogovskaya, F. Knorre and P. Sokolov arrived there and tried to persuade M.A. to start working at TRAM as a director. I was sitting in the bedroom, whilst M.A. spoke to them in his study. He kept running in every minute to ask for my advice, though. In the end, I came out, and we drew up a contract, which I then signed, on M.A. starting work at TRAM. And on 18th April, at 6 or 7 in the evening, he came running up to our apartment (mine and Shilovsky's) on Bolshoi Rzhevsky, in an agitated state, and said the following."

We shall break off from Y.S. Bulgakova's story at this point and briefly explain the contents of the letter. It was an extensive one and it was broken down into 11 sections. It began as follows:

"I am appealing to the Government of the USSR with the following letter," and after that came the 1st section: After all of my works were banned, one began to hear, among the many citizens to whom I am known as a writer, various voices offering me one and the same piece of advice: to write "a Communist play" (I am putting their quoted remarks in quotation marks), and, moreover, to appeal to the Government of the USSR with a letter of repentance, containing a rejection of the views I formerly held, as expressed by me in my literary works, and some assurances to the effect that from now on, I am going to work like a writer and fellow-traveller who is devoted to the idea of communism.

The aim: to save myself from persecution, destitution and inevitable death in the finale.

I did not heed this advice. I would hardly be likely to manage to come across in a good light before the Government of the USSR, after writing a deceitful letter, amounting to a dishevelled and naïve political curvet. I did not even make any attempt to write a Communist play, knowing as I did in advance that I would not be able to produce such a play.

The desire that has ripened within me to bring an end to the torments that have plagued me, as a writer, compels me to appeal to the Government of the USSR with a letter of justification."

He then presented some examples of reviews by critics, of the kind that were quoted earlier in this book. "I hasten to inform you that my aim, in quoting them, is not in any way to complain about the criticism or enter into any kind of polemics. My goal is far more serious. I am showing, with the documents in my hands, that the entire press of the USSR, and along with it all the institutions to whom control of the repertoire is entrusted, throughout all the years of my literary work, has unanimously and with *extraordinary fury* sought to demonstrate that the works of Mikhail Bulgakov cannot exist in the USSR." The letter was comprehensive, energetic and extremely frank. Quoting those who had written that *The Crimson Island* was "a call for freedom of the press", Bulgakov wrote: "I admit to this. The battle with censorship, of whatever kind and under whatever regime it may exist, is my duty as a writer, and the same is true of calls for a free press. I am an ardent admirer of this freedom and I would suggest that if one of our writers were ever to come up with the idea of proving that he did not need it, he would be like a fish declaring, in public, that it doesn't need water." When assessing the degree of frankness of this letter, one must keep in mind that Bulgakov may have felt that, after various people had become acquainted with his notes about day-to-day life in 1921-1926, he essentially had nothing to hide, nor any reason to keep anything hidden.

One must also keep something else in mind, however: if, by the time he wrote the letter, Bulgakov had had something new to say, then he had a wonderful opportunity to do so ("Over these years I have come to realise" etc.). And the price those words of his – "… deep scepticism with regard to the revolutionary process taking place in my backward country, and the juxtaposing against it of that beloved and Great thing, Evolution" – is not getting smaller, but growing, precisely because of the special situation in which the letter was written. These words show, beyond any doubt, that in the ten years and a bit that had elapsed since Bulgakov's first treatise in print, his view of the events which had turned the life of the country upside down remained fundamentally unchanged – and this was in stark contrast to many of his fellow-countrymen.

In the sixth section of the letter, its author wrote: "My literary portrait is finished and it is indeed a political portrait. I cannot say what depth of criminality can be found in it, but I ask only one thing: not to look for anything outside the perimeter of it. It was written in absolute good faith." And in section 8, he asked his correspondent "to take into account that I am not a political figure, but a writer, and that I have given my entire output to the Soviet stage", and also "that not being able to write, for me, is tantamount to being buried alive." Appealing to "the humanity of the Soviet government", the author asked: "The magnanimous thing to do with me, a writer who cannot be of use at home, in his homeland, would be to set me free." And the next section, the 11th, read: "If even that which I have written is unconvincing, and I am to be doomed to a lifetime of silence in the USSR, I ask the Soviet Government to give me some work that is suitable for my profession and to send me to work as an in-house director at the theatre." The author of the letter added: "I am asking, specifically and with emphasis, for a *categorical order on an overseas business posting*, because all of my attempts to find work in the solitary field in which I may be of use to the USSR as a uniquely qualified specialist have suffered a complete fiasco. My name has been made so odious that an offer to work from my side was met with *fear*, despite the fact that a vast number of actors and directors, and indeed theatre directors, are perfectly well aware of my virtuosic knowledge of the stage.

I am offering to the USSR an utterly honest, without the slightest hint of sabotage, expert director and author, who will take it upon himself in good faith to put on any play, from Shakespeare's plays right up until contemporary plays.

I am requesting that I be appointed as an assistant-director at the 1st Art Theatre – at the very best school, led by the masters K.S. Stanislavsky and V.I. Nemirovich-Danchenko.

If I am not to be appointed a director, I request the role of an in-house extra. If I cannot be an extra, I request the role of a stage-hand.

If even this is not possible, I ask the Soviet Government to act in relation to me howsoever it sees fit, but to act in some way at least, because *at the present moment*, I, as a playwright who has written 5 plays, and is famous in the USSR and abroad, am facing abject poverty, the streets, and death."

Over the last fifteen years, the letter has been quoted many times in the forewords to Bulgakov's works, and in 1987 it was finally published in full. Today, when we know what happened next, one cannot help but notice a certain lack of clarity in the way the letter is structured – though it was doubtless thought through intensively from every angle for a period of ten days (from 18th March). Specifically, in the letter, one notes the absence of a *third* alternative – it gets lost between the two outcomes that are energetically highlighted by the author (exile – or working as a director) – that the author had also had in mind whilst writing the text: the possibility of doing literary work in the Soviet Union, in his homeland.

One can only suppose that the author of the letter felt that this outcome made itself manifest by itself in his account of all the twists and turns in his career in the theatre. It may be that his literary interest in this account impeded him from clearly formulating his hopes, demands, requests.

Let us return to Y.S. Bulgakova's recollections about what Bulgakov told her on the evening of 18th April (let the reader pay particular attention to the remarks which help us to understand Bulgakov's condition at the time of the conversation): "he lay down after lunch, to have a little nap, as always, but at that moment the telephone rang and Lyuba called out to him, to say that the Central Committee were on the line for him. M.A. didn't believe it, and decided someone was playing a trick on him (that sort of thing used to happen back then) and, dishevelled and irritated, he grabbed the receiver and heard a voice say:

'Mikhail Afanasievich Bulgakov?'

'Yes, yes.'

'Comrade Stalin will speak to you now.'

'What? Stalin? Stalin?'

And immediately, he heard a voice with a distinct Georgian accent." After a few words of mutual greeting and the promise that Bulgakov would "receive a favourable answer" to his letter, the question that is already known to readers (as is the whole of the subsequent conversation) was asked: 'Is it, perhaps, true that you have asked to leave the country? What is it – are you really that fed up with us?'

(M.A. said that his surprise at being asked such a question – and at receiving the call in the first place – that he became utterly confused and did not immediately respond).

'I have thought a great deal lately about whether it is possible for a Russian writer to live outside the motherland. And it seems to me that he cannot.'

'You are right. I think so, too. Where do you want to work? At the Art Theatre?'

'Yes, I would like that. But I have said as much in the past, and I was refused permission.'

'You go ahead and make an application to them. My feeling is that they will agree to it. You and I ought to meet up, and talk.'

'Yes, yes! Iosif Vissarionovich, I very much need to talk to you.'

'Yes, we must find some time and meet up, certainly. For now, though, I wish you all the best.'

No meeting ever took place, however. And M.A. always asked me the same question, throughout his life: why did he change his mind? And I always gave him the same reply; what would he have had to talk to you about? After all, he understood perfectly well, after your telephone conversation, that the talk would not be of apartments, of money..."

This biographical theme of waiting for a second, 'real' conversation was one that made itself felt in Bulgakov's creative work throughout all the subsequent years.

"The day after the conversation," Y.S. Bulgakova's account went on, "M.A. went to the Art Theatre and was met there with joyful embraces. He muttered something about submitting an application…

'Ha, good God man! An application indeed! Write it on this, for all we care… (and they grabbed a scrap of paper, on which M.A. wrote his application).

And he was hired as an assistant director at the Art Theatre."

Bulgakov told a fairly large number of people about the telephone call that had changed his fate – and in such a significant way, as it seemed to him in those months – striving, it seems, to alter the atmosphere around his name. Evidence of this is seen in a diary entry by the well-known Moscow bookseller E.F. Zippelzon made on 12th June 1930: "Incidentally, about Bulgakov. Mikhail Afanasievich often pops into the shop [the bookshop owned by the *Nedra* publishing house on Kuznetsky Most – M.C.]. Knowing how much it irks me when people ask irritating questions like 'do you sell stationary?', he sometimes likes to put on a different voice and ask, loud enough for the whole shop to hear it: 'Do you sell ink-wells?' He says he likes the expression on my face and the answer I always give: 'No, and I never will.'

He told me about something far more serious than that a couple of weeks ago, though. He had been sitting in his study in an extremely bad mood. And one can see why. His work isn't being printed at all. All of his plays are banned. His efforts to appear on the stage of the Art Theatre as an actor (he even had a surname prepared – Narodov) came to nothing. And then suddenly... The telephone rings. Bulgakov walks up to it and cannot believe his ears. None other than J.V. Stalin himself was on the line. For obvious reasons, Bulgakov did not tell me exactly what was said, but a few days later he was hired as a director (and not as an actor!) at the Art Theatre. In this fact, one can immediately perceive the greatness of Stalin at play. To find the time, during the important preparations for the 16th party congress, to call Bulgakov, a writer whose name has been given such a kicking in every newspaper... [...] Admittedly, I later found out that Bulgakov had written an application to the Government, but all the same, Stalin's actions provide further evidence still that he is a big man, in such stark contrast to certain small-minded little men from Glavlit and Glaviskusstvo [this interpretation of the phone call shows us that the ideas that appeared in articles about Bulgakov several decades later were already widespread in 1930 – M.C.] ... I heard from Rayevsky (an actor at the Art Theatre) that Gorky chuckled – chuckled was the word, not laughed – when Bulgakov read his play *Flight* to him. And yet not even Gorky himself was able to save that play. All this only pushed Mikhail Afanasievich further away, to my great regret, from the only path worthy of such a great talent, the path of finally mastering the great epoch in which we have the happiness of living. And it is also indisputable that the remarkable step taken by Stalin is now bringing one of the most talented and sincere writers of our times closer to this path, and will, no doubt, continue to bring him closer to it."

On 15th July, Bulgakov departs for the Crimea with some actors from TRAM (he began working for the theatre group as a consultant in April). On 18th July, he sends a cable from Miskhor to Y.S. Shilovskaya, advising her, in his capacity as an old friend, to go to Miskhor and get a room at a guesthouse. Having received no answer from Y.S. Shilovskaya, he sends a cable to his wife: "Why no letters from Lyusetta probably sick." Meanwhile, the Leningrad Red Theatre sends him a cable asking him to write a play about the year 1905. On 23rd July, Bulgakov sends a cable from Miskhor: "Agree to write year o-five terms provide me choice of subject is epic task submit fifteenth December". On 3rd August, however, a cable arrives from the same theatre: "Play year o-five decided not to commission-Volf" (i.e. the director of the theatre, Volf).

On 6th August, Bulgakov writes to Stanislavsky: "Having returned from the Crimea, where I treated my sick nerves after the last two years, which have been very difficult for me, I am writing you a few simple, unofficial lines. [...] After the burden of the melancholy I felt over the death of my plays, I now feel better, now that I – after a long pause – and in a new role – have stepped over the threshold of the theatre created by you for the glory of the country."

On 4th September, Stanislavsky writes to Bulgakov: "You cannot imagine how glad I am to have you joining our theatre!

I have had occasion to work with you only at a handful of rehearsals for *The Turbins*, and I sensed there was a director (and perhaps an actor, too?!) in you back then.

Molière, and many others too, managed to combine these professions with literature!" That autumn, it appears that this was exactly what Bulgakov believed was going to happen.

At that point the Krasny Theatre once again got in touch with him, finding itself in urgent need of plays: Yekaterina Sheremetyeva travelled to Moscow with the literary department, especially in order to have a meeting with Bulgakov. "It was a risky step for a young, cutting-edge revolutionary theatre, which was what the Krasny Theatre aspired to be and, indeed, was," she writes in her memoirs. "There were vague rumours circulating about Bulgakov's letter to Stalin and about Mikhail Afanasievich's appointment at the Art Theatre, but who knew for sure whether they could be believed? And meanwhile everyone in the literary and theatre world knew beyond any doubt that *Zoya's Apartment*, *The Crimson Island* and even *The Days of the Turbins*, which had enjoyed a three-year run at the Art Theatre, had been taken off the repertoire and banned, and that Bulgakov was the 'wrong kind' of author.

At the meeting, it was agreed that the play "must be set in the present or the future", that the author would choose the subject himself, and that the money paid to the author as an advance would not have to be returned, "even if the play presented by the author is not accepted by the theatre, for whatever reason." "After each sentence, he paused, gave me a questioning look, and I would confirm that sentence; he pronounced the last line with a certain emphasis, sniggered and explained: 'After all, the author wouldn't be able to come up with the money, he will already have spent it!'" Bulgakov had acquired some experience; he no longer wanted to enter into the kind of agreement he had had with the Art Theatre; he looked at the future with caution and wariness – the first frenzy, apparently, had already passed.

Let us return to Y. Sheremetyeva's memoirs.

"Mikhail Afanasievich was always lively, jolly, in short – in a good mood. He was tired, of course, of the loneliness, of the atmosphere of distrust, wariness and simply malevolence that had been created around him. And now someone representing a theatre – albeit a small one – had appeared, someone representing a group of people working in the theatre, who valued his talent unconditionally and believed in him…

When we emerged from Bulgakov's apartment, the sweeper in the courtyard had started working with a broom, lifting up a cloud of dust in front of us. Mikhail Afanasievich's face grew tense – the change was barely noticeable – and he hurried to open the door to the carriage. As he stood beside it, he said, sounding very irritated: 'First he breaks his hat in humiliating fashion, now he gets dust in our faces.'

On many other occasions I observed that Mikhail Afanasievich was very sensitive to all manifestations of a lack of respect – whether for oneself or for others."

His secret love affair, meanwhile, was developing at quite a pace.

4

Winter was approaching; the 1930-1931 theatre season was in full swing. Just as before, not a single one of Bulgakov's plays was being performed; there had been no good news about the play about Molière, which was still lying in the author's writing desk.

On 10th November 1930, an exhibition opened at the Writers' Club entitled *The Writer and Collective Farms*. The lives of his fellow writers were moving along different paths than his own life.

On 11th November, the film *Dead Souls* appeared on the capital's cinema screens; as I.N. Rozanov wrote of it in his diary, "it is about the flirtation and bureaucracy of Doctor Ivanov, who disowned his daughter after she suffered burns and was mistakenly listed as deceased." The mass consciousness was being prepared, so that it would be ready to accept the future extravaganzas about "the sadist doctor Pletnev" and others. The entry about the film in the Moscow writer's diary was followed by a newspaper story about the Promparty and incidents of "its sabotage", 12th November: "News in the papers of the double-dealing of Srytsov and Lominadze"; 15th November: "Disgusting weather: rain, sleet"; at the Historical Museum, as at all of Moscow's institutions at this time, a signature sheet was put up "on the subject of the resolution on the Promparty. Several people did not sign it"; after a speech by one of the administrators "on apoliticism in science", there was a demonstration about the Promparty. Two days later, there was a discussion about the Promparty at FOSP; "Grossman said that the brain of the country had always been in favour of those who worked hard, i.e. all the best writers," I.N. Rozanov wrote. "Mstislavsky and others said that we must be at 100% not in our words, but in our actions," – i.e. one hundred percent dedicated to certain doctrines. A wholesale, blatantly aggressive politicization was taking place of those who had been dubbed "the workers of intellectual labour".

Tatiana Alexandrovna Aksakova-Sivers, describing in her remarkable memoirs her "fleeting encounter" with Bulgakov, which occurred that autumn "at Annochka Tolsto-Popova's home (she still lived in the basement at Nikolsky sidestreet)" tells of how, in Leningrad (the same things happened in Moscow too, but Bulgakov, who spent that autumn in Leningrad, perhaps observed the very same scenes that T.A. Aksakova-Sivers had seen), she "saw a vast crowd on the square in front of the Mariinsky palace. It was a procession of workers and officials from Leningrad, holding banners which read: "Death to Ramzin and his associates! We demand the most severe punishment!" The demonstrations preceded meetings at all institutions and there was only one place where such a resolution met with objections: the Military-medical academy. There, the neuro-pathologist Professor Mikhail Astvatsaturov said: "May I remind you that all of us swore a medical oath to protect life. We cannot and shall not hand out death sentences!" It later transpired that for Ramzin, the whole thing ended relatively favourably, but the demonstration… left a very heavy impression, it was a throwback to Pontius Pilate!" Both the position adopted by the medic, and the heavy feelings felt by the memoirist, were no doubt a close approximation of the feelings Bulgakov experienced in connection with these events.

On 25th November, the trial of the Promparty began. On 30th November, I.N. Rozanov described his thoughts on that day's proceedings in court (there was a real frenzy over the tickets to them; getting hold of one was considered a real slice of luck): "Striking impressions. One is struck above all by the theatricality of the whole setting."

In the first week of December, the congress of museum workers takes place at the Polytechnical museum (with talks by N.K. Krupskaya and N.Y. Marr). On 6th December, I.N. Rozanov describes how "the Adler affair" was discussed that day; one of the members of the special commission, on its behalf, "read out extracts from an article which had appeared in a German magazine about the state of science in the USSR. The article was written by Prof. Adler, a member of the congress. Running through it like a red line was the idea that science had flourished before the revolution, but that under Soviet rule it had decayed. Each time the author refers to the 'Red professors', he uses inverted commas. Adler says of the Academy of Sciences that it had proved to be "fairly elastic" and "had managed to adapt itself"… The commission, giving its verdict on this incident, decreed that the author must be excluded from the congress. The accused (!), Adler, requested the floor. "I admit my mistake," he said, "but in my defence I can say that the article was written in 1925, that I later realised how wrong it was and wrote to the editors asking them not to publish it, but the response from them was that the article had already been printed. Moreover," Adler added, "I would ask you to take into account that in Kazan, when the Czechoslovaks arrived, I was the only professor who immediately joined the side of the Soviet government.

So the Commission's [sentence?] is perhaps harsh." A ruddy-cheeked young man shouted out from his seat: "You were against the Czechoslovaks as a German: national enmity is at play here." […] One of the speakers proposes that Adler "be removed from all work everywhere". During the incident, Bubnov came in, prompting loud applause." Rozanov reported what he said in his speech: '… You have managed to punish a man who chose to stand on the other side of the barricades. I hope that in future, you will be able to identify class enemies just as well…"

These events must have put anyone who was not inclined to share the feelings of the judges and prosecutors in increasingly gloomy spirits.

On 2nd December, rehearsals began at the Art Theatre for *Dead Souls*, but Bulgakov's work on the text was by no means finished. The adaptation, which was being implemented not in the way in which it had been planned and begun, was now, one way or another, starting to look like the only end product from the year – and it was one that brought him little comfort.

Things had not improved much from a material perspective, either. In late December, Bulgakov writes a letter to the board of the Art Theatre asking for an advance: "I have been stealing time – between rehearsals for *Dead Souls* and my evening work at TRAM – to write the role of the First (Narrator), and I am forced to break off from it every day and every minute, to go walking around town in search of money. I consider it my duty to inform the board that my strength has run out." His request was refused – on account of the debt that Bulgakov owed to the Vsekomdram.

The trial of the Promparty lasted until 7th December and was accompanied by articles by Gorky which caught the public's attention, particularly the title of the first article: "If the enemy does not surrender, he is destroyed" (*Pravda* and *Izvestiya*, 15th November 1930), "To the workers and peasants" (*Pravda* and *Izvestiya*, 25th November); it was filmed for the cinema, complete with sound, and by the start of the next year it was already being shown at movie theatres. On 24th January 1931, the bookseller Zippelzon wrote in his diary: "I went to the talking cinema today and listened to the trial of the Promparty. It made a powerful impression on me, but all these people, or rather, "little people", even those famous Ramzin and Osadchy – what a petty matter all this is, what small fry… Krylenko generally seems to be the only interesting and significant person in the trial… Even in the cinema, Krylenko's speech was interrupted by applause." A comprehensive processing of the mass consciousness was taking place; from the autumn of 1929 onwards, this trial achieved significant success. The diary that we are quoting from duly reflected the congealing of the atmosphere in society.

The duller the colours of everyday life became, the more intensely, it seems, Bulgakov sensed that he was caught in a trap of his own making.

Bulgakov spent this year working on a manuscript of the kind he was not really used to. The writer's archive contains a sheet torn out of the *Notebook* in which he worked on both *A Cabal of Hypocrites* and on the stage adaptation of *Dead Souls*. The sheet is dated 28th December 1930 and headed Funérailles (Funeral). It contains some rough drafts of a poem that begins with the line "One must honestly admit...", revealing its confessional nature.

> At that very moment the underground rats
> Shall cease their flute-like whistle,
> I shall sink my flaxen-haired head
> Into the sheet that I have not yet written.

Some further lines are then added and then crossed out one by one (this work did not come to him nearly as easily as his prose!), developing the theme of a confession and a tragic end: "In all likelihood, the dog will start barking... and howling... The damaged table shall take pity... Many a time with an unclean lie have I stained a mouth that is dark and impure." The draft lines of verse reveal a proximity to some of the author's favourite themes:

> Why did you appear all twisted
> Why is your mouth fragmented
> You were killed in battle
> I shall be embraced by the monk.

The first three verses make one think of *The Red Crown*, in which the younger brother appears to the hero at night, his head tied up with a bandage reminiscent of a red crown or a bloody garland. The second line, moreover, uses a detail from the description of Berlioz's death. The "monk" is of the same ilk as the monks who give Molière a fright at the start of *A Cabal of Hypocrites* and appear at the hour of his death, and also Chekhov's *Black Monk* (Chyernyy Monakh), references to whom can be found in the writer's correspondence.

> I shall remember the angels, the scorching vodka
> And [I] shall be struck with gas
> On my gilded mouth.
> Why did you appear uninvited
> Why did you [not finish] not cry out

> Why has your boat been thrown
> Ahead of time onto the shore?
> Is there a punishment that is worthy
> Beneath your blows, lord, I collapsed
>
> Why did you not take care of me?
> Why did he lie in wait for me?

The theme of death was developed in later draft lines of verse (it may be that the poem was never finished), talking of "distant galaxies", in which "another candle will start burning."

Serving as a template of sorts for this poem, in my view, were some verses written by Mayakovsky shortly before he died (the second lyrical introduction to the long poem *In Full Voice* [*Vo Ves' Golos*]). The stanza included in the letter was addressed "To everyone" and was printed immediately after his death in the newspapers:

> As they say, the "incident is over"
> The boat of love
> crashed on the shore of existence
> Life and I must face the reckoning
> and there is no point to the list of shared pains
> woes
> and irritations

... was perhaps the first poem by Mayakovsky that touched Bulgakov, and it was reflected more than one-and-a-half years later in his own experiments with poetry – in the only two lines which come across as polished and complete:

> Why has your boat been tossed
> Ahead of time against the shore?

(M.A. Chimishkian tells of how, in the first few days after Mayakovsky's death, she walked in on Bulgakov when he was reading the newspaper. He pointed at the line: *The boat of love was broken on the shore of life*: "Tell me – surely it was not this? Because of this? No, it cannot be! There must be something else at play here!") Bulgakov must have been feeling a mixture of emotions as the New Year, 1931, arrived.

5

In December 1930 – January 1931, Y.S. Shilovskaya was at a rest home outside Moscow. Bulgakov went to see her several times. On one occasion, she told me, he came to see her on skis; he was freezing cold, but she was too afraid to let him stop there or even to give him some tea, and she immediately sent him home.

A piece of paper survives dated 3rd January 1931: "My friend! Forgive me for coming to see you so often. But today I…"

The relationship between them was blossoming and developing with increasing intensity. On the last page of the novel *The White Guard* there is an inscription written in Bulgakov's hand: 'For information. Serfdom was destroyed in the year… Moscow, 5.II.31." (On the same day, the inscription quoted earlier – "Muse, muse of mine" was made in a copy of the second part of the novel).

And much later, one-and-a-half years later, Bulgakov added: "A misfortune occurred on 25.11.1931."

Marika Chimishkian, who by that time had been married to S.A. Yermolinsky for around a year, told me: "In early spring, I think it was, I went to see Yelena Sergeyevna at Rzhevsky. She was friends with Lyubov Yevgenievna, you see, and we all knew her very well, she had been at the wedding when Yermolinsky and I got married. I arrive, and Shilovsky opens the door to me, then turns around swiftly and walks back into his room, having barely said hello. I walk into Yelena's room, she has the manicurist in there with her, and she speaks to me in a fairly bizarre way as well. I can't make head nor tail of it, I bid her goodbye, and I walk over to see the Bulgakovs on Pirogovskaya, and say: 'You don't happen to know what's going on over there, do you?'

They start laying into me: 'Why did you go and see them? They thought we had sent you!'

Lyuba says: 'Don't you know?'

'No, I haven't a clue what's going on.'

'What a scene there was! Shilovsky ran in and was waving a gun around…'

At that point they told me about how Shilovsky had somehow discovered Bulgakov's relationship with Yelena. Lyuba, by that point, had nothing against their affair, in my opinion. She had some plans of her own, too…"

Shilovsky had announced that he would not give up the children, and Bulgakov knew about this.

…Yelena had given her word that she would not try to arrange any rendez-vous with him, or go anywhere near the telephone.

It is possible that it was in the spring of that year (if not one or two years earlier) that a brief romance occurred, which is supposedly reflected in the plot of the novel that has now become a novel about a "poet" and his beloved Margarita. Although it is always a risky business to make assumptions about relationships of this kind, it may nevertheless be the case that in a writer's biography, some space ought to be found for them.

Over half a century later, in the spring of 1986, Margarita Petrovna Smirnova gave me her brief memoirs (along with a photograph showing her as a very beautiful young woman).

In her memoirs, as in her oral account, the things she remembered were to some extent merged with the things that she had read by that time in the novel: the very first time she read this work, signed with the name of a man she had long since forgotten, both she and her loved ones, who were referenced in some of the details of the story (Margarita Petrovna's sister worked at *Gudok* and knew Bulgakov), 'recognised' her in the novel's heroine…

We therefore have before us both part of a legend, and some real-life details from Bulgakov's life, from one of his adventures, which turned out to be related, at least, to the name of the novel's heroine.

Margarita Petrovna described how she had arrived back in Moscow one spring from her dacha ("What a pleasant feeling of freedom it was, I had all the time in the world. The children were at the dacha, my husband was on a business trip…") and was walking down the street holding some yellow spring flowers. She was caught up by a man dressed "very well, very smartly". She did not want to get to know him ("I am not in the habit of making new acquaintances on the sidewalk"), but he carried on walking after her, and eventually asked her to "slow down for a minute, so that I can introduce myself. He took off his hat, very respectfully, gave a bow, and said: "Mikhail Bulgakov". The name rang a bell, but who was he, who? I immediately sensed that he was a well-educated, extraordinary man." She did not think she had heard of *The Days of the Turbins* at that point. In her mind, the name was associated with a different Bulgakov – one that her father had told her about, who had been "one of those close to Tolstoy". […] When I met Mikhail

Afanasievich, I was sure that he was someone from Tolstoy's circle. What's more, the conversation soon turned to Tolstoy [...] He told me lots of interesting things about Tolstoy, and said that he had been going through his letters somewhere [this detail perhaps enables us to date the meeting to the time when he was working on a stage adaptation of *War and Peace* – i.e. the spring and summer of 1931 or 1932… - M.C.]

I found it terribly interesting to learn so many new things about Tolstoy. I had not yet read the memoirs of either Tatiana Andreyevna Kuzminskaya or Sergei Lvovich Tolstoy, and he spoke so knowledgeably about her and about the Behrs family. Mikhail Afanasievich said that Tolstoy was not respected in his own family, and that Sofya Andreyevna was forever nagging at him, scolding him, because he didn't understand that they had a big family, and the kids needed an education, yet he was spending money on his charitable works, on building schools, on publishing cheap books of folk stories. The children were all on the mother's side, with the exception of the youngest – Alexandra. Sometimes, they openly made fun of their father, of his asceticism, of his plebeian clothing.

Mikhail Afanasievich said: "That is what life can be like: a brilliant man, who is respected in his own country and further afield, is often misunderstood in his own family, and from his nearest and dearest gets neither support, nor empathy. Just think how difficult it must have been for him, how lonely he must have felt. I feel endlessly sorry for him!'

Mikh. Af. explored this theme of loneliness several times during conversations with me. I remember being struck by the pity he felt for Tolstoy. We have grown used to admiring Tolstoy, but the idea that one could, and indeed should, feel pity for him – that was new for me. [...]

I remember that at the end of the day, he asked me: 'Margarita Petrovna, have you read the Bible?' I replied: 'How fed up I am of Divinity lessons at school, and you expect me to want to read the Bible as well? That's all I need!' 'You'll read it, in due course!'

When we first met, he took certain liberties that I did not like very much. In response to some answer I gave, he burst out laughing and grabbed me by the shoulders in delight. I was terribly upset, I wanted to get away from him at once. He realised that, gave me a very serious look, apologised, and said: 'Believe me, that will never happen again!'

There was a second odd thing that occurred at the start of our friendship, too: he insistently asked me to join him at a café or restaurant, so that we could sit quietly together, and not have to walk and talk. He said he happened to have loads of money at the moment, which he had either earned or won, I forget – 'help me spend it!' I was very punctilious when it came to money, and I replied: 'To talk about money on the day we first meet one another – tut tut!' He was puzzled and said nothing for a long time, merely staring hard at me a number of times. He didn't take any more liberties, and our conversation was unusually engaging and frank. We simply couldn't seem to run out of things to say. I tried several times to say goodbye to him, but some new questions would come up, we would start talking again, and arguing, and, distracted by our conversation, we walked past the side-street that I should have turned into to get back home, and, step by step, without even noticing it, we arrived at the Rzhevsky station.

We turned back at 1 Meshchanskaya and once again, we couldn't find a way to part at the side-street, and without noticing walked on to Kolkhoznaya Square.

We walked that route from the station to the square several times. Neither of us wanted to part ways. In extraordinary intimacy had arisen between us, some sort of extreme, heartfelt attraction.

Just when we were getting on like a house on fire, he suddenly asked me why I had sad eyes? I had to tell him that I didn't have much in common with my husband, that I was bored in his company, and with his friends. Even in his rather noisy company I felt lonely. It was proving difficult to build a life for myself and with my husband, things were not only boring, but also difficult. Mikhail Afanasievich listened to me very attentively and with a degree of concern.

We stood on the embankment and strolled along it for a long time. There was a wind blowing from the Moscow river. I said that I loved putting my face under a warm breeze; I told him how nice it was to stand on a motor boat as it rushes across the sea, giving oneself up to the wind. I loved it very much when the warm breeze made my skirt billow, like a sail, and tousled and played with my hair: you feel like throwing your arms apart, you feel so good, so mischievous; you feel as though you're about to be whisked off your feet into the air. I remember how M.A. looked at me with gleaming eyes, when I talked about the warm breeze there, on the embankment. And suddenly, when I read the novel *The Master and Margarita*, I came across the words: 'She gave up her face to the wind.' What a remarkable way he had of remembering everything! That solitary line in the novel doesn't mean anything to anyone, and yet it inspired so many memories and emotions in me!

Our conversation turned to the sea, and the Caucasus. I told him that I had been to many cities in the south (my husband was a commissar-inspector for the railways of the RSFSR and immediately after our wedding, in

May 1921, he took me with him on an inspection trip across the Caucasus and the Trans-Caucasus. I helped with the secretarial work, and sometimes typed things up on the type-writer. We had been on a similar trip in the summer of 1923). Mikhail Afanasievich said that he had worked in the Caucasus too, in the same years. Suddenly, he took a step to one side, and his face somehow lit up, and he said, almost shouting: 'Margarita Petrovna! I saw you!' I couldn't help laughing. That took the biscuit – the idea that he'd seen me before! Where? When? Eight years had passed since then, at least, and he had suddenly remembered [...] he described my white dress fairly accurately (a Greek toga-suit which I had held onto after wearing it in a school play, Sophocles's *Trachiniae*). He said that he had seen me in the street, perhaps in Tbilisi or Batum, accompanied by two men (evidently my husband and his brother). He recalled a sensation of something light and bright, and I made fun of him: he had seen me once and that was enough for him to remember me! But perhaps it wasn't me at all; white dresses aren't exactly few and far between in the summertime. He looked me in the eyes, with a very serious expression and without the merest hint of a smile. He moved his face closer to mine and said to me, in a whisper: 'Margarita Petrovna! What is it, don't you realise that it would have been impossible not to remember you!' [...]

On that first day, he asked me why I was so well-dressed? Where had I got such nice shoes, such nice gloves (they were black silk ones, almost up to the elbow, with flared openings and a white hem)? I had no choice but to tell him that they had belonged to my mother, and that I had hung on to them. As for the shoes, I decided not to risk telling him that I had attached the bows and metal clasps to them myself, with my own hands.

Mikhail Afanasievich turned my handbag over in his hands for a long time, examined it carefully from every angle and gazed at me no less attentively and fixedly. I began to feel awkward: the handbag was a home-made one. I took it back from out of his hands.

A short while later he took hold of it again, glanced at me with a smile, and asked me who had sewn the yellow letter 'M' onto it.

'Margarita Petrovna, why won't you tell me? It's an interesting bag, who made it?'

I muttered something to the effect that I had done it of course, who else. And that only made me more embarrassed, since that wasn't altogether true: my mother had made the bag and given it to me as a gift.

Only later, when I found out more about Bulgakov's life, did I understand why that bag may have interested him so much. That bag must have reminded him of something, he had a sort of smile of understanding playing on the corners of his lips. [...]

We agreed to meet again in a week...

I went home, started doing some household chores, and after a while I went to the windows to water the flower and suddenly saw that M.A. was walking along the pavement opposite my home. I moved away from the window (I didn't want him to find out where I lived, I was afraid that might lead to all sorts of complications). But he didn't look at the windows, he just walked along lost in thought, with his head bowed. Then he almost came to a stop, lifted his head, gazed into the distance, and once walked slowly down the street.

When I had said goodbye to him in the street, I hadn't gone into the building via the main entrance, which could be seen from the street through the railings, but had instead walked from the gate into the courtyard, turned at the corner of the building and gone in via the tradesman's entrance. I thought that by doing so, he wouldn't be able to work out where I lived, which windows were mine. From the gate, you could see everything that is described on page 86 of book I: 'A little house in a garden... leading from the gate... Opposite, beneath the fence, there was a lilac tree, a lime tree, a maple...' There was also a little alleyway lined with poplar trees leading from the gate and, further along, a large white poplar.

One day, the following happened: I had arrived home from the dacha, and in the kitchen, my neighbour (Anna Ivanovna) says to me: "We were sitting in the courtyard, on a bench; some chap came along, not very tall, well-dressed; he walked around the courtyard, and looked at the windows, at the basement. Then he walked up to our bench and asked us: 'Is there a tall, beautiful young woman living here?' Laughing, we reply: 'Who is it you're after? The lady of the house, or the maid? They're both young and they're both beautiful. Only they're not here at the moment – they're at the dacha.' He walked around the courtyard, then came up to us again, and asked where exactly she lived? 'Right there,' we tell him, 'they live in half of this house; the windows are on both sides, overlooking the street and the courtyard. But tell us, who exactly are you looking for?' He said nothing in reply, and slowly walked to the gate. When we had said goodbye on the first day, I had asked him to stay on the other side of the street, and not to follow me. At the railing, he may have been able to see that I had turned at the corner of the building, but he wouldn't have known whether I had gone in via the porch, or perhaps walked down to the basement?

According to my neighbour, he came on two occasions, and that's why he writes that I lived in the upper part of a beautiful private house in a garden" (readers will forgive Margarita Petrovna, I hope, this simple-hearted identifying of herself with the character).

'Under the impression left on me by this encounter, I walked around in a sort of haze for several days and couldn't think about anything else. The meeting with him was so unusual, it had taken such a hold on us right from the very first minutes – it is hard to describe. It had been some sort of hallucination, as he put it. Even now, when so many years have gone past, I cannot recall that particular dream without a feeling of excitement. And at the time, I couldn't find my place in life, I kept thinking what is going to happen next? [...] I decided that whilst I was still capable of controlling myself, I had to part from him.' She remembers what he said to her: 'Margarita Petrovna, tell me, do you not like me? Am I bad in your eyes?'

I tried, of course, to convince him that things weren't so bad... [...] I said that now I would be even more lonely, that my soul felt drawn to him, that I had felt very good with him. I suddenly saw his face lighting up; he smiled, and said: 'Go on, keep talking, keep talking...' [...]

'Margarita Petrovna, if you should ever wish to see me, you shall always be able to find me. All you have to remember is this: Mikhail Bulgakov. And for my part, I shall never be able to forget you.'

When we parted, it was agonizing. Once again, we stood for a long time on the corner of the street. I asked him not to walk up to the gate.

He stayed on the other pavement. As I crossed the road, I looked back over my shoulder. And the last thing I remember is his hands, stretched out towards me. As though he was calling me, and was expecting me to go back to him right away. And what a wounded, insulted look there was on his face! He was looking at me and still saying something... And those arms on the other side of the railing, stretched out towards me...

It was all as he later wrote on page 94 of book II; only it was not Margarita and Woland, but him saying goodbye to me."

On 18th March, he writes a letter to Stanislavsky (who, a month earlier, after a long illness, had begun rehearsals for individual scenes from *Dead Souls* at his home in Leontievsky Side-street):

"Dear and greatly respected Konstantin Sergeyevich! I have left TRAM, since I cannot cope with TRAM work at all. I am writing to you to request that you include me, in addition to being one of the directors, as one of the actors at the Art Theatre, as well..."

On 19th April, in response to Bulgakov's letter of application, Stanisklavsky writes back with his decision: "I approve, that is agreed. I spoke to And. Serg. Bubnov about this. He has nothing against the idea." Bubnov had replaced Lunacharsky in 1929 as the people's commissariat for enlightenment and was in charge of the theatres.

What feelings did Bulgakov have that spring, on realising that a year after a conversation that had seemed to him to be so encouraging, his activities as a writer had been replaced by the profession of director and even actor? There are a number of documents that give us an idea of this. In this very period he starts writing a letter to the same person who had accompanied him with two epigrams from Nekrasov: "O muse! Our song is sung…" and "To the muse I shall return my voice."

After the opening line, he wrote: "Around one-and-a-half years have elapsed since I fell quiet. Now that I feel very sick, I want to ask you to become my first reader…" The letter was put aside at that point. An new draft of it was completed on 30th May, containing, on the right-hand side, a series of excerpts from Gogol's *Author's Confession* (*Avtorskaya Ispoved'*), including a long epigraph: "The further I go, the more strongly I feel the desire to be a modern writer. But I saw at that time, that when portraying modernity, one must not be in that lofty and peaceful state that is essential for a work of great and structured labour.

The present is too lively, it moves around too much, it irritates me too much; *the writer's pen insensitively moves into satire.*

… It always seemed to me that in my life, I would have to go through some great self-sacrifice, and that precisely so as to serve my country, *I would have to be educated somewhere far away from it.*

… All I knew was that I was travelling not in order to marvel at other lands, but rather so as to endure them, exactly as if I sensed that I would find out the value of Russia only outside Russia, and would achieve love for her by being far away from her." And immediately after the epigram, the letter began: "I ardently request that you petition the Government of the USSR, on my behalf, to send me on foreign leave for the period between 1st July and 1st October 1931.

I wish to inform you that after one-and-a-half years of silence, new creative ideas are burning within me with irresistible force, and that these ideas are wide-ranging and powerful, and I ask the Government to give me the opportunity to bring them to fruition.

Since the end of 1930, I have been suffering from a severe form of neurasthenia, with bouts of fear and sadness in my heart, and right now I am finished.

There are ideas in me, but there is no physical strength, none whatsoever of the conditions needed to carry out my work." This is the second document, after the poem, testifying to Bulgakov's condition one year on from that famous conversation. In it, he asserted: "The reason for my illness is known to me very distinctly.

In the broad field of Russian literary arts in the USSR, I was a lone wolf. I was advised to dye my fur. That advice was absurd. Whether a wolf has its fur dyed or has it shaved off altogether, it still does not look anything like a poodle.

People treated me as if I were a wolf, too. And for several years I was chased using all the rules of the literary holding cage, in an enclosed courtyard." One of his favourite books – N. Reutt's *Hunting with Hounds* (*Psovaya Okhota*, 1848) – seems to have prompted him with the hunting term he needed, signifying the baiting of a beast that has already been caught.

Bulgakov was not an outcast by nature, who feels like the person described above – "under all the executive powers of the world".

The image of a wolf being hounded took on a malevolent and to some extent challenging sense in the letter: having of course thought through such a powerful stylistic approach with great care, Bulgakov was implying, to the mighty recipient of his letter, that he saw the situation he was in as that of an animal caught in a trap, a situation that had last "several years already" (during which time he had submitted applications to leave the country on several occasions, none of which had elicitied a response – right up until April 1930). He now interpreted his consent to Stalin's suggestion in their conversation back in 1930 – that he stay here and go and work at the theatre – as follows: "The animal declared that he was no longer a wolf, no longer a writer. He rejects his profession. He falls silent. This, let us make no bones about it, is pusillanimity.

No such writer, who would keep silent, exists. If he kept silent, then he was not a real one. And if a real one were to keep silent – he would die. The reason for my illness is many years of being hunted down, and then silence."

... At this very time, a poem by Mandelstam is doing the rounds in Moscow's literary circles, written in the second half of March (1931) – with the same unexpected and powerful metaphor of the wolf:

... Onto my shoulders has leapt the age of the wolfhound,
And yet by blood no wolf am I...
... Because by blood no wolf am I
And only by an equal am I killed.

If one tries to understand the poem in a literal sense (which is hardly likely to be a good idea), the poet was striving to disown the humiliating and horrifying fate of the wolf: i.e. that of becoming, sooner or later, the prey of the dogs. As for Bulgakov, he assesses his rejection of his position as a wolf as a rejection of his "profession", as "pusillanimity". Mandelstam, who had written, just before this: "To the world of sovereign states I was only childishly related," "And to it not by a scintilla of my soul am I obligated", talks about the tragic mistake of the century: he, a poet, ought not to be the prey of wolf-hounds! This is expressed by him as early as in 1922: "The parasite merely trembles on the threshold of new days" (*Century* [*Vek*]) – in the same year in which Bulgakov was pondering that very same threshold: "...But am I going to live?" In 1931, Bulgakov proudly asserts his own blood-ties, different from those of other breeds, to a different state, one that has been destroyed. For the author of the tale *The Heart of a Dog*, which had been in someone else's hands since 1926 and had perhaps been read by Stalin, it was only natural to insist on how he differed from both the Sharikovs of this world, and the wolfhounds. He was not being bound by the role of a *miserable* that was prepared for all parasites, but did not consider it possible to refuse it.

Social life was being increasingly shaped in such a way that positions which were different at the outset were coming closer together, and when Mandelstam writes in May and early June, 1931: "... We shall die like infantrymen, But shall glorify neither potboilers, nor lies" – this is very close to the general meaning of Bulgakov's letter from 30th May, 1931.

The desperate condition of the author of the letter can be seen in the fact that felt it necessary to make the recipient fully acquainted with his activity in the period of just over a year that had elapsed since their conversation. "In the last year, I have done the following:

- √ despite great difficulties, turned N. Gogol's *Dead Souls* into a play
- √ worked as a director at the Art Theatre, at the rehearsals for this play
- √ was appointed a director at the Art Theatre for all campaigns and revolutionary festivities in the year in question
- √ worked at TRAM in Moscow, switching from daytime shifts at the Art Theatre to evening shifts at TRAM.
- √ left TRAM on 15.III.31, when I sensed that my brain was refusing to work and that I would not be of any use to TRAM
- √ undertook to put on a play at the Sanprosvet theatre (and I shall finish it by July).

√   And at night, I started writing.
√   But I overstrained myself."

Apparently, what he began to write was the novel about the devil that he had abandoned two years ago. Some paragraphs contained in two notebooks, entitled *Drafts of the Novel* (*Chernoviki Romana*), indicate that he did not manage to continue the novel that year: as the author suggested in his letter, he "overstrained himself" – one can assume this was by no means simply because of an abundance of work, including work that was utterly alien to him (the kind he always found it particularly painful to do), but also because of thoughts which had already acquired the nature of running around in a vicious circle to no avail.

On 30th May 1931, Bulgakov wrote: "… I have been given a very serious warning by great figures in art, who have travelled abroad, that it will be impossible for me to stay there.

I was warned that if the Government opens the door to me, I must be extremely cautious, so as not to slam that door shut behind me in despair and burn my bridges, and not to end up with problems that are a little worse than the banning of my plays." As we can see, the phrases he uses are now different from the ones in the previous letter. "… In conclusion, I wish to say to you, J.V., that my dream as a writer is to be summoned to see you in person. Believe me, this is not only because I see in this the most beneficial opportunity, but because your conversation with me over the telephone in April 1930 left a deep trace on my memory. You said: "Perhaps you do need, after all, to go abroad?" Touched by this sentence, I worked for a year not out of fear as a director at the theatres of the USSR." Here, Bulgakov is trying, for the first time, to play the situation out again, to return to a conversation that has alrady been completed; as he reminds his interlocutor about his question, he wants to give a different, more differentiated answer to it: no, he does not wish to go abroad, he has not lost hope of being able to work here, but he would like to go away just for a short time – to see the world.

We cannot say with complete certainty that this draft of the letter was the final one, but a letter to J.V. Stalin was, in any event, despatched on or around this date: it is mentioned in Bulgakov's correspondence with Veresayev.

So Bulgakov had sent his letter; and once again, like the previous year, he began waiting for an answer. The reply must have arrived no later than two weeks later – judging by the previous one and by the fact that Bulgakov asked for some time off starting on 1st July – meaning that a little time must have been required to lodge his request, something that, in the event of approval, the recipient of the letter would understand.

In the middle of June, he receives a telegram: Natalya Alekseyevna Venkstern, with whom he had established friendly relations in recent years, invites the Bulgakovs to Zubtsov (where the Vazuza meets the Volga) for the summer holidays, and on 17th June adds a note to a letter from Lyubov Yevgenievna: "I received the telegram, thank you for your friendly attention! I shall definitely try to visit you, but do not know when and how I will be able to (busy with the production at the Santheatre). If I intend to come over, I shall send a cable. Greetings, greetings! Yours amicably, M. Bulgakov."

Although the period in which the reply to his letter has already elapsed, he is still hoping, he does not leave Moscow.

On 29th June, he writes to Veresayev: "… the theatre has gobbled me up whole. I do not exist. Predominantly *Dead Souls*. In addition to the adaptations and corrections, to whose reign, apparently, there will be no end, the directors, and also the actors (I have been one of their number since the autumn – how do you like that, by the way?) […] This all ended in a very serious way: I fell ill, Vikenty Vikentievich. […] And a poisonous thought sometimes occurs to me: have I not perhaps already completed my circle? In academic terms this is known as neurasthenia, if I'm not mistaken. And then a miracle from Leningrad: a theatre there commissioned a play from me. I am making a final effort to get on my feet and show that my imagination has not run dry. Or perhaps it has."

On 1st July, he writes to N.A. Venkstern: "Everything depends on my affairs. If everything passes off successfully [the main failure by this time, essentially, had become obvious. – M.C.], I shall try in July, perhaps between 10th and 20th, to get to Zubtsov […] My plan: to sit in the wings on my own and write, delighting in high-brow literary chat with you. Besides writing, I am going to maintain a stripped-down lifestyle: a robe, slippers, sleeping, eating […] And those San-friends of yours! I shall tell you many funny things, and things intended especially for you, when I arrive."

In the first few days of July, Bulgakov concludes his negotiations with the Red Theatre and the Vakhtangov Theatre for a play on the subject of a future war.

On 7th July, he sends a cable to Natalya Venkstern in Zubtsov: "Cable me about whether there is an isolated room for me." 9th July: "I shall come on the twelfth."

No reply to his letter to Stalin was forthcoming: Bulgakov was not able to step into the same river twice.

With his hopes of a journey overseas dashed once and for all, he travels to the Volga – for a short time, apparently. Here, he puts all his energy into the play *Adam and Eve* – his only real hope, essentially, of getting his work back onto the stage.

On 22nd July 1931, he writes to Veresayev: "Today, on my return from Zubtsov, where I spent 12 days bathing and writing, I received your letter from 17.VIII and was delighted by it." Talking about the amount of work he has been doing lately, he described it as "unnatural", adding: "It stems from the darkest unrest, from a trade-off for all the trivial things which I ought not to have had to work on at all, from my utter hopelessness, from nervous exhaustion, powerless efforts. My wing is broken." On 25th and 26th August, continuing the same letter, Bulgakov explained the reason for his condition. The reason was rooted in that conversation from over a year ago and its consequences; or rather, from the absence of the consequences which, at first, he had confidently anticipated.

"There is a torturous unhappiness within me" – it was with these powerful words that Bulgakov defined his mood over the last year. "It is the fact that the conversation I had expected to have with the General Secretary did not take place. This is a horror and a black grave. I have a frenzied desire to see other countries, if only for a brief time. I get up in the morning with this thought and I go to bed at night with it.

For a year I racked my brains, trying to work out what had happened. After all, I wasn't hallucinating when I heard the words he uttered, was I? He did, after all, utter the line: 'Perhaps you do indeed need to leave and go abroad?'

He spoke those words! What happened? He wanted to invite me to see him…!"

In this letter, we see yet another version of the sentence spoken by Stalin, as Bulgakov remembered it (in his letter to Stalin from 1931 he had reproduced it as follows: '… You do, indeed, need to go abroad…')

Y.S. Bulgakova later offers two further versions of this sentence, in her diary for 1956 ("Perhaps it's really true – you are asking to go abroad?") and in the text of the entry when printed up.

This appears to suggest that this sentence, which became a source of agonizing thoughts for Bulgakov over the next few years and the subject of endless interpretations, in the condition that he was in the grip of during the conversation, was not one that he could remember verbatim.

The second, far more pertinent thing that stems from the letter to Veresayev is that the line uttered by Bulgakov himself, which, quarter of a century after his death, became a key one in terms of his official status ("I have thought a great deal lately about whether or not a Russian writer can live outside his motherland. And it seems to me that he cannot"), did not seem to Bulgakov, one year later, to have been one that brought the matter to a close. This means that it in no way sounded as definite and polished as it was recorded by Yelena Sergeyevna in 1956. One can only suppose that there were in fact several disconnected sentences, uttered in a flurry in his agitation, under the effect of that "shyness, which flew over me like a fainting fit" (remember that it seems fair to assume that these lines from his letter to P.S. Popov in 1932 describe the situation surrounding the conversation in 1930). They did not rule out the idea that this topic might be discussed in the new conversation that was cunningly promised to Bulgakov.

On 12th August, Veresayev wrote to Bulgakov:

"I received your letter – and not from your words, but from the letter itself, I sensed how ill you are and how crushed everything is in your soul. And for me, it is utterly beyond doubt that one of the reasons for your painful spiritual dejection is to be found in this abstention from writing."

To which abstention was he referring? What he appears to have meant, first and foremost, was the novel – i.e. something that was obligatory from an internal perspective. He thought of the play, on this occasion, as something he was doing to order, which had come into being outside his inner willingness to bring precisely these kinds of ideas to fruition, and it took him a considerable effort to write it.

Veresayev tried to persuade him to write independently of the situation that had been created, and even put himself forward as an example: "I am giving my judgement now based on my own experience. For two years, I worked on a novel, for 1½ years I worked at a factory in the most difficult conditions, and now, this spring, I worked out for myself, with utter certainty, that as regards getting it published now [...] there is no point even thinking about it. The question arises: why bother to write, then? But I pushed this question aside, and I have just worked devotedly all summer long, and it has given me an enormous amount of pleasure..."

It is highly unlikely he was able fully to understand Bulgakov's condition that summer – he had already some forms of living and working that were acceptable for him, that were balanced with reality, and he was calling on Bulgakov to do the same thing: "I am continuing to think that my hope of a holiday abroad is an utterly crazy hope. Yes, that is precisely it: 'who could believe it?' [...] I think that the thinking, there, is as follows:

'he wrote that he's dying of need, that he's even prepared to be a stage-hand at the theatre; and now he's got a job, and he earns very nearly the party maximum. So as far as anything else is concerned – I'm sorry, we've no time for it!'"[16]

---

[16] A commentary on this letter from Veresayev is provided by the memoirs of B.L. Leontiev: "For the whole winter he went off, for example, to the Moscow galoshes factory 'Bogatyr' in Bogorodsk. Abandoning a nice apartment and saying goodbye to the usual home comforts, he rented a shoebox of a room in a cramped worker's apartment. And he was 'hired' at the factory as a medical doctor… A year later, though, his interesting book about two Komsomol members appeared – *Sisters* (*Syostry*) (*Literaturnaya Rossiya* [*Literary Russia*], 1965, 8 Oct.)

6

That summer, Y.I. Zamyatin arrived in Moscow. After his travels in the years 1929-1930, he was in the same position that Bulgakov had been in a year earlier (and towards which he was now getting closer once again); on 15th July 1929, Zamyatin wrote to Bulgakov: "As you know, I no longer write plays," and a year later, on 25th October 1930, he joked: "To you – as a director and master of dramaturgy – I am sending a young female playwright…" In the summer of 1931, Zamyatin, like Bulgakov one year earlier, was pondering some decisive steps.

It was to Gorky that he once again appealed for help: on 3rd June 1931, he wrote to his wife in Leningrad: "Kryuchkov assured me that it is a matter of days. The day after tomorrow, probably, I shall go and see the old man at his dacha – it is better for him that way"; he spent some time with Gorky on 14th, and on 16th he informed Lyudmila Nikolayevna that Gorky "was very kind", "he agreed to take steps and today or tomorrow my letter will be "in the right hands"; an important addition: Gorky "is asking for some time to think" and, the next day, once again "asks for some time to think it over". "As for Mikhail Afanasievich, the two of us have only spoken on the phone so far; I shall probably see him only tomorrow." On 29th June, without waiting for a decision to be taken on his case, Zamyatin was getting ready to go home, to Leningrad, but Gorky's secretary, P. Kryuchkov, made him stay longer, promising that he would hear something soon. Thus, he spent almost the whole summer in Moscow, and on 9th June he wrote to his wife: "If I get delayed here any longer – come over, of course: it is not hard to arrange accommodation, with Mikh[ail] Af[anasievich] at least (he is alone at the moment) or with the Vakhtangov set."

He met up with Bulgakov a number of times that summer.

S. Yermolinsky recalled: the three of them went to Park Kultury, with the express purpose of talking about Bulgakov's letter from 1930 without any witnesses. Zamyatin knew about his second letter, of course, but the subject of their conversation was the first one. "You made an error – that was why your request was refused," said Zamyatin. "You did not construct your letter the right way: you got bogged down in discussions about the revolution and evolution, about satire…! You ought instead to have written concisely and clearly that you are asking to be released – full stop! No, I shall write the right kind of letter!" The difference, though, was that Bulgakov did not share the same goals and desires as Zamyatin at all, either that summer or at the time when he wrote the letter. One must assume, however, that the impression made by the fact that Zamyatin, with Gorky's help, soon received a positive response to his letter, was stunning.

Zamyatin had taken what he considered to have been Bulgakov's "error" into account. The tone of his letter was decisive, and his request was expressed very decisively.

He asked to be given permission "temporarily, for one year at least, to leave the country – so that I can come back as soon as it becomes possible here to serve great ideas in literature without having to kow-tow to little people, as soon as the view of artists of the word here starts to change at least a little. And this time, I am sure of it, is not so very far away, because once the material basis is successfully created, there will inevitably arise the matter of creating the superstructure: that of art and literature, which would truly be worthy of the revolution… I could have based my request to leave the country on more common motives, too, although they are less serious ones… All of these motives are obvious: but I do not want to hide the fact that the main reason why I am asking for permission to leave the country with my wife is the hopeless position I am in, as a writer, here, the death sentence handed to me, here. The particular attention that was given, on your side, to other writers who have appealed to you, allows me to hope that my request, too, will be respected" (this ending was a reference, perhaps, not only to Pilnyak, who had recently been allowed to do some foreign travel, but also to the conversation with Bulgakov).

On 22nd August, a handwritten draft of the play *Adam and Eve* was completed; over the next few weeks, an agreement was concluded with the Leningrad Dramatic Theatre for a stage adaptation of L. Tolstoy's *War and Peace*. One must imagine that Bulgakov cannot have been indifferent to the fact that exactly one year on, he was once again involved in an adaptation for the stage – albeit of a novel by one of his great teachers, this time.

On 30th August, Bulgakov writes to Stanislavsky, explaining that he has "received an offer from one of the theatres to write a play about a future war", that "an utterly iron necessity compelled me to deliver" the play to the Vakhtangov Theatre, and that in this case, it was fairly important to him that there should be no clause in the contract about the advance having to be returned in the event of a ban – a clause that was always included as standard in contracts with the Art Theatre ("I am eternally under the threat of a ban. Such a clause is unthinkable!"). "I am not physically capable of waiting until the autumn", he wrote, and he offered his play – "if you only have the desire to include it in the theatre's plan." "I say again: iron necessity now guides me in all my contracts."

In the early autumn of 1931, Bulgakov read *Adam and Eve* to the directors of the *Red Theatre*, and they immediately rejected the play – albeit with a great deal of embarrassment.

At roughly the same time, a reading of the play took place at the Vakhtangov Theatre – according to L.Y. Belozerskaya's memoirs, in the presence of the head of the Land and Air Forces, Alksin: "He said that he couldn't put the play on, because Leningrad perishes during it." At that, the whole matter was brought to an end.

Bulgakov spends the whole summer working on a copy of *A Cabal of Hypocrites* and on 30th September sends it to Gorky, with the following letter: "Esteemed Aleksei Maximovich! I am enclosing with this letter a copy of my play, *Molière*, with the corrections I made at the suggestion of the Main Repertoire Committee. One of the proposals was that I should replace the title *A Cabal of Hypocrites* with a different one. Yours respectfully, M. Bulgakov." The change of title (the fact that the initiative for this stemmed from the Glavrepertkom is in itself a striking fact – what reason could the Committee have had for wanting to protect the hypocrites exposed by the title?) complicated the fate of this play in many ways, as was to become clear in the future.

The text of the letter indicates, at any rate, the presence of a provisional agreement with Gorky, who was actively involved in the play's fate that autumn. And, sure enough, on 3rd October 1931, the long-awaited permission to put the play on arrived: just when all hope seems to be lost, a tiny slither of light at the end of the tunnel appears. Twists and turns of fate, such as these, would in later years become something akin to Bulgakov's permanent residence.

On 6th October, Bulgakov writes to the GBDT in Leningrad, offering the theatre *Molière*, now that it has been given the all-clear, and on 12th he signs the contract that they take over to him.

Towards the end of October, Bulgakov unexpectedly receives a letter from P.S. Popov; he had heard no news of him since his arrest in the autumn of 1930.

Popov wrote that he was in Leningrad (he had been given "minus one" – the least painful of the possible ways in which his fate could have been decided, which his wife was only able to secure for him thanks to the name of her grandfather, a great man) and was working on 22 "previously unpublished" notebooks that had belonged to Pushkin. "One doesn't feel drawn to the theatre here," he went on; we want to go to the opera house. At the Alexandrinka there's something called *Fear* being performed every day [a play by A.N. Afinogenov – M.C.], but word has it this fear is not particularly genuine. Leningrad is certainly a genuine city: there is something powerful, something solid about it by comparison with Moscow's little streets and sidestreets. There are untold numbers of people, though. It is hard to believe: in the month of September alone, 80,000 people moved here. We are in step with the times, it seems. [He was hinting to Bulgakov at the vast number of Muscovites who had been exiled to Leningrad; three years later, many of them would find themselves forced to make a far longer onward journey. – M.C.]. Is Kolya alive and well [N.N. Lyamin – M.C.] and what is he up to – I have been waiting to hear from him but haven't received any news." This was the way in which he delivered the news that had been bandied about in 1929-31 throughout the cities and towns by the Moscow intelligentsia. Bulgakov hurriedly wrote a reply: "have just received your letter dated 24th October. I was extremely pleased by it." And then he suggested: "If money is tight, please cable me."

Popov's letter was written on luxurious green vellum with white and gold lettering embossed in the left corner, prompting the following lines in Bulgakov's letter: "you knocked me down dead with the paper on which you write. Ah, what good paper! And look what sort of paper I have to write my reply on! And with a pencil, to boot. The ink I have is completely indelible. In a couple of days I shall have to devote my attentions fully to Anna Ilinishna's brilliant grandfather [the adaptation of *War and Peace* was begun one month earlier, but then postponed – M.C.]... I had planned to go to Leningrad yesterday, taking advantage of a short break at the Art Theatre, but I received a card asking me to appear at the Military Commissariat tomorrow. I imagine that this is a cross-examination. [...] Kolya is doing very well" (this meant that the Lyamins were still in place, in Moscow); my *Molière* was given the letter B (permission to be performed everywhere)."

"Dear Yevgeny Ivanovich," he wrote to Zamyatin on the very same day. "What sort of fashion is this – not writing to your old friends? When are you going abroad? I was told that at the end of October or the start of November, you are going to come to Moscow. Drop me a few lines to say when? My theatrical affairs are calling me to Leningrad, and I was all ready to go, but in addition to my Leningrad affairs, there are also, as you know, my Moscow ones, so I am putting off my trip until November." As we shall see later, this postponement proved to be fatal: Bulgakov's presence in Leningrad might perhaps have prevented the events which took place in the first half of November from unfolding. "So then, write to me quickly," Bulgakov continued, "and tell me when you are going to visit Moscow and where you will be staying. My *Molière* has been given the go-ahead. First of all for Moscow and Leningrad only, but then everywhere else (letter B). It's good news. Say hello from me to the famous traveller Lyudmila Nikolayevna!" And stressing once again that Zamyatin should let him know when he is going to arrive, Bulgakov finished off his letter like this: "It is pleasant for a provincial like myself to get the chance to admire a tourist's pipe and suitcase!" This jocular line spoke volumes both to the writer of the letter and its recipient.

On 28th October, Zamyatin writes his reply: "Well then, it's hurrah for the three M's: Mikhail, Maxim and *Molière*! […] It appears you are getting into dramaturgy, and I am getting into Ahasuerus."

These words identified the fork in the road, at which the literary paths and paths through life of these writers, bound by a friendship of 5 or 6 years, had diverged; both men might, with a large degree of confidence, have predicted that they had diverged forever. For Bulgakov at least, if not for Zamyatin, the words about Ahasuerus would have made him think about a line spoken by one of the characters from the play *Flight*, Charnota, who in the final scene of the play remains in Constantinople and bids farewell to Golubkov and Korzukhina, who are returning to Russia: "So then, our paths are diverging, fate has torn us apart. Some have been turned to ashes, some have been sent to Petersburg; where am I to go? Who am I now? I am the Eternal Jew from now on! I am Ahasuerus. I'm the Flying Dutchman! I'm a dog's devil!"

"Dear Ahasuerus!" Bulgakov began the letter he wrote to Zamyatin on 31st October. "Of the three M's in Moscow, there are now, alas, only two: Mikhail and *Molière*" (by that time, Gorky had long since been in Sorrento). In six months, he would once again start a letter with this greeting.

In the same letter, Zamyatin informed him of his departure date: "My onward journey will probably begin on 14/XI. I will be in Moscow on the 4th or 5th, I should think…" Sure enough, Zamyatin set off no later than at the end of November; they doubtless met up in Moscow and said their goodbyes to one another.

In November and December, Bulgakov is still firmly of the belief that, as Zamyatin had put it, he had got into dramaturgy: i.e. he was sure that *Molière* would be a success on the stage. On 25th December, he writes to Gorky: "My *Molière* has been given approval for performances – at first only in Moscow and Leningrad, but thereafter in accordance with the letter 'B' category.

Knowing how significant your good review of the play was in terms of securing permission, I wish to thank you, from my soul. I was given permission to send the play to Berlin, and I have sent it to Fisherferlag, with whom I usually sign contracts on the protection of my plays and on productions of them overseas." (Gorky soon sent his review of the play to the publishing house).

On 22nd December, Bulgakov resumes his work on the stage adaptation of *War and Peace*; on 31st December, he writes an ecstatic letter to Stanislavsky, who has been taking part in the rehearsals for *Dead Souls* throughout the last month: "The aim of this non-business letter is to express the admiration that I have been feeling these last few days. In the space of three hours, you transformed that key scene, which had become moribund and was going nowhere, into a vibrant scene! The magic of the theatre is alive and well…!"

Thus, at least two productions were in the pipeline: *Molière* in Leningrad and *Dead Souls* at the Art Theatre. And Bulgakov had promised to give the play *Adam and Eve* to the Bakinsky Theatre – it had not been banned, at any rate, the other theatres had rejected it before it was given permission to be staged.

7

The next year did not waste any time in throwing up some surprises, however – both of the pleasant and the unpleasant varieties. This year became a critical juncture in both Bulgakov's private life and his literary life. From the autumn of 1932 onwards, one can discern in his fate, when seen retrospectively, some sort of unified struggle, one that was no longer changing.

Fyodor Mikhalsky, who would be forever recorded for posterity some years later as Filipp Filippovich in *A Theatrical Novel*, recalled, in the 1960s, the events of mid-January 1932:

"I have a clear memory of the day when, in K.S. Stanislavsky's study, a telephone call came through from a member of the Commission for the management of the Bolshoi Theatre and the Art Theatre, A.S. Yendukidze, who asked: would the theatre be able to create a new version of the *Turbins* within roughly a month. "Yes, yes, of course!" The board of directors, the Directorial collegium and the Production department were all summoned, and they immediately set about bringing the play back to life.

I immediately called Mikhail Afanasievich at home. And in response, after a moment's silence, I heard a disconsolate, quivering voice: "Fyodor Nikolayevich, could you come over and see me right away."

... So there I am at Pirogovskaya Street, and I walk into the front room. Mikhail Afanasievich is reclining on the sofa, with his feet in some hot water, and cold compresses on his head and his heart. "Well then, tell me all about it, tell me!" I repeated the story about the call from A.S. Yenukidze and about the festive mood at the theatre. By making a great effort, Mikhail Afanasievich got to his feet. He had to do something, after all. "Let's go, let's go!" And we set off to the Union of Writers, to the Department of authors' rights and, finally, to the Art Theatre. Here, he was greeted with congratulations, friendly embraces and joyful words.

From that moment on, *The Turbins* was to remain in the theatre's repertoire for a long time; it was taken on tours to Leningrad and Kiev, with Mikhail Afanasievich often travelling to those places to join us. I can hear his jolly, teasing voice at the Palaces of Culture in Leningrad, and at the

Astoria, where we were all staying, and at the evening get-togethers in the little internal garden at the Continental hotel in Kiev... There is a long way to go before we hear that jolly voice, though. For the time being, as Mikhalsky himself tells me, Bulgakov has his feet in some hot water and cold compresses on his heart. A man who holds a degree in medicine, with honours, has a good idea of what exactly he ought to take in such cases. "Do you already know?" he writes to P.S. Popov on 25th January. "Has the news reached you in Leningrad and Tryalevo? No? Then allow me to tell you: on 15th January, I received a call from the Theatre in the afternoon, and they informed me that *The Days of the Turbins* is to be brought back to the stage, as a matter of urgency. I take no pleasure in admitting this: this news oppressed me. I began to feel physically sick. There was a flicker of joy, but right now I am feeling sad. My heart, my heart!" If we read the letter containing this message from the start, we see just how joyless it is: "Dear Pavel Sergeyevich! Here, at last, is the reply to your last letter. Insomnia, my faithful companion nowadays, is coming to the rescue and guiding my pen. And so, dear friend, what should one eat when drinking vodka, you ask?" The letter from P.S. Popov, dated 28th December 1931, to which he was replying, had read as follows: "Dear Mikhail Afanasievich! Sorry, but you are making a glaring error [a hint at the delay in the visit to Leningrad that had been promised back in November – M.C.]. You did not give any thought to what you should eat with your vodka. There can be nothing better than a strong, salty, fragrant gherkin. You will say that a mushroom is better. You are wrong. The gherkins were brought over from Moscow. But there is already a *sagginess* to be seen in them. You understand, I hope, that one can't get very far with sagginess. A good gherkin must be fragrant and *strong*, as stated above. You will say: ham. Yes – ham. That's right: the gammon will soon be cured with smoke. Our old landlady has already seen to everything at the smoke house in Pavlovsk. But ham is good with gherkins, too. So hurry up." The form of the letter served as a kind of literary challenge, defining to some extent the form of the reply and perhaps prompting a whole series of letters written in January – April 1932.

And so, Bulgakov replied firmly, "Ham. But that's not all. One must have one's vodka and the snack that goes with it at dusk, on an old divan with stains on it, surrounded by old and loyal things. A dog must be sitting on the floor beside your chair, and no sound of trams must be audible. As I write this, it is six o'clock in the morning, and the trams are already making a howl as they leave the depot. My accursed accommodation is creaking and groaning. But incidentally, I am not going to tempt fate, or else in the summer: what do you know, you've lost it – the contract is terminated.

... Here in my hole [the apartment was half in the basement – M.C.] I have some terrible residents to keep me company: bronchitis, rheumatism and a little black lady – neurasthenia. There is no way I can get them kicked out. To hell with it! I ought to move out myself.

Where would I go?

Where, Pavel Sergeyevich?

By the way, I suppose a letter like this won't give you much pleasure, and I am going to move on to other news." Only then did he inform the recipient of the letter about the events of ten days previously – the phone call from the theatre concerning *The Days of the Turbins*.

The prompts would go on being felt in each subsequent letter throughout those months. His personal life was starting to unravel. Lyubov Yevgenievna took a strong liking for horse-riding, then for cars; people for whom Bulgakov had no need began to barge their way into his home. A telephone hung over his writing desk, and his wife was forever chatting to her friends merrily. Yelena Sergeyevna told me about the following episode in 1969 (Bulgakov had told her about it): "He once said to her: 'Lyuba, this is impossible, I'm trying to work here!' And she replied, thoughtlessly: 'Well, it doesn't matter, you're no Dostoevsky!' He turned pale," Yelena Sergeyevna told me. "He was never able to forgive Lyuba for that." Marika Chimishkian, who often visited the Bulgakovs' home on Pirogovskaya at that time, told me, on 26th November 1969: "One day, I went in to see them – Lyuba wasn't there – and saw Mikhail Afanasievich in his dressing gown and cap, on all fours beside the wall, with a paraffin heater on the floor; that was his way of drying the apartment, he always thought it seemed damp. He was terribly embarrassed and asked me not to tell anyone." Such a story would undoubtedly have provoked roars of laughter in the company of Lyubov Yevgenievna, but for his part, this kind of merriment was already oppressing him. His wife loved pranks: he had been fond of them too until recently, but now, everything was somehow hitting a wrong note. Let us continue Marika's story: "One day, the maid opened the door and then came running back out: 'Lyubov Yevgenievna, what am I to do, Pyotr Ivanovich has arrived with bare feet!' In fact, this was Petya Vasiliev: he had attached some huge feet made of papier-mache to his boots... Lyuba said to me: 'Lie down on my bed at once, Maka will be here soon!' I lie down, she covers me with a blanket and my enormous bare feet are sticking out at the end of the bed. At that point Mikhail Afanasievich arrived, and he asked how things were going at home. Everything was fine, only something had happened to Marika – her feet had got all swollen.' He comes into Lyuba's room and sees my legs... Well, then, of course, he shouted at us an awful lot..." He seems to have found it particularly hard to bear "medical" pranks: his sense of responsibility as a doctor, which had stayed with him all that time, would spring to life in a flash, preventing him from assessing the situation properly.

For obvious reasons, one might call into question the objective accuracy of this story, and of other small but pertinent details. (He loved freshly-brewed tea, Yelena told me. He would leave his glass on the side and ask: "Could you brew some tea?" And the lady of the house would exchange winks with the maid, and the maid would say: "But I've only just brewed some!"). In the accounts of Lyubov's friends, however, one finds confirmation of this account: it appears that life in the building on Pirogovskaya Street really was unfolding as though its mantra were: "You're no Dostoevsky!" The lady of the house was a vivacious person, an extraordinary person; she had her own interests, her own circle of friends, and her friends loved her. Let us not try to judge how highly she assessed the talent of the man she lived with. His life was not, at any rate, at the centre of her attention.

In any case, any attempts to look for rhyme or reason would be senseless. Where things had once been pleasant and agreeable, suddenly things became unpleasant and odious. Their housing had started to creak and groan – and so had life itself.

There was plenty to think about, it has to be said.

The Days of the Turbins was being brought back to the stage, urgently, as we have seen.

But the period of waiting had probably been too long ("My heart, my heart!"). And no matter how hard the people at the Art Theatre tried, excitedly and ecstatically, to rephrase the question that had effectively been asked: why has there been no sign of *The Days of the Turbins* on the stage for so long? – after which it had returned instantaneously, he himself could remember perfectly well, and could have checked in his copy anyway, that back in March 1930 he had informed the government, in a letter, that all of his plays had been cut from the repertoire. One can imagine the tension he felt as he waited, that spring, for the return to the stage of at least one of them. The permission probably arrived at the very moment when he had got tired of waiting for it – and that was why it had "oppressed" him.

At this time, Popov was playing the role of an expert in Bulgakov's biography – and he refuted the rumours which, as we can see, had already come into being in literary circles in Moscow and Leningrad (and have continued right up until our times) about a "friendship" between Bulgakov and Stalin. The phenomenon of the grapevine, of the "Moscow rumour mill", was one that interested Bulgakov a great deal; it was these rumours that prompted him, one must suppose, to create a whole series of comic anecdotes about this friendship in later years.

... In response to the Muscovites' questions, Bulgakov gave the following answer in his long letter to Popov:

"I know.

Halfway through January 1932, for reasons which are not known to me and which I do not wish to go into, the Government of the USSR issued a remarkable order to the Art Theatre: it was to bring back the play *The Days of the Turbins*.

For the author of this play, this means that he – the author – has had part of his life returned to him. That's all there is to it."

In Bulgakov's own interpretation of "what this means", there is no great beauty in his epistolary language (although it is clear that he put a lot of thought into the forms of his letters to Popov), and there is reluctance (again, dictated by the circumstances of the correspondence) to hide what he is really thinking. Instead, there is a desire to draw a line under his own thoughts, which have now plagued him for almost two years.

People who worked at the Art Theatre and Yelena Sergeyevna herself later gave accounts to the effect that in January 1932, Stalin had gone to the Art Theatre to see the play *Burning Heart* (*Goryacheye Serdtse*). One of the senior directors – quite possibly Nemirovich-Danchenko himself – had somehow explained the situation to him in terms that were suitable for such a conversation, and something akin to concern was supposedly expressed. And the telephone call from A.S. Yenukidze followed the next day.

Did this provide a sufficient explanation to Bulgakov? In my view, it did not; he had not forgotten that in the letter he had written in 1930, he had stated clearly that *all* of his plays had been removed from the repertoires. Its recipient had done nothing to rectify the situation either that year or in the following one. And one can imagine how Bulgakov had longed, throughout all that time, for at least one of his plays to be brought back to the stage. This permission finally arrived at the very moment, one suspects, when he had stopped waiting for it: that is why "this news oppressed me". Permission for the play to go ahead had come exactly eighteen months after the letter was sent; as for the reasons for this, Bulgakov not only knew nothing of them, but, I believe, elected, after all his agonizing on the subject, to categorize them as phenomena for which it was senseless to try to seek an explanation.

The first showing of *The Days of the Turbins* took place on 11th February and the premiere was held on 18th February. "From Tverskaya all the way to the Theatre," Bulgakov wrote to Popov, "male figures were standing around, muttering mechanically: 'Anyone got a spare ticket?' It was the same on the Dmitrovka side. I didn't go into the auditorium. I went backstage, and the actors were so nervous that I was infected with their nervousness, too. I started moving from place to place, I let my arms and legs do as they please... When the Petlyurites, their excitement levels soaring, chased Nikolka away, a stage-hand fired a revolver right next to my ear, and that was the moment when I came to my senses. Space had appeared in the circle, a piano had appeared, and a boy had started singing the epithalamium in a baritone."

It is worth noting at this point that the letter was written on 24th April; the premiere is being described after the event – and through the prism of the deeply melancholic mood that gripped Bulgakov after the events that had occurred in the intervening months. This serves to intensify the bitterness expressed later in the description.

"A messenger appeared here, taking the form of a beautiful woman. Lately, I have perfected a special power that it is very hard to live with. It is the ability to know in advance what people who come to see me want from me. Clearly the covers on the tips of my nerves are already worn out completely, and interaction with my dog has taught me to be cautious at all times.

In a word, I know what people are going to say to me, and it is a bad thing that I know this, that they won't be able to say anything new. There will be nothing unexpected, I already know it all.

One glance at the tense smile on that mouth, and I already knew it: they were going to ask me not to go out onto the stage...

The messenger said that K.S. had called and was asking where I was and how I felt...?

I asked her to thank him: I felt fine, and I was currently back-stage and would not go out onto the stage for the audience's applause.

O, how the messenger beamed! And she said that K.S. thought this was a wise decision.

There is no particular wisdom in this decision. It was a very simple one. I do not want any bows, any summonses from the audience; I do not want anything at all, other than that people might, for Christ's sake, leave me in peace, so that I can enjoy some hot baths and not think every day about what I should do with my dog, when the contract for the apartment expires in June.

Generally speaking, there is absolutely nothing that I want.

There were 20 curtain calls. Then the actors and some acquaintances of mine tormented me with their questions: why didn't you go out there? Was that some kind of protest? So that's how it works: if you appear on stage, it's a protest; if you don't, that's a protest too. I don't know, I don't know what I am to do. Till the next letter, Yours, M. My greetings to Anna Ilinichna."

What had happened in those two months? At first, everything had been going well, and on a wave of tumultuous rehearsals for his restored play, Bulgakov finished the work that had been hanging over him since the autumn – the stage adaptation of *War and Peace*. On 27th February, he sends it to Leningrad (the deadline in the contract was 1st March). "I have thrown off the burden of the adaptation of *War and Peace*," he wrote to his brother Nikolai on 13th March. And on 14th March, the Bolshoi Drama Theatre (in Leningrad) informed him that it had decided to reject his play *Molière* and to terminate the contract.

This news was like a bolt from the blue for Bulgakov.

Over the next few days, he tried to gather information, to find out what had happened. On 19th March, he sat down to write a letter to P.S. Popov.

"Dear Pavel Sergeyevich!

I shall break this letter down into chapters.

Otherwise I'll get everything mixed up.

Ch. 1: *Stabbed in the back*

The Bolshoi Drama Theatre in Leningrad sent me a message informing me that Khudpolitsovet (the Artistic and Political Council) has rejected my play *Molière*. The theatre has relieved me of my obligations under the contract.

a) The play had been given the letter 'B' by Glavrepertkom, allowing it to be staged unconditionally.

b) The theatre had paid money to the author for the right to put on the play.

c) Work had already started on the play. What's this all about? First of all, it's such a blow for me that I won't even try to describe it. A painful and lasting blow. I had put everything on there being a premiere at the Fontanka in April (roughly). The summer has flown away in a puff of smoke... well, in a word, what can one say. I am telling you alone what a real blow this is. Do not tell anyone, so that nobody can try to play on this and cause me further harm.

The next thing: this means that, to my horror, the stamp of the Glavrepertkom really is on every play except my own.

I consider it a pleasant duty to declare that on this occasion, I can have no complaints whatsoever against the state bodies. As for the stamp: here it is. It was not the state, in the shape of its supervisory bodies, that cancelled the play. And the state is not responsible for the fact that the theatre is calling it off.

So who did cancel it? The theatre? For pity's sake! Why then did it pay 1,200 roubles and send that Board member to Moscow to draw up a contract with me?

Eventually, some information came through from Leningrad. It turns out that the play was not cancelled by a state body. No; *Molière* was destroyed by a very unexpected character! *Molière* was killed by a private, unofficial, non-political, crude and modest individual, and for reasons that are not political at all. This individual is a dramatist by profession. He appeared at the Theatre and frightened them so much that they got rid of the play.

My first reaction, when I was told about this dramatist, was to laugh out loud. I very soon stopped laughing, however. Alas, there can be no doubt about it. Various sources have told me this. What on earth is going on?!

I'll tell you exactly what's going on: at Fontanka, in broad daylight, I was stabbed in the back, whilst the audience stood around in silence. The theatre, incidentally, swears to God that it shouted out for help, but no-one came running to my aid.

I wouldn't be so bold as to question its claim that it shouted for help, but it did so very quietly. It ought to have shouted out over the telegraph lines to Moscow, to the People's Commissariat of Education, at least.

Two or three sympathetic souls have now attached themselves to me. They can see that their fellow-citizen is floating in a pool of his own blood. They say to me: 'kick up a fuss!' Kicking up a fuss is not easy to do when one is lying down. It is not something a dramatist does!

I would ask you, Pavel Sergeyevich: perhaps you have seen some trace of this matter in the papers in Leningrad. A caricature of some sort, or perhaps an article. Do let me know! Why? I don't even know myself. Simply for the bitter pleasure of staring those who tease me in the face once again." (It soon emerged that the events had been played out in November, when Vs. Vishnevsky's article *Who are you?* (*Kto zhe Vy?*) had appeared in *Vechernyaya Krasnaya Gazeta* (*Evening Red Newspaper*), accusing the theatre of poor judgment on the ideological front for having accepted the play *Molière*. The visit made to theatre by the playwright, in person – with his own play – did the rest. There is an intriguing detail that is forgotten nowadays but was familiar to all his contemporaries: before reading his plays, the playwright used to take a revolver out of a holster and place it beside him on the table. This was a theatrical gesture, of course, but it often had very untheatrical consequences.)

In his next letter too, dated 27th March, Bulgakov, responding to Popov's arguments, assures him that the play was killed off, "as I accurately reported to you, by a certain playwright, of whom I have already received numerous descriptions. And each of these descriptions is more tragic than the next. Outwardly: an open expression, works with a 'brotherly' manner, currently plying his trade in Moscow. I am assured that there is a hope that he will be caught up with at some fine moment by the corvette of the state, moving under a military flag, and then the filibuster will be sent to the bottom in one stroke. I can't say I really share this hope, however (the source is not a reliable one).

To hell with him, that filibuster! It's not him I'm interested in. For me, there's a more important question: what, at the end of the day, is going to become of *Molière* outside Moscow. There are some like that in every town, after all. […] What a bit of bad luck. In recent days, whenever I pick up my pen, my head starts to ache. I'm tired. I must leave this letter. To be continued."

So then, it is not the filibuster that concerns him; what concerns him is what to do next?

The condition in which Bulgakov finds himself in the spring of 1932 is similar to the one he was in two years earlier, and at the same time very different from that period. In the spring of 1930, he was utterly desperate and, without the slightest hope to cling to, was preparing for a decisive step that seemed only natural in that hopeless position. In the spring of 1931, he was gripped, it appears, by an unceasing inner anxiety, a desire to take some more essential action, a sense of an uncertain condition lasting temporarily, of waiting for a "real" critical juncture in his fate, the hope of that promised meeting, which he had directly expressed in his second letter. All of this interfered with his ability to work continuously on the novel, which he dreamed of writing that year; he wrote new scenes for it in outline. "New creative ideas have been lit up within me with an irresistible strength," he wrote; "…these ideas are broad and powerful…" In my view, these "ideas" relate first and foremost to the novel, which he had reimagined in those two years. In the notebooks from 1931, the first rough drafts appear for one of the final chapters: *Woland's Flight*. Margarita appeared – in the form of a comment in the first notebook ("Margarita began talking passionately…") and a solitary line in the second one: "No, no," Margarita shouted happily, "Let him whistle! I beg you! I haven't had this much fun in ages!" A new character had appeared, too – Margarita's anonymous travelling companion.

That spring, thorough work of this kind proved to be impossible: it was to an extent pushed to one side by attempts to take feverish action. In the year that had elapsed since the departure of Zamyatin, such a significant event in the general context, the deathly silence in response to his own letter, the unexpected, capricious return to the stage of *The Days of the Turbins* and the rejection by the theatre in Leningrad of *Molière*, after so much trouble had been taken to secure its approval (it was given approval again, just over a year after the first letter – mainly thanks to Gorky) – this entire chain of events, and of non-events which became significant events (the silence of the recipient of the letter, for example), led to that feeling of complete instability, of dependency, which can indeed become a support for work that is undertaken on one's own. Life had been returned to him only partially (one recalls the words in the letter to Popov about how "part of his life had been returned" to the author. There was no longer anything to calculate, to consider, to ponder over and resolve. Life was meant to unfold in this way, governed by unseen, uncontrollable forces, and it was time to submit himself, at last, to his fate and strive merely to make sense of it.

"Five o'clock in the morning. I can't sleep. I lay in bed, talking to myself, and now, Pavel Sergeyevich, allow me to talk to you" – so began a letter to Popov dated 14th April 1932. "One mustn't forget old friends – you are right. Just recently, a man who is close to me comforted me by predicting that, when I die in the near future and call out, nobody shall come to me, apart from the Black Monk. And just think – what a coincidence this is: even before this prediction, this story had got stuck in my head. And it's a little scary, after all, to think that nobody will come. What is one to do, though, that is how my life has unfolded." According to what Y.S. Bulgakova told me, these terrible words had been spoken that sad spring by his wife; life at Pirogovskaya had been unravelled, but was still continuing somehow. "Every night, now," the letter went on, "I look not forwards, but backwards, because in the future I see nothing for myself. In the past, I made five fateful mistakes. Were it not for them, were it not for the conversations about the Monk, the very sun in the sky would have shone differently, and I would have written works, not whilst grinding my teeth noiselessly at dawn, but at a writing desk, in the proper way. [...] *There is nothing to be done now though, you will not get anything back.* [Compare this with the recurring theme of bringing back a situation from the past that was "incorrectly" resolved in all the later drafts of *The Master and Margarita*. – M.C.]. The only thing I curse are those two fits of unexpected shyness, which flew over me like a fainting fit, due to which I made two mistakes out of the five. I have a justification: that shyness was accidental – it was the fruit of my exhaustion. I had grown tired after years of literary labour. There is a justification – but there is no comfort." It seems safe to assume that these two mistakes concern the relatively recent past ("years of literary labour" had elapsed prior to them, and his exhaustion had built up) and that one of them was the result of the conversation with Y.A. Shilovsky, who had demanded a complete split between Bulgakov and Yelena Sergeyevna Shilovskaya. By the time the lines quoted above from the letter to P.S. Popov were written, they had not seen one another, nor spoken on the telephone, for around a year, and Bulgakov was feeling this loss, which seemed irrevocable, badly. One can suggest with somewhat more certainty that Bulgakov may now have felt that the second "fateful mistake" committed out of shyness was the way he replied to certain questions in his conversation with Stalin, the one that caught him unawares on 18th April 1930; the erroneous nature of his replies did not become clear to him immediately, but over the next year to eighteen months.

"15th April.

I am picking up where I left off!

So then, feeling tired, and sensing that I must reach some conclusion, that it is high time I did so, that I must take all definitive decisions, I keep going over the life I have lived and recalling who my friends have been. And there are so few. I remember you, at any rate, I remember you firmly, Pavel Sergeyevich.

20.IV.

What is this punishment! It has taken me six days to write this letter. Some kind of devil has put me under its spell.

I shall continue: so then, take into your friendly arms part of the spiritual burden that I find difficult to bear alone. This, strictly speaking, is not a letter, but notes about the days…well, in a word, I am going to write to you about *The Turbins*, about *Molière* and about much else. I know that this is not the done thing, to talk only about oneself, but I cannot write anything about anything else, until I untie the spiritual knot I am in. First and foremost about the *Turbins*, for my entire life now hangs on this play as though by a thread, and every night I send up prayers to my fate, so that no sword might cut through that thread.

First of all, though, I am going to a rehearsal [rehearsals had begun at the Art Theatre at the end of March for *Molière*, which was to be staged there – M.C.], then I am going to sleep, and once I have had a good night's sleep, I shall write a letter." The next letter, written a few days later, described the premiere of *The Days of the Turbins*.

On 7th May, as he set about describing the story of the staging of *Dead Souls*, Bulgakov wrote to P.S. Popov: "So then, *Dead Souls*... In nine days' time, I shall be 41. That is monstrous! Yet it is nevertheless the case.

And at this time, towards the end of my work as a writer, I have been forced to write adaptations for the stage. What a scintillating finale, don't you think? I gaze at my bookshelves and feel a sense of terror: which of these authors, which one, will I have to adapt for the stage tomorrow? Turgenev, Leskov, Brokhaus-Efron? Ostrovsky? The last of these, though, happily, adapted his own work, clearly foreseeing what was going to happen to me in 1929-1931."

Thus, drawing a scarcely comforting conclusion about his life and without having taken any "definitive decisions", earning money on jobs that happened to come his way (rewriting the dialogue for the film *The Fishermen's Uprising* [*Vosstaniye Rybakov*] – a 'talky'), writing two applications to K.S. Stanislavsky asking for money (as his author's royalty) for his contribution "to the house of the writer as it grows higher" ("I shall have nowhere to live, if I do not move in by the winter"), and receiving a postcard from Zamyatin from Monaco, showing a port bathed in sunshine, and clearly without having commenced a single job that was essential to him from an internal perspective in the whole of the first half of the year, he greeted the summer of 1932. At that point, the editors of the series *The Lives of Remarkable People*, organised by Gorky, invited him to write a biography of Molière. The contract was concluded on 11th July; apparently, work began straight away – on 4th August, Bulgakov writes to Popov: "Dear friend Pavel Sergeyevich, as soon as Jean-Baptiste Poquelin de Molière lets go of my soul somewhat and I get the chance to think clearly again, I shall take a greedy enjoyment in writing to you. A biography – 10 pages – and in this heat – and in Moscow!" The correspondence with Popov, which had been born out of the impossibility of writing anything else – and the impossibility of not writing ("I fear that this letter is a long one," he apologized on 29th January. "But in my complete loneliness, my pen grew rusty long ago, after all, I have not quite died yet, I wish to talk in my own words!"), is at last replaced by some literary work that excites him.

That summer, an extremely significant event occurs in Bulgakov's life. Yelena Sergeyevna told me that they met up – for the first time after a separation lasting 15 months – at the restaurant Metropol, in the open, with the help of F.N. Mikhalsky, a long-standing friend of Yelena's (from her first year in Moscow). It became clear to both of them that they loved each other just as much as before. This was in June; Yelena Sergeyevna then went away to Lebdyan with the children.

She told me that she walked around in the fields and in the woods, thinking. And eventually, she wrote a letter to her husband: "Let me go…!" "I prayed to God for a reply – and an envelope came down from somewhere up above: the postman had thrown it through the window… I went to look for a place where I could read it without the children being around me. I read it in an outdoor toilet made of wood, with the sunlight coming through the cracks, and the buzzing of flies. I have loved the buzzing of flies ever since. Shilovsky let me go. He wrote: "I treated you like a child, I was wrong… Can I come and see you?" He arrived, and stayed for several days. Then, suddenly, he started beseeching me to stay at home. Like a fool, I agreed to do so," she recalled, regretfully. At the end of the summer, she went back to Moscow. "Misha said to me, when he found out that I intended to stay at home, 'Are you out of your mind?' I wrote to Shilovsky in Sochi. M.A. added a few words to the letter: 'Dear Yevgeny Alexandrovich, step out of the way of our happiness…' Shilovsky sent a reply – to me. There was a note added at the end: 'Mikhail Afanasievich, whatever I do, I do not for you, but for Yelena Sergeyevna.' Misha turned pale," – this was the phrase Yelena Sergeyevna always used to describe his condition when he had been deeply hurt by someone's words. "That burned on his face for the rest of his life, like a slap on the cheek."

The first page of Bulgakov's letter survives; it is not clear whether this is part of a letter that was sent back (returned to Yelena by Shilovsky) or a draft that was not sent; it perhaps relates to the first few days after their meeting, before she went to Lebedyan: "Dear Yevgeny Alexandrovich, I had a meeting with Yelena Sergeyevna after she summoned me, and we expressed our feelings to one another. We love one another just as we did before" (the rest of the letter is missing). The conversation that Yelena had with her eldest son – ten-year-old Zhenya, who idolized his beautiful mother – was extremely trying for her; Zhenya had to stay at the house that she was leaving; as for the younger son, five-year-old Seryozha, his mother took him with her to Pirogovskaya.

(As she told me about how her son died in her arms at the age of 35 in 1957, Yelena, who had been through so much, said to me with conviction: "That conversation with little Zhenya, and his death – those were the two most difficult things in my life.")

Shilovsky demanded that Bulgakov come to see him at home for a final conversation. He did not allow her to be present for it. She told me, in the autumn of 1969, that she had hidden on the other side of the street, behind the gate of the church ("The gate is still there today, you can see it," she added), and had seen him going into the house looking pale and downcast. During the conversation, Shilovsky, unable to restrain himself, grabbed hold of a pistol. Bulgakov, turning white as a sheet, said (Yelena told me this in a soft, restrained tone of voice): 'You wouldn't shoot an unarmed man, would you? ... if it's a duel you want – by all means!" One can easily imagine his memory duly digging out, from the recesses of his consciousness, his impressions from 1918-1920, and the disgusting sense of powerlessness felt by the unarmed man before the blind power of the armed one.

On 3rd September, Shilovsky wrote to Yelena's parents, in Riga: "When you receive this letter, Yelena Sergeyevna and I will no longer be husband and wife... We spent a whole host of years together and were very happy. I am forever grateful to Lyusya for the enormous happiness and *joie de vivre* that she gave me in that time..." On 7th September, on a damaged (darkened) photo of his study at Pirogovskaya, Bulgakov wrote, jokingly: "To Yelena, from Mikhail." "That's instead of an apartment, is it?" Yelena asked, adding: "Thank you." On 11th September, Bulgakov and Yelena wrote a joint letter to her parents, too.

Evidence of these events is a note made by Bulgakov on the final page of the Paris edition of his novel. It read: "The misfortune occurred on 25.11.1931. And we decided to wed early in September 1932. 6.IX. 1932." (The "misfortune" was, it seems, the events which led to them being separated).

Lyubov Yevgenievna, who at the time was engaged in a love affair of her own, according to her friends M.A. Chimishkian and N.A. Ushakova, responded to these events amicably. Yelena had this to say on her reaction: "When I went to see her and said that Misha and I had decided to get married (I was friends with her), she accepted it calmly. She had long known how close we were. All she said was:

'But I'm going to live with you!' And I replied:

'Well, of course, Lyubochka!'

(When I wrote about this to my parents in Riga, they decided I must have lost the plot).

But then she started saying nasty things to me about Misha: 'You don't know what you're getting into. He's greedy, miserly, he doesn't like children.'

And at that point I said:

'No, Lyubochka, I'm afraid we shan't be able to live together. I cannot bear to hear you saying bad things about him. Misha's not miserly...!'

And then we decided to buy Lyuba a little one-bedroom bachelor's apartment – right there, on the other side of the wall."

This is a view of the situation as seen through Yelena's eyes. An account of it from a different perspective also exists – in Lyubov's memoirs. A biographer's task is not, perhaps, to try to weigh up opposing accounts in search of some "truth" which probably cannot be found, but to draw the description of the situation closer to how it was perceived by the subject of this biography: to how it was seen by the man who made his decision that autumn.

… Tatiana Nikolayevna told me that Bulgakov said to her a number of times: "I must get married three times!" – he thought that this was the destiny ascribed to him at birth. She remembered that when Bulgakov repeated this, he said that Aleksei Tolstoy had told him it – Tolstoy considered this to be one of the actions that led a writer to literary success… As for Yelena, she remembered a different source behind this sentiment, which, during her life with Bulgakov, took on a new, happy meaning: she told me that Bulgakov had said that once, back in Kiev, a fortune-teller had told him this, and he found it amusing to think that her prediction had now come true. Curiously, Babel, according to memoirists (writing in a book of memoirs about him), used to tell people about a saying he had read in a diary from the early 19th century: "A man's first wife is from God, his second is from the people, his third is from the devil…" Perhaps Bulgakov knew this saying – might not that be the reason why he often repeated to Tatiana: "Will God punish me because of you…?" On 3rd October, Bulgakov's marriage to Lyubov Yevgenievna was annulled, and on the 4th, his marriage to Yelena Sergeyevna was registered.

"We signed the papers, but I had to live at Shilovsky's place for a while – Lyuba's apartment wasn't ready yet," Yelena told me, "she had nowhere to go. Bulgakov was terribly tormented by this. Then the theatres in Leningrad invited him to visit them, and we went away for two weeks. We stayed at the Astoria…"

Judging by some accounts, it was in Leningrad that he turned back to his novel once again.

CHAPTER FIVE

A Return to the Novel.

New Plays and Hopes (1932-1935).

1

In the exercise book in which the novel was started afresh, the date on the title page and the first page is "1932". Y.S. Bulgakova told me that Bulgakov had said to her in Leningrad that he wanted to return to the novel he had destroyed. "I said: 'How are you going to write it here – your drafts are in Moscow?' – and he replied: 'I can remember all of it.'"

He started the manuscript right from the first chapter, without any preliminary sketches; the first few pages come across as a final version, copied from some sort of draft text. There was no such text before the writer's eyes, incidentally – and not just because he had started the novel away from his writing desk: fragments from the early drafts were almost illegible and unsuitable for use, whilst the bits and pieces written in 1931 are only fragmentary, and there is no information about any fuller drafts that the author may have used in 1932. By this time, the novel had probably fully taken shape in the author's imagination, to the extent that he needed no additional material, and in the upbeat mood that he was in that autumn, it came pouring out onto the paper almost without any crossings out and, it appears, without any effort. It is unlikely the work continued when he returned to Moscow: he urgently had to finish his comedy *The Half-Wit Jourdain* (*Poloumnyy Zhurden*), based on themes from some of Molière's plays, for Y. Zavadsky's studio theatre, with which he had concluded a contract on 18th July for a translation of the play *Le Bourgeois Gentilhomme*.

"When we came back, I began moving house," Yelena Sergeyevna told me. "Shilovsky said to me: Lyolyochka, you did all this yourself, take all the furniture. I said:

'Zhenechka, why would I destroy the apartment? I'll just take my divan and Seryozha's wicker cot.'

'Nanny Anastasia (she called me 'Mummy') gave me her long, wooden chest.'

When we started loading all this into the car, Shilovsky ran out from the courtyard without his coat, so as not to see me leaving, and the nanny starting moaning loudly, so that people came running up to us. It was a 'love-interest' scandal in the truest possible sense.

… When we arrived – Mikhail Afanasievich was waiting for us, strolling beside the windows; I quickly gave Seryozha some *kasha* and put him to bed. Mikhail Afanasievich and I sat down beside the fire (the stove was on). I was finding it all very difficult, and he realised that. He started trying to make me laugh:

'Come on then, let's have a look in your chest!' He couldn't get the chest open.

'Did Shilovsky hammer the nails in?!'

… Then he told everyone in comic fashion the story of how he had spent ages trying to open it, then finally managed to do so – only to find a kilo of groats at the bottom…"

Yelena Sergeyevna's eldest son used to come over for lunch on Sundays; her sister, Olga Vokshanskaya, lived in one of the rooms at Shilovsky's apartment, helping the boy get over the traumatic experience.

Slowly but surely, life started to move in a new direction once again.

"When the four of us were sitting around the table – me, Mikhail and my sons," Yelena said to me on 28th October 1968, turning her eyes away from me to gaze into the distance, to a past that she alone could see, "and I was, of course, the happiest woman in the world, each of them would take turns to ask me, whispering into my ear: 'Which of us do you love the most?' (they were all terribly jealous!), and I would say to each of them in turn, in a whisper: 'You!'

Now there's only one of them left – Seryozha, although both of the others are always here (she gestured at the room with her hand), with me – and all my love is concentrated on him…

Mikhail Afanasievich was terribly fond of Seryozha. Rare is the biological father who has such a strong love for their child. He spent a great deal of time with him. He instilled courage and resourcefulness in him."

After the play was sent off to the theatre on 18th November, work began intensively on a biography of Molière, the deadline for which had been moved ("no later than 1st February 1933").

The year 1932 ended under the burden of this literary work; he found it entertaining but had to write it in a short space of time, and it required not only a huge effort of imagination but also a considerable amount of reading of the primary sources.

The woman that he loved was with him; rehearsals of his play *Molière* were taking place at the Art Theatre, and he was taking part in them. There was reason to hope that in the new year, 1933, both his play about Molière and his novel about the great writer of comedies would see the light of day.

"I am now finishing off a big job – a biography of Molière," he wrote to his brother Nikolai on 14th January, asking him to send him a description of the statue of Molière that had been put up on the corner of Richelieu and Molière – in a niche in the building where he was born. "I have to submit *Molière* by 1st February," Bulgakov added, "and give up all writing for a very long period of time, it seems." What he meant by that is not entirely clear – unless it is a prediction about his future fate as a writer whose work is not published.

It is possible that this was his chosen method of informing his brother that for the time being, there was no sign of any new takers for his prose or plays; it is also possible that he foresaw that over the coming months, he was going to be engaged in work for the theatre.

On 5th March 1933 (using the one month's grace period stipulated in the contract), Bulgakov submitted the novel *The Life of Mr de Molière* (*Zhizneopisaniye Gospodina de Moliera*) to the editors of ZhZL (*The Lives of Remarkable People*) and on 8th March he wrote to his brother: "To my great delight, I have finally finished my work on *Molière*, and I handed over the manuscript on 5th. It has exhausted me exceedingly and consumed all of my lifeblood. I cannot recall how many years it has been now, since I first began working on it, that I have spent living in the ghostly and magical Paris of the 17th century. Now, it seems, I am taking my leave of it forever.

If fate should take you to the corner of Richelieu and Molière – think of me! Say 'hello' to Jean-Baptiste de Molière from me!" These words paraphrase the last line of the novel: "And I, who am destined never to see him again, send him a final goodbye!'

On 7th April, Alexander Tikhonov, the editor of the series, wrote Bulgakov a long letter utterly tearing the novel apart. On 13th April 1933, Bulgakov informed P.S. Popov: "My *Molière* days have commenced. They began with

T.'s review [i.e. A.N. Tikhonov – M.C.]. It contains, dear Patya, a plethora of agreeable things. My narrator, who takes charge of the biography, is described as a presumptuous young man, who believes in witchcraft and devilry, has occult abilities, loves erotic stories, uses dubious sources, and, worst of all, is something of a royalist!

But that is not all. In my work, in T.'s opinion, "fairly transparent hints are made about our Soviet reality!!" Yelena, Bulgakov added jokingly, in a fit of rage, "had even rushed off to ask him to explain himself. Grabbing her by the skirt, I only just managed to persuade her not to engage in these familial actions. I then composed a letter to the editor. After thinking the matter through in great detail, I considered it for the best not to join battle. I bared my teeth at the form of the review only, but I did not take the bait."

The tone of his reply, written the previous day, is indeed restrained and peacable; the entire letter takes up only a page of text; in response to Tikhonov's suggestion that he replace the "presumptuous" narrator with "a serious Soviet historian", Bulgakov explains himself as follows: "I am not a historian, but a playwright, who at this moment in time happens to be studying Molière. Now that I find myself in this position, though, let me assure you that I see this Molière of mine very distinctly."

Bulgakov refused to rewrite the book – using concise and energetic phrases: "You surely understand that, having written my play the right way round, I certainly can't re-write it inside out. Have mercy!" And he ended his letter with a counter-proposal: the book wasn't suitable for the publishing house, "so perhaps you ought not to print it. Let us bury it and forget it."

The letter to Popov echoed this: "So then, I wish to bury Jean-Baptiste Molière. The more tranquil everyone is, the better. I am utterly indifferent to the idea of decorating a shop-window with the cover of my book. Essentially, I am an actor, not a writer. What's more, I love peace and quiet.

Here is a summary for you of the biography you were interested in. Call me on the telephone, please. We shall arrange a meeting, when we shall get together and recall, around the dinner table, the names of the great comedy writers, Messrs La Grange, Brequoir, Du Croissy and the commander himself, Jean Molière."

Tikhonov told him that he had sent the manuscript, together with his review, to Gorky in Sorrento: "let's wait and see what he says". On 28th April, Gorky wrote to Tikhonov: "with your negative – and justifiably so – review of the work by M.A. Bulgakov, I fully concur. He must not only add some historical content to it and give it some social significance – he must also alter its 'playful' style. In its current form, it is not a serious work, and – as you correctly note – it will be condemned vehemently." Bulgakov was apparently told about this review; for the first time, Gorky was fulfilling a role that took Bulgakov by surprise. Gorky left for Moscow on 9th May; Bulgakov began awaiting his arrival.

That spring, Bulgakov officially entrusted the management of all his publishing affairs to Yelena Sergeyevna. This was the first time he had done such a thing in his life, and he liked it enormously. He spent a lot of time teaching little Sergei, and together they wrote some playful notes to Yelena Sergeyevna ("Dear Mama, my worldview is well and truly lost…").

In May, the Music-hall in Lengingrad invited him to write "an eccentric three-act play" – by 15th October. On 19th May, Bulgakov writes to Popov, asking him to come round and say goodbye before he goes on vacation. "Bring with you that ill-fated *Molière* [the manuscript of the novel – M.C.].

"And as for me? The wind rustles the greenery beside the dermatology clinic [opposite Bulgakov's house on Pirogovskaya Street – M.C.], my heart stops at the thought of rivers, bridges, seas. There is a gypsy-like moaning in my soul." As we can see, his dreams of a summer holiday beside the Seine or the Mediterranean do not allow him a moment's peace. "This will pass, though. I predict that I will spend the entire summer here at Pirogovskaya, writing a comedy (for Leningrad). There will be heat, dust, knocking, *Narzan*."

The first surviving notes for the play *Bliss* were made on 26th May 1933. The play has no name at that stage, but the coloration of George Miloslavsky's speech patterns is already present, along with the theme of the boredom he feels in the 'golden age', and the lack of understanding between him and the men of the future. The play had been conceived several years earlier: it was later dated "1924-1934", and in one of the letters to Veresayev from 1934, the author talks of it as a play "that I thought up ages and ages ago." V. Sakhnovsky, the director of *Dead Souls*, who worked side by side with Bulgakov for several years, later stated that work had begun on the play in 1929, and claimed there was a link to a production of Mayakovsky's *The Bathhouse*, which, in his opinion, had influenced Bulgakov's plot. There is no doubt that both *The Bedbug* and *The Bathhouse* played a role in prompting the creation of a play about the future; Bulgakov wanted to portray his own particular version of it. In George Miloslavsky, one can see a connection to Prisypkin, in terms of his relations with the people of the future. Apparently, a comedy commenced in 1929 or 1930 is the one referred to as having been destroyed along with "a novel about the devil" in a letter to the government from 1930.

The work had to be postponed, however, until the winter.

On 3rd June, the final rehearsal for that season of *Molière* took place at the Art Theatre; an entry in the "Rehearsal Diary" states: "Livanov was 7 mins. late for the rehearsal and Bulgakov was 20 mins. late." A few days earlier, Bulgakov, at Stanislavsky's request, had drafted the text of a letter to Stalin about Nemirovich-Danchenko's foreign debts, which were preventing him from going to the Union, and requesting assistance. Bulgakov, it seems, was now considered an expert in writing letters to this particular individual; the letter was articulately written and very succinct – particularly in comparison with the strange version written by L.A. Markov.

In early June, a letter arrived from Tashkent, from someone involved in the theatre scene there: "I consider it my agreeable duty to inform you that your play *The Days of the Turbins*, after a public viewing organized by us on 18th May, has been given permission to be performed in Tashkent and is currently enjoying great artistic success."

The Art Theatre was showing signs of an intention to start work on *Flight* in the autumn. After receiving a letter from I.Y. Sudakov from Leningrad, where the Art Theatre were on tour with *The Days of the Turbins*, Bulgakov wrote to him, on 21st June: "As regards *Flight*, do not worry. Although I am as tired as a dog, I am still thinking it through and working on it. It is not beyond the bounds of possibility that I shall come to Leningrad for a couple of days, during the tour. And then we shall talk." On 29th June, he sent Sudakov "the final corrections for the play", promising to send him a truncated copy of the play soon, "which I ask you to use for the rehearsals." On the day when *The Days of the Turbins* was performed for the 400th time, he congratulated its director: "What a complicated fate this play has had, Ilya Yakovlevich! … We met at a most difficult and most frightening time, and all of us have been through a great deal, including me… and my rickety boat… [Lariosik's lines from the final scene of the play – M.C.]. Anyway, that's not the point… Times have changed, we are alive, and the play is alive, and more than that: you are now planning to rehearse *Flight* as well. Well, well!"

Ten days later, Bulgakov left for Leningrad with his wife; they stayed at the Astoria. By 22nd June he was back in Moscow, and he wrote to P.S. Popov: "Are you alive, are you well, dear Pavel? I have come back from Leningrad, after enjoying a significant amount of rest and relaxation over the course of 10 days at the Astoria… I am suffocating here at Pirogovskaya. Perhaps you could beseech my fate for me, so that they finally finish work on the house in Nashchekinsky? When, oh when, will it finally happen?! When?!"

On 2nd August, in a letter to Veresayev, who was spending the summer in Zvenigorod, Bulgakov writes of his attempts to obtain a royalty from the theatres in Leningrad at which the Art Theatre had performed *The Days of the Turbins* whilst on tour; he also writes that "Yelena Sergeyevna, armed with the power of attorney, descended upon the 2nd of the theatres – the Narvsky House of Culture," and that to date he has not received a kopeck, despite the best efforts of the woman energetically protecting his interests. "… And I dream only of that happy day, when she will accomplish her aim, and I shall return to you the debt that I still owe you, and I shall tell you once again what you did for me, dear Vikenty Vikentievich!

Oh, how I shall remember the years 1929-1931!" [He is referring to the money that Veresayev offered to Bulgakov in a year when he had nothing to subsist on – M.C.].

"I would have got back up on my feet, by the way, if it weren't for the need to quit this damn hole on Pirogovskaya…" The epithets given to this apartment are becoming more and more choice. Everything about it – from the roar of the trams passing beneath his window and the damp walls, to the difficulties, which soon became clear, of constantly having to talk to his ex-wife (Lyubov Yevgenievna moves into a little apartment in the same building, rented on her behalf, on 24th September) – irritates Bulgakov. His wife, having moved out of her own flat, is now forced to live in someone else's – her natural inclination to arrange everything exactly the way she wanted it could not be fully realised here. Uppermost in Bulgakov's mind is his eternal dream of the big, quiet apartment from his childhood. And although it had recently become clear that the apartment on Nashchekinsky was going to be much smaller than they had expected (47 square metres rather than 60, i.e. much smaller than the apartment on Pirogovskaya!), he continues to dream about it as a sanctuary that will come to his rescue. Here, one can see a particularity of his view of life coming to the fore: the need for some sort of expectation, hope for a change of fortune.

"… I have stayed up for two nights in a row over this Gogol of yours," his letter to Veresayev went on. "My God! What a person! What a character! [this is a reference to the collection of biographical documents, *Gogol in His Lifetime* (*Gogol' v Zhizni*), which the author had given to Bulgakov as a gift – M.C.]. A devil has made its home inside me. While I was in Leningrad, and now here, as well, as I suffocate in my tiny little rooms, I have begun covering page after page with the novel I destroyed three years ago. Why? I know not. I am soothing myself! Let it fall into the Lethe! I shall probably give this up soon, anyway."

On 5th August, Bulgakov writes to Gorky, who had come down with a lengthy bout of flu after returning to Moscow from Italy in May of that year: "Much esteemed Aleksei Maximovich! How do you feel now, after your illness? I should like to see you. Perhaps you would be so good as to tell me when this could happen?

I tried to call you at the apartment in town, but to no avail – there was no-one there." Apparently, Bulgakov wished to go back to discussing the fate of the novel about Molière, and perhaps also to talk about *Flight*. He received no answer to his letter.

On 1st September, "on the anniversary of my meeting with M.A. after our divorce," Yelena Sergeyevna starts keeping a diary – at her husband's request. Bulgakov himself, according to her, after destroying his diary for 1921-1926 soon after it was returned to him (seemingly at the end of 1929 or the beginning of 1930), never again kept a diary of any kind. Yelena began recording in her diary the writer's current literary activities and creative plans, his business meetings and meetings with friends, and occasionally brief notes about the content of conversations, never revealing very much and using cautious phraseology, and the writer's thoughts on certain events in public life, in literature and in the theatre scene. One should add that even in Yelena's own assessments of the plays and concerts that they went to see together, Bulgakov's views are present too, though they are hidden – for whenever their opinions differed, this difference was recorded. Eight exercise books containing these diaries survive, and the first two (covering the period from 1st September 1933 to 4th December 1934) survived in the archive only in the form of copies written out in the 1950s, so the reader should be aware, when encountering quotations later in the narrative from the diary for this eighteen-month period, of a certain flatness that was bestowed on these entries by the subsequent editing process (after 4th December 1934, I will quote the original diary, occasionally adding certain important lines from the later version).

On the day when Yelena started her diary, Bulgakov was already working on chapter 8 of the novel that he mentioned in his letter to Veresayev; he had filled up one exercise book with it and had now started on another. The plot, which had stayed with him over the last few years, was now drawing himself towards it powerfully, and would not release its hold on him until his dying day.

What sort of a novel was it, this book that almost literally rose out of the ashes in the autumn of 1933? It seems to me to be beyond doubt that the former plot was substantially restructured.

In Bulgakov's prose from his first 5-year period in Moscow, it is easy to identify two main currents: one of them takes the form of grotesque satire, from outside his autobiographical material, whilst the other amounts to a sort of fictionalized version of his biography (and these parts usually follow hot on the heels of the actual events on which they are based: when a particular biographical period came to an end – and Bulgakov was particularly fond of dividing his life into such periods – it was immediately described in his writing) in the form of *notes*, i.e. of an organised narrative, arranged chronologically and told in the first person, with a large number of milestones in time (the narrator keeps track of the passing years, seasons, months, days, times of day).

It is possible that the novel *The Engineer's Hoof* was not only started in 1928, but also devised as a continuation of the theme of grotesque satire (made dramatically more complex, of course, due to the inclusion in the novel, during the very first stages of work, of Christ and the Devil). In the 15 chapters that were written in 1928-1929, there do not seem to be any traces of autobiographical material, there is nobody writing any sort of work of a literary nature – there is only an academic (we can at least draw a parallel here with *The Fateful Eggs*, where one of the characters is an academic, a world-famous professor), who is interested mainly in the Middle Ages. Evidence of the change in the plot that undoubtedly took place, therefore, comes in the form of the new protagonist, who appeared in outline form in drafts from 1931, and who brought with him an autobiographical theme – as one can see by studying the first full draft of the novel (1932-1936). Thus, the two vectors of the subject matter in his creative work have been combined.

Supporting my theory that the hero, later given the name of the Master, does not appear in the plot of the novel any earlier than 1930-1931, is the fact that throughout the whole of the third draft, written from 1932 onwards, this hero does not come into contact with Ivan at all. Only during the phase when extensive sections are added to the third draft, after its completion in draft form, is the new hero "added in" by the author at the clinic (prior to that, he was certainly in a prison camp or in exile, as shown by the get-up in which he appears, after being summoned by Woland, in the manuscripts dated January 1934: "He wore a quilted men's jacket, with the buttons done up; soldier's trousers, and long, coarse boots…"), where he meets Ivanushka. The ties between the characters, and the interaction between them, are such an important feature of the novel's subject matter, that the fact that these two characters were not connected at all until the end of the third draft, and that this connection appeared in the additions made to it, must suggest that one of the two characters was introduced into the novel's plot at a comparatively late stage.

At the same time, one of the characters from the first draft – Fesya – disappears from the novel altogether.

The break-up of the "Prechistenka" humanities circle that occurred in 1929-1930 had an impact on the novel, in my view. The author had given his first readings from it to the group, when all its members were still around… It is perhaps the case that the author could no longer bring himself to portray the very specific biographies of these 'erudites' with irony – not even a gentle irony.

The new hero first appears in the novel and tells his story to Ivan in chapter 13 – *after Woland's evening at the Variety show*: i.e. *in the very same place*, in terms of the composition, in which Fesya's story was told in the first draft (chapter 11 in the first draft), providing further evidence that the Master *replaced* Fesya in the novel.

There is no doubt that a meeting with Woland was prepared for Fesya, *an expert in demonology*, in the novel as it took shape in 1928-29; Fesya was prepared for this meeting thanks to the activity he had been engaged in, just like the hero of the later drafts, the Master, and by contrast with Ivan and Berlioz. Fesya, with his "phenomenal erudition", was perhaps supposed to represent a contrast, in the structure of the novel, to Berlioz, whose superficial erudition was his abiding characteristic, preserved in all the drafts of the novel. In the first draft, Ivan Bezdomny was apparently supposed to disappear from the modern world by the end of the novel (one can interpret the scene in the third draft, in which the *dead* Ivan appears before Woland and Margarita, as a relic of his original place in the plot) – although one cannot rule out a meeting between him and Fesya (if one takes into account the theme of the intelligentsia and the people, which is present in chapter 11). As for Berlioz, he died at the beginning of the novel, just as in the later versions. It is fair to suppose that Fesya was originally supposed to stay in the field of modern life and perhaps play a role in the plot similar to Ivan's role in the novel's Epilogue (in the final version).

The manuscripts for the novel, chiefly the collated drafts from 1928-1929 and 1931-1933, compel one to suppose that in the interval between them, when work on the text came to a halt, there was some kind of impulse, some prompting, that brought about the rapid combining, merging of these two creative vectors. The second supposition we can make is that this jolt was not of a literary nature, but of a biographical one. An incident occurred of such biographical significance, that it destroyed the creative stereotype of a sequential retrospective reflection of his biography, calling for new forms in which that biography could be interpreted.

This event was, undoubtedly, the letter from 1930, the subsequent conversation with Stalin and, above all, the retrospective interpretation of the course of the conversation and of the eighteen months which Bulgakov saw as the consequences of his own actions unfolding before his eyes (the letter and the responses to it in the conversation).

His dark thoughts about the irrevocable nature of the past, about reaching a conclusion on his life, about the five fatal mistakes recorded in his letters to Popov in January to April 1932, the sense of some sort of diabolical trap, which he himself had involuntarily built – this is the psychological backdrop against which the new plot crystallized in his mind.

Contemporary researchers (B. Gasparov, L. Fleishman) rightly draw our attention to the significance of the death of Mayakovsky for this new stage in the plot of the novel. Indeed, having apparently become sure, as time went on, of the direct link between the portentous phone call and the tragedy of the death of Mayakovsky that had recently been played out (and let's not forget that, according to S.A. Yermolinsky, Bulgakov was "confident that there was a link between the permission granted to Zamyatin to leave the country, and Mayakovsky's suicide – along the lines of 'what if this one goes and shoots himself too'"), Bulgakov took an interest in the final months of Mayakovsky's life and perhaps noticed something he hadn't noticed before in his own travails.

It is worth recalling that on 23rd November 1929, Mayakovsky's play *The Bathhouse*, which he had just read in public to great acclaim, was submitted to Glavrepertkom, and its fate became more complicated. L.Y. Brik wrote in her diary:

"I had never seen Mayakovsky looking so lost, so crushed, before. [...] He, the first poet of the Revolution, seemed to have been knocked off his pedestal in an instant and transformed into a rank-and-file, inch-high, utterly run-of-the-mill writer, 'dragging up his dubious little play onto the stage'.

Mayakovsky did not want to give in, and with his beaming energy he fought for his six-act drama, which today, as I write these lines, has long been considered a classic, and rightly so.

'Listen, Kataich, what they want from me?' he asked, almost pitifully. 'You write plays, too. Do they slaughter you, too? Is this an everyday occurrence?'

O-ho!

I remembered seeing a copy of one of his plays that had been so defiled with red pencil that Stanislavsky had been reluctant to show it to me for several days, afraid that I might have a heart attack and drop down dead." In this sense, one can accept the assertions made by researchers to the effect that Mayakovsky's literary destiny turned out, fatally, to be a parallel to the situation in which Bulgakov found himself in the autumn of 1929, and that the fate of *The Bathhouse* might, in the circumstances of 1930, have proved similar to the fate of *The Days of the Turbins* (L. Fleishman); this parallel would have been striking from a chronological point of view – Bulgakov finished the first draft of *A Cabal of Hypocrites* (the play that later became *Molière*) on 6th December 1929, and on 16th January 1930 he told his brother, in a letter: "The torment from it has been going on for one-and-a-half months now…" The difficulties both writers faced were even linked to one and the same person – the chairman of Glavrepertkom, K.D. Gandurin, and in January 1930, Mayakovsky's epigram about him became famous. Soon after this, the parallels ceased, though: *The Bathhouse* was performed in Leningrad on 30th January, and at the Vs. Meyerhold Theatre on 16th March. By March, it was clear to Bulgakov that the situation regarding his new play was utterly hopeless, and he was compelled to pen his letter to the government, which he perhaps pondered over and gradually wrote during the whole of March, finishing it on 28th March 1930. At the very same time, Mayakovsky (on 25th March) gives a talk at an evening celebrating twenty years of literary activity, at which he complains to his audience and warns them: "perhaps I shall have to stop reading for a long time. Today is perhaps one of the last evenings…" In March and early April, Bulgakov is fully engaged by his own destiny, which from the side appears to be successful, and wholly involved in solving his own problems.

The event which occurred on 14th April must have brought about some change in Bulgakov's attitude to Mayakovsky and prompted him into making a retrospective reappraisal of his own fate. Having not been a poet as far as Bulgakov was concerned, the deceased immediately became less of a sufferer in his eyes. Let us not forget that during his younger days in Kiev, Bulgakov had suffered one of the biggest shocks of his life in just such a situation: a friend from his grammar school and student years shot himself in the chest with a revolver before his very eyes. Let us note that the revolver is an important object in Bulgakov's artistic world, and that a suicide involving a Browning is described in the story *Morphine*, along with one that is prepared but not carried through with in an unfinished story from 1929 and in *A Theatrical Novel*, the work that this story developed into. Thus, when Woland hands a revolver to the poet (along with some engagement rings) in the third draft, it is unlikely we should see this only as a reference to the theme of Mayakovsky (L. Fleishman); this section has its origins in a recurring theme in Bulgakov's work.

Let us also note that Bulgakov scrutinized the letter Mayakovsky wrote before his death, which was published in the newspapers. It was addressed not only to "Everyone", but also, specifically, to the same recipient as Bulgakov's letter ("Comrade government"); he can't have failed to notice that the author of the letter, unlike him, *did not ask for anything* for himself – only for his loved ones, after his death; the upshot was that into the contractual relations which one writer had terminated with his death, the other was now entering, whilst also binding himself, during the telephone call, to a very specific dependency (naturally, this aspect may only have been fully understood later – hence the barely perceptible tinge of bitterness in the final line of the letter from 1931: "… I worked for one year not out of fear, as a director at theatres in the USSR").

In the field of Bulgakov's creative process at this time, two opposing movements take place. On the one hand, his thoughts about important actions in his life and about his fate, acquiring the form of an autobiographical, artistic task, have to be adapted so that they fit within the confines of the plot that he already has. On the other hand, the novel itself, about Yeshua and Woland, with the issues it addresses and the atemporal nature of the events in which Pilate and Yeshua take part, could not fail to leave its imprint on Bulgakov's interpretation of his own problems in life – to have an impact on his awareness of his biography as a destiny, standing outside of time. The story of Yeshua and Pilate prompted his thoughts about the irreversible nature of the consequences of fateful steps, about the eternal payback for anyone who, like the new hero of his novel, the Master, has sought help from Satan and, in doing so, has tied his destiny to a diabolical force (this, above all, was the reason why he "did not deserve the light").

2

On 9th September 1933, Yelena Sergeyevna wrote down the following, after Bulgakov dictated it to her: 'At 12pm, Gorky read *Dostigayev* at the Art Theatre. It was greeted with applause, the actors gave him an ovation. The whole troupe was there. He did the reading in the upper foyer. Gorky: 'All the applause has deafened me. The only thing my ear can make out now is the shout of 'hurrah'.'

During the intermission, a meeting with Gorky and Kryuchkov. Kryuchkov said that M.A.'s letter had been received… that A.M. had been very busy, and that as soon as he had some free time… - 'And there I was thinking that A.M. didn't want to see me.' 'No, no!'

At the end of the play, there was no applause. Gorky: 'Well, tell me, what did I do wrong?' Nemirovich: 'You did nothing wrong. The play is wonderful, it is wise.' It seems that what was described in the diary as a "meeting" was in fact nothing more than an exchange of greetings. No dialogue with Gorky was forthcoming; so it was replaced by a dialogue with Gorky's secretary, P.P. Kryuchkov, who quickly assumed the role of the go-between for Gorky and those who wanted a private meeting with him.

The issue of *Flight* was discussed at the theatre and Afinogenov took an active part in this discussion; he had just returned from a long period spent travelling around various countries and was eager to dispense advise, as someone who had seen the world. This irritated Bulgakov; he did not allow many people to give him literary advice, and always reserved the right to hand-pick his advisers.

On the evening of 17th September, Bulgakov read two chapters of the novel to N.N. Lyamin. This was one of the first readings of the novel that he had set about writing once again.

An interesting document survives from that period. On 8th September, a questionnaire was brought to Bulgakov, containing questions about his views on Saltykov-Shchedrin (the questionnaire was drawn up by the editors of *Literaturnoye Nasledstvo* [*Literary Inheritance*]). On 19th September, Bulgakov fills in his answers; his reaction to some of the questions is just as interesting as his answers: he clearly pushes to one side any sentences that are alien to the language of his understanding of the world, his description of it. Addressing his letter "to the responsible editor comrade Averbakh", he was probably to some extent parodying even those questions that he answered:

"1. Extent and nature of your knowledge of Shchedrin's oeuvre, his role in the forming of your worldview.

Answer: I first began to get to know the works of Shchedrin when I was roughly thirteen years of age, and I was inordinately fond of these works. Thereafter I continued to read and re-read them, coming back to them again and again. I suppose that the extent of my knowledge of Shchedrin's oeuvre is fairly large, and his role in the forming of my worldview is significant. 2. Your assessment of Shchedrin as an artist. Answer: I consider him a first-rate artist.

3. Your assessment of Shchedrin as a classic writer of satire, in connection with the tasks faced by Soviet satire.

Answer: I would suggest that one cannot really create satire, it creates itself. I would suggest that all of the Soviet satirists, however, would do well to study Shchedrin carefully.

4. Shchedrin's artistic method in the light of our literary disputes today. Did Shchedrin have a purely literary influence on you.

Answer: The first part of the question is not clear. As far as Shchedrin's literary influence on me is concerned, I think this influence was pretty substantial.

5. Shchedrin as a type of writer (his involvement in practical life, level of his worldview).

Answer: The question is not clear, I am having difficulty answering it." These difficulties, openly admitted to, were the thing that, by the start of the 1930s, differentiated him from a great many of his fellow writers."

On 27th September, "Misha read to Kolya L. [Lyamin – M.C.] some new chapters of a novel about the devil, written in the last few days, or rather – nights." These past few days, he has spent the evenings playing chess with little Sergey, and before he goes to bed, he tells him stories about the brave pioneer Bubkin – about how he goes off to fight together with Voroshilov, and gets caught up in all manner of adventures. One of the relatively small number of visitors, L. Kantorovich, after hearing about this, tries to persuade Bulgakov to start working on a children's film, *Bubkin*. "But M.A. is busy with his novel," Yelena writes on 28th September, "and he doesn't think the task is a real one."

On 1st October, he sends a note to his sister Nadya, asking her to forgive him for failing to send his greetings the previous day, on her name day: "It's not that I've forgotten you. I am ill all the time and I'm not planning to go out until tomorrow. Please pass on to your dear little children 100 roubles to mark the occasion of your name-day yesterday. And I kiss you. Lyusya and I are now tackling the apartment issue with our heads together, damn the whole issue. Our apartment is still not ready and it's tearing me apart in all senses, but I've already set aside a room for Lyuba in the same building in which I live now. So don't get angry with me over the fact that I rarely reveal much about myself."

At 6.30pm on 5th October, Nemirovich-Danchenko talks to Bulgakov, Afinogenov, Vs. Ivanov, Faiko, Vishnevsky and the theatre critic Bakhelis, and Vishnevsky says, among other things: 'Bulgakov did a bad job on the stage adaptation of *Dead Souls*.'

That same evening, Bulgakov reads some excerpts from the novel at Popov's home.

On 10th October, Y.S. Bulgakova wrote: 'In the evening, Akhmatova, Veresayev, Olya and Kaluzhsky, Patya Popov and Anna Ilinichna were here. A reading of the novel. Akhmatova said nothing all evening.'

According to S.A. Makashin, Bulgakov himself wasn't happy with his answers to the questionnaire from *Literaturnoye Nasledstvo*, and on 11th October he writes some new answers. Altering his choice of words on how he first got to know the writer's works at an early age, he added: "When I grew up, I discovered an awful truth. At that point, my view of the world around me became one of mourning." In the new version, his answer to question three took on a new aphoristic energy of thought and expression: "I am convinced that any attempts to create satire are doomed to utter failure. It cannot be created. It creates itself, suddenly. It is created when a writer appears who considers life as it stands incomplete, and, in his indignation, sets about creating an artistic denunciation of it. I would suggest that the path travelled by such a writer will be very, very difficult." And as though in confirmation of these words he had just written, the next morning, as can be clearly seen from Yelena's diary, a call comes in from his sister Olya: "Nikolai Erdman and Mass. have been arrested. For some satirical cock-and-bull story, so they say. Misha frowned"; that night, as the same diary entry tells us, he throws part of the novel in the fire. It seems this was the chapter about Bosoi, which was on pages 117-292 of the version paginated by the author, but was almost entirely cut out by the author from the second exercise book in the new (third) version of the novel. Only four pages survived.

On 14th October, Bulgakov asks the editors of ZhZL to let him know whether or not the manuscript of *Molière* is free, and on 17th receives the manuscript, with a note from A.N. Tikhonov saying that they are not going to publish *Molière*. On the same day, Bulgakov starts a letter to Veresayev: "Dear Vikenty Vikentyevich, I seem to remember that I once treated you to a letter which left you utterly befuddled. That always happens, though: when my literary burden starts to oppress me too much, I give part of it to Yelena Sergeyevna. There is only so much that a woman's shoulders can bear, however. And then – I shall call on you.

I have not felt as much disquiet as I do now for a long time. I cannot sleep. At dawn, I start looking at the ceiling and I rub my eyes until life begins outside the window: a cap, a shawl, a shawl, a cap. Gosh, what boredom!

So what is the problem? The apartment. It all starts with that."

In the meantime, he works almost every day – or rather, every night – on the novel. On the night of 20th October he writes chapter 12, and on the 29th he starts chapter 14.

On 20th October, Yelena wrote: "M.A. went to see Blumenthal and to the X-ray room, about his kidneys – they caused him pain for a while. They say everything's okay now, though." Much later, his younger friend S.A. Yermolinsky would recall one of his pieces of medical wisdom, which he loved to dispense to other people from time to time: "Just so you know, the worst disease of all is disease of the kidneys. It steals up on you like a burglar. All quietly, without giving you any pain signals at all. That's usually what it's like. So if I were the head of all the police departments, I would replace passports with the requirement to show a urine analysis, and would only add my stamp of approval on the basis of that."

On 30th October, at a performance of *The Days of the Turbins*, V.M. Molotov praises the cast's acting – Yelena writes an entry to that effect in the diary.

On the night of 30th – work on the novel again.

Woland's story about Yeshua and Pilate, which had previously been contained within a single chapter, was now broken down into sections, which were intermingled with the other storylines. Fiello (who would later become Azazello) read an excerpt to Margarita from the novel by her beloved – at least in October he did; in November 1933, a new hero had been defined as the author of a novel, the text of which was the same as the Gospel according to Woland.

On 1st November, Sergei Budantsev called, and told Bulgakov about the experiments Bryukhonenko had been doing, trying to bring the severed head of a dog back to life; Bryukhonenko was invited to lunch the very same day, and talked about his experiments, assuring Bulgakov that this was "ready material for a play" (what follows is a direct quotation from Y.S. Bulgakova's diary).

N.A. Ekke called from the editorial offices of ZhZL and told me the following:

"Kamenev likes the biography of Molière very much, he doesn't agree with Tikhonov's assessment of it at all. He is awaiting his return from holiday…"

Bulgakov went to the construction site almost every day – he was curious to see how things were progressing, and would return home even more excited than before.

On 3rd November, some guests from the Art Theatre came for dinner. "Fedya [F.N. Mikhalsky – M.C.] predicted: *Molière* won't be accepted, but *Flight* will." On the 4th – "spent the evening with M.A. on his shift at the branch [of the Art Theatre – M.C.] – Kirshon's *Bread*. Before the play – the triumphal part, the stage was decked out in red, there were speeches, and after each one the orchestra played a little bit of the *Internationale*. But we weren't sitting in the auditorium, we were walking around the theatre looking for somewhere to get a glass of water. We watched the play, and were bored by it; the men weren't convincing; Kedrov performs his role well."

Just as before, the manuscript for the novel indicates that it was being worked on every day. 8th November: "M.A. slept through almost an entire day – he has had lots of sleepless nights. Then he worked on the novel (Margarita's flight). He is complaining of a headache."

9th November: "The issue of the apartment is a troubling one. We went to see Matei Zalka [from the board of the housing cooperative – M.C.] and he reassures us: we'll get it soon, by the end of the year.

It is cold. The first snow has fallen. A snowstorm."

10th November. "An afternoon concert at the Art Theatre – we went along to it. Golovanov and the orchestra – *Spanish capriccio*". A letter came from Zamyatin – "after a long interval". 11th November. "Meeting of the board in the new building", 12th: "Evening – Dmitriyev [the set designer V.V. Dmitriyev, who had already done the first sketches for the stage design for *Dead Souls* – with Rim. – M.C.]. He had just come from the Bolshoy Theatre. He had seen *Don Quixote* there from Stalin's box." 14th: "M.A. spoke to Kaluzhsky about his wish to try his hand at acting. He asked to be given the role of the judge in *The Pickwick Club* and of the Hetman in *The Turbins*. Kaluzhsky is favourably inclined to the idea. I am in despair. Bulgakov is an actor." 16th November: "M.A. was on duty at *Dead* [*Souls*]." This was to be the last day of his daily work on the novel – he stopped on page 506 of the manuscript – until 30th December 1933.

17th November: "Evening at the opening of Ruben Simonov's theatre in a new building on B. Dmitrovka – *Talents and Admirers* (*Talanty i Poklonniki*). A fresh, young play. Ruben gave M.A. a charming welcome, and invited us to the banquet after the play. Lots of the Vakhtangov set were there, they were all very nice."

22nd November: "At the Popovs house. There was a guitar being played, a gypsy waltz [many people recalled that A.I. Tolstaya had a remarkable aptitude for playing ballads on the guitar – M.C.]. Prior to our arrival, they had had some other friend over as a guest, but Annushka had said to him: 'Once Bulgakov arrives, you'll have to sling your hook, he can't stand having people he doesn't know around him.' M.A., on hearing about this, rushed off to try to stop him – but it was too late."

On 29th November, a meeting takes place at the Art Theatre, in Bulgakov's absence; the decision is taken to postpone *Flight*, and the author finds out about this the next day.

7th December. Evening – the doctor. "He found M.A. to be suffering from extremely severe exhaustion."

8th December: sketches for the play *Bliss*. He writes a note to Yelena Sergeyevna: "Love you very much. M." "Knorre [a director at TRAM – M.C.] came to the branch, summoned M.A. and very subtly, in a very round-about way, suggested a subject – a wonderful one – concerning the rehabilitation of criminals in the OGPU's labour communes; but M.A. doesn't want to work with him. In an equally round-about way, M.A. turned down the idea." This was a time when writers were going on trips to the White Sea Canal and countless stories and tales appeared on the subject of re-education through labour (M. Zoshchenko's *The Story of One Life*; this work was included in the anthology *The White Sea Canal*, as *The Story of One Correction*).

On 9th December, Bulgakov plays the role of the judge at a viewing of the first six scenes from *Notes from the Pickwick Club* (Bulgakov helped N.A. Venkstern with the stage adaptatation and even read the text of it at the Art Theatre). "He was a success. The first to congratulate him was Toporkov. Nemirovich said: 'Yes, a new actor has been discovered.' At the rehearsal, the cast were told that the rehearsals for *Molière* were going to resume' [*Molière* had not been rehearsed for six months].

With its frugal lines, Yelena's diary for the end of 1933 hints at a picture of alienation, of a mutual lack of understanding even with his loved ones, his family, who, by that time, had already completed their own corrective journeys and were waiting for those lagging behind to catch up. On 11th December, his sister, Nadezhda Afanasievna, arrived; she had come to ask for copies of the plays *Molière* and *Flight* for a friend of hers, the critic Nusinov; and she openly warns her brother that he is going to write negative reviews of his work. Bulgakov refuses to give her the plays, and she is displeased by this disservice on his part. Olga Bokshanskaya tells him about a call that was recently made to the theatre by the editors of the *Literary Encyclopaedia* (*Literaturnaya Entsiklopediya*): "A woman's voice: 'We're writing an article about Bulgakov – an unfavourable one, of course. But we'd like to know whether he was reformed after *The Days of the Turbins*.'

Misha: It's a pity the courier didn't pick up the phone, he would have told them: indeed he was, yesterday at 11 o'clock.' Over lunch or tea among a close family circle, there was more to come. 'Another story from N.A.: some distant relative of hers on her husband's side, a Communist, said of M.A. that he ought to be sent to Dnieprostroi (to work on the dam over the Dnieper) for three months, and not given any food, then he'd be reborn.

Misha:

'There's another way: feed him herring and don't let him drink.'

Thus, the tension, the sense that there was a distance in terms of the way of thinking and the language of those around him, did not leave him, even in a place where one would have thought he might be able to rest his mind – alongside those who had once been part of a single, shared home.

12th December: "In the afternoon, Misha and I tried to go out on skis. We went across the lake at Novodevichy and came back – a wild, icy wind was blowing.

There was a report in *Izvestiya* today about the new American ambassador, and a photo of him – he arrived in Moscow yesterday."

Directorial meetings about *Molière* were taking place every day; new actors were being brought in.

On 16th December, Bulgakov starts dictating the play *Bliss* to his wife, and on 17th he notes, on the printed text of a story from 1922, *No. 13 – The House of the Elpit Workers' Commune*, "For the collection and in memory of the woman who was my sole inspiration, my wife Yelena Sergeyevna. This story relates to a fearful time in my life." On 19th December, Yelena Sergeyevna's son, Zhenya, hands her a cutting from *Vechernyaya Moskva* for her to pass on to Bulgakov: it is a report stating that the new American ambassador, Bullit, had been to watch *The Days of the Turbins* and had written in the visitors' book: "A magnificent play, a magnificent performance."

At 11 o'clock on 23rd December, he reads *Molière* at the Art Theatre, to the new actors. "Veresayev called today, and complained that his book *The Sister*, published by GIKhL [the State Publishers of Fictional Literature – M.C.] had been put in the 'unwanted' window by GIKhL themselves, with a note saying that the book was harmful. One feels sorry for the old man."

25th December: Morning – a rehearsal of *Molière*. "Went to fetch M.A. from the theatre at 4 o'clock, drove to see Yakimanka at the Blood Transfusion Institute. Bryukhonenko was very sorry to tell us that he could not show us a severed dog's head coming back to life – he didn't have a suitable specimen. He showed us one or two of his achievements. Above all, though, he insistently suggested to M.A. that he should write a play – together with him – and base it on one of his scientific experiments.

Then some director from the Union of Cinema came to call and tried to persuade Bulgakov to write a film instead of a play, or to write both. At the same time, though, it was clear that the surname 'Bulgakov' frightened him. He kept muttering, with a bitter sigh:

'Yes... but the thing is, you're a satirist! I remember your work *The Fateful Eggs*... ye-e-s...' – and he shook his head sadly.

Then both he and Bryukhonenko, both dressed in thin jackets despite the extremely cold weather, came out into the yard to see us off, inviting us to go back and see them another time." Yelena Sergeyevna, who was sensitive to details like this, never failed to remember signs of such a respectful attitude towards Bulgakov.

29th December: "Today, Yegorov and Ripsi were at our place for the first time, and then Fedya too [N.V. Yegorov – the deputy director at the Art Theatre, R.K. Tamantseva – the secretary on the board of the Art Theatre; F.F. Mikhalsky. – M.C.]. Ripsi is one of the few people who welcomed the news of our marriage. Over dinner, Nik[olai] Vas[ilievich] began to demonstrate why M.A. was precisely the man to battle for the purity of principles in the theatre and for the artistic face of the Art Theatre.

After all, you are used to going hungry, what have you got to fear!' he said, deliriously.

'I am used to going hungry, of course, but I'm not particularly fond of doing so. So you'd better battle for it yourself.'

On 4th January 1934, Bulgakov returned to the novel; on that day, he writes the page on which Margarita, on meeting Woland not at the ball (which is not included in this draft), but at a Witches' Sabbath (described in far more

Rabelasian hues than in later versions), and asks him: 'Give me back my lover'.

Throughout the month of January, the author returns to the pages of the manuscript constantly. Fiello, pulling a fur hat down over his ears, set off to find the lover. The story of his disappearance, set out on two pages, is torn out of the exercise book (apparently for the same reason as the story about Bosoi), but the hero appearead in the pages of the novel in a padded jacket and *boots*, as stated above.

9th January: "M.A. – scene by scene – is crafting a play. For which theatre?
'With my surname, they won't take it anywhere. Even if it comes out well.' The play in question is *Bliss*. 'I have missed a few days. [Y.S. is trying to keep the diary carefully and regularly at this time – M.C.]. In that time, there have been two deaths: Lunacharsky and Andrei Bely." Both of these people meant something to Bulgakov: the first had a direct relation to his fate. Bulgakov's literary attitude towards Bely was negative, and from 1933 onwards he also felt some irritation with him – Bely had spoken out against *Dead Souls* being performed at the Art Theatre, claiming that neither the author nor the directors had properly understood Gogol.

"He spent his whole life, God forgive me, writing rudderless, broken nonsense. Lately, he decided to turn and face communism. But he was extremely unsuccessful in the way he turned… It is said that he was blessed in an extremely sad obituary." And in the same entry: "Rehearsals have begun at the Art Theatre for *Enemies (Vragi)* [the play by Gorky – M.C.]. At a recent performance of this play at the Maly Theatre, the following sentence was uttered in the government box: 'It would be good if this play were put on at the Art Theatre.' Thus, the repertoire at the Art Theatre was subject to unpredictable changes; this, in the eyes of Bulgakov and the other playwrights, meant that, on the one hand, plays which had already been rehearsed were in an unstable position, whilst on the other hand, they were constantly having to hope for miracles – such as the return of *Flight* to the stage.

Towards the end of January, work was taking place on the final chapters of the novel, as they were identified in a note called 'Chapter headings', back in October 1933: "17. Stepa's Return. 18. Bosoi is Released. 19. The Investigation at Ivanushka's House. 20. The Battle with Woland. The City Ablaze. Towards evening, a suicide. 21. The Flight. Pontius Pilate. The Resurrection."

Pages from the chapter which was evidently called 'The City Ablaze' have been torn out, and only a few fragments of the tale of how a locked car rolled up to house No. 10 can be made out. Its content can partially be restored, however, on the basis of an entry in Yelena's diary for 23rd January, which tells of how Bulgakov was working on the scene involving a fire in Berlioz's apartment, and of how that very night (i.e. the night of the 22nd to the 23rd), a fire broke out in their kitchen, and Bulgakov put it out himself, shouting out in desperation at one point: 'Call the fire brigade!', before managing to put out the fire after all…

Thereafter, work on the novel came to a halt again, on the scene at the Torgsin (this acronym stood for *torgovlia s inostrantsami*, 'trade with foreigners', and was the name of a type of hard-currency store); this time he was unable to go back to it until the summer of that year.

On 5th February, Bulgakov and his wife watch the dress rehearsal for Gorky's play *Yegor Bulychev* and Yelena Sergeyevna summarizes their thoughts about it in her diary: "A colourless play", and on 11th February, the day after the premiere, O.S. Bokshanskaya calls them and, as always, gives them *Posledniye Novosti* from the theatre: "Members of the government came to see the play, Stalin was there. It was a tremendous success. We've been ordered to create a production of *Lyubov' Yarovaya*."

Returning to the diary after a long break – from 11th February to 27th March – Yelena provides a special explanation: "At first I was ill for a long time (with an inflammation of the lungs), then we moved to a new apartment, and Misha took me over there with a temperature of 38 degrees; we got settled in etc. And also – M.A. has been working on a new comedy."

On 20th February 1934, the bookseller E.F. Zippelzon writes in his diary: "Met M.A. Bulgakov. When I asked him what he was looking for nowadays (in terms of books), he replied: 'what I'm looking for above all right now is gas for the bathroom.' He moved to the house of writers on Nashchokinsky side-street yesterday.

Rehearsals for *Molière* have now been going on for three years. *Flight* has once again been cancelled. For Bulgakov, the following is typical: I ask him: 'Has Bagritsky's funeral already happened?' Response: 'Who's Bagritsky? Honestly, I don't know who Bagritsky is!'

We talked about Talnikov's article, which set out to show that one should never try to rewrite the classics…"

On 6th March 1934 Bulgakov wrote to Veresayev about his new home: "It is a remarkable building, I swear! There are writers living here above and below me, and behind and in front and on either side.

I pray to God that the building will stand firm and be indestructible. I'm glad I got out of that damp hole in Pirogovskaya. What bliss it is to ride on the tram! Vikenty Vikentievich!" This was a huge advantage in the new apartment – the ability of go on foot in just 25-30 minutes along the boulevards, down Nikitskaya and the side-streets, and reach the Art Theatre or its affiliate. His route to the theatre from Pirogovskaya, by contrast, was inevitably associated with a journey on a packed tram. "Admittedly, it is chilly here, there's something wrong with the toilet and water leaks from the basin onto the floor, and there will probably be various other snags, but in spite of all that, I'm happy. If only the building stands firm!

Good heavens! If only spring would come quickly. O, how long and exhausting this winter has been. [Was Bulgakov aware that this part of the letter echoed almost exactly a line from Chekhov's story *The Peasants*: "O, how harsh, how long this winter has been!"? – M.C.]. I dream of opening the door of a balcony. I am tired, I am tired."

Roughly six months earlier than Bulgakov, O. Mandelstam and his wife had moved into the same building. It is unlikely that they met in the few short months that remained before May 1934 – unless perhaps by chance, on the street beside the building. Their brief acquaintance from 1921 was not, as far as I know, maintained in Moscow; there was too much dividing them (let us compare the recollections of the poet's wife about the Kiev days: "Mandelstam in 1919 was full of trust in people, he was jolly, his mood was light," with what we know about Bulgakov in the same period). Yet they were men from the same generation, who even had the same date of birth; they both belonged wholly to the 'urban' culture, and with hindsight one can see grounds for comparing their attitudes to the city as a focal point for culture, as the bearer of traditions.

A clue less to the personal interaction between Bulgakov and Mandelstam (of which, I shall say it again, there was practically none), than to the map of Moscow's literary life in the mid- and early 1930s, is provided by A. Akhmatova's memoirs: "In the winter of 1933-1934, when I was staying with the Mandelstams in Nashchokinsky Side-street, in February 1934, the Bulgakovs invited me to an evening at their place. Osip was worried: 'They want to bring us together with the literature of Moscow!' (he was clearly not *au fait* with the notion that by this time, Bulgakov was only very weakly linked to "the literature of Moscow" – M.C.]. To reassure him, I unfortunately said: 'No, Bulgakov himself is something of an outcast. There will probably be someone from the Art Theatre there.'

Osip got very irate. He ran around the room, shouting:

'How can one tear Akhmatova away from the Art Theatre…'"

Just over two and a half months later, at seven o'clock in the morning on 14th May, Mandelstam was arrested.

On 14th March, Bulgakov wrote to P.S. Popov: "This winter is truly interminable. You look out of the window and you feel like spitting on it all. And the damp snow goes on lying there on the rooftops. I'm fed up with winter!' The soul of this native of Kiev still had no patience for the harsh and lengthy winters of Moscow, despite having lived there for more than ten years.

"Little by little, the apartment is being made ready. But I am just as sick of the carpenters as I am of winter. They come and go, and do their knocking and banging.

A lantern has been hung up in the bedroom. As for the study, well, to the bog with it! What use are all these studies anyway."

The apartment was a three-room one. From the large dining room there were doors leading to the left, into a children's room, and to the right, into a small bedroom which also began to be used as a study.

"I have already forgotten Pirogovskaya Street. That is a sure sign that life there was not up to much. Although there were plenty of interesting things there. [...] *Molière*: well, what can I say, we're rehearsing it. But only rarely, and at a slow pace. And, I'll let you into a secret, I am observing all this with a gloomy feeling. Lyusya cannot talk about what the theatre has done with this play without getting worked up. For me, this period was over and done with long ago. And if it weren't for the thought that we need a new play for the stage, in order to keep on living, I would have stopped thinking about it. If it gets put on – all well and good, if it doesn't – so be it. I work hard at these rare rehearsals, however, and with abandon. There's no changing a man of the theatre, it's in the blood!"

He regularly took part in rehearsals for *Notes from the Pickwick Club*; he had lessons "with the the Art Theatre vocalists" – ahead of an anniversary concert, for which he was in charge of the preparations. "... And from time to time I write down, scene by scene, a comedy. Who am I trying to comfort by doing so? Why do it? No-one can explain that to me." On 23rd March, he signs a contract for the play *Bliss* with Moscow's Satire theatre.

On 27th March 1934, Yelena writes: "I went to the Art Theatre today to fetch M.A. Whilst I was waiting for him in the booking-office with Fedya, Nik. Vas. Yegorov came along. He said that Stalin had been at the theatre a few days earlier, and had asked among other things about Bulgakov, and about whether he was working at the theatre?

'Let me share with you, Y.S., that among the members of the government, the feeling is that the best play of all is *The Days of the Turbins*.'"

This new sign of attention from Stalin gave rise to new hopes in Bulgakov and just over two weeks later, on 13th April, Yelena wrote in her diary: "We have decided to submit an application for foreign passports for August – September."

On 28th March, Bulgakov finished the first hand-written draft of the play *Bliss*, which filled three and a half notebooks; part of the play was written in Yelena's hand, with him dictating it to her.

"I suffered a great deal there, in that life," said the play's female protagonist, Maria, to a man from the country of the future, to which she flies in a time machine. "Ah, God! What if it was just a dream? Your clear eyes reassure me. I am struck by the expression on the faces of the people here. There is a calmness about them.

Rodomanov: Were people's faces back then really so different?

Maria: Ah, how can you even ask. They were so very different from yours… They had terrible eyes."

Prefiguring the finale of *The Master and Margarita*, Bulgakov inserted into the play the motif of a longing for peace, of release from all anxieties – something that was not accessible, incidentally, to the protagonist, the inventor Rein, because he finds the reassurances of Rodomanov, who tries to persuade him to give the machine to him as a representative of the state, unacceptable: "Hold onto me, take out the mechanism, give it to me, I shall lock it away in the cash register… All the shops will be dealing in images of your bust."

No: the protagonists of these two plays, both creators, do not consent to the idea of surrendering the mechanism, not even in exchange for busts. Rodomanov's entreaties and Rein's reply: "I've got it. I'm a prisoner, you won't let me go" call to mind Konchak's aria from Borodin's opera *Prince Igor*.

"He was always endlessly troubled by that aria," Yelena said. "When he listened to it, he would turn pale and squeeze my hand…"

Rein and George Miloslavsky come running back from the future to the present, and the thief Miloslavsky gives the man who tries to restrain them a kick. The first draft of the play ended with this involuntary participation on the part of Rein in the murder which was the end result of his attempt to obtain peace and the freedom he needed for his creativity in *Bliss*.

His work on the second draft (most of which was dictated by the author to his wife), from which all traces of the musical comedy genre disappeared, took just two weeks. It was concluded on 11th April, after which the typing up process immediately began. On 12th April, the author read the play "for some of his closest friends," as Yelena wrote. "Kolya Lyamin was there, along with Sergei Yermolinsky and Bernet. They liked the comedy." The third, type-written version was dated 23rd April, and on 25th, the play was submitted to the theatre.

On 28th April, Bulgakov writes to Popov at Yasyana Polyana: "You can add one more chapter (half jokingly and half in earnest, the two are now discussing the idea of Popov working on a biography of Bulgakov – whether real or theoretical – M.C.], chapter 97, about how not a damn thing came of *Bliss*.

On 25th, I read the play to the troupe at the Satire. Everyone liked the first act and the last one a lot, but they didn't get the scenes in *Bliss* at all. They all, every last one of them, fell in love with Ivan the Terrible [in this play he was an episodic character, who only appeared in the first and last acts – M.C.]. Obviously I wrote something in completely the wrong way." A few days earlier, on the 26th, he complained in a letter to Veresayev: "… I have finished, at last, the play that I thought up ages ago. I dreamed of finishing it, submitting it to the Satire theatre, with which I have a contract, and then instantly forgetting about it and starting to write a screenplay for *Dead Souls*. (A contract was signed with the Union of Films on 31st March – he had to submit the screenplay for the director Pyrev by 20th August – M.C.]. But things didn't work out as I had thought they would… instead of forgetting about it, I've been lying in bed with neuralgia and thinking what a very odd sort of a playwright I am! I must have 'Olivier salad' for brains: one minute Chichikov's crawled into my mind, the next – this comedy."

It should not be forgotten that the play was thought up in 1929-1930, under the influence of Mayakovsky's plays and, of course, containing a polemical jab at them. In the few years that had passed, the very task of portraying the future had evidently lost its literary appeal. Bulgakov suffered what can only be described as the first total failure in his life as a dramatist.

"I feel disgusting from the point of view of my health. I am utterly exhausted. By the first of August, I must get rid of all work at any cost and have a break until the end of September, otherwise it is completely clear that by the next season, I will no longer be in a condtion to keep going."

On 31st April, a group of actors and directors from the Satire theatre have dinner at the Bulgakovs'. "M.A. greeted them from his bed, he had the most frightful headache. But he livened up later and got up for dinner. We had a pleasant evening. They all asked M.A. for changes, they agree to a long period, let's say 4 months (after all, M.A. now has to work on *Dead Souls* for the cinema). They are dreaming about a funny woman of some sort, with Ivan the Terrible, with a clip of the future. They think that this is already there, like a seed, in the play, in Ivan the Terrible's first appearance."

"I have decided to submit a request for a two-month journey abroad: in August – September," he wrote on 26th April to Veresayev. "I was lying in bed for a few days, thinking and racking my brains, trying to get some advice from someone. 'Don't cite the illness.' Very well, I won't. I can, and must, only cite one thing: I must and I have the right to see – albeit briefly – the world. I check myself, I ask my wife whether I have that right. She answers that I do. So am I, then, to cite that?

The matter is made incredibly complicated by the fact that I have to travel with Yelena. I feel unwell. Neurasthenia, my fear of loneliness would transform the trip into a sad agony. Now that's interesting, what can one cite in that case? Some of my advisers, on hearing the words "with my wife", waved their hands scoffingly. Yet there is no reason whatsoever for waving one's hands. It is the truth, and this truth must be defended. I do not need doctors, or leisure homes, or health spas, or anything else like that. I know what I need. For two months – a different city, a different sun, a different sea, a different hotel, and I believe that in the autumn, I will be in a fit state to rehearse at the Art Theatre, and perhaps to write, as well.

One fellow said to me: talk to Nemirovich.

No, I shall not do so! Neither to Nemirovich, nor to Stanislavsky. They won't lift a finger. Let Anton Chekhov appeal to them!

So then, my decision. I am appealing to Yelena Sergeyevna. She has a lucky hand.

It is time, it is time to make the move, Vikenty Vikentievich! Or else it will be somehow strange – it will be dusk!

Do not wish me luck; we have a superstition in the theatre, whereby it is not good to do so."

The application was submitted and handed to Y.L. Leontiev, a friend of the Bulgakovs, so that he could hand it in person to A.S. Yenukidze.

"The copy of my application to A.S. Yenukidze that is enclosed with this letter," Bulgakov wrote on 1st May 1934 to Gorky, "will explain to you that I am requesting permission for a two-month period of foreign travel. Mindful of your favourable responses to the plays *Flight* and *Molière*, which were so valuable to me ["valuable to me" is a well-decorated hint at the fact that *Flight* never made it to the stage – M.C.], I am taking the liberty of bothering you with a request to support me in this matter, which has a genuinely vital significance for me, and also has significance for me as a writer. I would ideally need a slightly longer period for my trip, but I am not asking for that, since I must be at the Art Theatre in the autumn so that I do not interrupt my work as a director on the plays with which I am involved (specifically, *Molière*). Such is my exhaustion that I am afraid to travel on my own, and I am therefore asking for permission for my wife to accompany me. I know for certain that this trip would result in me being fit for work again and would give me the opportunity, alongside my work at the theatre, to do some travel writing, an idea that I find very appealing. I have never been abroad. I would be extremely indebted to you if you were to reply to my letter."

Once again, he is enticed by the thought of foreign travel. Back on 28th April, whilst informing Popov that he had been forgiven, he writes: "I have long dreamt of the Mediterranean waves and the museums of Paris and a quiet hotel and no acquaintances whatsoever and Molière's fountain and a café and, in a word, the opportunity to see all this. I have spoken for so long to Lyusya about the kind of journey that one could write! And I recalled the unforgettable *Frigate 'Pallada'* and how Grigorovich set off for Paris eighty years ago! Ah, if only it could happen! Then, you could start preparing a new chapter – the most interesting one [another reference to the mooted biography of Bulgakov – M.C.]. I once saw a writer who had spent time abroad. He was wearing a beret on his head with a tiny tail. He didn't bring anything back with him at all, apart from that little tail! One got the impression he had slept through the entire two months, then bought that beret and travelled home.

Not a single line, not a single sentence, not a single thought! O, Goncharov, never-to-be-forgotten! Where are you?"

It is remarkable how Bulgakov looks upon the travels of Russian writers from the previous century for support, and refuses to accept the new language used to describe such journeys, one of the models for which was unquestionably Mayakovsky's *My Discovery of America* (*Moye Otkrytiye Ameriki*). "I urge you," Bulgakov warned, "not to tell anyone about this for the time being, nobody at all. There is no great mystery here, I simply wish to fence myself off from the untamed blathering of Moscow's gossipers.

… I simply do not want there to be idle chit-chat about such an important matter, which for me is the matter of a whole future, albeit a brief one, albeit in the evening of my life! … Ah, what letters I shall write to you, Pavel! Ah, when I arrive in the autumn, I shall embrace you, but I shall not buy myself a little tail. Nor shall I buy a pair of short trousers that end at the knees. Nor shall I buy any check stockings."

4th May: "… today, M.A. learned from Yakov Leontievich that Yenukidze has ordered that M.A.'s application should be sent to the Central Committee." Over the next few days, Bulgakov finishes writing the film-script for *Dead Souls*. On 10th May, in the evening, the directors I. Pyrev and I. Weisfeld come to see him. Yelena writes down an excerpt form their conversation:

"Pyrev: You ought, M.A., to come to the studio, you could have a look…"

"It's very noisy at the studio, and I'm tired, I'm unwell. You'd be better off sending me to Nice." K. Stanislavsky had recently been in Nice, receiving therapy.

11th May. "Intense heat.

There is a report in the papers about the death of the chairman of the OGPU, Menzhinsky."

12th May. *Literaturnaya Gazeta* (*Literary Newspaper*) reports on the death of Gorky's son – Maxim Peshkov. The Government sent a letter to Gorky. It is signed by Stalin. "We are mourning together with you and suffering the grief that has so suddenly and wildly descended on us all." The reason for his death is not clear. The report says: after a short illness."

Various complicated situations were constantly arising with regard to *Molière*: it suddenly emerged that Nemirovich-Danchenko was refusing to come and view a number of scenes and Bulgakov was already putting forward his own version, explaining that he was concerned about his own reputation: "He refuses to be associated with anything dubious! And I'll tell you this – Nemirovich, and *Molière* – I'm sick of the whole business! … I want only one thing: for the season to end." That same day, 13th May, one of the actors Bulgakov knew, L.M. Leonidov, says something to him that is in keeping with his current attitude to the rehearsals for *Molière*: "Art must be joyful, and its result must be joyful, like the result of childbirth. In our case, the baby is coming out rear-end first, then being shoved back in and amended…"

14th May: at P.S. Popov's place. "He tried – without success – to persuade M.A. to send his condolences to Gorky. It is true that he can't – after all, there was no answer to that other letter." Bulgakov considers it impossible to write to Gorky without having received a reply to his letter, which was so important to him, of 2nd May. At around this time, Popov gives him a copy of I.L. Tolstoy's *My Memoirs (Moi Vospominaniya)*, which he had published, with the inscription: "To dear Maka, with the wish that you do not fall prey to doubts and that you believe in your own strengths."

15th May: "in the morning, I accompanied M.A. to the theatre – he felt very bad, he was extremely worried.

At around 12 o'clock, a viewing of *Molière* began in the lower foyer. I stood by the closed doors and heard the music, and then, for the first time, the words spoken by Stanitsyn, who was playing Molière…"

16th May: "Today, M.A. has been lying in bed all day – he feels awful. He is reading Kipling to Sergei."

He loved Kipling, Yelena told me in 1969, and used to declaim, with particular feeling:

If you can talk with crowds and keep your virtue,
Or walk with kings – nor lose the common touch…

For him, these lines were saturated with biographical meaning.

And so 17th May arrived – they were summoned to collect their foreign passports. Yelena described what happened the next day. They were made to sit behind a desk in an empty room and fill in forms. "Whilst we were filling them in, M.A. was making me laugh so much, thinking up various funny answers and questions. We were giggling so much, and we didn't notice first a man, then a lady emerge from the doors near us; they sat down at the desk and started writing something. When we went upstairs, Boris Polets [the employee dealing with their documents – M.C.] said that it was too late: the woman who handled passports had left and the passports wouldn't be issued to us today. "Come back tomorrow," – "But tomorrow is the 18th" [a day-off according to the schedule – M.C.]. "Well, come on the 19th then." On the way home, M.A. said: "Hey listen, do you think those people who came into the room ruined our application?! Maybe they'd been eavesdropping on us? And they decided we can't leave, or come back? … No, surely not… Let's dream instead about going to Paris!"

And he kept repeating, gleefully:

"So I'm not a prisoner! I shall see the world!"

We were walking along feeling very excited. It was a hot day. The sun was shining. We walked along Trubny Boulevard. M.A. presses my hand against his side, laughs, and thinks up the first chapter of the book that he is going to bring back from our travels.

"Can it really be true that I'm not a prisoner?! That is the eternal, night-time question: 'I'm a detainee… I was artificially blinded…" At home, he dictated to me the first chapter of his future book."

19th May: "The response as to the foreign passports has been postponed until tomorrow."

23rd May: "The response has been postponed until the 25th."

25th May: "Again no passports. We decided not to go again. M.A. feels horrendously unwell."

29th May: "There is excitement among the writers – a reception is taking place at the new Union of Writers… Trenyov ran over to see us, all excited, and advised M.A. insistently "submit your application quickly!" That same day, Bulgakov submitted an application to the Union and filled in a questionnaire.

On 1st June, Yelena wrote that on those few days (26-29th May), "it had transpired that Yenukidze's secretary, Minervina, had said to Olya that she knew for certain that we would receive passports. They give them to lots of people from the Art Theatre, too, Olya included. They give the "old ones" 500 dollars each to take with them; Olya was given 400. Pilnyak had been given a passport and had gone away with his wife. I called Minervina, she promised to get us a certificate. We are losing control of all other matters due to this uncertainty," "Akhmatova came to see us. She has come here to take steps on behalf of Osip Mandelstam – he is in exile. Word has it there was an incident of some sort in Leningrad, during which Mandelstam struck Alexei Tolstoy across the face." It is hardly likely that Bulgakov felt any sympathy for Alexei Tolstoy. A. Akhmatova recalled that on the morning of the day when Mandelstam was supposed to set off for Cherdyn, accompanied by his wife, she had collected money for them and gone to see the Bulgakovs; Yelena "wept and gave me everything she had in her handbag"; the poet's wife also remembered that "Anna Andreyevna had gone to see the Bulgakovs and returned, touced by the behaviour of Yelena Sergeyevna, who had wept on hearing of the exile, and literally emptied her pockets."

It is not known whether Bulgakov knew about the circumstances of what had happened to Mandelstam, or whether he already knew about Stalin's call to Pasternak. If one supposes that he did know, then this may have once again stirred up in him illusory hopes, hopes which would soon prompt him to begin again his search for a connection to the man.

"M.A. feels awful – fear of death, loneliness," Yelena wrote in her diary that day.

1st June: "He lies in bed whenever he can." Dr. Shapiro, whom she summons, "found in him extreme exhaustion. His heart is in good condition."

2nd June: "We were at the Popovs' in the evening. M.A. and Patya thought up a game: when saying greeting each other or saying goodbye, you have to kiss each other's hand – when the other person's not expecting it. Patya managed to do so today. We had so much fun playing this game – like little children.

M.A.'s condition is better now – Shapiro had a good effect on him."

3rd June: "I called Minervina, she has had no luck in getting to see Boris Polets. It is cold, wet and windy outside." The official form refusing to grant them permission to leave the country was signed on 4th June, but Bulgakov only found out about this later. Y.L. Leontiev was still trying to help them; on 5th June, he said to Yelena, at a rehearsal for *The Pickwick Club*, that he had "added your surname in the the Art Theatre passport list", in the hope that they would be able to obtain passports along with the others, via the theatre's messenger.

The shock that they experienced on 7th June was a big one. Only one-and-a-half months later, on 20th July, did Yelena start to piece the events together in her memory: "What do I remember? On 7th June, we were waiting at the Art Theatre along with the others for Ivan Sergeyevich, who had gone to pick up the passports. He came back with a whole pile of them, gave them all out, and then to us, last of all, he gave some white pieces of paper – rejection letters. We left the theatre. Outside, M.A. soon began to feel ill, I had trouble getting him to the chemist. They gave him some pills and laid him down on a sofa. I went outside to see whether there were any taxis. There weren't, but there was a car parked near the chemist's, and standing beside it was Bezymensky. Not for anything in the world! I went back inside and called for a car using the telephone.

M.A.'s condition is very bad – fear of dying again, of loneliness, of open spaces."

Bulgakov describes the whole of that day in detail, in a letter to Veresayev sent a month later, on 11th July. Before this, however, a matter of days after receiving the refusal, Bulgakov once again writes a letter to Stalin – and on 11th June, Yelena takes it to the relevant office window in person. This letter is probably the most striking example of all the letters of this kind that he wrote. Into it there suddenly appeared, brightly and self-evidently, a connection to the literary and epistolary legacy of the prevous century; it is in many ways structured on old-fashioned turns of phrase ("In requesting permission... I wished to compose a book"), and one can detect a Gogolesque intonation in it; at times, the author seems to have forgotten about the recipient and to be addressing his text almost to himself, or to Pavel Popov – so uninhibited and freely emotional turns of phrase to which he resorts ("In a fit of joy...", "At that point, all doubts whatsoever fell away from me, and my joy became infinite", "... to which I already related with complete good humor..."). One gets the impression that the longer the time in which he had no connection whatsoever with the recipient went on (four years had already passed since the time of the telephone call), the more this recipient had lost, in the eyes of the man writing the letter, any kind of specificity; it was as though it had been preordained that he would perform the function of the providential interlocutor to whom, as Mandelstam once wrote, the poet appeals.

As he writes his letter, Bulgakov seems to be concerned chiefly with finding the best possible way of conveying – or rather, pouring out his feelings and thoughts; he is almost thinking out loud; the reason for the refusal, as he sees it, "could be only one thing: might there not be within the bodies which control foreign travel a supposition that I shall stay out of the country forever? I shall say nothing of the fact that, in order to get away from the border after a deceitful application, I would have to split apart my wife and child, putting her in a frightening situation, destroy the life of my family, with my own hand destroy my repertoire at the Art Theatre, bring shame upon myself – and, above all, do all this for no apparent reason. What is important here is something different: I cannot fathom why one would, after having designs to do one thing, one would request something different? And I have evidence for the fact that I do not understand this" – he was referring to the fact that in 1930, after planning "an indefinite departure, under the influence of my personal circumstances as a writer, I did not write requesting a two-month trip…"

"… *Or walk with kings – nor lose the common touch…*" This letter, just like the letter from 1931, was never answered. Thus, in the space of a year, two important correspondents had been lost – the first had been Gorky.

A curious detail: Bulgakov did not now start waiting for a letter or a call, and on 13th, he and his wife left for Leningrad, on paid leave from the Art Theatre. They stayed at the Astoria again. On 26th June, Bulgakov writes to Popov: "I couldn't write to you any sooner. After all that has happened, not only I myself, but also my mistress, to my great horror, is in very poor health. She started having some devillish migraines, then the pain crawled further down; she has suffered from insomnia and so on. Both of us have had to seek treatment, carefully and seriously. We are given shock therapy every day, and we are starting to get back on our feet." On 20th June, Bulgakov writes, the Art Theatre, which is on tour in Leningrad, performed *The Days of the Turbins* for the 500th time. The author was congratulated by V. Sakhnovsky and Y. Leontiev. "Nemirovich sent his congratulations to the Theatre, too. Turning it over in my hands, I became convinced that there was not a single letter in it that had anything to do with the author. I suppose that etiquette requires that no reference is made to the author. I didn't know this before, but I am obviously not one of the great and the good to a sufficient extent. The one thing I find annoying is that, without asking me, the Theatre sent him a thank you note, including the author in it. I would have given a great deal to delete the word 'author' from that note. […] I am writing *Dead Souls* for the screen and I shall bring the work with me when it's finished. Then all the fuss over *Bliss* will kick off. Oh, how much work I have! But my Margarita and the cat and the flights are wandering around in my mind… But I am still weak and broken. Admittedly, with each passing day I grow stronger.

Over the course of this summer, I shall gather every ounce of strength that I can muster.

Lyusya has given me the nickname Captain Kopeikin. Tell me what you think of this witticism – I think it's first-rate."

On 26th June, Bulgakov writes to P.S. Popov: "My health – alas! – has still not been fully restored, and, of course, one cannot expect to obtain that straight away. Yelena nonetheless feels much better. There is a certain amount of hope with regard to me as well. The shock therapy was very good indeed!" "There are many travails and much work ahead, but I don't think about that, I think about somehow securing tranquillity and a good state of mind," he writes to Leontiev on 6th July. On 4th July, however, he had already met his clients and handed them the first version of the screenplay for *Dead Souls*. "Lyusya assures me that the screenplay came out remarkably well. I showed it to them in draft form, and I was right not to redo it completely. All the parts that I liked best, i.e. the scene involving Suvorov's soldiers in the middle of the Nozdryovskaya scene, the big ballad about Captain Kopeikin, the funeral at Sobakevich's estate and, above all, Rome with the silhouette on the balcony – all that has been completely destroyed! All I can save is Kopeikin, and only then by compressing him a bit. But – God! – how sorry I am about Rome!" (This exclamation could equally have referred to the abandoned trip to Italy.). "I listened to everything that Weisfeld and his director said to me, and immediately said that I would redo it the way they wanted it, so that they were taken aback." He displayed such eagerness to please not because life was a bed of roses; he was economizing on his strength and counting on it; it was clear all the same that the script would have to be rewritten, and he had resigned himself to this, but lost none of his eloquence.

To the theatre which had once ordered an "eccentric, synthetic" play from him, he now brought *Bliss* – in its unrevised form, of course. He tells the story of what happened next in that same letter from 10th July:

"Something has happened here with *Bliss* that goes beyond the bounds of reality. The setting: our room at the Astoria. I am reading the play. The manager of the theatre, who is also the director, listens to it, expresses utter and, apparently, genuinely admiration; he intends to put the play on, he hands me some money and says that in 40 minutes he'll come back to have dinner with me. He arrives 40 minutes later, has dinner, says not a word about the play, and then vanishes without trace and there has been no sign of him since!

There is one school of thought that says he slipped into the fourth dimension.

These are the kind of wonders that go on in the world!"

On 12th July he starts writing in a new exercise book, giving it the title: "Novel. Ending" and he writes 20 pages by 16th July. Yelena, meanwhile, buys a desk and a mirror for their new apartment.

On 17th July they return from Leningrad; that day, he manages to write only a few lines of the novel: Woland and co. leave the Pashkov house and set off towards Pirogovskaya and Novodevichy – places which the author himself had only recently left. On 24th July, he receives a letter from Veresayev, sent in reply to one that he had sent from Leningrad; expressing deep sympathy over the "blow to his nerves" that he had had to endure due to the trip abroad that had to be abandoned, he exclaims at the end of the letter: "What do you need Italy for anyway! As if one can't secure peace and leisure for oneself here at home. Only not in Leningrad!"

On 1st August, he dictates to Yelena a letter to his brother Nikolai: "I am not well, I am suffering from nervous exhaustion. Tomorrow I must leave for about a week for the dacha outside Moscow, else I shall not be in a fit state to go on working. [...] Where did you get the idea that I was going away on holiday? I can't even remember the last time I went on holiday! ... I never go on holiday. [...] I can't write much more now, because the headaches are starting."

That same month, spending a week in Zvenigorod and writing the second draft of the script for *Dead Souls*, by invitation of Ukrainfilm, which had commissioned a script for *The Government Inspector* (*Revizor*) from him, Bulgakov left for Kiev with his wife. He had not been there for eleven years. A few months later, he wrote to A. Gdeshinsky, a friend from his childhood in Kiev: "When I walked in the parks in the afternoon, I was overcome by a strange feeling. This was my patch! Sadness, sweetness, excitement!"

On 23rd August, they returned to Moscow, and Yelena wrote in her diary: "We were there from 18th to the 22nd. [...]

Business matters: 1) *Molière* at the theatre of Russian drama. They both want it, and are hesitating [...] the theatre is afraid. He gave it to the People's Commissariat of Education for a review. The reviewer didn't approve of it: the theme of incest. How virtuous we are! Well, so be it. Let it be put on at the Art Theatre earlier, then. Maybe it's for the best. 2) *The Government Inspector* at the cinema. There were two meetings with the directors. M.A.'s plan went down well. Both directors have started trying to persuade M.A. to move to Kiev outright, and have even promised to get him an apartment. For M.A., the word 'apartment' is a magic word. There is nothing in the world he envies – but for a nice apartment! It's some sort of complex for him."

In the end, he was not able to force himself to step over the threshold of the house where he had grown up on Andreyevsky Hill there were simply too many ghosts inside it. He merely stood inside the deep entranceway to house No. 18 on the other side of the road, he later told his sister, and gazed across at the windows.

3

On the day of his return to Moscow, the 11th meeting of the Writers' Congress was taking place. Vs. Vishnevsky was one of the speakers. "Who knows how comrade Stalin conducted his work?" he asked, recalling the years of the Civil War. [...] "Who knows that he played a decisive role in the saga that was playing out in Siberia, when Kolchak was defeated? Who knows that Stalin silently directed the entire partisan movement? He ensured the crushing defeat of Kolchak's white front and the intervention in the far east of Russia (applause). The problem, the image of the Bolshevik proletarian leader is one that we are obliged to resolve, we are obliged to lift ourselves up higher than the 'regimental', 'divisional' level. A solution to this problem is essential. It not only has historical objectives, but also brings us out into the field of the very highest mental, ethical, moral and military categories." Bulgakov's attitude towards Vishnevsky after the autumn of 1931, when he rudely disrupted his production of *Molière* in Leningrad, was unambiguous. What must his feelings and thoughts have been as he read the report about his speech about the figure of the proletarian leader?

"We are seeing new forms of amicable relations between people," A. Fadeyev had said the previous day. "When we, as writers, are invited before the Central Committee of the Party, or are present at meetings of the Central Committee's bodies, or meet members of the Politburo, we see the exceptional bonds of friendship between these immense figures, the leaders of our party. They are bound by a courageous, principled, steely and jolly friendship, the friendship of Bogatyrs. Naturally, there has never been a collective such as this before, and there never could have been. Only our country engenders such forms of collective relations. But we have not yet learned how to express this."

He also talked about Stalin as a potential literary hero: "I am not suggesting that right now, one of us might feel they have the strength and ability to set about portraying such a mighty genius of the working class as comrade Stalin."

This might, perhaps, have set in motion – only vaguely, uncertainly, for the time being – the artist's competitive instincts… When the same kind of assertions are made again and again, designed to put people off an idea, they gradually start to have an effect through their immutability more than anything else.

25th August. "M.A. is still afraid to be out and about on his own. I took him to the theatre, then went to fetch him at the end. He told me how the meeting with K.S. had gone [Stanislavsky had returned to his homeland after a year spent at resorts in France and Italy – M.C.]. He arrived at the theatre at half past two. The actors greeted him with lengthy applause. K.S. had made a speech in the lower foyer. At first he talked about how things were bad abroad, and good at home. About how over there, everyone was dead and downtrodden, whereas here, one can feel the vitality of life. "One meets a Frenchwoman, and one wonders: where is her *chic*…?" Then came the pedagogical part of the speech. About how there was work to be done, because the Art Theatre was very highly thought of in other countries… In conclusion, he made everyone raise their hands and swear that they were going to do their work well. When he finished, he went to the exit, caught sight of M.A. – and they kissed one another. K.S. hugged his shoulder and the conversation started.

'What are you writing at the moment?'

'Nothing, Konstantin Sergeyevich, I'm tired.'

'You need to be writing… Here's a subject, for example: there isn't enough time to get everything done and be a well-ordered individual.'

Then he suddenly looked afraid and said:

'Don't take that the wrong way, mind you!' But he immediately added: 'I would take it the wrong way, too.'

The secretary of the theatre's party committee stopped them:

'I should like a word with you, Mikhail Afanasievich!'

'Not about anything unpleasant, I hope?'

'No! On the contrary. So that you don't feel lonely.'

A conversation with Afinogenov ensued.

'Mikhail Afanasievich, why haven't you been spending any time at the congress? [the First Writers' Congress was taking place at this time – M.C.].

'I don't like crowds.'

On the eve of the conversation with Afinogenov, Vs. Ivanov's speech had appeared in the papers. Recalling the early 1920s and the declaration by the *Serapionovy Brothers* (he himself had been one), Ivanov had said, at the congress: "I maintain that all those who signed and sympathized with the Serapionovy Declaration, without exception, have come along a path of such growth in consciousness over the last 12 years, that you could no longer find a single one of them who would not accept, in all sincerity, the phrase uttered by comrade Zhdanov, to the effect that we are in favour of the Bolshevik tendency in literature. [...] The old, capitalist world stands not far from us at all. And we are proud of the fact that our ever-growing attachment to the party compels us, teaches us, supports us, in the exasperation and in the constant animosity with which we look at that ancient world." A few days later, Y. Olesha's article *The Dramatists Have the Floor!* (*Slovo Dramaturgam!*) appeared in the newspaper *Trud*, with the sub-heading *From the Notepad of a Delegate at the Congress*. "Today, the dramatists are sitting around the table on the podium," he wrote. "The author of *Bread* (*Khleb*) – Kirshon. The author of *Fear* (*Strakh*) – Afinogenov. The author of *My Friend* (*Moy Drug*) – Pogodin. The author of *Lyubov' Yarovaya* – Trenyov. Masters of Soviet dramaturgy. One can discuss the quality of the various technical approaches used by each author, one can assess them in different ways, but the main thing is indisputable: all these masters create Soviet dramaturgy." Olesha himself had spent several years trying to bring to fruition an idea for a play about a writer, in which, as he wrote when publishing an excerpt from the play, he wanted "to discuss the issue of creativity." The play's protagonist, Modest Zand, dreamed of "being a writer from the aspiring class", but did not know how to reject "a whole host of topics" which "were perhaps remarkable, but were not needed for our times". This inner struggle, which was at the core of the hero's character, harassed the play's author too – and prevented him from completing it. Right from the start of the 1930s, the subject of creativity, the theme of the artist, had acquired a special significance: "How am I to exist, with my ribcage and with that which is duller than any dullness?" Pasternak had written at that time, about his creative capability as one of life's problems. Bulgakov's decision to address this subject – both in his plays, and in the novel that he starts writing, chapter by chapter, starting in 1932 – was not merely a fact from one individual writer's biography.

The difference was that in terms of his creative personality and social worldview, Bulgakov remained alien to the corrosive creativity of self-consciousness which prevented Olesha, for example, from completing a host of his ideas. Bulgakov felt external interference far more acutely than internal interference; that is why we do not know of any works in his creative lifetime that were not completed on account of internal reasons: once started, each of his works moves unrelentingly towards completion.

Let us return to the congress, though. The success of the playwrights about whom Olesha, his former colleague at *Gudok*, wrote in his "Delegate's notepad", was served up before Bulgakov once again in all its self-evidence and cannot have left him indifferent. The atmosphere created by the congress perhaps acted on his condition and prompted the birth of some new ideas for plays. On the very same day when he had the conversation with Afinogenov, Bulgakov comes up with a plan for a play about Pushkin and decides to invite a co-author to help him process the material – Veresayev; he felt grateful to him "because," as Yelena wrote, "in the most difficult days, he had come to visit him and offered to lend him money."

Veresayev's name had already been mentioned at the congress – in a speech by I.G. Lezhnev made on 21st August.

The former editor of *Rossiya* quoted a host of statements by writers in print relating to 1925, when he printed *The White Guard*, shortly before his exile: "V. Veresayev: 'There is a general moaning along almost the entire front-line of contemporary Russian literature. We cannot be ourselves. Violence is being done against our artistic consciousness all the time. Our creativity is becoming more and more two-storied: we write one thing for ourselves, and another thing for publication.' Ivan Novikov: '[…] A writer should not interfere, for here, the most well-intended stirrings on the part of the leadership do nothing but interfere.' "The late Andrei Sobol," the orator continued, "reflecting the mood of many like-minded thinkers not affiliated to the party, wrote: 'Custodianship and artistic creativity are incompatible things. Governors are needed by children, but when you have governors for a writer – that is more than sad." Lezhnev commented: "These talks speak for themselves. The 'shared democratic' demands put forward by the four writers are borrowed from the Menshevist-SR-cadet political daily life.' This was a direct denouncement on the living and the dead.

Governorship had, incidentally, by that time taken on forms which were not at all familiar to the uninitiated. One of the organisers of the congress, I.I. Gronsky, told me (in the early 1980s) that the writers who came under the closest attention from the government (there were a few of them) were "apportioned" among the members of the Politburo and authorised representatives, such as Gronsky: "Several members of the Politburo were assigned to each writer. Assigned to Gorky were Stalin, Molotov, myself and two others; assigned to Demyan Bedny were Voroshilov and me. It was very serious, difficult work. No-one knows about it and it is not yet time to talk about it."

"And how are you feeling, generally?" Afinogenov had enquired, during that same conversation.

"M.A. told him the story about the passports.
Afinogenov:
'How can I ensnare you, so that you come and see me?'
'No, it would be better if you came to see me – I'm forever bed-ridden.'"

That very same day, Yelena writes that Bulgakov came up with the idea for a play about Pushkin and that he deems it necessary to invite Veresayev to help him process the material.

On 28th August, the deputy director of a cinema production company, who had hosted them in Kiev, comes to stay; Bulgakov goes to see the Popovs with Kolya Lyamin, and Yelena and their guest "talk about M.A. until dawn.

'Why doesn't M.A. accept bolshevism? One can't be apolitical these days, one can't stand to one side and write stage adaptations…'

For some reason he said something along the lines of: 'From the dark woods… the sorcerer (the writer M.A.) emerges, and he doesn't want to sing songs in front of the Bolsheviks, not for anything.'

M.A. came home with a terrible migraine [...], lay down with a hot water bottle on his head and chipped in with a few words very occasionally. It was 5 o'clock in the morning."

At that time, an American theatre company was visiting Moscow to put on a production of *The Days of the Turbins*, and the director, a man named Wales, invited the Bulgakovs to come and see him. On 31st August, Yelena described this evening, going into the details which had caught *her* attention, but these functions did not escape Bulgakov's attention as a creative thinker either over the next few years, as he worked on passages of the novel dealing with the devil. "Stearic candles. Almost no furniture at all. On the table – cold snacks, vodka, champagne. The guests were all there already when we arrived. The American Lariosik is a rosy-cheeked fat man in glasses, fairly short. Aleksei is played by a well-built American, with a Slavic-looking face. Besides them, there was a slim American actress and two people form Bullit's embassy. Zhukhovitsky – he was there, of course [Emmanuil Zhukovitsky, who translated Bulgakov's plays, starts turning up at his home constantly from the beginning of the 1930s onwards, often without being invited. – M.C.] – tormented M.A., trying to persuade him to write a declaration saying that he recognises Bolshevism. There was a lady there whom Zhukhovitsky recommended in an utterly fantastical way, as he is wont to do:

'She's related to… (I forget who) from the State Duma…'

The Lady: I was at the premiere of *The Days of the Turbins* (putting the stress on '*Tur*'). Radek left after the first act.

O, lady! O, Zhukhovitsky!"

The atmosphere of fantastical, provocative conversations is getting thicker and thicker around him. It is as though the people speaking to him are talking in some special made-up language, coming to him with strange proposals (like writing some kind of declarations); it is getting harder and harder to achieve mutual understanding.

"The congress of writers ended a few days ago," Yelena wrote, "with a banquet in the Colonnade Hall. They say there was much drunkenness on display. That some drunken poet punched Tairov, after an opening gambit in which he shouted that he was an 'aesthete'..."

On 8th September, Bulgakov encounters his director I.Y. Sudakov in the street and hears yet another round of startling talk from him, which was carefully reproduced that evening by Y.S. Bulgakova in her diary: "Sudakov: 'You know, M.A., the situation with *Flight* is not bad at all, not bad at all. People are saying: put it on. J.V. is very much in favour, as is Avel Sofronovich [Yenukidze – M.C.]. All we need now is for Bubnov not to interfere (?!)" [A. Bubnov was the people's commissariat of education at that time]. Everything was unstable, vague and unreliable.

On 10th September, work resumed (after a break starting on the 13th August) on the novel: "In Vagankovsk side-street," wrote the author, thus recording with a literary device the Side-street where, in 1924, he had met some new friends at Zayaitsky's place, and all the places where the subsequent years had unfolded, "the group was subjected to some harassment. Some anxious citizen, on seeing them emerge, shouted:

'Stop! Detain the arsonists!' He stamped his feet and got all worked up, reluctant to throw himself on the four of them on his own. While he was trying to call people to help, however, the group disappeared in the bitter smoke that had settled on the side-street, and no-one ever saw them in that district again. [...]

It was clear which route they were taking. They were heading directly for the Moscow River. They were leaving the capital."

On 10th and 11th September, Bulgakov wrote the scene in which Margarita and the poet have a feast in the basement and Azazello appears – whilst Woland, with Koroviev and Begemot, is making his away alongside the Devichy Monastery. "Woland did not linger at the Monastery. [...]

The city no longer interested its guest, and, accompanied by his fellow-travellers, he strode quickly towards the Moscow River."

11th September: "We were at the Popovs' [the previous evening, apparently – M.C.]. Annushka sang some gypsy waltzes, with a guitar accompaniment. M.A. has been searching for some, for *Flight*. But will the play be put on at all?"

16th September: "Evening – Lyamin. Misha read a few chapters of the novel to him. And after he left – before 7 in the morning – the talk was all about one and the same thing: M.A.'s position"

On 17th September, in the evening, a director from the Satire theatre asks M.A. to turn *Bliss* into a comedy, featuring Ivan the Terrible transposed into modern-day Moscow. He described it as an overview. When M.A. said that he didn't want to write an overview, Gorchakov said that a comedy would suit them even better." Later, the American director of *The Days of the Turbins* came along, with an actress – they had come to say goodbye.

They are flying to Berlin tomorrow, then on to Bremen, and then going to America by steamship. They are travelling 3rd class on the steamer. They are very nice. They talk all the time about how good it's going to be when M.A. goes to New York."

18th September: "A day-off. Olya [Bokshanskaya – M.C.] and Patya Popov came to have lunch with us [...] In the evening we went to see Leontiev, but found only his sisters and the Shaposhnikovs at home... after dinner, M.A. and Boris Valentinovich went up to the grand piano and started singing some very old ballads. And we, the four ladies, were talking about all sorts of nonsense [...] It was an amusing atmosphere. The men's voices drifted over from the grand piano: 'Don't tempt me...', and at the same moment, from the ladies' table, the bass voice of Yev[geniya] Grigorievna entoned: 'I'll cut the cats' balls off!' – from some joke she was telling..."

Daily work on the novel continues: from 10th to 21st September, 45 hand-written pages are written – the poisoning of the lovers, the building being set on fire, the fires in the city, Margarita flying over it on a broomstick and the poet – on Azazello's coat, and the spectacle of the people dying. "... The poet said, moving his arms from side to side:

'But the children? Please! Children...!' A snigger distorted Azazello's features.

'I've been waiting a long time for that interjection, master.'

This was the first occasion on which this title appeared on the pages of the manuscript for the novel in connection with this character, although at this point it was only used almost by accident, like a test.

Then came a scene seeing out the storm in the empty Bolshoi Theatre; the meeting with Woland on the Moscow River, a confrontation with the pursuers (aeroplanes, ships, men in gas-masks). At last, on 21st September, he began the chapter describing the final night-time flight made by the poet and his beloved. "... Far beneath our feet, whole squares of light kept emerging form the darkness, and the fires floated in various directions.

Woland suddenly brought his horse to a sharp stop in the air and turned to the poet.

'You might perhaps be interested in seeing that?'

He pointed down to where millions of fires were gleaming, all aquiver. The poet spoke up.

'Yes, with pleasure. I have never seen anything. I have spent my life as a prisoner. I am blind and poverty-stricken.'

Woland sniggered and rushed downwards. His entourage, their horses' manes billowing, went after him, with a whistle." They hover above a square "on which a building was burning with a thousand fires.

"You perhaps wish to have a rest here, most valuable master," the former choirmaster whispered, 'we'll get hold of some evening dress and head to a café, to freshen up, so to speak, after our Ryazan sufferings'; there was a note of temptation in his voice… The poet's horse headed downwards; he jumped off it and darted in front of a car that was about to pull away, into the entrance-way."

The flight continued; at last, the poet saw the hero of his novel – Pilate – "seated at a stone table", bearing the burden of an eternal punishment. A transformed version of Azazello said: "Then is no sin more bitter than cowardice. This man was courageous and then got frightened by the Caesar once in his life, and he has paid for that." And he added, by way of explanation: "He dreams of one thing only – returning to his balcony, seeing the palms and having the prisoner brought to him, and being able to see Judas Hiscariot."

Thus, for the first time in all the years in which he worked on the novel, the biographical motif of waiting for the second (promised!) conversation with Stalin, to correct the first one – a period of waiting which at times (such as in the summer of 1931 and 1934) painfully acute, became part of the artistic fabric of the novel. In the novel, however, the roles had been reversed: there, the mighty procurator was doomed to eternal regret over his action and a passionate longing for a second conversation with the philosopher whose death he caused.

There also appeared the motif of forgiveness and release from sins (which in his later years of working on the novel acquired an increasingly destructive force: "'Forgiven!' Woland cried out above the cliffs, 'forgiven!'

He turned to the poet and said, with a laugh:

'He will be there now, where he wants to be, on the balcony and to have Yeshua Ganotsri brought to him. He will put right his mistake.

I assure you that there is no happier being in the world right now than this horseman. Such is the night we have had, my dear Master!'"

One can thus see with increasing clarity the link between the artistic structure of the novel and the images and motifs which came into being in the writer's earliest known experiments (the motif of a lucid dream in which the past is modified, a dead man seems to be alive and a redemption occurs, had already been seen in *The Red Crown* and was later seen in an unfinished story from 1929, in which shouts of protest were heard that had not been made in reality). Early ethical problems and artistic tasks are woven together with new ones which came into being and were formed in 1930-1932; the impossibility of changing what has happened and of being granted redemption is clarified more and more and the sole hope is portrayed more and more distinctly: hope for forgiveness, for a merciful release. *Night* – the penultimate chapter – is the kind of night when, in a surreal reality, fateful, irrectifiable mistakes, engendered by moments of cowardice or weakness, are corrected.

The exercise book that was begun in mid-July was finished, I would suggest, in October 1934, with a final chapter entitled "The Last Journey"; or rather, a rough outline of it, which took up just two and a half handwritten pages, but already contained within it the final conversation between Woland and the Master, the one that determined the fate of the latter forever afterwards.

"I received an order concerning you. Extremely favourable [In these lines one cannot help noticing a direct reflection of Bulgakov's work on the screenplay for *The Government Inspector*, and at the same time – an echo of Stalin's opening remarks in his telephone call from 1930 – M.C.]. Overall, I can congratulate you. You have been successful. I have therefore been ordered…"

"Can you really be given orders?"

"O yes. I have been ordered to take you away…" The sentence, and the entire draft of the novel, broke off there; we do not know where exactly Woland was to take the exhausted Master in the autumn of 1934. Let us note, however, that this name only appeared three times before the end of October 1934 – and only in remarks made to the hero by Woland and his entourage. The author was still referring to his hero as the poet.

13th October: "M.A.'s nerves are in a bad way. He has a fear of open spaces, loneliness. He is wondering about going to see a hypnotist."

15th October: "This morning I took M.A. to the affiliate-theatre for a rehearsal of *Pickwick* – a noisy one.

M.A.'s nerves are shot, but when we're walking together, he rescues himself by saying something funny." This time, he reports that someone had told him that "M.P. Galperin had translated *Tartuffe* and put it on at some small theatre in Moscow (I forget which one). The author's and director's "interpretation of the play is remarkable: Orgon is a representative of the disappearing bourgeoisie. Some sort of manufacturing is shown on the stage, so as to point out that Orgon has a factory, and all sorts of other nonsense. The whole thing ended in a huge row. Allegedly, everyone from the French embassy left after the first act – no, I tell a lie, after the second act. Catholic prayers were shown on the stage in a way that made fun of them."

16th October: "The day began as normal: I took M.A. to the theatre. Then I went to fetch him. [...] At the rehearsal, he found out that today, for the first time after a long gap, they were going to rehearse *Molière*, the scene in the cathedral. He says he was indifferent to this news when he heard it. But he believes that the play will be put on some day."

18th October: "In the afternoon, we were at V.V. Veresayev's. M.A. went there with a proposal that he and V.V. could write a play about Pushkin together. [...] The old man was very touched, and run around his cosy study several times, then hugged M.A. [...], got all excited, started talking about Pushkin, about how Natalya Nikolayevna had by no means been an air-head, but an unfortunate woman. At first, V.V. was flabbergasted that M.A. had decided to write the play without Pushkin (otherwise it would be vulgar), but after giving it a little thought, he agreed to the idea."

Getting ready to implement his new ideas was not all that easy, though. The progress made in the screenplay for *Dead Souls* was, as it turned out, a long way from completion: a letter came from the film studio on 18th October requesting fresh changes. And before doing that, he had to correct the script for *The Government Inspector*; between 18-24th October, he finished the second draft of it.

24th October: Bulgakov "decided to undergo a course of hypnosis to cure his fears".

30th October: a notebook of addenda for the novel was begun. At the top of the first page, near the margin, the author wrote: "Finish this before you die!"

3rd November: "There is chaos in the apartment – there are decorators here. Today, I was at the dress rehearsal for *Pickwick*. [...] The audience reacted to M.A.'s lines (he plays the judge) with laughter. Kachalov, Ktorov, Popova and others have told me that he plays the role just like a professional actor. His costume is a red cloak and a long white curly wig. Afterwards, in the interval, he told me that he had been terribly nervous – his cloak had brushed a stool as he sat down, and the stool had tumbled over. He had had to start the start off the scene hanging on by his elbows, on the lectern. And then someone helped him lift up the stool."

8th November: "In the evening, we sat among the chaos: M.A. dictated the novel to me – the scene at the cabaret. Sergei fell asleep on our ottoman. There was a telephone call – Olya [O.S. Bokshanskaya – M.C.]. A long conversation. At the end:

'Yes, by the way, I've been meaning to tell you this for a few days. You know, it looks as though *Flight* has been given the go-ahead. The other day, Vladimir Ivanovich [Nemirovich-Danchenko – M.C.] received a phone call […], they asked for his opinion on this play. Well, he praised it to the skies, of course, and said that it was a remarkable piece of work. The response he got was: 'We shall take your opinion into account.' And at the function that took place regarding the celebration (the 17th anniversary of the October Revolution – M.C.], Sudakov went up to Vladimir Ivanovich and said that he had secured permission for *Flight*. Today, Sudakov said to Zhenya (the actor Kaluzhsky – M.C.], that they needed to divide up the roles for *Flight*. Zhenya really wants to be given a part!"

In connection with this promising news, Bulgakov takes another look at the play on 9th November and finishes the final version of the 8th dream.

14th November: "A rehearsal for *Pickwick* with Stanislavsky… M.A. sat next to K.S."

17th November: "Akhmatova came over in the evening. Pilnyak had brought her over from Leningrad in his car. She told us about Mandelstam's bitter fate. We talked about Pasternak." Mandelstam was in exile at that time (and was already in Voronezh); in my view, the last line can only be read as a short record of Akhmatova's encoded story about Stalin's telephone call to Pasternak.

It was probably from Akhmatova that Bulgakov heard the details of the conversation; there is no doubt that he paid close attention to whatever she said. I would suggest that the words spoken about Mandelstam – "But he is a master, a master?" may have influenced the name he gave to the protagonist of his novel and the name he later chose to give the novel. As has already been stated, this name had appeared earlier in Bulgakov's manuscript, in sentences spoken to the protagonist (and also in the novel *Molière*, where it was associated with the main protagonist in the *Prologue*; "But you, my poor and blood-stained Master! You didn't want to die anywhere – either at home or outside your home!"). Yet it is only on the pages apparently written in the second half of *November* or December 1934 does the protagonist tell Ivan, who has appeared in his ward, "that, strictly speaking, only one person knows that he is the master, but that since she was a married woman, he could not reveal her name…" Thus, a woman which was clearly recorded in oral stories as being part of the vocabulary of the recipient of Bulgakov's letters and the supposed recipient of the novel (one remembers the idea that he had in 1931 to ask to be the "first reader"), went into the novel as a title for the nameless hero – and later secured its place in it.

As for the conversation between Ivan and his night-time guest, in the manuscript from the late autumn of 1934 it continued as follows: the guest admitted that he had tried to read his novel "to a certain someone, but that this person hadn't even understood half of it. That he hadn't seen her for one-and-a-half years and didn't intend to see her, since he considered that his life was over and that appearing before her in such a state would be awful.

'Where is she?' Ivan asked, very pleased with this night-time chat.

The guest said that she was in Moscow. But circumstances had unfolded in an extremely curious way. I.e. he hadn't even had time to write half his novel, when…" The manuscript then contains four lines of dots: the omission of some excerpt that was clear to the author but was not written in by him. One cannot help noticing the fact that what the guest says coincides with the actual volume of the part of Bulgakov's novel to which the author had brought his narrative in the first draft from 1928-1929. Let us quote K.M. Simonov's words: "I am sure that the burning of the first draft was brought about as a result of a betrayal by someone." Without wishing to go further into the circumstances, unknown to us, of the author's work on the novel and its subsequent burning, let us return to the story told by Ivanushka's guest:

"'But, naturally, they didn't prove anything to me by doing this,' the guest continued, and said that he had been mournful in his head and had begun to have a fear of crowds, which he hadn't been able to bear earlier either, incidentally, and now he had been brought here and that she would of course visit him, but he was not letting anyone, and would not let anyone, know about him… That he even rather liked it here, because, essentially, things were wonderful here and, above all, there were no people."

19th November: "After the hypnosis, M.A.'s fits of fear are starting to disappear, his mood is even and cheerful and he is fit to do his work. If only he could now go out and about on his own."

On 20th November, the family celebrate Bulgakov's name-day: he is given the music for his favourite operas: *Tannhäuser* and *Ruslan and Lyudmila*.

21st November: "Today, I gave him a writing desk – an Alexandrine one. In the evening, Berg [the doctor – M.A.]. Persuaded M.A. to go and see

Leontiev on his own tomorrow. Before that, there was a call from Olya – congratulating him [on his name-day – M.C.] and informing him that *Flight* had not been given the go-ahead. M.A. accepted this news with the utmost tranquillity."

22nd November: "At ten in the evening, M.A. got up, got dressed and went to see Leontiev on his own. *He hadn't been out on his own for six months*" [my italics – M.C.].

25th November: "The refurbishment is coming to an end. M.A. has a lot of work to do. Moreover, people are coming for advice from time to time. In the evening, a seat attendant came to see him to ask for help – he has written a play. Rehearsals are taking place at the theatre for *Molière*.

26th November: "In the evening – Ilf and Petrov. They came to M.A. to ask for advice about a play they have had an idea for. After that, M.A. went to see Veresayev; on his way back, V.V. took him to Smolensk Square, and then he continued on his own [i.e. no more than ten minutes – M.C.]. He says his fears have been blunted."

On 27th November, the cinema studio sends Bulgakov a letter informing him that it is rejecting the changes he made to the screenplay for *Dead Souls*. He had begun work on this project six months earlier with great enthusiasm, for it involved his favourite writer; now, the project had reached a dead-end, and the feeling was all too familiar.

28th November: "In the evening: Dmitriyev. He had just come from the Art Theatre and says there was a great fuss and commotion there, someone from the government had probably turned up – the General Secretary, one must suppose (to see *The Turbins*)."

29th November: "Sure enough, yesterday the General Secretary was there for *Turbins*, along with Kirov and Zhdanov. I was told this at the theatre. Yanshin said that the cast did a great job and that the General Secretary applauded a great deal at the end of the play."

Startlingly, the sustained success of the play was having less and less of an impact on its author and on his fate.

Work had begun on *Ivan Vasilievich* (the re-write of *Bliss*); on 30th November, news arrived from the Art Theatre to the effect that *Molière* was scheduled to start its run in March. Word was, wrote Yelena, "that it will be a lavish production; Stanislavsky is insisting upon it."

1st December: "Yermilov called in the afternoon, the editor of *Krasnaya Nov'*, and offered to print one of M.A.'s works in his journal. M.A. told him about the play *Molière*.

'Wonderful!'

He talked about an excerpt from his biography of Molière – 'That would be wonderful too!'

He asked for permission to put M.A.'s name in the brochure for 1935. M.A. gave his consent. They agreed that Yermilov would call him again, and M.A. would start collecting material.

The premiere of *Pickwick* took place in the evening. I took M.A. to it in a taxi. He stayed until the end of the play. He came home and said that the news that Kirov had been killed in Leningrad had broken during the play.

A huge number of people had left the theatre immediately, Rykov among them."

4

On 2nd December 1934, Bulgakov no doubt opened the morning newspaper with a great deal of impatience and anxiety. In it, he read that Kirov had died "at the hand of a murderer sent by the enemies of the working class", and that the man who shot him had been arrested and "his identity is being established". Accustomed as he was to thinking clearly and soberly, he cannot have failed to notice the fact that contradictory information was being presented here: the identity of the murderer had not yet been established, and yet the identity of those who had sent him had been…

The newspaper also contained the text of a newly published directive from the Presidium of the VTsIK, signed by M.I. Kalinin and A.S. Yenukidze, on alterations to the country's criminal and procedural codes relating to cases of terrorism: the investigation was to be completed within ten days, the case was to be heard without the parties being present, no appeals or petitions for leniency were to be admitted and sentences involving the highest degree of punishment were to be implemented as soon as the sentence was handed down. Anyone who still had an understanding of what legal standards were supposed to be, could not have failed to sense that something new was beginning.

Bulgakov read and collected literature on the law. He had in his collection, for example, V. Spasovich's *Handbook on Criminal Law* (*Uchebnik Ugolovnogo Prava*, St. P., 1865). Whilst Yelena was still with him – i.e. perhaps in the year in question – he had bought the *Charter on the Punishments Imposed by Justice of the Peace* (*Ustav o Nakazaniyakh, Nalagayemykh Mirovymi Sudiami*, 15th edition, St. P., 1904), containing special explanations about appeals practices… Yelena Sergeyevna told me that Mikhail Afanasievich "was terribly proud and happy with this purchase."

He read the book attentively – there were a huge number of markings in the text.

3rd December: "At half past three, I took M.A. to the theatre. A rally was taking place there among some of the mourners. […] Yanshin, Batashov and Dmokhovskaya issued a statement to the effect that they accepted him among the mourners," she wrote, reporting what Bulgakov told her when he returned home. A period of mourning was declared; the performances scheduled for the 3rd, 4th and 6th were cancelled. [...] "it is possible that the last play he [Kirov – M.C.] ever saw in his life was *The Days of the Turbins*.

9th December: "At Vikenty Vikentievich's place in the afternoon. We took him the final thousand of Misha's debt. We both feel more at ease in our souls now."

On 10th December, for the umpteenth time, employees from the cinema are once again at Bulgakov's house in connection with *The Government Inspector*, bringing new advice and requests. "All these conversations have an oppressive effect on Misha," Yelena wrote: they are boring, unnecessary and give him nothing, since they are not artistic... These people come to see a writer who is intelligent, who is an expert on Gogol – and they are unartistic, they have no taste, and yet in a self-assured tone of voice they set out their requirements with regard to the artistic work that this writer is working on, exhausting him beyond measure and bringing with them boredom."

His mood changed the next day, however. 11th December: "A wonderful evening: the Leontievs, the Arendts, the Yermolinskys; I made pelmeni for them, and ice cream. After dinner, Misha read out the cockroach races and the scene in Paris from *Flight*.

And on 13th December, they stay up until 4 am with the Lyamins: "we ate tangerines and talked excitedly about the Art Theatre."

... Whenever friends came to call in the evening, dinner would be served; with the dishes served in an order known in advance (and carefully selected by the lady of the hosue); and an amicable conversation would start bubbling away, so that the guests didn't notice the time flying by and only started getting ready to go home as morning approached – this did not cause him any kind of bother, disrupting the rhythm of life, the norm. On the contrary: therein lay the norm, the norm he so yeared for, which he had never quite been able to enjoy, neither after the "frightening, thundering years" in Kiev (as he defined them in his sketch *Kiev-city* [*Kiyev-gorod*]), nor after his life in Moscow in the early 1920s, which was not comparable to anything else (from his perspective) and which he had occasionally called *frightening* as well. The poorly served table of the overly noisy, non-creative feast of the 'Pirogovskaya' years had gone against his norm, too. As for the current phase in his life, he still could not become sated on the lifestyle at home that had come along just when he needed it.

Not all these evenings were equally cosy. Occasionally, there were guests who were not particularly welcome or who were invited by the master of the house because of acute feelings, in order to study the way they behaved. From time to time, E. Zhukhovitsky would come round, either asking questions – what were people saying in their letters from Paris? – or bringing some news. "An exceedingly spicy bit of news," writes Yelena on 14th December: "it turns out that Anatoly Kamensky, who left the country four years ago, became a non-returner, and defamed the USSR – is now in Moscow! Misha couldn't contain himself at that, and said: 'Well, this is nothing short of mysticism, comrades!' Zhukhovitsky was all in a dither, he kept lying about something, his eyes darting around, and he was terribly embarrassed. I now see quite clearly what he is; Misha and I have caught him out telling lies several times." The impressions left by this guest were reflected in various ways on the pages of his manuscripts, including in the scene in which Azazello appears in the basement to which the lovers wanted to return: "They are asking for you," he croaked, squinting at the window, towards which the vernal twilight was already floating up in waves, "with us. In short, we're off. [...]

"Me?" the poet asked in a whisper.

"You."

[...] "Aha... traitor..." the word flashed up in his head. He stared straight into the twinkling eye.

"Where are you inviting me to go?" the poet asked drily.

"We'll find a place," Azazello croaked seductively.

[...]

"Traitor, traitor, traitor..."

Signs of treachery will also be shown by the figure of Bogokhulsky (a surname which sounds a little like "Zhukhovitsky"), who in later drafts turns into Aloisius (compare with "Emmanuil") Mogarych. Let us remember: "I had never met, and I am sure that I shall never meet, a man with the intellect that Aloise had. If I did not understand the meaning of some story in the newspaper, Aloisius would explain it to me literally in one minute, and it was clear that this explanation cost him absolutely nothing. [...] Aloisius stunned me with his passion for literature. He would not calm down until he had convinced me to read to him the whole of my novel, from cover to cover... He explained to me in very precise terms, and I perceived that what he said was flawless, why my novel could not be printed." He was painting the portrait of a man who had complete mastery of the language of modernity, which he himself had not only failed to learn, but did not want to study.

The rest of the diary entry from 14th December is worthy of attention: "Everyone left, but Dmitriyev stayed for a long time, and in fact made us sad.

Misha thinks that he has a nervous disposition, he can't sleep. It is clear that he is exhausted: he has been doing an insane amount of work."

It is possible that this entry contains an encoded version of Dmitriyev's account of the difficult situation into which his wife, the beauty Yelizaveta Isayevna Dolukhanova, had fallen.

We know from accounts by a number of contemporaries that in the mid-30s, she was summoned to the offices of the NKVD and asked to become a permanent informer. From the late 1920s, she and her sister had enjoyed great success in literary circles in Leningrad, and had been charming hostesses of literary salons. Tynyanov was in love with Yelizaveta, and Mayakovsky and Olennikov used to visit the sisters' apartment. She was now the wife of V.V. Dmitriyev, and she was being invited to be more active in hosting guests... Seeking a good reason to refuse the offer, she said that they only had a small apartment. "Don't let that worry you – we'll help you out on that score!"

Dmitriyev's nervous disposition was, it seems, related to the fact that there seemed to be no way out of this situation.

18th December. "A wonderful evening: working on *Pushkin* at Veresayev's. Misha has a plan. The most eye-catching bit should be at the start: Natalya, covered by a light coming from outside at night, and the secret arrival of Dantes that night, there in the apartment; in the middle of the play – lunch with Saltykov (an eccentric book-lover), and at the end – the arrival of Danzas, bringing the news that Pushkin has been wounded."

19th December. "In the evening, Dina Radlova [an artist, the wife of N.E. Radlov – M.C.]. A remarkable conversation. She started talking about Misha's work on *Pushkin* herself (I don't get how she knew about it) and advised him not to work with V.V.: 'now if you were to team up with Tolstoy, Maka (i.e. with A.N. Tolstoy – M.C.], what a force that would be!' Misha: 'I don't understand, what sort of force? How can Tolstoy and I team up? Are we going to walk down Tverskaya holding hands?' Dina: 'No! The point is, you're the better playwright, and he, it's fair to say, is the better writer...'" She asked about the content of the play. Misha said it was a secret." Secrets, mysteries, suspicions... all of these things crop up constantly in Yelena's conversations with her husband and are reflected in her diary entries. In all things, they were prepared to see – and more intensively with each passing year – mysteries, bad omens, and occasionally they were proved right. As far as A. Tolstoy was concerned, Bulgakov's strong opinion of him only became more intense as the years went on; he was put off mainly by his lifestyle (the carousing and so on) and his behaviour as a writer: Tolstoy did not shy away from writing complete codswallop, particularly in the genre of drama, and their subjects in this field sometimes overlapped. Thus, the play by Tolstoy and Shchegolev, *The Empress's Plot* (*Zagovor Imperatritsy*), was, in essence, the realisation of one of Bulgakov's plots from his early years in Moscow: an historical drama about Rasputin, Nikolai II and so on (at the moment being described, an overlap also arose on the subject of Pushkin). On top of this, Bulgakov was certainly irritated by the lack of attention to sources, and the overly dramatic evolution of his views about a historical figure.

22nd December. "Misha has spent all these past days in an agony, he is afraid that he won't be able to cope with the work: *The Government Inspector*, *Ivan Vasilievich* and now *Pushkin* is coming along.

On 24th December, a New Year's tree is installed at the Bulgakovs' for Yelena Sergeyevna's children, reminding him, it seems, of the house on Andreyevsky Descent, his younger brothers, with whom he had had to part so early and forever. "At first, Misha and I took the tree away, put all the presents for everyone underneath it, turned off the lights and lit the candles on the tree – Misha started playing a march – and the kids came dashing into the room.

Misha had written the text, basing it on *Dead Souls* – two short scenes – one set at Sobakevich's place, the other at Sergei Shilovsky's. I played Chichikov, Misha played Sobakevich. Then I played Zhenka, and Misha played Sergei… for the role of Seryozha, Misha put on a pair of drawers, and Sergeyev's coat, which barely went up to his belt, and a sailor's jacket. A huge red mouth." Everyone in the household watches the play. "A success. Then dinner, with dumplings and Christmas treats."

And once again, on 28th December, Yelena Sergeyevna writes, bitterly: "I can sense how much the work on *The Government Inspector* is beyond Misha, how he is tormented by this. Working on other people's ideas because of money. And it is interfering like crazy with his work on Pushkin. He is overloaded with ideas which torment him. Towards 9 in the evening: the Veresayevs. Work on the play. Misha told us what he had thought up, and the play can already be seen. One can picture Nikolai, one can picture Alexandrina and the most powerful thing that has stayed in my memory today is the scen at Gekkeren – the arrival of the blind Stroganov, who decides the issue of whether Dantes should fight Pushkin or not." And then a later note added to the diary: about the author's interpretation of the scene – from memory: "It is a symbol: blind death, with its code of the duel, kills."

Blindness is one of the most important characteristics in Bulgakov's artistic world; it arose back in the early 1920s in the form of one of his favourite portraits (the horseman with unseeing eyes in *The Red Crown*), and at the start of the 1930s it is interpreted mainly as the blindness of rulers, who do not see the significance of creators – the artist, the philosopher. One remembers the author's meditations on Louis XIV in the novel *Molière*: "He was mortal, like everyone else, and consequently – blind. Had he not been blind, he would perhaps have gone to the dying man, because in the future he would have seen interesting things and would perhaps wish to come closer to actual immortality."

That same day, on the 28th, Yelena Sergeyevna writes: "the people from the Vakhtangov are inviting us [they are already interested in the play about Pushkin – M.C.] to see in the New Year with them. We don't want to, though; we're going to be at home." 31st December. "The year is ending. And now, as I move through our rooms, I often catch myself making the sign of the cross and I whisper to myself: "Good Heavens! If only things could go on like this!"

Thus ended a year in which there had been the joy of acquiring their own home (guests praised the apartment and said it was "very European", which Yelena found very flattering), and a shock, one that had proved too powerful and lasting, and the completion – albeit in the form of a rough draft – of a novel which had become more and more important for him, and hopes for new productions of plays: *Molière*; the play about Pushkin, as yet unwritten but already visible to the author in his mind's eye; and the comedy *Ivan Vasilievich*, which promised to be a barrel of laughs.

A diary entry made on 1st January 1935 reveals, however, that New Year's Eve found the Bulgakovs at the home of the Leontievs, a place they liked very much. "On the table: an incredible abundance. They are extraordinarily kind and cordial. Everything was wonderful, but at around three, the group that had been with the Shervinskys [i.e. in the same building on Pomerantsevy Side-street – M.C.] descended upon us. [...] When they arrived, everything fell apart, and it became noisy and not much fun. One of the guests was in evening dress. To look at him, you would have thought he had spent the last twenty years asleep in a naphthalene chest in those clothes!"

She was always disparaging about the 'Prechistenka set'. As is usually the case in her diary, though, her own emotions are tinged with the attitude of Bulgakov himself, whatever it might be; one can hear an echo of his words. What was that attitude? It would be the simplest thing in the world to say that what prevented him from fitting in with the former crowd was his talent – it is always talent that distinguishes the artist from clans, from camps, from an overly specific environment. This explanation is somehow inadequate, however. Why was the evening dress so irritating? After all, Bulgakov himself was keen to emphasize his conservatism: conservatism in his habits, in his questions, in certain aspects of his home life. And he himself would put much thought into his preparations for the reception at the American embassy. What was it that irritated him – about not all, but some of the representatives of that environment? What specific combination of "bourgeois behaviour" (in the old, pre-Revolutionary sense) and at the same a split from the new way of life? Was is not perhaps the case that the author's long-held attitude to the characters from *The Séance*, his story from 1922, was present here too? The conviction that he knew and sensed the nerves of life more acutely than they did?

4th January: "A frightful cold snap! -32° Celsius. In the afternoon I was with Misha at the theatre – we had our photos taken in the make-up and costumes for *Pickwick*, with the stage decorations.

I was wearing skiing breeches, and that attracted a lot of attention from the actors.

In the evening, the Lyamins and the Shaposhnikovs came to see us. Bor[is] Val[entinovich] and his wife are remarkably nice too."

… From the very first sketches of the play about Pushkin, which Bulgakov is writing on a daily basis in January and early February 1935, alternating between writing it in his own hand and dictating it to Yelena, a treatment of Natalya Nikolayevna emerges that was pround and very new for the literature of the time. In Bulgakov's view, the heroine is not blameworthy; rather, she is blind. Her life and that of Pushkin are shown in the play as two fates, moving in parallel, but unable to join together as one, and only intersecting in a fatal manner. "Why has no-one ever asked me whether I am happy?" "I cannot give any greater love", "What else is expected of me? I gave birth to his children and I've spent my whole life hearing poetry, only poetry…" One is struck by how close Bulgakov's interpretation of the heroine's character and of her role in Pushkin's fate is to that of M. Tsvetayeva: in her sketch of the artist Natalya Goncharova (in the chapter *The Two Goncharovs*), which was written in 1929 and with which Bulgakov was unlikely to have been familiar: "Pushkin entered into this marriage with his eyes not closed but wide open, with no eyelids; Goncharova did so blindly or half-blindly, with eyelids that were like veils, as one might expect of a girl and a beauty. All blame is removed from Natalya Goncharova right from the very outset. […] Whether Goncharova was unfaithful to Pushkin or not, whether she kissed another man or not, she is blameless all the same. She is blameless because she was a puppet, she is blameless because of fate, she is blameless because she did not love Pushkin." There is a reason why Bulgakov emphasizes Natalya's short-sightedness in her very first appearance. The other characters who are pitted against Pushkin in the play are either blind or malevolent: Kukolnik and Benediktov see his genius but feel a brutal envy of him. The theme of jealousy over someone else's talent, seen by the author as one of the human characteristics that is most to be despised, cropped up in a story in 1929, then in 1931, in Ryukhin's vague thoughts about Pushkin, and then becomes a regular feature of Bulgakov's creative output.

At the start of February, there are a few sessions of hypnosis; on the evening of 9th February, the Bulgakovs host Dr. Berg and his wife, the Leontievs, the Arendts and Marusya Topleninova. "They are all very favourably disposed towards us," Yelena wrote, "and for that reason we had a good time." On 12th February, in the evening, Bulgakov reads from the 4th and 8th scenes of the play (written at around this time) at Veresayev's house and, evidently, soon breaks off his work on it, to throw himself energetically into the rehearsals for *Molière*, which have resumed. On 15th February, in the evening, Zhukhovitsky comes round. "An endless, delicate conversation about the same subject yet again: Misha's fate. Zh. said that Misha must express his view on a contemporary subject and show his attitude to modernity. M. said: we will play out a draw! I am not going to set out my thoughts, people ought to leave me in peace."

On 23rd February, the doctor writes to him (stating that he refuses to accept a fee: "For going as a guest to some old friends I can certainly not take any money"), apparently after obtaining the results of a medical check-up: "I am infinitely glad that you present a clean bill of health; things could not have been otherwise, incidentally – you have such firm foundations, such prerequisites for absolute and durable good health!"

5th March. "Misha had a difficult rehearsal… He came home broken and enraged. Stanislavsky, instead of sorting out the cast's acting, started trying to sort out the play, in front of the actors. He speaks naively, he has a schoolboy's notion of Molière in his mind and therefore he is demanding that changes be made to the play." A note recording the conversation between Stanislavsky and Bulgakov, made by an assistant director (and published in Stanislavsky's *Manuscripts* [*Letopisi*]), clearly shows that the director and the playwright each talk about this play in a different kind of language, and that mutual understanding is simply impossible in this case. Stanislavsky "believes that the production and the play require changes. The main flaw, in S.'s view, is the one-sidedness of the portrayal of Molière's character, in the denigrating of the image of the brilliant artist, the ruthless denouncer of the bourgeois, the clergy and charlatanism of all kinds… In the play, there is "too much intimacy, petty bourgeois life, and there are no flashes of genius." S.

enters into a dispute with M.A. Bulgakov, who asserts that Molière "did not recognise his great significance", his brilliance. And Bulgakov "strove to give life to an ordinary person" in his play. "It is of no interest to me at all, that someone got married to his own daughter," S. objects... Molière [...] may be naïve, but that does not mean that one cannot show the ways in which he was brilliant."

... A few days later, describing this rehearsal to P.S. Popov, Bulgakov wrote: Stanislavsky "started telling me that Molière was a genius and how this genius ought to be described in the play.

The actors took a predatory delight in this and started asking for bigger roles.

I was overcome by a wild rage. I was intoxicated by the desire to throw away the exercise book and say to them all: you go ahead and write about geniuses and non-geniuses, but don't go teaching me, I won't be able to do it anyway. I would be better off playing one of the roles for you.

But I cannot, I cannot do that. I forced that into me, I started defending myself."

10th March. "With Stanislavsky again. [...] He began by stroking Misha's sleeve and saying: 'You are the sort that needs to be stroked.' He had clearly already been told that Misha had lost his temper over his conversation in front of the actors. They negotiated matters for three hours. Stanislavsky's idea consists of showing at every opportunity that Molière was a creator of brilliant theatre. There is therefore a need to include things which Misha considers to be trivial or unnecessary. A furious row with Stanitsyn and Livanov. But Misha came home in a livelier mood, because he had calmed down. He said that Stanislavsky had made a very witty remark about a diminutive actor who plays a monk serving the cardinal: that he was the priest from the early mass, not from the late one."

In the same letter to Popov, dated 14th March: "In brief, I need to include something about Molière's significance for the theatre, to show somehow that he is the brilliant Molière and so on. All this is primitive, helpless, unnecessary. And now I am sitting over a copy, and I cannot lift my hand. Not including it is not an option – it would be a declaration of war – so am I to tear up all this work, wreak havoc in terms of its form, harm the play itself, and put green patches on genteel black trousers! Devil knows what I am to do!

What on earth is this, dear citizens?

And outide, alas, it is spring. The light snow either falls at an angle, or disappears, and there is sunlight on the dining table. What will the spring bring?

I listen and listen to the voice inside me: and I hear nothing!"

20th March. "Working through *Molière* with Stanislavsky is taking up so much time. Misha is exhausted." Stanislavsky "is trying to get rid of all the best bits: the poem, the duel scene and so on. He's too greedy by half. It's reached a point where Misha and I have decided the matter: we shall write a letter to Stanislavsky refusing to make the changes, take the play and leave. Misha always says: 'I can't prove that the play is good; perhaps it is bad. But then why did they accept it…? So that they could later cripple it as only they know how?' I have no doubts at all about this play, though, and Stanislavsky only sends me into a rage." Against the backdrop of these strong emotions, and her wholehearted sympathy for her husband, the ardent Yelena went on: "Misha told me, Olya and Kaluzhsky yesterday how all this happens at Leontievsky. It is simply incredible!

He calls the 17th century the "middle century" and also uses that name for the "18th" one, and fills his speeches with long jokes and tangents, muttering something about Stakhovich, about French actors, and tries to prove that we mustn't have men with swords coming on stage, i.e. he attacks everything on which the play rests. His biggest bit of Jesuitism and his merchant manner lies in the fact that, even as he ruins some part of the play, he tries to convince Misha to 'learn to love' this distortion. […] Misha compared his torments with *Molière* and Stanislavsky in a very figurative way: 'Imagine that someone started twisting Seryozha's ears with a pair of pliers and assuring you that this was necessary, that Chekhov's daughter had had it done to her too and that you must learn to love it'. […] And today he went further: he thought up the idea of trying to frighten Misha by talking about the French ambassador. 'What will you do if the ambassador ups and leaves after the second act?!!'

He has a naïve understanding of Molière and he thinks that he must be portrayed the way he is in a reading-book.

Sick of writing about it!"

The female emotion aside, this mirrors the feelings of Bulgakov himself; he felt worn down by the sluggish pace of the theatre's work on *Molière*, which to some extent reflected the disintegrating artistic life of that era and the inexorable freezing of it by public life.

"The preparations for the play had already been going on for four years, with lenthy pauses. These pauses not only disrupted the working rhythm, but also put the play in a constantly changing "historical and aesthetic context," a student of the relations between Bulgakov and the Art Theatre would later observe. He quotes an entry in Afinogenov's diary about the premiere of

La Belle Dame aux Camelias (*Dama s Kameliyami*) at Meyerhold's theatre, which struck many with its "luxuriously refined packaging" – an entry which recorded "the fact of the dramatic change in theatrical tastes", and connects to this the order that was given to the costume department for *Molière* to "sew using gold brocade, so that everything gleams like the sun." They strove, the researcher says, quoting something the artist P.V. Vilyams said on the day of the premiere, to convey "the heavy, dusty atmosphere of the epoch."

The epoch was moving its face close to the mirror but was ready to jump back from it at any moment, crushing with this sharp movment those who had moved the mirror forward.

Yelena Sergeyevna takes a voluptuous pleasure in recording, in her diary, the thespians' stories about Stanislavsky's eccentricities, which at times bordered on petty tyranny. A young actor was once brought to him, "to be an understudy in *Dead Souls*.

Stanislavsky: 'What is your surname?'

The actor: 'Konsky, Konstantin Sergeyevich...'

Stanislavsky: 'Well that can't be right! Surnames like that are unheard of!'" (20th March 1935). The previous day, Konsky himself had told the Bulgakovs of another incident, from the rehearsals for *A Bride for the Tsar (Tsarskaya Nevesta)*. "One young actor was terribly afraid of Stanislavsky and kept trying to hide behind the stove (in the room at Leontievsky).

St.: 'Who's that hiding behind the stove? What's your surname? Who are you playing? You ought to conduct yourself on the stage as though you're playing the main part. Do you know the opera?'

'Yes I do, Konstantin Sergeyevich...'

'Then conduct the whole thing, from the top.' The actor starts to sweat; he picks up the baton and starts conducting. After the overture, which the actor conducted without making any mistakes:

'Remove him from the cast!'

Let us turn once again to the rather strange diary entry made by Yelena on 20th March 1935: 'B.I. Yarkho has translated *Le Bourgeois Gentilhomme* and sent an inscribed copy to Misha.

Roughly three days ago, we found out that he and Shpet had been arrested. We don't know what for, of course."

The carefully considered construction of the diary entry is typical: the edition of Molière's *Le Bourgeois Gentilhomme* (L., 1934) remained in Bulgakov's library right up until 1970, with an inscription by B. Yarkho dated 22nd February 1935: "To the deeply esteemed Mikhail Afanasievich Bulgakov;

remember me fondly, from the translator." After the news came out about his arrest, less than a month later, there was a need to provide some justification for the inscription.

These arrests were associated with the so-called "case of the German dictionaries", or the "case of the dictionaries". Also arrested at this time were D.S. Usov, the son of professor Chelpanov, M.A. Petrovsky (his brother had been arrested back in the autumn of 1929 but had returned home two years later). Mariya Vakhtereva (the wife of F.A. Petrovsky) said that on the morning after their home was raided, she had called the Yarkho brothers. Grigory Isaakovich had picked up the phone.

"Can I speak to Borya?" Mariya had asked.

"Not any more. And I already know that Misha's not available either, because when they left our place, they were headed to your place…"

The "case of the dictionaries", according to the accounts of those alive at the time, was fabricated in the following way: some linguists – Germanists – were doing some work on a freelance basis for a publishing house specialising in dictionaries, preparing some German-to-Russian dictionaries. A member of the publishing house's in-house staff, Yelizaveta Meyer – who was of German ancestry – was given the money for all those involved in the work, and handed each of them their share, after they had signed for it. Her brother was accused of spying for the Germans: the pieces of paper signed by the linguists were found at her home, and served as the evidence on the basis of which they were arrested.

M.A. Petrovksy was the investigator and heard what the accused had to say for himself. He later said to his brother, when they met up in Tomsk:

"You all say that's what happened – but the spy said that this was money paid for espionage!"

All three of them left Moscow forever. From 1935 to 1937, M.A. Petrovsky and B.I. Yarkho lived in Tomsk, where they worked at the library; in 1937, they were detained and sentenced to "10 years without the right to send or receive letters", and before long they were dead.

On 25th March, the Bulgakovs were "at a Wagner concert in the Large hall of the Consevatorium. Senkar was conducting, and Reizen was singing (Wotan's Farewell and Magic Fire music). We liked Senkar, he has a good feel for Wagner. The orchestra was a small one, only 80 people, no more. Reizen sings awfully badly, although he has a very powerful voice. The only part that he sang well was the last line of the incantation. We were sitting in row 6. I was wearing a black dress with a cutout at the back, which attracted a lot of attention. I heard one lady say maliciously: 'I hate things like that!'

"It is warm and sleety one minute, then there's a snowstorm the next," Yelena wrote on the same day, 26th March 1935; she also wrote down some of her thoughts about the behaviour of a young actor who had made overtures to them: "… he appeared at our house today at 3 o'clock, without having called in advance. I have been taking a very good look at him – what a character. I cannot work him out. He asks a neverending stream of questions. He talks about exactly the same subjects and in exactly the same way as K. and Zh. Today, by the way, Zh. Called and said that Vels had written an article about Soviet theatre in one of the American newspapers. He says in it, according to Zh., that Soviet theatre, after leaving agitprop behind, has now set off on a different track. First of all, Soviet comedy has appeared, or rather, farce; secondly, the classics are being put on; and, thirdly, there is Mikhail Bulgakov. If there were several playwrights like him, one would be able to say that Soviet drama was alive and well."

That same day, Bulgakov returned to his work on the play about Pushkin, dictating the 9th scene to his wife.

29th March. "Lord Eden is in Moscow, the Keeper of the Privy Seal. There was a portrait of him in *Izvestiya* – he's a relatively young man, 38 years of age." (in the 1950s, whilst editing the diary, Yelena added the following note: "M.A. does an uproariously funny send-up of the "keeper of the seal", in which he hides the seal in his pocket, then, glancing to either side as he takes it out, hastily uses it and immediately hides it again.) […] An envelope was brought to us from the American embassy, containing an invitation for Misha and me on the 23rd April"; the invitation said "dress-suits or a black jacket. I shall sew a black suit for Misha, he doesn't have one. How interesting it is to spend time there!"

On 30th April, Bulgakov writes to the doctor S.M. Berg, who had recently treated him using hypnosis: "To be brief, I feel wonderful. Thanks to what you did, that damned fear no longer torments me. It is far away and silent."

On the same day, Yelena wrote: "Today, Misha and I went to see the tailor. We then went to the hard-currency store to get the material for the suit and the other things. We bought some very nice material, the shop-assistant told us it was made in England and was intended specifically for evening dress and dinner jackets, but it's terribly expensive. Then we bought some black shoes for Misha to go with the same suit. They didn't have any starched shirts."

On 5th April, Bulgakov reads the last two scenes of *Pushkin*, which he has written in draft form, at Veresayev's house.

7th April. "Misha and I went to pick up some books this afternoon at Cuba – the bookbindery on Prechistenka. I bought him the letters of Tchaikovsky and some material on Dost[oevsky] [apparently, this was *F.M. Dostoevsky. Material and Studies* [*F.M. Dostoyevskiy. Materialy i Issledovaniya*], which was published in 1935 – M.C.].

"Akhmatova had lunch with us. She had come to the city to take steps to assist some friend of hers, who has been exiled from Leningrad." Later that day, Yelena calls *Krasnaya Nov'*, and the editor "informed me very politely, that on 10th or 12th, the issue of the printing of the biography of Molière in their newspaper would be resolved. Misha said: 'You will never hear from him or see him again in your life' (he made a fair few such predictions, he had a taste for them – and, remarkably, judging by Yelena's stories but also by her diary, one can see that a considerable portion of them turned out to be right: the manuscript for *Molière*, for instance, was sent back from *Krasnaya Nov'* "without the slightest trace of an accompanying letter" on 26th April 1935 – after Yelena sent them a cable). On the same day, Yelena records – over and over again – records everything that has to do with the theatrical destiny of *Molière*: "Stanislavsky is leading rehearsals for *Molière* at the Leontiev, and Misha is at the end of his tether. Rather than rehearsing scenes from the play, he [Stanislavsky – M.C.] – is carrying out pedagogical studies with the actors and saying a load of irrelevant things, which aren't moving the play forward at all. Misha has been seeking to show me that no system or special measures exist, by means of which one can force a bad actor to act well. When he is in a good mood, he does an impression of how K. acts – it is very funny. It is hopelessly repulsive!" On the 9th, V.V. Dmitriyev and a young actor from the Art Theatre, G. Konsky, are at the Bulgakovs'. "Misha was on extraordinarily good form, he talked about the rehearsals for *Molière*, and did impersonations of Stanislavsky, Podgorny, Koreneva and an absolutely classic one of Sheremeteva in the role of Rene – Molière's nanny." When he began doing an impression of the one of the staff at the theatre, "I noticed that there were tears of mirth streaming down Dmitriyev's cheeks and that he was almost choking with laughter… It really was incredibly funny." On an almost daily basis, he was either telling stories, filled with irritation, or doing hilarious impressions, and through them, the material for *A Theatrical Novel* was taking shape of its own accord, even though the idea of writing the novel may not have occurred to him in that year. It is a novel in which the director, Ivan Vasilievich, asks an actor to "ride around on a bicycle for the girl you love," and at another rehearsal, to "take a bouquet of flowers to your beloved. This was how things began at twelve o'clock, and it went on like that until four. And it was not just Patrikeyev that had to deliver the bouquet, but everyone, taking turns: Yelagin, who was playing the general, and even Adalbert, who was playing the leader of the gang of bandits. I was extremely amazed by this; but Foma reassured me again, explaining that Ivan Vasilievich was making sure that his lesson was accompanied with interesting and engaging stories about how exactly one ought to present a bouquet of flowers to a lady, and about how each of the actors had done so. [...] Ivan Vasilievich was the best of all at doing so. He got carried away, came out onto the stage and demonstrated thirteen times how one ought to deliver this pleasing gift. In short, I began to feel convinced of the fact that Ivan Vasilievich was a remarkable and a truly brilliant actor."

At around this time, on 8th April, the Bulgakovs are invited to the home of K.A. Trenyov; he lives above them, in the same apartment block. "I liked Pasternak," Yelena writes, on her return home, "he is unique, unlike anyone else… after we had drunk the first toast to the hostess, P. said: 'I wish to drink a toast to Bulgakov.' Our hostess suddenly said with conviction: no, no, we shall drink to Vikenty Vikentievich now, and then to Bulgakov – in response to which P. declared stubbornly: 'I want to drink to Bulgakov. Veresayev is a very great man, of course, but he is a legitimate phenomenon, whereas B. is an illegitimate one.' Bill-Belotserkovsky and Kirpotin lowered their gaze – virtuously."

On 11th April, Zhukhovsky called and said that the secretary of the American embassy, Boolen, wanted to invite them for lunch and was asking them to choose a day. "Instead of replying," Yelena wrote that day (apparently at night, as always), "Misha invited Boolen, Tef (Bullitt's private secretary) and Zh. to visit us this evening.

We had dinner: caviar, salmon, home-made paté, radishes, fresh gherkins, fried mushrooms, vodka, white wine." (She loved preparing food for guests and describing what was served to them; it is easy to detect a fondness for a table laden with good food in Bulgakov's works, too: in *The Heart of a Dog* and *The Master and Margarita*, this was to have a challenging, ideologized nature.) The Americans speak Russian – Bollen's Russian is very good. The dinner began with Misha showing them his photos, for the questionnaires, and saying that he was going to submit his application for a foreign passport the next day, for he wanted to go abroad for 3 months.

Zh. almost choked on his food. The Americans say that he ought to go. The dream of America…

B[oolen] wants to translate *Zoya's Apartment* with Zhuk. We sat together for a long time, and it seems that they had a good time with us. Bollen invited us to lunch on the 19th."

12th April. "We went over to see the Zaposhnikovs in the evening. Misha played chess with them. Then Serg[ei] Yerm[olinsky] walked us home, came in with us and sat up with us till 3am."

13th April. "Misha went to see Akhmatova this afternoon; she is staying with Mandelstam.

They want to print Akhmatova's book, but with a very selective approach". (There follows an account of what Nadezhda Mandelstam said about their first meeting in Batum, the account that can be found in the first chapter of this book).

18th April. "In the morning, I called Rzhevsky; Yev[geny] Al[exandrovich] told me that Irina Svechina has been arrested. I went to see Alex[andr] Andr[eevich] right away. He is in an awful state: he says he has lost his ability to work altogether, and that his home has become like a coffin…"

Yelena had had a connection to the Svechin family for almost nine years by that time: on 9th November 1925, she writes to her sister about having recently met them: "I am very glad about this. They are both very interesting people." Alexander Andreyevich Svechin (1877-1938), a nobleman (like Shilovsky), who graduated in 1903 from the Academy at the General Headquarters and had fought in the world war; he joined the Red Army in March 1918 and in the 1920s was a professor at the Military Academy of RKKA (later renamed the M.V. Frunze Academy). He was one of the most intelligent and knowledgeable military experts of that period. Yelena mentioned his name in passing during our conversations in the autumn of 1969: she was talking about where exactly she had met Bulgakov. They met, as her words made clear, at the Svechins' home.

Y.A. Shilovsky, at the very same time – from October 1928 to February 1931 (by a strange quirk of fate, just before the moment when Bulgakov's affair with Yelena was discovered, and Shilovsky forced them to separate) – was chief of the headquarters of the Moscow military district, and after that began teaching at an Academy with Svechin, with Tukhachevsky as his director. A short time earlier, in 1930, the so-called *Spring* operation, organised by Menzhinsky, was carried out, according to military historians: in one night, in the central military apparatus and in the districts, around 5,000 old experts were arrested. After this, a campaign of denunciations was rolled out, and one of the key points was Svechin's opinions on military theory; M.N. Tukhachevsky spoke out particularly vehemently against him.

Svechin soon went back to teaching at the Academy; Bulgakov spent time with him – evidence survives which establishes that he had a direct connection (and not just a vicarious one, through Yelena's acquaintances and stories) with the military milieu, and this is significant in terms of hypotheses about his attitude to the events of later years. Let us quote this evidence: "At the Art Theatre – a banquet, the old men are being honoured," Yelena writes on 25th November 1933. M.A. did not go, for we had been invited to the Svechins." The very fact that he preferred this invitation over the banquet at the Art Theatre would seem to indicate that the relationship between them was a serious one. Note the date of this diary entry, too. This was a time when Yelena's new marriage had been going for only a year. Judging by the diary, this was one of the few households from her "old" life that she feels comfortable going to with Bulgakov.

There was also another 'military' household that Bulgakov found himself tied to in the 1930s, apparently through the agency of Yelena: it was the home of the family of Ivan Troitsky, a family that remained close to her for many years, even after her split from Shilovsky. On 12th January 1970, she wrote in her diary: "… in 1922, we moved into an apartment on Vozdvizhenka, in a wing of the house and courtyard, where the Hunters' Club had once been. We moved in with Yevgeny Alexandrovich and Ivan Alexandrovich Troitsky (also from the headquarters) with his mother, Marya Ivanovna Khanykova. Despite the age gap, she and I became friends. Then, after her death (and indeed before it), I made friends with her daughter, Lidia Alexandrovna Ronzhina, and again after her death, with her daughter, Nina Georgievna Ronzhina-Chernysheva…" (we will come across these names again later in the narrative).

… On 19th April 1935, Yelena described a lunch at Boolen's home: "an ap[artment] in the ambassador's house: bright, very nice, an electric gramophone, also known as a radio. Zhukovitsky was there, of course. Then some oth[er] Americans arrived from the embassy, they were nice people, they do not put on airs and graces. Cocktails were served before lunch. We had no soup with our lunch.

Misha and I were both surprised when Lina S. appeared.

When we said goodbye, Misha invited the Americans to call on him. Lina S. said: 'I should like to come and see you, too.'"

22nd April: "Today, Misha and I read the minutes of the rehearsal for *Molière*… One can see from it that Stanislavsky intends to break the whole play up and write it afresh. In the 'Cabals' scene, for instance: "d'Orsini should put on a mask and join the cabal, out of vengeance." [A year later, we have these lines in *A Theatrical Novel*: "Ivan Vasilievich kept asking me, more and more insistently, to write a scene involving a duel with swords in my play" – a play about the time of the civil war! – and as the author, he initially "treated this as some kind of bad joke", and then "was driven into a frenzy". – M.C.] The cup of his patience was running over, and Misha immediately dictated to me a letter to Stanislavsky and Gorchakov, saying that his proposals were "leading to the writing of some sort of new play, which I cannot write, since I fundamentally do not agree with it." If the play, in the form it is in now, is not suitable for the theatre, the author asked for it to be returned to him.

On 23rd April 1935, they set off for a ball at the American ambassador's residence.

Yelena wrote down a detailed description not only of the ball itself, which proved to be rather unusual, but also of the preparations for it, the next day, in detail. "In the afternoon, I went to the hairdresser's; on the Arbat, I walked up to the cars to hire a cab, and the driver got out. I told him I would give him 40 r. to take us in the evening, and then to come and fetch us at 3 in the morning.

He readily agreed.

I was dressed up for the evening by the tailor and Tamara Tomasovna. My gown was an evening one, black and blue with pale pink flowers, it came out very nicely.

Misha wore a black suit – a very good one.

At 11:30, we set off. Once again, our chauffeur refused to take the money in advance. He said he would come and fetch us. We said: at 3 o'clock. He said: 'isn't that too early for you?'

Never in my life had I seen such a ball," Yelena wrote, almost echoing Margarita's words. "The ambassador stood at the top of the stairs, greeting the guests. Everyone was in tails, there were only a handful of jackets and dinner jackets. Litv[inov] was in tails, Bubnov was in uniform [the people's commissariat for education still had the same uniform, familiar to Bulgakov from Kiev in 1919 – M.C.], and there were a handful of our soldiers.

Boolen stood there with another American, who turned out to be a military attache – the former in tails, the latter in a smart red uniform with gold fourrageres. They came down the steps towards us and were very welcoming.

There was dancing in the hall with the collonade, projectors lit the scene from the choir, and behind some netting that ran down the middle of the orchestra, there were live birds and pheasants. Dinner was served at separate little tables in a vast dining room, with live bear-cubs in the corner, along with baby goats and caged cockerels. After dinner, there was music from some accordion players." With a womanly, disapproving intensity of gaze, she notes: "Among the guests I caught sight of Bersenev, looking tense and lost. Afinogenov was there, wearing a jacket and for some reason holding a stick."

She herself for some reason feels utterly at home at this ball, enraptured. Bulgakov, too, gains self-confidence through having this beautiful, well-groomed and magnificently dressed lady by his side. He does not feel lost: for him, this is undoubtedly a legitimate part of that "norm" in life that he had dreamed of "restoring" back in the autumn of 1921. At the same time, the rather unusual spectacle and extravaganza, in which they themselves were participants, stirred his imagination. "We had dinner in a hall," Yelena's description went on, "in which the table with the food on it was bedecked with a transparent green material and lit from underneath. There was a huge number of tulips and roses. There was an inordinate abundance of food and champagne, of course. Some Caucasian dances were danced. We were treated in a very welcoming way, I danced with many of the people I knew…"

Herein, perhaps, lie the origins for the hall "with columns made of some sort of yellowish, gleaming stone," the "low wall of white tulips", the "white chests and black shoulders of the men in tails", the "red, pink and milky-white walls of white roses on one side, and on the other – a wall of Japanese double camellias", the champagne, which was bubbling "in three decorative basins", the "grandiose, carpeted staircase", the "green-tailed parrots", the "chimpanzee accordionists", the spectacle of the "Polar bears playing harmonicas and dancing the Kamarinskaya on the stage" – everything that was soon to make such a striking impression on the first people to hear the novel, and, a quarter of a century later, on the first people to read the novel about the master and his beloved.

"They are very flattering towards Misha," Yelena continued. "The ambassador is very kindly among his guests, he makes a very agreeable impression. We wanted to leave at 3:30 am, but they were having none of it. Then Misha went out and found his chauffeur, who emerged as though from beneath the ground [all these details seem to have been recorded by her for a reason, and provide pause for thought – M.C.], and told him he could go home.

We didn't leave until 5:30 am, in one of the embassy's cars, after inviting one or two of the American embassy staff to visit us… Someone got into the car with us whom we didn't know, but who is known to all Moscow and always spends time among foreigners – Shteiger, I think it was.

We arrived home and day had already broken. Katerina Iv. [Yekaterina Bush, or 'Lolichka', Sergei Shilovsky's maid – M.C.], who was staying with us, came out to see us in a blanket and listened in, with awful curiosity, as we talked about the ball."

25th April. "Misha, although he was loath to do so, went to a meeting of writers with Godon Craig, after receiving an invitation from the Union of

Soviet Writers. It was terribly boring, there weren't many people there. Vs. Ivanov gave a speech."

On 28th April, there is an entry in the diary of the assistant director, to the effect that Bulgakov's letter about *Molière* had been read out to the actors at the Art Theatre prior to the rehearsal and that "S[tanislavsky] called on the actors to keep their morale up, and, through their acting and directorial resources, to make a success of the chosen direction and to defeat the author, without departing from his text. "It will be harder, but it will also be more interesting."

The rehearsals continued in accordance with the former text.

Relations with the Americans were maintained and strengthened, with one or other of the informers and spooks always present.

29th April: "In the evening – the wife of Whiley's adviser, and Bollen", then the names of a few more Americans, "and, of course, Zhukhovitsky. Whiley brought me some roses, and Boolen brought Misha some whisky and some Polish *zubrovka*. Misha read the first act of *Zoya's Apartment*, the final version". After giving the play to Zhukhovitsky and Boolen so that they could translate it, he made Zhukhovitsky sign a note stating that he "would assume responsibility himself for obtaining permission from the relevant bodies of the USSR for it to be sent abroad […]. Much fun was had over dinner. Madame Whiley invited us to visit her in Turkey, she is leaving in a few days with her husband to spend a month in Turkey.

We parted at around 3 o'clock."

It was pleasant to talk about the possibility of such a trip, at least, to tempt himself and to tease Zhukhovitsky. The Americans could not imagine, of course, what complex emotions they must have been feeling.

30th April. "We arrived at the embassy on foot at 4:30. Misha was dressed in a black suit, I was wearing a very, very worn black dress.

Boolen invited us to watch a film with him yesterday. Everyone was in black tie, we were given a very nice welcome. The only Russians there were Nemirovich and Kotik [his wife – M.C.].

The film was remarkable! It was about the lives of the British cavaliers, somewhere on the border with India. After the screening, we were invited into the dining room, where we were treated to champagne and all sorts of sweetmeats. We were introduced to lots and lots of people, including the French ambassador and his wife, and the Turkish ambassador. He is a portly, very jolly character! Madam Whiley invited us to call on her at 10:30 tomorrow. Boolen said he would send a car to pick us up.

So then, these are our American days!"

1st May. "Sergei went along with his father [Y.A. Shilovsky – M.C.] to the parade and came home looking delighted. He said the parade was terrific.

We woke up in the afternoon, and in the evening, when the car came for us, we did a lap, along the embankment and through the city centre, to look at the illuminations. The embankment has been made to look very beautiful. The same is true of the Bolshoi Theatre.

There were 30 people at Whiley's place, including the Turkish ambassador, some French writer [this was apparently St.-Exupery – M.C.], who had just arrived in the Soviet Union, and, of course, Shteiger. All our acquaintances were there too – the secretaries of the Amer[ican] emb[assy]. In our seats, we were served champagne, whisky and cognac. Then we had a buffet dinner, sausages and beans, macaroni and spaghetti and then a compte. And fruit. I wasn't very hungry. Misha, though, the poor dear, didn't have a chance to get a mouthful of anything. He was having questions thrown at him constantly by a certain American woman. The Frenchman – who turned out, among other things, to be a pilot – talked about some of the dangerous flights he had been on. He showed us some extraordinary card tricks. I thought at first that our hostess was in on the act. Later, though, when he did a magic trick right in front of me, he convinced me. And I was frightened – I couldn't get my head round it.

We sat up till half-three, then took a taxi home."

This was how Bulgakov saw in 1st May 1935.

A ride in a taxi, a table laden with good food, guests in tails from various corners of the world, the ever-present baron Shteiger, magic tricks, the return home during the night…Alongside the pages of the novel about the devil and the master, the flow of events taking place in his life was a far cry from the everyday reality in his homeland and was close to the world that came into being on these pages.

2nd May. "… Zhukhovitsky came to call in the afternoon – he brought a translation of the agreement with Fisher [the foreign publishing house which bought the rights from Bulgakov to the translations of his plays – M.C.] about England and America (*The Days of the Turbins*). He recommends excluding America, of course. He had some very bad things to say about Shteiger, saying that he would not wish to meet him here for the world.

He even squirmed as he told us that."

Material for his play about Pushkin, on which he was still working, in order to create the atmosphere of surveillance (which he modernizes in the play, giving it traits taken from modernity) was constantly being provided by his own life, by the people who came to his home.

Yelena told me (on 12th November 1969) that Bulgakov, who could clearly see that his role was to be a permanent visitor at their house, once said to her: "Invite that scoundrel over!" Shteiger duly arrived – "fat and carnivorous, and Bulgakov began playing a game with him. 'I want to go overseas.'

'You ought to go to the factories first, Mikhail Afanasievich, and write a play about the working class, and then go overseas.'

'I've decided to do it the other way around, you know – first the overseas bit, then the bit about the working class. Together with Yelena Sergeyevna, here.'

'Why would you wish to go with Yelena Sergeyevna?'

'Oh well, you know, we've sort of grown used to the idea of travelling abroad together, just the two of us.'

'No, you will probably be given an interpreter…'

She said that their guest made haste so that he could leave by evening (he was clearly required to 'put in an appearance' that same day), and was nervous, but Bulgakov intentionally made him stay until eleven o'clock, then said to Yelena that she was "never to let him over the threshold again:

'It takes the biscuit, after all! He graduated from Oxford, so as later to…' And he struck the table with his fist, so as to demonstrate what had happened 'later'.

"Two or three weeks later, though," Yelena went on, "he wanted something spicy again, and he said:

'Well, invite that scoundrel over again.'"

9th May. "Versayev, Angarsky, Dmitriyev and the Trenyovs, in the evening. […] Angarsky asked, over dinner: 'I don't understand, why is it that writers are now writing about historical themes, and avoiding modernity?'

Angarsky had been doing diplomatic work for a long time; he spent far more time in Greece and other countries than at home. Yelena does not comment in her diary on this matter, which, around the table at the Bulgakovs', probably sounded too clerical, cerebral.

Bulgakov had spent the whole of the previous week correcting *Zoya's Apartment* – for Zhukhovitsky's translation – and he gave it to him on 1st May, in the evening.

V.Y. Volf, from the Krasny Theatre in Leningrad, came to visit the Bulgakovs; on learning of his work on the play about Pushkin, he urged Bulgakov to give it to him for the theatre. One of the Moscow theatres asked for "a play about the civil war, by the year 1937". A few days later, Bulgakov called them and said no, "explaining that there was no way he could start work on something new, since he already had two big, unfinished works on the go – *Pushkin* and a comedy. To say nothing of *Molière* (entry from 13th May).

On 16th May, they celebrated Bulgakov's birthday at home: he was given some sheet-music for one of Wagner's works and a book by Lesage (apparently, it was *The Lame Devil*).

On 18th May, Bulgakov reads his play about Pushkin to the people at the Vakhtangov theatre, at 12 noon. "… They listened to it very well," Yelena wrote. After the reading, we had breakfast – caviar, salmon, ham and gherkins." Over breakfast, Yelena's son, Zhenya, called, and told her about the air disaster involving a plane called the *Maksim Gorky*. "They say 42 people died."

9th May. "At the Sechins' in the evening. Irina was let out on the 16th, at 5 pm. She has grown pale and apathetic and has had a temperature for 10 days. She no longer laughs."

On 22nd May, Yelena's sister told her about "a list of those who have applied to go abroad. She herself, along with Nemirovich, Stanislavsky and Podgorny, are definitely going."

24th May – at the premiere of Pogodin's *The Aristocrats* (*Aristokraty*), at the Vakhtangov Theatre, "The audience gave the play an ardent reception. The play is a hymn to the GPU."

28th May – "Misha has been dictating *Pushkin* these past few days. Seryozha Yermolinsky and Konsky liked the play ever so much," Yelena wrote on 31st May, the day after the reading. They can't find the words to express how much they enjoyed it… Zhukhovitsky said a lot of things about Misha's high mastery, but he had a deflated look on his face: what is this, does everyone understand?! … When Misha read scene four [in which the figure of Bitkov is outlined with particular brilliance – M.C.], the temperature in the room dropped significantly, many people froze." And in the same entry: "I am happy with this play. I know it almost by heart – and every time, I feel a strong sense of excitement." This womanly capacity for wholehearted and impassioned empathy was an important and apparently beneficial part of Bulgakov's life at this time.

3rd June. At Trenyov's. "Misha liked Malyshkin a great deal. He says he is witty and pleasant in conversation."

On 4th June, they fill in questionnaires once again for a trip abroad in the summer months. In this period, Bulgakov is enduring a strained relationship with his co-author, Veresayev, who does not agree with many of the things in the play about Pushkin and is asking to have his name taken off it.

Bulgakov returns to the novel – not for long though, it seems – and writes the chapter about Bosoi on 21-22nd June. The summer was already well under way. Little Seryozha had been packed off to the dacha with his maid. On 29th June, Yelena wrote to her sister in Leningrad, saying that they were enjoying the "silence and the peacefulness. He is resting, not working, we have gone on lots of walks, and been sleeping and chatting." She had not given up her efforts to furnish the apartment: "Write soon, and tell me whether you've seen anything nice made of mahogany? Perhaps a nice mirror for the hallway, or a trumeau with side-holders for the candlesticks, old-style lanterns for the corridor, or rugs?"

The chapter about Bosoi reflected events which affected specific, yet fairly broad sections of the urban population, and which were dubbed the "gold fever": the forcible confiscation of gold and valuables from the population.

When the exchange rate for the Soviet *chervonets* currency was restored, people were supposed to hand in their "gold desyatoks" ("zolotyye desyatki") and exchange them for the currency that was in effect; failure to do so was looked upon as the stashing of currency and a sign of disloyalty. Judging by the reminiscences of contemporaries, there were at least two waves of this "fever" that spread throughout the country, one in 1928-29 and one in 1931-33. The people who, in 1970-80, could still remember exactly how this confiscation had happened, disapproved of the chapter "Bosoi's dream", in the printed text of the novel. "I can't imagine how Bulgakov could have described it in comical tones," an academic in his seventies, M., said to me; he told me that in 1932 (or 1933), his entire family had been rounded up, and the investigator had said to him: "What, you're refusing to give it up are you, you're waiting for us to go away? We'll go away, but we'll slam the door so hard that heads will roll" (contemporaries attributed this mysterious phrase to Trotsky, supposing, in the political fog of those years, that it was repeated by his secret supporters…). "Do you know how they used to do it?" the academic said. "They would squeeze 10 people into a tiny room, so that no-one could sit down. The things that went on! The children were screaming to their parents: 'Give them the gold! Make them let us out! We can't take it any more…!' No, I cannot fathom how he could portray that in the form of a parody!" From those who witnessed the events of those years, I heard about methods of extortion that would not look out of place in a novel by George Orwell. T.A. Aksakova-Sivers includes in her memoirs a frightening episode from the winter of 1931-1932 in Leningrad, when the "confiscation of valuables and currency from people who were suspected of having them in their possession was taking place (handicraftsmen, doctors with large practices, etc.)"; this episode was related to the well-known Leningrad doctor Boris Ivanovich Akhsharumov: "After a two-day stay at Nizhegorodskaya Street [i.e. at the NKVD's internal prison – M.C.], Boris Ivanovich returned home accompanied by two agents and pointed out to them a door on the balcony that had been locked for the winter. The agents forced the door open, picked up a buried casket full of valuable items and went away. After this, Boris Ivanovich, who had previously been communicative and even good-humoured, was unrecognisable. He said nothing at all for two days, and then: "After what I have been through, what I have had to endure, I cannot live any longer!" He took morphium that night. On that occasion he was saved, and taken to the Mariinsky hospital, but a week later, seizing an opportunity when his wife was briefly absent, he threw himself from the ill-fated balcony. The balcony overlooked Ligovskaya Street and was on the 4th floor. He died instantly." If one takes the risk entering into conjecture as to the events of his spiritual life, hidden from view, one can perhaps suppose that in this case, which reflected the widespread social and psychological clash of the era – a collision that is significant in terms of understanding the specific background against which Bulgakov's creative life and that of his contemporaries was played out – a catastrophic rift had arisen between man and his own identity. Extreme degrees of physical and psychological influence on a person caused the kind of behaviour in him that, once he was set free again, were no longer compatible with his customary self-respect. For those who could not conceive of life without that feeling, this resulted either in their identity being utterly broken (and all the values they once held dear being rendered worthless), or in death.

On 26th July, Bulgakov wrote to Veresayev: "I am alternating between the dacha and the city. I have already started working. I am cleaning up the language [this refers to the play about Pushkin – M.C.], and am busy transforming Arendt into Dal... My application for overseas travel was rejected (You will no doubt be holding up your hands in amazement!), and I know find myself not beside the Seine, but beside the Klyazma instead. Oh well, it's a river, too... I wish you the best, the most valuable thing that there is in the world – good health." He had not, it seems, been altogether convinced by the favourable results of the medical studies.

In early August, the play, as he informs Veresayev, "is completely ready".

On 22nd August, Yelena wrote that I. Lezhnev had appeared – after so many years.

The former editor of *Rossiya*, in whom Bulgakov, in 1923, had placed such serious hopes, was, as has become clear from some relatively recent studies of Russia's political history, an important figure in Stalin's political game. Exiled from the country in May 1926, "from the autumn of 1926 onwards he worked as an economist in the Soviet trade delegation in Germany, remaining a correspondent for several Soviet newspapers. In 1929, I.G. Lezhnev wrote to the Central Committee of the Communist Party asking for permission to return to the USSR. The letter was read out at one of the district party conferences in Moscow and seen as an important symptom of the reappraisal by the 'landmark' intelligentsia of their position. In March 1930, I.G. Lezhnev returned to his native land. [...] In December 1933, he was allowed into the party by decision of the Politburo." We know that his recommendation for party membership was given to him by Stalin.

It was only then, it seems, that Bulgakov discovered that Lezhnev had also made use of Stalin's patronage, so unambiguously revealed in this unprecedented fact, in the years when he had been publishing *Rossiya*. On 16th May 1934, *Literaturnaya Gazeta* reported that Lezhnev had been admitted to the Writers' Union; from the following year, he took up a post as the director of a department at *Pravda*. At the same time as he held this post, so close to state power, almost all those who had thought, on returning to Russia in 1922-1923, that they were fleeing, whereas in fact their later, deadly flight had merely been put off by twelve to fifteen years, were put to death.

On 5th September, *Vechernyaya Moskva* reported: "The dramatist M.A. Bulgakov has finished a new play about Pushkin. The play is to be put on at the Vakhtangov Theatre." Yelena Sergeyevna writes to her sister and mother on 7th September (they are in Riga): "I have so much work to do right now, with Misha, with Seryozha, his schooling. It is autumn, everything needs to be sorted out. I am terribly tired... In a couple of days I shall finish a big job (the copying out of *Pushkin*). I shall be a bit freer." On 10th September, the play, copied out by her, is submitted to the Vakhtangov Theatre, and just over a week later – to the Krasny Theatre in Leningrad.

On 17th September, the Bulgakovs apply to swap their apartment for a four-bedroom one in the writers' house in Lavrushinsky Side-street: they complain that the walls are too thin, and ask for a lower floor.

On 20th September, they learn that *Alexander Pushkin* has now been granted permission to be staged, from the Repertkom. "It's worth offering up a prayer to God – a happy day, at last!" Yelena writes. It was hoped that rehearsals for *Ivan Vasilievich* would begin in October.

27th September. "Misha is anxious about what sort of a reception he will get from the theatre."

2nd October. "What a joyful evening! Misha read *Ivan Vasilievich* with uproarious success – here in the flat [...] everyone was in fits of giggles. [...] They want to start work on the play right away. Everyone was pleased...It was terribly pleasant. We had a very merry dinner."

3rd October. "In the evening – Sergei Prokofiev, with Dmitriyev. He makes a pleasant impression on one. We discussed the idea of an opera based on Misha's play (*Pushkin*). He took the play away with him."

On 7th October, Bulgakov submitted a comedy to the Satire theatre, and on 17th October, Yelena wrote: "Remarkable news about *Ivan Vasilievich*. Five people in the repertkom read the play, they all tried to find something suspicious in it. And they didn't find anything. Misha says: 'What are they looking for in it?!' A remarkable line: couldn't we have Ivan the Terrible saying that things are better now than they were then...? In the evening, we took a spontaneous decision to go and see *Faust*. We met Melik [the chief conductor at the Bolshoi Theatre, A.S. Melik-Pashayev – M.C.], he was conducting... I was ever so happy, as I've liked him for a long time. ...*Faust* gave me a pleasant feeling..." For Bulgakov himself, *Faust* was the ever-present background to his works and almost a constituent part of the novel he worked on that year – far less than he would have liked, it seems.

That same evening, Y.L. Leontiev (he was now on the board of the Bolshoi Theatre, and the Bulgakovs were often guests of his in the director's box) "showed us today's copy of *Pravda*, in which Afinogenov blessed the Theatre [i.e. the Art Theatre – M.C.] with a satirical article about how the rehearsals for the plays go on endlessly, sometimes for as long as 4 years. It feels like a celebration for the soul: they deserve as much, the scoundrels!" She was gripped by a feeling of rage, hurt, vengeance for her husband, but more important than this was something else: her belief in the idea that the hand of the Nemesis would definitely come to rest as soon as it had struck their enemies.

On 20th October, people from the Satire theatre came to see Bulgakov, along with a representative of the Repertkom (he was ill). "A trying, heavy, unpleasant conversation, although it was held in fairly pleasant tones. Mlechin cannot bring himself to allow the play to go ahead. First of all he tried to find some sort of damaging idea in it. When he didn't find one, he started getting upset about the idea that there is no idea in it at all. He exhausted Misha with all his questions. It is inexpressibly tortuous to have such conversations. He left, saying that they would read the play again that evening." Apparently, the theatre was covering its own back – Yelena writes down something that Mlechin said to his representative: "'You have some concerns, don't you…' Nonsensical cowardice and sycophancy – that's the reason for all these issues!" Yelena concluded decisively, as always reflecting in her diary entries, to some degree, the mood and assessments of Bulgakov himself.

On the night of 29th October, there was a call from the theatre: *Ivan Vasilievich* had been "given the go-ahead, with a few small modifications. What a joy."

30th October. "We received a phone call in the afternoon. I walked out, and Akhmatova was there, her face looking so terrible, so emaciated, that I didn't recognise her, and nor did Misha. It turned out that in one night, both her husband (Punin) and her son (Gumilyov) were arrested. She had come to Moscow to hand a letter to Josef Vissarionovich. Clearly distraught, she was mumbling something to herself."

31st October. "Anna Andreyevna copied out, by hand, her letter to J.V. S. In the evening, a car took her to Pilnyak's place." According to Yelena's oral account, Bulgakov offered to write out Akhmatova's letter – composed with his help and already typed up on the type-writer – in neat handwriting; to do so seemed to befit a poet, in his opinion. When Akhmatova came to see them on 4th November holding a cable from her husband and son – evidence that the letter had been successful ("I am happy for Akhmatova", Yelena wrote), Bulgakov attributed this success, in part, to his advice.

On 5th November, Bulgakov began translating Molière's *The Miser* into Russian – to earn some extra money. Once again, an activity had emerged that was distracting him from his own plans.

7th November. "I accompanied Misha to the demonstration in the morning. He told me afterwards that there were columns of them walking around the square, several lines thick. He saw Stalin standing on the tribune – in a grey overcoat and a peaked cap." On 10th November, they were at the Bolshoi Theatre again, to see the opera *Carmen*. After the performance, Yakov Leontievich and Melik-Pashayev had dinner with us."

18th November – the first rehearsal for *Ivan Vasilievich*. On 23rd November, they saw the opera *Sadko* at the Bolshoi. Bulgakov reads both *Ivan Vasilievich* and *Pushkin* to guests at their home. Stanislavsky had refused to put on *Molière*; "I have many objections as to the author, and also about you, and the actors," he said to the director, N. Gorchakov, and suggested: "Put the show on yourself, if you're prepared to take responsibility for it." Bulgakov hoped that this would accelerate the staging of the play.

22nd December. "Misha was at a rehearsal for *Molière* in the afternoon, I was at the Bolshoi for the dress rehearsal for *Lady Macbeth* [Shostakovich's opera, Lady Macbeth of the Mtsensk District – M.C.]. The music is very powerful and original. I met Shostakovich. After the theatre, I went to see Misha together with Yakov Leontievich and Dmitriyev [set designer at the Art Theatre by this time – M.C.], then we went back home for lunch, and bought champagne on the way home. Melik-Pashayev came after us, and there was much laughter over lunch. The fact that I didn't invite Shostakovich is gnawing away at me, though. Melik played on the grand piano with Seryozha, then on his own, and he sang and had a good time."

The year was coming to an end, to the accompaniment of hopes which, at long last, seemed realistic. The new year ought to bring with it the staging – for the first time in seven years – of three of his plays: *Molière*, *Alexander Pushkin* and *Ivan Vasilievich*.

On 31st December, Nemirovich-Danchenko watched the rehearsal for *Molière*, and afterwards got actively involved in the work required to put on the play. His proximity to the Bolshoi Theatre gave rise to new ideas: Bulgakov was already thinking about some possible directorial work on his favourite operas, *Faust* and *Aida*, the current productions of which were very old. On 1st January 1936, Pasternak's poem about Stalin appeared in *Izvestiya*, influencing, in my view, Bulgakov's decision to turn his attentions to this very subject.

CHAPTER SIX

*A Fresh Failure. "What Can I Say,
It's a Libretto Like any Other!"*

1

On 2nd January 1936, Bulgakov and his wife set off for the Bolshoi Theatre to see the opera *Lady Macbeth*. They had been invited by Y. Leontiev and A. Melik-Pashayev. This was the second performance of the opera. They then had dinner at the Masters of the Arts Club (a place they had often visited over the last year) with Melik-Pashayev and Shostakovich.

On 6th January, the directors of the Bolshoi, Meli-Pashayev and Shostakovich, called on the Bulgakovs in the afternoon. "At their request, Misha read *Pushkin* to them (an idea for an opera). Shostakovich told Misha how grateful he was to him, said he had liked the play ever so much and asked for a copy of it. We then had lunch, and our pies were a resounding success… It was generally very good. Shostakovich played his polka and the waltz from *The Bright Stream*, and Melik also played one of Shostakovich's waltzes, *The Golden Mountains*. All three pieces are remarkable!' Thus, two of the greatest composers of the day had expressed a desire to write an opera based on Bulgakov's play, and Yelena Sergeyevna, surrendering herself with ardour to the most joyful hopes, had already written down: "My preference, if *Pushkin* were to be made into an opera, would be for Shostakovich to do it." "Our lives are wonderful at the moment," she wrote to her mother, in mid-January. "Admittedly, we have become very tired over the last two months, since Misha has taken on the task of translating a comedy by Molière from the French and had to do an awful lot of work. We only finished it yesterday – or rather, I finished the writing up of it – and we gave a huge sigh of relief. We have missed a whole load of wonderful days because of that translation – we weren't able to do any skiing." In the middle of the season, with his plays on the point of being performed, Bulgakov already felt very tired.

On 25th January they bought him a grey fur coat to mark the occasion – it had been made using the hide of an American grizzly. Everyone who met him that winter and the next remembered him wearing it.

The final rehearsals for *Molière* were taking place.

28th January. In *Pravda*, Yelena Sergeyevna wrote, "there is an unsigned article with the headline 'Instead of music, a mess'. The article talked of an "unstructured, messy flow of sounds", and said that this opera was the expression of leftist monstrosity. I think Shostakovich was wrong to take on this gloomy, difficult subject. I can imagine what sort of mood he's in now!" Behind the distinctive language of her diary, it is hard to get a sense of Bulgakov's attitude to these events, which had an acute social resonance. Could he detect, in these peals of criticism, the storm that was approaching him? Or was he completely sure that they were only talking about some 'leftist deviations', which he had nothing to do with?

6th February. "Yesterday, after the torments that have lasted so many years, was the first dress rehearsal for *Molière*. A much livelier atmosphere at the dress rehearsal – and I love that... It is not the play I have been waiting for since 1930, but it went down well with the audience at this dress rehearsal. It will probably continue to enjoy success. I am struck by the precision of Misha's predictions as to how the actors would perform their roles. Yanshin (Bouton) and Bolduman (the king) are magnificent... Koreneva, Gerasimov and Podgorny are monstrously bad. It is criminal to provide such [word cut out] actors. I should very much like to know how Koreneva managed to spread a rumour all over Moscow to the effect that she is the best actor in the entire cast.

Vilyams is good. There were times when the audience applauded the set designs. The first ripple of applause rolled around the auditorium when Larin (Charlatan) stopped playing on the harpsichord.

There was applause for the king's line: "You shall sit – if you're capable of sitting – for three months in Father Varfolomey's prison" [...] A roaring success... At the end of the play Misha left, so as not to have to go up on stage, but they went and found him in the vestibule and brought him on stage. Nemirovich came out to give a bow too (he was very content, frightfully so). [...] People generally made their presence felt very well. Many of the Art Theatre people who were watching the play had gloomy expressions on their faces. This was plainly a case of jealousy.

After the dress rehearsal, we had lunch at a kebab-house, and then Misha persuaded me to join him for a trip to Sadko, for he wanted to listen to some music.

Late in the evening – Dm[itriyev]. There is an article in *Pravda* about *The Bright Stream* today, under the headline *Falsehood in the Ballet*. It is very powerful stuff and, according to many, it is absolutely right. I feel very sorry for Shostakovich. They made him get involved in something that was a load of tosh. The authors of the libretto were aiming to please." The carefully thought-through, calibrated language of the diary entries masks the conversations that must have taken place at their home at this time. Did the success of *Molière* determine the mood of Bulgakov himself? We have very little material to go on when trying to form an opinion on this. That evening, Melik-Pashayev and Y. Leontiev came to see them. "Misha has made up his mind once and for all to write a play about Stalin. Melik played a small excerpt from *The Valkyries*. We had a very merry dinner." The order in which the events are described in this entry enables us to suppose that the plot of the play must have been discussed with the guests in some way. 8th February. "Another dress rehearsal tomorrow. Success and happiness!"

The first private performance of *Molière* was held on 11th February, for the proletarian students. "At the end, there was an endless number of curtain calls – I think there were 21 in total. The audience were very keen to see the author on stage. Misha duly obliged." That same day, a sharp-tongued piece about *Molière* by O. Litovsky appeared in *Sovetskoye Iskusstvo* (*Soviet Art*). "His writing is fuelled by malice! He doesn't even try to hide it. One can see so clearly that this is dictated by the personal hatred he feels for Mikh. Af. Among those watching the play was Poskrebyshev, J.V.'s secretary. He liked it a lot, Olya informed me…"

Let us examine the tone of the letter that Bulgakov writes that day to A.I. Tolstaya and P.S. Popov at Yasnaya Polyana. There is no triumphalism in it; it contains hints of uncertainty and doubts that are almost not expressed. "Here, after the thaw, the weather is odious once again, with wind and a devilish frost. I hate it and I curse it. Of course, if it were possible to move over there without any effort, to the snow banks of Yasnaya, I would sit by the fire, trying to forget it all – *Molière*, *Pushkin* and comedy. […] *Molière* has opened. The dress rehearsals were on the 5th and the 9th. Word has it they went down well. At both rehearsals, I had to go out on stage and bow, which is agonizing for me. Today, in *Soviet Art*, the first swallow arrived: a review by Litovsky. He writes disapprovingly about the play, with a malevolence which, though restrained as much as possible, is nonetheless great. ... Rehearsals are under way for *Ivan Vasilievich*, but I haven't been at the Satire for a very long time. I am trying not to think about *Alexander Sergeyevich*, and the burden is so great. I think the people at the Vakhtangov are starting work on it. It is clear that it won't be put on at the Art Theatre. I'm not feeling very well; I am so tired that I can't do anything now; I just sit and dream about felt boots. I don't have to sit here forever, though – this evening I am going to see the play (the first, private performance)."

16th February. And so, the premiere of *Molière* has taken place. We had been waiting for this moment for so many years! The auditorium was absolutely stuffed full, as Molière puts it, with prominent people. Akulov was there, and Boyarsky, and Kerzhentsev, Litvinov, Mezhlauk, Mogilny, Rykov [...] I can't recall all of them now. What's more, the entire audience was a very well-educated one: there were loads of professors, doctors, actors and writers.

Afinogenov listened to the play with a mysterious look on his face, but very attentively. And at the end, his applause was long and loud.

Olesha uttered some unpleasant absurdity at the play during the interval.

In the intermission, people were invited to take tea; all of the 'crème de la crème' were there, apart from the government ones, of course.

The play was an enormous success; yet again, there must have been around 21 curtain calls, perhaps 23. The audience called the author on stage, very eagerly. [...] We invited Arendt, the Yermolinskys and the Lyamins into our box. After the play, we waited for Misha for a long time, since Akulov had gone backstage and was talking to the cast."

The secretary of VTsIK said to Bulgakov "that the play was superlative, but – would it be understood, was it suitable for a Soviet audience member?" Bulgakov listened to his advice to get rid of the scene with the nun.

The nun appeared on stage twice in the play, as a premonition of Molière's death. Did Bulgakov perhaps see the conversation backstage as a premonition of the death of the play?

The same entry, for the 16th, reads: "At 4:30, we were there, by invitation of the embassy and of the American ambassador. He had just returned from America. He conducts himself charmingly.

The guests were the diplomatic corps. Budyonny was there, in his new uniform, with long trousers.

There was a screening of the film *Benv[enuto] Cellini*. The Americans were awfully nice to us."

Having been deprived by the government of the ability to see the world, he was making up for this with his visits to a small corner of the New World in Moscow.

On 17th February, a harsh negative review of the play appeared in *Vechernyaya Moskva*, along with a "short, unfavourable review" in *Za Industrializatsiyu (For Industrialization)*. Accustomed as he was to the scorn that the newspapers poured on him, Bulgakov may not have noticed the context of it, which had changed over the course of the last year.

On 18th February, he talks to the new director of the Art Theatre, Arkadyev. "He said that the only subject that interests him, for a play, is the subject of Stalin. The conversation we had was extremely interesting, but Misha thinks he won't be given any material for the play." According to the oral accounts given by Yelena Sergeyevna, he could not initially contemplate doing the work without being able to call on archived materials.

… Perhaps in the very year when the idea came to him of writing a play about Stalin, the hero of this future play started to be embodied in the stories he told orally – his comic novellas. Yelena Sergeyevna later wrote them down from memory and read them out, reproducing the author's intonation and gestures.

"The story has it that Mikhail Afanasievich, feeling utterly desperate, wrote a letter to Stalin, saying: I'm writing plays, but no-one's putting them on, and no-one's printing any of my work – in a word, a short letter, written very well, and he signed it: 'Yours, Trampazlin'.

Stalin receives the letter and reads it.

S: What's this then…? Tram-paz-lin… I don't understand a word! (Misha always put on a Georgian accent when reciting Stalin's lines).

S: (*Presses a button on the desk*). Tell Yagoda to come in and see me! *Yagoda comes in and salutes Stalin.*

S: Listen, Yagoda, what on earth is this? Look at this letter. It's from some writer – but it's signed: Yours, Tram-pa-zlin. Who on earth is that?

Y: I can't say that I know.

S: What do you mean by that – I can't? How dare you give me an answer like that? You'll certainly see what's what when you're buried three miles beneath the ground! You're to tell me, within the next half an hour, who this is!

Y: Yes, your majesty!

Yagoda walks away and reappears half an hour later.

Y: Well, your majesty, the writer is Bulgakov!

S: Bulgakov? What on earth is going on? Why is my writer writing a letter like that? Send for him at once!

Y: Right away, your majesty! *(He walks out).*

The motorcycle zooms off – vrrooom! Straight to Furmanov Street. Ding-a-ling! There's a ring at the door, and a man appears in our apartment.

The man: Bulgakov? I am to take you to the Kremlin right away.

Misha is wearing an old pair of white, faded canvas trousers and his torn house-slippers, with his toes sticking out, and an unbuttoned shirt with a hole at the shoulder; his hair is dishevelled.

B: B-b-but… How can I possibly… I don't have any boots…

The man: My orders are to take you there right away, there's no time to get changed!

Misha takes off his slippers, looking frightened, and goes off with the man. The motorcycle roars – vvrroom! And they're already at the Kremlin. Misha walks into a hall, and sitting before him are Stalin, Molotov, Voroshilov, Kaganovich, Mikoyan, Yagoda. Misha stops at the door and bows.

S: What's this?! Why are you wearing nothing on your feet?

B: *(waving his arms around, looking grief-stricken)* Well, what can I say… I haven't got any boots…

S: How can that be? My writer – and he has no boots? What chaos! Yagoda, take off your boots, give them to him!

Yagoda takes off his boots, and gives them to Misha, looking disgusted. Misha tries to stretch them a little – they're not a comfy fit!

B: They don't fit me…

S: What sort of legs do you have, Yagoda, I just don't understand! Voroshilov, take off your books, perhaps they'll fit him.

Voroshilov takes off his boots, but they are too big for Misha.

S: Look – they're too big for him! Your legs are gigantic, they're like a quartermaster's!

Voroshilov faints.

S: Look at that, one can't even tell a little joke! Kaganovich, why are you just sitting there, can't you see the man needs some boots!

Kaganovich hurriedly takes off his boots, but they don't fit Bulgakov either.

S: Well, of course, what would you expect of a Russian man…! I ask you…! Get out of my sight!

Kaganovich faints.

S: It's nothing, it's nothing – he'll get back up. Mikoyan! There's no sense in asking you, come to think of it – you've got chicken-legs!

Mikoyan starts to wobble from side to side.

S: Don't even think of falling over!! Molotov, take off your boots!

At last, Molotov's boots slip over Misha's feet.

S: Ah, there we are! All right? Now tell me, what's the matter with you? Why did you write me such a letter?

B: Well, what am I to do…! I've been writing play after play, but it's never any good…! Just now, for instance, I've a play lying at the Art Theatre, and they won't put it on, or pay me any money…

S: So that's how things are! Well, you just wait there! Wait a moment.
He makes a telephone call.
S: That's the Art Theatre, right? This is Stalin. Get Konstantin Sergeyevich on the phone for me *(Pause)*. What? He dropped down dead? When? Just now? *(Softly)* You know what happened? He dropped dead when they told him.
Misha sighs deeply.
S: Wait, wait, don't start sighing.
He makes another call.
S: That's the Art Theatre, right? This is Stalin. Get me Nemirovich-Danchenko on the line. *(Pause)*. What? He's dead?! He's dead too? When did it happen…? You know what, he dropped dead just now, as well. Oh well, it doesn't matter, wait a moment.
He makes another call.
S: Get me someone else on the line then! Who am I talking to? Yegorov? All right then, comrade Yegorov, there's a play lying around at your theatre *(he winks at Bulgakov)*, a play by the writer Bulgakov… I don't like putting pressure on anyone, of course, but it seems to me it's a rather good play… What? You think it's rather good, too? And you intend to put it on? And when are you thinking of doing so? *(he covers the phone with his hand and asks Misha: when do you want them to put it on?)*

B: Good heavens! In three years' time, that would be fine!

S: Ah… *(to Yegorov)*. I don't like interfering in a theatre's affairs, but it seems to me that you could put it on… *(winks at Misha)* in three months… What's that? In three weeks? Well, good, that's settled. And how much are you planning on paying him for it…? *(he covers the receiver with his hand, and asks Misha: how much do you want?)*

B: Well, I suppose… well, five hundred roubles, at least.

S: Aaaaaah! *(to Yegorov)*. I'm no expert in money matters, of course, but it seems to me that for a play like that one, you ought really to pay fifty thousand. What's that you say? Sixty thousand? Well, very good, so be it, so be it! *(to Misha)*. There you are, you see – and there you were saying…

After this, life goes on in such a way that Stalin simply cannot live without Misha – they do everything together. One day, though, Misha comes up to him and says:

B: I would very much like to go to Kiev for three weeks or so.

S: Well, look what sort of a friend you are! What am I supposed to do?

But Misha makes the trip, all the same. Stalin, left on his own, starts to miss him.

S: Ah, Mikho, Mikho...! He's gone away! My Mikho's not here! What am I to do, it's so boring, it's simply awful...! Should I go to the theatre or something...? Zhdanov keeps shouting all the time – "Soviet music! Soviet music!" ... I ought to go to the opera.

He starts calling everyone on the phone, one after another.

S: Voroshilov, is that you? What are you up to? You're working? Nothing good will come of your work anyway. No, no, don't fall over! Come over and see me, we'll go to the opera together. And bring Budyonny with you!

S: Molotov, get over here now, you're going to go to the opera! What? You're stammering so much I can't understand a word you're saying. Get over here, I say! And bring Mikoyan too!

S: Kaganovich, stop playing those Jewish games of yours, and get over here, we're going to go to the opera.

S: Well then, Yagoda, you've of course been eavesdropping on us all, so you know perfectly well that we're going to the opera...Prepare a car for us!

A car is brought round. Everyone climbs inside. At the last minute, Stalin remembers:

S: What are we thinking, we've forgotten the biggest expert of all! We've forgotten about Zhdanov! Send the fastest plane we've got to Leningrad, to pick him up!

Vvrroom! The plane whizzes through the air and lands a few moments later – with Zhdanov inside.

S: There he is, good man! Always quick, aren't you? We've decided to go to the opera, you see – you keep shouting like that all the time, after all...about the flourishing of Soviet music! Well, show us! Get in. Ah, you've nowhere to sit? Well, sit here on my lap, you're only little.

The car drives off – vvrroom... and they all head into the government box at the branch of the Bolshoi Theatre. And there, at the theatre, there is a terrible fuss; everyone knows that the top brass are on their way. Yakov L. called Samosud on the phone – he had tonsillitis; then he called Shostakovich. Samosud arrived at the theatre 5 minutes later, his throat bandaged and with a high temperature. Shostakovich – white with fear – came running along too, immediately. Melik, wearing evening dress and with a little red carnation in his buttonhole, is getting ready to conduct – *Lady Macbeth* is being performed for the 2nd time. Everyone is anxious, but it is a pleasant kind of anxiety, since a short time before this, the top man and his entourage were at *Quietly Flows the Don (Tikhiy Don)*, and the next day all the main participants in the performance were awarded with titles and medals. So today, everyone – Samosud, Shostakovich, Melik *et al.* – is poking a little hole in the left side of their jackets.

The government box has settled in, Melik waves his baton furiously and the overture starts up. Licking his lips at the thought of his medal, and feeling the leaders' gazes on him, Melik is frantic, he jumps around, striking at the air with his conductor's baton, and mouthing the words silently as the orchestra plays. He is sweating buckets. 'What does that matter,' he thinks, in his ecstasy, 'I'll change my shirt in the interval.'

After the overture, he squints in the direction of the box, expecting applause... yet nothing happens.

After the first act, the same thing happens. There is no reaction at all. In the directors' box, by contrast, everyone is on their feet: Samosud, with a towel on his neck; Shostakovich, white and trembling; and Yakov Leontievich, majestic and tranquil – he has no hope of getting anything. Stretching out his neck, he is gazing tensely at the government box opposite.

There, things could not be calmer.

The whole show goes ahead in the same vein. No-one is thinking about the holes in their lapels any longer. Their only wish is to stay alive...

When the opera ends, Stalin gets to his feet and says to his entourage:

'I would like my comrades to stay here. Let's step into the ante-room, we need to have a chat.'

He walks into the ante-room of the box.

'Well then, comrades, we must have a collegiate meeting. *(They all sit down).* I don't like putting pressure on other people's opinions, I am not going to say that in my view, this is a cacophony, a musical mess; instead, I would ask my comrades to express their opinions completely independently. Voroshilov, you are the eldest, tell us what you think of this music?'

V: Well you see, your-yourship, I think that this is an utter mess.

S: Sit here next to me, Klim, sit down. Well, what about you, Molotov, what do you think?

M: I, y-your m-mightiness, th-think that this is a c-cacophany.

S: Well, all right, all right, you've started stammering, I hear! Sit down here, next to Klim. Well, and what does our Zionist think about this?

K: I think, your mightiness, that this is a cacophony and a mess mixed together!

S: I shall not bother asking Mikoyan, the only thing he's knowledgeable about is pickling jars… Well, all right, all right, only don't fall over! But what about you, Budyonny, what do you say?

Bud. *(stroking his moustache)*: They all ought to be eaten alive!

S: Well what good would that do now, to eat them all alive? What a hot-head you are! Sit here, closer to me! Well then comrades, so everyone has expressed their opinion, and we have come to an agreement. The collegiate meeting went very well. Let's go home.

They all get into the car. Zhdanov, at a loss as to why his opinion was not asked for, moves to and fro between everyone's legs. He tries to sit in his old place, i.e. on Stalin's knee.

S: Where do you think you're going? Are you out of your mind? On the way here, you nearly crushed my legs! Soviet music…! The dawn…! You're going back on foot!

The next morning, an article appeared in the paper: *Sumbur v Muzyke* (*A Musical Mess*). The word 'cacophany' appeared in it several times."

These stories are one of the scarce but important sources for reflections on Bulgakov's attitude towards Stalin, both from an artistic perspective and a personal perspective.

19th February. "The second reception with a movie, at Bullit's place. Diplomats again. Bullit was wearing a jacket, not morning dress, like the first time.

We went to the house on foot.

It was a very good movie. A comedy about Americans, about how an Engl[ish] servant stayed in America, charmed by Americans and their lives." The Americans are very nice.

Lunch with the Kunikhols in the evening. A very nice evening. Derbroy showed us a movie, he had filmed it himself (his travels in America).

Among the Russians, there was also the artist Konchalovsky and his wife.

The daughter of the Fr[ench] ambassador was there, Mademoiselle Alphon, she is very pretty and extraordinarily attractive."

It is all very similar to the glitzy, glamourous life that might be led by a very successful dramatist.

On 21st February, some unfavourable reviews of *Molière* were published in the the Art Theatre newspaper *Gorkovets* by Afinogenov, Vs. Ivanov, Y. Olesha and several actors, and Yelena's diary, we find an entry that comes as a surprise on these days of triumph: "Misha's fate is clear to me, he is going to be lonely and persecuted until the end of his days." (A few days later, however, she writes: 'Misha said that Slavin [the writer L.I. Slavin – M.C.] came up to him and expressed admiration for *Molière*. This is a rare thing. No playwright has ever praised any of Misha's works"').

On 29th February, a sharply-written article about the Art Theatre II appears: 'On imaginable achievements and excessive pretentions', and on 1st March – an editorial: 'On pen-pusher artists'. On 2nd March, Yelena writes:

"The sensation that all Moscow is talking about is the death of Ivan Bersenev's theatre. The government directive on the liquidation of his theatre [the Art Theatre II – M.C.] was written in a very harsh tone... Bersenev evidently made some massive error... One article after another has appeared in *Pravda*, into which they are flying headlong, one after the other." She lists, with barely concealed rapture, those who have "had their comeuppance", and notes, about one of the victims: "This one in particular got what was coming to him." Is this blindness, or an attempt to keep their assessments and possible concerns over the fate of the play completely hidden from prying eyes? Or is it an attempt to implore fate to be on their side?

On 4th March, *Molière* is performed again; they arrive at the theatre near the end. "The theatre was full, in the box on the right I could see Litovsky in the gloom, writing something down. There were a lot of curtain-calls. Misha came out to take a bow. A competition was announced today for the best textbook on the history of the USSR. Misha said that he was going to write one. *I* am struck by him. In my view, this is an impossible task." On 6th March, Yelena notes that Bulgakov was supposed to have a meeting with the director of the Art Theatre today, "but for some reason it was cancelled". On 9th March, an article appears in *Pravda* headed 'A gleaming exterior and false content' – about *Molière* at the Art Theatre. As soon as we had read it, Misha said: 'That's that – no more on *Molière* or *Ivan Vasilievich*.' In the afternoon, we went to the theatre. *Molière* has been cancelled. In the evening, a call came from F. [F.N. Mikhalsky – M.C.]: 'You have to write a letter justifying Misha's actions.' Justifying what? I said that Misha did not intend to write any such letter." She was passing on Bulgakov's response when she said this, of course; it appears that he took this decision straight away and irrevocably. "In the evening, Olga, Kaluzhsky – and, later, Gorchakov. The same thing again: a letter! And Markov said the same thing on the phone [P.A. Markov, head of the literary department at the Art Theatre – M.C.]. Some friendly pressure. What sort of people are these!"

Many years later, F.N. Mikhalsky wrote in his memoirs that the decision to cancel the play was taken by the director of the Art Theatre that very day. "Such hastiness!" writes V.Y. Vilenkin in his memoirs, published in 1982; "to many [how many really, one wonders? – M.C.] it seemed incomprehensible. Bulgakov could never forgive the Art Theatre for its failure to protect him."

On 10th March, an article by B. Alpers, entitled *M. Bulgakov's Reactionary Plots* (*Reaktsionnyye Domysly M. Bulgakova*), is published in *Literaturnaya Gazeta*. "Misha went to the theatre to see Markov, and told him that he would not, under any circumstances, write a letter of repentance. They are clearly going to cancel *Ivan Vasilievich*. It has now transpired that rumours were flying around the city in the first days of March to the effect that *Molière* was going to be cancelled. We have fallen upon very difficult times."

11th March. The director of *Ivan Vasilievich* summons Bulgakov to a rehearsal. "Why torture myself? The Satire Theatre is torn, they are afraid to put it on, they clearly had the play ready. We refused to go." On 13th – Zhukhovitsky: "… he comes over to ask all his questions, and I can sense that he is causing harm. There is no doubt as to what his role is." 14th: "… we were invited today to see the American ambassador. We hesitated for a long time, wondering whether or not to do. In the end, we decided against it. We are afraid of the sympathy, the questions and so on and so forth. In the evening, we were at the Bolshoi Theatre for *Natalka-Poltavka*… Before the start of the second act, Stalin, Ordzhonikidze and Molotov appeared in the government box. I was thinking about Stalin the whole time and dreaming that he might think about Misha and that our fate might change. At the end, the cast were all on the stage. There was an ovation for the government box, for Stalin, in which the whole theatre took part. I saw Stalin applauding as he waved his hand at the actors in greeting."

On 16th March, P.N. Kerzhentsev talks to him for half an hour, "criticising *Molière* and *Pushkin*. Misha realised that *Pushkin* is going to be cancelled; he showed Kerzhentsev a photocopy of an old review of *Molière* by Gorky. "Misha didn't argue, though, didn't ask for anything, and didn't complain about anything."

"Don't ever ask for anything," he would soon write in his novel, "particularly from those who are stronger than you…"

In response to a question about his future plans, he "deemed it necessary to mention the play about Stalin and his work on the textbook". The conversation did not really come to anything.

On 16th March, there is an article in the papers by the Art Theatre actor M.M. Yanshin, *An Instructive Failure* (*Pouchitel'naya Neudacha*). Although it was far softer in tone than the other repenting articles ("It seems wrong to me to hold the playwright alone responsible for this failure," wrote Yanshin), it had a very dispiriting effect on Bulgakov. He harboured a soft spot for this actor, who had played Lariosik in *The Days of the Turbins*. Many years later, Yanshin spoke at a memorial evening in honour of Bulgakov, and said that he had called him that day and tried to explain that the editor had altered his text, and had not shown it to him; that he, Yanshin, had written it differently… Bulgakov had heard him out and then hung up without a word. They had never met, nor spoken to each other, again. When Yanshin reached that part of the story, his voice shook, he began to weep and he left the podium.

17th March: In *Soviet Art* there is "a report about *Pushkin* that is monstrous in tone. Misha called Veresayev and suggested sending a letter to the editorial office to the effect that the play had been signed by Bulgakov alone, so as to rescue Veresayev from attacks, but V.V. said there was no need to do so."

In two empty lines in Yelena's diary, left between entries for 28th March and 5th April, a line was written in – at a later time, that much is obvious – dated 3rd April: "Kolya L. has been arrested" – the Kolya in question was Nikolai Lyamin.

"He was in prison for six months," his wife, Natalya Abramovna Ushakova, tells me. "The transfer was bearable, they allowed me to see him before his departure. It had been decided that he would be exiled for three years, but then there was a change at the top [Yezhov replaced Yagoda in the NKVD in September 1936 – M.C.], they crossed out what was on the slip of paper – and instead sentenced him to a camp, Chipya in the Komi Soviet Socialist Republic. I was allowed to travel there to see him, but one could only find out whether the meeting itself would be allowed once one got there. On one occasion I went there with the mother of another prisoner, and we talked about how of the Decembrists' wives had had it much easier. That woman was a singer, and she managed to stay there, working for a club – they needed her…" On 5th April – "Misha is dictating *Ivan Vasilievich*, making corrections as he goes. A few days earlier, the Satire theatre invited him over – they want to put the play on, but are afraid (it's not clear what they're afraid of). They are asking about corrections. Gorchakov has come up with God knows what crazy ideas – such as putting some kind of female pioneer into the comedy – a positive one. Misha rejected the idea of going down this cheap route outright. He said he would do everything he possibly could to amend the role of Timofeyev."

In mid-April, there was suddenly talk at the Art Theatre of resurrecting *Molière*; the directors began discussing amendments with Bulgakov, but this hope was soon destroyed.

In mid-May, meanwhile, the fate of another play was very quickly sealed. 11th May: "A rehearsal for *Ivan Vasilievich*, in make-up and costumes [judging by Y.S.'s diary, Bulgakov sees the play for the first time on this occasion –

M.C.]. Without an audience. In terms of sheer bad taste and chaos, this is a one-in-a-million play… The humour has been killed dead… The role of the thief has been turned by the director into I know not what! The make-up looks like it was done by a piglet or something. What a foul thing to have to write about," she concludes. 13th May: "Dress rehearsal for *Ivan Vasilievich*, without an audience. My impression of the play just as off-putting as before." The play is watched by a handful of officials; "towards the end of the play, without even taking off his coat, another one came in; "Immediately after the dress rehearsal, the play was banned."

One can only try to imagine how Bulgakov must have felt on learning of this latest incident in his destiny as a playwright; his feelings would have been mixed, but they would not have been any less unpleasant for that. His birthday followed three days later – he turned 45.

On 19th May, the Vakhtangov Theatre asked him to make changes to the play about Pushkin; he categorically refused to do so.

2

They spent the first half of June in Kiev, where the Art Theatre had taken *The Days of the Turbins* on tour. They enjoyed some much-needed leisure time after what had been a difficult year.

They stayed for a while with a friend from Bulgakov's childhood in Kiev, Sasha Gdeshinsky. (Generally, Mikhail was very quick to abandon people – he was very exacting," Nadezhda Afanasievna told me, "but he loved Gdeshinsky.").

He hosted them at his wife's apartment, on Artyom Street (formerly Lvovskaya Street). Many years later, on 8th October 1980, Larisa Nikolayevna Ilina-Gdeshinskaya told of how she could remember the warnings Bulgakov gave to the lady of the house: "He said: 'Don't go cooking anything, mind: I can't eat anything spicy, any conserves, or herring; and you should know that the only thing I can drink is white wine.' That was enough for me to know that he was already sick…". It may be that this was only a temporary indisposition; more pertinent is another detail that tells us about Bulgakov's condition after the theatre season that had just ended: "When Alexander Petrovich went to see them at the Continental, Yelena soon had to go off somewhere. She asked my husband to wait for her: "You know, Misha mustn't be left on his own." At one of the performances of *The Days of the Turbins*, Bulgakov was sitting next to Larisa Nikolayevna. "When they took the curtain-call, he said to me very quietly: 'Shout 'author'!' I did so, but no-one joined in. Going out onto the stage in his native city, and taking a bow before a packed house containing the nearest and dearest of the people with whom he had once walked up and down the same streets, sat at the same schooldesk, was something he was never quite able to do. Although the play was performed in Kiev without the scene involving Petlura, it was impossible fully to dispel the sense of caution that pervaded the auditorium.

The weather was unwelcoming, gloomy; it was not typical summer weather. A few days after their return, on 17th June, Gdeshinsky wrote: "Someone is poking fun at us, what wonderful weather we have here now." And yet when they arrived in Moscow, the feelings that had been stirred up in Bulgakov by this encounter with his native city – the look of the city had remained the same, in some way that he could not quite put his finger on – seemed positive. On 12th June, Yelena wrote in her diary: "We came back from Kiev today. The city gave us a comforting feeling – joyful, merry. [...] The rain was the only thing that spoiled it. [...] Some villain spread a rumour that the *Turbins* was going to be cancelled, and poisoned the day for us. As it turned out, it wasn't true. The first performance went ahead on the 4th."

On the Kiev – Moscow train, they bought the 4th edition of the journal *Teatr i Dramaturgiya* (*The Theatre and Dramaturgy*); in the leader, *Molière* was described as a "low-brow bit of fakery"; in the same edition they saw Meyerhold's speech before theatre workers in Moscow from 26th March 1936, dedicated not only to self-criticism, but also to the critics. The following was written about the Satire theatre: "In this theatre, laughter is transformed into sneering. This theatre is starting to look for the kind of actors who, in my view, ought not to be allowed to join it in any way. Bulgakov has crawled his way in there, for example." This was said long before the dress rehearsals for the play.

That summer, Bulgakov undertook two new jobs – side-projects in relation to his main ideas, a translation of *The Merry Wives of Windsor* for the Art Theatre and a libretto for the opera *Minin and Pozharsky* for the Bolshoi Theatre. B. Asafiev undertook to write the opera.

He also continued his work on the novel, although there are no references to it in Yelena's diary, nor did the author give any readings of the new chapters for his friends.

On 6th July 1936, he started a new notebook of additional material – the last one. In it, he wrote the final chapter of the third draft – *The Final Flight*, which he had previously outlined in a two-page sequence. The protagonist was referred to as the "master" throughout this entire chapter; his fable-like conflict was resolved here for the first time. "You have been rewarded," Woland said to him. "Be thankful to the Yeshua, wandering across the sand, whom you created, but do not think of him ever again. You have been noticed, and you will get what you deserve. You are going to live in a garden and walk out onto the terrace each morning; you will see wild grapevines criss-crossing your home in thick clusters, as it climbs up the wall. [...] The house on Sadovaya will vanish from your memory, as will the frightening Bosoi, but thoughts of Ha-Notsri and of the hegemon, now forgiven, will disappear as well. This matter is not one that your mind can comprehend. You shall never rise higher, you shall not see Yeshua, you shall not leave your refuge." The liberation of his memory was associated with the extinguishing of his creative power.

The dream of seeing his hero (the one that the Master's novel was about) was attributed here to the Master – by contrast with the later versions, in which it was attributed to Pilate alone. It is not inconsequential that in the previous chapter, Pilate had set off in good spirits to meet the one to whom he had "not said all he had to say", whereas the master was deprived of this opportunity forever. At this stage of his work on the novel, two themes which took turns to take a prominent position in the writer's creative work became intertwined, for the first time: the power of people and circumstances, crushing a personal human fate, including the fate of an artist (a subject which is predominantly outward-looking); and personal guilt, resulting in agonizing reflections and a dream of redemption (a subject which looks inward). The destinies of these characters, who had hitherto not crossed paths with one another in the novel, became incredibly tightly interwoven. The guilt of someone who has displayed cowardice, a cowardice that destroys his own fate or causes the death of another person, now seemed to be shared between Pilate and the Master – characters who are so different, but who are brought closer by their dream of redemption and peace.

The novel was completed and, apparently, put to one side for a while.

26th July. "Tomorrow, we are leaving Moscow – we will be staying at the Sinop, outside Sukhumi. *Minin* is now finished. M.A. wrote it in one month exactly, in intense heat. Asafiev liked the libretto enormously. He is promising to start writing the music right away."

"The Sinop is a marvellous hotel," Bulgakov wrote to Y.L. Leontiev on 17th August 1936. "One can have a very good holiday here. There's a park. Billiards. Balconies. The sea is very close. It's spacious, clean… At first, I didn't read anything, and tried not to think about anything, to forget everything, but now I've started working on the translation of the *Windsors* for the Art Theatre… Ah, dear Yakov Leontievich, will anything happen to me in the autumn? Ought I to go to a fortune-teller?"

Before long, however, the the Art Theatre director N.M. Gorchakov arrived at the Sinop and started giving Bulgakov advice on how to translate the play; he was the man who was going to put it on at the theatre. This advice had such an effect on Bulgakov, who was by no means well-disposed towards the theatre at the time, that he stopped working on it and informed Gorchakov that he refused to go ahead with the translation. Naturally, nobody had expected a playwright in the position in which Bulgakov found himself, with the new season around the corner, to take such a step.

On 1st September, they returned to Moscow. 9th September: "M.A. is feeling sad about the fact that he gave up his role in *Pickwick*, and he thinks it would be better if he stayed in the actors' studio, so as to avoid all the bullying on the part of Gorchakov and others"; he is still working at the Art Theatre as before, but any work as a director or adapter for the stage at this theatre has become unbearably burdensome for him this autumn.

On 14th September, after an annoying and fruitless conversation with the director of the Art Theatre, Bulgakov went home at a complete loss as to what to do. "There is no knowing what is to be done. In the evening, M.A. lit some candles and started looking at the *Windsors*, and writing something down." Late in the evening, some people arrived from the Bolshoi Theatre, including Samosud – to try to persuade Bulgakov to write a libretto for an opera about Perekop. "M.A. said that he doesn't know what to do; would he not have to quit the Art Theatre. Samosud said: 'We'll hire you, we'll give you any position you like' ['you can be a tenor, if you want?' Y.S. later added to this entry, from memory – M.C.]. That day, Bulgakov wrote two notes on the manuscript of the translation: his work was "resumed on 14th September 1936 in Moscow", and "Curtailed on 14th September 1936, once and for all".

On 15th September, he wrote a letter to the director of the Art Theatre, informing him that he wished to leave his job at the theatre and that he was not going to do the translation, and containing a statement for the board. He took the letter to the theatre with his wife and "left it with the courier's wife". It was the end of a job that had been given to him six years ago in the form of a special favour and that had cost him massive disappointments (in spite of all the 'stage-blood' he had spilt!). On 10th October, he began work at the Bolshoi Theatre – as a librettist. "What can I say, if I'm to write a libretto, then so be it!!" he had written to Veresayev on 2nd October. A new period in his life had begun, and it was to be the final one.

The final months of this ill-fated year were a torment. As though it were in pursuit of him, *Vechernyaya Moskva* reported on A. Globa's play in an article entitled *The Pushkin Season* (the preparations for the centenary of Pushkin's death were in full swing), in which "Pushkin is brought out onto the stage in his final, tragic years. This alone distinguishes it from the play by M. Bulgakov, who has tried to convey the tragedy of the poet without the involvement of…Pushkin himself." The critic M. Zagorsky added: "We can say with pride that in our era, neither theatre-goers, nor Soviet society as a whole, will accept a play about Pushkin that is not written at the artistic level required, with the right level of ideas…"

Arriving at the Writers' Union to pay his fees, Bulgakov "suddenly," as Yelena wrote on 9th October, "decided to go and see Stavsky – the secretary of the SSP. A difficult, unpleasant conversation about Misha's position ensued. The impression that Stavsky made on me was a difficult one, he wants to get out of having to resolve this matter. He is a civil servant, insincere down to the very marrow in his bones."

Yelena makes an important entry in her diary on 14th October, after another conversation with Stavsky; he had come to see them briefly on a formal matter, but they kept him talking – at her initiative, it seems. "When I invited him to take off his coat, he did so. We talked. This conversation was sad and horrific. Essentially, it is the conversation that should have happened before, from Misha's side: he ought to have said that in his own homeland, he wasn't being allowed to work. He said this. But some conclusion is needed. No-one is providing one. Least of all Stavsky. Everything he says is a either a dodge, a non-committal answer or a bit of cunning. He talked about how right now, someone somewhere would be discussing M.A.'s works. Who? Where? Why? This won't lead to anything."

With a womanly impatience, she prompted him into decisive words and actions. But was he ready to put his fate on the line once again, as he had done 6 years ago?

3

"We have been going to the opera and the ballet ever so often lately," Yelena wrote to her mother on 19th November 1936. At this time, Bulgakov had began the novel that he had first had the idea for back in 1929; he referred to it in a letter to the government as the novel *Theatre*, but now decided to call it first *A Theatrical Novel*, then, soon after he began work on it, on 26th November, *Notes of a Dead Man*. His desire to tell of how he had "become a playwright" had come true (just as in the autumn of 1929!) in a year in which the author himself had given up writing plays – forever, as he supposed. (It is worth noting that in Y.S. Bulgakova's diaries, there are no more mentions of the idea of a play about Stalin from the spring of 1936 onwards).

They were stunned by some of the things they saw in the first few plays of the new season.

On 2nd November, Yelena wrote: "The dress rehearsal for *Bogatyrs* at the Kamerny Theatre in the afternoon. It is a monstrous disgrace." This was a production of A.P. Borodin's comic opera *Bogatyrs*, with the text written by Demyan Bedny. On 13th November, at a reception hosted by the American ambassador at a beautiful house in Spasopeskovsky Side-street, the chairman of VOKS, the writer A.Y. Arosev, asks Bulgakov whether he is "writing anything to mark the 20th anniversary of October" (Arosev himself was arrested just over two months before the anniversary and soon died in prison), and the next morning, Yelena methodically recorded, "Misha said: 'Read that' and handed her the newspaper. It was a bit of news about the theatre scene: under a directive from the Committee for Matters of the Arts, *Bogatyrs* was to be cancelled, specifically for deriding the Christianization of Rus. I was amazed!"

This event, which Yelena accurately described as pertaining to the theatre scene, was one that turned out to go far beyond the footlights of the Kamerny Theatre. There is no doubt that it hurt Bulgakov to the quick and that he took it personally. Firstly, his own account against Demyan Bedny had been opened, as we saw, back in his first few years in Moscow, but far more important than that, perhaps, was the fact that these new tendencies might also affect the fate of his novel about Yeshua and Pilate, the draft version of which he had completed that summer.

What did the author of this novel think about the wording of the official statement, which he could not even have imagined in, let's say, the winter of 1922-1923? Did he link it to the common chain of events of that year, such a dramatic one for him personally, and the two subsequent years – at least from the spring of 1934, with the historic opening of the history departments at the universities (which had been closed in the first years after the revolution), since the directive 'On the introduction at initial and middle schools of an elementary course of universal history and the history of the USSR' – right up to that competition to write a history textbook, which he had decided to enter six months earlier? We cannot answer these questions. All one can do is assert that this event gave him food for thought and was the focus of his attention over the next few days – there is evidence of that, as we shall soon see.

"We went to see *The Fountain of Bakhchisarai*. After the show, M.A. stayed behind for a gala evening," Yelena wrote in her diary on 15th November 1936. "Samosud proposed that he should tell Kerzhentsev the contents of *Minin*, and M.A. stayed up until half past three in the morning in the office beside the director's box, telling Kerzhentsev not just the plot of *Minin* but also of *The Black Sea (Chernoye More)*.

The idea of officials acquiring such a close and thorough knowledge of the theatre's artistic ideas had long since ceased to surprise anyone, and had become part of daily life, but these officials also reflected on them, and considered in their minds versions which were intelligible only to them – at home, in their offices, and at the plays, which they never failed to attend. On 17th November, after watching two films at the same house in Spasopeskovsky, they went to see the premiere of *The Marriage of Figaro* at the branch of the Bolshoi (the famous F. Shtidri was conducting). "After the show, Kerzhentsev came up to M.A. and said that he was having doubts about *The Black Sea*. Oh, how tired we are of all this!

We had been given a ride to the theatre from the embassy by Afinogenov. Prior to that, he had spent the whole reception stubbornly interrogating M.A. about what he had been doing and how he was feeling." This unique lack of ceremony, inability to hear half-tones, and coarseness of approach in 'professional' interaction gradually overtook all of his peers in the industry, one by one.

Irritated by the pep talk he had been given by the chairman of the Committee for Matters of the Arts, Bulgakov finished the typewritten draft of the libretto for *The Black Sea* on 18th November. Yelena was overjoyed to see in the papers that a campaign had started up in support of *The Bogatyrs*, and she confessed to being "glad that Litovsky has received his comeuppance", after he "wrote a fawning review praising the play to the skies." They hadn't forgotten about Bulgakov either, though: the press started writing about *The Crimson Island* once again, reproaching the author of a play that had been taken off the stage eight years earlier.

Hope was growing stronger for a production of *Minin and Pozharsky*, however: on the evening of the 19th, Yakov Leontievich called from the Bolshoi Theatre "and said with gladness in his voice that Kerzhentsev had talked about *Minin* in the government box and that it had been met with approval. There was obviously a conversation with Iosif Vissarionovich," Yelena explained, in her diary entry. The incentive provided by a respectful focus on the historical past was becoming clear. Bulgakov's thoughts on this new turn of events led him to a new idea at this time. It is easy to imagine that it whilst he was influenced by the text of the directive on *The Bogatrys*, on 23rd November, that he wrote down some sketches for the libretto *On Vladimir*, dealing with the time of the Christianization of Rus and the historical figure with whom Kiev was associated for him, and the memorial to whom occupied such an important place in the novel *The White Guard* (as reflected in the first versions of this novel's name). His work on this libretto was not continued, however.

Premieres of the opera *Carmen* were taking place at the Bolshoi, and at one of Moscow's theatres, performances of Afinogenov's new play, *Salud, Espana!* had begun; the 'Spanish' subject became a very topical one in the summer of 1936.

Among Bulgakov's peers – the writers of Moscow – the literary life of the early 1920s had long since been replaced by new forms of existence in their profession. Bulgakov himself had not grown together with them, did not think of himself as anything other than at one remove from them.

"In the evening, we met some Spanish guests at the DSSP club," I.N. Rozanov wrote in his diary on 18th November. "There were slogans on the walls; Ksenia had spent hours working on the Spanish translations of them the night before (she had returned home at 2 am). In the morning, some changes were discovered. On the advice of the writer Fink, the question marks had been taken down and put at the start of the sentences, upside-down. Ksenia objected to this display of illiteracy." A Spanish plasterer gave a speech; "he talked about the 9 months he had spent in prison for having read *The Iron Flood*. There was a touching moment when he handed the badge of the Spanish people's militia to Serafimovich [...] We all sang 'We were born to turn fairy tales into reality'. Among the Russians that spoke was Tamara Ivanova – from the Council of Writers' Wives, and Vishnevsky."

A diary entry written by Yelena a few days later sounds polemical when compared with the diary of her contemporary, which was not known to her, and incorporates a call for a broader social context. "We gather together on a daily basis. We talk about this frightful life of ours. We read the newspapers. The events in Spain hold no interest for me. I have enough to deal with in my own life. In the evening, M.A. went to see *Carmen*."

On 26th November, Bulgakov had some visitors: I. Ilf, Y. Petrov and Sergei Yermolinsky, with their wives. "Over dinner, they persuaded Misha to read out the script (of *Minin*)", Yelena wrote. "M.A. read out the first two acts. I liked the way they listened to him. I like Petrov very much. He is very witty. That's the first thing. And on top of that, he talks in an extraordinarily serious and ardent way, when a subject starts to interest him. Both of them (but Petrov above all, I think) are very favourably disposed towards M.A. And besides that, they are genuine writers. And that is a rare thing."

At the end of November, the Bolshoi Theatre sent Bulgakov on a business trip to Leningrad with Melik-Pashayev, to listen to the vocal score for *Minin and Pozharsky*. For the first time since he had started living with Yelena, he was going away on his own; his wife saw him off at the station. He was away for two days, and in that time she sent him three funny telegrams: such was the nature of their relationship. "It feels empty at home without him," she wrote in her diary on 30th November.

Bulgakov came home on 1st December. Leningrad, a city he had not visited since the summer of 1933, had this time "had an utterly dispiriting effect on him. The general public seemed somehow very provincial and backward there." There were numerous shades of meaning in these words, besides their literal meaning. The relocation of a substantial number of the city's populace to places which were a long way from Leningrad, in the winter of 1934-1935 and the spring of 1935, and the fact that new residents moved into the apartments that were left vacant, according to many accounts, had very visible consequences: the very physiognomy of the city's population had changed, and wherever one looked, the people and faces were no longer the same as they had been in 1933. Even the ones who had managed to stay in their apartments had changed markedly in the intervening years, a period that was so difficult for the city. "He took an exceptional disliking to the R[adlov]s," Yelena wrote. "The only bright moment was when they went to see an opera. Asafiev is an incredibly strong, expressive actor, according to

M.A... M.A. was ever so keen on the music, and on the way Asafiev sang it." At last, some joyful expectations had appeared. On 20th December, the score was brought over from Leningrad, and Bulgakov made the final amendments to the text of the libretto. On 27th December, Kerzhentsev, Angarov, S. Gorodetsky and the theatre's directors listened to the music. Yelena wrote down what Bulgakov told her about their "messy and confused objections.

Angarov: But there's no opera!

Gorodetsky: The music is no good for anything.

Kerzhentsev: Why does the hero only feature at the beginning and at the end? Why is there no sign of him in the middle of the opera?

They each set out their own formula for an opera, and all of these formulae were different."

It now appeared, however, as though nothing could either surprise or annoy Bulgakov: he had been through hell and high water, and there was little that scared him now. "What I liked very much was the fact that M.A. came back from there at 3 o'clock in the morning – in a very good mood, and kept saying: 'No, I liked them very much.' I asked him, 'But what will happen now?' 'I'll tell you honestly, I don't know. It looks as though they won't let it go ahead.'"

For Bulgakov, the year 1937 began to the accompaniment of the orchestra of the Bolshoi Theatre, where he was now part of the furniture.

"We saw in the new year at home... There were gifts, masks, surprises, big balloons. Misha and Sergei smashed some cups with 1936 inscribed on them... At 2 am, Sergei Yermolinsky came to give us his best wishes, and there were phone calls from the Leontievs, the Arendts... the Meliks. May God grant that '37 is a happier year than last year!"

On 9th January 1937, Bulgakov writes to Afanasiev: "I am currently sitting here putting in a new scene in *Minin* and making the changes they've asked for. I'm having a hard time of it, I feel rotten. I can't get out of my head the thought of the demise of a literary life, of a hopeless future, and this gives rise to other dark thoughts. What else can I write to you in this letter? What? I value your work and I wish you, with all my soul, that which is being exhausted within me – strength."

On 29th January, he informed P.S. Popov via a very brief note that he had grown "utterly bored", and would like to meet up, adding: "It is quiet, sad and hopeless here, after the death of *Molière*." At that particular time, the hopelessness of the situation had become self-evident. Several months later, the speech made recently by P.M. Kerzhentsev at the All-Union Repertoire Conference was printed in *Soviet Art*; in it, he had expressed a high opinion of Kirshon's play *The Big Day* (*Bol'shoy Den'*) and reference was made to the cancelling of *Molière* and the banning of the play *Alexander Pushkin*.

On 7th February, recalling the events of the last month, Yelena wrote: "The most important thing of all, though, is the novel. M.A. is writing a novel based on life at the theatre. He has already written quite a lot of it. He read it to Yermolinsky – everything he's written so far. Sergei was full of praise for it, and picked up on all the subtle things that M.A. wanted to say in it."

18th February. "In the evening: the Vilyamses and Lyubov Petrovna Orlova [an extremely popular movie star – M.C.]. Late at night, when we were finishing our dinner, we heard from Alexandrov [the film director, L. Orlova's husband – M.C.] over the telephone that Ordzhonikidze had died of a heart attack. We were all deeply shaken by this news." 19th February. "Went into town with Sergei and Misha during the day; thought we might get into the Colonnade Hall, but that proved impossible…"

18th March. "After M.A. had finished the crazy work he was doing on *The Black Sea* (the libretto for the very opera about Perekop, talk of which had led to him moving to the Bolshoi the previous autumn). 21st March. "M.A. told me that he had heard that Zamyatin had died in Paris." (Y.I. Zamyatin died on 10th March).

On 24th March, Bulgakov writes to Popov: "I haven't written to you until now because we are incredibly busy all the time, bogged down in extremely difficult and unpleasant travails. Many people told me that 1936 was a bad year for me because it was a leap year – some people believe in that superstition. I assure you that is a bogus superstition. I can now see that '37 is going to be no better than its predecessor as far as I am concerned.

Among other things, on the second of April I shall be appearing in court: some wheeler-dealers from the Kharkov Theatre are trying to get some money out of me, by playing on my misfortune with *Pushkin*. I cannot hear that word now – Pushkin – without uttering a groan, and I curse myself every hour of every day for having had the ill-fated idea of writing a play about him" ["…in addition to the theatre, he began to hate the poet Pushkin…" – this line would crop up a few years later in the epilogue to his novel about the former chairman of the residents' association, Nikanor Ivanovich Bosoi…]. A day earlier, Bulgakov wrote to the chairman of the Committee for Matters of the Arts, Kerzhentsev, that he had received a summons to appear before the Moscow city court from the Kharkov Theatre that day; the theatre was demanding that he return the advance he had received for the play about Pushkin that had been banned. "In notifying them that I had in no way assumed the obligation to put on a play that was banned, as was utterly clear from the contract, and that, under the provisions of the law, I was entitled to demand money from the theatre for the play that was never put on, rather than the other way round – what I am protesting about, above all, is the discrediting remark that I 'led the theatre into a state of confusion', for never in my life have I led a theatre into a state of confusion. Generally, as far as I understand it, my position is becoming harder and harder. I'm not talking about the fact that I can't put a single one of the plays I have written in the last few years onto the Russian stage (I have fully resigned myself to this); but now I must, as though it were a reward for my dramatic works, including for the play about Pushkin, not only fend off unfounded attempts to extort money from me (the case described here is not the first), but also suffer the discrediting of my literary name. It is on this score that I am appealing to you with this complaint. M. Bulgakov."

What is noteworthy here is Bulgakov's concern for the honour of his name – a concern that has not been diminished in all the years that have elapsed.

On 2nd April, the court rejected the theatre's claim. "I am very weary, and have been doing much thought," Bulgakov wrote to V. Veresayev on 4th April, in a letter informing him that they had won their court-case. My latest attempts to write something for the theatres were sheer Quixotism on my part. And I shall not make that mistake again… I shall no longer appear on that front, that of the dramatic theatres. I have some experience, I have endured too much."

7th April. "A call from the Central Committee, Misha is summoned to appear before Angarov. He went to see him. He said they had a long, difficult conversation that came to nothing. Misha talked about what had been done to *Pushkin*, and Angarov replied in a way that made it clear that he wanted to point Misha towards the right path. He said of *Minin*, incidentally: 'Why don't you like the Russian people?' and kept saying that the Poles were very handsome in the libretto. The most important thing of all was left unsaid… he will probably have to write to the CC or take some sort of action. But Misha sees no hope in his situation. He has been crushed, they want to force him to write in a way that he is not going to." On 10th April, they found a list in *Vechernyaya Moskva* of the plays that the Art Theatre was taking to Paris. "So the rumours about *The Turbins* weren't true. Misha will never get to see Europe."

14th April. "Misha has been told that Vishnevsky gave a speech… and said 'It is wrong that we have lost a dramatist of the calibre of Bulgakov.' And Kirshon said (at the same meeting, apparently) that *The Turbins* was a good play. Both of them are monstrous characters! They were among Misha's most biting critics. They have no conscience, no opinion of their own. We had dinner at the House of the Actor. I got the unbearable sense that this was by no means a "place of leisure for masters of the arts", as it said in the invitation, but rather an awful and dubious group of people." 14th April. "Bad news: Ilf has died." Bulgakov stands in the guard of honour the next day.

... As she recalled those years, Yelena told me, on 28th October 1968: "He barely had any time to write. We would get up in the morning, have some coffee, and he would go out to rehearsals – until half past ten. In the evening we almost always had guests round – and at the same time we went out all the time, we went to all the new shows! We didn't have many friends, but the ones we did have were the ones who couldn't live without M.A. He used to joke and tell us stories, and act out little scenes – he was an endless source of fun, of *joie-de-vivre*. We would eventually disperse at 5 or 6 in the morning, and I would always beg him beforehand: 'Let's at least start saying goodbye to people at 3!'

And just occasionally, when our guests had gone home and we were left alone, he would get all gloomy and say:

'What is this, anyway? After all, all of this will disappear into thin air, will vanish, and yet it could have lived on, it could have been written.'

At times like that I would start to cry, and he would get scared and his mood would change instantly."

It was perhaps as a result of this desire to give words some sort of reinforcement, words which would otherwise melt into thin air, that the plot for *Notes of a Dead Man* came into being.

He found it particularly easy to write. "He would come home from his job at the Bolshoi Theatre," Yelena recalled, "go into his room and, while I laid the table, he would sit at his desk and write a few pages. Then he would come out and, wiping his hands, say: 'I'll read you what I've come up with after lunch!' He wrote that novel in one go, from start to finish, without any drafts..."

In February, March and April, Bulgakov read chapters of his novel about the theatre to close friends and actors from the Art Theatre; each reading was a success. And a very small number of friends knew about the other novel, the one he had completed in rough draft form the previous summer.

There were assemblies of the Union of Writers taking place; Stavsky gave a speech at the Polytechnical Museum. On 3rd April, I.N. Rozanov wrote in his diary: "This morning there were talks by Lyashko and Chumandrin. The former read out some information about how many contracts people had for 1937, and some had 4 or 5 book deals. Surely these cannot all be new books? (There is a battle going on against re-editions)."

This battle did not affect him personally; he had not had anything published for more than a decade, nor were there any new editions of his books in the pipeline.

"If we did not have the Union of Writers, could literature exist?" one of the speakers asked, before answering his own question: "It could. And if we did not have literature?" There were a few unexpected shouts of "It could!" from the audience at that point, Rozanov noted, which "provoking laughter and glee". 19th April. "The wife of the poet Mandelstam came to see M.A. He was exiled and is now into his third year in Voronezh. She is in a very difficult position, with no work." 20th: "A sensational event at the Bolshoi – Mutnykh (the director) has been arrested."

On 23rd April, Yelena writes, with unconcealed satisfaction: "Yes, retribution has come. There are very unfavourable reports in the papers about Kirshon and Afinogenov, and *The Big Day* is already being described as a bad play." 27th April. "We were walking down Gazetny Street [now Ogarev Street – M.C.], and Olesha catches up with us. He tried to talk Misha into going to the assembly of Moscow playwrights that is opening today, and at which Kirshon is going to face his reckoning. Kirshon has contrived to provoke universal hatred." Her hatred and rancour is looking for a way out. Bulgakov, however, goes to the evening not in order to exact retribution on anyone, but to listen to *Yevgeny Onegin*. 28th April. "Misha has been feeling down for the last few days, which kills me. I recognise, incidentally, that our future is utterly dark."

("A number of my well-wishers," Bulgakov wrote to Popov in his letter of 24th March, "chose a fairly strange way of consoling me. I have already heard, several times, some suspiciously unctuous voices: 'it's nothing, after your death, everything will be published!' I am most grateful to them, needless to say!"). 29th April. An acquaintance "fervently tried to talk Misha into going to the Moscow playwrights' conference and speaking against Kirshon, trying to prove that by doing so, Misha would do himself a colossal amount of good. He was wasting his breath." 30th April. "Nice sunny weather, we went for a ride on the river tram along the Moscow River. It is a most soothing trip. On our way back, we bumped into Trenyov. He told us that at the playwrights' conference, Litovsky had been hauled in to give his response…" 1st May. "Sergei Yermolinsky and Shaposhnikov came for lunch. Sergei said that Mlechin had been hauled in at the conference. He had begun his speech like this: 'It has been said here that I poisoned Bulgakov…'"

Doing precious little to improve Bulgakov's spirits, these stories reopened old wounds, forcing him to think about taking new action of some sort – in connection with the undoubtedly changed circumstances. The view of an observer, located within his own time, could not clearly distinguish or foresee the direction these changes were taking.

"During the day, M.A. went through the old newspapers on his bookshelves.

In the evening, the Troitskys invited us over. We set off at a very late hour. Besides Lida and Iv[an] Al[exandrovich], their daughter Nina was there with her husband, a journalist apparently, and Ivetta, on catching sight of whom I immediately felt irritated. I have told Lida dozens of times that I do not want to spend any time with her, since I consider her to be an obvious informer.

The journalist told us about the meetings held by the playwrights in connection with the Kirshon affair.

Lida asked M.A. to add an inscription to her book *The Turbins* (she has the Concorde edition, published in Paris), and Ivetta tried to find out, by means of impudent and stubborn probing, whether or not Misha had that edition and if so, where from, who had brought it for him. Today, Misha took the firm decision to write a letter about his fate as a writer. In my view, this is absolutely the right thing to do. We cannot go on living like this. I have said to M.A. all this time that he is merely devouring himself with what he is doing."

3rd May. "M.A. lay in bed all day, he feels poorly, he didn't sleep last night. I feel utterly broken, too. And that stupid evening yesterday! Sure enough, we went there as guests. One person bothered us with pushy questions about why M.A. wasn't going to the writers' conference, another asked why M.A. wasn't writing the kind of thing he ought to be writing, and a third kept asking him where he had got a copy of his own book from?!"

5th May. In the evening – with the Vilyams. Shebalin was there too. We had a very nice time, sitting up until three in the morning in the candlelight, and then we went home on foot through the empty city at night. When we got home, day was already dawning. I love these spring-time sunrises and empty streets so much."

6th May. M.A. is working on his letter to the government a great deal at the moment."

Yelena's diary recorded the daily vibrations of public life, the jolts taking place in which seemed to reverberate through the very air of their home.

7th May. "Today, when we were walking to the Moscow River to take the river tram, we met Trenyov, and he looked extremely upset. The word is that *The Big Day*, according to the papers, has not been cancelled. So that whole story about Kirshon, with all those speeches against him by the writers, seems slightly strange now. They cursed him furiously, yet nothing has happened!"

That day, P.A. Markov, in an article about the Art Theatre marking the occasion of the theatre being awarded the Order of Lenin, left Bulgakov's name out of a list of dramatists whose plays had been performed at the Art Theatre over the past 39 years. "In the evening, we were with the Kaluzhskys [...]," Yelena wrote in the same diary entry. "Misha asked: 'Did you read that article by Markov in today's paper?' In response, Olga hurriedly said 'No' [...] and Kaluzhsky said: 'I read it. What an anaemic piece.'"

The theatre people maintained a strong solidarity, regardless of any family ties.

9th May. "The Vilyamses and Shebalin [the composer – M.C.] were here in the evening. M.A. read the first few chapters (not in full) of his novel about Christ and the devil (he hasn't got a title yet, but that's what I've decided to call it for now). They were infinitely keen on it, and over dinner the conversation kept going back to the novel again and again..."

On 10th May, F.N. Mikhalsky reports to Yelena on what P. Markov told him about the course of the discussions about an overseas tour by the Art Theatre: "Stalin said ardently that *The Turbins* should be taken on tour, but Molotov objected."

It was as if a giant magnet were somehow constantly holding him within its force-field.

On 11th May, in the evening, they went to see the Vilyamses after Bulgakov's working day at the Bolshoi Theatre. "Petya says that he can't work, he wants to know what happens next in the novel ('about the devil'). M.A. read a few chapters. They took an extraordinary liking to it. Their feedback was that it was a work of immense power, interesting because of its philosophy, in addition to the fact that it is appealing because of its plot and stunning from a literary perspective... We sat up talking till half-three in the morning. Then we went home on foot and went to bed at 6 – still deep in conversation." 12th May. "Evening – at home. M.A. is sitting over a letter to Stalin." Two days earlier, he had dictated a letter to B. Asafiev to Yelena: "For a month now, I have been suffering from complete nervous exhaustion. A new factor has appeared on the horizon, and it is *Ivan Susanin*, about which people are starting to talk obstinately about at the theatre. If it is put forward – one must look the truth in the eyes – then *Minin* will not be accepted." Self-evidently, it would not be possible to have two operas about very similar historical subjects going on simultaneously. Bulgakov must surely have pondered, however, over the fact that circumstances had indeed taken shape in a way that was not advantageous to him – even in places where, it would seem, there were no direct grounds for them to do so. 15th May. "In the afternoon, Dmitriyev was here. He says: write an agitprop play! Misha says: tell me, who sent you here? Dmitriyev started laughing. I am very pleased to see him. In the evening, Anusya [Vilyams's wife – M.C.], Vilyams, Dmitriyev. Misha read more from his novel about Woland." That same day, Yelena met the actress N. Litovtseva, Kachalov's wife. "She too says: 'You must do something. Appeal to those up above.' With what though, what? M.A. is in a terrible mood. He is afraid to go outside on his own again." 16th May. "In the evening, Dmitriyev came round, before taking the 'Red Arrow' [the fast night-train from Moscow to Leningrad – M.C.]. He kept harping on over dinner about how we should appeal to those above us, but that before doing so we should iron out the start of the history textbook." Bulgakov had not apparently spent much time on the textbook since the spring of 1936, when he had worked on it actively.

The backdrop for his state of being in those months was formed of incessant conversations which were summed up by a diary entry on 17th May. "Everyone who reads the papers is of the opinion that now, in connection with all kinds of events in the literary environment, M.A.'s position simply has to change for the better." That evening, he "worked on the novel (about Woland)," and Yelena Sergeyevna goes to the Art Theatre, to see Mikhalsky, and for one-and-a-half hours, as they stroll around the courtyard outside the theatre, they talk about "Misha's impossible position". On 19th May, Y. Leontiev, after a conversation with Kerzhentsev, tells Yelena that *The Turbins* could now be given the green light in all other cities too (prior to then, and since 1926, the play had only had permission to be shown by the Art Theatre), and that all Bulgakov needed to do was go to Kerzhentsev "and talk to him about all his literary affairs – the banned plays and so on, and ask him why *The Turbins* could only be shown by the Art Theatre. When I told Misha all this over lunch, he refused outright to do any of it – as I expected; he rejected the idea of going to have a talk about it, and he rejected the idea of asking about *The Turbins*. He said that none of that would help him resolve the unbearably burdensome position in which he found himself." On the 20th, he got another call from the dramatists' division inviting him to tomorrow's conference ("It's about Kirshon, Yasensky and so on, again"), and again he refuses to settle the score with his literary enemies in the circumstances that have arisen in these months, citing his poor health. In the evening, he gets a call from Adrian Piotrovsky, who has arrived from Leningrad: "He wanted to commission a script from M.A. M.A. said no. But I was curious to know what subject they had come up with. As it turned out, it was an anti-religious one!! That's clever!" 20th May. "Stories in the papers today about Afinogenov being expelled from the party". O.S. Bokshanskaya tells them that over at the Art Theatre, people are saying "what a harmful organisation the RAPP is, what sort of characters are operating there. And look what they've done, for instance: they've poisoned… Bulgakov, so that instead of being at the Art Theatre now and writing plays, he's at the Bolshoi Theatre writing librettos for the opera. That Bulgakov and Smidovich [V.V. Veresayev – M.C.] had written a good play about Pushkin, but that company had sunk the play and taken the liberty of making pejorative references to Bulgakov and Smidovich in the press. So I think we will now see a sharp turn in favour of Maka. So my advice to you is to write a play about Frunz as quickly as you can!" "This playful joke," Yelena explained, "meant that Misha should turn his libretto for *The Black Sea* into a play.

All of this literally permeates the air around him, smothering him and causing him anxiety and irritation.

22nd May 1937. "Dmitriyev came for lunch. How I love the conversations M.A. has with him. He's not like that with anyone else. He is clever, interesting, witty, he knows what's what; he's generally a magnificent sparring partner for M.A."

On the evening of 28th May, they go out for a walk and pop into the pharmacy; and there, they meet a journalist they know, who strives to convince them "that Misha's position at the moment is very good, because he did not sell himself and did not take part in all that hullaballoo", meaning "the latest stuff involving Kirshon, which has shaken up all those in and around the literary world." 31st May. "A report in *Pravda* saying that Kuprin is coming back to the motherland." 1st June. "A report in the newspapers about the suicide of Hamarnik. Kuprin came over yesterday. There's a photo of him in *Izvestiya*…"

2nd June 1937. "Dmitriyev called in and stayed for lunch […]. We talked about Yelizaveta Isayevna – she is leaving for Borzhom." Reading between the lines, Dmitriyev no doubt told them about the ongoing harassment of his wife and her attempts to save herself by leaving town.

4th June. "Dmitriyev and Akhmatova were here in the evening. She read 3 or 4 of her lyric poems." 5th June. "A report in *Soviet Art* states that Litovsky has been fired as chairman of Glavrepertkom" – and then some powerful epithets that Yelena bestows on this man, whom she saw as one of Bulgakov's most indefatigable literary enemies. 6th June. "I went to get the newspapers in the morning, glanced at *Pravda*, and rushed off to wake up Misha. A stunning bit of news: Arkadiev has been fired from the Art Theatre; according to the story in the paper, it's for repeatedly providing false information about a tour", etc. "Dmitriyev came over in the evening. We congratulated him on his new apartment. Arkadiev had spoken to him just yesterday, in the evening, and invited him to work at the Art Theatre full-time and promising him an apartment in Moscow; Dmitriyev roared with laughter, then told of how Knipper [his aunt O.L. Knipper-Chekhova, with whom he stayed whenever he travelled from Leningrad to Moscow – M.C.] had woken him up and shoved the newspaper article about Arkadiev into his hands. Misha kept acting out the scene, with old Knipper in a white negligee, wringing her hands…"

8th June 1937. "Some monstrous story involving Professor Pletnev. There is an anonymous article in *Pravda* entitled *Professor-Offender-Sadist* (*Professor-Nasil'nik-Sadist*). In 1934, he had allegedly taken a female patient and bitten her on the bust, and she had come down with some sort of incurable disease. The patient is now harassing him. On a steamship – with Misha and Zhenyushka, in Kuntsevo.

Zhenka and Misha went bathing, the water is cold and dirty."

… The flow of this water, which for many years had washed over the woods and valleys, getting tinged with the colour of blood to a greater and greater extent, was now rushing through the city streets, and could be seen from his window.

10th June. "Dobranitsky was here; he brought M.A. some books about the civil war. He asked M.A. lots of questions about his convictions and is clearly trying to provoke him. It is a mystery to us, who is he?"

11th June. "A report in *Pravda* in the morning: the prosecutor of the Union on the committal for trial of Tukhachevsky, Uborevich, Kork, Aidelman, Putna and Yakir in a case about the betrayal of the motherland.

M.A. is at the Bolshoi for a rehearsal of *Virgin Soil Upturned* (*Podnyataya Tselina*) […] There was a meeting after the rehearsal. The resolution called for the maximum penalty for the traitors."

Did he vote on this matter? Or did he somehow manage to get out of the hall before the vote?

In order to recreate, to some extent at least, the atmosphere which must have prevailed in those days at Bulgakov's home, we have no choice but to examine some rather delicate material.

Before doing so, however, let us look again at the words of F.A. Stepun, mentioned earlier, about the "revamped Russian officerhood", about the desire for a victory over Denikin's officers – and the aversion that there was to this victory. In Bulgakov's attitude towards the top brass of the Red Army, with whom life had made him cross paths predominantly after he met Yelena Sergeyevna Shilovskaya, around whose table Tukhachevsky, Voroshilov and many others had dined in those years, this duality of opinion was certainly present, though it ebbed away as the years went on.

His attitude towards Tukhachevsky and to what now awaited him may have been made more complicated by a strictly personal matter. Accounts have survived which imply that several years before Yelena met Bulgakov, she may have had an affair with Tukhachevsky.

I shall venture onto even shakier ground now (on which my sole support is the decisiveness of Bulgakov himself, in putting the subject of incest into his works on Molière), and share with the reader a theory that is not mine, but which does not seem to be without foundation, according to which Tukhachevsky was the father of Yelena's youngest son. My female readers may share my own personal view on this matter, which is that if this was indeed the case, Yelena probably would have admitted it to Bulgakov at the point when she joined her fate to his and brought her son into his house (as a woman, she may have felt that it would be easier for him if he knew that the boy was not the son of Shilovsky). If one admits that this theory does seem to have some currency (and many people noticed the similarity between S.Y. Shilovsky and Tukhachevsky), our reading of the following entry in her diary may be slightly different: "A report in *Pravda* about how Tukhachevsky and all the others are to be put before the firing squad.

In the morning, Misha suggested driving over to see Seryozha at the dacha. We took a cab, drove to Yeliseyev's for some groceries and set off. The dacha is like everything in the suburbs of Moscow. It is dingy, both in terms of the surrounding nature and in terms of the amenities.

I was so happy to see Seryozhka, though! […] We didn't spend much time there; we had some coffee and came home for lunch."

4

… In his own home, the guests still gathered just as before, music was played, and there was always much merry-making. Such was his life in those months, filled with unexpected news stories on an almost daily basis – with transitions from amazement and horror or deep gloominess to fun and laughter, practical jokes, funny scenes being acted out. The fact was that the fast-flowing events taking place – that aspect of these years – did not affect him: all the major events of his own life had somehow already happened. On 22nd June, F. Mikhalsky came to see him, a couple of days before setting off for Paris with the Art Theatre. "Well, the conversation soon turned to Misha's affairs, of course. The same *leitmotif* cropped up yet again: he ought to write, not sink into despair. Misha said that he felt like a drowning man: he is lying on the shore and the waves are rolling over him. Fedya protested fiercely."

Vague rumours reach Bulgakov's ears to the effect that "in the autumn, they will start work on *Pushkin* at the Art Theatre. I am not refusing altogether to believe this story," Yelena writes, "because I can feel it in the air – I can feel that there has been some shift with regard to *Pushkin*."

Let us not forget that this was the year in which the centenary of the death of Pushkin was celebrated with great pomp and ceremony. It may well be that the fact that a play had been written by a famous playwright, but was not being staged, became a source of irritation, an annoyance.

The Vakhtangov Theatre proposed, meanwhile, that Bulgakov write the script for a stage adaptation of *Don Quixote*. Bulgakov occasionally worked on his novel "about the devil" that spring and summer, starting to write it out again from the beginning in May.

The entire month of June was exceptionally hot. They drove to the Moscow River several times, to go bathing and canoeing. They often spent their evenings at the Club for masters of the arts restaurant. It emerged that there were plans to stage the opera *Ivan Susanin* at the Bolshoi Theatre, to mark the 20th anniversary of the October Revolution. For Bulagakov, this was "the final nail in the coffin for *Minin*," as Yelena wrote in her diary. Yet another work that had involved a huge amount of organisational effort (the endless correspondence with Asafiev, the trip to Leningrad, the exhausting conversations and so on), had come to nothing. And yet he now had to start work on the next libretto – for the opera *Peter the Great*.

12th July 1937. "The day of the physical culture parade." As they drove around town going about their business, the Bulgakovs stopped at Arbat Square. "We looked at the proponents of physical culture as they marched past. From a distance, it was a very beautiful sight: the tanned bodies, the brightly-coloured shorts. When we moved closer, we saw that there were hardly any beautiful faces among them.

We spent the evening with the Vilyamses. M.A. read out half of his story *The Heart of a Dog*. It is a witty, lively satire. M.A. says it is rough around the edges."

"… We are staying outside Zhitomir, in a village," Yelena wrote to her mother on 19th July. (They were at a guesthouse owned by relatives of the the Art Theatre actor V.A. Stepun). "I'm frightfully glad that I managed to persuade Misha to get away from Moscow. He was tired, and so was I, we were both overstrained, but here we are completely at our leisure, with no newspapers in sight, no chores to do, no telephones ringing." Bulgakov worked on the libretto about Peter the Great, and also on *Notes of a Dead Man*. They returned to Moscow on 14th August. While they were away, a sad fate had befallen S. Klychkov, who lived in the same building as them, as well as Zarudin, B. Yasensky and Ivan Katayev. "Seryozha Yermolinsky called us at 5 o'clock – he had heard that we were back in town and was very glad. That was nice. Everything else is very gloomy." Over the next few days, Bulgakov heard similar news about A. Bukhov, A. Piotrovsky and many others – though the news was not always true. 20th August. "Cold, non-stop autumnal rain. After a telephone call – Dobronitsky arrived. It turns out that Angarov has been arrested. In Misha's opinion, he played a very difficult role both in the case of *Ivan Vasilievich* and generally in Misha's latest literary affairs, particularly in *Minin*. Dobranitsky is stubborn in his prediction that there will be changes for the better in M.A.'s literary destiny, and M.A. is equally stubborn in his refusal to believe this. Dobranitsky asked the following question: 'do you regret the fact that in your conversation in 1930, you didn't say that you wanted to leave the country?' M.A. replied: 'It's for me to ask you whether you pity me or not. If you put it to me that writers lose their voice when they are in a different country, then is it not all the same to me where I am dumb – in my homeland or in a different country." On 29th August, Bulgakov attended a meeting with Samosud and the authors of the opera

Virgin Soil Upturned at the Moscow hotel. "The poet Churkin was there too; he came up to M.A. and asked:

'Tell me… there was a writer once named Bulgakov…'

'Oh? And what did he write, who are you talking about?'

'I read a book by him, the press poured scorn on him…'

M.A. grew cautious, and asked: 'Did he write plays, as well, by any chance?'

'Yes, there was a play called *The Days of the Turbins*.' M.A. said:

'That would be me.'

Churkin stared at him with bulging eyes and said: 'You weren't even one of the *poputchiks*, does that mean you were even worse?!'

M.A. replied: 'Well now, what could possibly be worse than the *poputchiks*?'

Thus it turned out that he was already something akin to those 'monstrous excavated dinosaurs', as his long-time billiards partner had described himself in his last long poem.

On 30th August, they get a call from VOKS and Yelena writes down what the caller tells her: "Arosev is gravely ill and will not be coming back again" – it is clear that the former chairman of VOKS, Arosev, has been arrested. […] In the evening, M.A. played chess here with Topleninov."

2nd September. "A marvellous sunny day. […] We called on Melik in the evening […] There is a report in the newspaper about the suicide of the chairman of the Council of People's Commissars, Lyubchenko."

5th September. "Misha has been told that Abram Ephros has been arrested. We don't know whether it's true, there are many lies being told.

In the evening, Misha played chess at Sergei Topleninov's place.

6th September. "M.A. is working on Peter."

On 13th September, he finished dictating the libretto of *Peter the Great*, and by the 19th the author had already received 10 comments on the typed-up version from P.M. Kerzhentsev, which concluded with the words: "So then, this is the very first approach to the subject. A great deal of work is still required." He had once again fallen into the clutches of re-writes and delays. With increasing frequency, he compared himself in conversation to a factory that is forced to produce lighters. 23rd September. "Agonizing attempts to find a way out: a letter to those at the top? Abandoning the theatre? Finalizing the corrections for the novel and submitting it? There is nothing that can be done, it is a hopeless situation! Spent the day with Sergei on the river tram, the weather was wonderful. It soothes the nerves." 24th September. "Took the river tram with M.A. during the day. It is already foggy, though, there was a drizzling rain."

Bulgakov was suddenly called upon to work on a copy of *Flight* for a few days (28th September – 1st October) – the Committee of Arts had expressed an interest in the play. 3rd October. "M.A. and I are talking about *Flight* all the time now. What is this? Has something changed from a political perspective? Why is the play suddenly needed?" The previous day, on 2nd October, Bulgakov had dictated a letter to B. Asafiev to his wife: "I shall start at the end: my play *Peter* is no more, i.e. the libretto is lying in front of me, re-written, but it is going nowhere" – and then he writes about Kerzhentsev's comments: "On that score, I can tell you that they are, above all, extremely hard to implement and, at any rate, they signify that all the work has to be done again right from the start, delving into the historical material once again… I have now reached a critical juncture. Do I redo it or not, do I have a go at something or give it all up? I expect that necessity will require me to redo it, but as to whether I will achieve success, I can't vouch for that at all. […] I am sitting here now and seeking a way out, and it would appear that there is no way out open to me at all. It is not just about *Peter* that I need to come to a decision. In the last seven years, I have written sixteen works of various genres, and they have all perished. Such a position is impossible, and the prevailing mood at home is one of hopelessness and gloom."

… The events around him at home had increasingly lost any kind of meaning that he could make sense of. The internal purpose that they had, which can hypothetically be guessed at when they are looked at retrospectively (why was it, for example, that when the preparations for the Pushkin publications were in full swing, in the autumn of 1936, was one of the most active experts on Pushkin had been snatched away? – evidently, the 'plot' now included an ever greater complicating of the lives of those who remained free, who worked until they reached breaking point, in consternation and fear, in a condition that gradually began to border on madness), could not be revealed to the 'observers' of that time, thinking in accordance with their usual logic, seeking normal cause-and-effect connections.

The editors and authors who worked for the newspaper *Nakanune*, and who had returned to Russia in 1923 hoping for better things, had disappeared, one by one.

Back in 1935, Alexander Bobrishchev-Pushkin – the eldest of the *smenovekhovtsy* – was arrested; he was shot (as was later established, during the rehabilitation process) in 1937 "at the site where he was imprisoned"; in 1937, Vasilevsky Ne-Bukva was arrested (he died in prison the following year), as were Y.V. Klyuchnikov (he also died the following year) and N.V. Ustryalov, who had returned to Russia in 1935 and spent some time working as a professor at Moscow University. In the same year, it seems, Y.N. Potekhin was arrested, and he too died in circumstances that could not be established. Yelena wrote in her diary on 4th September 1937: "Misha is at Sergei Popov's place [the brother of P.S. Popov – M.C.], playing vint. It is quiet at home, I am reading Y. Potekhin's book *Men of Dusk* (*Lyudi Zakata*); in form, it is a rotten book, in content – an adventure story." There mere fact that she mentions this book, going by the laws of her narrative style in the diary in those years, probably suggests that Potekhin was still a free man on that day.

5th October: "Samosud is proposing that he write about the year 1812, based on Tolstoy… I am horrified by all this. It is awful that M.A. is going to be writing another libretto…! He ought to send a letter to the top. But that is a scary step." This letter makes it clear that Bulgakov never sent the letter he wrote in the spring; predicting what the upshot of such a move would now be far more difficult than it had been in 1930; he realised, particularly after the events of the summer, that it would now be dangerous to refer to himself directly. 23rd October. "The decision to leave the Bolshoi Theatre is now almost fully-formed in Misha's mind. This is awful – having to work on the libretto. He should iron out the novel and submit it." The word 'submit' makes one think that in the author's eyes, the novel would essentially be some sort of substitute for a letter.

Over the next few days, the decision became a firmer one and was put down on paper. All the vague hopes he had fostered had fallen away one by one (the interest in *Flight* had faded away again; by mid-November, the bullishly optimistic Dobranitsky had himself vanished from the horion (a very brief entry in Yelena's diary on 11th November recorded this event: "I went to see the Troitskys in the afternoon. It turns out that Dobranitsky has been arrested."); the destiny of the librettos that he had already written had become bogged down in endless additional requirements). 5th November. "Pilnyak has been arrested. In the evening, we had Melik, Minna [his wife – M.C.] and the Yermolinskys here." 12th November. "In the evening, M.A. worked on his novel, *The Master and Margarita*" – this was the first time that the new name, the one that was settled upon, appeared in Yelena's diary and on the title page of the exercise book containing the start of the new draft of the novel. Thus, in the autumn of 1937, in one of the periods his search for a way out of the position he was in, both in a literary sense and a biographical sense, was at its most intense, Bulgakov makes a choice that is significant for his creative life. He decides that he should complete his work on the novel, deeming this to be his most important and decisive literary step of all. "This year is coming to an end," Bulgakov's wife wrote on 31st December 1937. "It has left a bitter taste in my mouth."

In the middle of January 1938, lovers of the arts in Moscow were interested in two key events: the closure of Meyerhold's Theatre and the first performance of Shostakovich's 5th symphony. On the 20th, Yelena wrote that Bulgakov, who had had an extremely hostile attitude to this 'lefty' director ever since the '20s, had assured her "that the loss of Meyerhold's Theatre didn't bother him at all (though the loss of Stanislavsky would shock him, and perhaps kill him, because he was definitely the creator of his theatre), but that what bothered him was the thought that he might have his party membership ticket taken away from him and that they might do something to him."

The 5th symphony was due to be performed in the Great hall of the Conservatoire on the 29th. "We intend to go. M.A. said that he couldn't care less about the symphony, but that he's interested in seeing the hall" (25th January).

30th January. "God, what was that at the Conservatoire yesterday…! I came away feeling awestruck! What a brilliant piece it is! The audience were on their feet applauding, they called for the composer; he came out looking pale and anxious…" Yelena's diary entry only goes some way towards conveying the electrifying atmosphere in the auditorium, when, two years on from the events of the early spring of 1936, the brilliant composer appeared before an audience once again.

Eyewitness accounts describe how Nemirovich-Danchenko, walking into the orchestra pit, hammered on the rail with the conductor's baton whilst calling for the composer, and how the audience roared and was reluctant to leave at the end of the concert. Bulgakov left the Conservatoire in very high spirits, together with Vilyams, Sergei Yermolinsky and Boris Erdman. "We didn't want to just go straight home after the concert," Yelena writes. They set off for the Metropol and sat in the far room for a long time, feeling happy, excited and full of hope. On 31st January, riding the wave of these hopes, perhaps, Bulgakov set about writing a letter to Stalin requesting leniency in the case of Nikolai Erdman (he finished writing it on the 4th and posted it on the 5th). The same wave of optimism, I would suggest, also prompted him to return to the novel.

On the morning of 6th February, there was a phone call from V.V. Dmitriyev. "… I asked him to come over at once," Yelena wrote. "He came, looking like a broken man. It turns out that his wife, Yelizaveta Isayevna, has been arrested. He wants to see if something can be done for her."

The poor woman's attempts to get away from the NKVD's networks had not succeeded. She had been torn away from her two little twin daughters.

The malevolent shadow of evil had now almost reached the windows of their home.

9th February. "In fits and starts, between *Minin* and Soloviev, who refuses to budge, Misha is moving his novel about Woland forward.

In the evening he went to see the Yermolinskys."

At this point in the diary, Yelena writes: "Dmitriyev came to call this afternoon. He has an idea on how to do something for his wife. The poor man!" A day later, the diary reveals how frightened she is by these frequent visits – whether on purpose, for any third parties who might happen to read it, or so as openly to convey her own frustration (and probably for both of these things together), she writes, on 11th February: "Dm[itriyev] came here before taking the train to Leningrad. He has irritated me lately, I don't like it when conversations turn into idle chatter about such squabbles." These were the sorts of words she used when referring to the subject of the tragic fate that befell Dmitriyev's wife, and that drove him out of his mind at the time and in the days that followed.

1st March. "Misha went to Angarsky's today [in his final years, he met this benevolent editor from his first years in Moscow several times. – M.C.], and they agreed that he would read the start of the novel. Misha now seems to have settled on the name *The Master and Margarita*. The idea of it being printed is hopeless, of course. Misha is ironing it out and racing ahead, he wants to finish the job in March."

On 5th March, Dmitriyev arrived from Leningrad once again. "He is still overwhelmed by his wife's arrest," Yelena writes, "and thinking about what he should do to find out about her fate or to help."

5th March. "Misha has been working on the novel all of these past days – he spends all his free time on it."

8th March. "The novel." 9th March. "The novel. Misha read the scene in which the bartender is at Woland's house to me." The trial of Yagoda was taking place. 10th March. "I pick up the newspaper every morning; what a monstrous character Yagoda is! [...] At 6 pm, I looked through the window, and in the sky I caught sight of a huge, light-yellow loop (left by an aeroplane)."

CHAPTER SEVEN

"The Final, Twilight Novel".

The Final Play. (1938-1940).

1

From the late autumn of 1937 to the spring of 1938, there was no longer any let up in Bulgakov's work on the novel – on the contrary, for the sake of this work, *Notes of a Dead Man* was apparently brought to a halt right at the start of the second part (the book was never completed). Busy every day with his day-to-day duties at the Bolshoy Theatre (not only writing reviews and editing other people's librettos, but also tense participation in rehearsals), and constantly troubled by the lack of success of his own librettos, Bulgakov systematically pushes the sixth draft of the novel further and further, chapter by chapter. The composition of the work had been decided upon: in the novel he was finishing off in the winter and spring of 1938, he himself was reflected – the novel about Pilate and Yeshua was communicated to the reader not all at once, not in the form of a unified, inserted novella; instead, it seemed to finish itself off before his very eyes. The Master's novel was assuming the characteristics of some sort of pre-text, which had existed right from the outset and had only been pulled out of the darkness of oblivion into the light field of the contemporary consciousness through the artist's brilliance. As a result of the composition itself, the reader was compelled to believe that the creator of the Master, too, the author of the "other" novel, which replaced this one, had grasped the life that was contemporaneous with him, and its prospects, with exactly the same strength of foresight and truthfulness in every detail. Creativity itself came across as the process of achieving, without fail, a true image of reality.

On the evening of 30th March, the author reads the *On Bald Mountain* to Yermolinsky. The latter "says that the chapters from the ancient world are at an extraordinary high level," Yelena Sergeyevna writes in her diary, adding: "I too am endlessly fond of them." We now see just one word frequently appearing after the date in the diary: "Novel". Work on it takes place almost daily. On the evening of 7th April, various guests come over to listen to the chapters of the novel relating to Ivanushka and his illness: the doctor Samuil Tseitlin (apparently, a psychiatrist – the reading was specifically intended for him), A.A. Arendt, Y.L. Leontiev and his wife, Yermolinsky, N. Erdman, Vilyams and his wife. "The reading made an enormous impression on them… The chapters set in the ancient world particularly captured the interest of the audience and captivated them; I am madly in love with those chapters. Everyone was struck by the remarkable extent of M.A.'s knowledge of that epoch. But how well he managed to convey it! Kolya Erdman stayed at our place. He and Misha have had some remarkable conversations about literature. I could have killed myself, so annoyed was I at not knowing the art of stenography – I'd have written down every word."

22nd April. "Nikolai Radlov came to see us today… Radlov said to Misha: 'You are the finished article as a writer… former writer… everything is in the past…' That was the running theme. Then came a suggestion: 'why don't you write some little stories for *Krokodil* (*Crocodile*), they've a new editorial team now, do you want me to speak to Koltsov?' Misha – 'I beseech you never to mention my name in front of Koltsov.'"

Thus, his life, which had forked out in two directions long ago, very definitely began flowing along two parallel channels from that year onwards, and one of them was only visible to a handful of people.

On 2nd May, N.S. Angarsky came over (he was a prominent figure in publishing once again) and asked straight away: 'do you agree to write a Soviet adventure novel? A huge print-run, I'll have it translated into all languages, heaps of money, in foreign currency, if you want I'll give you a cheque now – as an advance?' Misha said no, he said – I can't do that. After trying to persuade him, Angarsky asked M.A. to read his novel (*The Master and Margarita*), and M.A. read the first 3 chapters. Angarsky immediately said: 'that can't possibly be published' – 'Why?' – 'It can't.'"

The final handwritten draft of the novel was finished on 22nd-23rd May. After the draft from 1932-1936, it was rewritten from start to finish and amounted to 30 chapters, contained in six thick exercise books, ready to be typed up.

The novel now ended with the Master and Margarita flying off to their final haven on horseback: "The Master pressed his beloved to him with one hand and spurred the horse on towards the moon, wither the fifth procurator of Judea, Pontius Pilate, had just flown, after being forgiven during the night on Sunday."

On 26th May, after accompanying Yelena Sergeyevna and Seryozha to Lebedyan, where they were to spend the summer, in the morning, Bulgakov began preparing the text of the novel for typing up. Fortunately, the letters he sent to his wife on an almost daily basis survive, and we are now able to imagine how his work progressed. On 27th May he writes to her: "At night – Pilate. Ah, what difficult, confused material!" 30th May. "The novel is already being typed up. Olga is working well. I am waiting for her now. I am nearing the end of the 2nd chapter." He was not dictating a finished text: a comparison of the manuscript and the typed version shows how many things were changed in the text during the process of typing it up. We can get a sense of how this work was done by turning to *A Theatrical Novel (Notes of a Dead Man)*, in which Olga Bokshanskaya is immortalized as the character Toropetskaya: "Toropetskaya had mastered the art of typing on a type-writer to perfection. I had never seen anything like it. One never needed to dictate the punctuation marks to her, or to repeat the indications about which character was talking." The author, "whilst dictating, would pause, ponder something over, then say: 'No, wait a moment…' – I would change what had been written… I muttered at times and then spoke loudly, yet no matter what I did, from out of Toropetskaya's hand, a perfectly smooth page of the play would flow out, almost entirely without corrections – you could have handed it to the printers there and then.'"

On 31st May: "I am writing the 6th chapter. Olga is working quickly… I am tired beyond belief."

1st June: he writes that he is cancelling the 4-day trip to Yalta that was mooted: "It is exhausting, and yet I don't want to stop work on the novel for a single day. I am starting the 8th chapter today." On the night of the 2nd: "I wanted, immediately after the dictation came to an end, to start writing my long letter, but I had no strength left in me. Even Olga, with her unheard-of endurance as a typist, flew off the handle today… 132 pages have now been typed up on the typewriter. Roughly speaking, around 1/3 of the novel (taking the reductions of long bits into account)." 2nd June: "We are writing for many hours in a row, and in my head is the soft moan of fatigue, but this fatigue is of the right kind, it is not one that torments me." He is afraid lest Nemirovich-Danchenko should take his secretary away from him – even for a day. "The rewrite must be brought to an end, at any cost"; "The novel must be finished! Now! Now!"

"'What is going to happen?' you ask? I don't know. You will probably put it away in the bureau or in a cupboard containing those plays of mine that were killed, and you will sometimes think of them. We do not know our future, incidentally.

I have already passed judgement on this thing, and, if I can manage to improve the ending a little, I will feel that the work is worthy of being proof-read and of being put away in a dark drawer.

What interests me now is your judgement; as for whether I shall ever know what readers think of it, nobody can say."

An answer to the question about who the novel was intended to be for – both specifically and non-specifically – (i.e. an ordinary reader of a literary work) – a matter that assuredly changed during the process of working on the text – is perhaps given by the author more clearly in this letter than anywhere else.

15th June: "At dawn: tomorrow, I mean – tut, tut – today, I am renewing my work. I am going to finish the chapter *By Candlelight* and I shall move on to the ball. Yes, I am very tired, and to tell the truth I don't feel very well." 15th: "Early evening": "I feel tired beyond measure. I am dictating the 23rd chapter." 19th: "The 26th chapter is being written (Niza, the murder in the garden)." On the night of the 21st: "I feel under the weather, but I'm working. I am dictating chapter 28." 22nd June, in the morning: "If Olga comes a little earlier today, I shall try to dictate a large chunk, and then the end of the typing will become very close indeed. The one bad thing in all this is that I keep feeling unwell. But that doesn't matter!"

On 24th June 1938, the typing up of the novel was finished, and its ending was now very close to the one that we know today from the final version of the text.

The next day, on 25th June, Bulgakov travelled to Lebedyan and set to work on a new task – the adaptation of *Don Quixote* for the stage, which he had commenced on 8th December 1937, stopping on page 15 of the manuscript – evidently for the sake of *The Master and Margarita*.

2

On 21st July 1938, Yelena Sergeyevna wrote to her mother: "Misha has spent almost a month here now… He has written a play in that time, a stage adaptation of *Don Quixote* [the first draft was completed by 18th July – M.C.], and it has turned out very well. He is now travelling to Moscow, because he has to work with a composer on a libretto for the Bolshoi Theatre. On top of that, he wants to iron out his novel once and for all, the one he finished this summer; it is a very original work, a philosophical one, that he has been working on for almost ten years." On 24th July, Bulgakov writes to his wife, from Moscow: "Once I had settled a most tiresome matter involving the papers for the apartment, I felt splendid and the work on *Quixote* is coming easily. The conditions here make me feel very comfortable. There is no din coming from upstairs for the time being, the telephone has stayed silent, my dictionaries are ranged in front of me. I have been drinking tea with a marvellous jam, and polishing off Sancho, so that he gleams. After that I shall give Don Quixote the once over, and then all the others, so that the characters can play with one another like those dragonflies beside the river, remember?"

23rd August. "We met up with Katayev at Lavrushinsk – Valentin. Drank carbonated water. Then we were walking along, and Katayev slowly turned the conversation towards Misha's position. The sense of what he was saying was clear: Misha had to write, in Katayev's opinion, a short story, to present it, and generally make his return to the writing world with something new – "The dispute has dragged on too long" and so on and so forth. We've heard it all before, we know it all, we understand it all too well! It's all very boring!"

On 4th September, the people from the Vakhtangov Theatre listen to Bulgakov reading *Don Quixote* at his house. "It was clear that they liked it…! And, of course, the conversation was about it being wonderful, but that such-and-such a scene needed to be replaced with something different… On their faces, one could see the question: how will it get past the censors, how will it need to be served up, what will the directors think of it, and so on."

By now, in his fourteenth year of working in the theatre, all this must have been all too familiar, and perhaps almost unbearable as a result.

Bulgakov "categorically refused" to read the play to the entire theatre group or to the Arts Council… "he said that he didn't want to open himself up to harrassment. He would rather they took a copy to have a look at and gave him their answer." At V.V. Kuza's request, he agreed to read it to some of the leading actors only (an entry on 8th September tells us).

On 9th September, in the evening: P.A. Markov and V.Y. Vilenkin came round. "They came after 10 pm and stayed until five in the morning… They came to ask Misha to write a play for the Art Theatre. 'I shall never do that, it is not in my interests to do that, it is dangerous for me. I know in advance what will happen… Misha told them everything he thinks about the Art Theatre, in respect of him… He added that now, all that was in the past, and that he had forgiven and forgotten. But that he would not write anything.'

All this went on for at least two hours. And when we went through to have dinner at around one in the morning, Markov's expression was black and gloomy. Over dinner, the conversation somehow turned to more general matters concerning the Art Theatre, and at that point their mood improved. They complained amicably about Yegorov. And then they talked about a play again. 'The theatre is dying… We have no play, the theatre is showing only an old repertoire. It is dying a death, and the only thing that can save it and resurrect it is a remarkable, modern play.' Markov described this as *Flight* on a contemporary topic, i.e. in the sense of something with the same import as that work, which had been the best-loved play at the theatre. And only Bulgakov, of course, could deliver such a play. He spoke for a long time, and it seemed as though his anxiety was genuine. 'You wanted to write a play on the subject of Stalin, didn't you?' Misha replied that things were very difficult as regards the material: it was necessary, but where could one get it? They suggested that they could get the material too, via the theatre, and that Nemirovich would write a letter to J.V. asking about the material. Misha said: 'It is very hard, although there is much about this play that I can already glimpse. As long as there is no play, one ought not to talk about it or ask for anything.' They left at 5 am, with difficulty – and as Valenkin said to Olga the next day – 'It was pretty interesting.'"

On 10th September, a note was made in the manuscript for the play about Stalin, which was initially given the name *The Shepherd*, saying that work began on it; no more work was done on it that year, though.

On 12th September, Bulgakov tells his wife that "the actors arrested a few months ago have been returned to the Bolshoy Theatre; apparently they were taken there in a Lincoln. They are now going to receive a salary for 8 months and trips to a relaxation and leisure home.

And at the Art Theatre, they say, Stepun has been arrested." (This was the brother of Fyodor Stepun, who had been exiled in the autumn of 1922, V.A. Stepun, a good friend of Bulgakov's).

On 14th September, Yelena Sergeyevna wrote: "After a very long interval [these words were included in the diary for a reason: if necessary, they could be used as documentary evidence – M.C.], Lida R[onzhina] called and said that Ivan Al[exandrovich] and Nina R[onzhina] had been arrested and that she still had Nina's little Andryusha to look after. She asked me to pop round." This was about Troitsky and the wife of Dobranitsky, who had been arrested just over a year earlier.

In September, Bulgakov was busy all the time working on the ballet *Svetlana* – he got home late each night, either from the ballet school or the theatre. "My tiredness, the hopelessness of my own position!" (17th September 1938).

On 19th September, in the evening, he "sat down to do the author's corrections for the version of *The Master and Margarita* that was finished in June.

23rd September – he starts work on a new libretto, based on Maupassant's novella *Mademoiselle Fifi*.

27th September. "… We stayed up talking till late. Markov and Vilenkin came round and tried to demonstrate that everything was different now – bad plays weren't satisfying anyone, everyone wanted to see something real. Now was the time for Misha to write something. Misha replied that since Litovsky had resurfaced again and been given a job and a rank again – everything would be as before. Litovsky was a symbol. After dinner, Misha read them the first three chapters of *The Master and Margarita*. They listened to him in a remarkable way, particularly Markov… Markov spoke very well afterwards about these chapters, he had understood everything correctly. He said: 'I could see it all so clearly.' It was agreed that they would come back on the 1st to hear more. 28th September. "This morning, Misha read the libretto of *The Battle on the Ice*, so that he could provide feedback on it… The plot is messy, absurd, ponderous. Oh, the things Misha has to read and bust his brains over!" He gets home late at night almost every day, broken by his duties at work, which bear no relation to his own creative work. His strength already seems to have been gnawed away at, to a considerable degree. On 4th October, Yelena writes in the diary about the "deadly" mood that both she and he have been in since the early morning; "One cannot go through all this of course, naturally, without being able to see the fruits of one's labours."

That autumn, everyone was following the military events that were occurring in Europe, reading about them in the newspapers, and thinking about the future. 9th October. In the evening, A. M. Faiko and Volkenshtein were here, we played vint until three in the morning, then "the conversations began. We started off with L.A. [the wife of the dramatist Faiko – M.C.] asking: 'Why did you put up all these articles on the walls – 'We'll deal a blow to Bulgakov-ness', 'Down with *The Days of the Turbins*', and so on?' We talked about Misha's literary life until half past five… Misha was in a gloomy mood.' On 14th October, though, they spent the evening with Leontiev, Melik-Pashayev and Dunayevsky, and Yelena Sergeyevna wrote: 'We had fun over dinner. Misha did an impersonation of Melik directing, which had everyone dying with laughter, and Dunayevsky played his waltzes and sang his little songs.' 19th October. A conversation at home with F. Mikhalsky "about how Misha ought to write a play for the Art Theatre. It all makes perfect sense. the Art Theatre needs a play about Lenin and Stalin at any cost, and since the plays by other playwrights are incredibly weak, they are hoping that Misha will bale them out. The awkward conversation about *Flight* was sad for us, too; among other things, Misha said that his horizons had been closed off, that he would never see the rest of the world outside his own country and that this was a very bad thing. F., looking lost, replied: 'No, no, you will go travelling, of course you will!' – though he didn't believe a single word, of course, of what he was saying.'

There were negotiations over the telephone with the Vakhtangov theatre about *Don Quixote* and about the Repertkom's attitude – negotiations which led to nothing; and the worldy-wise Bulgakov said to the theatre's director: "favourable reviews of the play are no good to me, what I need is a piece of paper telling me whether this play has been approved or not" (22nd October).

The Art Theatre was celebrating an anniversary at around this time; "The very thought of it!" Yelena wrote impetuously on 26th October. "They didn't include *The Turbins* among the plays put on to mark the anniversary, even though it's in its 13th year – it's already been performed more than eight hundred times! No mention is made in any of the articles about the anniversary of his name, or of the title of that play." On the evening of the anniversary, Bulgakov did not go to the Art Theatre, nor indeed did he attend any of the plays put on to celebrate the anniversary. On 5th November, V. Kuza told him that Don Quixote had been approved both by the Repertkom and by the Committee for matters of the arts, and the coveted official piece of paper arrived on the 9th. On the 10th, the author read the play to the people from the Vakhtangov theatre; there was much applause; "After the final scene, the applause lasted even longer. Then Kuza stood up and announced triumphantly: "That will be all!", i.e. no further discussion was needed. They had clearly planned this surprise in order to please Misha and rescue him from having to listen to all manner of utterly groundless opinions."

He really had grown tired, over the course of his literary life, of having to listen to people discuss his works.

They went home, and at half past midnight, some emissaries from the Art Theatre arrived – Sakhnovsky and Vilenkin. "This was the start of Sakhnovsky's speech: 'I have been sent to you by Nemirovich and Boyarsky [Y.O. Boyarsky, the director of the Art Theatre from 1937-1939. – M.C.] on behalf of the Art Theatre to say to you: come and work for us again…I was ordered to kneel down before you…We are holding out our hands to you… I understand how much beastlinless and thuggery the Art Theatre has done to you, but you were not the only one…'"

The whole of November was consumed by tense work at the Bolshoi Theatre, which often went on until two in the morning. Nikolai Erdman would sometimes arrive from Kalinin, and they would talk until 6 in the morning, and then in the day-time – if he was free – they would play billiards until they could no longer stand up; on 20th November, during an evening at the restaurant in the Writers' Club, the writer Chicherov, who was head of the playwrights' division, came over to Bulgakov: "Why have you forgotten us, M.A., gone away from us?" And in response to what Misha said about '36, when everything had been cancelled, he said: 'there you go, there you go, we need to talk about all this, we need to get together, the four of us – you, Fadeyev, Katayev and myself, and discuss everything; you ought to go back to writing plays, and not entrench yourself at the Bolshoi Theatre."

On 12th December, *Soviet Art* publishes an article (signed 'A. Kut', the pseudonym of the critic A.V. Kutuzov) called *A Play about Cervantes* (*Piesa o Servantese*), which provided a favourable opinion of E. Mindlin's play *Cervantes*. "At the start of the article," Yelena wrote, "were some lines about hack playwrights, who had come up with hundreds of reworkings of *Don Quixote*. 13th December. "Misha called Chicherov today and asked him who Kut was. Chicherov said that he didn't know. He asked Misha to come to a meeting about the plays and the repertoire. Misha said that he wouldn't come and that he would not be going anywhere until people stopped harassing him in the newspapers." S. Yermolinsky writes about this episode in his memoirs, too. "Who is this A. Kut? Yet another pseudonym?" "You see," said Bulgakov, "I am surrounded by pseudonyms…"

On 20th December, he is ill. "He doesn't want to lie in bed, of course; he wanders around the apartment, sorts through his books, puts his archived documents in order. Over dinner – just the two of us – we talked about some important things. When he works at the theatre (regardless of which one, Misha says, but in my view this is particularly true of the Bolshoi), it is impossible to work at home – to write his own things. He comes home from the theatre so worn out by his work on other people's librettos, that, naturally, he is not in a fit state at all to work on his own things. Misha is wondering what to do. What should he say no to? Perhaps he ought to switch to a different job? What can I say? For me, when he isn't working, isn't writing his own things, life loses all meaning." 21st December. "Sorting through Misha's archive in the evening. It has made Misha sad. Yes, he cannot go on working like this! But as to what he should do – we don't know." And again – on 24th December: "We are now going through the archive in the evening. Misha said: "You know, all this (pointing at the archive) is making me lose the will to live."

At the end of the year, they acquired some new friends: the couple living on the next floor up, Sergei Mikhalkov and his wife Natalya Konchalovskaya. On 25th December, Yelena Sergeyevna wrote: "He is witty, observant, evidently talented, a wonderful story-teller… She is a very lively, passionate person, a good person." On 26th December, the Bulgakovs hosted the Mikhalkovs at home – "We sat talking till late at night."

On 31st, they saw in the new year, 1939, with the Erdman brothers and the Vilyamses.

5th January. Mikhalsky called in the evening: "We had some dear guests for your play, again" – that meant that Stalin had once again come along to see *The Days of the Turbins*; "there was a conversation about Chulkov, who died the other day [G.I. Chulkov – an author of historical works and works of literary history – M.C.]. Misha says "he was a good man, a real writer, not a great one, but a writer." In the evening – N.R. Erdman; conversations through the night again, until six in the morning; "When N.R. started advising Misha, in a friendly way, to write a new play, not to feel down and so on, Misha said that he was preaching to him like a 'local archpriest'. The conversations they have – because of their wit and acuity – give me endless pleasure." 8th January – M.A. "is in a very burdensome, pessimistic state of mind at the moment."

On 9th January there is an entry stating that V.V. Dmitriyev had been to see them; "he did not look well at all, and said that he had been summoned to the offices of the NKVD. He was racking his brains trying to work out why."

Negotiating with civil servants over foreign productions of Bulgakov's plays became a regular activity. "Misha and I went to talk to Umansky at the Literary Agency," Yelena Sergeyevna wrote on 10th January. "How absurd all this is! Not to see the fate of one's plays, not to receive any royalties for them, and on top of that they're sending letters from VOKS, which do nothing but cause irritation."

On 14th January, she is at Mossovet, in connection with the change of apartment. The secretary "said that the form [sent with Molotov as the recipient – M.C.] had probably been sent to the inspectorate of apartments, and that was the office that he should go to."

Every day, no doubt, she was saying to her husband that different, more effective measures were needed.

On 20th January, Yelena Sergeyevna, after accompanying Bulgakov to the Writers' Club for an electoral meeting, "went up to the gallery and looked down on the meeting from there. I found it terribly unpleasant: there is such a tumult, so much bickering all the time, and it is not a place that breathes literature, in my view."

There is a record of a mysterious episode from this period in her diary. On 21st January, she takes the manuscript of *Don Quixote* to *Literaturnaya Gazeta*, to give it to Yevgeny Petrov; he hoped to publish an excerpt from the play in the paper and had promised to give the manuscript to Olga Voitinskaya (the editor of the newspaper). On 27th January, Yelena wrote that Voitinskaya had called them; she had liked the play, "and we agreed that Misha would go to the editorial offices at 10 in the evening [in those years, work was still in full swing at the institutions in Moscow, in accordance with Stalin's customary working regime – M.C.], so as to discuss which excerpt to print." On 28th January, Yelena writes: "What a story that was! We arrived at exactly 10 o'clock, and there was a janitor sitting in the hall of the editorial offices, who for some reason had nothing on his feet; a young woman with a confused look on her face emerged and said that "Voitinskaya's already left…She won't be back again today… She fell ill yesterday…", and the best advice she could give us was to consult the secretary… We did so, and he said that he was prepared to make his excuses on behalf of Voitinskaya, that the reason for her absence was of the kind that we would have to forgive her – and we never managed to work out what had actually happened to her."

On 29th January, Yelena writes that while she was at the Art Theatre, she had said to F. Mikhalsky and O.S. Bokshanskaya "that our apartment building is probably going to be demolished. This news had a powerful impact on Fedya and even on Olga." Whereupon Mikhalsky asked her, "isn't Misha perhaps writing a modern play? [the question contained a direct link to what she had said – and all three of them understood this. – M.C.]. *I said that he had an idea for a play about Stalin, but that he didn't have enough material. He immediately started giving me advice about how to get some material.*

Yevgeny Petrov said to me over the phone: 'With Voitinskaya, you see, it was a case of *force-majeur*.' What kind of force-majeur could it be?!

We can't make head nor tail of it, but it appears they are going to print a small excerpt."

The circumstances truly were exceptional.

Let us first of all try to imagine what the Bulgakovs may have supposed had happened. An arrest? No, in that case it would have been out of the question for the secretary to have declared his willingness to apologize on her behalf – her name would have had to cease to be used from that moment on, to disappear, under the regulations of those years.

The incongruous nature of the circumstances, however, and the strange respect with which they were spoken of at the newspaper, and the small dose of humour in the statement made by Y. Petrov may have suggested to them, well-versed as they were (like all those who, for one reason or another, somehow came into contact with the 'powers that be') in the finer points of Kremlin-related etiquette – in the same way that the courtiers of French kings were well-versed in court etiquette – that the name of Stalin was somehow involved in the incident.

Word of this mysterious force-majeure event soon spread throughout the literary world in Moscow.

It transpired that Voitinskaya had unexpectedly (as was always the way in cases like these) received a telephone call from Stalin. The moment the poor woman realised who was on the other end of the line, she lost the power of speech – not in the figurative sense, but in a very literal sense.

Having been unable to utter a single word on the phone, she remained in this state of paralysis for another week or two.[17]

This was how Bulgakov's fellow citizens played out, in life – and in the most unintended ways – the scenarios which he thought up in his grotesque stories about fictitious encounters with Stalin.

This real-life anecdote must, of course, have been discussed in detail in the Bulgakov household: although the impact of his own phone call with Stalin in 1930, which he went over and over in his mind and re-imagined a

---

[17] The author was told this on 16th January 1977 by L.I. Slavin; it was later confirmed by V.A. Kaverin.

hundred times, had by now, one must surmise, been lessened, any news about a similar situation must, without question, have captured his attention and his imagination. Furthermore, the figure of Stalin had now taken its place, so to speak, directly at his writing desk.

16th January. "… In the evening, Misha started work, after a long interval, on his play about Stalin… I have just read the first scene. I liked it very much! All the characters are vividly brought to life!"

Thereafter, all of Yelena's diary entries about the work on this play are jubilant. Her dream had come true; new hopes had emerged.

18th January. "Both yesterday and today, Misha has been writing the play, thinking up situations and images for future scenes, and studying the material. May God grant that it will be a success!"

On 19th January, there was a phone-call from Ilya Sudakov: "I cannot let the matter rest as regards *Flight*, I want there to be a production of it without fail, I have already brought it up before the Committee…" He was also interested in *Don Quixote* and, as Yelena wrote, "basically M.A.'s entire output," and a few days later Yudkevich from the Pushkin Theatre in Leningrad asked for a play, any play at all… Bulgakov, according to Yelena's diary entry for 24th January, replied that he was "overwhelmed with work – let them write to him in March – and see whether the play he is working on now will be ready…"

On 24th January, R. Simonov called and said "that he was starting work on *Don Quixote*, and that the new director was very keen on the play indeed, and that Simonov was going to be the director…Besides that, he also said: 'As for *The Turbins* – what a good play! Anastas Ivanovich praised it to the skies! Now there's a real play!'" (Anastas Ivanovich was Mikoyan).

His work on *Batum*, which had apparently run its course in the quiet atmosphere of his study, was already having an electrifying effect on the very air around him.

Let us comment on the decision taken by Bulgakov with some excerpts from the memoirs of S. Yermolinsky: "In the 1930s, when almost all the theatres in the country started including plays in their repertoires about events related to Stalin's role in history or about the man himself, the Art Theatre, which was considered the role-model for our entire theatrical life, could not, of course, avoid this subject. The directors of the Art Theatre realised that he, Bulgakov, was capable of coming to their aid, in a way that no-one else could, because he would not write an official play, or a false one. … They visited him at home and sat up talking about it until dawn. They talked about how putting on a play such as this would signify a complete turn-around in his fortunes. The men from the Art Theatre touched his most sensitive nerves; how could he not now dream about the resurrection of his works...

Secretly, he had been thinking for a long time about the man whose name was inextricably linked with everything that happened in the country...

For the play, he selected a romantic story about a young revolutionary, about his tumultuous youth. In his imagination, the image of a protagonist with a single-minded determination and stubbornness took root. The impudent young man is expelled from the seminary in Tbilisi, and he immediately gets stuck into revolutionary work, and leads the famous mass strike in Batum (in 1902). The strike is violently brought to an end and he is exiled to the Turukhansk Region."

V.Y. Vilenkin would later write: "The first time I spoke to him about the subject of the play, he said to me: 'No, that is risky for me. It will end badly.' And nonetheless he started working on it."

On 1st February, their application to exchange their apartment for a four-bedroom one was rejected (Bulgakov had sent a letter to Molotov; the request had been put through the usual channels and had been refused). On the same day, there was a story in the papers about the awarding of medals to a very large group of writers, and the next day – to cinema workers; Yelena records these events dispassionately in her diary.

On 16th February, Bulgakov goes to the Bolshoi Theatre, to see *Swan Lake* with Galina Ulanova. Some women try to talk to him, Yelena writes, saying: "'You were the first!' What does all this mean? It turned out that the women wanted to console Misha for the fact that he was not given a medal. Good heavens, good heavens! What would Misha want with a medal? Why would he want one?" The incident concerned her and irritated her, if nothing else because of the fact that for long months, it had remained the subject of the day, a subject of discussion in literary circles. There is an entry in I.N. Rozanov's diary recording a story told by N.N. Aseyev's wife: "Oksana told of how the assigning of orders had passed off. Of Lebedev-Kumach, Stalin had asked whether he was the one who "writes couplets".

Utk[in]. Molotov was in favour of him. Utkin was discarded. He cried when he found out.

Of Aseyev, Stalin said: 'Why do you idolize him so much!' 'He had a number of biases,' someone said, it may have been Fadeyev. 'Who didn't? He's ours, though, after all...'"

On 9th February, N.N. Lyamin writes to Bulgakov: "Returning from my wandering in distant lands, I have found a tranquil refuge in Kaluga."

In late February and early March, he resumes work again on the novel *The Master and Margarita*.

On 4th April 1939, Yelena wrote that on the previous evening, "Misha was at the Bolshoi, where *Susanin* was put on for the first time with the new epilogue included [the epilogue had been re-written on the basis of Stalin's comments, and in its new form was an image of the necessary moral and political unity among all sections of the population. – M.C.]. He came home after the play and told us that before the epilogue, the government had moved from their customary government box to the big one in the middle (formerly the Tsar's box) and had watched the opera from there. The audience began applauding as soon as they noticed this, and the applause went on throughout the musical interlude before the epilogue. Then when the curtain was raised and, most of all, towards the end, when Minin and Pozharsky appear – there was applause from those at the top. This intensified and, in the end, was transformed into grand ovations; the government was applauding those on the stage, those on the stage were applauding the government, and the audience were applauding both at the same time.

Today I was at the Director's office at the Bolshoi, and then at one of the studios, and I was told that something extraordinary had happened in terms of the enthusiasm on display; that some old woman, on seeing Stalin, started crossing herself and muttering: "Well I never, I've seen him, after all!" and that people had been standing up on their chairs.

It is said that Leontiev and Samosud were summoned to the box after the play, and Stalin asked them to pass on his gratitude to the entire staff of the theatre who worked on the play, and said that this play would become part of the history of the theatre.

There was a meeting at the Bolshoi today on this subject."

On 8th April, Bulgakov writes to V.V. Kuze: "The situation with *Don Quixote* is starting to trouble me seriously, and I would request that you write to me and tell me what you are going to do with this play. When will it be put on? And will it be put on at all?" The play, having been granted permission to go ahead and secured everyone's approval, had not yet moved forward at all.

On 26th April and 1st May, he reads the novel *The Master and Margarita* (from the start) to the Faikos, P.A. Markov, V.Y. Vilenkin, and the Vilyamses, who came to the second reading, about which Yelena wrote: "It was very good. The audience were fabulous, M.A. read very well. There is a colossal amount of interest in this novel. Misha said over dinner: 'I shall submit it soon, and it will go to the printers.' Everyone giggled bashfully." 14th May. "… A reading – the end of the novel… We listened to the final chapters, frozen to our seats for some reason. It frightened them – Pasha [Markov – M.C.] said to me in the hall afterwards, with fear in his eyes, that he mustn't submit it to the publishers under any circumstances – for the consequences could be terrible."

The memoirs of V.Y. Vilenkin, published not long ago, contain details of the impressions made by the novel on those who attended the reading: "At times, the tension became inordinate, and it was hard to bear. I remember that when he finished reading, we were silent for a long time, it was as though we felt crushed. And it was quite a while before I grasped the philosophical and moral meaning of this striking work... The final reading lasted until the morning. At the table, which had been hastily covered with a cross between dinner and breakfast, I was sitting next to Mikhail Afanasievich, and he suddenly leaned in towards me and asked: "Well, what did you make of it – do you think they'll print that one?" And when I said, somewhat at a loss for words: 'In my view, they won't,' there was suddenly a strong reaction on his part, and he said, in a loud voice: 'But why not!'"

Yelena told me about this episode as well, in 1968-1969: after the reading, as he poured out vodka for the guests from a small decanter, the author said – not in a quiet voice, but in a loud one, so that the whole table could hear: 'Well, there we are, I'll get it published soon!' And glanced around merrily at the embarrassed looks on the faces of his guests.

S. Yermolinsky wrote in his memoirs that some of the audience members then said to him, "in a little whisper: 'It is a piece that shows extraordinary talent, of course. And it must have required a vast amount of work. But judge for yourself, why is he writing this sort of thing? What is he expecting? And it might be the thing that... brings him down! How can one go about telling him this in a cautious way, so that he understands? So that he doesn't waste his time and his strength so wastefully and intentionally in vain...' Back then they said, looking frightened and distressed, 'intentionally in vain', but now I hear ecstatic reminiscences about that unforgettable reading of a startling novel."

3

The fact that work on the novel dragged on for so many years had consequences not only for the text itself (in the final draft, one can see how the layers from the extremely late transformations of the plot come floating in over the previous ones), but also for how it was received by readers. There are hardly any detailed accounts left of the reactions of those who listened to readings of the first drafts, which apparently took place in 1928-1929 (I mentioned them in chapter three), but none of the listeners from that time, among the ones I spoke to, said anything about any kind of lack of clarity, or mystery, in the hero of the opening scene – Woland. The insertion of the storyline from the Gospels, though it may have come as a surprise, was hardly likely to have been shocking; on the contrary, it provoked a professional conversation about the sources that the author had used.

Fast-forward a decade, and a different reaction was provoked. The first few chapters of the novel came across to audiences as something that needed demystifying. There was no spontaneity of reactions – there was an enormous tension, a desire to work out "what this might mean". There is no doubt that the author sensed this tension – and met it head-on. Evidence of this is provided by Yelena, who wrote, on the day after the first reading: "Misha asked, after the reading: who is Woland, then?' Vilenkin said that he had guessed who he was, but that he wouldn't say – not for anything."

Quoting this diary entry, V.Y. Vilenkin adds the following: "No-one was prepared to answer the question directly, to do so seemed risky." The audience members therefore wrote their answers down on slips of paper, exchanged their slip of paper with someone else's, and Vilenkin recalls: "Mikhail Afanasievich couldn't wait any longer, and he came up behind me while I was writing 'Satan', like everyone else, and, glancing at the piece of paper, patted me on the head."

Thus, on the one hand, the situation described in the novel, whereby nobody besides the Master and Margarita recognises Woland, was repeated. And not only that: as though foreseeing the reaction of the first people to hear the novel, its author, back in the late autumn of 1934, whilst describing the meeting between Ivan and the Master, told of how the latter had admitted to Ivan that he had tried reading his novel "to a few people, but they didn't understand it – not even half of it."

On the other hand, it is obvious that the author noticed the flaws in the way the novel was received by his contemporaries: it was precisely because they failed to recognise him that they were so excessively focused on trying to work out who Woland was, and frightened by the inevitable associations to which they were brought by the all-powerful might of this character as he punished some and encouraged others. Moreover, all those who heard his reading, or almost all of them, as one can see from all the surviving accounts, experienced a kind of bewilderment on account of how different the novel was from what they were used to seeing in the literature of the day.

Bulgakov strove to take his audience back to the spontaneous interpretation that they had lost, as a prior condition for the completeness of that interpretation. He wanted to turn the attention of his listeners (there were no readers as such – for Bulgakov did not, it seems, allow anyone to *read* the novel at this time) in the novel. Yermonlinsky remembered Bulgakov saying: "… There are no prototypes for Woland at all. I strongly request that you keep that in mind."

The difficulties experienced by the audience were also related to the fact that in the later drafts, the author freed up the figure of Woland from any direct associations with the devil (the limp, the cloven hoof – one thinks of the original titles for the novel: *The Engineer's Hoof (Kopyto Inzhenera)*, *The Cloven-Hoofed Consultant (Konsul'tant s Kopytom)*) – and yet expected people to identify him.

Approximately two years earlier, Bulgakov, Yelena told me, had read the novel (or part of it) to I. Ilf and Y. Petrov. Pretty much the first thing they had said after the reading had been this: "Take out the chapters set in the ancient world, and we'll undertake to publish it." Yelena recorded Bulgakov's reaconi to this using her favourite expression: "He turned pale."

What struck him was the inadequacy of the reaction to the text they heard on the part of those people whom he considered to be highly-qualified listeners. The goodwill they felt towards him was beyond doubt, but this only served to worsen, one imagines, the state the author was in: his listeners' speculation about the possibilities and conditions for printing the novel not only went too far ahead of an objective reader's interpretation (which he was no doubt expecting), but also, to a considerable extent, knocked the stuffing out of him. In the very first readings of it, the novel had proved to be incomprehensible. The author's reaction was one of mockery, with a carefully concealed sarcasm ("surely they'll publish this one?").

The pragmatic, business-like nature of some listeners, and the confusion (no less pragmatic in its origins) of others, both suggested the same thing: that there was some breach of the connections between the novel that was being completed, or was already complete, and contemporary readers. Typical is this feeling of being almost physically broken, recorded by V.Y. Vilenkin: here, too, as with Ilf and Petrov, the aesthetic reaction was crushed and deformed by some other reaction, which his listeners were not capable of overcoming.

Yet nonetheless the novel captivated those who heard it, thrilled them, left them restless. It was on the day of the last reading, according to Yelena, that the epilogue to the novel was typed up on the typewriter. Yelena stressed how sudden this decision on the part of the author had seemed to her: "I liked the last words of the novel so much! I couldn't understand why there was a need to add anything after them."

From the summer of 1938, when the novel was typed up on the typewriter in its entirety, Bulgakov's attention must have been caught by the shuffling of officials from one position to the next, which seemed significant: on 20th July, Beria became Yezhov's deputy, and on 8th December he replaced him in the post of people's commissar; "in the middle of February 1939, Yezhov disappeared without trace" (R. Conquest. *The Great Terror*. 1974. P. 858). One can sense the taste for solving riddles that was typical of Bulgakov in the epilogue, which was written in the spring of 1939, and one can also see signs of psychological fatigue caused by both the events themselves and the constant guessing games.

The verbal fabric of the epilogue is different from that of the novel: the author puts forward one explanation after another for everything that has happened, yet distances himself from these explanations, refusing to acknowledge any of them as being accurate and entrusting the entire field of supposition and conclusions "to the most well-developed and cultured people", who "have not taken part in any stories about an impure force and have even laughed at them and tried to outwit those who told such stories." When he put a full-stop at the end of the novel, the author subsequently distanced himself from the events set out in it, just as he distanced himself from explanations based on prototypes taken from real life. "What's done is done" is the running theme of the epilogue.

The epilogue to the novel is a place that is devoid not only of Woland and his entourage, but also of the Master. It is also missing the parallel aspect of the two different time-periods in the life of humanity, the connection between which was created through the creative will of the Master. Here, too, a special significance was acquired by the role that was set aside in the epilogue for Ivan Nikolayevich Ponyrev – the man who had been Ivan Bezdomny in the novel.

There was a reason why the part of the epilogue that is dedicated to him began with a return to the square where the novel opened (the bench in Patriarch's Ponds) by the only one of the three characters involved in that scene who was still present within the space of the novel. This time, though, the description begins not with the words "One day …" but "Every year…"

Before us is bleak infinity, the idea of going round in a circle. The 'Continuation' that the Master advises the Master to write cannot possibly be written, since "everything has ended, and everything ends…" – these, the final words spoken by Margarita, talk of the conclusion of some sort of cycle of movement in historical time, some kind of period, within which the entire creative life of the novel's author was contained.

With the departure of the Master, the integrity of his novel was lost; not only could no-one continue it – they could not even reproduce it in any meaningful way; in the consciousness of Ivan Nikolayevich, however hard he might try to make a creative effort, there were merely fragments of visions, which had lost their coherent shape forever. The Master leaves the novel together with his line about peace; no other words are spoken by him in the epilogue. Without this character, no-one can assemble into a single whole the pieces of his novel or the novel about him – which had disintegrated into the consciousness of those who heard it (or saw it – like Nikolai Ivanovich, who was present at the orgy in the form of a boar), nor could they continue it, nor indeed add anything new to it. The Master's novel about Yeshua and Pilate described – in the form of a meta-novel – life as it was in the Master's time, served as the key to it; this life itself could not describe either itself, or history.

At the same time as the epilogue, the page of the novel in which Levy Matvei appeared with a final decision on the Master's fate was also dictated: "He does not deserve the light, he deserves peace" (referencing, as I have already mentioned, Dante's *Divine Comedy*). These words also shed a different light on the final pages of the novel, which had already been written, the Master's farewell to the city. "His anxiety was transformed, as it seemed to him, into a feeling of deep hurt, one that he could feel in his blood. That hurt was not lasting, though; it disappeared and was for some reason replaced by a proud indifference, which was itself replaced by a presentiment of continuous peace."

The novel, "regrettably, is not finished", Woland says to the Master, pointing at Pilate. The novel cannot be finished until all the loose ends related to the theme of guilt have been tied up; this theme ran through the writer's entire oeuvre and underwent a deep transformation during the final decade of his life; the mental labour he had done for so many years would remain unfinished until this knot, which had been twisted horribly around plenty of other people too, not just the hero of the writer's last novel, was untied. As he sets Pilate free, with this gesture of mercy the Master is also asking for release for himself, and for all those who are in need of forgiveness and reassurance. Redemption is only to be found in the length of the torments itself, and in nothing else, and the ending is to be found in one thing – forgiveness. "The punishment has already happened"; a memory that is pricked can torment a person far more powerfully than anything else, and seeks oblivion. Pilate will see Yeshua and will speak to him, but the Master will not, because nobody can give themselves full redemption. And if we turn away again from the text of the novel to the context of his biography, then in the spring of 1939, the author of the novel perhaps recognised with particular clarity the fateful irrevocability of both his previous actions in life and his current ones, the way in which man is imprisoned in the ring of his own life.

Without knowing any specific details about the decision taken on high, the Master blindly goes in the direction that Woland sends him. Even if had known it, though, he would not have tried to argue with it. The romantic Master, too, is wearing a cloak with a bloody lining, but this lining remains invisible to everyone but the author.

15th May. "Faiko called and came round – he said that the novel is captivating and touching." On 16th May, Bulgakov had sent a photograph to his wife, in which he is gazing into the distance at the unseen onlooker, with knitted brows and a rather fierce expression, one that could also be described as courageous yet hopeless: "This is what a man can look like after he's spent several years hanging around with the likes of Aloizy Mogarych, Nikanor Ivanovich and the others. In the hope that you will recognise this face, I am giving you this postcard Yelena; I kiss you and embrace you."

18th May. "Misha has had an idea for a play (Richard the First). He told me the plot – it's remarkably interesting, exactly as a pure 'Bulgakov play' should be." If the play in question was the one whose plot was later developed under the title *The Swallow's Nest (Lastochkino Gnezdo)*, which was to feature a writer, a grandee who was his benefactor and a man in boots and with a pipe standing over all of them, then the name 'Richard' may have been connected to one of the most fervent haters of Bulgakov's plays, who had disappeared from literary life in 1936: Richard Pickel, and also with the name 'Genrick', i.e. with Yagoda.

20th May. "... Dmitriyev called on us with news of Veta. It appears she is no longer in the land of the living. There is a rumour going about town that Babel has been arrested."

21st May. It is Yelena's name-day, and the apartment is filled with roses from her friends. "At around 8 in the evening it began to get dark; at 8, the first claps of thunder came, and lightning. The storm began. It was a very brief one. And then everything was lit up in an extraordinary way – the sky was red.

Misha is now (at 10 in the evening) sitting over his play about Stalin."

22nd May. "Misha is writing a play about Stalin." On this day, he receives a rejection in response to his request to order a typewriter from abroad. "This is not life! This is torture!" Yelena wrote down in irritation. "Whatever we try to do, it never comes to anything! Whether it's a play, an apartment, a typewriter, it makes no difference!" On the 27th, Bulgakov joins his wife as she tries to take measures to sort out this matter: "It's not diamonds from overseas that I'm asking for, after all. For me, a typewriter is a necessity, the tool of my trade."

4th June. V.Y. Vilenkin goes to see Bulgakov, with an insistent offer from the Art Theatre that he enter into an agreement for a play about Stalin. "Misha told them about the scenes he has written so far, and read part of them out. I shall never forget how V. listened with rapt attention, trying to get to the bottom of this." (Vilenkin, quoting this diary entry in his memoirs, also adds one from his own diary: "I was with Bulgakov yesterday. His play is almost written. There were none of those 'Ah!' moments, perhaps because M.A. did not read any of the key scenes... But it is all well-written, subtle, without too much strain. There are some real *roles* in it, not to mention the central, most interesting one (Khmelev?). I stayed at their place till three in the morning.").

6th June. "... we had a pleasant evening, Faiko, Petya and Anusya [the Vilyamses – M.C.] were here, Misha read to them the draft of his prologue from the play about Stalin (his expulsion from the seminary). They liked it ever so much, and their reaction was genuine. They liked it because it's original, and because it's unlike all the plays that are being written on these subjects, and because of the remarkable role of the protagonist." Yelena Sergeyevna is particularly thorough as she goes about the task of collecting favourable reviews of this play.

On 9th June, Bulgakov goes to the Art Theatre to agree on the terms on which he will give the play that he is writing to the theatre, which he left three years earlier.

They greeted him very cheerfully, and promised "to sort you out with an apartment and, if possible, 4 rooms, by November or December…" They asked him "which actor he could envisage playing Stalin, and who he thought would be right for all the other roles. When we had just arrived at the Art Theatre, a storm was coming…" On their return home, "Misha was sitting up, writing the play. I've just read another scene – a new one. It will be accepted!" 14th June. "Misha working on the play. He's written the start of the scene in the governor's office. What a part…! It is stuffy. Even though it was pouring with rain this afternoon – it has not brought any relief."

He wrote, relying as he did so on two or three works which had just come out – no archive material, of the kind he had thought about while pondering over the play, had been provided to him.

On 2nd July, Bulgakov reads a few scenes to Khmelev and a few other listeners. "Then we had dinner, with a long period sitting down afterwards. Conversations about the play, about the Art Theatre, about the system [Stanislavsky's one – M.C.]. We only dispersed when the sun had already well and truly come up." Yelena could remember a story told by Khmelev, who was extremely excited by the idea of this new role: "Stalin had once said to him: 'You play Alexei very well. I even see your shaven moustache in my dreams. I can't forget it.'"

9th July. "A whole crop of phone calls today: 3 from Kalishyan [the deputy director of the Art Theatre – M.C.]. He is asking Misha to read his play at the Committee on the 11th… Khmelev called – saying that the play was remarkable, that he could almost remember it by heart, and that if he was not given the role of Stalin – it would be a tragedy for him." On the 11th, Bulgakov reads the play to the directors of the Committee for matters of the arts. "They listened with rapt attention. They liked the play very much"; "During the reading of the play – an extremely powerful storm".

On 14th July, Bulgakov wrote to Vilenkin, who had gone on holiday: the results of this reading "I can profess, it seems, without risk of erring, to be favourable (altogether). After the reading, Grigory Mikhailovich [Kalishyan – M.C.] asked me to speed up my work on the corrections and re-writing, so that we can submit the play to the Art Theatre by 1 August. And today (we had a meeting today), he asked to move the deadline to 25th July. I have 10 days of very intensive work ahead of me. I hope that if I put all my strength into it, I shall submit the play to him on 25th… I am tired. From time to time I travel to Serebryany bor, go for a bathe and now I am returning. As for what we'll do for a real holiday – we don't know anything about that yet… Exhausted, I'm putting my exercise book to one side, and I'm thinking about what the fate of the play will be. Your guess is as good as mine. A great deal of work has gone into it."

He was not destined ever to enjoy a "real holiday" again.

How cautious, uncertain, superstitious the tone of the letter is!

17th July. "A hasty writing up of the play… There is a rumour that Zinaida Reich has been stabbed in a most brutal way." 20th July. "The dictation is continuing uninterrupted. The play is being cleaned up, condensed, embellished."

21st July. "Misha is dictating." 22nd July. "Today, Misha dictated scene nine – with Nikolai [Nikolai II – M.C.] – in draft form… he has decided to call the play *Batum*. 23rd July. "He re-did scene 9. Very successfully. Then he went to Pestovo [a holiday home owned by the Art Theatre outside the city – M.C.] with Kalishyan. The the Art Theatre group are now sticking to Misha like glue, they went around with him like shadows." His wife was struck by this change.

V.Y. Vilenkin did indeed recall how Kachalov "was interested in the role of the governor of Kutais, which he thought seemed made for him", and "V.O. Toporkov was attracted, right from the outset, to the scene with Nikolai II, receiving an extremely lyal report about the terrifying events in the Caucasus at the Livadisky palace, standing in a red silk tunic beside a cage containing a dressed up canary, which he is enthusiastically teaching "to sing *God Save the Tsar*."

All those involved in this situation realised, it seems, that times had changed, that Bulgakov was once again a beloved playwright, who had brought them a play promising nothing but success, just as he had done thirteen years ago.

No-one was more enthusiastic than the author's wife. 24th July. "The play is finished! Misha has done an absolutely incredible amount of work: inside 10 days, he wrote scene 9 and cleaned up and edited the entire play…I can't for the life of me understand how he had the strength to do so. In the evening, Kalishyan came here and Misha gave him three completed copies."

26th July. "Kalishyan called; he said he had read the play in its current form, and he liked it very much. He reminded Misha about the reading on the 27th." The author was due to read the play at an open session of the Sverdlovsk district committee, which would be held at the Art Theatre.

27th July. "There was a storm at 4 o'clock. Kalishyan sent a car to pick us up. At the theatre, in the new rehearsal room, the district committee met, along with party members among the theatre's staff and a handful of actors… They listened to the reading remarkably well, and after it they stood and gave Misha a very long ovation. Then they expressed their opinions of what they had heard. It was all very good. Kalishyan said, in his last speech, that the theatre ought to put it on by 21st December." (i.e. in time to celebrate the 60th birthday of the hero of the play).

Thirty years later, on 10th December 1969, Yelena told me: "When we arrived at the theatre, we saw a poster for a reading of *Batum*, painted in watercolours – and the rain had ruined it.

'Give it to me!' Misha said to Kalishyan.

'Whatever for, what use is it to you? Do you realise what kind of posters you're going to have put up for you? An altogether different kind, let me tell you!'

'I won't see the other ones.' (The poster on which the colours had run was present among the writer's archived documents).

On 28th July, Bulgakov writes a funny note to F.N. Mikhalsky on Yelena's behalf: "… Misha asked me in advance to allocate places for his acquaintances at the premiere of *Batum*. I am sending you the first list (artists and playwrights, composers). Be so good, Fedinka, as to do it like this:

B.R. Erdman – director's box
P.V. Vilyams – Row 1 (left)
V.Y. Shebalin – Row 3.
N.R. Erdman – Row 7.

Dmitriyev – in the dress circle, standing. And Fedinka! If Olesha comes and starts asking for a place, do me a favour, tell a policeman that he's involved in ticket scalping." 1st August. Kalishyan reports that the Committee for matters of the arts "liked the final draft of the play very much and sent it to those above them." 5th August. "Nikolai called and came here, along with Boris Erdman. Nikolai had some depressing news – he is not allowed to live in Moscow. Vilenkin called – he was very nice."

7th August. Kalishan tells them over the telephone that Nemirovich-Danchenko "liked the play very much, and called the Secretariat, and spoke to Stalin apparently, to find out about the play; he was told that the play has not returned yet."

The man to whom Bulgakov had not dared to send a letter in the last few years, and whom he had occasionally imagined reading his novel, was now reading the play that Bulgakov had written about him.

At that point, they find out from Olga that the theatre is sending a brigade to Tbilisi and Batum, with Bulgakov included. 8th August. In the morning, "Misha said that after giving it some thought during a sleepless night, he had come to the conclusion that he ought not to go to Batum right now." 9th

August. He is with Nemirovich-Danchenko; they talk about how to put on the play. The doubts that Bulgakov is experiencing go unnoticed this time by his wife, it seems, though she is usually so sensitive to his mood. On 11th August, she writes to her mother: "I am in a wonderful condition, both spiritually and physically. This is probably in connection with Misha's work. Life for us is full to the brim, interesting, wonderful!" Never before had her letters to her mother, which were always joyful and painted a picture that was more pleasant than the reality, expressed such an upbeat mood and a belief that success was inevitable. Even more expressive was a letter she sent on the same day to her sister: "I am shaking with impatience, I can't wait to leave, everything's ready for the departure and I only have to wait until the 14th, or perhaps a little longer." 13th August. "We have packed our things. Telephone calls… *Soviet Art* is asking M.A. to give them some information about his new play. 'Our newspaper is following all *Posledniye Novosti* with such interest… The Committee is praising the play so much…' I said that M.A. could not give them any information, the play had not yet been given permission. 'You know what, let him write it and give it to me. The piece of paper will lie in my room. If permission is granted, I'll print it. If not – I'll return it to you.'

I tell him that that would be a bit like writing an obituary for someone who was gravely ill, but still alive.

'What on earth do you mean?! On the contrary…'

Can it really be that we are leaving tomorrow!!

I can't believe how happy I am." 14th August. "The last bit of packing. The car leaves at 11. And then – the railway car!"

V.V. Vilenkin, who was going to be travelling to Batum and Kutaisi with Bulgakov and the assistant director, wrote in his memoirs: "We were collectively known as a 'brigade', and Mikhail Afanasievich was our 'brigadier' on that trip. I remember he was clearly very happy with his new name and he took it very seriously, without a smile.

At last, the 14th arrived, and we set off, in complete comfort, in an international railway car," in two private compartments. "It was terribly hot. Everyone changed into their pyjamas. In the 'brigadier's compartment', Yelena Sergeyevna immediately set up a farewell 'banquet', with pies, pineapples dipped in cognac and so on. It was great fun. Paying no heed to superstition, we drank to our success. The train stopped in Serpukhov and stood there for a few minutes. Some woman came into our carriage and stood in the corridor, shouting: 'Telegram for the accountant!' [*bukhgalter* in Russian]. Mikhail Afanasievich said: 'It's not for the accountant, it's for Bulgakov' [Yelena told me, with a sense of horror that the last thirty years had not dispelled, that he had said that, turning pale, at the very second when that strange shout had been heard from the corridor – as though he had been expecting it to come at any moment. – M.C.].

He read the telegram out loud: "Need for trip gone return to Moscow". After an initial minute of confusion, Yelena said firmly: "We're not turning back. We'll just go and have a holiday…"

Their fellow travellers, barely managing to change back out of their pyjamas and chuck their suitcases onto the platform in time, got off at Serpukhov. The Bulgakovs stayed on the train, stunned by the message. It quickly became clear that they had to return to Moscow, after all. They got off the train at Tula. They had difficulty finding a car that would take them back to Moscow, but eventually managed to do so. Yelena described this journey in great detail. Bulgakov was tormented by a searing pain in his eyes, he covered them with his hand. "In the car, we thought: what are we travelling towards? To something completely unknown?" (When she looked through her diary in the 1950s, Yelena had written in something that she remembered Bulgakov had said: 'What are we rushing towards? To death, perhaps?') "After three hours of driving like crazy, i.e. at 8 in the evening, we were at our apartment. Misha didn't let me turn on the lights, we lit candles instead." In the evening, there was a call from the Art Theatre; they asked Bulgakov to come in for an official conversation. "Misha's condition is awful. Early in the morning, he said to me that he couldn't go anywhere. He spent the day in a darkened room, the light irritates him." For the second time in Bulgakov's life, his hopes had been crushed by Batum. He began writing in a new exercise book that day: 'Foreign language learning' (French and Italian). 16th August. "… At three in the afternoon – Sakhnovsky and Vilenkin." First of all, Sakhnovsky declared that "the theatre is not changing its attitude towards M.A., under any circumstances, nor its opinion of the play; the theatre will keep all its promises, i.e. – about the apartment, and shall pay everything, as set out in the contract. He then started to convey the news: the play had garnered an extremely negative response from the powers that be. An individual such as Stalin could not be turned into a literary image (Yelena, clarifying the meaning of the phrases used at the time, replaced this with 'a romantic hero'); one could not put him in made-up positions and put made-up words into his mouth. The play was neither to be performed, nor published. Secondly: that the powers that be looked on the fact that this play had been put forward by Bulgakov as a desire to put down a bridge and to smooth over the way he was thought of [one can imagine how Bulgakov, on hearing this, might have thought about the words spoken by Khludov to the messenger Krapilin in his own play: 'You're a bad soldier! You started off well but ended badly." – M.C.]. This is such a baseless accusation," Yelena writes; "what an unsubstantiated claim. How can one possibly prove that M.A. wasn't intending to build any bridges at all, but simply wished, as a dramatist, to write a play – one that he finds interesting, because of the material, with a hero; and wished that this play would be brought to the stage, not left lying on his writing desk?! In the evening, Yakov called on us [Y.L. Leontiev. – M.C.]. He talked to Misha; Misha is thinking about writing a letter to the powers that be."

The news that was brought to him from the theatre probably affected him just as powerfully as the failure of the play itself.

18th August. "This afternoon, Sergei Yermolinsky arrived from Odessa and heard the news. He asked Misha to read him the play. Once he had finished, he gave Misha a big kiss. He thinks the play is remarkable. He says that the figure of the hero is written in such a way that when he leaves the stage, you can't wait to see him appear on stage again. He generally said a great deal and was full of admiration, as a professional who understands all the difficulties of the task and the virtuosity of the execution. [...] In the whole day – not a single call. [...] Misha is agonizing over a letter to the powers that be all the time." In the evening, he goes to see Sergei Yermolinsky. On 19th August, Vilenkin came round again. "Misha told him that he has some specific documents, that he had the idea for this play early in 1936, when both *Molière* and *Pushkin* were due to be performed on stage at any moment. It was 1 am. Kalishyan did not come. Nothing but silence from the telephone, Misha is sitting over his Italian language exercises. I am doing household chores."

22nd August. A visit from Kalishyan. "He tried to convince us that the phrase about the 'bridge' was never spoken. He tried to persuade Misha to write a play about Soviet people. He asked: will it be ready by the 1st of January?

He asked Misha to give him *Flight*, although he promptly warned that there was now no hope of it being staged. Misha's mood was ruined after this conversation… Vilenkin came in the evening, then Misha went to call on Seryozha Yermolinsky."

Yermolinsky recalled this visit as follows: "It is hard to forget his first appearance at my home after what had happened. He lay on the divan for quite some time, gazing at the ceiling, then said:

'Remember how they banned *The Days of the Turbins*, how they cancelled *A Cabal of Hypocrites*, how they rejected the manuscript about Molière? And you remember – however hard all that was to take, I never let my hands rest for a moment. I carried on working, Sergei! And now look at me: I'm lying here in front of you, bullet-ridden...'

I retained a very clear memory of that rather peculiar word: bullet-ridden. But I understood very well what he was talking about. He was condemning writerly indifference, in whatever way it was manifested, particularly if it was related to a calculating approach, that of a mercenary or someone hungry for fame, not to mention cowardice. He condemned himself all the more mercilessly and talked about this directly, without the slightest bit of condescension... In those years, the people around him, even those closest to him, looked on his act as the right move, strategically. His friends were stunned by the catastrophe with the play, they felt sympathy for the author, they were bewildered. Yes; in those years, his behaviour was not condemned by anyone, it seemed utterly normal and natural. Yet now, when I tell people how it all was, they say to me: don't talk about that." To those who fear that this casts a shadow over the "flawless image of the writer", Yermolinsky has the following objection: "The unhappy incident involving the play *Batum*, which he experienced as a tragedy, in no way lessens his image, or diminishes it; on the contrary, it enlarges it."

23rd August. "Misha is stubbornly forcing himself to sit over his languages, clearly with the same goal that I have in doing the cleaning."

26th August. "Today – the theatre company gathered at the Bolshoi for the first meeting... Misha was there. Samosud said (about *Batum*): couldn't we turn it into an opera? Operas are supposed to be romantic, after all..."

26th August. "... On the whole, I would say that I have seen so much concern, tenderness, love and respect for Misha lately, that I never thought he would get that much. It is very valuable...

Misha's spirits are broken. He says he has been knocked out of the saddle once and for all. He has never been like this before."

"Nemirovich cannot calm down about this play," Yelena wrote on 30th August, recording what Bokshanskaya had told her, "and he is determined to ask for a meeting with J.V. and to talk about this."

Essentially, this no longer concerned Bulgakov himself. He was now engaged in settling scores with himself – in a far more brutal manner than had been the case in 1930-1931.

September 1939 was under way and the newspapers were full of reports about military action taking place in European countries. These were read and discussed in Bulgakov's home. There was vague talk of a trip to the south, to Batum – that place again – for some rest and relaxation. On 7th September, Khmelev came to see him along with Kalishyan, who "tried very hard to talk him out of going to Batum… He spoke to Misha about a new play, very insistently, and offered to sign a contract. Then he started talking about an adaptation of *The Spring Tide* (*Veshniye Vody*) for the stage. (One can imagine what Bulgakov must have felt, as it was proposed to him that he should start all over again a life-cycle that he had already been through).

"All the talk is of war, of course," Yelena wrote on 8th September… We went to the theatre for a chat with Y. (Leontiev). He does not recommend going to Batum (we had already ordered tickets for 10th September). His conclusions are convincing. It's the wrong destination and the wrong time to go. He urged us instead to go to Leningrad. He promised to get us the tickets and a room at the Astoria."

On 9th September, as she prepared for the trip to Leningrad, Yelena wrote: "We are terribly disappointed not to be going on our trip to the south. We were so looking forward to going bathing and seeing all those beautiful places." This was the last entry in her diary before it broke off; the next one would be made some twenty days later – under altogether different circumstances.

4

A small desk calendar for 1939 survives, with short notes on it written by Yelena Sergeyevna. She may have written them when she was back in Moscow, looking back on those fateful days. 11th September. "The Astoria (Len.). A wonderful room, wrote a joyful telegram to Yakov. Took a stroll. Couldn't make out the words on the shop-signs, all very irritating – came home. Searching for an eye specialist." They found a doctor the next day: Bulgakov was complaining of a dramatic worsening of his eyesight. "He is stubbornly trying to persuade me that we should leave… A terrible night. ('I am in a bad way, Lyusenka. He has signed my death sentence')." It seems that the doctor in Leningrad had suggested that this could be the very illness that sent his father to his grave at the age of 48. Bulgakov himself was now in his 49th year. On 15th September, five days after they had set off (Bulgakov was not due back at the Bolshoi until 5th October), they went back to Moscow, shaken by this misfortune, which was unexpected and clearly beyond repair now. "I asked Arendt to come over," Yelena told me on 4th November 1969. "He invited the neuro-pathologist M.Y. Rapaport and the kidney expert Vovsi to join him. They confirmed the diagnosis: 'That telegram dealt him a blow in the smallest capillaries: the eyes and the kidneys'). They told him he ought to go to hospital straight away. He looked at me with entreaty in his eyes. When we had decided to get married, he had said to me: 'When I die, it is going to be a painful affair. Will you promise that you won't pack me off to a hospital?' He was serious. I made the promise. I now said:

'No, he'll stay at home.'

And the doctor, as he was leaving, said to me:

'The only reason I'm not going to insist is that we are talking about a mere three days…'

He heard this remark… I am certain that if it weren't for those words, things would have been different with the disease… That killed him. And in any case, he didn't live for just three days after it, but for six months…"

On 16th September, Y.S. Bulgakova starts writing notes in an exercise book about the course of the disease and the appointments with doctors, later making daily entries in it.

On 29th September, she resumes her diary entries. "I have no desire to return to that which has been lost. I shall therefore turn straight to Misha's terrible disease: the headaches are his main scourge…

Events are reaching boiling point all around us, but they fall on deaf ears when they reach us, because we are stunned by our own troubles.

The Union has entered into a pact of friendship with Germany."

On 4th October, Bulgakov dictates a letter to Popov to his wife: "Thank you for your kind letter, dear Pavel. My letter cannot, unfortunately, be very detailed, for I am plagued by headaches. I therefore simply embrace you and send my greetings to Anna Ilinishna. Yours, …" – and the signature is almost impossible to make out. That day, he starts dictating some corrections for the novel *The Master and Margarita*. Yelena puts some of them into the type-written text from 1938, and others into a special notebook.

On 10th October 1939, Bulgakov, certain of the hopelessness of his situation, summoned a notary to his house and drew up a will with his wife as the beneficiary, and also a draft power of attorney for the management of his affairs; on 14th October, the notary added a huge number of provisos to it, which were required by the standard form, but had already lost their material meaning as far as the mandatory was concerned. He entrusted to his wife the right to enter into "agreements with publishing houses and production companies for the publication, staging and public performance of my works." Yet there was no prospect of his works either being published or performed publically. On 18th October, A. Fadeyev called – "to say that he would come to visit Misha tomorrow". There was a call from the Art Theatre saying that theatre had had a visit from "the government, and the General Secretary, whilst talking to Nemirovich, said that he considered the play *Batum* to be very good, but that it must not be performed. This prompted a flurry of phone calls from the folks at the Art Theatre." No favourable reviews could now reverse the flow of events. By an irony of fate, a typewriter – procured from America after all – was delivered to the apartment at around this time.

There were ups and downs in his condition; on 23rd October, he dictated a fairly lengthy letter to P.S. Popov, in response to his interesting letter about the prose of Apukhtin, yet the entire first half of November was agonizing, with a half-delirious condition. On 10th November, the doctors insisted that he ought to be taken to hospital; he woke up at 4 am and said to his wife: "I sense that I shall die today." Yet death was in no hurry. 15th November. "Vilenkin. An unusual mood. A conversation about the new play." On 18th November, Bulgakov and his wife went to the Barvikha sanatorium outside Moscow. On 1st December, he dictates several letters to her – to P.S. Popov,

N.P. Khmelev and A.M. Faiko, to whom he wrote: "This is how things stand with me: my health has improved here, such that some hope has even awoken within me. An extremely significant improvement has been discovered in my left eye. The right eye, the worst afflicted of the two, is slowly dragging itself after it." To Popov, he wrote: "hope has arisen within me that I shall return to life"; "When you are sitting in your study, reading a book – think of me. I have been deprived of that happiness for two and a half months now." On 3rd December, he wrote to his younger sister, Yelena: "Based on what the doctor says, it seems that since there's been an improvement in my eyes, then there's also an improvement in the process of the kidneys. And since that's the case, I am starting to hope that I shall get away from the old woman with the squint and finish one or two things that I should like to finish." During his brief strolls, he told his wife about his new play. On 10th December 1969, Yelena recalled how, on hearing about one of the characters, she had been frightened: "You're writing about him again!" His cool reply had been: "I shall include him in all my plays from now on." These words are telling. The dialogue was continuing, even though one of the participants in it could not hear the other and had no intention of seeing him.

On 18th December, they returned to Moscow. There was a letter waiting for Bulgakov at home (dated 5th December) in which one could clearly perceive the desire of the author, P.S. Popov, to say some important and essential words to the dying man, which he would not have been able to utter under normal circumstances:

"Dear Maka, I was very touched by your little letter. I think about you all the time. Now, in the past, and always. At the dinner table, when I'm in bed, when I'm out and about. Whether I see you or do not see you, for me, you embellish life. I fear that you may not have any inkling of what you mean to me. When a Russian was once asked whether he hailed from a barbarian clan, he replied: "since Pushkin and Gogol lived in my people's past, I cannot consider myself a barbarian." A certain Aleutian bishop, who had come to Moscow from his snowy wildernesses, was once asked: how did he like Moscow? He said: "there are no people", i.e. there were no real people. What I want to say is that, as a contemporary of yours, one doesn't get that feeling, that there are no people; when one reads lines written by you, one knows that genuine literary culture exists; as one moves with one's imagination into the places described by you, one understands that the creative imagination has not dried out, that the light that was lit by the Romantics, Hoffman and so on, will keep shining and glistening, that the art of the word has not left people. For me, you are on a pedestal that not a single artist has reached – those masters at feeling as though they are not just at the centre of the auditorium, but at the centre of the whole universe. I even find it scary at times that I know you, that I can use the familiar form of 'you' with you – it feels like a profanity against the reverenetial feeling that one has…"

On 28th December, O.S. Bokshanskaya described what it was like at their home in a letter to her mother: "… Maka's all right, he's holding up and in lively spirits, but Lyusya has changed frightfully: though she's pretty, and always looks prim, there is such a trembling in her eyes, such sadness and so much inner tension being expressed, that one is afraid to look at her. The poor thing – when people come to visit Maka, he livens up, of course, but she has to endure his darkest moments alone, and she hears all his most gloomy forebodings, and when she does, she constantly feels this incredibly tense desire to fight for his life. "I shan't give him up," she says, "I shall pull him out of this, for life." She loves him so powerfully that it is not like the notion one usually has of love between spouses who have already spent many years together…"

On the same day, Bulgakov writes to Gdeshinsky: "I could not write to you until now, dear friend, and thank you for the information you kindly passed on." Gdeshinsky answered in extremely great detail all his questions about life in Kiev in their younger days – which concerts were being performed at the Merchants' Garden, which books the Spiritual Academy had in its library, etc.; deprived of the ability to read and write, Bulgakov hoped to dictate some memoirs, and apparently wanted to adopt a systematic approach. "I have now come back from the sanatorium," he went on. "If I'm to be completely open with you and let you into a secret, I am plagued by the thought that I have come back here to die." It was in this letter that he contrasted an "agonizing" and "long-drawn-out" death caused by disease with "one agreeable form of death: being shot with a fire-arm, but sadly I do not possess one."

On 31st December, as he enters his final year, clearly aware that it will be his final year, Bulgakov wrote to his younger (and favourite) sister: "Dear Lyolya, I got your letter. I hope that both you and your sister will get better soon. And since the New Year is upon us, I am also sending you other joyful wishes, better ones.

I do not wish for anything for myself, because I have noticed that nothing ever works out as I wished it to… What will be, will be. I feel joy at the fact that I have come home."

On 1st January, his friends and acquaintances sent their best wishes for the new year – Nikolai Erdman, N. Radlov, B.V. Shaposhnikov…

In the first few days of the new year, his condition was very bad. On 6th January, he makes some notes about the play which he thought up over the course of the last year; "it was thought up in the autumn of 1939. I started writing it on 6.1.1940. A play. A cupboard, an exit. A swallow's nest. The Alhambra. Musketeers. A monologue about impudence. Grenada. The death of Grenada. Richard I.

It's not coming easily at all, my head's like a cauldron… I'm in pain, I'm in pain…" He received a letter from Gdeshinsky, from Kiev: "For some reason, winter is the most poetic time, and brings with it memories… The snow falls and it caresses one's face lovingly. The coachmen's sleigh-bells ring… And there are fir trees everywhere. And you have them too, and someone is singing…" This letter was a final greeting for Bulgakov from his youth in Kiev, before the grave which now awaited him.

By mid-January, there had been something of an improvement in his condition.

13th January. "A fierce cold spell, we went to Povarskaya, to the Union of Writers. Misha wanted to see Fadeyev, but he wasn't there. We made it to the writers' restaurant and had something to eat… Misha was wearing dark glasses and his hat [his wife had sewn him a black hat – like the one his hero wore. – M.C.], as a result of which the people around us (we wre sitting by the buffet) were gawping at him – I can't put into words the kind of stares they gave us. We went home through a freezing mist."

14th January. "Aseyev. He had some terribly ecstatic things to say about both of us, he wishes to strengthen this friendship at any cost. He read out an excerpt from *Mayakovsky*. Misha is lying down, the cold is having a bad effect on him." The work in question was *Mayakovsky is Beginning* (*Mayakovskiy Nachinayetsya*), a long poem that Aseyev had recently completed. They must have talked about Mayakovsky that evening; Bulgakov perhaps asked Aseyev some questions about him. In the last year of his life, his thoughts returned to a man whose fate had been intertwined with his own in such a strange way, at the time of its tragic conclusion; in a notebook that she had started writing in at Barvikha, Yelena wrote down the subjects which he hoped to think about (he dictated them to her), the areas of knowledge which he wanted to examine: "Geography. Geography?", "Medicine, the history of it? The mistakes made in it? The history of its mistakes?", "Philosophy, philosophy!" And among these notes was this one: "Read Mayakovsky properly".

One can assume that his thoughts were returning to Mayakovsky now, in an effort to imagine what Mayakovsky's own condition prior to death had been like; we shall never know this; but certain similarities can be seen in some of their philosophical and creative ideas. As early as in the novel *The White Guard*, some encouraging words are uttered by the man at whose altar the sergeant-major collapses, and dies: "*Live* a little, enjoy yourself" – the very words, it seems, on which, many years later, the unusual building in the concluding chapters of *The Master and Margarita* is erected – words which identify the next life as *life*, as existence in the same physical form and even alongside the woman one loves. R. Yakobson, recalling something Mayakovsky said about the theory of relativity: "I am utterly convinced that there will be no death. The dead will be resurrected," said he was certain that the title of the poem *Petition in the Name of... (Please, comrade chemist, fill in the name yourself!)* was, for Mayakovsky, "not a literary heading at all, it was a genuine, reasoned petition to the quiet chemist of the 20th century, with the high forehead," and that here, as in the plays *The Bedbug* and *The Bathhouse*, "faith was the down-payment for resurrection". This is similar to the value system expressed in *The Master and Margarita*; one could also attribute to Bulgakov the words that the same researcher said about Mayakovsky: "there is no resurrection for him without embodiment, without flesh" – a trait which in my view brings these two very different creative worlds closer together. In her memoirs, Y. Lavinskaya recorded the following words spoken by L.Y. Brik the day after the poet's funeral: "He did not understand what he was doing at all, did not understand that death meant a grave, a funeral. Had he really understood that, he would have been disgusted, and he would not have shot himself, not for anything." Bulgakov, as a former doctor, had a good idea of what death was, and told several of his friends back in the autumn of 1939 how his disease and death would occur. As for his notion of the modern funeral ritual, it is insistently described, with all the accessories which the author found distasteful, from the first draft of his novel *The Master and Margarita* to the last.

A profound and, as yet, undeciphered account of the relationship between Bulgakov's creative work and his life and death was left in some lines written by A.A. Akhmatova, who knew the poet well: "And you let in the frightening guest yourself and you stayed with this guest, alone together." (She brought this poem to Yelena Sergeyevna on 16th April). Bulgakov continued to perfect his novel until his final days, resembling in some sense the poetry Mayakovsky wrote just before he died.

15th January. "Misha is working on the novel with all the strength he can muster, and I am copying it out." She read it to him out loud, he stopped her, dictated corrections and improvements, and this new text was either written down in the notebook for corrections, begun on 4th October, or was included in a typewritten text in the form of separate sheets. 16th January. "42 degrees…! Work on the novel. Yermolinsky came over in felt boots, I read a little bit of the novel to him – the little sparrow. Misha demonstrated the sparrow." This was the episode he had just dictated, in which the buffet attendant meets Professor Kuzmin, which covered 5 large pages of text in tiny handwriting. "… As he stared at it, the professor immediately became convinced that this sparrow was no ordinary sparrow. […] It was dancing a foxtrot to the sounds coming from the gramophone, like a drunken man at the bar. It tried to be as rude as it could, glancing impudently at the professor." In such vivid, fun ways did the dying man's creative imagination occasionally flicker into life. On the same day: "In the evening – corrections to the novel… dinner at Misha's writing desk. I believe he is getting better." 24 January. "Vilenkin was here yesterday. A conversation about the new play. Then about an apartment. A conversation which troubled Misha. He is complaining about his heart. At 8 o'clock, we went outside, but came back in immediately: he couldn't do it, he is tired." 25th January. "He dictated a page (about Stepa – Yalta)"; that day, they went out for a walk – apparently, for the last time. 28th. Once again, there was work on the novel. On 29th, there was a worsening of his condition. On 13th February, however, Bulgakov worked on the novel yet again – for the last time, it seems. Y.S. Bulgakova said of this: "In 1940, he made some more corrections to the first part; I read it to him. But when we moved on to the second part and I started reading about Berlioz's funeral, he was about to start making corrections, but then he suddenly said: 'Oh well, all right then, that's enough, I suppose.' And he did not ask me to read it to him after that." The extent of the corrections and additions made to the first part and the start of the second part suggests that he had wanted to do just as much work on the rest of the novel, but the author did not have time to do it.

15th February. "Fadeyev called yesterday asking to see Misha, and he came today. The conversation they had covered two subjects: the novel and a trip Misha could make to the south of Italy, to restore his health. He said that he would go about getting all the permits and call in a few days." They were already finding it hard to turn Bulgakov over in bed by now; he felt pain when people touched him.

19th February. "For three days now, Misha has been in a very bad state. He is deep in his thoughts and looks at those around him with a distracted gaze. On top of the physical suffering – or rather, the physical suffering has led to mental suffering that is equally painful." Thoughts about the novel returned to him. The internal task of his work on the final drafts had ended, it seems, in the author's *biography* being kept utterly private in it, reinterpreted as having come to an end and having already been assessed from the point of view of *fate*. In the light of this, in the final months of his life, he perhaps saw that an attempt to give new movement to a novel which had already come to a stop, or, to use the author's words, "go chasing after the clues for something that is already over", whilst reaching out for new ideas, could not fail to have catastrophic consequences, which were his disease and death, tortuous and long by contrast with the quick, easy death of the Master. On the other hand, this attempt was explained *in advance* in the novel itself, interwoven with the theme of tragic guilt. "As he lay dying," Yelena recalled, "he said: 'Perhaps this is as it should be... What could I write after *The Master*?'..."

On 1st March, Fadeyev came to their home; on the same day, K. Venets took the last photographs of Bulgakov (notable for his dramatically changed, yet peaceful, and sometimes smiling face) – this speaks volumes about the strength of character of the dying man and his wife. On 5th March, Fadeyev comes to see him again. "They talked (he made out as much as he could)," Yelena wrote; she later told me how moved Fadeyev had been whilst talking to the dying man. Bulgakov, gazing at him with unseeing eyes, had said:

"Alexander Alexandrovich, I am dying. If you should ever decide to publish – she knows all about it, it's all with her..."

Fadeyev said, in his high-pitched voice:

'Mikhail Afanasievich, you lived courageously and you are dying courageously!'

There were tears streaming down his face; he darted out into the corridor and, forgetting his hat, ran out of the apartment and rushed down the stairs with a thunderous noise..."

On 8th March, O.S. Bokshanskaya wrote to her mother: "The news from Lyusya is sadder and sadder... today an artist they know came to call, a friend of theirs [V.V. Dmitriyev. – M.C.], who stayed there with them last night. He was very deeply affected by what he saw: Maka has barely been able to speak for a day, he just shouts out occasionaly, with pain, so they think... He seems to recognise Lyusya, but not the others. He only uttered one sentence that entire time, not one that could be made sense of, and then 10 hours later, he repeated it; his brain is probably still working in some way." His wife alone was able to work out what he was saying; the nurse who took her place beside his bed brought in a notebook, in which Yelena Sergeyevna meticulously recorded how each day unfolded, and the strange words she heard; "Donkey khod...donky khod". These words were: *Don Quixote*; his characters were still alive in his memory, as it faded away. On 6th March, Yelena wrote: "I decided to say to him (for it seemed to me that he was thinking about this): 'I swear to you that I will write out the novel [i.e. that she would reprint it in full – he knew that his corrections had not yet been inserted into it. – M.], and that I'll submit it – you will be published!' And he listened to this fairly attentively, as though he understood it, and then said: 'so that people might know…so that people might know!' In the final days, in a near-delirious state, it seemed to him, Yelena Sergeyevna told me on 3rd November 1969, that "they were taking away his manuscripts; he kept asking anxiously, 'Is there someone there?'" And on one occasion he made me lift him out of bed and, leaning on my arm, in his robe, with bare feet, he walked from room to room and made certain that the manuscript for *The Master* was where it ought to be. He lay down high up on the cushions nice and rested his right hand on his thigh – like a knight." On the night of 9th – 10th March, Yelena Sergeyevna told me on the same day, "I sat on a little cushion on the floor the whole time, beside his head, and held his hand… Then I went out into the other room, and V.V. Dmitriyev asked my permission to draw him. He did his drawing, and tears were running down his cheeks." These drawings survived to the present day.

A letter from O.S. Bokshanskaya to her mother dated 12th March left, for biographers of the writer, a detailed description – the most accurate one that exists, it seems – of his final day: "He died on the 10th, at 20 to five, in the afternoon. After the extremely powerful torments which he had suffered in the final stages of the disease, the day of his death was quiet and peaceful. He was oblivious… he fell asleep just before morning, and they woke Lyusya up as well, and gave her some sleeping pills. She said to me: 'I woke up at two o'clock; it was unusually silent and from the next room I could hear Misha's even, calm breathing. And it suddenly seemed to me that everything was all right, that that terrible disease had gone, that Misha and I were simply getting on with our lives, the way we had done before it came, and there he was asleep in the next room, and I could hear his even breathing. But that only lasted for a second, of course: that happy thought.' He went on sleeping peacefully, breathing evenly. At 4 o'clock, she went into his room with a great friend of theirs, who had arrived just then. And his sleep was so peaceful again, his breathing so even and deep, that – Lyusya tells me – 'I thought it was a miracle (she constantly expected this of him, of his unusual nature, not like that of ordinary people) – that it was a turning point, he would start to get better now, he would fight the disease.' He went on sleeping, only at around half-past four a slight cramp passed over his face, he somehow 'ground his teeth, then his breath was even, though growing weaker, and, every so softly, the life departed from him."

"When he had already died," Yelena Sergeyevna told me, "his eyes suddenly opened very wide – and light, light poured out of them. He was looking straight ahead and upwards, in front of him – and he could see, he could see something, I'm sure of it (and everyone who was there later confirmed as much). It was beautiful."

In Yelena Sergeyevna's diary, which contained details of all the visits that took place over the next month (Pasternak, Akhmatova, Fadeyev…), there are a few blank pages and then this entry: "Walt Whitman: '… something pernicious and dread! Something far away from a puny and pious life! Something unproved! Something in a trance! Something escaped from the anchorage and driving free.'"

ACKNOWLEDGEMENT

The author wishes to express her heartfelt thanks to all those who, over the years, have helped and are continuing to help reconstruct the life of Mikhail Bulgakov.

I would like to mention, first and foremost, the names of those whose silent voices can be heard, I would like to think, in this book:

Y.S. Bulgakova, T.N. Kisel'gof, L.Y. Belozerskaya, N.A. Zemskaya, A.A. Tkachenko (Barkhatova), Y.B. Bukreyev, S.A. Yermolinsky, M.G. Nesterenko, N.K. Shaposhnikova…

I would like to express my gratitude to N.A. Ushakova and M.A. Chimishkian-Yermolinskaya, M.N. Angarskaya, M.V. Vakhtereva, Y.P. Kudryavtseva, to the writer's nieces I.L. Karum, Y.A. Zemskaya and V.M. Svetlayeva, to K.A. Martsishevskaya, A.A. Shiryayeva, Y.I. Abyzov, R. Yangirov, N. Filatova, D.E. Tubel'skaya, N.A. Klykova, T.Y. Gnedina, Y.M. Galach'yan, B.V. Anan'ich, R.S. Ganelin; to the writer's fellow Kievans – S.I. Belokon', N.Y. Bukreyeva, V.G. Kirkevich, V.V. Kovalinsky, T.A. Rogozovskaya, K.N. Pitoyeva, A.N. Konchakovsky, A. Yershov, M. Kal'nitsky, A. Lyagushchenko, V.P. Zakurenko. I am grateful to all my friends and colleagues in my homeland and abroad for the kind advice and practical assistance they have given me, and to the readers of the journal version of *Mikhail Bulgakov: The Life and Times* (*Zhizneopisaniye Mikhaila Bulgakova*), for their corrections and comments.

INDEX

A

Adam and Eve (*Adam i Yeva*) (Bulgakov) 113, 304, 342, 435, 439, 440, 443
Admiral Kolchak (Auslander) 235
Adventure of the Dancing Men, The (Conan Doyle) 298
Afanasieva, Stepanida 171
Afinogenov, A. N. 441, 472, 474, 497, 498, 499, 500, 519, 527, 536, 542, 548, 559, 560, 566, 570
Ageyev, K. M. 40
Ailment, The (*Nedug*) (Bulgakov) 76, 77, 156
Akhmatova, Anna Andreyevna 160, 171, 172, 181, 207, 334, 335, 474, 482, 490, 506, 523, 525, 537, 570, 615, 619
Akhsharumov, Boris Ivanovich 534
Aksakova-Sivers, Tatiana Alexandrovna 418, 419, 533
Alekseyev, G. 284
Alekseyev, M. P. 90
All-Russian Church Committee (organisation) 213-214
All-Russian Committee (organisation) 213-214
All-Russian Union of Writers (organisation) 172, 205-206, 214, 222, 223, 225, 327, 328, 334, 335, 342, 386, 396, 444, 489, 565, 566, 614
All-Ukrainian Congress of Soviets 81
Alpers, B. 550
Amfiteatrov, V. 145
Andreyevsky Hill 43, 55, 59, 62, 80, 89, 107, 109, 119, 279, 495
Angarsky, N. S. 257, 275, 276-277, 297, 298, 299, 302, 303-304, 305, 306, 318, 319, 320, 321, 324, 326, 331, 332, 531, 579, 581
Annenkov, Pavel Vasilievich 18
Archbishop Antony of Volynsk 40
Arkhipov, Nikolai 208-209
Asafiev, B. 554, 555, 561, 562, 568, 574, 576

Aseyev, N. N. 229, 231, 593, 614
Ashukin, N. S. 173, 207, 223, 258
Asmus, V. F. 90
Auslender, Sergei 221, 228, 229, 230, 231, 233, 234, 235, 236, 241, 271, 272
Author's Confession (*Avtorskaya Ispoved'*) (Gogol) 430

B

Bathhouse, The (*Banya*) (Mayakovsky) 393, 399, 401, 463, 469, 470, 615
Batum (Bulgakov) 592, 603, 604, 608, 611
Bedbug, The (*Klop*) (Mayakovsky) 391, 393, 401, 463, 615
Belinsky, Vissarion G. 18
Belozerskaya, Lyubov Yevgenievna *see* Bulgakova, Lyubov Yevgenievna
Bely, Andrei 170, 172, 207, 210, 224, 229, 295, 300, 301, 302, 308, 321, 322, 480
Berberova, N. N. 222, 343
Berdyayev, N. A. 172, 204, 214, 223, 225, 344
Berg, S. M. 507, 517, 522
Beridze, Lyudmila 155
Beseda (*Conversation*) (journal) 343
Bezymensky, Benedikt Illyich 348
Big Day, The (*Bol'shoy Den'*) (Kirshon) 563, 566, 568
Binshtok, V. L. 363
Birzhevyye Vedomosti (*News of the Stock Exchange*) (newspaper) 172
Black Sea, The (*Chernoye More*) (Bulgakov) 559, 560, 563, 570
Bliss (*Blazhenstvo*) (Bulgakov) 28, 401, 463, 477, 478, 480, 483, 484, 485, 492, 493, 502, 508
Bobrishchev-Pushkin, Alexander 273, 576
Bobrov, Sergei 171
Bogatyrs, The (Borodin) 558, 560
Bogdanov, Boris 60, 64-65
Bogdanov, Pyotr 86
Bogdashevsky, D. I. 44
Bogoborets (*The Theomachist*) (journal) 381
Bogolepov, N. P. 29
Bohemia (*Bogema*) (Bulgakov) 155, 157, 158
Bokshanskaya, O. S. 478, 590, 608, 613, 617-618
Bolsheviks 9, 80, 81, 90, 95, 97, 98, 103, 108, 110, 112, 113, 114, 115, 117, 121, 123, 125, 127, 129, 133, 137, 142, 164, 175, 177, 178, 199, 200, 201, 204, 212, 218, 219, 256, 337, 350, 351, 353, 362, 392, 500

Bolshevism 113, 138, 175, 228, 392, 500
Bolshoi Theatre 183, 444, 502, 530, 536, 537, 538, 539, 546, 550, 554, 556, 560, 561, 562, 565, 568, 570, 573, 577, 584, 588, 593
Bourgeois Gentilhomme, Le (Molière) 459, 520
Breitman, G. N. 99
Brezhnev, Leonid Ilyich 7
Brik, L. Y. 399, 469, 615
Brik, Osip M. 330
Brusilov, A. 68, 69
Bubkin (Bulgakov) 473
Budyonny, S. M. 89, 542, 546, 548
Bukreyev, Boris Yakovlevich 26
Bukreyev, Yevgeny Borisovich 26, 27, 28, 29, 31, 33, 34, 35, 41, 42, 48, 54, 61, 67, 112
Bulgakov, Afanasy Ivanovich 25, 40, 43-44, 45, 49, 54
Bulgakov, Ivan Afanasievich (Vanya, Vanka, Vanyusha) 25, 51, 55, 83, 84, 87, 105, 122, 125, 129, 130, 194, 195, 394
Bulgakov, Ivan Avraamovich 25
Bulgakov, Konstantin Petrovich (Kostya) 46, 51, 60, 83, 86, 129, 141, 147, 153, 154, 156, 158, 161, 168, 191, 249, 259
Bulgakov, Nikolai Afanasievich (Kolya) 55, 80, 83, 87, 95, 102, 105, 122, 125, 130, 142, 143, 144, 161, 190, 194, 195
Bulgakov, Sergei Ivanovich 26, 29, 43, 99
Bulgakov, Valentin Fyodorovich 178
Bulgakova, Irina Lukinichna 43, 46, 56, 63
Bulgakova, Kseniya Alexandrovna 129
Bulgakova, Lyubov Yevgenievna (Lyuba, Lyubasha; née Belozerskaya) 108, 289, 292, 293, 305, 308, 309, 310, 311, 315, 319, 321, 323, 324, 325, 329, 332, 333, 341, 365, 366, 369, 371, 394, 395, 397, 413, 423, 424, 434, 440, 446, 457, 458, 465, 474
Bulgakova, Nadezhda Afanasievna *see* Zemskaya, Nadezhda Afanasievna
Bulgakova, Olympiada Ferapontovna 25
Bulgakova, Tatiana Nikolayevna (Tasya; née Lappa) 28, 41, 50, 51, 53, 57, 58, 59, 60, 61, 64, 67, 83, 84, 85, 109, 115, 122, 128, 129, 130, 131, 146, 151, 154, 155, 158, 159, 160, 161, 162, 163, 172, 180, 186, 190, 193, 195, 197, 198, 220, 226, 243, 245, 266, 269, 286, 291, 292, 309, 323, 366, 376, 377, 458
Bulgakova, Varvara Afanasievna (Varya; married Karum) 25, 50, 59, 63, 64, 65, 78, 83, 87, 105, 115, 122, 156, 194, 195, 261, 266
Bulgakova, Varvara Mikhailovna (née Pokrovskaya) 25, 46, 54, 56, 65, 66, 83, 143, 162, 193, 195

Bulgakova, Vera Afanasievna 25, 46, 46, 55, 63, 83, 119, 142, 156, 196, 260, 272
Bulgakova, Yelena Afanasievna (Lyolya) 43, 45, 46, 49, 50, 56, 83, 86, 162, 261, 309, 613
Bulgakova, Yelena Sergeyevna (née Shilovskaya) 8, 12, 17, 19, 21, 24, 55, 69, 105, 132, 145, 153, 156, 160, 191, 280, 301, 332, 350, 352, 355, 397, 400, 404, 410, 413, 414, 415, 423, 424, 435, 453, 454, 459, 463, 466, 472, 474, 476, 477, 480, 483, 501, 514-515, 520, 531, 539, 540, 543, 556, 558, 570, 572, 576, 578, 581-586, 590, 592, 597, 610, 616, 618, 619
Burmistrov, A. 75
Burning Heart (*Goryacheye Serdtse*) (Ostrovsky) 448

C

Cabal of Hypocrites, A (*Kabala Svyatosh*) *see Molière* (Bulgakov)
Capital in a Notepad, The (*Stolitsa v Bloknote*) (Bulgakov) 245, 254, 256, 262
Cardboard King, The (*Kartonnyy Korol'*) (Slezkin) 239
Carmen (opera) 61, 537, 560, 561
Cervantes (Mindlin) 588
Changing Landmarks (*Smena Vekh*) (magazine) 173-174
Chayanov, Alexander 206, 380
Chenier, Andre 171
Chevkin, S. M. 257
Chichikov's Shenanigans (*Pokhozhdeniya Chichikova*) (Bulgakov) 255, 330, 334, 336
Chimishkian, Marika 366, 368, 369, 371, 422, 423, 446, 457
Chudakov, Aleksandr 11
Chudakova, Marietta 7-13
Clay Bridegrooms, The (*Glinyanyye Zhenikhi*) (Bulgakov) 154
Cloven-Hoofed Consultant, The (*Konsul'tant s Kopytom*) (Bulgakov) 597
Cold Summer, The (*Kholodnoye Leto*) (Mandelstam) 201
Collective Novel: The Circle of Thirteen (*Kollektivnyy Roman: 'Kruzhok Trinadtsati'*) 258
Crimson Island, The (*Bagrovyy Ostrov*) (Bulgakov) 325, 330, 336, 354, 355, 370, 371, 372, 373, 391, 392, 393, 396, 407, 411, 416, 560
Cuff-notes (*Zapiski na Manzhetakh*) (Bulgakov) 146, 150, 151, 155, 156, 157, 160, 161, 162, 163, 172, 184, 193, 203, 208, 209, 216, 219, 220, 246, 250-251, 253, 254, 258, 262, 263, 265, 267, 271, 273, 294, 301, 319, 320

D

Days of the Turbins, The (*Dni Turbinykh*) (Bulgakov) 17, 58, 86, 97, 110, 153, 154, 156, 158, 160, 231, 232, 260, 281, 345, 346, 347, 349, 350, 352, 355, 356, 358, 360, 362, 363, 364, 368, 369, 371, 391, 392, 393, 396, 399, 407, 416, 424, 444, 445, 446, 447, 448, 453, 454, 464, 465, 470, 475, 476, 478, 479, 483, 492, 500, 502, 508, 511, 530, 551, 553, 554, 564, 567, 568, 569, 575, 587, 589, 592, 607
Dead Flight: A Tale about Foreign Years (*Mertvyy Beg. Povest' Zarubezhnykh Let*) (Alekseyev) 284
Dead Souls (*Myortvyye Dushi*) (Bulgakov) 330, 418, 420, 421, 429, 432, 434, 443, 455, 463, 474, 476, 480, 485, 487, 492, 493, 494, 505, 508, 514, 520
Denikin, Anton Ivanovich 93, 94, 95, 97, 108, 123, 125, 132, 219, 227, 256, 340, 572
Derman, A. 350
Diaboliad (*Dyavoliada*) (Bulgakov) 241, 243, 272, 274, 276, 277, 279, 289, 290, 293, 294, 300, 301, 309, 320, 324, 325, 328, 330, 331, 334, 342, 343
Diamond Wreath, My (*Almaznyy Moy Venets*) (Katayev) 249, 281, 290
Dmitriyev, V. V. 476, 508, 512, 513, 523, 531, 536, 538, 569, 570, 571, 578, 579, 589, 601, 604, 617, 618
Dolgoruky, Yury 267
Don Quixote (Bulgakov) 573, 583, 584, 587, 588, 590, 592, 594, 617
Donskoi, Boris 92
Dostoevsky, Fyodor Mikhailovich 46, 125, 172, 232, 302, 304, 305, 320, 322, 446, 447, 523
Double Death (*Dvoynaya Smert'*) (Mozalevsky) 209
Drafts of the Novel (*Chernoviki Romana*) (Bulgakov) 433
Dramatists Have the Floor! (*Slovo Dramaturgam!*) (Olesha) 498
Dynnik, Valentina 250, 253

E

Eccentric of Moscow, The (*Moskovskiy Chudak*) (Bely) 300
Ehrenburg, Ilya 27, 28, 90, 91, 108, 112, 208, 224, 258, 302, 377, 378
Eichenwald, Y. I. 172, 173
Ekho (*Echo*) (journal) 237
Ekke, N. A. 476
Ekonomicheskoye Vozrozhdeniye (*Economic Regeneration*) (newspaper) 220
Ekzemplyarsky, Vasily Ilyich 39, 40, 45, 46, 50, 52, 53
Elshanskaya, N. 45

Empress's Plot, The (*Zagovor Imperatritsy*) (A. Tolstoy and Shchegolev) 230, 514
Engineer's Hoof, The (*Kopyto Inzhenera*) (Bulgakov) 291, 389, 467, 597
Erdman, Boris 578, 604
Erdman, Nikolai R. 474, 578, 581, 588, 589, 604, 613
Etinhof, B. Y. 285, 286
Evacuation, The (*Evakuatsiya*) (Shestakov) 235
Extraordinary Adventures of the Doctor, The (*Neobyknovennyye Priklyucheniya Doktora*) (Bulgakov) 111, 114, 116, 118, 208, 236

F

Fadeyev, Alexander Alexandrovich 496, 588, 593, 611, 614, 616, 617, 619
Faiko, A. M. 231, 474, 587, 594, 600, 601, 612
Faiman, G. 149, 168
Fantastic Tales (*Fantasticheskiye Rasskazy*) (Mozalevsky) 236
Fateful Eggs, The (*Rokovyye Yaytsa*) (Bulgakov) 113, 278, 295, 298, 299-300, 301, 312, 313, 314, 318, 319, 325, 327, 330, 336, 467, 479
Fedorchenko, Sofya 90, 324, 328, 331
Fialkova, L. L. 257
Fictions in Geometry (*Mnimosti v Geometrii*) (Florensky) 206
Fiery Snake, The (*Ognennyy Zmey*) (Bulgakov) 55
First Blossom (*Pervyy Tsvet*) (Bulgakov) 156
First Meeting, The (*Pervoye Svidaniye*) (Bely) 172, 173
Flight (*Beg*) (Bulgakov) 77, 137, 220, 227, 259, 271, 354, 356, 357, 358, 359, 360, 362, 364, 365, 367, 368, 369-370, 371, 372-373, 391-392, 393, 396, 407, 415, 442, 464, 466, 472, 476, 477, 478, 480, 481, 486, 501, 506, 508, 511, 576, 577, 585, 587, 592, 607
Forty Forties (*Sorok Sorokov*) (Bulgakov) 201, 210, 220, 248, 264, 267
Frank, S. L. 174
Frankfurt, S. I. 93

G

Gabrichevskaya, Natalya A. 324, 404
Gabrichevsky, Alexander G. 314, 324, 329, 404
Galati, Yekaterina Alexandrovna 210, 221, 230, 231, 350
Ganetsky, Y. S. 372
Gasumyanits, Tamara 147

Gavrilova, Larisa Dmitriyevna 131, 148
Gdeshinskaya, Larisa Nikolayevna 48, 49, 553
Gdeshinskaya, Nina Polikarpovna 47
Gdeshinskaya, Sofya 55
Gdeshinsky, Alexander (Sasha) 47, 48, 51, 55, 60, 266, 272, 494, 553, 613, 614
Gdeshinsky, Platon 47, 60, 64
Gdeshinsky, Polikarp Petrovich 47
Gdeshinsky, Pyotr 47, 48
Gerasimov, Mikhail V. 72, 78, 79
Gerasimov, Osip P. 72, 73, 74, 76, 176
Gerasimov, Vasily O. 72, 73
Gershenzon, M. O. 172
Gireyev, D. 153
Gladyrevsky, A. 89
Gladyrevsky, Nikolai Leonidovich 85, 86, 160, 162, 192, 194, 248
Glagolev, A. A. 54
Glagoleva, Tatiana Pavlovna 45, 46, 55
Glagolin, Sergei 112
Gogol in His Lifetime (*Gogol' v Zhizni*) 465
Gogol, Nikolai Vasilievich 18, 231, 255, 300, 334, 399, 401, 430, 432, 480, 491, 511, 612
Goldebayev, Alexander Kondratievich 164, 165
Golden City, The (*Zolotistyy Gorod*) (Bulgakov) 277
Golodolinsky, P. 138
Golos Minuvshego (*Voice of the Past*) (journal) 225, 226
Golos Rabotnikov Prosveshcheniya (*Voice of the Workers of Education*) (publication) 262, 264
Goncharova, Natalya Nikolayevna 516
Gorbachev, Mikhail Sergeyevich 12
Gorchakov, N. M. 502, 527, 537, 549, 551, 555, 556
Gorkovets (newspaper) 548
Gorky, Maksim (Aleksei Maximovich) 158, 170, 211, 284, 289, 317, 328, 336, 343, 354, 364, 367, 368, 369, 371, 372, 395, 396, 397, 400, 401, 409, 415, 420, 438, 439, 440, 442, 443, 453, 455, 462, 463, 466, 472, 480, 481, 486, 488, 492, 499, 432, 550
Gornfeld, A. 350
Gornung, Boris Vladimirovich 231, 291, 295
Gorodetsky, Sergei 206, 257, 258, 562
Gotfried, A. P. 164

Government Inspector, The (*Revizor*) (Bulgakov) 494, 504, 505, 511, 514
Grasshopper, The (*Poprygunia*) (Chekhov) 198
Great Evening, The (*Velikiy Vecher*) (Bulgakov) 149
Green Snake, The (*Zelyonyy Zmiy*) (Bulgakov) 75, 156
Grossman, Leonid Petrovich 206, 418
Groznyy (*Fearsome*) (newspaper) 131, 132, 137
Grushevsky, M. S. 80, 81
Gudok (*The Hooter*) (newspaper) 233, 248, 261, 265, 268, 282, 283, 285, 286, 287, 292, 296, 304, 307, 308, 309, 314, 424, 499
Gudzy, N. K. 90, 253, 254
Gulag 7

H

Half-Wit Jourdain, The (*Poloumnyy Zhurden*) (Bulgakov) 459
Handbook on Criminal Law (*Uchebnik Ugolovnogo Prava*) (Spasovich) 510
Heart of a Dog, The (*Sobachie Serdtse*) (Bulgakov) 10, 192, 270, 278, 295, 315, 318-320, 325, 326, 331, 332, 333, 375, 432, 524, 574
Heavy Lyre, The (*Tyazhelaya Lira*) (Khodasevich) 222
History of the Pugachev Rebellion (*Istoriya Pugachevskogo Bunta*) (Pushkin) 389
Hugo's Wedding (*Svad'ba Khiuga*) (Globa) 253
Hunting with Hounds (*Psovaya Okhota*) (Reutt) 431

I

I Killed (*Ya Ubil*) (Bulgakov) 113, 114, 357, 358
Ignatovich, Z. A. 84, 126
Ilf, I. A. 165, 292, 508, 561, 565, 597, 598
Iliad, The 384
Instructive Failure, An (*Pouchitel'naya Neudacha*) (Yanshin) 550
Iron Flood, The (*Zheleznyy Potok*) (Serafimovich) 276, 560
Istoricheskiy Vestnik (*The Historical Herald*) (journal) 226
Ivan Susanin (opera) 568, 573
Ivan Vasilievich (Bulgakov) 508, 514, 515, 535, 536, 537, 538, 542, 549, 550, 551, 552, 574
Ivanov-Razumnik, R. V. 301
Ivnev, Ryurik 121
Izmailov, N. 133

Izvestiya (*Reports*) (newspaper) 189, 215, 216, 267, 368, 370, 396, 420, 478, 522, 538, 570

J

J.V. *see* Stalin, J. V.

K

Kagansky, Z. 327, 363, 364
Kalinin, M. I. 178, 214, 215, 395, 410, 510, 588
Kareyev, Nikolai Ivanovich 72, 73, 76, 78, 176
Karum, Irina Leonidovna 87, 89
Karum, Leonid Sergeyevich 80, 87-88, 89
Karum, Varvara Afanasievna *see* Bulgakova, Varvara Afanasievna
Kasyanyuk, S. A. 47
Katayev, Valentin Petrovich 245, 247, 249, 260, 272, 273, 281, 282, 290, 292, 307, 308, 309, 324, 368, 399, 400, 584, 588
Kazin, Vasily 229
Kerensky, Alexander Fyodorovich 34
Kerzhentsev, P. N. 542, 550, 559, 560, 562, 563, 569, 575, 576
Khan's Flame, The (*Khanskiy Ogon'*) (Bulgakov) 73
Khiryakov, A. M. 178
Khmelev, N. P. 369, 601, 602, 608, 612
Khodasevich, Vladislav Felitsianovich 175, 179, 207, 222, 224, 343-344, 361, 362
Khristianskaya Mysl' (*Christian Thought*) (journal) 45
Khrushchev, Nikita Sergeyevich 7
Kiev Types (*Kiyevskiye Tipy*) (Kuprin) 61
Kiev-city (*Kiyev-gorod*) (Bulgakov) 63, 212, 266, 272, 376, 511
Kiryakova, Lidiya 230, 231, 291
Kiselgof, David A. 243, 247
Kiselgof, Tatiana Nikolayevna 19, 89
Kiyevlyanin (newspaper) 124, 125, 126, 127, 137, 142
Kiyevskoye Ekho (*The Kiev Echo*) (newspaper) 108, 110, 126
Klyuchnikov, Y. V. 216, 217, 224, 273, 289, 576
Koltsov, Mikhail 100, 101, 122, 167, 305, 385, 581
Kommunist (*The Communist*) (newspaper) 149, 150
Komorsky, Vladimir 243-245, 247, 269, 287, 290, 292
Komsomolskaya Pravda (newspaper) 348, 373

Konchakovskaya, Inna Vasilievna 56
Konchakovsky, Valery 57
Kondratieva, M. L. 45
Kozhich, I. P. 42
Kozhich, Platon Grigorievich 29, 42
Kozhich, V. P. 42
Kozyrev, Mikhail Yakovlevich 222, 230, 250, 251, 258, 295, 319
Krasnaya Gazeta (The Red Newspaper) (newspaper) 325, 334, 365
Krasnaya Niva (The Red Cornfield) (magazine) 257
Krasnaya Nov' (Red Soil) (journal) 300, 404, 508, 523
Krasnaya Panorama (Red Panorama) (journal) 318, 325
Krasny Zhurnal Dlya Vsekh (Red Journal for All) (magazine) 245
Krechetov, Sergei 137
Kreshkova, Vera 197
Krichevskaya, E. 245
Krug (publisher) 297, 328, 331
Krupskaya, Nadezhda Konstantinovna 181, 419
Krymsky, O. E. 117
Kryuchkov, P. P. 368, 438, 472
Kudryavtsev, Pyotr Pavlovich 19, 39, 40, 41, 45, 50, 226
Kudryavtseva, Yekaterina Petrovna 19, 39, 50
Kurennoi, Alexander 284
Kuza, V. V. 34, 326, 329, 331, 349, 585, 587, 588
Kuze, V. V. 51, 594
Kuzmin, M. 239, 334
Kuzminskaya, Tatiana Andreyevna 176, 425
Kuznetsov, Stepan 366

L

La Belle Dame aux Camelias (Dama s Kameliyami) (Dumas *fils*) 520
Lady Macbeth (opera) 537, 539, 546
Lappa, Elizaveta 57
Lappa, Tatiana Nikolayevna *see* Bulgakova, Tatiana Nikolayevna
Lappa, Yevgeniya Viktorovna 64
Lavinskaya, Y. 615
Lenin, Vladimir 125, 174, 183, 199, 211, 287, 288, 340, 587
Leonidov, L. M. 408, 488
Leontiev, Y. L. 317, 486, 490, 536, 539, 541, 555, 569, 581, 607, 609

Letters to Friends (Pis'ma Druziam) (Gorky) 368
Levitsky, O. I. 91
Levshin, V. 179, 180, 194, 329,
Lezhnev, I. G. 211, 246, 262, 274, 275, 293, 296, 303, 321, 322, 323, 324, 327, 333, 499, 534, 535
Life of Mr de Molière, The (Zhizneopisaniye Gospodina de Moliera) (Bulgakov) 461, 463, 466, 475, 476, 506, 509, 515, 523
Linnichenko, I. A. 89
Lisinevich, Ksavery Antonovich 198, 200
Listovnichy, Vasily Pavlovich 56, 57, 59, 109, 122, 124
Literary Encyclopaedia (Literaturnaya Entsiklopediya) 478
Literaturnaya Gazeta (Literary Newspaper) 488, 535, 550, 590
Literaturnaya Mysl' (Literary Thought) (almanac) 234
Literaturnoye Nasledstvo (Literary Inheritance) (journal) 472, 474
Literaturnoye Prilozheniye (Literary Supplement) 220, 237, 245, 258, 271
Literaturnyy Yezhenedel'nik (Literary Weekly) 257, 258
Litovtseva, N. 569
Lives of Remarkable People, The (Zhizn' Zamechatel'nykh Lyudey) see ZhZL
Lord Curzon's Benefit (Benefis Lorda Kerzona) (Bulgakov) 266
Lukianov, Yakov Pavlovich 30
Lunacharsky, A. V. 183, 223, 326, 346, 347, 348, 350, 352, 353, 355, 385, 430, 480
Luzhsky, V. V. 321, 326, 327
Lyamin. Nikolai N. (Kolya) 291, 295, 311, 315, 325, 341, 404, 441, 472, 473, 484, 500, 502, 511, 516, 542, 551, 593
Lyamina, Alexandra 314, 315
Lyubishchev, A. A. 202
Lyubov' Yarovaya (Trenyov) 352, 364, 481, 498

M

M. Bulgakov's Reactionary Plots (Reaktsionnyye Domysly M. Bulgakova) (Alpers) 550
Magical Tales (Magicheskiye Rasskazy) (Muratov) 175
Magnanimous Cuckold, The (Velikodushnyy Rogonosets) (Crommelynck) 264
Makashin, S. A. 474
Malgasova, T. 157
Mandelstam, Nadezhda Yakovlevna 160, 202, 482, 525, 566
Mandelstam, Osip Emilyevich 12, 121, 123, 159, 160, 179, 201, 207, 223, 431, 432, 482, 490, 491, 506

Markov, L. A. 464
Markov, Pavel A. 369, 371, 399, 549, 550, 568, 585, 586, 594, 595
Mary from Vladivostok (*Meri iz Vladivostoka*) (Venediktov) 234
Maslov, G. 231, 234
Master and Margarita, The (Bulgakov) 8, 17, 18, 20, 47, 48, 146, 166, 171, 204, 209, 212, 240, 279, 290, 291, 335, 349, 355, 365, 374, 426, 453, 484, 524, 577, 579, 581, 583, 586, 594, 611, 615
Matveyev, Boris Stepanovich 313
Mayakovsky (Aseyev) 614
Mednyy Vsadnik (*The Bronze Horseman*) (literary society) 233
Melik-Pashayev, A. 536, 537, 538, 539, 541, 546, 547, 562, 575, 577, 587
Memory of Gogol, In (*Pamyati Gogolya*) 33
Memory of Pushkin, In (*Pamyati Pushkina*) 33
Mendelson, N. M. 226, 254
Meshcheryakov, N. 284
Meyerhold, V. E. 183, 193, 194, 230, 248, 263, 264, 301, 352, 354, 366, 391, 399, 400, 401, 470, 520, 554, 578
Mikhalsky, F. N. 444, 445, 455, 476, 549, 568, 569, 573, 587, 589, 590, 604
Mindlin, E. 232, 352, 263, 588
Minin [*and Pozharsky*] (Bulgakov) 554, 555, 559, 560, 561, 562, 564, 568, 573, 574, 579
Miotiyskaya, Maria Fyodorovna 87
Miser, The (Molière) 537
Missing Eye, The (*Propavshiy Glaz*) (Bulgakov) 72
Molière (also *Cabal of Hypocrites, The*) (Bulgakov) 400, 401, 407, 408, 409, 418, 421, 440, 441, 442, 443, 450, 451, 453, 454, 455, 470, 476, 477, 478, 479, 481, 483, 486, 488, 494, 496, 505, 508, 515, 517, 519, 520, 523, 526, 529, 532, 537, 538, 540-541, 542, 548, 549, 550, 551, 554, 562, 563, 607
Molière see Life of Mr de Molière, The (Bulgakov)
Molière, Jean-Baptiste de 316, 399, 400, 401, 405, 406, 407, 416, 459, 461, 462, 487, 517, 518, 520, 537, 539, 572
Monina, V. M. 171
Moritz, V. E. 315, 402, 403
Morphine (*Morfiy*) (Bulgakov) 65, 70, 75, 76, 77, 86, 470
Moskovskiy Al'manakh (*Moscow Almanac*) 207
Moskovskiy Ponedel'nik (*Moscow Monday*) (newspaper) 221-222
Moskva (*Moscow*) (journal) 8, 9
Mozalevsky, Viktor 206, 208, 209, 230, 231, 233, 235, 236, 295
Muguyev, Khadzhi-Murat 155

Muizhel, V. 167, 207
Muratov, P. P. 175, 206, 207, 229
Muse of Vengeance, The (*Muza Mesti*) (Bulgakov) 167, 168, 182, 255
My Discovery of America (*Moye Otkrytiye Ameriki*) (Mayakovsky) 487
My Memoirs (*Moi Vospominaniya*) (I.L. Tolstoy) 488
My Sister, Life (*Sestra Moya Zhizn'*) (Pasternak) 229
Myshlayevsky, Alexander Zakharovich 260
Myshlayevsky, Zakhary Yakovlevich 260

N

Nabokov, V. D. 216
Nakanune (*On the Eve*) (newspaper) 208, 211, 216, 217, 220, 227, 237, 242, 245, 246, 249, 254, 256, 258, 263, 264, 265, 266, 267, 269, 271, 272, 273, 274, 275, 277, 278, 289, 291, 293, 576
Nash Ponedel'nik (*Our Monday*) (newspaper) 284
Nasha Gazeta (*Our Newspaper*) 336, 346
Nedra (*The Depths*) (almanac) 222, 257, 275, 276-277, 279, 289, 293-294, 296, 297, 298, 300, 301, 302, 303, 305, 310, 318, 319, 320, 325, 330, 331, 414
Nemolodyshev, Mikhail 33
Nesterenko, M. G. 402
Neverov, A. S. 222, 230, 284, 285
Nikitina, Y. F. 285, 286
Nikitinskiye subbotniki (*Nikitinskiye Saturdays*) (literary circle) 171, 175, 207, 222, 250, 252, 284
Nikolayev, N. I. 37
Nikulin, L. 90, 122, 262
NKVD 12, 513, 534, 551, 579, 589
Notes from the Pickwick Club (adaptation) 476, 477, 483, 490
Notes of a Cavalry Officer (*Zapiski Kavalerista*) (Gumilyov) 172
Notes of a Cossack Officer (*Zapiski Kazachiego Ofitsera*) (Sayansky) 286, 287
Notes of a Dead Man (*Zapiski Pokoynika*) (Bulgakov) *see Theatrical Novel, A*
Notes of a Miscreant (*Zapiski Merzavtsa*) (Vetlugin) 226, 227
Novaya Rossiya (*New Russia*) (newspaper) 211
Novaya Russkaya Kniga (*New Russian Book*) (journal) 224, 225, 227, 235, 239, 252
Novaya Zhizn' (*New Life*) (almanac) 207, 210
November, the 7th Day (How Moscow Celebrated) (*Noyabrya 7-go Dnya (Kak Moskva Prazdnovala)*) (Bulgakov) 282

O

Ob'yedineniye (*Association*) (newspaper) 126, 127
Oblomki (*Fragments*) (Sobol) 229, 379
Ogonyok (*Little Flame*) (journal) 201, 352, 385
OGPU 333, 367, 477, 488
Oksman Y. G. 208, 234
Olesha, Y. K. 292, 308, 309, 341, 353, 399, 400, 498, 499, 542, 548, 566, 604
One Day in the Life of Ivan Denisovich (*Odin Den' Ivana Denisovicha*) (Solzhenitsyn) 7
Orlinsky, A. 346, 347, 352, 353
Orwell, George 533
Osorgin, M. M. 177, 214
Ostroumova-Lebedeva, A. 325
Ovchinnikov, I. S. 248, 282, 304

P

Paris Communards, The (*Parizhskiye Kommunary*) (Bulgakov) 154
Pasternak, B. L. 33, 173, 207, 222, 224, 226, 229, 230, 295, 321, 331, 490, 498, 506, 524, 538, 619
Paustovsky, Konstantin Georgiyevich 31, 311
Pavlovich, Nadezhda 204
Pechat' i Revolyutsiya (*Print and Revolution*) (journal) 38, 227, 257
People at War, A (*Narod na Voyne*) (Fedorchenko) 90
Peshkova, Y. P. 367, 368, 369, 395
Peter the Great (Bulgakov) 574, 575
Petlyura, S. V. 80, 84, 92, 94, 96, 97, 99, 100, 101, 102, 103, 104, 107, 108, 110, 111, 113, 117, 118, 120, 124, 129, 133, 331, 337, 338, 339, 357, 358
Petrov, N. I. 39, 40, 91
Petrov, Yevgeny 165, 292, 508, 561, 590, 591, 597, 598
Petrovsky, A. 260, 521
Petrovsky, M. A. 312, 403, 521
Petrushevskaya, Sofya 48
Phantasmagoria (Slezkin) 236, 259
Pikel, R. 396, 409
Pilnyak, Boris 206, 207, 222, 225, 229, 232, 245, 258, 272, 302, 308, 369, 374, 397, 439, 490, 506, 537, 577
Piotrovsky, Adrian 570, 574

Plantain (*Podorozhnik*) (Akhmatova) 171
Play about Cervantes, A (*Piesa o Servantese*) (Kutuzov) 588
Poet's Barge (*Barka Poetov*) (literary circle) 234
Pokrovskaya, Alexandra Mikhailovna 66
Pokrovskaya, Anfisa Ivanovna (née Turbina) 24, 45, 46
Pokrovskaya, Varvara Mikhailovna *see* Bulgakova, Varvara Mikhailovna
Pokrovsky, Mikhail Mikhailovich 63
Pokrovsky, Mikhail Vasilievich 24
Pokrovsky, Nikolai Mikhailovich 24, 46, 63, 69, 83, 175, 176, 182
Politbiuro 8, 13
Pomoshch' (*Help*) (newspaper) 212
Ponyrev, Ivan Nikolayevich 599
Popov, Leonid Viktorovich *see* Sayansky, L.
Popova, Anna Ilinichna 176, 450, 474
Poroshin, Alexander 159
Posadsky-Dukhovskoy 33
Posledniye Novosti (*The Latest News*) (newspaper) 90, 92, 96, 97, 98, 99, 100, 101, 102, 104, 110, 112, 115, 293, 481, 605
Potekhin, Y. N. 216, 224, 273, 289, 292, 319, 323, 324, 407, 577
Pototsky, Pavel 260
Pravda (*Truth*) (newspaper) 183, 215, 372, 420, 535, 536, 540, 541, 549, 570, 571, 572
Pribludny, Ivan 279
Prospects for the Future (*Gryadushchiye Perspektivy*) (Bulgakov) 131-132, 137, 138, 139, 170
Prosvita (club) 39
Proust, Marcel 232
Prudkin, M. I. 345
Pushkin (*Alexander Pushkin*) (Bulgakov) 349, 499, 500, 505, 513, 514, 515, 516, 517, 522, 530, 531, 532, 534, 535, 536, 537, 538, 539, 541, 550, 551, 552, 556, 563, 564, 570, 573, 607
Pushkin, Alexander 18, 90, 150, 152, 169, 170, 172, 206, 209, 231, 253, 322, 380, 389, 399, 401, 441, 505, 514, 556, 563, 573, 576, 612
Pyatakov, Leonid Leonidovich 35

Q

Quietly Flows the Don (*Tikhiy Don*) (Sholokhov) 547

R

Rabochiy (*The Worker*) (newspaper) 194, 196, 278
Raid, A (*In a Magic Lantern*) (*Nalyot (V Volshebnom Fonare)*) (Bulgakov) 46, 285
Rapaport, M. Y. 610
Rastorguyev, Alexander 72
Ravich, N. 120
Red Army 89, 120, 121, 123, 148, 151, 201, 219, 227, 256, 265, 525, 572
Red Army Officers, The (*Krasnoarmeytsy*) (lubok) 149
Red Cross 67, 68, 70, 84, 104, 248
Red Crown, The (*Krasnaya Korona*) (Bulgakov) 76, 128, 130, 133, 356, 357, 358, 421, 504, 514
Red Tree, The (*Krasnoye Derevo*) (Pilnyak) 397
Red-stone Moscow (*Moskva Krasnokamennaya*) (Bulgakov) 201
Renaissance in Trade, The (*Torgovyy Renessans*) (Bulgakov) 187
Repair of Love, The (*Remont Lyubvi*) (Breitman) 99
Resurrection (Tolstoy) 404
Rodionov, K. S. 347
Romashov, Boris 51
Rossiya (*Russia*) (journal) 163, 223, 245, 246, 254, 262, 274-275, 293, 309, 310, 318, 320, 321, 323, 324, 327, 333, 336, 362, 363, 499, 534, 535
Rozanov, Ivan N. 171, 173, 175, 206, 222, 224, 225, 226, 229, 230, 250, 254, 284, 285, 319, 418, 419, 420, 560, 565, 566, 593
Rupor (*Mouthpiece*) (journal) 198, 208, 249, 335, 377
Russkaya Starina (*Russia in Past Times*) (journal) 226
Rybinsky, V. I. 39, 40

S

Sadovsky, B. A. 210, 229, 230
Sadyker, Pavel Abramovich 245, 263, 265, 266,
Samogon Lake, The (*Samogonnoye Ozero*) (Bulgakov) 271, 310
Savich, O. 224, 229, 253, 284, 285, 379, 380
Sayanskaya, Yulia 309
Sayansky, Leonid (Popov, Leonid Viktorovich) 249, 286, 287
Scarlet Stroke, The (*Aly Makh*) (Bulgakov) 245, 259
Séance, The (*Spiriticheskiy Seans*) (Bulgakov) 198, 200, 201, 203, 204, 208, 218, 242, 377, 516

Self-defence (*Samooborona*) (Bulgakov) 119, 149, 156
Selivanov, A. 335
Selvinsky, Ilya 250, 251, 253
Sentimental Journey, A (Sentimental'noye Puteshestviye) (Shklovksky) 337, 338, 339, 340, 359
Serapionovy Brothers (literary group) 229, 497
Severtsova, N. A. 312, 313
Shaposhnikov, B. V. 312, 402, 502, 516, 566, 613
Shaposhnikova, Natalya Kazimirovna 312, 402, 516
Shervinsky, S. V. 207, 315, 316, 317
Shestakov, N. Y. 231, 232, 234, 235, 236
Shilovskaya, Yelena Sergeyevna *see* Bulgakova, Y. S.
Shilovsky, Y. A. 397, 423, 424, 454, 456, 457, 458, 460, 525, 526, 530, 572
Shilovsky, Y. Y. 410
Shklovsky, V. 112, 224, 303, 330, 336, 337, 338, 340, 342, 343, 353, 359
Shlet, G. G. 172
Shpet, G. G. 223, 312, 403, 520
Shtorm, Georgy Petrovich 165, 166
Shulgin, V. V. 37, 38, 39, 68, 124, 125, 142, 359
Sibirskaya Rech' (*Siberian Speech*) (newspaper) 235
Simonov, K. M. 507
Skabalanovich, Lyubov 49, 50
Sketches of the Russian Unrest (*Ocherki Russkoy Smuty*) (Denikin) 93, 94
Slezkin, Yury Lvovich 141, 145, 146, 147, 148, 149, 151, 152, 153, 155, 157, 158, 197, 203, 210, 221, 224, 230, 231, 233, 236, 237, 238, 239-241, 242, 243, 245, 258, 259, 269, 271, 272, 273, 274, 280, 281, 286, 289, 291, 330, 349
Smekhach (*The Laughter*) (journal) 341
Smidovich *see* Veresayev, Vikenty Vikentievich
Smirnova, Margarita Petrovna 424, 425, 427, 429
Smrchek, Leopold Leopoldovich 71
Sobol, Andrei 90, 207, 222, 223, 229, 250, 253, 258, 285, 335, 379, 499
Sobolev, Yury V. 225, 237, 258
Sokolov, Yury 253, 254
Soloviev, Sergei 204
Solzhenitsyn, Alexander 7, 8
Sons of the Mullah, The (*Synovia Mully*) (Bulgakov) 155, 157
Sopov, Y. 234
Sovetskoye Iskusstvo (*Soviet Art*) (newspaper) 541, 551, 562, 570, 588, 605
Sovremennyye Zapiski (*Contemporary Notes*) (journal) 173

Spring Tide, The (Veshniye Vody) (adaptation) 609
Stalin, J. V. 7, 8, 13, 181, 365, 366, 391, 392, 395, 410, 413, 415, 416, 431, 432, 433, 434, 435, 447, 448, 454, 464, 469, 476, 481, 483, 488, 490, 491, 496, 499, 501, 503, 504, 506, 535, 537, 538, 541, 543, 544, 545, 546, 547, 548, 550, 558, 568, 578, 585, 587, 589, 590, 591, 592, 593, 594, 601, 602, 604, 606, 608
Stanislavsky, Konstantin Sergeyevich 325, 331, 335, 344, 345, 346, 355, 369, 370, 371, 408, 412, 415, 416, 429, 439, 443, 444, 445, 449, 455, 464, 469, 486, 488, 497, 506, 508, 517-520, 523, 526, 527, 532, 537, 545, 578, 602
Starokadomsky, M. Y. 39
Startsev, Ivan Ivanovich 165, 166, 279
Stechkin, V. 110,
Steel Nightingale, The (Stal'noy Solovey) (Aseyev) 229
Stenich, Valentin 122
Stepun, Fyodor A. 207, 217, 218, 219, 225, 256, 571, 586
Stolovaya Mountain, The (Stolovaya Gora) (Slezkin) 151, 152, 230, 231, 237, 238, 259
Stolypin, P. A. 53
Stonov, D. 197, 207, 230, 231, 233, 241, 243, 245, 258, 289, 349
Streltsov, Kornei Lukyanovich 46
Struve, P. B. 174
Student-Dragoon, The (Student-Dragun) (Kuprin) 61
Stui, Adolf Frantsevich 354
Sudakov, I. Y. 325, 326, 369, 404, 464, 501, 506, 592
Sudzilovskaya, Varvara 89
Sudzilovsky, Nikolai 89
Sviderksy, A. I. 372, 373, 395
Svobodnaya Rech' (Freedom of Speech) (newspaper) 284
Svobodnyye Vesti (Free News) (newspaper) 92, 102, 103, 167
Swallow's Nest, The (Lastochkino Gnezdo) (Bulgakov) 600

T

Talberg, Nikolai Germanovich 260
Talberg, V. G. 127, 259
Tale of a Man, The (Povest'o Cheloveke) (Arkhipov) 209
Tan-Bogoraz, V. 167, 321, 322
Teatr i Dramaturgiya (The Theatre and Dramaturgy) (journal) 554

Theatrical Novel, A (*Teatral'nyy Roman*) (Bulgakov) (also *Notes of a Dead Man*) 8, 20, 38, 48, 184, 195, 209, 237, 242, 245, 269, 272, 274, 287, 325, 327, 329, 336, 345, 374, 444, 470, 523, 526, 558, 565, 574, 580, 582
Third Russia, The (*Tretia Rossiya*) (Vetlugin) 227
Tikhonov, Alexander Nikolayevich 304, 317, 328, 334, 354, 461, 462, 475, 476
Tkachenko, Alexandra Andreyevna (née Barkhatova) 19, 47, 66
To a Secret Friend (*Taynomu Drugu*) (Bulgakov) 246, 263, 268, 273
Tolstaya, A. I. 477, 541
Tolstaya, Alexandra Lvovna 176, 177, 178, 179, 226
Tolstaya-Yesenina, Sofya Andreyevna 175
Tolstoy, Aleksei 101, 173, 216, 224, 230, 269, 272, 273, 308, 334, 353, 374, 458, 490, 513, 514
Tolstoy, Lev Nikolayevich 52, 53, 175, 176, 178, 231, 232, 305, 308, 320, 389, 404, 424, 425, 439, 577
Torgovo-Promyshlennyy Vestnik (*The Trade and Industry Courier*) (newspaper supplement) 184
Towel with the Cockerel, The (*Polotentse s Petukhom*) (Bulgakov) 71, 75
Tragedy of Atilla, The (*Tragediya ob Atille*) (Zamyatin) 334, 367
Tretyakov, Sergei Mikhailovich 229, 231, 265
Trivolskaya, Katerina 171
Troitsky, Ivan Alexandrovich 526, 586
Troitsky, Yevgeny Alexandrovich 526
Trotsky, Leon 81, 122, 125, 135, 178, 211, 533
Trubetskoy, G. N. 85
Trud (*Labour*) (newspaper) 254, 498
Tsenzor, D. 145
Turbin Brothers, The (*Bratia Turbiny*) (Bulgakov) 151, 153, 360
Turgenev, Ivan 18, 305, 455
Two Worlds (*Dva Mira*) (Zazubrin) 294

U

Ulukhanova, Lyubov 147
Umansky, D. 327, 590
UNU (Ukrainian National Union) 94, 96
Urod (*An Ugly Person*) (magazine) 99
Ushakov, Abram Abramovich 316
Ushakov, Nikolai 51, 101, 112, 121
Ushakova, Natalya A. 291, 292, 295, 311, 315, 325, 329, 369, 380, 402, 403, 457, 551

Ustryalov, N. V. 174, 274, 576

V

Vakhterera, M. V. 403, 404
Vechernyaya Moskva (*Evening Moscow*) (newspaper) 321, 323, 330, 355, 368, 393, 404, 478, 535, 543, 556, 564
Venediktov, A. I. 231, 234, 380
Venets, K. 617
Venkstern, Natalya Alekseyevna 434, 477
Vensky, Y. 145, 210
Veresayev, Vikenty Vikentievich (Smidovich) 207, 222, 225, 250, 276, 296-297, 298, 299, 301, 328, 336, 433, 434, 435, 436, 437, 463, 465, 466, 474, 475, 479, 481, 485, 491, 494, 499, 500, 505, 508, 513, 517, 522, 524, 532, 534, 551, 556, 564, 570
Vernadsky, Vladimir Ivanovich 91, 92, 116
Vetlugin, A. 226, 227, 228, 258, 359
Vilenkin, V. Y. 549, 585, 586, 588, 593, 594, 595, 596, 598, 601, 602, 603, 604, 605, 606, 607, 611, 616
Vilyams, Pyotr Vladimirovich 520, 540, 563, 567, 568, 569, 574, 578, 581, 589, 594, 601, 604
Vinnichenko, V. K. 94, 96, 106, 107, 125
Virgin Soil Upturned (*Podnyataya Tselina*) (Sholokhov) 571, 575
Vishnevsky, Vs. 451, 474, 496, 561, 564
Visions of Life (*Videniya Zhizni*) (Auslander) 235
Volf, V. Y. 415, 531
Voloshin, M. 324
Volunteer Army 92, 96, 97, 98, 106, 125, 126, 127, 129, 134, 138, 143, 145, 167, 190, 202, 286
Voronsky, A. K. 297, 300, 330, 404
Voroshilov, K. Y. 355, 473, 499,
Voskresensky, Ivan Pavlovich 49, 51, 63, 115, 190
Voyna Zolotom (*War Fought in Gold, A*) (almanac) 378

W

Walking through Torments (A. Tolstoy) 173
War and Peace (*Voyna i Mir*) (Bulgakov) 439, 443, 450
White Army 9, 130, 137, 219, 234

White Guard, The (*Belaya Gvardiya*) (Bulgakov) 8, 28, 30, 34, 39, 43, 51, 54, 56, 76, 82, 85, 86, 87, 89, 92, 93, 94, 98, 101, 102, 103, 104, 105, 106, 108, 109, 110, 116, 119, 125, 126, 151, 160, 166, 167, 204, 209, 211, 233, 242, 261, 262, 275, 279, 280, 290, 291, 293, 296, 297, 298, 303, 304, 307, 309, 317, 318, 319, 320, 323, 324, 325, 326, 327, 329, 330, 331, 335, 336, 337, 338, 339, 340, 344, 346, 347, 354, 356, 358, 359, 360, 362, 363, 374, 375, 376, 407, 423, 499, 560, 615
Working May (*Rabochiy May*) (Kazin) 229
Wright, A. Colin 12

Y

Yanovskaya, L. 77
Yanshin, M. M. 508, 509, 540, 550, 551
Years, The: Memoirs of a Former Member of the State Duma (*Gody. Vospominaniya Byvshego Chlena Gosudarstvennoy Dumy*) (Bulgakov) 37
Yenukidze, Avel Sofronovich 178, 395, 400, 444, 448, 486, 490, 501, 510
Yermolenko, Alexander 103, 118, 119
Yermolinsky, Sergei 352, 423, 438, 469, 475, 484, 532, 561, 562, 563, 566, 574, 578, 581, 588, 592, 595, 607, 608, 616
Yesenin, Sergey 90, 165, 166, 175, 229, 278, 279, 303
Yeshua Ha-Notsri. An Impartial Revelation of the Truth (*Iyeshua Ganotsri. Bespristrastnoye Otkrytiye Istiny*) (Bulgakov) 257
Yevgeny Onegin (Bulgakov) 167
Yevgeny Onegin (opera) 183, 566
Yevreinov, N. N. 90
Young Doctor's Notebook, A (*Zapiski Yunogo Vracha*) (Bulgakov) 71, 183, 184, 325

Z

Zabludovsky, P. Y. 352, 353
Zaglushkin, Polikarp Ivanovich 235, 236
Zagorsky, M. 556
Zaitsev, B. K. 207, 208, 210, 214, 222, 223, 225, 229
Zaitsev, P. N. 221, 223, 276, 277, 295, 296, 298, 299, 300, 301, 310
Zakharov, V. M. 285
Zamyatin, Yevgeny Ivanovich 207, 258, 289, 290, 300, 334, 335, 365, 367, 368, 370, 396, 401, 408, 438-439, 441, 442, 443, 455, 469, 476, 563

Zavitnevich, V. Z. 39, 40
Zayaitsky, Sergei S. 207, 291, 295, 311, 314, 316, 317, 402, 501
Zazubrin, Vladimir Y. 234, 294
Zelensky, K. 294
Zelyonaya Lampa (literature circle) 178, 231-235, 236, 237, 245, 269, 291, 314, 324, 350
Zemskaya, Maria 179
Zemskaya, Nadezhda Afanasievna (Nadya) (née Bulgakova) 9, 24, 25, 39, 43, 46, 50, 54, 55, 59, 60, 62, 63, 64, 69, 75, 77, 78, 143, 156, 158, 159, 161, 167, 179, 182, 184, 186, 187, 193, 194, 196, 197, 279, 287, 310, 355, 474, 478, 553
Zemsky, Andrei Mikhailovich 39, 179, 186. 196
Zemsky, Boris Mikhailovich 186, 194, 195,196, 197, 203, 211, 243
Zhukhovitsky, Emmanuil 500, 512, 517, 529, 530, 531, 532, 550
ZhZL (*The Lives of Remarkable People*) 21, 455, 461, 475, 476
Zippelzon, E. F. 266, 414, 420, 481
Zoshchenko, Mikhail Mikhailovich 304, 330, 477
Zoya's Apartment (*Zoykina Kvartira*) (Bulgakov) 326, 329, 330, 331, 341, 342, 349, 352, 360, 363, 368, 372, 396, 407, 416, 524, 529, 531
Zozul, E. 91

Nikolai Gumilev's Africa

Gumilev holds a unique position in the history of Russian poetry as a result of his profound involvement with Africa. He extensively wrote both poetry and prose on the culture of the continent in general and on Ethiopia (Abyssinia, as it was called in Gumilev's time) in particular. During his abbreviated lifetime Gumilev made four trips to Northern and Eastern Africa, the most extensive of which was a 1913 expedition to Abyssinia undertaken on assignment from the St. Petersburg Imperial Museum of Anthropology and Ethnography. During that trip Gumilev collected Ethiopian folklore and ethnographic objects, which, upon his return to St. Petersburg, he deposited at the Museum. He and his assistant Nikolai Sverchkov also made more than 200 photographs that offer a unique picture of the African country in the early part of the century.

This volume collects all of Gumilev's poetry and prose written about Africa for the first time as well as a number of the photographs that he and Nikolai Sverchkov took during their trip that give a fascinating view of that part of the world in the early twentieth century.

Buy it > www.glagoslav.com

I Want a Baby and Other Plays
by Sergei Tretyakov

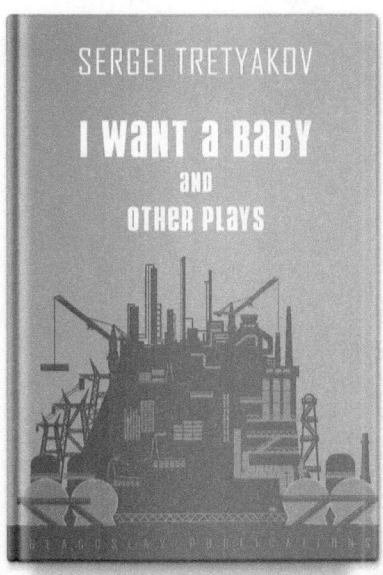

When Sergei Tretyakov's ground-breaking play, *I Want a Baby*, was banned by Stalin's censor in 1927, it was a signal that the radical and innovative theatre of the early Soviet years was to be brought to an end. A glittering, unblinking exploration of the realities of post-revolutionary Soviet life, *I Want a Baby* marks a high point in modernist experimental drama.

Tretyakov's plays are notable for their formal originality and their revolutionary content. *The World Upside Down*, which was staged by Vsevolod Meyerhold in 1923, concerns a failed agrarian revolution. *A Wise Man*, originally directed by the great film director and Tretyakov's friend, Sergei Eisenstein, is a clown show set in the Paris of the émigré White Russians. *Are You Listening, Moscow?!* and *Gas Masks* are 'agit-melodramas', fierce, fast-moving and edgy...

Buy it > www.glagoslav.com

A Brown Man in Russia
Lessons Learned on the Trans-Siberian
by Vijay Menon

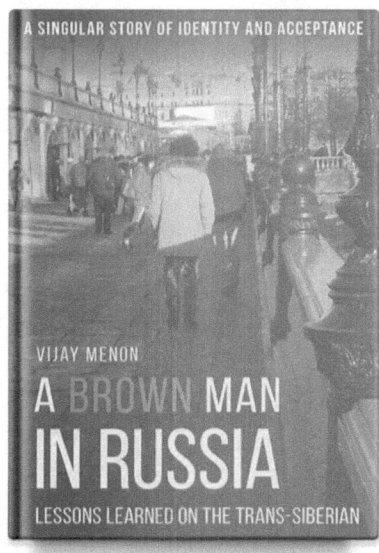

A Brown Man in Russia describes the fantastical travels of a young, colored American traveler as he backpacks across Russia in the middle of winter via the Trans-Siberian. The book is a hybrid between the curmudgeonly travelogues of Paul Theroux and the philosophical works of Robert Pirsig. Styled in the vein of Hofstadter, the author lays out a series of absurd, but true stories followed by a deeper rumination on what they mean and why they matter. Each chapter presents a vivid anecdote from the perspective of the fumbling traveler and concludes with a deeper lesson to be gleaned. For those who recognize the discordant nature of our world in a time ripe for demagoguery and for those who want to make it better, the book is an all too welcome antidote. It explores the current global climate of despair over differences and outputs a very different message – one of hope and shared understanding. At times surreal, at times inappropriate, at times hilarious, and at times deeply human, A Brown Man in Russia is a reminder to those who feel marginalized, hopeless, or endlessly divided that harmony is achievable even in the most unlikely of places.

Buy it > www.glagoslav.com

Dear Reader,

Thank you for purchasing this book.

We at Glagoslav Publications are glad to welcome you, and hope that you find our books to be a source of knowledge and inspiration.

We want to show the beauty and depth of the Slavic region to everyone looking to expand their horizon and learn something new about different cultures, different people, and we believe that with this book we have managed to do just that.

Now that you've got to know us, we want to get to know you. We value communication with our readers and want to hear from you! We offer several options:

– Join our Book Club on Goodreads, Library Thing and Shelfari, and receive special offers and information about our giveaways;

– Share your opinion about our books on Amazon, Barnes & Noble, Waterstones and other bookstores;

– Join us on Facebook and Twitter for updates on our publications and news about our authors;

– Visit our site www.glagoslav.com to check out our Catalogue and subscribe to our Newsletter.

Glagoslav Publications is getting ready to release a new collection and planning some interesting surprises — stay with us to find out!

Glagoslav Publications
Email: contact@glagoslav.com

Glagoslav Publications Catalogue

- *The Time of Women* by Elena Chizhova
- *Andrei Tarkovsky: The Collector of Dreams* by Layla Alexander-Garrett
- *Andrei Tarkovsky - A Life on the Cross* by Lyudmila Boyadzhieva
- *Sin* by Zakhar Prilepin
- *Hardly Ever Otherwise* by Maria Matios
- *Khatyn* by Ales Adamovich
- *The Lost Button* by Irene Rozdobudko
- *Christened with Crosses* by Eduard Kochergin
- *The Vital Needs of the Dead* by Igor Sakhnovsky
- *The Sarabande of Sara's Band* by Larysa Denysenko
- *A Poet and Bin Laden* by Hamid Ismailov
- *Watching The Russians (Dutch Edition)* by Maria Konyukova
- *Kobzar* by Taras Shevchenko
- *The Stone Bridge* by Alexander Terekhov
- *Moryak* by Lee Mandel
- *King Stakh's Wild Hunt* by Uladzimir Karatkevich
- *The Hawks of Peace* by Dmitry Rogozin
- *Harlequin's Costume* by Leonid Yuzefovich
- *Depeche Mode* by Serhii Zhadan
- *The Grand Slam and other stories (Dutch Edition)* by Leonid Andreev
- *METRO 2033 (Dutch Edition)* by Dmitry Glukhovsky
- *METRO 2034 (Dutch Edition)* by Dmitry Glukhovsky
- *A Russian Story* by Eugenia Kononenko
- *Herstories, An Anthology of New Ukrainian Women Prose Writers*
- *The Battle of the Sexes Russian Style* by Nadezhda Ptushkina
- *A Book Without Photographs* by Sergey Shargunov
- *Down Among The Fishes* by Natalka Babina
- *disUNITY* by Anatoly Kudryavitsky
- *Sankya* by Zakhar Prilepin
- *Wolf Messing* by Tatiana Lungin
- *Good Stalin* by Victor Erofeyev
- *Solar Plexus* by Rustam Ibragimbekov

- *Don't Call me a Victim!* by Dina Yafasova
- *Poetin (Dutch Edition)* by Chris Hutchins and Alexander Korobko
- *A History of Belarus* by Lubov Bazan
- *Children's Fashion of the Russian Empire* by Alexander Vasiliev
- *Empire of Corruption - The Russian National Pastime* by Vladimir Soloviev
- *Heroes of the 90s: People and Money. The Modern History of Russian Capitalism*
- *Fifty Highlights from the Russian Literature (Dutch Edition)* by Maarten Tengbergen
- *Bajesvolk (Dutch Edition)* by Mikhail Khodorkovsky
- *Tsarina Alexandra's Diary (Dutch Edition)*
- *Myths about Russia* by Vladimir Medinskiy
- *Boris Yeltsin: The Decade that Shook the World* by Boris Minaev
- *A Man Of Change: A study of the political life of Boris Yeltsin*
- *Sberbank: The Rebirth of Russia's Financial Giant* by Evgeny Karasyuk
- *To Get Ukraine* by Oleksandr Shyshko
- *Asystole* by Oleg Pavlov
- *Gnedich* by Maria Rybakova
- *Marina Tsvetaeva: The Essential Poetry*
- *Multiple Personalities* by Tatyana Shcherbina
- *The Investigator* by Margarita Khemlin
- *The Exile* by Zinaida Tulub
- *Leo Tolstoy: Flight from paradise* by Pavel Basinsky
- *Moscow in the 1930* by Natalia Gromova
- *Laurus (Dutch edition)* by Evgenij Vodolazkin
- *Prisoner* by Anna Nemzer
- *The Crime of Chernobyl: The Nuclear Goulag* by Wladimir Tchertkoff
- *Alpine Ballad* by Vasil Bykau
- *The Complete Correspondence of Hryhory Skovoroda*
- *The Tale of Aypi* by Ak Welsapar
- *Selected Poems* by Lydia Grigorieva
- *The Fantastic Worlds of Yuri Vynnychuk*

- *The Garden of Divine Songs and Collected Poetry of Hryhory Skovoroda*
- *Adventures in the Slavic Kitchen: A Book of Essays with Recipes*
- *Seven Signs of the Lion* by Michael M. Naydan
- *Forefathers' Eve* by Adam Mickiewicz
- *One-Two* by Igor Eliseev
- *Girls, be Good* by Bojan Babić
- *Time of the Octopus* by Anatoly Kucherena
- *The Grand Harmony* by Bohdan Ihor Antonych
- *The Selected Lyric Poetry Of Maksym Rylsky*
- *The Shining Light* by Galymkair Mutanov
- *The Frontier: 28 Contemporary Ukrainian Poets - An Anthology*
- *Acropolis: The Wawel Plays* by Stanisław Wyspiański
- *Contours of the City* by Attyla Mohylny
- *Conversations Before Silence: The Selected Poetry of Oles Ilchenko*
- *The Secret History of my Sojourn in Russia* by Jaroslav Hašek
- *Mirror Sand: An Anthology of Russian Short Poems in English Translation* (A Bilingual Edition)
- *Maybe We're Leaving* by Jan Balaban
- *Death of the Snake Catcher* by Ak Welsapar
- *A Brown Man in Russia: Perambulations Through A Siberian Winter* by Vijay Menon
- *Hard Times* by Ostap Vyshnia
- *The Flying Dutchman* by Anatoly Kudryavitsky
- *Nikolai Gumilev's Africa* by Nikolai Gumilev
- *Combustions* by Srđan Srdić
- *The Sonnets* by Adam Mickiewicz
- *Dramatic Works* by Zygmunt Krasiński
- *Four Plays* by Juliusz Słowacki
- *Little Zinnobers* by Elena Chizhova
- *We Are Building Capitalism! Moscow in Transition 1992-1997*
- *The Nuremberg Trials* by Alexander Zvyagintsev
- *The Hemingway Game* by Evgeni Grishkovets
- *A Flame Out at Sea* by Dmitry Novikov
- *Jesus' Cat* by Grig
- *I Want a Baby and Other Plays* by Sergei Tretyakov
- *Duel* by Borys Antonenko-Davydovych

More coming soon...

www.ingramcontent.com/pod-product-compliance
Lightning Source LLC
Chambersburg PA
CBHW020036120526
44589CB00032B/354